FRANCE
WINE COUNTRY
ACCESS®

W9-DEW-022

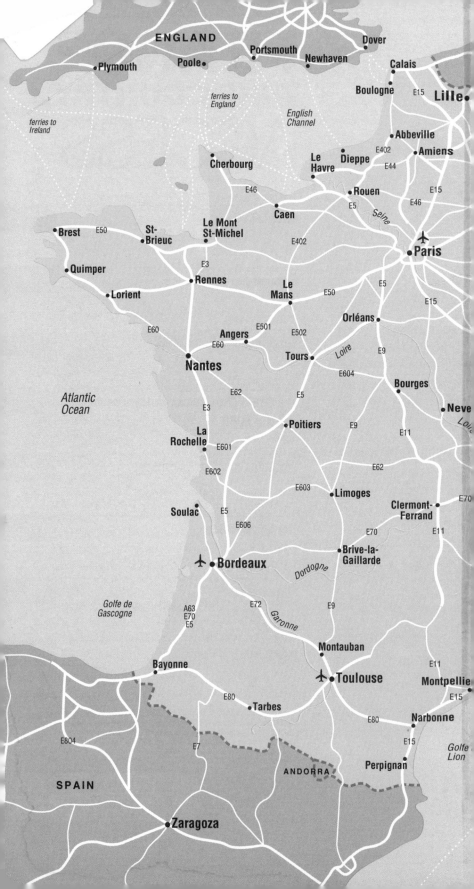

Orientation

France is the source of the world's greatest wines. The yardstick against which other nations' wines will be judged, France's wine and grapes have a long and rich history. And no other country's wine areas have such beguiling associations: noble châteaux built by aristocrats enamored of the grape; eternal, sun-drenched fields crowded with vine rows and wild anemones; and the varied and rich cuisines, many of them wine-based, of the French countryside.

Wine has been made in France (or Gaul, as the Romans called it) for over 2,000 years. In ancient France, the Gauls and other local tribes were probably already making wine for their own use, rough country wines which in leaner times made up a large percentage of the rural population's caloric intake. When the Romans conquered Gaul in the first century BC, they established the practice of producing fine wine for consumption in faraway places. Between conquests, the Romans kickstarted the nascent wine industry. Later, between prayers, medieval monks became wine makers after discovering that much of their land holdings would produce nothing but wine grapes; in fact, monks were the primary cultivators of the better varieties of wine through the Middle Ages and the Renaissance. In the 18th century, some of France's best wines were bought by the case and shipped back home by francophiles Thomas Jefferson and Benjamin Franklin, among others; Thomas Jefferson was one of the first Americans to travel along French wine routes.

But while 19th-century wine writers in England and the United States were extolling the virtues of France's burgundies, champagnes, Clarets (Bordeaux reds), and Sauternes, disaster struck: The American vine louse *Phylloxera vastatrix* got to France in the 1870s, devastating its vineyards. The only means of salvaging the country's renowned vines was by grafting European *Vitis vinifera* grape varieties onto American rootstock which was resistant to the louse. This was done, and the continuation of France's role as the world's greatest wine producer was assured.

French wines are made, categorized, and judged above all else according not to type but to *terroir*. *Terroir* literally means "soil," but refers not only to soil content but also to the vineyard's overall character—its sun exposure, moisture, temperature, drainage, and incline, all of which must be taken into account by the individual *vigneron* (vintner) who manages the vineyard. A *terroir* can be barely an acre or much larger, but no two *terroirs* are ever the same. A vineyard visit will let you see the microclimate of a *terroir* up close, and learn from the *vigneron* something of the precision and the passion that go into making the wine. French wine makers are the poets of the agricultural world: They keep their eyes anxiously on the vines and the sky while keeping their senses alert to nuances of taste and character. The best of them have a touch of genius that gives their wines qualities the rest of us can only sense, but not explain.

There are wine co-ops (which run 40 percent of French vineyards) and wine makers in lesser-known regions who have tried to compete better by abandoning traditional processes and local grapes. (Use of artificial yeasts is among the shortcut methods employed.) But no one with a good name is going to risk such tactics, and there are probably now more great wines being made in France than ever before. With western economies at a low ebb and more competition from foreign producers, France once again has been concentrating on quality over quantity production. This means that the good wines are often better than they used to be, the medium-quality wines are more affordable, and the wines at the lower end of the market are as they have always been—some are true bargains, and some give you just what you pay for. Overall, these are good times for the wine lover.

Today's *vignerons* toil throughout the year to meet a world audience's demand for wine from France, and many have opened their vineyards to the thousands of French and non-French tourists who arrive each year to taste the wine at its source and to see the glorious countryside and castles. July and August are high season for visitors, who come by car, train, jet, or bicycle. Some just make it a day out from Paris—to champagne-making **Reims**, for instance, only 144 kilometers (90 miles) from the capital, while others stay a week—or a lifetime. Wine routes within each region vary hugely in complexity and accessibility to the vineyards themselves. Between the **Pays Nantais** (Nantes country) in the western **Loire Valley** to vineyards in **Provence**, the wine areas with the greatest distance between them are nearly 1,500 kilometers (930 miles) apart. It is no wonder each Frenchperson refers to his or her home region as *"mon pays"*—my country.

Five principal wine regions cover vast stretches of this Texas-sized European nation. To behold them is to see France in all its variety: flat, mountainous, lush, dry, empty, crowded, rugged, civilized. Moving clockwise from Paris, they are **Champagne** and **Alsace**; **Burgundy** and **Beaujolais**; the **Rhône Valley**, Provence, and the **Midi**; **Bordeaux** and the **Southwest**; and the Loire Valley. Each region is unique in how its wine areas are divided; the chapters in this book are arranged accordingly.

Less than two hours' drive east from Paris is the heart of Champagne, the region that gave the golden, bubbling wine of celebration its name. This is the northernmost place in France where grapes will ripen on the vine. Farther (about four more road hours from Paris) into northeastern France is mountainous Alsace, ruled for centuries by bordering Germany and today producing some of the world's richest still white wines. Its timbered medieval villages have seen a long history of border wars between France and Germany, but today's Alsace is one of France's most open and friendly places to visit, and its great wines become more popular each year.

Several hours south of Alsace are Burgundy and Beaujolais, producing some of the world's favorite wines. Burgundy (Bourgogne in French) wines include great whites like Chablis and Meursault, famous reds like Romanée-Conti, and many lesser-known wines. To the south is the hillier, more ruggedly rural Beaujolais, where red tile roofs and warm sunshine pouring over western hills covered with pine forests introduce a taste of the Mediterranean.

The South really begins on the sloped sides of the Rhône Valley below Lyons, where the vine rows grow in banked terraces, producing historic wines like Hermitage and Châteauneuf-du-Pape. To the southeast, oven-hot Provence covers a huge, mostly mountainous hinterland that in addition to grapes produces lavender, herbs, olives, honey, and flowers before it sweeps down to the Mediterranean Sea at the **Côte d'Azur**, opposite North Africa. West of the Rhône delta is the Midi, which builds in elevation through the **Languedoc-Roussillon** to the rocky **Pyrenees** mountains and the Catalan areas of the French-Spanish border; the region's full, dry reds, rosés, and rarer whites bear a range of local place names.

Bordeaux and the Southwest include great geographic variations, from the dense oak-covered hills of the southern part of the region to the marshes and maritime pines north of Bordeaux. Altogether, this region is one of the world's largest producers of quality wines, yielding an incredibly wide variety from the favored white dessert wine, Sauternes to the great reds of the **Médoc** such as Château Margaux.

The most famous combined château-and-wine trails in the world are in the Loire Valley in northwest France, which produces such high-demand white wines as Muscadet and Sancerre. Dozens of magnificent castles brood over the riverbanks of the Loire and its tributaries. Some castles are set amidst forests, others in open formal gardens or moats, and many have been converted to wineries or fine hotels.

Throughout the rest of French wine country, castles, simple and elaborate inns, farmhouses, and bed-and-breakfasts abound to accommodate travelers. Some have mandatory in-hotel meal charges, mainly in the summer. At other than peak season, rules and prices relax a little, and there are still many reasons to come to explore the many vineyards, *caves* (wine cellars), museums, and other historic landmarks of this enormous wine-making land.

How To Read This Guide

FRANCE WINE COUNTRYACCESS® is arranged by region so you can see at a glance where you are and what is around you. The numbers next to the entries in the following chapters correspond to the numbers on the maps. The text is color-coded according to the kind of place described:

Restaurants/Clubs: Red   **Hotels:** Blue

Shops/🌳 Outdoors: Green **Sights/Culture:** Black

Rating the Restaurants and Hotels

The restaurant star ratings take into account the quality of the food, service, atmosphere, and uniqueness of the restaurant. An expensive restaurant doesn't necessarily ensure an enjoyable evening; however, a small, relatively unknown spot could have good food, professional service, and a lovely atmosphere. Therefore, on a purely subjective basis, stars are used to judge the overall dining value (see star ratings at right). Keep in mind that chefs and owners often change, which can drastically affect the quality of a restaurant, for better or for worse. The ratings in this guidebook are based on information available at press time.

The price ratings, as categorized at right, apply to restaurants and hotels. These figures describe general price-range relationships among other restaurants and hotels in the area. The restaurant price ratings are based on the average cost of a meal including tax and tip but excluding wine. Hotel price ratings reflect the base price of a standard room for two people for one night during the peak season.

Restaurants

★	Good	
★★	Very Good	
★★★	Excellent	
★★★★	An Extraordinary Experience	
$	The Price Is Right	(less than $20)
$$	Reasonable	($20-$50)
$$$	Expensive	($50-$150)
$$$$	Big Bucks	($150 and up)

Hotels

$	The Price Is Right	(less than $50)
$$	Reasonable	($50-$125)
$$$	Expensive	($125-$200)
$$$$	Big Bucks	($200 and up)

Map Key

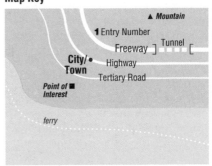

To call France from the US, dial 011-33, followed by the eight-digit local number, except for Paris in which case you must also dial 1 before the local number. In France, when calling from Paris to one of the provinces, dial 16, wait for a dial tone, and then dial the eight-digit local number; when calling from outside Paris to another province, dial only the eight-digit local number. To call a number within Paris, dial the eight-digit number. To dial a Paris number from within France but outside Paris, dial 16, wait for the tone, then dial 1 followed by the eight-digit number.

Getting to France Wine Country

Airports

Most Americans who travel to France choose to fly into one of Paris's two airports—**Charles-de-Gaulle** or **Orly.** Other French cities with international airports are **Bordeaux, Lyons, Marseilles, Montpellier, Nice, Strasbourg**, and **Toulouse.** For more airline information and local phone numbers, see the orientation sections for your desired destinations in the chapters to follow.

Aéroport Charles-de-Gaulle (1/48.62.12.12, 1/48.62.22.80) is in **Roissy,** 30 kilometers (18.6 miles) northeast of Paris. The **Aérogare 1** terminal services international flights; **Aérogare 2** handles domestic lights. A free shuttle bus connects the two terminals.

Airport Emergencies	1/48.62.30.00
Currency Exchange	1/48.62.87.62
Customs and Immigration	1/48.62.35.35
Damaged Baggage	1/48.62.52.89
Information	1/48.62.12.12, 1/48.62.22.80
Lost and Found	1/48.62.20.85
Medical Emergencies	1/48.62.28.00, 1/48.62.53.32
Paging	1/48.62.22.80
Police	1/48.62.31.22
Security	1/48.62.31.22
Traveler's Aid	1/48.62.22.80

Aéroport d'Orly (1/49.75.52.52, 1/49.75.15.15) is 15 kilometers (9.3 miles) south of Paris. The **Orly Ouest** terminal handles primarily domestic travel as well as flights to Geneva, Switzerland; the **Orly Sud** terminal services international flights. A free shuttle bus connects the two terminals.

Airport Emergencies.........................1/49.75.45.12

Currency Exchange 1/49.75.78.40

Customs and Immigration 1/49.75.78.60

Ground Transportation 1/49.75.15.15

Information 1/49.75.52.52, 1/49.75.15.15

Lost and Found 1/49.75.42.34

Medical Emergencies........................1/49.75.45.12

Paging...1/49.75.15.15

Parking 1/49.75.56.50

Police..1/49.75.43.04

Security...1/49.75.43.04

Tourist Information 1/49.75.00.90

Traveler's Aid 1/49.75.00.90

Airlines

The French phone numbers listed below are for the airlines' Paris offices. The 800 numbers are for calls within the US only.

Air France 1/44.08.22.22, 800/237.2747

American Airlines 1/42.89.05.22, 800/433.7300

Continental Airlines......1/49.75.10.80, 800/525.0280

Delta...1/49.75.54.04, ...05.35.40.80 (toll free in France), 800/221.1212

Lufthansa ....1/42.65.37.35, 1/48.62.59.60, ...800/645.3880

Northwest Airlines 1/42.66.90.00, 800/225.2525

TWA 1/49.19.20.00, 800/221.2000

United Airlines ....1/48.97.82.82, 1/48.62.96.50, ...05.01.91.38 (toll free in France), 800/241.6522, ...800/538.2929

US Air 1/49.75.40.31, 800/428.4322

Getting to and from Paris's Airports

By Bus

Air France airport buses (1/42.99.20.18, multilingual recorded message 1/49.38.57.57) carry passengers to and from **Aéroport Charles-de-Gaulle.** The buses are available to passengers of all airlines and arrive and depart frequently from 5:40AM to 11PM. Convenient stops in Paris include the **Palais des Congrès** (*métro* stop **Porte Maillot** on the *Pont-de-Neuilly/Château-de-Vincennes métro* line), the **Arc de Triomphe** (*métro* stop **Charles-de-Gaulle/Etoile**), and the **Gare Montparnasse** train station where transportation to and from outlying areas can be found. **Roissybus,** operated by the **Réseau Autonome des Transports Parisiens (RATP);** (1/48.62.12.12, 1/48.62.22.80), also brings passengers to and from the airport with frequent daily departures and arrivals from 5:45AM to 11:30PM. **Roissybus** stops in Paris at the **Place de l'Opéra** (*métro* stop **Opéra**) as well as **Gare du Nord,** where trains convenient to other locations around the city can be found.

From **Aéroport d'Orly, Air France** buses will take you to the **Invalides Air Terminal** (Esplanade des Invalides; *métro* stop **Invalides**) in the center of Paris. **Orlybus,** operated by RATP, carries passengers to **Place Denfert-Rochereau** in southern Paris; frequent departures begin at 5:45AM and continue to 11:30PM. Both **Air France** and **Orlybus** also make frequent return trips via the same routes.

By Car

To get to Champagne and Alsace from Paris, take the **A4E 50** autoroute, which leads from the eastern edge of Paris to Reims and from there heads south in the direction of **Epernay** before turning east (near Chalons-sur-Marne) toward **Metz.** In Metz, the autoroute turns into **A4E 25** which goes to **Strasbourg.** Alternatively, to reach **Troyes** and the champagne vineyards of the **Aube,** you can take A4E 50 to **A26** (near Chalons-sur-Marne) and take A26 south. From **Aéroport Charles-de-Gaulle,** take **A3** toward Paris, turning left onto the **A104** spur autoroute that will take you to A4E 50 near the village of **Croissy-Beaubourg.** From **Aéroport d'Orly,** the simplest route is to take **A6** to Paris, turn right onto the **Périphérique** (the road that circles central Paris), and turn right again onto A4E 50 at Porte de Bercy on Paris's eastern edge.

To arrive at Burgundy and Beaujolais, take A6 south from Paris to Lyons. On the way, you'll pass **Beaune** on the **Côte d'Or, Mâcon,** and **Villefranche-sur-Saône** (just east of Beaujolais). From **Aéroport Charles-de-Gaulle,** take A3 to the Périphérique, turn left (southwest), and turn left again just after the Porte d'Italie, following the signs to Lyons. From **Aéroport d'Orly,** take A6 south, away from Paris.

To get to the Rhône Valley, Provence, and the Midi, take A6 south past Lyons, where A6 becomes **A7.** Then take A7 to **Valence,** and continue on it to **Montélimar** and **Orange.** At Orange, continue on A7 southeast to **Avignon** (the official end of the Côte du Rhône wine region), then on to **Aix-en-Provence,** Marseilles, and **Perpignan** through Languedoc and Roussillon.

If you're traveling to Bordeaux from the Mediterranean coast, take **A61** from near **Narbonne** to **Toulouse** (where it turns into **A62**) and then continue on to Bordeaux. From Paris, take **A10** which begins just south of **Aéroport d'Orly;** the autoroute south from Orly divides at this point with A10 going west to Bordeaux (via Tours and Poitiers) and A6 going south to Lyons and the Mediterranean.

To get to the Loire Valley from Paris, take A10 to **Tours,** or toward Bordeaux, or turn right off A10 onto **A11** in the direction of **Chartres** to **Le Mans, Angers,** and **Nantes.** To get from Bordeaux to Nantes, take A10 north to **Niort,** then head north on the *routes nationales* (N roads); at press time, an autoroute connecting Niort and Nantes was under construction.

Renting a car in France is expensive because of the *TVA* (VAT, value-added tax) of almost 20 percent that's added on to car-rental bills, as well as a special "luxury" tax. These taxes are often not included in the price car-rental agencies quote you; always ask if the price you are given is *TTC (toutes taxes comprises,* or tax included). US residents can usually pay much less by renting the car from the US. The following car-rental companies have networks in France (the numbers for France are for the companies' offices in Paris), as well as offices in the US. All except **Europe by Car** have offices near major train stations and airports in several locations in France. For more car-rental information and local numbers, see the orientation sections for your desired destinations in the chapters to follow.

Avis	1/46.10.60.60, 800/331.1084, or dial 3615 code Avis on the Minitel
Budget	1/45.72.11.15, 800/472.3325
Dollar Rent a Car	1/34.29.03.01, 800/800.4000
Europe by Car	212/581.3040, 800/223.1516
Hertz	1/47.88.51.51, 800/678.0678, or dial 3615 code Hertz on the Minitel
Thrifty	800/367.2277

By Taxi

There are taxi stands outside the terminals at the airports, and at the train stations. In Paris, taxis cluster at special stops marked with a blue and wite "taxi" sign. Hailing a cab can be time-consuming. If you need to get to a train or the airport by a specific time, call ahead for a cab (49.36.10.10, 47.39.47.39, or 49.00.05.55). The meter starts running the moment the cabdriver receives the call, but the dispatcher will tell you how long it will take for a cab to arrive (it's usually less than 10 minutes).

By Train

From the new train station in the basement of the **Aéroport Charles-de-Gaulle**'s main terminal building, you can take a fast direct train to Paris's **Gare du Nord** railroad station, or the *TGV* directly to Burgundy (Dijon), the Rhône Valley (Lyons), Provence (Avignon), or the Mediterranean coast (Marseilles), bypassing Paris. Return trains depart from the same stations. At press time, *TGV* trains were scheduled to begin servicing the Loire Valley (Tours, Angers, and Nantes) and Bordeaux in 1996 but there were no plans to extend train service from this station to Champagne or Alsace.

From **Aéroport d'Orly,** the *métro* line, **Orly Rail** (information 1/49.75.15.15), will take you to the **Gare d'Austerlitz** railroad station. Return trains to the airport depart from the same station.

Getting around France Wine Country

Airlines

France is well served by the domestic airline **Air Inter** (119 Ave des Champs-Elysées, near Pl de l'Etoile, Paris, 1/45.46.90.90). Until mid-1994, **Air Inter** had a monopoly on domestic air travel in France, and flights were extremely expensive. At press time, **Air Inter** was starting (though unwillingly) to open up certain routes to competition, a great boon for air travelers within France. Keep in mind that traveling

by the *TGV (Train à Grande Vitesse)* is less costly than traveling by plane—and in many cases actually quicker, given the traffic problems of getting from airports into city centers. For more airline information and local phone numbers, see the orientation sections for your desired destinations in the chapters to follow.

Bicycles

Cycling is a wonderful way to see the countryside, and bicycles can be rented at most of France's larger train stations or at local bike shops. For more bicycle information and local phone numbers, see the orientation sections for your desired destinations in the chapters to follow.

Buses

Buses in France outside of the cities are generally slow, indirect, and expensive. Trains are much better alternatives.

Driving

US citizens may drive legally in France with a US driver's license for up to six months, but to avoid hassles with French officials who get confused and suspicious when confronted with the wide variety of US state licenses, the American Automobile Association recommends you obtain an international driver's license from one of their US branches before departing.

Driving in France can be a hair-raising experience in cities and on major autoroutes, but less so if you keep certain rules in mind. The basic system involves *priorité à droite* (priority to the right)—whoever is on your right has the right-of-way, even if the car is entering a larger thoroughfare from a smaller road; exceptions to this rule are indicated by the sign *"vous n'avez pas la priorité"* (you don't have priority here). Driving is on the right side of the road. Speed limits are given in kilometers-per-hour in signs along every road, but the limits are often exceeded on autoroutes (although France has vowed to crack down, given the country's high number of automobile accidents each year). Be forewarned: French drivers have a frightening tendency to tailgate, even at high speeds.

France's autoroutes (marked "A" on maps) require you to pay *péages* (tolls), which can get very expensive, but it's certainly the fastest way to travel (although not the most scenic). The *Routes Nationales* (marked "N") and the smaller *Routes Départementales* (marked "D") are free. Every part of France is covered by superb local or regional road maps produced by the Michelin company. If you're planning to tour a large part of the country, you might want to buy Michelin's *Atlas Routier France*, a book that contains detailed maps of the whole country, as well as of some cities. It's available in bookstores throughout the country.

Seat belts are required in the front and back seat in France, and children under 10 are required to ride in the back seat even if they are in a car seat. There are strict laws against driving while inebriated, and intoxicated drivers can lose their licenses on the spot. So if you plan to tour a number of wineries, be sure to designate a driver.

Professional wine organizations have mapped out specific wine routes to almost all of France's wine regions, usually along small roads leading past major vineyards. The maps are available at *maisons de vin* (wine centers) and tourist offices. While it's fun to follow such routes occasionally, many of them are poorly signposted and you can waste time trying to find the proper road when another road might do equally well. Another problem is that local feuds and jealousies often come into play when wine routes are being organized, so that you might miss many great wineries that have been left out. And some wine areas, including **Chablis**, have decided not to organize official wine routes because they don't want tourists tromping around through the vines. Wherever you go, make a point of getting out of the car often to stroll about in the countryside; it's the only way to get a feel for each region.

Hiking

The best way to see France's great vineyards is up close, although it's obviously not a good idea to march through the vines—the soil between grape vines is carefully worked to achieve the best possible drainage, and hikers who disturb the soil (or worse, sample the grapes) are definitely not welcome. But all vineyards are crisscrossed by small access roads used by vineyard workers and their tractors, and these are great places to hike. Along Burgundy's Côte d'Or, for example, small gravel roads wind through tiny vineyards, each surrounded by ancient stone walls, and if you follow the roads to the top of the slopes, you're certain to find a great spot for a picnic overlooking the vines. Some wine-producing parts of the country have constructed *sentiers viticoles* (vineyard paths) specifically for tourists; look for these particularly in Alsace.

France also has a very well organized system of pedestrian trails, called *grandes randonnées* (long-distance hiking trails), many of which pass through wine country. All Michelin maps indicate these trails with the abbreviation "GR" followed by a number; each part of France has its own set of numbered trails. Most of the GR routes are partly pedestrian trails and partly small roads that are also open to cars; the pedestrians-only sections of the trails are indicated by dashes on the Michelin maps. Most GR trails are well maintained. Any local tourist office can provide detailed information on the GR trails in the area, or you can write or visit France's national office for hiking trails, the **Fédération Française de la Randonnée Pédestre** (French Hiking Trails Federation; 64 Rue Gergovie, at Rue Raymond Losserand, 75014 Paris, 1/45.45.81.02; fax 1/43.95.68.07). The office is open Monday through Saturday. Detailed maps of each of the GR trails, along with information (in French but with symbols) about the difficulty of the trail, and about camping or other facilities available along the way, can be found at local *papeteries* (newspaper and magazine stores), in tourist offices, or through the **Fédération Française de la Randonnée Pédestre** (see above).

Rustic huts where hikers can camp overnight have been built along some of the trails.

There are many picturesque GR trails in France's wine country. In Champagne, **GR14** leads from the village of **Hautvillers** (home of Dom Pérignon), just north of **Epernay,** to the wine village of **Reuil,** around 20 kilometers (12.4 miles) to the west, offering good views of the Marne Valley; although some stretches are long ascents, it's not a difficult hike. In Burgundy, **GR76,** a relatively easy, although occasionally steep, trail winds for around 40 kilometers (24.8 miles) through the rugged **Hautes-Côtes** area west of the Côte d'Or (passing near the great wine villages of **Pommard, Volnay,** and **Auxey-Duresses,** and ending in the wine village of **Chassagne-Montrachet**). In Beaujolais, a steep trail for hardy hikers, the **GR76a,** leads from the village of **Pierreclos,** 15 kilometers (9.3 miles) west of **Mâcon** (by the **N79**), passes through the hills to the west of the villages of **Pouilly** and **Fuissé,** and continues to the town of **Beaujeu,** the ancient capital of the province of Beaujolais, before heading on for points south; this 30-kilometer (18.6-mile) stretch of trail, however, is through pine-covered hills rather than near vineyards. In Provence, **GR4** leads from the ancient village of **Vaison-la-Romaine** to the village of **Séguret,** an artist's colony, and from there it crosses the crest of the **Dentelles de Montmirail** mountains before descending to the wine village of **Gigondas.** This 20-kilometer (12.4-mile) trail has some steep ascents. In France's southwest, **GR36** leads from the historic town of **Cahors** along the banks of the **Lot** in the heart of Cahors wine country to the village of **Bonaguil** (45 kilometers/27.9 miles) and beyond; this trail offers some great views of the **Lot Valley** and has no steep ascents. Along the Loire Valley, **GR48** runs 15 kilometers (9.3 miles) along the north bank of the **Vienne River** from **Chinon** to the village of **L'Ile Bouchard,** passing through pine and oak forests and then through some of the Chinon area's best vineyards; it's an easy hike with no steep ascents.

Trains

The government-owned French national railroad, the **Société Nationale des Chemins de Fer (SNCF;** information 1/45.82.50.50, reservations 1/45.65.60.60) is one of the most complete in the world; almost every village in France is served by it. There are six **SNCF** train stations in Paris. Each serves a different region of the country: for northern destinations, go to the **Gare du Nord** (15 Rue de Dunkerque, between Rue du Faubourg-St-Dénis and Rue de Maubeuge, 1/49.95.10.00); to go east, **Gare de l'Est** (10 Pl du 11-Novembre 1918, at Blvd de Strasbourg, 1/40.18.20.00); southeast, **Gare de Lyon** (Pl Louis-Armand, at Blvd de Lyon, 1/40.19.60.00); southwest, **Gare d'Austerlitz** (53 Quai d'Austerlitz, between Rue Buffon and Blvd de l'Hôpital, 1/45.84.14.18); west, **Gare Montparnasse** (Pl Bienvenue, at Rue du Départ, 1/40.48.10.00); west and northwest, **Gare St-Lazare** (20 Rue St-Lazare, between Rue de Rome and Rue d'Amsterdam, 1/42.85.88.00).

Most trains have first- and second-class service, and you can specify a smoking *(fumeur)* or nonsmoking *(non-fumeur)* car. Reservations are required for the special *Train à Grande Vitesse (TGV)* trains, the super-fast network that now serves most of France's major cities from Paris, including Angers, Avignon, Bordeaux, Dijon, Lyons, Strasbourg, Toulouse, Tours, and others along the wine route. Seat reservations are required for *TGV* trains, and it's a good idea to book a seat on trains on major routes during peak travel periods. If traveling overnight, you can reserve a *couchette* (bunk bed in a second-class compartment that holds six beds, or first-class compartment with four) or a more comfortable and more expensive *wagon-lit* compartment with its own sink. Special *trains-auto-couchettes* allow you to travel overnight with a car.

Information about specific trains and schedules *(fiches horaires)* is available in all train stations, including blue and orange leaflets—each covering a specific route—near the ticket booths. You can also dial 3615 code SNCF on any Minitel electronic directory (available in post offices and in some hotels) anywhere in the country. In the US, contact **Rail Europe** (800/438.7245) to make reservations on any **SNCF** train (including the *TGV*) prior to departure.

FYI

Accommodations

There's a wide range of hotel facilities throughout France's wine regions, from the most luxurious châteaux to the simplest bed-and-breakfast establishments to out-of-the-way campgrounds. You can usually find a hotel room without a reservation, as long as you arrive at the hotel before 6PM. In July (when France is overrun with foreign tourists) and August (when the French go on vacation), however, it's essential to reserve in advance. Note that many hotels with restaurants require you to pay for *demi-pension* (breakfast and either lunch or dinner) during the high season. Continental breakfast is typically included at bed-and-breakfasts, but not at hotels. Many less-expensive hostelries in France offer some rooms without private baths. Guest rooms with bath facilities have either a bathtub *(bain)* or a shower *(douche);* the latter is always cheaper. Many older hotels don't have air-conditioning, but you usually won't miss it—they have high ceilings, big windows with shutters, and other means of keeping out the heat.

Three organizations provide information about luxury accommodations throughout France:

Relais & Châteaux (11 E 44th St, between 5th and Madison Aves, Suite 707, New York, NY 10017, 212/856.0115; fax 212/856.0193) is a central information center for the small, high-quality (and expensive) hotels that belong to the prestigious Relais & Châteaux chain. It won't arrange rentals, but will send you a guide (in English) to all the Relais & Châteaux establishments; it costs around $10. The Paris office (15 Rue Galvoni, at Rue Vernier, 75017

Paris, 1/45.72.90.00; fax 1/47.23.38.99) can also supply information.

Châteaux-Hôtels Indépendents et Hostelleries d'Atmosphère (Independent Châteaux-Hotels and Hotels with Atmosphere; 15 Rue Malebranche, between Jardin du Luxembourg and the Panthéon, 75005 Paris, 1/43.54.74.99) publishes *Châteaux et Hotels Indépendents,* a free 272-page book (in French) which can be ordered by mail. The guide details private châteaux offering rooms, as well as particularly charming hotels.

A free guide listing châteaux-hotels of all kinds located in France's wine regions can be ordered through **Châteaux, Demeures de Tradition et Grandes Etapes des Vignobles** (Châteaux, Traditional Domaines and Fine Hotels in Wine Country; Pont de Joux, B.P. 40, 13717 Roquevaire Cedex, 42.04.41.97; fax 42.72.83.81).

To be assured of a tranquil stay in France, check into a *Relais de Silence* establishment (2 Passage du Guesdin, at the intersection of Ave Suffren and Rue Duplex, 75015 Paris, reservations 1/45.66.53.53, information 1/45.66.77.77; fax 1/40.65.90.09). These hotels have been classified by the French government as places that guarantee peace and quiet; they are usually well-maintained old monasteries, abbeys, or inns, typically in a very calm natural setting, such as the woods or the hills.

One of the best ways to see France's wine country is by staying at *gîtes*—accommodations in private houses, châteaux, or farmhouses. There are two types: *gîtes chambres d'hôtes* (bed-and-breakfast lodgings) and *gîtes ruraux* (fully furnished farmhouses or apartments created from farm buildings in small villages or rural locations). All have private owners who have agreed to rent the *gîtes* for a minimum of ten years in return for a low-cost loan from the government to renovate them. It's a great system for preserving rural dwellings and increasing the income of France's rural residents. *Gîtes* owners are often good sources for information about the local wines and regions.

Gîtes are ranked from one to three stars; the top-of-the-line places usually have dishwashers and washing machines, and a few three-star *gîtes chambres d'hôtes* are located in elegant châteaux. *Gîtes chambres d'hôtes* are rented by the night; *gîtes ruraux* are available by the week or, in some cases, the weekend. To rent a *gîte,* choose the *département* (region) where you would like to stay, and then contact the **Maison des Gîtes de France** (35 Rue Godot de Mauroy, near Rue de Mathurim, 75439 Paris Cedex 09, 1/49.70.75.85, 1/49.70.75.97; fax 1/49.70.75.80) and request the catalog of that *département's gîtes* (the catalogs are in French, but they use pictures and symbols to describe the rentals). Each catalog costs around $10. You can reserve a *gîte* through an English-speaking operator by dialing 1/49.70.75.75. US branch offices of the **French National Tourism Board** land tourist offices in the main towns of all France's wine regions can also provide information about *gîte* rentals. Also available is *French Country Welcome,* an English-language guide to bed-and-breakfast *gîtes* throughout the country, which costs 95 francs and can be ordered through the **Maison des Gîtes de France** (see page 10) in Paris. Again, if you want to stay in a *gîte* in July or August, be sure to make a reservation months in advance.

France also has many campgrounds with excellent facilities near the GR routes, and many farmers have organized camping areas on their properties. Check with local tourist offices for information about camping facilities; reservations are not required, but in July and August it's best to arrive at a campground before 6PM. Camping *sauvage* (outside a campground) is usually tolerated except in forests in summer where there is a danger of fires; do not plan to camp in a vineyard or on a farmer's field in the middle of a carefully tended crop. Be on the lookout for *attention chasse* (hunting area) signs in forests, and avoid these areas at all costs, even if you're simply going for a short stroll through the woods. Don't always take the *chasse interdit* (hunting forbidden) sign literally—not all hunters obey the laws (nor are they all crack shots).

Climate

Since France has a temperate climate with rare extremes in temperature, you can plan your visit for virtually any time of year. However, a wine tasting tour should be planned around the best times for the wine makers. Many *vignerons* will refuse to see visitors during harvest time—their busiest period. For most, that's in September, but in regions where late-harvest sweet white wines are produced (Alsace, Sauternes, parts of the **Entre-Deux-Mers** in the Bordelais, and the **Layon Valley** in Anjou) wine makers will still be harvesting in October. Otherwise late October is a wonderful time to go: high temperatures average in the 50s and 60s, grape leaves are golden, and village streets are filled with the aroma of fermenting wine. Bright green vine leaves make all wine regions picturesque in late spring, when high temperatures are in the 60s and 70s, and summer, when highs generally reach the 80s. But hotels and restaurants can be very crowded during the summer, and some wine makers tire of casual tourists. This is especially true in July and in August, when almost all French people take their annual holiday. High temperatures in January range from the 30s to the 50s, and winter is the time to enjoy peace in the wine country; restaurants and hotels are uncrowded, and the gnarled vines are starkly beautiful denuded of their leaves.

Customs

Given the complexity of US customs regulations involving wine imports—each state has its own laws—be sure to verify the import rules in your area. Many wineries in France can relate horror stories about cases of wine they have sent to the United States that were held up in hot or cold storage areas in US airports, finally refused entry, and sent back to the winery in France in undrinkable condition. Though some states will let you bring in up to six bottles, one or more of which will be duty-free, it's best to check out your state's regulations before leaving home.

Drinking

The legal drinking age in France is 18.

Electric Current

France uses 220-volt or 230-volt current; a converter is necessary to operate US appliances. Pick up a converter in the US, where they cost much less than in France.

Embassies and Consulates

The US Embassy operates a **Citizens' Emergency Center** hot line (1/42.96.12.02, 1/42.61.80.75) that will try to help you with any extreme problems you encounter abroad. The following embassies and consulates can also help in case of emergencies:

American Consulates:

22 Cours Maréchal-Foch, between Pl de Tourny and Esplanade des Quinconces, Bordeaux. 56.52.65.95

12 Blvd Paul-Paytral, at Cours Paul-Puget, Marseilles. 91.54.92.00

31 Rue du Maréchal-Joffre, between Rue du Congrès and Rue Maccarani, Nice. 93.88.89.55

2 Rue St-Florentin, at Pl de la Concorde, Paris. 1/42.96.12.02 (Office of American Services)

15 Ave d'Alsace, at Ave des Vosges, Strasbourg. 88.35.31.04

American Embassy:

2 Ave Gabriel, at Pl de la Concorde, Paris. 1/42.96.12.02

Australian Embassy:

4 Rue Jean-Rey, at Quai Branly, Paris. 1/40.59.33.00

British Consulates:

353 Blvd du Président-Wilson, between Ave Carnot and Ave d'Eysines, Bordeaux. 56.42.34.13

11 Sq Dutilleul, Lille. 20.57.87.90

24 Rue Childebert, off Pl de la République, Lyons. 78.37.59.67

24 Ave du Prado, one block south of Pl Castellane, Marseilles. 91.53.43.32

British Embassy:

35 Rue du Faubourg-St-Honoré, between Rue d'Agnesseau and Rue d'Anjou, Paris. 1/42.66.91.42

Canadian Consulates:

74 Rue de Bonnel, at Rue Garibaldi, Lyons. 72.61.15.25, 72.61.16.49

Rue du Ried, La Wantzenau (near Strasbourg). 88.96.65.02

30 Blvd de Strasbourg, Toulouse. 61.99.30.16

Canadian Embassy:

35 Ave Montaigne, at Ave des Champs-Elysées, Paris. 1/44.43.29.00

New Zealand Embassy:

7 Rue Léonard da Vinci, off Pl Victor-Hugo, Paris. 1/45.00.24.11

Holidays

Almost all businesses, including wineries, are closed on major holidays. Banks, gas stations, some businesses, post offices, and other essential offices may even be shut the day before the major holiday, especially if it falls on a Saturday or Sunday. Most French schools have two-week holidays in November and in February (the weeks are staggered throughout the country) and many businesses close for these periods. The following are the country's leading holidays:

Jour du Nouvel An (New Year's Day)

Pâques (Easter Sunday)

Lundi Pâques (Easter Monday)

Fête du Travail (Labor Day), 1 May

Ascension (Ascension Day), the Thursday 40 days after Easter

Pentecôte (Whitsunday), the seventh Sunday after Easter

Fête Nationale (Bastille Day), 14 July

Assomption (Assumption), 15 August

Toussaint (All Saints' Day), 1 November

Armistice 1918 (Armistice Day), 11 November

Noël (Christmas Day), 25 December

Hours

Most shops and almost all wineries are closed on Sunday. Food-related shops are generally closed on Sunday afternoon and on Monday. The French take lunch very seriously; all sites and stores in this book are closed midday unless stated otherwise. Even city office workers with lunch breaks of only an hour eat a big midday meal (no doubt partly because most French people's breakfast consists of just coffee and bread). In the countryside, lunch is often the primary meal of the day, and a family's main chance to be together. Days begin very early at a winery; throughout the year, there are endless chores to do in the vineyard and cellars. Wineries that are not marked "no midday closing" are in most cases closed for three or four hours, not merely from noon to 1PM. Avoid visiting a winery between noon and around 3PM, regardless of the stated visiting policy; use this time to live as the French do and have a long lunch. And many shops are also closed from noon or 1PM to around 3PM or 4PM every day. (However, most stores remain open until 6:30PM or 7PM, and most wineries accept visitors until around 6PM or even later.)

Medical Services

Proof of medical insurance is not needed in order to be treated in a French hospital, and fees are much lower than in the US. Check before leaving home to find out whether your policy covers treatment in France, and if so, in which hospitals. Almost all French towns have *pharmacies* (drug stores), and at least one in each locale is open 24 hours (different pharmacies rotate this task). A green neon cross denotes a drug store, and each pharmacy posts the address and phone of the nearest store on 24-hour duty.

Money

The basic unit of currency in France is the franc (FF), which is made up of 100 centimes. Coins come in five, 10, and 20 centimes, and one-half, one, two, five, 10, and 20 francs. Bills are 20 francs, 50 francs, 100 francs, 200 francs, and upward. It's best to change money in larger cities. Banks that exchange foreign currency display a *"CHANGE"* sign. In general, banks are open Monday through Friday from 9AM through 4:30PM. Some close for lunch (usually between 1PM and 2PM). Most are closed Saturday morning, except for **Crédit Agricole,** which is usually open 9AM through 1PM, even in small towns.

Visa and Mastercard credit cards are accepted throughout France by most restaurants, hotels, and shops; other cards are accepted by major establishments. Most businesses in France now use a code system to verify credit cards rather than a time-consuming call to credit-card companies. Check to see whether your credit card offers the possibility of an international code; this will greatly speed up validating the card in France. *Gîtes* and *chambres d'hôtes* (bed-and-breakfasts) do not accept credit cards. Some large wineries accept credit cards, but most small wineries do not.

Personal Safety

In general, France is very safe, but some precautions should be taken to ensure a hassle-free vacation. Women should not walk alone on country roads at night (daytime is usually fine), venture into poorly lit sections of large cities, or hitchhike. Men should also be careful when they are alone on dark streets in big cities. Pickpockets are everywhere, and prey on tourists, particularly in train stations, in the *métro,* and along crowded shopping streets. Don't put your wallet in a back pocket and keep a good grip on handbags. Beware of children or groups of women who may try to distract you in order to pick your pockets. Although this is rare, robbers have been known to rob night trains while people are sleeping, especially in southern France. Avoid sleeping in your car in picnic areas near autoroutes, particularly in the south of France. Lock your car and avoid leaving belongings inside; if you must leave something in the car, store it in the trunk.

Post Offices

Most post offices in France—**Bureaux de Postes, Télécommunications et Télédiffusion (PTT)**—are open Monday through Friday and Saturday morning. In addition to buying stamps and sending packages, you can make local and international calls, purchase phone cards, and send faxes (the fees are outrageously high for the latter service) at **PTTs.** Most larger post offices have public Minitels. Stamps are also available from *tabacs* (tobacco shops), hotels, and some newsstands. Mailboxes in France are yellow.

Publications

The International Herald Tribune, an English-language daily published in Paris, is available at *papeteries* (newspaper, magazine, and stationery stores) in cities all over the country. The major French-language, Paris-based daily newspapers are *Le Monde, Le Figaro,* and *Libération.* Most regions have their own French-language dailies.

Restaurants

Each region of France has its own cuisine; in fact, each area within a province has its own special dishes. Make a point of seeking out restaurants that feature regional cooking, and be sure to order local wines that go with the dishes you've chosen. Red burgundy has an affinity for beef, Pauillac from the Médoc goes best with Pauillac lamb, and nothing goes better with the river fish from the Loire than a bottle of white Loire Valley wine. Let the sommelier guide your choice; you may find your ideal wine this way! Most wine lists include some wines that haven't made it into wine books, as some small producers sell their entire production to a single restaurant. Avoid ordering very high priced, big-name wines in a restaurant; the markup will probably be almost as high as in the US. Buy the "big" wines at the wine makers or in a wine shop, and stick to lower-priced regional wines when dining out.

All French hotels, from the simplest to the most luxurious, serve a continental breakfast, which ranges from a croissant and coffee to an elaborate choice of pastries, fruits, and coffee or tea. Some luxury hotels cater to American and British tastes by offering a full breakfast as well. You can find good croissants and coffee at any simple cafe anywhere in the country; most cafes open around 7AM or earlier. When traveling the wine routes of France, follow the French habit and eat a big meal at lunch, or have a picnic. Restaurants begin to serve lunch around noon and dinner at 7:30PM or 8PM. Many eating establishments offer an economical fixed-price menu, which often includes the day's special.

Reservations are essential at most three-star restaurants listed in this book—not because they won't have the room to seat you, but because they only buy enough food to serve as many people as expected. Reserving ahead is always a good idea, particularly on Friday and Saturday evening and at lunch on Sunday. Restaurants generally have one seating per meal (your table is yours for the duration), so you will not find the turnover typical of US restaurants. No reservations are necessary in sidewalk cafes, bars, *crèperies,* or casual eateries.

Shopping

A *taxe à la valeur ajoutée (TVA,* Value Added Tax or VAT) of about 20 percent is included in the puchase price of many items. You can get a refund if you obtain a VAT refund form from the store where you make your purchase; be prepared to produce the items and forms at the airport *détaxe* (refund) desk. A minimum purchase of 2,000FF is required to get a refund. Americans can bring $400 worth of goods into the US duty-free.

For information on store schedules, see "Hours," on page 12.

Smoking

French law restricts smoking in all enclosed public places. Restaurants generally have smoking and nonsmoking sections, and long-distance trains have *fumeur* (smoking) and *non-fumeur* (nonsmoking) cars. Some hotels have designated nonsmoking rooms.

Telephones

To make a phone call, most public telephone booths in France require a *télécarte,* a magnetic card which can be bought in any post office, in some *métro* stations in Paris, or in any establishment that displays a red *"tabac"* sign. The cards are available in different *unités* (number of minutes of calling time). In some villages, phone booths still require coins; a few cafes still sell *jetons* (tokens) at the bar that you use to make a call from the cafe. Rates are lower in the evening and on Sunday. To reach an English-speaking AT&T operator, dial 19/00/11; no coins or *télécartes* are required from public phones. The first two digits of toll-free phone numbers in France are "05"; no coins or *télécartes* are required from public phones.

The Minitel—France's computerized phone directory network—is often available at hotels and large post offices. Using this service usually costs the same as making a local call to directory assistance, and is infinitely quicker.

Tipping

A 15-percent service charge is almost always included in restaurant bills; leave an additional five percent if you feel the service was extraordinary. Taxi drivers get 15 percent of the fare. In hotels, tip baggage carriers and breakfast servers 10FF each. Tips are not expected in *gîtes chambres d'hôtes* or gîtes *ruraux.*

Visitors' Information Offices

The **French Government Tourist Offices** (900/990.0040; there is a 50¢ charge per minute for this call) in the US can be helpful when planning your trip. Offices are located at 628 Fifth Ave (between 50th and 51st Sts), New York, NY (212/757.1125); 9454 Wilshire Blvd (at S Beverly Dr), Suite 715, Beverly Hills, CA (310/271.6665); 676 N Michigan Ave (between Chicago Ave and Ontario St), Suite 3360, Chicago, IL (312/751.7800).

The **American Express toll-free English-language hot line** (05.20.12.02) in France provides a wealth of valuable information.

Phone Book

Emergencies

Ambulance 15

Fire 18

Police 17

Hospital:

    American Hospital near Paris............1/46.41.25.25

Poison Control....................................1/40.37.04.04

METRIC MEASUREMENTS

In France	In the US
1 kilometer	.6214 miles
1 meter	39.3 inches
1 centimeter	.394 inches
1 square meter	10.76 square feet
1 hectare	2.471 acres
1 liter	1.06 quarts
1 liter	.2642 gallons
1 kilogram	2.2 pounds
1 degree Celsius	1.8 degrees Fahrenheit

Tastings

Wine tasting is a sensual experience and should be approached with a spirit of curiosity and pleasure. Though connoisseurs have more knowledge and may express their opinions more eloquently, all the novice needs to enter the realm of the initiated is tastebuds. Below are some facts you should know before you and your palate embark on a journey of delight.

There are basically two kinds of *dégustations*: rather impersonal tastings held regularly by larger wine operations, and more individual ones given by smaller wine makers. The first kind are offered by some of the big châteaux around Bordeaux, almost all the well-known champagne houses, the big *négociants* (wine dealers) in Burgundy, local wine co-ops, and local *maisons de vin* (centers designed to promote the local wines). Some of these have organized tours that end with a tasting. (If you would like an English-speaking guide, make sure you specify that when reserving.) You can learn a lot in such visits about how a particular wine is made and how it tastes, but you will learn little about *terroir* and even less about the individual wine maker's philosophy.

For this, you will want the second type of tasting, which usually takes place in the wine maker's *cave* (cellar). Some wine makers require that you make an appointment in advance (a phone call a few days earlier is usually enough). Others schedule visiting hours or display signs advertising *"cave ouverte"* (cellars open) or *"dégustation de vin"* (wine tasting), but it's always a good idea to call ahead. Rarely is there someone on staff whose only job is to greet visitors. The wine maker, a family member, or an employee will greet you. You will be given several wines to taste, told the background of each, given some information about the *terroir,* and usually told what foods go best with the wine (always remember a French wine-maker's advice on this last point, it's worth having!). There is no charge for tasting (except for very rare and expensive wines, or in-depth tastings of many wines), but it's good manners to buy a bottle or two, in recognition of the gift of professional time you've been given. Unlike at many American wineries, wines bought at a winery in France are actually cheaper than they would be in a wine store (even a local one) and infinitely less than in a restaurant.

A few wine makers speak some English, but most do not, so even if you don't speak French, try to learn a few useful phrases before you go tasting. Guided tours of the winery or of the producer's house are considered a treat. If the wine maker does not offer to show you around, respect his or her individual style: Requesting a private tour is considered rude. And do your homework about the producer's wines; nothing pleases a wine maker more than an informed visitor.

Some of the wines you taste may be offered before their time, especially in the Bordeaux area where the red wines made from cabernet sauvignon grapes are designed for long aging. Because of French tax laws, it's expensive for wine makers to keep many bottles of their older wines on the premises. To taste older wines, you may need to buy them in a wine shop or order them in a restaurant. Always ask the wine maker if there is something you can taste that is already at its peak. If there is not, let the wine maker guide you through a tasting of a younger wine, explaining what you're tasting and how the wine is expected to evolve. Many officially too-young wines are very enjoyable even if they would be better, or at least more complex, after a few years in the bottle.

When you are given a glass of wine, take time to look at it to judge its color, swirl it in the glass a bit and sniff it, and only then put some wine in your mouth. Roll it around vigorously as though you were chewing it; the flavor will expand in your mouth. You are then expected to spit it out. The wine maker (usually a model of sobriety) will either give you something to spit into or point to a drain or other suitable spot. If you find this truly distasteful, have one taste, swallow, and throw the rest away. You can't taste if you're too drunk, and driving around tiny country roads in France with several glasses of wine under your belt is not a safe way to spend your holiday!

The goal of wine tasting is not to put on a buzz, but rather to savor the tastes, and exercise your discretionary talents. There is art in recalling an accent of oak or cinnamon that was found in one vineyard and not in another. As you fill your brain with knowledge, you also fill your tastebuds with delight—and what a painless way to learn more about all that life has to offer.

Fêtes et Foires (Festivals and Fairs)

France has perfected the art of organizing a festival—they've been having celebrations such as these since the Middle Ages. Nearly every town or village has at least one event that displays its costumes, food, wine, traditions, and culture. Here are just a few of the most enjoyable:

January

St-Vincent Festival, Patron Saint of Wine, Franche-Comté

St-Vincent Festival, Patron Saint of Wine, Burgundy

Sound-and-Light Show in the St-Pierre-aux-Nonnains Basilica, Lorraine (January-May)

February

Wine and Food Fair, Tain-l'Hermitage

Wine Fairs, Chalonnes-sur-Loire, Fondette, and Vouvray

March

Music Festival, Epinal (March-May)

Strasbourg International Film Festival

Wine Fair of the Loire Valley

Wine Fairs, Bourgueil, Chinon, and Thouars

Wine Festival, Nuits-St-Georges

Wine Festival, Cassis

April

Wine Fair, Saumur and Montlouis

Daffodil Festival, Lorraine

Marionette Festival, Lorraine

May

International Music Festival, Sarrebourg

Joan of Arc Festival, Domrémy

Medieval Festival, Vic-sur-Seille

Pentecost Folklore and Gastronomy Festival, Alsace

Wine Fair, Cadillac

Wine Festival, Mâcon

June

Festival of the Rosés, Tigne

Anjou-Saumur Art of Living Festival

Champagne Fairs, Troyes

Festival of the Jurade and of the Wine Blossom, St-Emilion

International Ballooning Festival, Villersexel (June-July)

International Music Festival, Strasbourg

Joan of Arc Festival, Reims

Wine and Regional Products Fair, Fronsac

July

Cahors Wine Festival

Aix Wine Festival, Aix-en-Provence

Grand Crus Musical Festival "From Bach to Bacchus" (mid-July–early August)

International Baroque Music Festival, Beaune

Jazz Festival, Strasbourg

National Street Artist Festival, Chalon-sur-Saône

St-Nicolas de Bourgueil Wine Fair

Traditional Folklore Festival, Obernai

Wine Fair, St-Chinian

August

Gaillac Wine Festival

Provençal Wine and Food Fair, Carpentras

Wine and Food Fair, Saulieu

Wine Fair, Vouvray

Wine Festival, Madiran

Garlic Festival, Mauvezin

September

Festival of Bonnezeaux, Thouarcé

Champagne Fairs, Bar-sur-Aube

Harvest Festival, St-Tropez

Harvest Festival, Tain l'Hermitage

Wine Festival and Médoc Marathon

October

International Gastronomy Fair, Dijon (late October–November)

International Jazz Festival, Nancy (Lorraine)

New Wine Festival, Itterswiller (Alsace)

Wine Harvesting Festival, Narlenheim (Alsace)

November

Les Trois Glorieuses de Bourgogne Wine Festival & Wine Auction, Beaune

Wine and Food Fairs, Dijon, Fleurie, and Brouilly

December

Christmas Market, Alsace

St-Nicolas Festival, Lorraine

Champagne and Alsace

The northernmost wine-growing regions in France, Champagne and Alsace (separated by non–wine-producing Lorraine), share similar weather conditions. Both are cooled by westerly winds, and are prone to mists. The bright green landscapes of hillsides in these cool lands are accentuated by bright colors in the fall, when the vine leaves transmute from green to gold to red. Both regions are fed by great rivers. The Champagne region's viniculture depends on the **Marne River** and its offshoots, while Alsace depends on the **Rhine**. Despite the regions' similarities, the wines they produce are very different in character. Champagne's famous products, among them Veuve Clicquot and Taittinger, are everywhere associated with celebratory toasts and the sounds of popping corks, and champagne is most often dry. Fruity, flowery Alsace wines—like

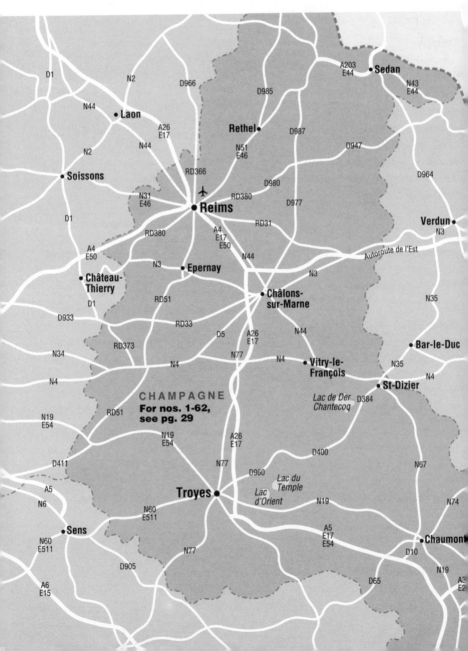

CHAMPAGNE
For nos. 1-62, see pg. 29

Gewürztraminer and Riesling—are still rather than bubbly and usually dry (except for late-harvest Sauternes-type sweet wines). Served up in their slim green bottles, they are full-bodied and substantial on the tongue, in contrast to Champagne's light, effervescent products.

Champagnes are made using an elaborate technique known as the *méthode champenoise* from select pinot noir, chardonnay, and pinot meunier grapes that thrive in a sometimes muted landscape of rolling green hills with white, chalky soil only 144 kilometers (90 miles) east of Paris. Champagne villages around **Reims** and **Epernay** tend to be built of pale gray stone, the houses cheered by brimming gardens. In the southern Champagne region are some timbered houses surrounded by lush vineyards and pine forests. About 300 kilometers (180 miles) east, on higher elevations near the German border, Alsace cultivates most of the same grape varieties found in Champagne, but adds other valued wine

fruits like the riesling, gewürztraminer, and muscat. Its vineyards lie between **Strasbourg** and **Mulhouse,** with **Colmar** the center of Alsatian wine country. Alsatian wine-making methods are conventional compared to Champagne's, and are carried out in Rhenish villages with lots of timber-beamed houses and geraniums; between towns lie mountain-shadowed valleys with crystal lakes and pine groves. The object of a long tug-of-war between France and Germany, Alsace has been continuously French since the end of World War I. But proximity to Germany and a lack of significant natural barriers have given it a German flavor—and have historically laid Alsace and the whole of northeastern France vulnerable to attack, most recently in the heavy aerial bombardments by the Germans in World Wars I and II. Many monuments remain, however, that date to Roman times.

Champagne's landscape can be austere, with pale green hills and open plains. The **Montagne de Reims** ("Mountain" of Reims), really just a craggy hill fringed with oak and nut trees, is northern Champagne's topographic high point and one of its most important vine growing areas. But the Champagne region's human touches—its sophisticated cities, Renaissance manors, tree-lined villages tucked into river bends, plus wine-associated landmarks like the elegant Moët-et-Chandon orangery with its reflecting pool at Epernay—enliven and prettify it. Alsace's beauty is more immediately inviting because it is both more dramatic and more accessible; its hill towns have the intimacy of mountain villages and its vineyards are concentrated in a tighter group. The region's soaring medieval citadels, like the one at **Haut-Koenigsbourg** (**Château du Haut-Koenigsbourg**), are reminders of the vicious border wars that plagued France and Germany for so long. Both now members of the European Union, the two countries no longer even check passports at their Rhineland frontier.

Ecclesiastical architecture varies enormously throughout Alsace and Champagne, from the Gothic pantheon in Reims (the **Cathédrale de Notre Dame de Reims**) to a Dominican monastery in Colmar. In the countryside between lie Romanesque and Benedictine chapels. Around **Hautvillers,** just north of Epernay, churches show a great influence of Napoleonic Imperial style, their square bell towers topped with bulblike turrets.

Meanwhile, the agricultural and dairy products of the Champagne region, like its native brie, make for some bountiful markets and excellent restaurant meals. Alsace's foods tend to be flavored by Germanic influences, but regional preparations of smoked trout or wild mushrooms are distinctly Alsatian, and are as much loved by the French as any other of their native cuisines.

Getting to and around Champagne and Alsace

Airports

The **Aéroport Reims-Champagne** (26.07.15.15) is in Bétheny, seven kilometers (four miles) from Reims. A limited number of regional flights and charters fly through this airport.

Airport Services

Airport Emergencies 26.09.01.12

Currency Exchange 26.07.03.60

The **Aéroport International de Strasbourg-Entzheim** (88.64.67.67) is about 13 kilometers (8.1 miles) from the center of Strasbourg. The airport services domestic and European flights. All major car-rental companies have offices here, and several flights travel daily to Paris and other destinations on **Air Inter** and other carriers.

Airport Services

Customs 88.68.81.65

Parking 88.68.95.86

Police 88.68.90.80

Car Rental

Colmar

Ada Location 89.23.90.30

Avis 89.23.21.82

Europcar 89.24.11.80

Hertz 89.41.18.41

Loca Plus 89.71.72.02

Reims

Ada 26.50.08.40

Avis 26.47.10.08

Budget 26.82.20.02

Citer 26.04.68.56

Europcar 26.88.38.38

EuroRent 26.47.15.80

Hertz 26.47.98.78

Strasbourg

Allocar 88.84.00.55

AS Location 88.28.97.97

Avis 88.32.30.44

Budget 88.75.68.29

Century 88.35.34.88

Europcar 88.22.18.00

Hertz 88.32.52.62

Rent a Car 88.52.25.52

Trains

Several trains make the trip each day between the **Gare SNCF** in Colmar (Rue de la Gare, at Rue Messimy, 89.24.50.50) and Paris's Gare de l'Est. The trip takes about five hours.

Several trains also travel daily between Reims's **Gare SNCF** (Blvd Joffre, at Rue Thiers, 26.88.50.50) and Paris's Gare de l'Est. The trip takes about 1.5 hours. Several trains make the 25-minute trip between Reims and Epernay daily. There's an **Avis** office (26.47.10.08) in the Reims train station.

In Strasbourg, the **Gare Centrale SNCF** (20 Pl de la Gare, at Rue Maire-Kuss, information 88.22.50.50, reservations 88.32.07.51) is west of the Old City. This hub has good connections to several European cities, including Brussels, Frankfurt, and Zurich. Although the *TGV* doesn't yet travel between Paris and Strasbourg, regular trains depart daily from Paris's Gare de l'Est and make the trip to Strasbourg in less than four hours (connections available to other French and international destinations). There is an **Avis** office (88.32.30.44) in the Strasbourg train station.

FYI

Visitors' Information Offices

Colmar's **Office de Tourisme** (4 Rue des Unterlinden, between Rue du Rempart and Rue de Ribeauville, 89.20.68.92) is open daily. It has many useful maps and brochures in English on the city's attractions.

Epernay's **Office de Tourisme** (7 Ave du Champagne, between Pl de la République and Rue J.-Chandon-Moët, 26.55.33.00) is open daily from Easter to mid-October, Monday through Saturday from mid-October to Easter. It provides information on the city's champagne houses in French and English.

The **Office de Tourisme** (2 Rue Guillaume-de-Machault, at Pl du Trésor, 26.47.25.69; fax 26.47.23.63) in Reims is open daily. Most of the brochures, maps, and other documents are available in English.

Strasbourg's efficient **Office de Tourisme** (17 Pl de la Cathédrale, between the Cathedral and the Rue des Hallebardes, 88.52.28.22) is open daily from April through October and Monday through Saturday November through March. The staff will arrange dinner cruises down the **Ill River** and tours of the city.

Wine Organizations

The **Comité Interprofessionnel du Vin de Champagne** (5 Rue Henri-Martin, between Rue Maurice-Cerveaux and Rue des Jancelins, 26.54.47.20; fax 26.55.19.79) in Epernay is a professional wine organization that has tons of material on Champagne: its history, economy, lists of wineries that welcome visitors, and so forth. Some of the brochures are available in English. It is open Monday through Friday.

The principal Alsace wine group is the **Comité Interprofessionel des Vins d'Alsace** (Maison des Vins, 12 Ave de la Foire-au-Vin, 89.20.16.20; fax 89.20.16.30) in Colmar. (It's signposted.) Only the reception area, with fact sheets on the classifications and history of Alsatian wine, is open to the public; the organization's main function is to service wine professionals.

Phone Book

Hospitals		Police (nonemergencies)	
Colmar	89.80.40.00	Colmar	89.24.75.00
Epernay	26.58.70.70	Epernay	26.54.11.17
Reims	26.78.78.78	Reims	26.61.44.00
Strasbourg	88.16.17.18	Strasbourg	88.32.89.08

Champagne

The people of Champagne have a reputation for reserve, not ebullience; even tourist literature published in English acknowledges this. Villagers seem to retreat behind their shuttered windows at midday, leaving the flower-filled squares to birds and passing tourists until early evening. Their compatriots have found that by respecting this natural distance, contact can eventually be made—especially when it involves mutual interest in champagne.

The four main vineyard areas in Champagne are the **Montagne de Reims**, **Vallée de la Marne**, **Côte des Blancs**, and the **Aube.** The Champagne region's center is the city of **Reims**, where many of France's great champagne houses are clustered; the surrounding growing region is known as the Montagne de Reims. **Epernay** and **Ay**, to the southwest, are the other great champagne centers, and are within the Vallée de la Marne (Marne Valley). The Côte des Blancs, a hilly region where only white grapes are grown, lies just south of Epernay. **Troyes**, Champagne's ancient capital, is the southernmost champagne center. The area east and south of Troyes is known as the Aube (Dawn), after the river. The landscape here is more elevated, and crossed by swaths of oak and pine forest. Villages in this area typically contain a few medieval half-timbered houses set off with flowered window boxes. This part of Champagne makes a lesser-known, fruitier champagne than the northern Champagne region, as well as a good rosé (the rare, still Rosé de Riceys, from **Les Riceys**), and is far less visited.

Real champagne comes only from Champagne. A combination of limited high-quality vineyard land (the rare great *terroirs,* or vineyard terrains, of the Champagne vineyards have chalk subsoil going down hundreds of feet in places), rising prices for fine grapes (most major houses buy their grapes from growers), and an expensive process has driven prices of the best champagnes to unheard-of heights in recent years. The good news is that, faced with declining sales in their biggest export markets (England and the United States) and increased competition from cheaper bubblies made with the *méthode champenoise,* producers of real champagne have recently determined to keep prices under control. Many have started offering special deals to restaurants throughout France so that the wines will actually be affordable to restaurateurs and their customers.

Most producers also have been stepping up efforts to attract visitors to this wine taster's paradise. Possibilities range from the highly organized, instructive tour of **Moët-et-Chandon**'s splendid headquarters in Epernay to a cozy chat in the cellars with one of scores of small-scale village wine makers whose product may be superb but little known—and half the price of the "greats." This is *the* only place to see real champagne in the making, and to purchase varieties you might never see at home.

France cultivates a total of 35,000 hectares (86,500 acres) of vineyards within the Champagne appellation, two percent of France's total acres under vines, with most of them concentrated around Reims and Epernay in the Marne *département* east of Paris. The vineyards of Champagne are among Europe's oldest; native vines grew here in the Tertiary era, from one to 60 million years ago. The Romans were responsible for expanding wine production here, as elsewhere in France.

Dom Pierre Pérignon (1638-1715), cellar master at the **Abbaye de St-Pierre d'Hautvillers** (St. Peter of Hautvillers Abbey), north of Epernay, is usually credited with "inventing" champagne, although a slightly bubbly, very fresh-tasting wine was already being made in Champagne before his time. But Dom Pérignon did come up with the concept of *cuvée,* in which wines from different vineyards and vintages are blended to achieve the best possible taste, a practice that all champagne makers still follow. The still-revered Dom supposedly could identify any grape by taste alone, down to the vineyard it came from, and knew with what other grapes it should be pressed to achieve the best *cuvée.* Today's champagne producers aren't required to make such split-second decisions; they blend the grapes' juices only after the first fermentation.

Surprisingly, one of the most prized grape varieties used in making champagne, particularly in northern Champagne around Reims, is the pinot noir, Burgundy's great red wine grape. The black pinot meunier grape (which generally gives roundness, but not heavy coloration, to a wine) and white chardonnay (for finesse) are also used, and the juices from these different grape types (sometimes from different vintages) are usually combined to produce a *cuvée.* What distinguishes one brand of champagne from another is partly the proportions of grape varieties in a particular *cuvée,* or whether the *cuvée* is made from one type of grape alone. But what many outside the champagne industry do not understand is that not only is the choice of grape variety crucial to a *cuvée,* so is the choice of *terroir.*

Vineyard quality is as important for champagne as for any other wine. There are 17 official *grand cru terroirs* in Champagne, each one named for the particular village around which the great vineyards lie; the term indicates the finest possible conditions and methods for grape cultivation. Next down the scale (some would say the difference is small, others say large) are the *premier cru* vineyard sites, of which there are 42. Some top champagne producers make *cuvées* derived totally or partially from the fruit of either or both of these select vineyards, which explains why certain bottles of champagne taste so good—and cost so much. If the champagne is neither *grand* nor *premier,* it will show only its *commune* (village or locality) on the label.

In the champagne process, grape juice is fermented without the skins. (Skins give the red color, as in red burgundy made with the pinot noir grape, for example.) After this first fermentation and the *cuvée* blending, the wine is bottled and made to ferment again, which causes carbon dioxide gas to form in the bottle (hence the bubbles). This second fermentation produces sediment that is removed in an ingenious process called *remuage,* in which bottles are placed on slanting racks, cork down, and turned (usually by machine nowadays) every day for two or three months, until the sediment has collected into a lump against the bottom of the cork. The necks of the bottles are then dipped into an ice-cold solution and the bottles opened so that the frozen lump of sediment shoots out with the cork, propelled by the gases within. The bottles are then usually topped up with aged champagne and cane sugar (the amount determines the sweetness of the final product), and recorked. Then the champagnes are aged in the bottle before being sold, a year for ordinary champagne and a minimum of three years for the great vintage bottles. Many top champagne houses age their wines much longer before releasing them; aging makes the bubbles finer and the taste more harmonious. Wines aged with their lees (before the sediment is popped out) for a longer than usual time are labeled "R.D." for *récemment dégorgé* (recently disgorged), and usually have exceptionally rich flavor.

Reims

This large provincial city (whose name rhymes with "lance") 144 kilometers (90 miles) east of Paris is home to many of the biggest champagne houses in the world. Beyond its city center are bucolic fields of wheat and sugar beet, but the city itself is a sophisticated place of modern business and ancient landmarks. Wine bars, fine restaurants, and chic fashion boutiques flourish, but the city's focal point is the magnificent, Gothic **Cathédrale de Notre Dame de Reims** (Our Lady of Reims Cathedral) and the historic district that surrounds it. The kings of France were crowned here for centuries, from 1137 (Louis VII) to 1825 (Charles X). That tradition was inspired by the fact that the city's patron saint, St. Remi, crowned Clovis King of the Franks here in AD 496. Before then, the site had been the capital of a Gallic tribe, the Remi, and then became a major Roman trading center. Another fine old landmark is the **Porte de Mars,** a Roman arch dating from around AD 200, on the **Place de la République.** The city is built above a labyrinth of champagne caves, most of which were dug in Gallo-Roman times. The Romans dug for chalk in the *crayère* (a local white limestone) and left cone-shaped caves that were broad at the bottom and rose to airholes at the top. These caves were probably used for centuries to store perishable foods; today they make ideal wine cellars because they remain at stable chilly temperatures throughout the year. A local treat is *croquignolles,* sweet, dry biscuits designed to accompany champagne. Try them at any local pastry shop. Other than the champagne houses described in the entries below, good champagne houses in Reims that accept visitors—by appointment only—include **Lanson** (12 Blvd Lundy, at Pl Aristide-Briand, 26.78.50.50); **Henriot,** whose cellars were dug by the Romans (3 Pl des Droits-de-l'Homme, between Blvd Diancourt and Ave du Général-Giraud, 26.89.53.00; fax 26.03.53.10); **Roederer** (21 Blvd Lundy, between Rue du Champ-de-Mars and Rue Coquebert, 26.40.42.11; fax 26.47.66.51), and **Bruno Paillard,** founded in 1981 and already known for its stringent grape selection and excellent wines, particularly the vintage bruts (Ave de Champagne, at Allée du Vignoble, 26.36.20.22; fax 26.36.57.72).

1 Cathédrale de Notre Dame de Reims
(Our Lady of Reims Cathedral) Designed by 13th-century master builder **Jean d'Orbais,** this cathedral is one of the purest examples of 13th-century French Gothic architecture in the world. Note especially the beautiful western facade—it's spectacular around sunset—with its many statues, including the *ange au sourire* (the smiling angel). Also known as the *sourire de Reims* (smile of Reims), the statue stands next to scalped St. Niçaise in the left portal. Although the 13th-century stained-glass windows were destroyed in a disastrous bombing during World War I, many of them have been restored; a set of stunning modern stained-glass windows designed by Marc Chagall was installed in 1974. For almost 800 years the cathedral was the site of most coronations in France. Saturday and Sunday evenings in July bring the excitement of son et lumière (sound-and-light shows) featuring laser imagery, music, and commentary (in French) on great events in the cathedral's past. ♦ The main entrance is on Pl du Cardinal-Luçon (on Rue des Fuseliers, between Rue Cardinal-de-Lorraine and Rue Rockefeller). 26.82.49.49

Colmar has the lowest rainfall in France.

Restaurants/Clubs: Red	**Hotels:** Blue
Shops/ 🌳 Outdoors: Green	**Sights/Culture:** Black

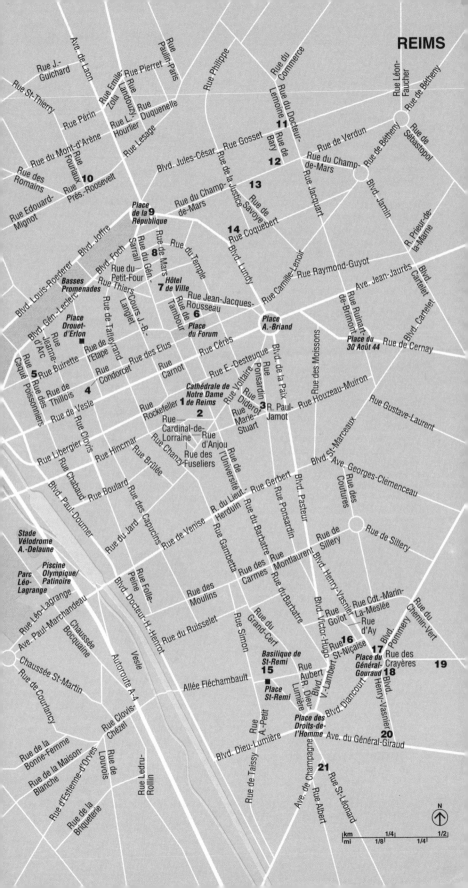

2 Palais du Tau This building was once shaped like the letter it is named for: the Greek tau, which is our "T." It has gone through so many changes, you would never spot the "T" today. The original structure, an episcopal palace, was built in 1138. In the 13th century a chapel was added, and in the 15th century a large rectangular room replaced the 12th-century structure and became known as *Salle de Tau* (Tau Room). The kings of France celebrated here with elaborate feasts immediately following their coronations, which took place in the cathedral next door. The main building you see today was built in 1690, and within it are the 13th-century chapel, the *Salle de Tau*, and a collection of medieval and Renaissance art, religious relics, statuary, and tapestries, including a ninth-century talisman carried by Charlemagne and an 11th-century crystal reliquary belonging to St.-Epine. ♦ Admission. Daily (no midday closing) July-Aug; daily Sept-June. Rue Cardinal-de-Lorraine (between Ave France and Rue d'Anjou, next to the cathedral). 26.47.74.39

3 Le Vigneron ★★$$ Hervé Liégent's passion for his region and its wines really shows in his restaurant—the whole place is decorated with antique posters on Champagne and he cooks nothing but authentic regional fare. Try the *brochet aux escargots au beurre de champagne* (pike with snails in champagne-butter sauce). Local wine makers have made this place their hangout; with a superb wine list, including 300 champagnes, it's no wonder! ♦ M-F lunch and dinner; Sa dinner; closed late December–early January, first two weeks in August. Reservations recommended. Pl Paul Jamot (between Rue Diderot and Rue Ponsardin). 26.47.00.71; fax 26.47.87.66

4 Eglise St-Jacques This small stone church contains architectural features from many different periods. It is most famous for its 13th- to 14th-century nave with a triforium, an arcaded gallery above the ground floor. It also contains an early 16th-century choir in the Flamboyant Gothic style, which is flanked by two mid-16th-century chapels that feature Corinthian columns. The original stained-glass windows, destroyed during World War I, were replaced by modern windows with geometric designs by the artists Viera da Silva and Sima. ♦ Rue Condorcet (at Rue Drouet-d'Erlon). No phone

The Impressionist painter Pierre-Auguste Renoir and his wife are buried in the churchyard in Essoyes, along with their progeny—Pierre (the actor) and Jean (the filmmaker). The house on the edge of town in which the family lived from 1897 to 1916 is marked by a plaque.

5 Holiday Inn Garden Court $$ All the modern comforts and good value you'd expect from the famous chain. This 80-room contemporary hotel also has a seventh-floor restaurant, **Le Jéroboam,** that has a great view of the entire city of Reims and the surrounding countryside; unfortunately, the view is far better than the food. An added plus: Many rooms are nonsmoking, a rarity in France. ♦ 46 Rue Buirette (at Rue Caqué). 26.47.56.00; fax 26.47.45.75

6 Hôtel le Vergeur/Musée du Vieux Reims (Museum of Old Reims) Once a private home, this half-timber building dating to the 13th-century now houses Reims's historical museum. Along with paintings and sculptures relating to the history of Reims, the museum showcases works by Flemish and Dutch artists, including a noteworthy collection of engravings by Albrecht Dürer. There are also period rooms filled with antiques from the 19th century. ♦ Admission. Tu-Su afternoon. 36 Pl du Forum (between Rue du Marc-Pluche and Rue de Tambour). 26.47.20.75

7 Hôtel de Ville Appropriately enough for a city with so many architectural treasures, Reims's City Hall—or at least its facade—is a historic landmark. Originally a 17th-century aristocratic residence, the multistoried white stone building was almost completely destroyed by fire in 1917. Its impressive facade, now the entrance to a more modern building, boasts many decorative carvings, including a huge representation of Louis XIII on horseback above the main entrance. The interior houses the offices of various city government organizations. ♦ Pl de l'Hôtel-de-Ville (between Rue de Tambour and Rue du Général-Sarrail). 26.40.54.53

8 Au Petit Comptoir ★★$$ The exceptional cooking of Reims's star chef, Gérard Boyer, should not be missed. But if a meal at his **Restaurant Les Crayères/Gérard Boyer** (see page 28) will leave you without a sou, come to this friendly bistro for a taste of his fine cuisine at affordable prices. The decor in this ancient stone building is very traditional—exposed-beam ceilings, plain white tablecloths, and bouquets of fresh flowers—and the kitchen excels in the simple fare your grandmother might have made had she grown up in Champagne. The menu changes regularly, but you'll find dishes like *tourte de lapereau* (two-crust rabbit pie), *mousseline de brochet* (pike mousse), and *crumble* (apple crumble). The wine list is short, but well chosen. Prices are very low for the high quality, and the fixed-price menu is a steal. ♦ M–F lunch and dinner; Sa dinner; closed in late December and mid-August. Reservations recommended. 17 Rue de Mars (between Rue du Temple and Rue du Petit-Four). 26.40.58.58

9 Porte de Mars Once a gate in the city's walls, this monumental triumphal arch dating back to the third century is a fine example of Gallo-Roman architecture. The arch, built of stone that has weathered to shades of dark gray and creamy yellow, looks like a smaller version of Paris's Arc de Triomphe (Arch of Triumph) and, like the capital's, was constructed to celebrate military might, in this case Julius Caesar's. In the Middle Ages the arch was incorporated into a defensive wall built around the city and made into a *porte* (gate). Though time has taken its toll, take a look at what's left of its once exquisite, now very eroded, bas-reliefs. A constant stream of exhaust-spewing traffic may prevent this monument from lasting another 1,800 years. ♦ Pl de la République (at the intersection of Blvd Foch, Blvd Joffre, Ave de Laon, Blvd Jules-César, Rue du Champ-de-Mars, and Blvd Lundy)

10 Salle de Reddition (Hall of the Surrender) World War II history buffs should take a look at the simple schoolroom here. Although the rest of this former school is now office space, this room has been kept exactly as it was when General Eisenhower used it as his headquarters during the last days of the war. It was here that the German Army signed its treaty of surrender a half century ago, on 7 May 1945. The battered desk on which the treaty was signed, maps showing troop movements, and various 1940s memorabilia are a vivid reminder of the past. ♦ Admission. M, W–Su. 12 Rue Président-Roosevelt (at Rue Fouriaux). 26.47.84.19

11 Jacquart This forward-thinking cooperative's powerful, full-flavored wines—many of which are dominated by pinot noir—are the basis of its success at home and abroad. The winery is housed in a contemporary building notable for a colorful modern mosaic on its facade that depicts the champagne-making process. The nonvintage Tradition label tends to be fruity, while the nonvintage Sélection is more powerful. The well-named Onctueuse (Unctuous) pink champagne goes well with desserts, and the La Nominée *blanc de blancs* has a high percentage of chardonnay, with overtones of vanilla and toast. The tour takes you through ultramodern cellars and a video (in French) explains the champagne process. Be sure to pick up the informative brochure (also in French) to learn more about the wines. ♦ Free. M–Sa by appointment. 5 Rue Gosset (at Rue du Docteur-Lemoine). 26.89.54.40; fax 26.07.12.07

12 Chapelle Foujita (Foujita Chapel) Also known as "Notre-Dame de la Paix" (Our Lady of Peace), this Romanesque chapel was designed by the Japanese painter Léonard Foujita and built by his godfather, René Lalou, in 1965-66 following Foujita's conversion to Catholicism in Reims. The frescoes by Foujita and the stained-glass windows are strikingly beautiful. ♦ Admission. M–Tu, Th–Su; closed during very cold weather. 33 Rue du Champ-de-Mars (at Rue de Bary). No phone

13 Mumm This house is known for fruity champagnes with very little acidity. The expensive Cuvée René Lalou 1985, made from half pinot noir, half chardonnay grapes, is one of their best. It has a powerful, mouth-filling taste. Surrounded by trees, the winery is housed in a huge building dating from 1920, which was built to replace an earlier structure destroyed during World War I. Bas-reliefs on the facade illustrate wine making. With the exception of the *crayère* (a local chalky limestone) cellars, which date from Gallo-Roman times, everything inside the winery is ultramodern, from the video projection room to the tasting area. The tour begins with a video, followed by an hourlong walk through the cellars—wear comfortable shoes and a sweater—which house 35 million bottles. Multilingual guides explain how champagne is made. There's also a look at a little museum of wine makers' tools, and a tasting at the end of the tour. ♦ Free. Daily Mar-Oct; M–F Nov-Feb. 34 Rue du Champ-de-Mars (at Rue de Savoye). 26.49.59.69; fax 26.40.46.13

14 Krug This prestigious house has been owned by the Krug family for six generations and is on most people's lists as one of the greatest champagne producers of all time. But unlike its competitors, the Krug family does not go out of its way to attract tourists. Their efforts are clearly focused on making great wine, rather than on making a great impression. The winery itself is a simple, medium-sized white building that dates from 1860 but has been completely rebuilt in modern style. The building is so discreet-looking that you may have trouble spotting it; even the "Krug" sign over the door is very small. Quality rather than quantity is the emphasis here—they produce only around 500,000 bottles per year, all top class, such as the very dry Grande Cuvée and the very rare single-vineyard Clos de Mesnil, a masterpiece of finesse. All the wines are aged in the bottle a minimum of six years before being released. The Krug Grande Cuvée illustrates the kind of effort Dom Pérignon's notion of *cuvée* can involve if perfection is the goal: It's a blend of 40 to 50 wines from 20 to

25 *crus* and six to 10 vintages. Although this house is not geared toward tourism, the family will allow visits by very small groups (in English on request) if arrangements are made well in advance. The tour gives a look at the small oak barrels still used for the wine's first fermentation, another factor that sets **Krug** apart from the rest. ♦ Free. M-F by appointment. 5 Rue Coquebert (between Blvd Lundy and Rue de la Justice). 26.89.44.20; fax 26.84.44.49

15 Basilique de St-Remi (St. Remi Basilica) Built mainly in the 11th century and restored in the 12th century in Gothic style, this basilica is the city's oldest surviving church. Its stained-glass windows, carvings, and decorative elements date from many different centuries, but all were restored after the basilica was bombed during World War I. Try to attend one of the Saturday evening concerts performed here during the summer. ♦ Pl St-Remi (between Rue Simon and Rue du Grand-Cerf). No phone

Next to the Basilique de St-Remi, across a small courtyard:

Musée St-Remi (St. Remi Museum) If you thought Reims was just a great place to sample champagne, this museum will change your mind. Installed in an 18th-century stone structure that contains some elements of the 13th-century Benedictine abbey that once stood on this spot, the museum was used as a field hospital during World War I and was heavily bombed. Now lovingly restored, it contains a remarkable collection of objects and artworks related to the life of St. Remi and to the town of Reims itself. Among the treasures on display are many archaeological finds dating from the city's Gallo-Roman period, including a mosaic of a gladiator and a third-century Roman tomb. There's a lovely 17th-century stone staircase leading to a spacious room where the *Dix Tapisseries de St-Remi* (Ten St. Remi Tapestries) are displayed. These still-vivid, intricately designed tapestries created in 1531 illustrate scenes in the life of the saint. Another room in the museum houses a collection of sculpture from the 11th to the 16th century that clearly shows the evolution of medieval art. ♦ Admission. M-F 2PM-6:30PM; Sa-Su 2PM-7PM.26.85.23.36

The ideal temperature at which to serve champagne is 45-48 degrees Fahrenheit. The preferred way to achieve this ideal is to chill the bottle in an ice bucket for 30 minutes. If you don't have an ice bucket, the next best choice is to place the bottle in the warmest part of a refrigerator (never the freezer!) for three to four hours.

16 Taittinger Housed in a sprawling modern building surrounded by a large garden filled with trees and flowers, this winery is known for the high percentage of chardonnay used in most of its wines. The exceptions are the Comtes de Champagne rosé, with its overtones of raspberries, which is made entirely from pinot noir, and the fruity Prestige, made from one-third each pinot noir, chardonnay, and pinot meunier. Their chardonnay-dominated wines usually have a rich aroma and a full taste, with hints of almonds and apricots. The visit takes you through some of the loveliest cellars in the region: You'll see white limestone cellars carved out in Gallo-Roman times, as well as the vestiges of a 12th-century chapel and parts of the 15th-century crypt of the **Abbaye de St-Niçaise** (Abbey of St. Nicaise). The cellar's gleaming white walls are dramatically lit to emphasize every angle and ancient quarry mark. Tastings and sales are in a modernly decorated room. ♦ Admission. Daily Mar-Nov; M-F Dec-Feb. 9 Rue St-Niçaise (between Rue d'Ay and Blvd Victor-Hugo). 26.85.45.35; fax 26.85.44.39

17 Piper-Heidsieck Set in two elegant stone-and-stucco buildings dating from the 1950s, this prestigious champagne house offers one of the most sophisticated tours around. You cruise through the miles of underground cellars in little train cars guided by laser beams, and watch a media extravaganza on the life of champagne grapes and how the wine is made. The tour is so Disneyesque that you may suspect the quality of the wines to be inferior, but they are actually among the region's best. Some people say Piper-Heidsieck champagnes are more appropriate for toasting an occasion than for accompanying a meal, because they are particularly delicate. The outstanding rosé will convert you if you've never liked pink champagne, and the frightfully expensive Brut Sauvage 1982 (super dry), made from 70 percent pinot noir, is the essence of finesse. The tour concludes with a tasting. ♦ Admission. Daily Mar-Nov; M-Th Dec-Feb. 51 Blvd Henry-Vasnier (at Pl du Général-Gouraud). 26.84.43.00, 26.84.43.50, 26.84.43.44; fax 26.84.43.49

Restaurants/Clubs: Red   **Hotels:** Blue
Shops/ ♀ Outdoors: Green   **Sights/Culture:** Black

18 Pommery In 1858 Madame Pommery, a 39-year-old recent widow with children to raise, decided to turn her small champagne dealer's business into a champagne production house, even though she knew nothing about making champagne. She succeeded. Among the first to recognize the importance of the quality of the vineyards from which champagne grapes come, she began to buy vineyard land. The rest is history. This famous champagne house not only makes excellent wines; it's also one of the most distinctive-looking local wineries and it has extraordinary cellars. The huge Victorian–Neo-Gothic building has tall crenellated towers and arched windows; as if the design weren't unusual enough, it is built of redbrick and dark gray stucco with bands of white stone. It's not elegant, but it certainly stands out.

Known for fine, delicate champagnes, **Pommery** is among the few champagne houses that still grow most of their own grapes. It has 300 hectares (741 acres) of prime vineyards, most of it near Reims. The 1988, made from half pinot noir and half chardonnay grapes, has a slightly toasty taste with the finesse typical of **Pommery** wines. The Cuvée Spéciale Louise Pommery vintage champagne is at the top of the line; it's made from Avize and Cramant chardonnay, and Ay pinot noir.

An hourlong trek leads through magnificent cellars, part of which date from Gallo-Roman times. (Wear comfortable shoes and bring a sweater; the cellars are quite chilly.) To enter the cellars, you descend 116 steep steps. Once there you're led past some famous underground landmarks. First there's a giant oak wine cask created in 1904 that holds almost 20,000 gallons; it's adorned by an elaborate carving by Emile Gallé of three women in Victorian dress (all representing Madame Pommery) picking grapes and making wine. There are also two bas-reliefs carved into the limestone walls of the cellars: One, which dates from 1883, depicts an 18th-century dinner party at which fancily clad guests drink from tall, cone-shaped glasses; the other, which dates from 1986 but is Neo-Classical in style, depicts Madame Pommery as a goddess with grapes in her hair. Overhead, throughout the gleaming white cellars, are long, conical skylights that were hollowed out of stone in Gallo-Roman times. ♦ Free. Daily May-Oct; M-F Nov-Apr. Many guides speak English. English-language tours are offered in summer; inquire ahead for times. 5 Pl du Général-Gouraud (between Rue des Crayères and Blvd Henry-Vasnier). 26.61.62.63; fax 26.61.63.98

19 Ruinart This venerable champagne house, supposedly the oldest commercial winery in Champagne, was founded in 1729 by Nicolas Ruinart, the nephew of Dom Thierry Ruinart, a Benedictine monk who learned about champagne making from his friend Dom Pérignon. The winery is housed in a U-shaped two-story stone-and-stucco building, with white shutters at each of its seemingly endless number of windows, surrounding a wide cobblestone courtyard. Chardonnay dominates the wines here, and is the only grape used in the Cuvée Dom Ruinart. The grapes come from the Montagne de Reims, particularly from vineyards near Sillery, and from the Côte des Blancs district. These elegant wines have a powerful, flowery aroma when they're young, which becomes even more intense, with hints of honey, as they age. The incredibly beautiful cellars, carved out of *crayère* (limestone), are dramatically lit to show off the elegant curves and angles of the sculptured stone. Reputed to be Reims's oldest, these *caves* (cellars) date from the second century BC and are classified a historic landmark. ♦ Free. Daily by appointment. Tours are limited to 10 people; ask whether an English-speaking guide will be available. 4 Rue des Crayères (at Rue du Chemin-Vert). 26.85.40.29; fax 26.82.88.43

LES CRAYÈRES

GERARD BOYER

20 Hôtel Les Crayères/Gérard Boyer $$$$ Champagne is a wine to splurge on, so where better to splurge on a great hotel and restaurant than in Champagne? Of all France's top auberges, Gérard Boyer's establishment is one of the few that never seem to hit a false note. Surrounded by its own 14-acre park, this elegant, white, turn-of-the-century château has 16 splendid rooms and three huge suites. Each room is unique, and despite the fact that every nook and cranny exudes luxury, the warm, cozy atmosphere makes guests feel at home. You'll find beautiful fabrics, several nice pieces of antique furniture, paintings, good lighting, big windows with views of the park, and completely equipped bathrooms. All rooms have air-conditioning and satellite televisions, among other amenities. Sit out on the terrace and sip (what else?) fine champagne, or if the weather doesn't cooperate, convene with other guests in the glass-enclosed terrace, whose potted plants and wicker armchairs will make you feel as though you've stepped right into a Proust novel. It costs a fortune, but this establishment gives excellent value for the money. And the management makes a point of being friendly. ♦ Closed Christmas–mid-January. 64 Blvd Henry-Vasnier (between Ave du Général-Giraud and Blvd Diancourt). 26.82.80.80; fax 26.82.65.52

Within the Hôtel Les Crayères/Gérard Boyer:

Restaurant Les Crayères/Gérard Boyer

★★★★$$$$ Gérard Boyer is one of France's most famous chefs, and his restaurant is one of the country's most highly rated. The menu continuously evolves, but you'll find treats like *ravioli de petit gris au jus au basilic* (ravioli filled with tiny snails and served with a light basil sauce), *filet de bar rôti sur sa peau au Bouzy rouge et à la moelle* (whole sea perch roasted in a sauce of Bouzy wine—Champagne's only red—and beef marrow), *panaché de poissons grillés, au beurre de truffes* (mixed grilled fish with truffle butter), *côte de boeuf "angus d'aberdeen" poêlée sauce à la moelle* (Angus beef sautéed with a beef marrow sauce), and *noix de ris de veau braisé, ses légumes, une galette croustillante de pommes de terre* (braised veal sweetbreads with vegetables and a crispy potato cake). Dessert lovers will go wild over the made-to-order delights here. You can choose from the simple (apple tart with vanilla ice cream) to the exotic (caramelized mangoes with passion-fruit juice accompanied by ice cream flavored with pepper and anise). The wine list, with 650 labels, includes 200 champagnes from a wide range of producers, served at lower prices here than at many other places. ♦ W-Su lunch and dinner; Tu dinner; closed Christmas–mid-January. Reservations required. 26.82.80.80

21 **Veuve Clicquot Ponsardin** The *veuve* (widow) was Nicole Barbe Ponsardin, who had wed François Clicquot in a wine cellar in 1798; after her husband's death, Nicole Clicquot took over the family champagne operation and invented the ingenious process of *remuage*, in which bottles of champagne are kept cork down, at an angle, and gradually turned so that the sediment collects around the cork. Madame Clicquot used a table with holes cut into it, but today most champagne houses use turning machines. With vineyards in 12 of Champagne's 17 *grand cru* sites, this house is known for powerful, full-flavored, fruity wines made with a high percentage of pinot noir. The excellent nonvintage brut is a great buy, but the vintage wines are the real stars. The Grande Dame 1985 is a perfect example of the importance of *terroirs:* Chardonnay grapes from vineyards near the village of Avize give it a slightly flowery taste, while the same grape grown near the village of Mesnil gives it mineral overtones. The winery is housed in a large 19th-century manor house surrounded by a garden. The tour includes a video, a visit to a museum of wine tools, a look at the cellars, and a tasting. ♦ Free. Visits and tastings M-Sa by appointment Apr-Oct; closed January-March, November-December. Reservations required for the tour 48 hours in advance; ask whether an English-speaking guide will be available. 1 Pl des Droits-de-l'Homme (at the intersection of Rue Albert and Rue St-Léonard). 26.40.25.42; fax 26.40.60.17

Reims Environs

22 **La Garenne** ★★★$$$ In a little village just outside Reims, this quintessential French country restaurant offers a warm welcome and excellent traditional cuisine. The pistachio-colored walls and lots of gleaming antique furniture add to the atmosphere. Try chef Laurent Laplaige's *fricassée de rognons et ris de veau aux champignons de bois* (fricassee of veal kidneys and sweetbreads with wild mushrooms) or *asperges et girolles en sauce légère* (asparagus and wild chanterelle mushrooms in a light sauce). The *nougatine à la menthe glacé* (caramel and mint ice cream) is a delicious way to end any meal. The very reasonably priced wine list has a fine selection of champagnes. ♦ Tu-Sa lunch and dinner; Su lunch; closed the first three weeks of August. Champigny (7 km/4.3 miles northwest of Reims on N31-E46). 26.08.26.62; fax 26.84.24.13

Auberge du Val des Bois

23 **Auberge du Val des Bois** ★$ This friendly family-run auberge in the countryside northeast of Reims is perfect for those on a budget—just stick to the fixed-price menus; ordering à la carte can prove costly. The restaurant serves regional dishes like *feuilleté d'escargots au beurre vert* (puff pastry filled with snails and herb butter) and *escalope de ris de veau Rossini* (veal sweetbreads with a rich mushroom sauce); there's chocolate cake for dessert. Most of the 21 simple guest rooms upstairs have private bathrooms; all are comfortable and quiet. ♦ M-F lunch and dinner; Sa dinner; Su lunch; closed late December–early January. Reservations recommended. In the center of Warmeriville (from Reims take N51-E46 northeast about 17 km/10.5 miles and follow the signs to Warmeriville). 26.03.32.09

24 **Auberge Le Cheval Blanc** $$ The same family has run this charming, old-fashioned inn for five generations. It is in an ancient, vine-covered stone house that makes a good base for touring champagne country. The 18 simple but very comfortable guest rooms have private bathrooms and views of the surrounding garden. There are also seven luxurious (and expensive) suites; some have private terraces overlooking the tranquil Vesle River. This is an official *Relais de Silence*, meaning peace and quiet are guaranteed. ♦ Closed mid-January–mid-February. Rue du Moulin, Sept-Saulx (from Reims follow N44 southeast about 18 km/11.16 miles to D37, then go northeast about 2 km/1.2 miles). 26.03.90.27; fax 26.03.97.09

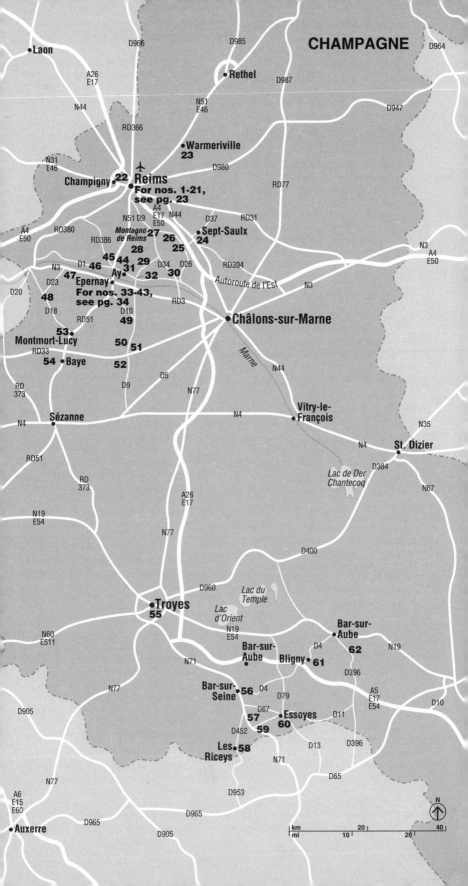

Within the Auberge Le Cheval Blanc:

Restaurant Le Cheval Blanc ★★$$$
The cooking is as traditional as the pretty dining room's decor. The chef seems to prefer heavy cream sauces—delicious, but not for the cholesterol-conscious. The *paillard de veau, sauce au romarin* (veal with a creamy rosemary-flavored sauce) is particularly tasty. The outstanding wine list will tempt you to run up your bill fast. Although the fixed-price menus are good deals, ordering à la carte is expensive. There's a view of the garden and bouquets of fresh flowers on every table. In summer, reserve a table on the terrace. ♦ Daily lunch and dinner; closed mid-January–mid-February. Reservations recommended. 26.03.90.27

25 **Champagne A. Margaine** A great find, this small, family-run winery in the Montagne de Reims area is housed in a big yellow stucco mansion with gray shutters. The winery has its own vineyards (90 percent chardonnay, the rest pinot noir and pinot meunier). Its excellent Cuvée Spéciale Club vintage *blanc de blancs,* made exclusively from chardonnay, has a mouth-filling taste and delicate aroma with a hint of quince; it's a real bargain, too. The Margaines also produce a light Pinot Noir red wine, pink champagne, ratafia (unfermented grape juice with alcohol added, drunk cold as an aperitif), and a brandy made from distilled champagne. The family produces about 60,000 bottles of champagne per year, and sells solely to individuals. Tastings and sales are given by a family member in a small room in the house, which is surrounded by gardens and vineyards. ♦ Free. Tastings and sales M-Sa. Appointment recommended. 3 Ave de Champagne, Villers-Marmery (from Sept-Saulx follow D37 southwest 5 km/3.1 miles, then drive north on D26 about 2 km/1.2 miles). 26.97.92.13; fax 26.97.97.45

For a champagne to be labeled "Vintage Champagne," 90 percent or more of its grapes must have been harvested in a single year, and it must have been aged a minimum of three years.

Champagne has 17 officially designated *grand cru* villages. Those producing red grapes are Ambonnay, Ay, Beaumont, Bouzy, Louvois, Mailly, Puisieulx, Sillery, Tours-sur-Marne, Verzy, and Verzenay. Those producing white grapes are Avize, Chouilly, Cramant, Le Mesnil, Oger, and Oiry.

Restaurants/Clubs: Red   **Hotels:** Blue
Shops/ 🌳 Outdoors: Green   **Sights/Culture:** Black

26 **Champagne Mailly** Based in a village edging the Montagne de Reims, this excellent wine cooperative groups 70 wine growers whose grapes come exclusively from Mailly's *grand cru terroirs.* Their wines include an unusual *blanc de noirs,* a fresh-tasting, intensely flavored champagne made exclusively from pinot noir grapes; and a delicate, fruity Brut Réserve (75 percent pinot noir). The delicate Brut 1988 made from chardonnay and pinot noir is a great deal. The facade of the modern building that houses the winery is decorated with two colorful frescos: One depicts the grape harvest, the other the process of making champagne. Tours of the cellars are available on request. ♦ Admission. Tastings and tours M-Sa, Su afternoon July-Aug; M-F Sept-June. 28 Rue de la Libération, Mailly-Champagne (6 km/3.7 miles northwest of Villers-Marmery on D26). 26.49.41.10; fax 26.49.42.27

27 **Montagne de Reims** Not a mountain at all, but steep vine-covered hills that *seem* like mountains compared to the flat landscape around here. Topped with bands of dense oak and pine, the hills rise up just south of Reims. The area has been designated a natural landmark, the **Parc Régional de la Montagne de Reims** (Reims Mountain Regional Park); its eastern edge is near the village of Verzy; southward it reaches to Ay; and its western edge is near Châtillon-sur-Marne. Some of the area's best vineyards are here, and many scenic and wine routes in champagne country overlap patches of designated park area. Near the village of Verzenay two kilometers (1.2 miles) northwest of Verzy is a working 1820 windmill, one of the last to survive in a region once covered with them. This one was used as an observation tower during World War I. Seven kilometers (4.3 miles) due west along the D26, near the village of Rilly-la-Montagne, is the well-named Mont Joli (Pretty Mountain), 273 meters (888 feet) high. The view from its summit of vineyards, pine groves, and villages on the slopes and valleys below is well worth the hourlong (round-trip) hike. ♦ From Reims take N44 southeast 13.5 km/8.4 miles, then take D326 south 2.5 km/1.5 miles to Villers-Marmery, on the eastern edge of the Montagne de Reims. From Sept-Saulx take D37 southwest about 5 km/3.1 miles to D26. Turn right (north) and follow the scenic little D26 along the flank of the slopes beyond Villers-Marmery.

Within Montagne de Reims:

Les Faux de Verzy Just south of Verzy is a famous beech forest, Les Faux de Verzy (*"faux"* here does not mean false, but comes from the Latin *fagus,* for beech). Some of the beeches here are 500 years old. They have short trunks with branches that spread rather than soar, like fruit trees against a garden wall; some even coil into corkscrew shapes. The **Observatoire du Mont Sinaï,** the highest point in this forest, offers a great view of the surrounding countryside. Leave the car in the parking lot and take the easy one-hour (round-trip) hike up to the 283-meter (928-foot) summit.

28 La Ferme des Boeufs ★★$ This friendly family-run farmhouse restaurant nestles in the hamlet of Germaine in the middle of the Montagne de Reims forest. The prix-fixe menu lets you select from three first courses and three main courses; a salad, cheese assortment, dessert, and coffee are included, and just about everything except the coffee comes from this or nearby farms. And all for around $20 per person (wine extra)! There's a half-price children's menu, too. ♦ Sa lunch and dinner; Su lunch; closed mid-October–mid-April. Reservations required. From Mailly-Champagne follow D26 5 km (3.1 miles) west to Rilly-la-Montagne, then go south another 5 km (3.1 miles) along D71E and follow the signs to Germaine. 26.52.88.25

29 Chambres d'Hôte Au Beau Sarrazin $$ Savine Villain offers five comfortable guest rooms, all with private bathrooms, in her farmhouse with a flower-filled interior courtyard. One of the rooms is in the ancient vine-covered family house; the other four are in an elegantly converted stone farm building nearby. All rooms are on upper floors and have the partly slanted ceilings typical of farmhouse bedrooms in France. The complimentary breakfast features homemade cake and jams. There's a tennis court on the premises and good walking trails nearby; the family is also a good source for information on the local champagne houses. ♦ 6 Allée des Seigneurs, Fontaine-sur-Ay (from Germaine follow D71E south 6 km/3.7 miles to Avenay Val-d'Or, then go east about 5 km/3.1 miles on D201). 26.52.30.25; fax 26.52.03.99

Champagne Bottles

Quart: 18.7 cl

Demi: 37.5 cl

Bouteille: 75 cl (bottle)

Magnum: 2 bottles (1.5 liters)

Jéroboam: 4 bottles (3 liters)

Mathusalem: 8 bottles (6 liters)

Salmanazar: 12 bottles (9 liters)

Balthazar: 16 bottles (12 liters)

Nabuchodonosor: 20 bottles (15 liters)

30 Champagne Herbert Beaufort Champagne has only one red wine appellation—Bouzy (an official *grand cru*)—and this highly rated family-run winery makes one of the best. Their version of this light Pinot Noir red wine is aged in wood and has a bouquet of peaches and ripe red fruit. Bouzy *rouge* is meant to be drunk at a cool cellar temperature, and should be served (according to the winery) with white meats or cheese. The great champagnes produced here are made almost completely from pinot noir grapes, and always with old wines blended in. The Carte d'Or has a powerful, spicy aroma and mouth-filling taste, and the pink champagne is deliciously fruity; all the wines are well priced. The top of the line is the vintage Cuvée Spéciale La Favorite brut, made only in great years. The winery, marked by a large sign, is in an elegant stone mansion dating from 1845. Tastings are offered in the spacious, modernly decorated sales area or, weather permitting, outside in the large cobblestone courtyard filled with blooming flowers. ♦ Free. Visits and tastings M-Sa. 28 Rue de Tours, Bouzy (from Fontaine-sur-Ay take D19 east about 6 km/3.7 miles). 26.57.01.34; fax 26.57.09.08

30 Auberge St-Vincent ★★$$ This is the kind of family-run village auberge that you stumble on by accident and want to keep to yourself. The simple white stucco building is covered with vines, and flowers fill the window boxes. Owner and chef Jean-Claude Pelletier serves such excellent regional dishes as *cassolette de petits gris* (casserole of local snails), *rognons et foie de veau sauce à la truffe* (veal kidneys and liver with truffle sauce), and a crusty fruit gratin for dessert. The fixed-price menus are among the best deals in Champagne. ♦ Tu-Sa lunch and dinner. Reservations required. Rue St-Vincent, Ambonnay (from Bouzy follow D19 east 3 km/1.9 miles). 26.57.01.98; fax 26.57.81.48

Above the Auberge St-Vincent:

Hôtel St-Vincent $ Anne-Marie Pelletier is in charge of the 10 very comfortable bedrooms above the restaurant. The rooms are small and simple, but all have private bathrooms, TVs, and telephones; most have views of surrounding vineyards. *Demi-pension* (breakfast and one other meal) is required in summer. ♦ Closed Monday and Sunday night. 26.57.01.98

"De vignes en caves, de caves en bouteilles, de bouteilles en verres" (from vines to cellars, from cellars to bottles, from bottles to glasses) is a slogan often used by French wine makers to point to their wines' authenticity.

31 Manoir de Montflambert $$$ The Rampacek family offers six luxurious guest rooms, all with private bathrooms, in their beautiful 17th-century manor house. It's just outside the village of Mutigny and only minutes from the Montagne de Reims vineyards. The house is surrounded by a huge private park with formal French gardens for strolling. The restaurant is very popular, so if you want to dine here, reserve in advance. Typical offerings include *feuilleté de cuisse de grenouilles* (puff pastry with frogs' legs) and *coq au champagne* (chicken in champagne). ♦ Closed January–mid-February. From Avenay-Val-d'Or take D201 west 2 km (1.2 miles). From Epernay take D201 east 5 km (3.1 miles) northeast and follow the signs to Mutigny. 26.52.33.21

31 Ay This village (pronounced Ah-*ee*) on the banks of the canal across the Marne is surrounded by some of Champagne's best vineyards, but the most famous wineries here accept visitors by advance appointment only. Although World Wars I and II devastated the town, a number of well-preserved half-timber houses and 15th- and 16th-century churches remain. ♦ From Reims follow N51 south 23 km (14.3 miles) to D1, then take D1 east 2.5 km (1.6 miles). From Mutigny take D201 west 2 km (1.2 miles)

Within Ay:

Bollinger Although champagne producers are not known for praising the competition, they admit to believing this to be one of the top champagne houses (the other is **Krug,** in Reims)—so you know it's one of the best. The winery is housed in a small 18th-century brick-and-white-stucco manor house with a distinctive double staircase. Each staircase, lined with wrought-iron railings, rises in a curve from a stone-paved courtyard to either side of the building's main entrance, above which is a window with an ornate wrought-iron balcony. The overall effect is harmonious elegance, a characteristic shared by champagnes produced here. The winery itself reflects the family-owned company's solid, traditional values. A combination of grapes from *grand cru* and *premier cru* sites, and painstaking care in the cellars (including a commitment to aging in oak), have made pricey Bollinger champagnes consistently top-notch. Don't miss splurging on a Bollinger vintage "RD" (*récemment dégorgé,* meaning the wine has been aged on its lees for seven to 10 years, much longer than usual, and consequently has a special intensity of flavor). In addition to its reputation for impeccable wine making, Bollinger's claim to fame is its vineyard with vines that have pre-phylloxera root stock, taken from a section of vines that miraculously survived the late-19th-century vine scourge. Their grapes produce wines with such powerful flavor that, according to a Bollinger spokesman, they'd be too strong on their own to suit the contemporary predilection for a delicate champagne. The grapes from these priceless vines are used in some of Bollinger's top *cuvées* (blends). You can have a tasting of some of the wines and take a tour of the underground cellars. Free. ♦ Visits and tastings by appointment. 16 Rue Jules-Loubet. 26.44.21.31; fax 26.54.48.29

32 Philipponnat The Philipponnat family has owned vineyards in the Ay area since the 17th century. They began bottling their own champagnes a century ago, and have become a prestigious champagne house. The top Philipponnat wines are among the scarcest of all champagnes on the market: Only 15,000 bottles from their celebrated Clos de Goisses, one of the best *grand cru* champagne *terroirs* of all, are released per year. The great Goisses vineyard is planted with two-thirds pinot noir and one-third chardonnay, and any wines made from its grapes are guaranteed to be splendid (and costly). Clos de Goisses champagne, always aged in wood, is proof in itself of the power of *terroir.* The winery also produces excellent nonvintage brut, such as the Royal Réserve, made primarily from pinot noir, that has a full, fruity taste; it's a good buy. The vintage Grand Blanc, made from chardonnay grapes from six different *grand cru* vineyards, is superb. Their pink champagne is also very good. The elegant two-story brick and peach-pink stucco winery—an Italianate style atypical of the region—is surrounded by a wide cobblestone courtyard. Take a look at the winery's collection of ancient champagne tools. ♦ Free. Daily June-Oct; M-F Nov-May. For a tour of the cellars, advance reservations are required. 13 Rue du Pont, Mareuil-sur-Ay (3.5 km/2.2 miles east of Ay on D1). 26.52.60.43; fax 26.52.61.49

32 Billecart-Salmon Although not well known abroad, this champagne house is highly respected in France. A family-run operation founded in 1818, the winery has only three hectares (7.4 acres) of its own vines, but has long-established contracts with the best local growers. The winery's credo is to "make wine rather than just champagne," which seems to mean that all the wines here are designed to be very full-flavored, particularly the brut pink champagne. You can purchase a sample box of one pink and two regular champagnes for around $50. The winery—a large, vine-covered 19th-century mansion—is surrounded by a lovely park. ♦ Free. M-F. 40 Rue Carnot, Mareuil-sur-Ay. 26.52.60.22; fax 26.52.64.88

Epernay

Unimpressive at first sight, Epernay soon wins over any champagne pilgrim with its important champagne houses. With about one-fifth the population of Reims, Epernay makes nearly as much champagne. An estimated 100 kilometers (60 miles) of *caves* (cellars) run about 20 to 30 meters (65 to 100 feet) under the streets and hold millions of bottles of champagne-in-the-making. Epernay lost most of its historic buildings to World War I raids, but several opulent 19th-century houses and a few Renaissance structures remain, especially around the **Avenue de Champagne** quarter at Epernay's center, where most champagne houses have their sales rooms. In addition, the town has excellent wine information resources and museums, and many parks and gardens.

33 Chez Pierrot ★★$$ This cozy bistro attracts Epernay's chic set, including many local wine makers. The regional home-style cooking includes such specialties as *truite saumonée avec une sauce au champagne* (salmon trout with champagne sauce) and *andouillette de Troyes à la moutarde* (chitterling sausage with mustard sauce). The wine list offers a superb choice of champagnes served by the glass, many at very reasonable prices. ♦ M-F lunch and dinner; Sa dinner; closed two weeks in February and the last two weeks of August. Reservations recommended. 16 Rue de la Fauvette (at Rue des Nommois). 26.55.16.93; fax 26.54.51.30

34 Les Berceaux ★★$$$ In an ancient brick-fronted building with big windows and flower boxes, right in the heart of Epernay, this friendly restaurant-hotel has been serving guests for over a century. You'll receive a warm welcome at the bar, which offers many champagnes by the glass. Very good regional cuisine is on hand in the restaurant; try the *cassoulet d'escargots au champagne* (snail casserole with champagne sauce), *caille au ratafia* (quail with a sauce made with ratafia, the local aperitif), or *oeufs de caille au foie gras* (quail eggs with foie gras). In addition to the wide choice of champagnes, you'll find a selection of bordeaux and burgundies.

♦ M-Sa lunch and dinner; Su lunch; closed in February. Reservations recommended. 13 Rue des Berceaux (at Rue Jean-Pierrot). 26.55.28.84; fax 26.55.10.66

Above Les Berceaux:

Hôtel Les Berceaux $$ After dining, head upstairs to one of the 29 simple but comfortable guest rooms above the restaurant. All the rooms have TVs, direct-dial phones, and private bathrooms (the cheapest have showers instead of tubs); one room has a mini-bar. You can choose a continental breakfast (coffee or tea and breads) or a more copious, pricier buffet breakfast. ♦ Closed Sunday night and in February. 26.55.28.84

35 Hôtel de Champagne $$ This modern 35-room hotel lacks the charm of some of the region's older establishments, but it's clean, quiet, and a good value. All rooms are air-conditioned and have TVs, telephones, and private bathrooms. There is an elevator, but no restaurant. ♦ Closed the first two weeks of January. 30 Rue E.-Mercier (between Rue des Archers and Passage du Jard). 26.55.30.22; fax 26.51.94.63

36 Le Petit Comptoir ★★$$ The Epernay branch of superchef Gérard Boyer's Reims bistro is just as charming as the original. The old stone building has an antique bar, where you can sample champagnes by the glass. The excellent traditional cuisine includes *rillettes de saumon avec coulis de poireau froid* (salmon spread served with leek sauce), *sauté de thon en ratatouille au thym* (sautéed fresh tuna with thyme-flavored ratatouille), *escalope de veau pommes dauphines* (veal cutlets with eggy potato puffs), or the *sauté de cuisse de poulet aux épices avec riz sauvage* (spicy sautéed chicken thigh with wild rice). For dessert, try the delectable hot soufflé of caramelized pears with chocolate sauce. ♦ Tu-Sa lunch and dinner; Su lunch; closed the last week of December and most of August. Reservations recommended. 3 Rue du Docteur-Rousseau (between Rue du Docteur-Verron and Rempart Perrier). 26.51.53.53; fax 26.51.53.53

> The beech trees in the Faux de Verzy twist in a unique shape seen in no other beeches. There is no known botanical explanation for their appearance, but legend offers one: While traveling through the forest, Joan of Arc rested on one of the trees, and they have bent under her saintly weight ever since.

Restaurants/Clubs: Red   **Hotels:** Blue
Shops/ ♥ Outdoors: Green   **Sights/Culture:** Black

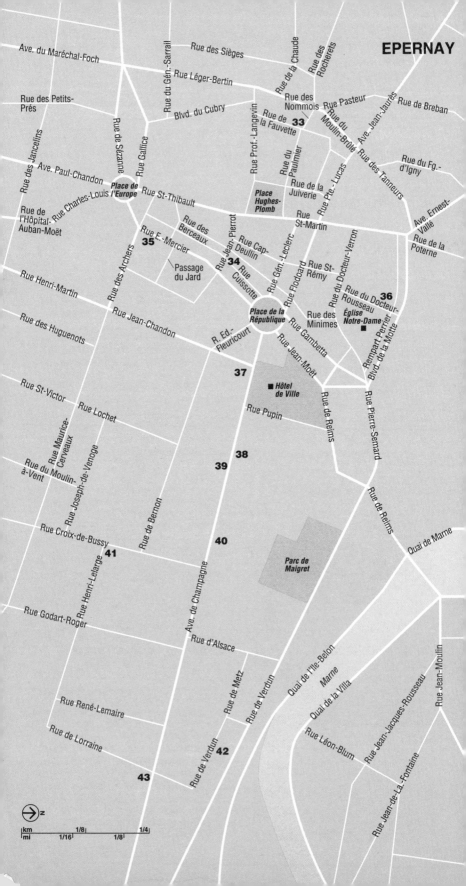

MOËT & CHANDON

37 Moët et Chandon Claude Moët founded this venerable house in 1743, but it certainly isn't resting on its laurels. It produces 20 million bottles per year and sells about 80 percent of them abroad. The Brut Imperial is the biggest seller; the nonvintage *cuvée*, made from a third each of the major grape varieties, contains 20 percent aged champagnes blended in. The vintage champagnes have more body and taste, especially the pinks, which are full of pinot noir fruitiness. Unquestionably the best bottle, though, is the complex, elegant, vintage Dom Pérignon, such as the wonderful 1985. Several buildings on or near the Avenue de Champagne constitute the winery. Tastings and tours are given in an imposing stone building that dates from 1919 (it replaced an earlier structure that was destroyed during World War I). The building has a huge walled courtyard opening onto the Avenue de Champagne; a statue of Dom Pérignon greets visitors at the entrance. The tour here is one of the best in the Champagne region; well-informed multilingual guides lead visitors through the whole champagne-making process, concluding with a tasting. If you have never really understood such things as *remuage* or how they get the corks into the champagne bottles, you will after taking this excellent 45-minute tour. ◆ Admission. Daily Apr-Nov; M-F Dec-Mar. 18 Ave de Champagne (at Rue Jean-Chandon). 26.54.71.11; fax 26.54.84.23

38 Musée Municipal du Vin de Champagne et d'Archéologie (Municipal Museum of Champagne and Archaeology) Exhibits devoted to local traditions and archaeology are housed in the **Château Perrier**, a 19th-century château. Many paintings demonstrate how champagne is made, and other displays detail the long history of the region. ◆ Admission. M, W-Su (no midday closing). 13 Ave de Champagne (between Rue Pupin and Rue d'Alsace). 26.51.90.31

39 Perrier-Jouët This winery is famous for one of the world's most distinctive champagne bottles: It is beautifully painted with flowers and turn-of-the-century motifs designed by Emile Gallé, a prominent French artist of the Belle Epoque. These bottles contain the winery's most famous *cuvée* (blend), the Belle Epoque (marketed in the US as "Fleur de Champagne"), which is produced in white and pink versions. Both are full-tasting, fruity wines, although some people

feel the *dosage* (addition of sugar) is too extreme for contemporary tastes. They need some aging; the 1985s or 1986s—both good years—are treats that should not be missed. If you ever thought that the pretty bottle was just a gimmick to sell an inferior champagne, you will change your mind upon tasting the excellent wines here. Another suberb *cuvée* is the Blason de France, also made in white and pink versions; both are made from 30 percent white grapes and 30 percent dark ones. The fruity but balanced pink variety is considered one of the best pink champagnes around. The winery itself is an elegant stone château dating from the 18th century with a wide cobblestone courtyard surrounded by flowers and trees; it's a delightful setting for tasting champagne. Across the wide Avenue de Champagne from the main winery at 11 Avenue de Champagne is another 18th-century château that **Perrier-Jouët** also owns; its interior was completely redone in 1990 in Belle Epoque style, but it is open only to professionals. ◆ Free. Visits and tastings by appointment. 26 Ave de Champagne (between Rue Croix-de-Bussy and Rue Jean-Chandon). 26.55.20.53; fax 26.54.54.55

40 Besserat de Bellefon Dating from 1843, this reputable winery illustrates the kind of change always going on in the high-powered world of big-time champagne operations. It moved from Ay to Reims in 1970 when it was sold to a new owner; it came to Epernay when it was sold again in 1993 to the huge Marne & Champagne conglomerate. Its distinctive style of wines hasn't changed, however; made mainly from pinot noir, they are full-flavored and designed, most people say, to accompany a meal rather than to be drunk as an aperitif. Best-sellers are the Cuvées des Moines, one white, the other pink. The Grande Cuvée vintage champagne is the top of the line; it is made from both chardonnay and pinot noir and has a more delicate, slightly flowery flavor than their other wines. The winery is housed in a late-19th-century mansion built in Neo-Classical style; a large cobblestone courtyard spreads before the entrance. The **Espace Besserat de Belfond** is one of the most ambitious visitors' centers in the region; it includes a big tasting room where you can try Besserat de Bellefon wines as well as those of two other champagne houses owned by the

Marne & Champagne group (Lanson and Alfred de Rothschild). ♦ Free. M-Sa. 19 Ave de Champagne (between Rue Pupin and Rue d'Alsace). 26.59.51.00; fax 26.59.51.19

41 Pol Roger This winery is housed in a big, elegant, turn-of-the-century brick mansion surrounded by a garden. Growing in front is an extremely rare tree, an odd variety of beech known as the *faux de Verzy* (Verzy beech), which is native to the village of Verzy in the nearby Montagne de Reims vineyard area. According to the winery, the tree here is one of only 10 growing outside the Faux de Verzy forest. The interior of the winery is decorated in the cozily elegant style that the French always describe as "very British": lots of dark woods, heavily upholstered chairs, and fine paintings on the walls. **Pol Roger** champagnes are known for their delicate, slightly floral taste and elegant balance. The vintage *blanc de blancs* (made only from white grapes) champagnes are considered to be the winery's best; try the 1985 or 1986. The nonvintage champagnes are also very good, and very reasonably priced. **Pol Roger** markets a Cuvée Winston Churchill in the United Kingdom (it's not available elsewhere), reciprocating the honor that Churchill once paid in naming one of his horses Pol Roger. ♦ Free. Tastings and visits by appointment. 1 Rue Henri-Lelarge (at Rue Croix-de-Bussy, just west of Ave de Champagne). 26.59.58.00; fax 26.55.25.70

42 De Castellane One of the region's most interesting winery tours is given here; it includes a look at a collection of antique champagne labels, a butterfly garden with many species living in a heated greenhouse, and a good museum on the history of champagne making. This champagne house buys all its grapes already pressed, then gives the task of producing coherent wines out of all that juice to its cellar master, Marc Fournier. He generally succeeds in creating several wines that are very different from each other, but that all have a certain roundness. Try the chardonnay-dominated vintage Cuvée Royale, or the pinot noir–dominated vintage Commodore. The view from the 19th-century white stucco tower with a pointed roof (visible from anywhere in Epernay) is fabulous—if you don't mind hiking up 237 steps to get there. ♦ Admission. Tastings daily May-Oct; daily afternoon Easter-May, Nov-Dec; closed January-Easter. 57 Rue de Verdun (off Ave de Champagne). 26.55.15.33; fax 26.54.24.81

43 Mercier Epernay's most futuristic building is the setting for a reliable champagne house founded in 1858. It's a salmon pink, round structure with something resembling a huge silver flying saucer on its roof. Several nations' flags fly from the roof: In addition to the French flag, there are flags of other European Union nations and the US to show recognition of the champagne's international audience. The two top wines here are the vintage brut, made from chardonnay and pinot noir, and the vintage Cuvée Bulle d'Or (golden bubble). The winery uses a high percentage of pinot meunier grapes in some of its less-expensive wines, which gives them a very round, winey taste that some feel lacks finesse. The tour is one of the most popular in Champagne. Visitors first view a film (in French), then descend into the cellars in a glass-sided elevator past tableaux of automated figures acting out the champagne-making process. Next comes a trip through miles of cellars in a laser-guided train. There's even a very interesting collection of ancient wine presses, and a huge barrel that can hold 200,000 bottles' worth of champagne, which was towed (full) to Paris by 42 horses for the 1889 World's Fair! ♦ Admission. Visits and tastings daily Apr-Nov; M, Th-Su Dec-Mar. 70 Ave de Champagne (at Rue de Lorraine). 26.54.75.26; fax 26.55.12.63

Epernay Environs

44 Royal Champagne $$$$ For high-class pampering, you can't beat this Relais & Châteaux establishment, one of the most luxurious in Champagne. The white former *relais de poste* (stop on the stagecoach route) sprawls on a hill overlooking Epernay and its vineyards; the road it is on was a Roman route, and apparently some sort of inn has operated on this spot since AD 458! The 27 rooms and three suites—all big, bright, and sumptuous—are housed in separate modern bungalows with terraces and great vineyard views. Every room is equipped with a mini-bar, direct-dial telephone, TV, and air-conditioning. The traditional French Provincial decor features flowery wallpaper and fabrics, and dark wood furniture. The hotel management will meet you at either of Paris's airports, and will organize private tours of the Champagne region, flights above the vineyards in a hot-air balloon, cruises down the Marne, and other special activities. ♦ From Epernay follow N51 6 km (3.7 miles) north to the village of Champillon. 26.52.87.11; fax 26.52.89.69

Within the Royal Champagne:

Restaurant Royal Champagne
★★★$$$$ Excellent renditions of traditional dishes such as *jarret de veau à l'ancienne* (long-simmered veal stew) or *sandre cuit sur*

sa peau, réduction au Bouzy (whole pickerel cooked in a sauce of Bouzy red wine) are accompanied by innovative treats like truffles and *choux vert* (green cabbage) braised with fresh coriander. For dessert, either go the traditional route with *gratin de fruits de saison au sabayon de Champagne* (fruit gratin with an egg-based champagne sauce), or try the unusual fig-and-grapefruit ravioli. Don't miss the excellent cheeses, particularly the local brie. The selection of champagnes (and other wines) is outstanding. The only drawback: The prices are out of sight, except for a fixed-price menu served at lunch on weekdays. ♦ Daily lunch and dinner. Reservations required. 26.52.87.11

45 Abbaye de St-Pierre d'Hautvillers (St. Peter of Hautvillers Abbey) Just north of Epernay is the medieval abbey where Dom Pérignon lived and experimented with champagne making; it's open to a few lucky visitors who make an appointment well in advance through the abbey's current owner, Moët et Chandon. The abbey is a simple complex of creamy yellow stone buildings with gray slate roofs and beautiful gardens. Moët et Chandon established a small museum on Dom Pérignon's life and on the history of wine making (several ancient vineyard tools are on display), but the most moving part of the visit is the abbey's small church, which contains many ornate medieval wood carvings and the tomb of Dom Pérignon himself. A wide terrace in front of the abbey provides a wonderful view of the surrounding vineyards and the little village of Hautvillers, a sleepy place with many 15th- and 16th-century half-timber houses. The village is worth a stroll; some of the shops have interesting intricate wrought-iron signs advertising their wares. ♦ Free. By appointment M-F Apr-Nov; closed December-March. From Epernay take RD386 6 km (3.7 miles) north to Hautvillers. Reservations 26.54.71.11

46 Excursion Along the Marne In slightly different countryside now, take the tiny, scenic D1 west of Epernay along the north bank of the Marne River for a close look at other typical Champagne landscapes. The slow-moving Marne is lined with willow trees and a few ancient villages; above it rise vineyard-covered slopes topped with pine and oak forests. To really explore the countryside, get out of your car in the village of Hautvillers and pick up the Grande Randonnée hiking trail No. 14, which parallels this road. You can hike along it to just north of Damery four kilometers (2.4 miles) west; from there it winds ten kilometers (6.2 miles) through the countryside to the village of Reuil on the Marne. Good picnic spots abound along both the car and hiking routes.

Decoding Champagne Labels

RM *(Récoltant-Manipulant):* A grower producing champagne from his or her own grapes.

RC *(Récoltant-Coopérateur):* A grower selling wine made by a cooperative.

R *(Récoltant):* A small-scale grower producing up to a maximum of 500 bottles a year under his or her own name.

ND *(Négotiant-Distributeur):* A *récoltant* wishing to become more commercial can use these initials.

SR *(Société de Récoltant):* A company created by growers from the same family.

NM *(Négotiant-Manipulant):* A champagne house.

CM *(Coopérative de Manipulation):* A champagne co-op.

MA *(Marque d'Acheteur):* The term used for shops' and restaurants' private-label brands.

brut-de-brut (or brut sauvage or brut zéro): extremely dry

brut: very dry

sec: dry

demi-sec: semisweet

doux: sweet

47 Tarlant Housed in an ancient stone mansion on top of a vineyard-covered hill overlooking the Marne Valley, this operation grows its own vines—50 percent pinot noir, 30 percent chardonnay, and 20 percent pinot meunier. This excellent small champagne house was founded in 1687 by Pierre Tarlant, a grape grower in the Aisne province. It has been in Oeuilly ever since Louis Tarlant established vineyards here in 1780. Today it is run by a friendly couple, Jean-Mary and Micheline Tarlant. The Tarlants are committed to preserving the individual characteristics of each of their *terroirs,* and carefully separate the grapes before pressing. Each of their champagnes has a special character: the nonvintage Réserve has a fruity roundness derived from the pinot meunier grape; the Tradition has the full, strong taste of the pinot noir, more subtle however than the taste of pinot noir grapes from around Reims; while in the elegant Prestige vintage brut, the chardonnay grape dominates. The vintage Cuvée Louis brut (in honor of Louis Tarlant) is aged partly in oak. It's made from half pinot noir, half chardonnay grapes from vines at least 25 years old; it is lovely, full-flavored, and well balanced. In a small room in the house, an ancient wine press has been converted into a table for wine tasting. The wine cellars beneath the winery date from the 18th century, when Louis Tarlant set himself up here. The Tarlants also offer two very comfortable guest rooms with private bathrooms on the top floor of their home at an exceptionally low price; staying here is a great way to learn more about the traditions of Champagne, but you must reserve well in advance. ♦ Free. Daily; tours M-Sa 10:30AM, 2:30PM, 3:30PM, 4:30PM. Oeuilly (from Epernay take N3 15 km/9.3 miles west). 26.58.30.60; fax 26.58.37.31

48 Château du Ru Jacquier $$ A stay in this high-class bed-and-breakfast will make you feel like royalty. The Granger family offers six guest rooms in this golden stone-and-brick 18th-century château near Epernay; all the rooms are big and comfortable and have private bathrooms. Meals are served on request in a dining room with a beamed ceiling, fireplace, elegant furniture, and formal table settings. The cuisine matches the refined surroundings: *truite aux amandes* (trout with almonds) and *pigeonnaux au champagne* (squab with champagne sauce) are usually on hand. Other amenities include a fishing pond, bicycles, and a horse-drawn carriage; an 18-hole golf course is nearby. ♦ From Oeuilly follow N3 west 5 km (3.1 miles) to Port-à-Binson, then take D23 south 9 km (5.6 miles) and follow the signs to the village of Igny-Comblizy. 26.57.10.84; fax 26.57.11.85

New Perspectives on Champagne

Rent a bike: With its quiet country roads, Champagne is great bicycle country, and **Reims** has three reliable bike-rental shops: **Dubau** (26 Ave de Paris, at Ave Eperny, 26.08.53.12); **Boulanger** (5 Blvd Lundy, at Rue Jean-Jacques-Rousseau, 26.47.47.59); and **Cycles Hubert** (82 Rue Neufchâtel, between Blvd des Belges and Blvd Robespierre, 26.09.16.93). Along the **Montagne de Reims** vineyard route, try **Cycl'o Vert** (34 Rue Carnot, Verzy, 26.97.97.77).

Champagne from the air: Two Reims companies offer balloon trips over Champagne's vineyards: **Champagne Air Show** (15 *bis* Pl St-Niçaise, at Blvd Victor-Lambert, 26.82.59.60; fax 26.82.48.62), and **Club Tonus Montgolfières** (36 Rue Léo Lagrange, between Canal de L'Aisne-à-la-Marne and Parc Léo-Lagrange, 26.82.80.04; fax 26.49.08.52).

By horse-drawn carriage: Calèche Evasion (26.74.05.85), an Epernay-based company, offers this unusual way to tour Champagne's vineyard-covered countryside. The pleasant trips are given only in the summer, by reservation.

Cruising the Marne: Two companies operate cruise boats on the Marne. **Champagne Vallée** (Pl du Kiosque-à-Musique, Cumières, 26.54.49.51; fax 26.51.87.56) offers a 90-minute cruise, which leaves from **Cumières** just north of Epernay Tuesday through Sunday at 3:30PM and 5PM from May through September. Reservations are recommended. The **Coche d'Eau** (at Quai de la Matine on the right bank of the Marne, 26.74.05.85) offers cruises that last anywhere from one hour to 4.5 hours—the latter includes dinner. Boats leave daily from the **Pont de la Marne** in Epernay at 4PM from May through September.

The Côte des Blancs

Some of Champagne's *grand cru* vineyard sites are found on the **Côte des Blancs** (Slope of the Whites), an open-sky, densely cultivated landscape spread over a nearly flat apron of land south of Epernay. Its name derives from the fact that only white grapes are grown in the area—and in abundance. The ocean of vines can go on uninterrupted for miles, until an isolated chapel or windmill breaks the flow. The towns, most just a handful of creamy white houses with red or black roofs, sit in low bowls of land, leaving the only slightly higher elevations to the grapes. Several small wine villages here are worth a visit, including the *grand cru* village of **Cramant,** known for its chardonnays (here the grape is often called blanc de cramant); **Avize,** a *grand cru* village with a 12th-century church; **Oger,** another *grand cru* village with a beautiful 12th-century church and great views of the surrounding countryside; **Le Mesnil-sur-Oger,** also a *grand cru,* with a Romanesque church and several good champagne houses; and **Vertus,** a picturesque village filled with ancient homes, a few *lavoirs* (the old-fashioned version of launderettes), and a 12th-century church that was almost destroyed during World War II, but has since been lovingly rebuilt. At noon every day, a group of swans are fed on a little pond behind the church.

49 Pierre Moncuit Founded in 1889, this winery is one of the "musts" in a tour of the Champagne region. The Moncuit family has long been known for its excellent champagnes made from the local *grand cru* chardonnay, which here produces a fresh, slightly mineral-tasting, almost nutty wine. They have many vintage *blanc de blancs* on hand from the 1980s; try the 1986, with its full, rich aroma. The 1989 *blanc de blancs* won the gold medal at the 1994 Concours des Vins de la Foire de Paris (a wine contest held at Paris's annual gastronomy fair). Don't miss the superb Nicole Moncuit vintage *cuvée* made from grapes off old vines. All the champagnes here are great bargains, especially since all are made from *grand cru* grapes. The winery is housed in a graceful 18th-century manor house with white shutters and a gray slate roof. Visits to the *crayère* (limestone) cellars are available on request. The oak barrels that line the cellars fill the place with the wonderful aroma of wine. The tasting room is especially well designed, with wicker chairs around little tables where you can sit down while you sip (not the case in most other wineries). ♦ Free. Visits and tastings M-F; Sa-Su by appointment. 11 Rue Persault-Maheu, Le Mesnil-sur-Oger (from Epernay take D10 south about 15 km/9.3 miles and follow the signs to the winery). 26.57.52.65; fax 26.57.97.89

49 Restaurant Le Mesnil ★$$ At this cozy place, the good traditional cooking includes a generous *filet de boeuf sauce au poivre* (beef fillet in pepper sauce), *terrine de poisson et homard chaud, beurre cerfeuil* (warm terrine of fish and lobster with chervil-butter sauce), *cassolette d'escargots au champagne* (a stew of snails in champagne sauce), and *poulet de Bresse aux morilles* (fine chicken from the Bresse region, with morel mushrooms). Try the Grand Marnier soufflé for dessert. The very reasonably priced wine list is exceptional, with many local producers represented. ♦ Tu, Th-Su lunch and dinner; M lunch; closed late February–early March, mid-August–early September. Reservations recommended. 2 Rue Pasteur, Le Mesnil-sur-Oger. 26.57.95.57; fax 26.57.78.57

49 Musée de la Vigne et du Vin (Museum of the Vine and Wine) A wonderful small museum that is a work of love. Bernard and Dany Launois, husband and wife, have put together a collection of wine-making tools and other objects related to wine, including some superb wine presses from the 17th, 18th, and 19th centuries. ♦ Admission includes tour and wine tasting. M-F. 7 Rte d'Oger, Le Mesnil-sur-Oger. 26.57.50.15

"In considering the 1855 classification, it should be emphasized that a Second, Third (*Troisième*), Fourth (*Quatrième*), or Fifth Growth (*Cinquième Cru*) is not a second-, third-, fourth-, or fifth-rate wine. Actually, only sixty-two among approximately two thousand vineyards were considered worthy of being listed Great Growths (*Grands Crus*)—whether First or Fifth—and they are the absolute cream of the vineyards which, as a group, are probably the world's finest in red wine. To be second after only Lafite, Latour, Margaux, and Haut-Brion is very far from being second-rate. Moreover, it is only on an average that the first are the best; in certain years, others equal and even surpass them."

Alexis Lichine, *New Encyclopedia of Wines and Spirits*

Restaurants/Clubs: Red   **Hotels:** Blue
Shops/ 🎋 Outdoors: Green   **Sights/Culture:** Black

50 Guy Larmandier This excellent wine maker produces 70,000 bottles a year—a colossal amount for a small operation. The quality never suffers, though; Larmandier's champagnes have won gold medals in several recent wine tastings. Several generations of Larmandiers have grown fine grapes in Champagne, and Guy Larmandier began producing his own champagne in 1977. The wines are made from grapes from two local *grand cru terroirs* (Cramant and Chouilly) and the *premier cru* Vertus vineyards. Made from 80 percent chardonnay, all the wines here have an appealing, slightly acidic freshness typical of the local grape; the vintage Cramant Brut is rounder, almost creamy, and very elegant. Larmandier also produces an excellent pink champagne. All these wines are inexpensive, and the good news is that they're now being distributed in the US. The winery is in an ancient half-timber house with a blue slate roof in a tiny village; sales and tastings are in a room in the house. ♦ Free. M-Sa. 30 Rue du Général-Koenig, Vertus (from Le Mesnil-sur-Oger follow D9 5.5 km/3.4 miles; watch for signs to the winery). 26.52.12.41; fax 26.52.19.38

51 Hôtel Le Mont Aimé $$ Located in a tiny wine village, this establishment has 29 guest rooms and one suite which are all spacious, quiet, and comfortable, with private bathrooms, mini-bars, direct-dial telephones, and satellite TVs. Each has either a terrace or a balcony with a view of the garden, big windows, white walls, and cheerful floral fabrics. The management is very friendly, and the continental breakfasts are very good. Guests can use the swimming pool in the summer. ♦ Closed Sunday night. 4-6 Rue des Vertus, Bergères-lès-Vertus (from Vertus go 3.5 km/2.2 miles south along D9). 26.52.21.31; fax 26.52.21.39

Within the Hôtel Le Mont Aimé:

Restaurant Le Mont Aimé ★★$$ The inventive dishes here include *magret de Barbarie au Bouzy* (Barbary duck breast in red Bouzy wine sauce) and *gâteau de lapereau à la confiture d'oignons* (terrine of young rabbit with caramelized onions). Dine on the pleasant garden terrace in summer. ♦ M-Sa lunch and dinner; Su lunch. Reservations recommended. 26.52.21.31

52 Mont Aimé Drive up the tiny road that leads to the top of this hill for an unforgettable view of the Côte des Blancs. Prehistoric, Roman, and feudal structures have all been found here, and bits of some of them remain. ♦ From Bergères-lès-Vertus take D39 1.5 km (0.9 miles) southwest

53 Auberge Le Cheval Blanc ★★★$$ This friendly place housed in a 16th-century brick manor house is a real find. The labyrinth of tiny alcoves that make up the restaurant should enable those so inclined to isolate themselves from smokers—a difficult thing to do in France. The dishes are generous and traditional. Try the salad with foie gras, the *rognons de veau à l'ancienne* (veal kidneys in a rich sauce), and the great *charlotte au poires* (pear charlotte) for dessert. Ordering à la carte can get expensive, but there are some excellent deals among the fixed-price menus. ♦ Daily lunch and dinner Easter-Oct; M-Th, Sa-Su lunch and dinner Nov-Easter; closed two weeks in February. Reservations recommended. From Epernay take RD51 for 15 km (9.3 miles) southeast and follow the signs to the village of Montmort-Lucy. 26.59.10.03; fax 26.59.15.88

Above the Auberge Le Cheval Blanc:

Hôtel le Cheval Blanc

Hôtel Le Cheval Blanc $$ There are 19 simple but comfortable guest rooms, all with private bathrooms. Floral fabrics and muted wallpaper (pale blue in most rooms) lend a romantic air to the place; several rooms have slanted ceilings and dormer windows. Although all rooms are on the small side, each has a TV and direct-dial phone. The countryside around the inn is perfect for strolling, bicycling, and fishing. ♦ Closed Friday November-Easter, and two weeks in February. 26.59.10.03

54 Ferme de Bannay $ Muguette and Jean-Pierre Curfs operate an excellent bed-and-breakfast on their farm deep in rural Champagne. The two guest rooms can sleep three each; both have private bathrooms, and one has a private entrance by way of an outside staircase. The complimentary breakfast is delicious, featuring farm cheese, homemade jams, and fruit juice. Dinner is served in a cozy dining room on request, but bring your appetite: A typical meal might include homemade rabbit pâté, *pintade aux pommes et raisins* (guinea hen with apples and grapes), and a *marc de Champagne* cold soufflé—all this (wine included) for about what you would pay for a sandwich and a Coke in Paris. This is a great place to stay if you have children; they can visit the farm animals and watch milking in action. The Curfs give classes in bread baking, organize guided tours of champagne houses, and sell homemade edibles, including fresh cheeses with herbs and delicious jams and jellies. Take some time to walk in the countryside around the farm. ♦ From Montmort-Lucy follow RD51 9 km (5.6 miles) south to Baye, then go west about 3 km (1.86 miles) along D343 to Bannay and follow the signs to the farm. 26.52.80.49; fax 26.59.47.78

Southern Champagne: The Aube

The quiet Aube (Dawn) region, which lies southeast of **Troyes,** is lightly dotted with farmhouses and minute, half-timbered villages. It is the kind of area the French call "La France Profonde" (deep or backcountry France) for its peace and isolation. However, the Aube has good champagne-producing areas that are fighting to make a name for themselves in the shadow of the houses of Reims and Epernay. Its vineyards were cast out of the Champagne appellation in the late 1800s due to some difficult production years, but a 1911 protest at Troyes got them restored, and the Aube has been strengthening its production ever since. The region has around a third of France's champagne vineyards, a percentage that is expected to grow in coming years. The best vineyards are located around the pretty villages of **Bar-sur-Aube** (where several Marne champagne houses buy grapes), **Bar-sur-Seine** to the southwest, and the triple *commune* of **Riceys.** The Aube vineyards are not far north of Burgundy and suffer the same climate that wine makers in Chablis have to contend with: extremes of temperatures and occasional vintage-destroying late frosts. About 80 percent of these vineyards are planted in pinot noir. The Aube champagnes tend to be softer than the Marne wines and are usually a pale straw yellow. The region's famous nonchampagne wine is the rare Rosé des Riceys, a dark, dry, still rosé with a pronounced taste described as suggesting mint, chocolate, or gooseberries; it's made

from pinot noir, yet another illustration of how *terroir* counts for more than grape variety in France. It is very rarely seen outside the Aube, and makes a good accompaniment to the mild, local chaource cheese in rustic village restaurants. The local farm-raised meats and orchard fruits are wonderfully fresh, and you may discover a new favorite champagne from any one of the scores of tiny, family-run outfits that sell bottles at bargain prices here.

55 Troyes On top of a hill with the Seine looping around its base, this modern, bustling city was originally a fortress built by a Gallic tribe called the Tricasses. In the Middle Ages Troyes became the official capital of the province of Champagne, and huge trade fairs were held here. Troyes also gained a reputation as a center for the arts, particularly in the Renaissance, when its stained glass and textiles were widely praised. Traces of this illustrious past linger in Le Vieux Troyes, the old part of the town, which is filled with lovely half-timber houses, especially along Rue Champeaux and the tiny Rue des Chats. ♦ From Epernay follow RD51 southwest 40 km (24.8 miles) to Sézanne, then go south on RD373 about 35 km (22.3 miles) to the exit for N19-E54, and take N19-E54 south another 25 km (15.5 miles) to Troyes

Within Troyes:

Cathédrale St-Pierre et St-Paul (St. Peter and St. Paul Cathedral) Among the city's landmarks well worth a visit is this Flamboyant Gothic golden stone cathedral, built from the 13th to the 17th centuries. The facade contains many lovely carvings, though most of the figures above the portals were destroyed during the Revolution. Happily, the magnificent stained-glass windows have survived, and provide a history of stained glass from the Middle Ages to the Renaissance—from the intensely vivid but naive 13th-century glasswork to the intricately designed 16th-century windows. The cathedral's most famous window—a work of art that depicts the city's past as a wine capital—is the *Pressoir Mystique* (Mystical Wine Press), created by Linard Gontier in 1625. You can get a great view of the town from the cathedral's tower, if you don't mind the climb. A 13th-century chapel within the cathedral houses a collection of religious relics, highlighted by a 14th-century red bishop's cape embroidered with gold medallions, a missal cover adorned with various jewels, an illuminated manuscript from the ninth century, and other priceless items. ♦ Cathedral free; chapel admission. Cathedral daily sunrise to sunset; chapel 2PM-6PM mid-Apr–Oct. Pl de la Cathédrale. 25.80.58.46

Basilique St-Urbain (St. Urbain Basilica) The stained-glass windows in this 13th-century basilica are unusually large for their era. Taking up almost all the wall space in the chancel, they are stunningly delicate nonetheless. Complemented by the basilica's other treasure, the amazingly lifelike 16th-century statue *Vierge au Raisin* (Madonna with Grapes), this church is certainly worth a stop. ♦ Daily July-Oct. For visits at other times, contact Troyes's Syndicat d'Initiative (16 Blvd Carnot, at Ave Maréchal-Joffre, 25.73.00.36; fax 25.73.06.81). Pl Vernier. No phone

Eglise Ste-Madeleine (St. Madeleine Church) This 12th-century stone church is the city's oldest. Its stained-glass windows date from the 16th century and are brilliantly colored and intricate. Note the window in the apse representing the creation of the world: It verges on the abstract and looks almost contemporary, but dates from 1500. The church's greatest treasure is the magnificent *Jubé*, a gallery in magnificently carved stone that is suspended several feet above the floor of the church between two of the huge support pillars. The Flamboyant Gothic–style gallery was created between 1508 and 1517 by **Jean Gailde,** a renowned Troyes-based sculptor and architect. The pale gray stone is so festooned with carved detail and has so many see-through lacework sections that it looks like spun brown sugar. ♦ Daily Easter-Oct. Rue de la Madeleine. No phone

Musée d'Art Moderne (Modern Art Museum) Just to the right of the cathedral is one of France's best collections of modern art, including works by Braque, Bonnard, Cézanne, Gauguin, Matisse, and Picasso. The collection was assembled by a local industrialist named Pierre Levy. In 1976, he bequeathed his collection to the city, which remodeled an office building—once an episcopal palace—to house it. The renovation preserved the loveliest features of the palace, which dates to the 15th century: vast rooms with high-beamed ceilings, a 17th-century carved stone staircase, and several huge, elaborately carved fireplaces. Levy also collected African art, and many rare samples of Bambara carvings are also on display. ♦ Admission. M, W-Su. Pl St-Pierre (at Rue de l'Evêche). 25.42.33.33

Hôtel Le Relais St-Jean $$ This stone mansion, dating from the Renaissance, is in the heart of Troyes. All of the 22 rooms are spacious (two very large ones are called suites), quiet, and well equipped with direct-dial phones, satellite TVs, and large bathrooms. Given the historic setting, you'd expect something a bit more in line with the styles of the 1700s, but the decor is resolutely contemporary, with spare-lined furniture and fabrics in geometric designs. At least it's all in good taste, and the staff is friendly. There is no restaurant. ♦ Rue Paillot-de-Montabert (at Rue R.-Salengro). 25.73.89.90; fax 25.73.88.60

Restaurant Le Valentino ★★★$$$ The city's best restaurant is set in an ancient stone mansion on a tiny alley in the medieval heart of the city. It has atmospheric turn-of-the-century decor, with lots of big mirrors, bright lighting, brass railings along the top of the red banquettes, and potted plants. The best place to sit in summer is on the flower-filled patio—the tables in the main dining room are so close together that you may find yourself engaged in your neighbors' conversations whether you want to be or not. Not perfect for a cozy tête-à-tête, but it's a great place for dinner in elegant but relaxed surroundings. Try the *saumon grillé aux herbes* (grilled salmon topped with fresh herbs) or the grilled *marcassin* (baby wild boar) in the fall or winter. The wine list is excellent, with an especially good selection of chablis. Meals can get expensive if you order à la carte, but the fixed-price menu is a bargain. ♦ Tu-Sa lunch and dinner; closed mid-August–early September. Reservations recommended. 11 Cour Rencontre (at Rue Paillot-de-Montabert). 25.73.14.14; fax 25.73.74.04

56 Champagne Veuve Devaux Just outside the picturesque half-timber village of Bar-sur-Seine, this high-class wine co-op of about 750 growers is best known for its Veuve Devaux and Léonce d'Albe labels. The Veuve Devaux 1985 has won numerous awards; it's a mouth-filling champagne that's a surprising yellow-green color and has an aroma of hazelnuts. The co-op also produces excellent Rosé de Riceys; the 1985 has an intense taste of raspberries. The co-op isn't really geared to tourism, but offers sales and tastings to individuals who call ahead. ♦ Free. M-F by appointment. Domaine de Villeneuve, Bar-sur-Seine (from Troyes take N71 southeast about 33 km/20.5 miles). 25.38.30.60; fax 25.29.73.21

56 Hôtel Barséquanais $ Sitting almost on the banks of the Seine (which is just a small river here), this cozy village auberge offers 28 simple but comfortable rooms. All have pine-paneled walls, big windows, dark wood furniture, and cheerful floral fabrics, as well as private bathrooms, televisions, and direct-dial telephones. The management (Monsieur and Madame Bongard) is very friendly. All in all, a great place to stay. ♦ Closed Monday and Sunday night, and mid-February–early March. 12 Ave du Général-Leclerc, Bar-sur-Seine. 25.29.82.75; fax 25.29.86.27

Within the Hôtel Barséquanais:

Restaurant Barséquanais ★★$ With generous servings of local specialties like *canard aux girolles* (duck with wild chanterelle mushrooms) and *ris de veau au champagne* (veal sweetbreads in champagne sauce), plus a great cheese assortment (including creamy chaource from a famous cheese village near here), this restaurant offers a good deal. Eat outside on a shady, flower-bedecked terrace in summer, or inside in a cozy dining room with a fireplace and beamed ceiling. Champagnes are offered by the glass at the bar. ♦ Tu-Sa lunch and dinner; Su dinner; closed mid-February–early March. Reservations required. 25.29.82.75

57 Champagne Moutard Père & Fils This excellent family-run winery produces one of the Aube's best champagnes. They have planted about 80 percent of their vineyards in pinot noir, but are using more and more chardonnay, which gives the wine a definite chablis taste, according to François Moutard. They keep many old vintages on hand, and you may even be able to buy a bottle of the superb 1975 brut for the same price you'd pay for a young and mediocre champagne in Reims. The family also produces luscious fruits preserved in eaux-de-vie. Sales and tastings are in the ancient golden stone family house in a village just outside Bar-sur-Seine. ♦ Free. Sales and tastings M-Sa. Rue du Pont, Buxeuil (from Bar-sur-Seine follow N71 south 7 km/4.3 miles). 25.38.50.76; fax 25.38.57.72

58 Domaine Morel Père & Fils This small family-run operation is the only one in the region dedicated exclusively to the production of the rare Rosé de Riceys. It takes a real art to make this wine. The pressed pinot noir grapes are macerated about four to five days before being barrel-aged; the trick is to let them develop enough tannin, but not too much, lest the special Rosé de Riceys taste be lost. They are richer and redder than usual rosés, but aren't quite reds, and they taste like no other wine in the world; however, they need some time in the bottle to develop. The wines here have pronounced aromas of raspberries, licorice, and violets. Adjacent to the Morel residence, an elegant white stone 18th-century manor house with a red tile roof and geraniums in window boxes, is an inviting tasting room with a marble table and bistrot chairs on a white tile floor. Both the house and the tasting room overlook a walled garden with a huge chestnut tree. Tours of the nearby cellars are available on request. ♦ Free. Sales and tastings M-Sa. Appointment recommended. 93 Rue Général-de-Gaulle, Les Riceys (from Buxeuil follow D36 west 2 km/1.2 miles to Polisy, then take D452 south

about 8 km/5 miles and follow the signs to the winery). 25.29.10.88; fax 25.29.66.72

58 Alexandre Bonnet The Bonnets are known for their fine Rosé de Riceys, considered by many to be the appellation's best, as well as their excellent champagnes. Their Rosé de Riceys has a pronounced taste of wild raspberries and wild strawberries, a luscious wine with finesse. Their champagnes are a bit more elegant than many in the Aube; one reason is that they are made partly from grapes the Bonnets buy in the Marne. Their pink champagne is very fruity and delicious. The winery, a large, elegant, creamy white stone château built in the 17th and 18th centuries, is just beyond an elaborate wrought-iron gate. ♦ Free. Sales and tastings M-F. Appointment recommended. 138 Rue Général-de-Gaulle, Les Riceys. 25.29.30.93; fax 25.29.38.65

58 Ferme-Auberge St-Sébastien ★★$ This cozy farmhouse restaurant is an absolute-must stop in the Aube region. Almost everything the friendly Fagiolini family serves is raised on their farm, from the meats and poultry to the just-out-of-the-garden vegetables and the freshest possible fruits. Andrée Fagiolini offers two fixed-price menus; specialties include *gougères forestières* (cheesy cream puffs), *salade aux chèvres chauds* (salad with warm goat cheese), *gâteau de foies de volailles à la sauce tomate* (chicken-liver terrine with tomato sauce), *poule au vin blanc* (young chicken cooked in white wine), *boeuf bourguignon, lapin à la moutarde* (rabbit with mustard sauce), and *tarte tatin* (upside-down caramelized apple tart). The reasonably priced wines are Rosé de Riceys and local champagnes. ♦ Tu-Su lunch and dinner. Reservations required 48 hours in advance. No credit cards accepted. 31 Rue du Magny, Les Riceys. 25.29.35.10

The famous Talmudist Shlomo Yitzhaqi, known as Rashi, lived in Troyes in the Middle Ages.

Restaurants/Clubs: Red   **Hotels:** Blue

Shops/ 🌳 Outdoors: Green   **Sights/Culture:** Black

59 Champagne Fleury Yet another small, family-run champagne house, this winery has garnered several prizes, among them *GaultMillau*'s prestigious *vigneron de l'année* (wine maker of the year) citation for Jean-Pierre Fleury in 1993. The full-flavored Fleury Champagne is made using strict biodynamic techniques; no insecticides or artificial fertilizers are ever used, and vineyard tasks are timed to celestial rhythms. The Fleurys have a tradition of being ahead of the times; Jean-Pierre's grandfather was the first in the region to plant pinot noir grafted onto resistant American root stock after the phylloxera scourge. A couple of decades ago neighbors laughed when Jean-Pierre and his wife decided to make their wines organically, and laughed even harder when they went biodynamic in the early 1980s. But they are not laughing now, because the Fleury vineyards are visibly healthier than they have ever been, and the Fleurys' pink champagne came out tops in a recent blind tasting, just ahead of Ruinart. Not bad for a little family winery in the Aube. No wonder some of their neighbors are now switching to biodynamic agriculture. The winery is a simple modern building built in the typical style of the region, with a beige stucco facade and a gray tile roof. ♦ Free. Visits and tastings by appointment. 43 Grande Rue, Courteron (from Bar-sur-Seine follow N71 south 14 km/8.6 miles). 25.38.20.28

60 Essoyes Here is a picturesque little village of half-timber and golden stone houses, designated by the French government as an official *ville fleurie* (flower-filled village). It is surrounded by ancient forests of oak and pine, and the old-fashioned beauty of the place is no doubt one reason painter Pierre-Auguste Renoir chose to live and be buried here. The Grande Randonnée hiking trail No. 24 cuts right through the village and is lined with good picnic spots, as are the little D79 and D67 roads that cross the trail. The **Musée du Vigneron d'Autrefois** (Museum of the Wine Maker of the Past; no phone) on D70 in the center of the village honors the area's history of wine making. The museum is open Monday afternoon and Wednesday through Friday from mid-June through mid-September; there is an admission charge. ♦ Take D70 11 km (6.8 miles) east of Courteron

---

Sculptor Frédéric-Auguste Bartholdi, who designed the *Statue of Liberty*, was born in Colmar.

Alsace produces one-fifth of France's total output of white wine, and a half of France's beer.

61 Drappier Drappiers have been growing grapes in the village of Urville, near Bar-sur-Aube, since 1808. This excellent family-run winery produces only champagnes, mainly from pinot noir grapes, although they are beginning to use more chardonnay. Their wines have an intense aroma (often of apricots) and are very fruity, especially the 100 percent pinot noir brut rosé vintage champagne with the Val des Demoiselles label; it has a raspberry bouquet. Try the rich Signature *blanc de blancs,* made from chardonnay; it's almost creamy in the mouth, with hints of honey. The fruity Carte d'Or brut is the winery's top seller; it's made mainly from pinot noir and is, according to the winery, best served with food rather than as an aperitif. The top of the line is the Grande Sendrée vintage brut champagne made with 45 percent pinot noir and 55 percent chardonnay grapes from vines planted more than 70 years ago, the cream of the winery's crop; the 1985 has a full, fresh taste. **Drappier** wine labels are marked "Reims," and the winery maintains cellars in that city, but the wines are made here. Tastings and sales are in the winery's beautiful, labyrinthine, and dramatically lit 12th-century cellars, which were dug out of the local golden stone by the monks of nearby **Abbaye de Clairvaux** (Clairvaux Abbey). The cellars are the only part of the winery open to the public. ♦ Free. Sales and tastings M-Sa. From Bar-sur-Seine follow D4 east 27 km (16.7 miles) to Bligny, then take D44 east about 3 km (1.9 miles) to Urville. 25.27.40.15; fax 25.27.41.19

62 Cristalleries Royales de Champagne Founded in 1866, this factory is a well-known source for fine crystal and glass, including carafes, champagne flutes, and wine glasses, many of which can be purchased in the on-site retail shop. Also on the premises is a museum devoted to crystal.♦ M-Sa; Su afternoon. Factory tours M-Sa 9:30AM. Make appointment for factory tours (not necessary for museum or shop) with tourist office (25.92.42.68, 25.92.05.02). La Voie Basse, Bayel (7 km/4.3 miles southeast of Bar-sur-Aube along D396)

Restaurants/Clubs: Red	**Hotels:** Blue
Shops/ 🌳 Outdoors: Green	**Sights/Culture:** Black

Alsace

All appearances to the contrary, Alsace is not Germany—as its residents will be the first to point out. It's no accident that it looks like it, though. Alsace was German for seven long centuries and was French for more than two before the post–World War I Treaty of Versailles confirmed the region to be part of France. Typical Alsace scenery includes orderly, 17th-century half-timbered villages with cobblestone streets that extend from central fountains; dense evergreen forests spread up the mountainsides above fields of thickly planted vine rows. In contrast to Champagne's dusty, chalky hillocks, Alsace has steep fields and darker soil.

Alsace's wine-growing area extends from the **Vosges Mountains** to the **Rhine Valley.** It is usually referred to by its main divisions, the **Haut-** and **Bas-Rhin** (Upper and Lower Rhine). The terms correspond to the river's south-north directional flow, which explains why "Haut" is below "Bas." Most good Alsatian vineyards lie in a 75-kilometer (47-mile) belt along the Vosges foothills. This area stretches southward from just west of **Strasbourg** to just west of **Mulhouse,** roughly following the flow of the river **Ill** and its tributaries, **Giessen** and **Fecht.** The midpoint of Alsace's wine-producing area, the historic city of **Colmar,** is 447 kilometers (268 miles) from Paris and 303 kilometers (182 miles) from Reims in Champagne. The **Rhine River** lies just east, at the French-German border, and Switzerland is to the south.

Alsace's wines have more flavor and are much drier than their cousins produced across the Rhine, although the grapes here are also commonly cultivated in Germany. Many of the region's still, robust whites have traditionally been named for the grapes from which they are derived (for example, Alsace Riesling, Muscat, Gewürztraminer, and Pinot Noir)—a naming practice that is common in Germany (and California), but rare in France.

Since 1983, official French *grand cru* appellation status has been accorded to top Alsatian *terroirs;* there are now about 50 of them (many shared by several wine makers/owners), and the *grand cru* names appear on labels along with the name of the grape. There are no *premier cru* nor *commune* (village) designations in Alsace. Almost all Alsace's wines are dry whites, but some growers are beginning to make rosés and even red wines from pinot noir grapes; excellent *vendanges tardives* (late harvest) Sauternes-type wines are also produced. The region's rarest wines are a dry Muscat, a great aperitif wine, and Klevener de Heiligenstein, a delicate dry, white made from the uncommon savagnin rosé grape.

Despite the assertively French modern-day population, many building and place names remain German or German-influenced. Nevertheless, Alsace has a dialect (Alsatian) and a vibrant, living culture all its own. Alsatians are generally known to be hearty and good-spirited, which is nowhere more evident than in that cherished Alsatian institution, the *winstub* (wine bar/tavern-style restaurant). Here heavy wooden tables are set around large fireplaces, where people typically consume melted muenster cheese and potatoes, onion tarts, and glasses of the luscious local Gewürztraminer; main courses are heavy on meats and sauerkraut. Alsatian buildings are bedecked with geraniums and with elaborate wrought-iron signs advertising the profession of a current or past occupant. Almost every village has an ancient tower housing nests of storks, a traditional symbol of Alsace and of good luck. Many of the sharply sloped roofs of the centuries-old beamed houses are adorned with black-and-red tile patterns. Mixed among these houses are remnants from Alsace's Gallo-Roman, Gothic, German Baroque, and Neo-Classical French periods.

In addition to its scenery and friendly ways, Alsace appeals to wine lovers for its easily traveled, clearly signposted "official" wine route. The key vineyards (the best of them on hillsides facing east) are compactly clustered to the north and south of the pretty town of Colmar. Several villages have *sentiers viticoles,* pedestrian paths overlooking or even running though the surrounding vineyards. But be warned: In summer, Alsace's *Route du Vin* (wine route) can get extremely crowded.

On the Road to Colmar

63 Maison Albert Seltz The Seltz family has been making wines since 1576, but that's a mere drop in the bucket in the long history of Mittelbergheim, the picturesque village of half-timber houses where their winery is located. Known for its wines since AD 388, the village has carefully kept a *Weinschlagbuch* (book of wine prices) since 1456. Pierre Seltz's 1992 entry in the book notes the price of sylvaner, a grape he champions in spite of the fact that it doesn't have a "noble" standing. His Sylvaner Zotzenberg is not to be missed; made from old vines, it's powerful, full-flavored, and very dry—an illustration of what can be achieved with a combination of this grape, a great *terroir,* and care. The winery also uses six other grape varieties—riesling, gewürztraminer, pinot blanc, tokay–pinot gris, muscat, and pinot noir—and produces excellent Riesling and Pinot Gris wines. All the wines here are fermented slowly and naturally, and aged in oak. Visits and tastings are given in limestone cellars under the family's half-timber house. With its intricate wood carvings, large wooden balcony, and window boxes filled with geraniums, this is one of Alsace's prettiest wineries. ♦ Free. Visits and tastings M-F. 21 Rue Principale, Mittelbergheim (from Strasbourg take N422 southwest 36 km/22.3 miles just past Barr, then take D62 2 km/1.2 miles south). 88.08.91.77; fax 88.08.52.72

63 Domaine Marc Kreydenweiss Wines have been produced in the village of Andlau since 70 BC; they were praised in writing by Pliny, the first-century Roman wine scholar and historian. And this highly respected wine maker's family has been making wines in the area for three centuries. It's not surprising, then, that Marc Kreydenweiss decided to adopt biodynamics, a system his ancestors must have understood by tradition and instinct. He uses no artificial chemicals, and times vineyard tasks according to solar and lunar rhythms. As in other great biodynamic vineyards in France, the approach is working; all the wines produced here achieve what Kreydenweiss says are his three main goals: finesse, purity, and a long finish (meaning that the taste lingers in the mouth). Grapes are picked in relays and rigorously selected. The Vendanges Tardives (late harvests) and Sélections de Grains Nobles (of "nobly rotten" grapes) wines are spectacular, but all the wines are good. Try the wines from the three *grand cru* vineyards in which Kreydenweiss has vines: Grand Cru Kastelberg Riesling, the Grand Cru Wiebelsberg Riesling, and the Grand Cru Muenchberg Tokay–Pinot Gris. The wine labels are designed by contemporary artists, a sign of the link Kreydenweiss believes exists between wine and art. The winery is in an Alsatian half-timber house, typical, except for its yellow (rather than white) stucco and pale gray shutters. A steep vine-covered slope rises from the edge of a flower-filled courtyard next to the house. ♦ Free. By appointment. 12 Rue Deharbe, Andlau (2 km/1.2 miles west of Mittelbergheim along D62). 88.08.95.83; fax 88.08.41.16

Since 1648 Alsace has changed its nationality five times.

Louis Pasteur's disovery of yeast as the source of fermentation provided the key to consistency in wine making.

Restaurants/Clubs: Red   **Hotels:** Blue
Shops/ 🌳 Outdoors: Green   **Sights/Culture:** Black

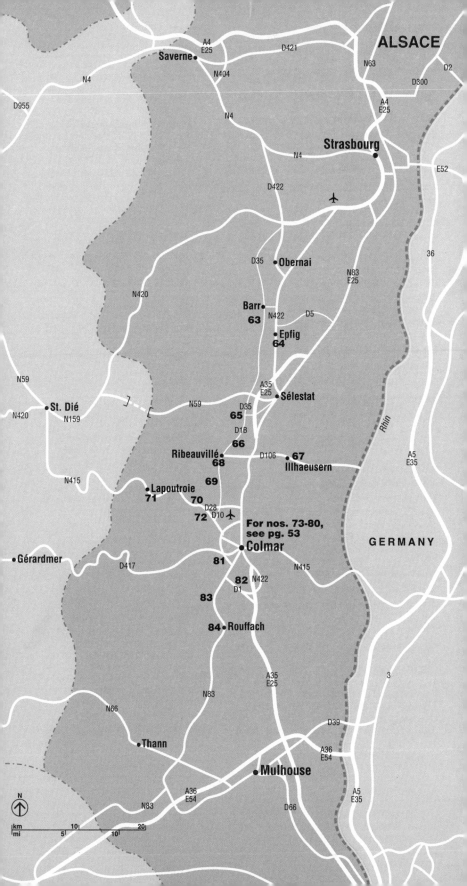

Eat, Drink, and Be Merry in Champagne and Alsace

Key grape varieties: In Champagne: pinot noir, chardonnay, pinot meunier. In Alsace: riesling, gewürztraminer, muscat, pinot noir, sylvaner, pinot blanc, Auxerrois blanc (klevner), tokay–pinot gris.

Classification: There is just one appellation in Champagne and one in Alsace, called simply champagne or Alsace. Champagne has 17 *grand cru* villages; Alsace has around 50 *grand cru* wine vineyard sites. Four types of wine are made in Champagne: vintage, nonvintage, *cuvée de prestige* (the firm's best), *coteaux champenois* (still red or white wine made in Champagne); also made is *ratafia* (grape juice with added alcohol).

Culinary specialties: Brie is a specialty of Champagne, and foie gras and muenster cheese are specialties of Alsace. Here are a few others you may not be familiar with:

Champagne:

andouillettes: tripe sausage

blanquette de veau: creamy veal stew

boudin blanc: white blood sausage

chaource: creamy white cheese made from cow's milk

matelote champenoise: a fish stew using white wine

mousseline de brochet au champagne: pike mousse in champagne sauce

pieds de cochon: pigs' feet

potée champenoise: a hearty meat and vegetable soup

tarte aux raisin: grape tart

Alsace:

choucroute: sauerkraut with meats

tarte flambée: cream, bacon, and onion tart

truite au bleu: lightly poached mountain trout

64 Domaine Ostertag André Ostertag knows his *terroirs* and cherishes their uniqueness; the 26 wines he makes are as distinct from each other as different vineyard conditions and grape varieties can make them, but all are excellent. He grows six types of white grapes (sylvaner, pinot blanc, riesling, pinot gris, gewürztraminer, and muscat) plus pinot noir on three very different, prime vineyard sites: Muenchberg, Heissenberg, and Fronholz. Try the unfiltered Riesling from the Fronholz vineyard, with a rich taste but great finesse, or the late-harvest Riesling from the *grand cru* Muenchberg vineyard, with a delicate mineral taste that balances out the sweetness. The

wine maker's love of his land shines through in his wine. The winery is in Ostertag's house, an ancient gardener's cottage with a slope of vines rising behind it. ♦ Free. M-Sa by appointment. 87 Rue Finkwiller, Epfig (from Mittelbergheim take D62 east 2 km/1.24 miles, then take N422 south 3.1 km/1.92 miles; from Andlau take D603 5 km/3.1 miles southeast). 88.85.51.34; fax 88.85.58.95

65 Auberge St-Martin ★★$$ This friendly *winstub* (wine bar/restaurant) serves regional specialties in its rustic dining room with a fireplace. Try the *choucroute* (sauerkraut) with salmon, beef cooked in Pinot Noir, big ham steaks grilled over a wood fire, and *flammkuchen* (a thin-crusted cream, onion, and bacon tart, also called *tarte flambée*). Chef Toussaint's more sophisticated offerings include *saumon poêlé au miel* (salmon sautéed with honey) and *salade de choucroute au foie gras d'oie* (sauerkraut salad with foie gras). An excellent fixed-price *menu alsacien* provides a low-cost introduction to the region's cuisine. The wines are very reasonably priced too. ♦ Daily lunch and dinner July-Aug; M-Tu, F-Sa lunch and dinner, Th dinner Sept-June. Reservations recommended. 80 Rue de la Liberté, Kintzheim (from Epfig follow N422 14 km/8.9 miles south to Sélestat, then take D159 west 5 km/3.1 miles). 88.82.04.78

65 Hôtel du Haut-Koenigsbourg $ Film buffs might want to check out this formerly elegant, now rather kitschy (but still comfortable) place, which Jean Renoir used as a setting in his classic film about war, *Grande Illusion*. The hotel overlooks a beautiful valley; be sure to ask for a room with a view. The 26 rooms all have private bathrooms. Be careful if you drive up to the hotel in the evening, when many deer cross the road. ♦ Rte du Haut-Koenigsbourg, Orschwiller (from Sélestat follow D159 southwest 6 km/3.7 miles). 88.92.10.92; fax 88.82.50.04

Within the Hôtel du Haut-Koenigsbourg:

Restaurant Hôtel du Haut-Koenigsbourg ★$$ The hotel's rustic dining room is the place to go for hearty regional cooking, including *potée alsacienne*, a stick-to-your-ribs soup. The wines are local, and many are offered by the glass from the small bar. ♦ Daily lunch and dinner; closed in January. Reservations recommended. 88.92.10.92

65 Château du Haut-Koenigsbourg This grandiose castle, the largest in the Vosges, is perched on a high cliff on the Haut-Koenigsbourg Mountain, overlooking vineyards and the Rhine Valley. Built in the 12th century, the château was destroyed in a 1462 siege, but was rebuilt in 1479 by the Thierstein family, then the rulers of Hapsburg. The château gradually fell into ruins, like many châteaux in the Vosges mountain range. In

1889 the residents of the village of Sélestat, who had become the château's owners, offered it to Kaiser Wilhelm II, the ruler of Alsace. The château was completely rebuilt between 1901 and 1908, and the result is more Neo-Gothic than Gothic: There's something a bit too tidy about its massive gray-pink walls and rounded towers with sharply pointed roofs. At the time of the reconstruction, many Alsatians complained that the château had been more attractive as a vine-covered ruin than as an extremely expensive monument to the power of the German emperor. In any case, the view from the terraces is sensational: The high peaks of the Vosges and miles of vineyard- and pine-covered countryside sloping down to the Rhine spread out before you. ♦ Admission. Daily. Rte du Haut-Koenigsbourg, Orschwiller (from Sélestat follow D159 southwest 6 km/3.7 miles; then, at the Hôtel du Haut-Koenigsbourg, take the steep, narrow road through the pine forests). Reservations 88.82.50.60, recorded information 88.92.11.46

65 Aux Ducs de Lorraine $$$ Also called **Hôtel Restaurant Munsch,** this hotel in a half-timber building is an official *Relais de Silence,* meaning it guarantees peace and quiet. The guest rooms open onto the flower-filled balconies that line each floor of the hotel; unfortunately, the balconies are not particularly private, as they are divided by almost transparent panels. The 42 comfortable, spacious rooms and four suites are decorated in contemporary style; be sure to ask for one with a view of Haut-Koenigsbourg and the castle. The hotel itself is located in a pretty wine village. ♦ Closed the first two weeks in December. 16 Rte du Vin, St-Hippolyte (from Sélestat take D35 southwest 6 km/3.7 miles). 89.73.00.09; fax 89.73.05.46

Within Aux Ducs de Lorraine:

Restaurant Aux Ducs de Lorraine
★★$$$ Delicious regional dishes with inventive touches are featured here, like *foie d'oie au gingembre confit* (goose foie gras with candied ginger), *pigeonneau rôti aux oignons confits* (roast squab with caramelized onions), *pot-au-feu de saint-jacques au Riesling* (sea scallops "stewed" in Riesling), *côte de boeuf au Pinot Noir* (beef in Pinot Noir wine sauce), assorted local cheeses, and such luscious desserts as a cold kirsch soufflé.

There's a good choice of Alsatian wines, too. ♦ Tu-Su lunch and dinner Mar-Nov, mid-Dec–mid-Jan; closed the first two weeks in December and mid-January–February. Reservations recommended. 89.73.00.09

66 Bergheim Don't miss this wine village's **Porte Haute,** a 14th-century fortified gate; near it is a linden tree that was planted ca. 1300. The village, a collection of lovingly maintained half-timber houses with geraniums cascading from window boxes, also has a scenic *sentier viticole* (pedestrian path through the vineyards). ♦ 4 km (2.4 miles) south of St-Hippolyte on D1B

Within Bergheim:

Domaine Marcel Deiss This wine maker is known for his very rich, concentrated wines (he makes almost 50 different ones), which need a long time in the bottle for their sugars to break down. The star of the house is the Riesling from the Schoenenbourg vineyard, especially the magnificent (and costly) 1989. Other excellent wines are the Riesling Engelgarten de Bergheim from old vines, full of finesse; a fruity, inexpensive Pinot Blanc; and a full-flavored Pinot Gris. The winery also makes some late-harvest wines. You can tour the world of Alsatian wines right here in this one winery. The building dates from the 1960s, but was built in traditional Alsatian style with half-timbering and stucco. ♦ Free. Tastings M-Sa Apr-Dec; M-F Jan-Mar. Appointment recommended. 15 Rte du Vin (in the center of Bergheim). 89.73.63.37; fax 89.73.32.67

Winstub du Sommelier ★★$$ With a name like this, how could you go wrong? Needless to say, the selection of local wines is outstanding, and the simple regional specialties are very good—try the *cuisse de canard confite en choucroute* (duck with sauerkraut) and the fruit tarts. The place is quintessential Alsace, with a beamed ceiling, big stone fireplace, flower boxes in the windows, and a display of copper cooking utensils. ♦ Tu-Sa lunch and dinner; M dinner. Reservations recommended. 51 Grande Rue (in the center of Bergheim). 89.73.69.99

Though champagne stored at home does not improve with age, if you shelve your champagne bottles horizontally and away from light, heat, and vibration, the contents will keep for several years.

Champagne is best when served in long-stemmed tulip or flute glasses; saucer-shaped glasses allow the bubbles and aroma to escape too quickly.

Restaurants/Clubs: Red   **Hotels:** Blue
Shops/ 🌳 Outdoors: Green   **Sights/Culture:** Black

67 Auberge de l'Ill $$$$ Alsace's great splurge address, one of the best hotels in France, is a little off the wine route, but well worth the detour—if you can afford it. The very luxurious hotel run by the Haeberlin family is housed in a former tobacco-drying hall, but you would never know it. There are nine huge rooms, each as large as some apartments, and two opulent suites, all decorated with light wood furnishings and Italian paintings. The only Alsatian touches are the pretty glazed ceramic wood-burning heaters and the embroidered comforters on the very comfortable beds. All rooms have views of the tranquil countryside; the best choice is the suite in a sumptuously converted fisherman's cabin right at the edge of the picturesque Ill River. All rooms are equipped with mini-bars, direct-dial telephones, TVs, air-conditioning, and grandiose bathrooms. ◆ Closed February–early March. Rue Collonges, Illhaeusern (from Sélestat follow N83-E25 8 km/4.9 miles south, then take D106 3 km/1.8 miles east). 89.71.87.87; fax 89.71.82.83

Within the Auberge de l'Ill:

Restaurant Auberge de l'Ill ★★★$$$$ Marc Haeberlin raises regional cuisine to new heights here. Try his *cuisses de grenouilles à la truffe blanche du Piémont avec pâtes fraîches* (frogs' legs with white truffles from the Piedmont and fresh pasta), *colvert laqué aux épices avec chou rouge* (wild duck with a spicy glaze, served with red cabbage), or *carré d'agneau aux pommes de terre et olives noires* (rack of lamb with potatoes and black olives). A spectacular dish is *ragoût de coquilles saint-jacques aux oursins* (sea scallops with sea urchins), flavored with *curcuma* (turmeric). The wines, particularly those of Alsace, are outstanding, and the sommelier is one of the best in France. Prices are very, very high, but there are some fixed-price menus to help you avoid blowing your whole travel budget on a single, albeit superb, meal. ◆ W-Su lunch and dinner, M lunch Apr-Oct; W-Su lunch and dinner Nov-Mar. Reservations required weeks in advance. 89.71.83.23

68 Ribeauvillé This wine village of half-timber houses and tiny squares dominated by elaborately carved stone fountains is the site of one of Alsace's most ancient and colorful celebrations, the *Pfifferdaj* (day of the fife players), held on the first Sunday of September. There's music, a parade, and a free wine tasting at the *"Fontaine du Vin"* (Wine Fountain) set up on the Place de l'Hôtel de Ville. Any time of year, try to see the storks nesting at the top of the two ancient towers at the town's south and east entrances; storks' nests are a symbol of Alsace, and throughout the region efforts are now being made to boost the declining stork population. The tourist office is in the center of town (1 Grand' Rue, 89.73.62.22; fax 89.73.36.61). ◆ From Sélestat follow N83 south 8 km (5 miles), then take D106 west about 5.5 km (3.4 miles)

Within Ribeauvillé:

Clos Ste Hune

Maison F.E. Trimbach The Trimbach family has been making wine in this area since 1626. Their winery, one of the most highly respected in Alsace, is a collection of ancient half-timber buildings at the foot of the steep slopes on which one of the family's great vineyards is located. If you like dry, pure-tasting, elegant wines with a hint of minerals, you'll love these. The Rieslings are the stars here; they're all well aged in the bottle before being released on the market. Try the Riesling Cuvé Frédéric-Emile, with a mouth-filling, pleasantly mineral taste, or any of the Rieslings from the prestigious Clos Sainte-Hune *grand cru* vineyard, of which the winery is the sole owner. The Clos Sainte-Hune is said to produce one of Alsace's finest Rieslings—its nickname is *"Roi des Riesling"* (King of Riesling). Sylvaner, chasselas, pinot blanc, tokay–pinot gris, gewürztraminer, muscat ottonel, and muscat à petits grains are the other grape varieties grown here. Besides the great Clos Sainte-Hune, the Trimbachs have vines on three other *grand cru* vineyards: Geisberg and Osterberg in Ribeauvillé, and Rosacker in Hunawihr. The Trimbachs also make some luscious late-harvest sweet wines when conditions allow. ◆ Free. Sales and visits by appointment. 15 Rte de Bergheim. 89.73.60.30; fax 89.73.89.04

Les Seigneurs de Ribeaupierre $$$ In the center of the picturesque wine village of Ribeauvillé, this hotel is housed in a half-timber, typically Alsatian structure built in 1727. Madeleine and Marie-Cécile Barth, two sisters who run the place, have carefully chosen the beautiful antique furniture in the larger (and more expensive) rooms and suites; the smaller rooms are very comfortable, but their decor is less elegant. All rooms have private bathrooms and are very quiet. There's no restaurant. ◆ 11 Rue du Château. 89.73.70.31; fax 89.73.71.21

Hôtel de la Tour $$ This hotel in the heart of medieval Ribeauvillé was built in the last century as a winery. It's a four-story white building with blue shutters and a tile roof, but its interior decor is more 1990s than 19th century. There are 35 comfortable rooms decorated in contemporary style, all with private bathrooms. Many of the rooms are on the small side, but all have TVs and direct-dial phones. There's a sauna, Jacuzzi, and tennis court on the premises. The hotel's simple *winstub* offers snacks and local wines by the glass. ♦ Closed January-March. 1 Rue de la Mairie. 89.73.72.73

Au Zahnacker ★$ It's no surprise that this friendly, crowded *winstub,* owned by a local wine co-op, offers a good selection of wines. The prices are low, too. The simple regional fare includes onion tart and *poussin rôti au pinot noir* (roast young chicken with Pinot Noir sauce). Summertime meals are served on a terrace with masses of blooming geraniums; winter meals are in the rustic dining room, where huge planks suspended by chains serve as tables. ♦ M-W, Sa-Su lunch and dinner; closed January-February. Reservations recommended. 8 Rue du Général-de-Gaulle. 89.73.60.77

69 **Riquewihr** This entire tiny wine village has been declared a historic landmark and officially dubbed one of the *plus beaux villages de France* (most beautiful villages in France). Almost all the houses date from the 17th century or well before. And almost every one of them contains something to attract tourists: wine shops; wine-tasting centers; boutiques of various kinds, including many food shops; *winstubs* and other restaurants; and hotels. That's why you can barely move for the crowds here in July and August. Try to come in the off-season. The tourist office (2 Rue de la Première-Armée, 89.47.80.80) is open daily April through mid-November. ♦ 4.5km (2.8 miles) south of Ribeauvillé on D1B

Within Riquewihr:

Le Sarment d'Or $$ The name means "golden vine shoot." This rambling hotel in the center of Riquewihr comprises three former wine maker's cottages and a 13th-century structure. There are seven tiny (claustrophobes, beware!) but romantic rooms and three slightly larger suites; some of the rooms have hand-painted furniture typical of Alsace. All have private bathrooms and direct-dial telephones. ♦ Closed January–early February. 4 Rue Cerf. 89.47.92.85

Within Le Sarment d'Or:

Restaurant Le Sarment d'Or ★★$$ Alsatian tradition reigns here, in decor and food alike. The cozy dining room features heavy ceiling beams, paneled walls, a fireplace, and lots of fresh flowers. Among the good typical offerings, try the *presskopf* (a hearty, meaty casserole), the *magret de canard au pinot noir* (duck breast with Pinot Noir sauce), and the local muenster cheese. ♦ Tu-Sa lunch and dinner; closed January and the last week in June. Reservations required. 89.47.92.85

Maison Hugel & Fils The Hugel family has run this winery since 1639. It is one of the few wineries in Alsace that have made *vendanges tardives* (late-harvest) wines commercially for almost a century. Their 1989 late-harvest wines are among the best anyone at the winery can remember, especially the Gewürztraminer and Pinot Gris. The *vendange tardive* Gewürztraminer 1989 from the Sporen *grand cru* vineyard is spectacular. The winery's Jubilee label signifies wines made from *grand cru* vines; try the full-flavored 1988 Jubilée dry Riesling. The Sélection des Grains Nobles wines are made from "noble rot" grapes (on which botrytis bacteria has been allowed to develop, intensifying the grapes' sugar content and taste); they are incredibly lush and delicious. Two 16th-century half-timber houses make up the winery; take a look at the elaborately carved wooden pillars on their facades. The interiors have been totally remodeled to hold modern wine-making equipment. Hansi, the beloved Alsatian artist known for his scenes of nesting storks on rooftops and other images typical of the region, made the sign that hangs in front of the sales and tastings shop. In the cellars sits what is believed to be the world's oldest wine cask still in use; it dates from 1715 and holds more than 2,000 gallons. ♦ Free. Sales and tastings daily Easter-Nov. 3 Rue de la Première-Armée. 89.47.92.15; fax 89.49.00.10

70 **Kaysersberg** This picturesque village halfway between the official wine route and the Vosges Mountains is filled with half-timber houses. There are several churches, an ancient stone-and-wood covered bridge over the Weiss River, and a great view of the surrounding countryside from the castle ruins above the town (reached by a steep path). An open-air food market is held on Place Gouraud every Monday morning. Albert Schweitzer was born here in 1875. ♦ From Riquewihr take either spur of D3 east to D1B; follow D1B south 3 km (1.9 miles) to Sigolsheim, then take D28 west about 5.5 km (3.4 miles)

Within Kaysersberg:

Au Péché Mignon Pastry shops all over France are thus dubbed; the name means "besetting sin." If sweets are your weakness, you'll love the rich breads, cakes, and pastries on hand here. If you visit at Christmastime, don't miss the bakery's *berawecka,* a fruit-filled yeast bread made only during the holidays. ♦ Tu-Su; closed a week in January. 67 Rue du Général-de-Gaulle. 89.47.30.40

71 Les Alisiers $$ This auberge in the Vosges Mountains is reached by a road that winds through pine trees and past trout streams. The 20 small but comfortable guest rooms all have private bathrooms; ask for one with a view of the valley. The management is very friendly. Good picnic spots dot the area, especially along the scenic D48, which runs through the mountains south of the village. ♦ Closed three weeks in January and the first week of July. 5 Rue Faudé, Lapoutroie (7 km/4.3 miles west of Kaysersberg on N415). 89.47.52.82; fax 89.47.42.38

Within Les Alisiers:

Restaurant Les Alisiers ★★$$ A fireplace and a beamed ceiling are just two of the reasons for this restaurant's cozy ambience. Others are the regional dishes served, like *pommes de terre au muenster* (potatoes with bits of melted muenster cheese on top) and smoked salmon served with blinis and horseradish mousse. There's also a superb selection of Alsatian wines. This place has one of the best quality-price ratios in Alsace. ♦ W-Su lunch and dinner; M lunch; closed three weeks in January and the first week of July. Reservations required. 89.47.52.82

71 Fromagerie Jacques Haxaire A great source for muenster, the rich golden cheese of Alsace. Add some dark rye bread and a bottle of Gewürztraminer, and you've got the makings of a wonderful picnic. ♦ Daily. 18 Rue du Général-Dufieux, Lapoutroie. 89.47.50.76

72 Domaine François Schiélé Wine maker François Schiélé has seven hectares (17.2 acres) of prime vineyards on lovely slopes west of Colmar where he cultivates all the main Alsatian grape varieties, but especially favors riesling, gewürztraminer, and tokay–pinot gris. He says his best terroir is on the Kaefferkopf vineyard site, renowned since the 14th century (it's mentioned in archives dating from 1328). This vineyard is known for producing wines that have both powerful flavor and finesse. All grapes are picked manually here, and the wines are aged in wood. These wines age well, 15 to 20 years. Schiélé says his goal is to "faire apprécier à tout amateur le fruit de ma passion" (to make any wine lover appreciate the fruit of my passion), and he succeeds. He also advises, "Laisser mes vins s'exprimer et vous entendrez les anges chanter" (Allow my wines to express themselves, and you will hear the angels sing). Try it. Much of the elegant mansion, built of light gray stone from the Vosges Mountains, was reconstructed after sustaining damage in World War I, but the tastings and sales room, with paneled walls that date from the house's earliest days, is pure 18th century. ♦ Free. By appointment. 1 Rue de l'Aigle, Ammerschwihr (4 km/2.4 miles northwest of Colmar on N415). 89.78.24.90

Colmar

Handsomely set on a plain at the foothills of the **Vosges,** the Alsatian wine region's central town was once the royal residence of the Emperor Charlemagne. Great sections of it have been restored, mostly those with half-timber 15th- and 16th-century buildings. Among them are the **Maison Pfister** (1537), with a beautiful wooden gallery and a magnificent facade decorated with allegorical figures in bright colors; the **Maison des Têtes** (1608), whose facade is decorated with carved wooden heads; and the **Ancienne Douane** (Old Customs House, or *Koifhus;* 1480), with a colorful diamond-patterned roof. Throughout the city are statues by Frédéric-Auguste Bartholdi—the sculptor of the *Statue of Liberty*—who was born here; one is the *Monument du Vigneron* (Wine Maker's Monument) on Rue des Vignerons (at Rue des Ecoles). The historic neighborhood of **La Petite Venise** (Little Venice)—so dubbed for its 16th-century buildings and many bridges—comprises picturesque homes, stores, and artists' studios perched along the banks of the **Lauch River. Pont St-Pierre** (St. Peter Bridge) overlooks the tranquil scene. The city also boasts the great **Musée d'Unterlinden,** housed in 13th-century Gothic cloister buildings, to which whole books have been dedicated. In addition to the celebrated church art (such as Matthias Grünewald's 16th-century *Issenheim Altarpiece,* transported here in 1793) in the cloister's chapel and a vast store of Renaissance and other art treasures, the museum has good displays on wine culture through the ages; it is the most visited museum in France outside Paris.

A little train takes visitors through the heart of Colmar from June to mid-September; check at the tourist office (4 Rue d'Unterlinden, at Rue du Rempart, 89.20.68.92) for times and stops, and also for information on Colmar's food, wine, and music festivals.

73 Eglise St-Martin (St. Martin's Church) In the heart of ancient Colmar, this 13th- to 14th-century church was to have had two towers on either side of its main (west) entrance, but only one was built, the south. It is capped with an odd pinnacle resembling a Chinese rice paddy hat. Its stained glass windows depict the life of Christ. The most famous entryway is the *Portail St-Nicolas* (St. Nicholas's Portal) which tells of the saint's life in a series of 13 figures carved in the red-gold stone arched over the door. The fourth from left, however, signed "Maistres Humbret," is apparently a self-portrait by the stonecarver. The church's sundial is inscribed with the warning *memento mori* (remember death). ♦ Pl de la Cathédrale (at Rue des Serruriers). No phone

74 Eglise des Dominicains (Church of the Dominicans) This golden stone church, once part of the town's (no longer functioning) Dominican monastery, is known for its 1473 painting *Vierge au Buisson de Roses* (Virgin of the Rose Bush) by Martin Schongauer. The lifelike Madonna is in a flowing red gown against an elaborate background of red and white flowers, birds, intertwined leaves, and two robed angels. The baby Jesus she holds has his arm across her in what many intepret as a protective gesture. Although the first stone of the choir was laid in the late 13th century, the rest of the structure was not built until the 14th and 15th centuries; some interior details date from as recently as the 18th century. Over the south portal is a portrait of King Solomon, one of many stunning depictions rendered in stained glass. ♦ Rue des Serruriers (between Rue de Reiset and Pl de l'Etoile). 89.41.44.96

75 Le Fer Rouge ★★$$$ This popular eatery in a 17th-century half-timber building is pure Alsace, from the decor to the cuisine (which is good, but overpriced unless you stick to the cheapest fixed-price menu). Try the *sandre avec choucroute* (pickerel with excellent, buttery sauerkraut) or the *foie gras cru au ciboulette et navets glacé* (raw foie gras with chives and glazed turnips). There's a great selection of Alsatian wines. ♦ Tu-Sa lunch and dinner; Su lunch. Reservations required. 52 Grand' Rue (at Pl de l'Ancienne-Douane). 89.41.37.24; fax 89.23.82.24

Tomb paintings from ancient Thebes depict the grape harvest and wine making.

Restaurants/Clubs: Red   Hotels: Blue

Shops/ 🌳 Outdoors: Green   Sights/Culture: Black

76 Hôtel Le Maréchal $$$$ This quiet, luxurious hotel in the ancient heart of Colmar known as Little Venice is definitely the city's most picturesque. It is housed in a half-timber mansion that dates from 1562. The 28 rooms and two suites are huge and equipped with all the modern amenities—some even have Jacuzzis and/or saunas. The decor combines the rustic (exposed beams) with the very elegant (velvet-upholstered Louis XVI–style furniture and gilded mirrors); some rooms have canopy beds. The management is friendly, and the continental breakfasts are excellent. The catch: The prices are very high, especially for a city hotel that you'll probably be away from all day long. ♦ 4 Pl des Six-Montagnes-Noires (on Rue du Manège at Rue Turenne). 89.41.60.32; fax 89.23.73.61

Within the Hôtel Le Maréchal:

Restaurant L'Echevin ★★$$$ The exposed beams, tile floors, comfortable chairs, widely spaced tables, and elegant table settings add to the beauty of this restaurant. There's also a terrace overlooking the Lauch River. The chef prepares inventive variations on regional dishes, such as *salade de lentilles verts aux filets de rouget à la crème de raifort* (green lentil salad with fillets of red mullet and horseradish cream) and *ris de veau aux endives et lamelles de truffe* (veal sweetbreads with endives and truffles). Try the flaky *chausson aux pommes* (apple turnover) for dessert. There's an excellent wine list. 89.41.60.32; fax 89.23.73.61

77 Food Shopping in Colmar Stroll along the Rue des Boulangers and the nearby Rue des Têtes, which are lined with tempting food shops. Try **Glasser** (18 Rue des Boulangers, 41.23.69) and **Sigmann** (6 Rue des Boulangers, 41.33.27) for great charcuterie and salads—perfect for picnics. **La Ferme** (34 Rue des Têtes, 23.43.55) is a fine cheese shop. A colorful open-air food market is held in Colmar on the Place St-Joseph on Saturday morning all year. ♦ Both start at Rue Kléber and continue two blocks east

78 Restaurant Jean Schillinger ★★★$$$$ Colmar's best restaurant by far is decorated in a style that's as un-Alsatian as possible: the furniture and artwork on the rice paper–lined walls are contemporary, with the added touch of Venetian mirrors, and there's not a ceiling beam or hanging copper pot in sight. The cooking, though, has regional touches. There's excellent foie gras, an Alsatian specialty, and *filet de sandre peau croustillante au raifort et son choucroute* (pickerel with a crisp crust, served with horseradish and sauerkraut); while *sandre* is often served in area restaurants, it is not usually combined with these beloved Alsatian condiments. The cheese assortment and the wine list are superb. ♦ Tu-Sa lunch and dinner; Su lunch; closed most of July. Reservations required. 16 Rue Stanislas (at Pl Jean-de-Lattre-de-Tassigny). 89.41.43.17; fax 89.24.28.87

79 Musée Unterlinden (Unterlinden Museum) Housed in a 13th-century former convent, this museum is considered one of France's greatest. It contains a spectacular collection of medieval and Renaissance art, including works by Schongauer and the priceless 16th-century Issenheim altarpiece by Matthias Grünewald; there are also many exhibits related to wine, including some ancient wine presses. ♦ Admission. Daily. Pl d'Unterlinden (between Rue d'Unterlinden and Rue Kléber). 89.41.02.29

80 Hôtel Mercure $$ A member of the reliable French chain, this place has 72 rooms and four suites; they're all smallish, but comfortable, and decorated in a cheerful contemporary style. The good continental breakfast is served either buffet-style or in your room. The location is ideal, near the heart of the city and the **Musée Unterlinden,** and prices are very reasonable. There's a restaurant, but it's not the city's best by any means. ♦ Rue Golbery (at Rue du Rempart). 89.41.71.71; fax 89.23.82.71

Colmar Environs

81 Josmeyer Jean Meyer, the head of this highly respected winery, is a great believer in vintages: He says each vintage has its own charm, which should be accentuated rather than hidden. He also avers that the trend of judging wines in comparative tastings causes many wine makers to try for effect, rather than allowing their wines to be delicate, if that's what the vintage calls for. Another approach that sets Meyer apart from the crowd is his defense of planting less "noble" grape varieties, even on great *terroirs*. Among the top wines here are elegant Rieslings from the *grand cru* Hengst and Les Pierrets vineyards, a very dry 1989 Pinot Gris Cuvée du Centenaire, and several wonderful Gewürztraminers from the Folastries, Archenets, and Hengst vineyards, each with its special character. The winery is in a half-timber house with a red tile roof. Tastings and sales are in the wine cellars, which are carved from golden stone; enter them through the garden, which is shaded by a huge, ancient linden tree. ♦ Free. M-F; Sa 10AM-noon. 78 Rue Clemenceau, Wintzenheim (5 km/3.1 miles southwest of Colmar on D417). 89.27.01.57; fax 89.27.03.98

The tomb of King Tutankhamen (who died in 1352 BC) included 36 amphoras of wine meant to accompany his spirit on its journey to the afterlife.

Recommended Reading

Whether you'd like to travel to France from your armchair, prepare for an actual trip, or learn more about wine before you go, there's a wealth of literature that can help. Gerald Asher, *Gourmet* magazine's wine editor, writes highly informative articles each month giving background on wines, wineries, and wine regions. He often writes about France. The following are a few of the many books available to whet your appetite for a wine-tasting journey through the French countryside. Some are about French wines, others about France, and others are simply literary works set in the French countryside.

The Food Lover's Guide to France, by the *International Herald Tribune*'s restaurant critic Patricia Wells (1987; Workman Publishing Company), gives information on several lesser-known regional wines, as well as the typical foods of each part of France and where to find them.

Lexiwine, by Paul Cadiau (1987; French & European Publications), is a pocket-size English-French wine dictionary. Written and published by a Burgundy-based winery owner, it lists all sorts of wine-related terms, from the most technical—*égrappoir* (destalker)—to the most subjective terms used by wine tasters—*voilé* (dim). You can order the book directly from the author: Paul Cadiau, Pernand-Vergelesses, 21420 Savigny-les-Beaune, France (80.21.53.72). The book is also available at W.H. Smith & Sons (248 Rue de Rivoli, Paris), an English-language bookstore.

Alexis Lichine's Guide to the Wines and Vineyards of France (1989; Alfred A. Knopf) provides detailed information on the wines and wineries of France.

The Lily of the Valley, by Honoré de Balzac (1989; Carroll & Graf Publishing), is a classic of French literature set in 19th-century France. Balzac tells the story of an ambitious young man who wins the affections of a highly placed older woman.

Lulu's Provençal Table, by Richard Olney (1994; HarperCollins), is a portrait of a Provençal wine-making family, with typical Provençal recipes.

Michelin Green Guides (1995; Michelin and Co.), a series of regional guidebooks, provide historical background and include listings of museums and other places to see and visit. An overall guide to France is also available. Some of the regional titles are available only in French.

Toujours Provence, by Peter Mayle (1992; Random House), is the follow-up to his tremendously popular *A Year in Provence* (see below). The English journalist continues his adventures in the French countryside, and provides more insights into life in Provence.

The Wine Atlas of France, by Hugh Johnson and Hubrecht Duijker (1993; Mitchell Beazley), delivers an overview of all of France's wine regions. Hugh Johnson has another book, *Vintage: The Story of Wine* (1992; Simon & Schuster), which is a great study of the history of wine making in France and elsewhere.

Wines of Burgundy (1990; Simon & Schuster) is one of three exhaustive books on French wines by Robert Parker. The other two, *Bordeaux: The Definitive Guide for Wines Produced From 1961-1990* (1991; Simon & Schuster) and *The Wines of the Rhône Valley and Provence* (1987; Simon & Schuster), are also important works. *Robert Parker's Wine Buyer's Guide* (1993; Simon & Schuster) details wines from all over, but features many French wines. His newsletter, *The Wine Advocate,* is available by subscription only; write to: The Wine Advocate, Box 311, Monkton MD 21111.

The Wines of Languedoc-Roussillon, by Liz Berry (1992; Ebury Press), is an excellent guide to the wines of this up-and-coming area.

The Wines of the Loire, Alsace, The Rhône, and Other French Regional Wines, by Roger Voss (1992; Mitchell Beazley), introduces France's smaller wine regions (those not among "the big three") and lists wineries, with descriptions of the wines and details on visiting policies.

A Year in Provence, by Peter Mayle (1991; Random House), is an autobiographical account of the adventures this English journalist and his wife had in Southern France. The story welcomes readers into the Mayles' house bought in Provence and shares all their joys and travails.

The following titles are in French:

GaultMillau Le Vin (1995; Editions Médiazur) is published yearly by the famous gourmet food magazine. It is available in any French bookstore. The focus is on wines sold by the case at reasonable prices. Useful information is also given about individual wineries throughout the country.

Le Guide Hachette des Vins (1995; Editions Hachette), a useful book, comes out annually. It lists about 17,000 wines from all over France, all from a particular vintage and sampled in blind tastings by 500 reliable tasters. The 1995 edition covers wines from the 1991 vintage. Although information is in French, easy-to-follow symbols indicate such information as how the wine rated in the tastings, what its price-quality ratio is, and whether the winery accepts visitors. Wines are grouped by appellation. Also, listed in the beginning of the book are excellent wine stores throughout France, restaurants with great wine lists, wine schools, and other useful information. The book is available in any French bookstore.

Les Routes des Vins de France, by Antoine Gerbelle (1995; Ediguides), is revised each year and gives detailed portraits of individual wineries throughout France.

Michelin France (1995; Michelin and Co.), with its famous red cover, is an indispensable guide to hotels and restaurants in France. Although it is in French, easy-to-follow symbols are used. This book is available at any bookstore in France, and is revised every year. Restaurant reputations in France are made or broken by the gain or loss of a *Michelin* star.

Strasbourg

Strasbourg, the ancient capital of the province of Alsace, is a bustling, modern city, the sixth largest in France. It retains a cozy feel, however, perhaps because the city's heart (and most of its major landmarks) are found in a city-within-the-city: **La Cité Ancienne,** a little island bounded by the **Ill River** and the **Fossé du Faux-Rempart,** a narrow canal that once was a moat. The island is filled with ancient half-timbered houses—tall, narrow structures from the 15th, 16th, and 17th centuries—with steep, red tile roofs. It also has, in addition to some traffic-choked boulevards, a maze of pedestrian-only streets lined with *winstubs* (wine bars/restaurants), pastry shops, and cafes tempting you to stop for a gooey pastry or a glass of Gewürztraminer and watch the world go by. The world you see will most likely be international: Strasbourg, strategically located on France's German border, has been the headquarters of the Council of Europe since 1949 and of the European Union's Parliament since 1979. Most residents of Strasbourg speak both French and German, as well as the Alsatian dialect (which is more German than French). The **Université de Strasbourg** was founded four centuries ago and is considered one of France's best, attracting students from all over the world. Strasbourg has, in fact, been an international crossroads since it was founded by Romans in the first century BC; its name is derived from the Latin *strateburgum* (city of the roads).

The city's chief landmark is its beloved **Cathédral Notre-Dame de Strasbourg** (Our Lady of Strasbourg Cathedral), a Gothic masterpiece carved out of pink sandstone from the **Vosges Mountains** west of the city. Though it was built between the late 12th century and the early 15th, its main portions, including the facade, date from the 13th century. The architect **Erwin de Steinback** was in charge of most of the 13th-century construction, including the central portal, which has an amazingly lifelike biblical chronicle carved into its stone facade. On the *portail de l'horloge* (clock portal) on the south side of the cathedral is a 13th-century carving, *La Mort de la Vierge* (Death of the Virgin), that is considered one of the cathedral's masterpieces. Inside are some stunning medieval stained-glass windows, a collection of 17th-century tapestries, and the *Horloge Astronomique* (Astronomical Clock), an ornate 16th-century clock whose animated cherubs tell the days of the week and positions of the stars, as well as the hour (actually, it runs a half hour late). Visitors may watch the clock strike every day at 12:30PM (admission).

The cathedral's spire is a fragile-looking marvel, with open spaces crowned by tiers of carved stone in the shape of a wedding cake. The spire's height made the cathedral the tallest building in the Christian world, a title it held for 400 years after its erection in the 15th century. An observation platform on the spire offers stunning views of the

city and nearby mountains. Admission is charged to the observation platform, which is open daily. Sound-and-light shows are held every evening at 9:15 from April to October.

For the best view of the cathedral from the city, stand on the **Rue Mercière** west of the cathedral's main entrance, between the **Place de la Cathédrale** and the **Place Gutenberg** (named for the printer, who lived in the city). Here you will also see the **Maison Kammerzell,** a 16th-century town house with elaborate wooden carvings, now the **Restaurant Maison Kammerzell** (★$$; 16 Pl de la Cathédrale, 88.32.42.14), and the 13th-century **Pharmacie du Cerf,** said to be the oldest pharmacy in France.

Among Strasbourg's many fine museums is the **Château de Rohan** (2 Pl du Château, 88.52.50.00) just south of the cathedral, an 18th-century episcopal palace now filled with sumptuous period furnishings; it is open on Monday, as well as Wednesday through Sunday, and there's an admission charge. The **Musée de l'Oeuvre Notre-Dame** (Our Lady's Work Museum; 3 Pl du Château, 88.52.50.00) houses what is considered to be the world's best collection of medieval and Renaissance Alsatian art; it is open daily and there's an admission charge. By contrast to those museums' focus on opulent objects once owned by church figures or aristocrats, the charming **Musée Alsacien** (Alsatian Museum; 23-25 Quai St-Nicolas, at Rue de Bouchers, 88.52.50.00) contains a cozy collection of folk art and everyday objects from Alsace's past. Exhibits include a re-creation of a 19th-century farmhouse living room, complete with a rocking horse, hideaway bed, and chamber pot. Admission is charged to the museum, which is open Monday and Wednesday through Sunday.

Don't miss a stroll through what many say is Strasbourg's most picturesque neighborhood, **La Petite France.** The district is filled with half-timbered houses lining the tranquil Ill River and is crisscrossed by several small canals; walk along the cobblestone streets next to the water and watch swans and small boats glide by. Wander along the **Rue des Moulins** and the **Quai de la Petite France** to the **Ponts Couverts** (Covered Bridges), remnants of the city's 14th-century fortifications. The bridges originally were built of wood, and were covered later; they were rebuilt in stone in the 19th century, and now make up a scenic pedestrian walkway. Near the bridges and across the Ill is the **Barrage Vauban** (Vauban Dam; Quai de l'Ill, between the Ponts Couverts and Rue des Frères-Matthis, no phone), which also was once part of the city's defensive fortifications. Today, for the price of admission, you can climb up it to a terrace, from which you will have a spectacular view of the willow-lined Ill, ancient houses along its banks, and the cathedral's spire hovering over it all. The dam is open daily until 9PM.

81 Auberge du Père Floranc $$ Colmar's coziest hotel is actually in a village just outside the city. The sprawling modern pink stucco building is adorned with hundreds of window boxes filled with colorful blooms, and the hotel is very quiet; it's classified as a *Relais de Silence*. The 32 rooms and one suite are all spacious and comfortable, with private bathrooms, direct-dial telephones, TVs, and views of either a flower-filled garden or mountains and vineyards. ♦ Closed the first two weeks of July and November–mid-December. 9 Rue Herzog, Wetolsheim (3 km/1.9 miles south of Wintzenheim on N83). 89.80.79.14; fax 89.79.77.00

Within the Auberge du Père Floranc:

Restaurant du Père Floranc ★★$$ An elegant spot that offers such typical Alsatian dishes as *filet de sandre lardé* (pickerel fillet with bacon), *tourte de caille* (quail pie), and praline ice cream. The wine list is one of the best in the region, and the pretty garden provides a nice backdrop. ♦ Tu-Sa lunch and dinner; Su lunch; closed the first two weeks of July and November–mid-December. Reservations required. 89.80.79.14

82 Hôtel Au Moulin $ This simple 17-room hotel is located in a quiet village just outside Colmar. The modern building has traditional Alsatian half-timber architecture and a small garden. The rooms are small but very comfortable, and the price is definitely right for this expensive area. There's no restaurant. ♦ Rte de Herrlisheim, D1 (from Colmar follow N422 south 6 km/3.7 miles to the exit for D1 west, then take D1 about 3 km/1.9 miles and follow the signs to the hotel). 89.49.31.20

83 Domaine Pierre Frick One of the best versions of one of Alsace's rarest wines, a dry Muscat, is produced by this small winery housed in the Frick family's half-timber house. The clear golden wine, made from grapes grown on the *grand cru* Steinert vineyard, has a bouquet of green apples and flowers; it has a rich, grapey taste with overtones of peaches—amazing flavors for a dry wine. Pierre Frick has cultivated his vineyards using biodynamic principles since 1981, which certainly seem to have paid off. The authentic taste of grapes carefully grown on prime *terroir* clearly comes through here. ♦ Free. Visits by appointment. 5 Rue de Baer, Pfaffenheim (14 km/8.6 miles south of Colmar on N83). 89.49.62.99

84 Restaurant Philippe Boher ★★★$$$ This auberge's excellent fare is based on market offerings. Try the *côtelette de caille aux rouelles de salsifis frais et au jus de truffe* (quail cutlets with slices of fresh salsify and truffle juice), followed by the puff pastry with apricot filling for dessert. The wine list is sensational. The bad news: This place is housed in a contemporary building and lacks the great charm of the region's older spots. Upstairs are 43 reasonably priced guest rooms in the **Hôtel à la Ville de Lyon.** They're decorated in a banal contemporary style, but are comfortable, with all the modern conveniences. ♦ Tu-Su lunch and dinner; restaurant and hotel are closed the first three weeks of March. Reservations required. 1 Rue Poincaré, Rouffach (15 km/9.3 miles south of Colmar on N83). 89.49.62.49; fax 89.49.76.67

84 Maison René Muré The Murés have been wine makers here since 1648, and are the sole owners of the Clos St-Landelin *grand cru* Vorbourg vineyard. This winery is a perfect example of how a vineyard's unique combination of sun exposure, rainfall, soil, and climate—collectively known as its microclimate—can affect the quality of the wine. Through an unusual combination of factors, the grapes on the Vorbourg *grand cru* vines almost always ripen early, and botrytis, the bacteria that causes the "noble rot" necessary for fine Sauternes, almost always forms here. The Sélection de Grains Nobles Grand Cru Vorbourg is a superb wine, worth the splurge. The winery also makes dry wines, including a powerful Pinot Gris, but the luscious late-harvest Rieslings and Gewürztraminers are the stars. Ask to see the winery's magnificent 13th-century wine press. ♦ Free. Tastings and sales M-F; Sa 9AM-noon. Clos St-Landelin, Rte du Vin, Rouffach. 89.49.62.19; fax 89.49.74.85

Bests

Bernard Robert

Hotel/Restaurant Owner, Le Cheval Blanc, Sept-Saulx

Visit the **Faux de Verzy,** where you can walk through an ancient forest and discover its unusual trees with twisted branches. Visit a sacred site, **Cathédrale de Notre Dame de Reims.** Additional riches—once housed in the cathedral—are on display at the **Palais du Tau.** Take a cruise down the **Marne River** and discover the **Marne Valley** and its vineyards. Visit the wine cellars of the town of **Bouzy,** and taste champagne in the cellars of a grower/producer.

Claude Jaillant

Chef/Owner, Restaurant Le Mesnil, Le Mesnil sur Oger

Visit the **Côte des Blancs** and wineries in **Le Mesnil sur Oger;** **Epernay**'s champagne cellars (10 kilometers away) and the **Cathédrale de Notre Dame de Reims** (35 kilometers away). See the reproduction of the grotto at **Lourdes** in Le Mesnil. Les Vendanges (the grape harvest) takes place over 10 days between September and October every year in Le Mesnil.

Burgundy and Beaujolais

Wine lovers would probably make a pilgrimage to this region, source of some of the world's best wines, even if it had nothing else to entice them. But Burgundy and its southernmost region, Beaujolais, offer the visitor beautiful scenery and fascinating historical sites as well as spectacular wine.

Stretching from **Chablis** in the north to **Villefranche-sur-Saône** in the south, Burgundy and Beaujolais are fertile and hilly regions, with huge forests of oak, beech, and pine; great rivers, lakes, and canals teeming with fish; cattle farms; orchards; and, of course, vineyards. Dotting this lush landscape are countless villages of golden stone houses hidden in the hills, some of France's most beautiful Romanesque and Gothic churches and monasteries, and opulent honey-colored palaces, once the homes of the fabled dukes of Burgundy.

Cultivating mostly pinot noir, chardonnay, and gamay grapes, the area's vineyards are contained on prized plots of land nestled in *côtes* (slopes or hillsides) and surrounded by orchards and fields of sunflowers. Unlike in France's other wine-producing regions, acres of vines do not rule the landscape here. In fact, you could drive straight through the heart of the area on the truck-clogged *Autoroute du Soleil* ("Highway of the Sun," or A6) without ever glimpsing a single vineyard. To discover the region, you must get off the autoroute and the crowded N74, the main road from **Dijon** to **Beaune**, and explore the small "D" roads leading through the hills west of the **Côte d'Or.** And really rural France is quite close; one need not venture

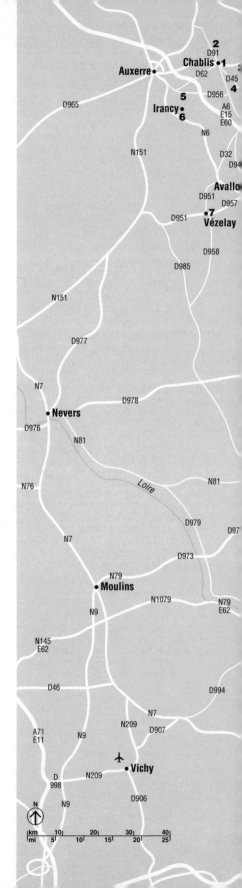

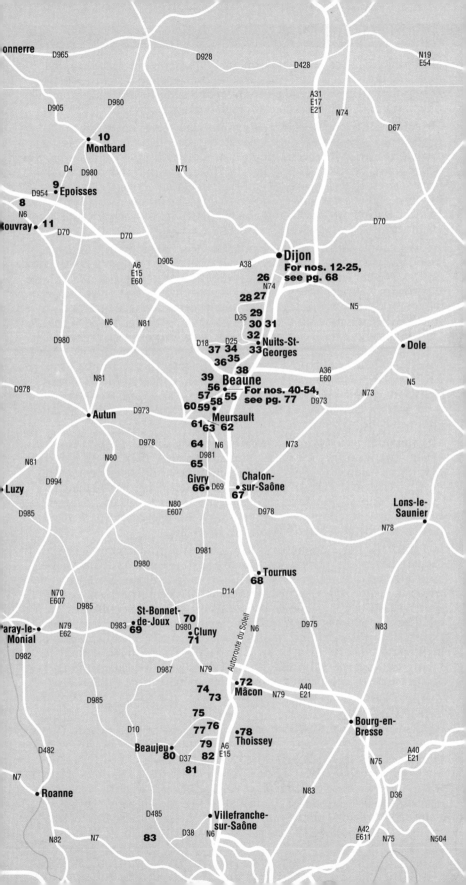

any farther than the **Côte Chalonnaise** and **Mâconnais** regions to find quiet and unspoiled countryside, where postage stamp–size wine villages nestle among vineyards and pine-covered hills. Here, wine makers happily offer tastings in the cellars beneath their homes.

Two interesting ways to explore Burgundy are to barge down one of the region's placid rivers or to take a gustatory tour and sample the region's many delicacies. Whether in simple bistros or multistarred restaurants, you will rub shoulders with ruddy-cheeked *vignerons* (wine producers) while feasting on such local specialties as snails in butter redolent with garlic, poached eggs in a red wine sauce served on garlic-infused toast, hearty *boeuf bourguignon* and coq au vin, and pungent local cheeses such as époisses and chambertin.

It is not known who originally planted vines in Burgundy. The Romans found vineyards here when they arrived to fight the Gallic Wars in the first century BC. But we have the 12th-century Cistercian monks at the **Abbaye de Cîteaux** (Cîteaux Abbey) to thank for creating the first fine wine—Clos de Vougeot—from the fruit grown from the desolate chalk, flint, and clay soil along what is now known as the Côte d'Or. From this "slope of gold," a 150-kilometer (93-mile) belt of vineyards stretching between the towns of Dijon and **Chagny**, come some of the world's most famous and expensive wines: Gevrey-Chambertin, Chambolle-Musigny, Aloxe-Corton, Corton-Charlemagne, Richebourg, Pommard, Meursault, Puligny-Montrachet, Chassagne-Montrachet, and, rarest of all, Romanée-Conti. Most experts agree that the great wines of the Côte d'Or have no serious rivals in France, although wine makers from Bordeaux would beg to differ.

The Burgundy region also encompasses four other famous wine areas: Chablis in the north, the Côte Chalonnaise south of the Côte d'Or, and the Mâconnais vineyards in southern Burgundy, home of the popular white, Pouilly-Fuissé. Just south of the Mâconnais is Beaujolais, where many excellent wines are produced (mainly in the northern part of the region), as well as a seemingly endless river of fruity, inexpensive *vins ordinaires,* particularly the now famous Beaujolais Nouveau.

In spite of its fame, Burgundy's total annual wine production is just a drop in the world's wine bucket: The region comprises 23,000 hectares (56,800 acres) of vines, making up only about five percent of France's total wine production. The typical Burgundian *vigneron* cultivates a mere 10 hectares (24.7 acres) of vines, most of them scattered along hillsides. Each bit of land has its own special soil and microclimate. That explains why there are more than a hundred official *Appellations d'Origine Contrôlée (AOC)* in Burgundy, most of them in the Côte d'Or. Made up almost entirely of *grand cru* and *premier cru* vineyards, the Côte d'Or is divided into two distinct regions: The **Côte de Nuits**, which stretches from Dijon south to **Nuits-St-Georges**, and the **Côte de Beaune**, which runs from **Aloxe-Corton** to Chagny.

Just remember: A wine with a famous village name isn't necessarily a great one. Burgundy's whites often are better buys than the reds, because many of the reds need to age longer, which adds to the price and cuts down on availability. As elsewhere in France, you will need to go to dealers or special wine stores to find wines from older vintages that are ready to drink. At the wine maker's own cellars you'll most likely find mainly recent vintages; some may be ready to drink, but others will only be suitable for stocking up.

The good news is that, by exploring Burgundy, you will be able to taste wines so rare that you might never find them back home, and you can buy great wines that don't cost a month's pay. That, coupled with the stunning landscape and intriguing historic sites, places Burgundy among France's best regions to tour.

Getting to and around Burgundy and Beaujolais

Airport

The **Aéroport Dijon-Bourgogne** (80.67.67.67) is approximately seven kilometers (4.5 miles) southeast of Dijon. It is used primarily for domestic flights; the only international flights available here are to and from London.

Car Rental

Dijon and Beaune are significant cities, but Chablis is so tiny that it doesn't have a car-rental office or a train station. The closest are in Auxerre, which is 15 kilometers (nine miles) away; and there are some in Villefranche-sur-Saône, the capital of Beaujolais.

Auxerre

Avis	86.46.83.47
Europcar	86.46.99.08
Hertz	86.46.57.30
Eurorent	86.46.00.00

Beaune

Avis	80.24.96.46
Budget	80.24.10.23
Citer	80.22.28.14
Europcar	80.22.32.24

Dijon

Avis	80.43.60.76
Hertz	80.43.55.22
Europcar	80.43.28.44

Villefranche-sur-Saône

Avis	74.02.27.77
Europcar	74.09.07.90
Hertz	74.60.02.36

Trains

Auxerre's **Gare St-Gervois** (Rue Paul-Doumer, 86.46.50.50) is the nearest train station to Chablis. The *TGV* (*Train à Grande Vitesse*, France's "very fast" train) does not service Auxerre, but the trip takes only about two hours from Paris's Gare de Lyon by ordinary train. An **Avis** office is across the street.

Beaune's train station, **Gare SNCF** (Ave du 8-Septembre, 80.22.13.13), is 2.5 hours from Paris's Gare de Lyon by *TGV* and four hours by ordinary train. **Avis** and **Budget** have offices across the street from the station, on Blvd Jules-Ferry.

The **Gare de Villefranche-sur-Saône** (Blvd Louis-Blanc, at the intersection of Rue de la Gare and Rue Arnaud, 78.92.50.50) is not served directly by *TGV,*

but you can take the fast train from Paris to Lyons—a two-hour ride, then switch to the local train, which will take 45 minutes to travel to Villefranche-sur-Saône.

In Dijon, the **Gare de Dijon-Ville** (Ave Maréchal-Foch, at Rue du Docteur-Rémy, information 80.41.50.50, reservations 80.43.52.56) is the central station, where the *TGV* trains arrive from Paris's Gare de Lyon (about an hourlong trip) and elsewhere. Within the station is a well-equipped *salon des affaires* (business lounge), complete with a fax machine, telephones, and other business services (for a fee). Train tickets, as well as the obligatory seat reservations for *TGV* trains, can be purchased at windows or from machines. **Avis** and **Hertz** have offices on Avenue Maréchal-Foch next to the station.

FYI

Visitors' Information Offices

Beaune's **Office de Tourisme** (Rue de l'Hôtel-Dieu, between Pl de la Halle and Rue Rolin, 80.26.21.30; fax 80.26.21.39) is in the center of town. The office offers many brochures on Beaune in both French and English, organizes tours and wine tastings, finds hotel rooms, and recommends restaurants and wine-tasting centers. It is open daily.

Chablis's **Office de Tourisme** ("Le Petit Pontigny," 1 Rue de Chichée, 86.42.80.80; fax 86.42.80.16) is open Monday through Saturday.

The **Office de Tourisme de Dijon** (Pl Darcy, at Ave Maréchal-Foch, 80.44.11.44) offers numerous publications in English on Dijon. Services include guided tours of the city in English, help finding hotel accommodations, and arrangements of luxurious barge trips down the Canal de Bourgogne. The office is open Monday through Saturday, and Sunday from 9AM-noon.

Also in Dijon, the **Comité Régional du Tourisme de Bourgogne** (12 Blvd Brosses, at Rue du Temple, 80.50.10.20; fax 80.30.59.45) has many publications in French and English on Burgundy's wine regions, landmarks, gastronomy, and other attractions. Brochures on special kinds of sightseeing include details on barge-hotel tours, ballooning adventures, fishing, and horseback riding. The office is open Monday through Saturday.

Wine Organizations

Beaune is home to the head office of the **Bureau Interprofessionel des Vins de Bourgogne** (Interprofessional Office of Burgundy Wines; 140 Blvd Bretonnière, between Rue Maufoux and Rue Louis-Very, 80.24.70.20; fax 80.24.69.36); it has branches in Mâcon (520 Ave de Lattre de Tassigny, 85.38.20.15) and Chablis (see "Délégation Régionale du Bureau Interprofessionel des Vins de Bourgogne" below). The organization publishes several useful brochures in French and English, including the "Guide to Lovers of Burgundy Wine"; cards that list the special characteristics of each Burgundian *AOC;* and "De Vigne en Cave," which lists and describes wine makers who open their cellars to visitors (look for the "De Vigne en Cave" sign next to private wine cellars thoughout Burgundy; it guarantees they accept visitors). Many wine maps are for sale, as are several videos on Chablis (one is in English, and formatted on the US VCR standard, so you'll be able to play it at home). The center also organizes wine tastings and special classes and tours. It is open Monday through Saturday.

In Chablis, the **Délégation Régionale du Bureau Interprofessionel des Vins de Bourgogne** (Regional Office of the Burgundy Wine Professional Association; "Le Petit Pontigny," 1 Rue de Chichée, 86.42.42.22; fax 86.42.80.16) is housed with the local tourist office in a restored 17th-century abbey. This branch of the serious, well-organized association sets up wine tours, classes, and tastings all year. It hosts such special events as formal initiations into Chablis's own wine society, the Piliers Chablisiens, plus many events linked to Chablis's annual wine festival (the fourth Sunday in November). The center, which is open Monday

through Saturday, also has general info for wine route travelers.

In Beaujolais, the **Union Interprofessionnelle des Vins du Beaujolais** (210 Blvd Vermorel, Villefranche-sur-Saône, 74.65.45.55; fax 74.60.02.32) has a wealth of material on Beaujolais, but almost all of it is in French. Their booklet, *"A la découverte du patrimoine beaujolais"* (Discovering Beaujolais Heritage) details 11 routes through the region, with descriptions (in French) of sites along the way. The office is open Monday through Friday.

Phone Book

Hospitals

Auxerre	86.48.48.48
Beaune	80.24.44.44
Dijon	80.29.30.31
Villefranche-sur-Saône	74.65.82.50

Police (nonemergencies)

Beaune	80.24.64.00
Chablis	86.42.10.17
Dijon	80.44.55.00
Villefranche-sur-Saône	74.65.45.71

Northern Burgundy and Chablis

As a wine-route traveler, you'll make your way to northern Burgundy primarily to visit Chablis, the town where one of the world's most famous white wines is produced—one so widely known that the word "chablis" is often used generically in the United States to refer to any white wine. The prominent wineries spread from Chablis proper to its environs—**Maligny, Fleys,** and **Poilly-sur-Serein.** After you've seen Chablis's wineries and explored its specialty shops, you should spend some time exploring the surrounding picture-postcard countryside.

Venturing south from the Chablis area, you'll come to a town on a hilltop, **Vézelay,** famed for its jewel of Romanesque architecture, **Basilique Ste-Madeleine.** And don't miss the grand medieval monastery, **Abbaye de Fontenay** (Fontenay Abbey).

1 Chablis This small, flat town of austere houses, located on the banks of the pretty Serein River, offers no remarkable landmarks, although the city park and public campground along the Serein (just east of Quai Paul-Louis-Courrier) is a pleasant picnicking spot. The compelling reason to go to Chablis is not the scenery, but the wine. True Chablis, a flinty, dry white made solely from chardonnay grapes (known locally as beaunois), is produced in an area of about 1,000 hectares (2,470 acres) on a thin layer of hard topsoil. The climate can be a curse: Chablis often contends with harsh winters, rainy summers, and damaging frosts. These difficulties, combined with the wine's international renown, have led to a large amount of inferior wine being produced just near enough to the

great vineyards to be dubbed Chablis. ♦ At the junction of D965 and D91, midway between Auxerre and Tonnerre

Within Chablis:

Le Cellier Chablisien

Le Cellier Chablisien In this low-slung, modern white building, knowledgeable ex-sommelier Bernard Guyot purveys a variety of wines from Chablis and elsewhere in Burgundy. He has everything from high-priced *grands crus* (all ready to drink) to more modestly priced *petit* Chablis, an appellation within Chablis whose reputation and taste is not quite up to the standards of its big brother. That said, you must try the rich-tasting selections from Domaine Pisse-Loup that belie the winery's name, which means "wolf piss." In addition, the shop has a selection of wine-serving accoutrements, such as a fine sommelier's knife made by the Laguiole knife company in central France. Guyot also organizes vineyard tours and tastings for small groups; he speaks English, and the programs are available in English on request. ♦ M-Sa. Tours and tastings by appointment. 7 Rue Jules-Rathier. 86.42.15.64; fax 86.42.82.06

Hostellerie des Clos $$$ Chablis's finest hotel is a simple, pink stucco, 12th-century former convent right in the center of town, with its own large garden and an elegant restaurant. The decor is modern, but floral-patterned fabrics and pink walls warm it up. All 26 large rooms have private baths, televisions, and phones; most have views of the peaceful garden. The buffet breakfast is a real treat, with homemade jams and fresh croissants. ♦ Closed late December–early January. Rue Jules-Rathier. 86.42.10.63; fax 86.42.17.11

Within the Hostellerie des Clos:

Restaurant Hostellerie des Clos
★★★$$$ Highly rated chef Michel Vignaud offers rich, elaborate dishes like *rouget à l'émulsion d'huîtres* (red mullet with oyster essence). All the food is perfectly set off by the outstanding Chablis on the wine list. ♦ M-Tu, Th-Su lunch and dinner June-Sept; M-Tu, F-Su lunch and dinner, Th dinner Oct-May; closed late December–early January. Reservations required. 86.42.10.63

La Chablisienne A wine co-op with real class. The 280 growers represented here produce a third of Chablis's wine; some three million bottles are stocked, representing six different vintages. The organization was created in 1923 and is one of the most reliable wine co-ops in France—the group even owns

parts of some *grand cru* vineyards, such as **Château Grenouille.** You'll find bottles in a wide range of prices, many of them ready to drink now, and made to very high standards. Try the Premier Cru Beauroy 1991, whose aroma suggests citrus fruits, toast, and butter, and whose price is more than reasonable. Helpful and friendly staff are a plus. ♦ Daily. English spoken. 8 Blvd Pasteur. 86.42.11.24; fax 86.42.47.51

Domaine Jean Collet & Fils Don't be put off by the yellow neon that outlines this modern winery's pointed roof. Inside you'll find a warm welcome, probably from Gilles Collet (Jean's daughter-in-law), and tastes of the high-quality wines this family has produced since 1792. Collet wines have been ranked highly by Hachette's annual *Guide des Vins* and other prestigious wine publications. The family has 30 hectares (74.1 acres) of vines, including three *premiers crus* and one *grand cru,* Vaumur. The fine Premier Cru Le Montmains 1988 is ready to drink in 1995, although all the *premier cru* wines here are long-lived. The Montmains is the color of gold, with a complex taste that includes overtones of honey, greengage plums, and almonds. The superb Vaumur is pale and has an almost citrus bouquet. ♦ Free. M-F; Sa-Su by appointment; closed the first two weeks of August. 15 Ave de la Liberté. 86.42.11.93; fax 86.42.47.43

La Maison de l'Andouillette Artisanale If you like tripe, try the Chablis version of a French culinary specialty: *andouillette,* a strong, smelly tripe sausage. The best way to cook it is on a grill over a wood fire, but kitchen facilities will do. The specialty here, Chablis *andouillette,* is long and thin, and decidedly not for fat-content watchers. Also featured here are wine's accoutrements: glasses, corkscrews, cheese, you name it. ♦ Tu-Sa; Su 8AM-1PM. 3 *bis* Pl du Générale-de-Gaulle. 86.42.12.82

2 Domaine de l'Eglantière With 170 hectares (420 acres), this winery run by Jean Durup and his son is the largest vineyard in the Chablis area. (It also offers a perfect view of gently sloping vineyards, separated by green trees.) Jean *et fils* produce several award-winning *premiers crus* and an assortment of fruity *petit* Chablis to be drunk young. The Durup family has been making wines in Chablis at least as far back as the village's written records go. Much of the current estate was purchased by Jean Durup's father after the phylloxera scourge drove other local grape growers off their land. The winery's *premiers crus* include Chablis's top vineyard names: Fourchaume, Vau de Vey, and Montée de Tonnerre; any Durup Chablis with one of these names on its label is bound to be spectacular. Tastings and sales are in the small, simple office building; nearby is the family's red-turreted, 12th-century **Château de Maligny** (closed to the public), which Jean Durup has been restoring for almost 20 years. ♦ Free. ♦ M-F; Sa morning. 4 Grande-Rue, Maligny (from Chablis go 7 km/4.3 miles north on D91). 86.47.44.49; fax 86.47.55.49

3 Domaine Grossot Jean-Pierre and Corinne Grossot have been producing fine Chablis since 1979. They have vines in five *premier cru* vineyards—Fourchaume, Vaucoupin, Côte-de-Troëmes, Les Fourneaux, and Mont-de-Milieu—all top quality and completely reliable. Most of their wines are kept in stainless-steel tanks, but the simple Chablis is aged in wood and has a delicate yet full taste, at an excellent price. Corinne Grossot greets visitors and offers tastings in an attractive room with vaulted ceilings, designed to resemble an ancient wine cellar. ♦ Free. ♦ Daily by appointment. From Chablis follow D965 east about 5 km (3.1 miles) to Fleys and follow the signs to the winery. 86.42.44.64; fax 86.42.13.31

4 Le Moulin de Poilly-sur-Serein $ This bed-and-breakfast in a tiny village along the Serein River southeast of Chablis is run by a friendly Franco-British couple, Pascal and Hester Moreau. They have five simple guest rooms with flowered wallpaper and 19th-century furnishings. The Moreaus make their own Chablis wines (which can be sampled), as well as lovely pottery. This is a great base for touring the countryside on foot or bicycle, and the Moreaus are excellent sources of information on the area. ♦ From Chablis take D45 southeast about 10 km (6.2 miles) and follow the signs to Poilly-sur-Serein. 86.75.92.46; fax 86.75.95.21

5 Grand Cru View One of the most beautiful views in the Chablis area is along a narrow, peaceful road that runs east of the village of Irancy toward the village of St-Bris-les-Vineux. Stop by the two picnic tables atop the hill. All you'll hear is the wind rustling—but, oh, what you'll see: rows of vines, expansive fields of corn and brilliant yellow sunflowers, and—to the west, in the valley far below—the white stone houses and tapering church steeple of Irancy, nestled among pine trees and fruit orchards. ♦ From Chablis take D62 southwest about 18 km (11 miles), then follow D956 south 2 km (1.25 miles) to the top of the hill where D956 intersects with D38

6 Domaine Anita & Jean-Pierre Colinot Jean-Pierre Colinot, the friendly wine maker at this small, family-run winery, uses pinot noir and césar grapes to produce his Irancy reds. They are all treated in the traditional manner, with lengthy contact between skins and juice and no aging in wood. Most Irancy wines need aging in the bottle, but the very fruity 1992s can be drunk in 1995. Colinot is also a gold mine of information about the local wine-making scene, and the unspoiled village of Irancy is worth a visit on its own. ♦ Free. ♦ M-Sa 9AM-8PM; Su 9AM-3PM (no midday closing). By appointment. 1 Rue des Chariats, Irancy (from Vincelottes take D38 north 4 km/2.5 miles and follow the signs to the winery). 86.42.33.25

7 Vézelay Although Vézelay is off the Burgundy wine route, it's worth the detour: Its **Basilique de la Madeleine** is justifiably one of the most famous sites in France. The village itself, although touristy, is lovely, with steep, narrow cobblestone streets, restored stone cottages, and medieval ramparts and gates. Treat yourself to a walk early in the morning or just before dusk, when the sun casts a glow over the surrounding valleys. ♦ From Irancy take D38 south 5 km (3.1 miles), then follow N6 south 29 km (18 miles) to D951, which goes south 10 km (6.2 miles) to Vézelay. From Avallon take D957 13 km (8 miles) southwest to Vézelay

Within Vézelay:

Basilique de la Madeleine For centuries (construction began on this edifice in AD 860), the basilica was renowned for housing the remains of Mary Magdalene (Sainte Madeleine), and pilgrims trekked up the steep hill to Vézelay in search of miracles. (They still do every 22 July, the saint's feast day.) In 1122, disaster struck: Fire broke out in the church and its roof fell in, killing many pilgrims. The basilica was rebuilt over the next century, and it became a principal stop on the pilgrim route to Santiago de Compostela in Spain. In 1146, Saint Bernard set off on the second crusade from here, and King Philippe-Auguste of France and Richard the

Lionhearted of England met here to launch the third crusade; Saint Francis of Assisi founded the first Franciscan monastery in France on Vézelay's hillside. From these illustrious beginnings, Vézelay went into a long decline, and the basilica was looted during the Revolution. In 1840, crusading architect-restorer **Viollet-le-Duc** took charge of the renovation, using old drawings as his reference. He restored the facade, the Gothic pediment, and the tympanum of the center Romanesque portal. Flying buttresses support the nave which intersects the **Tour St-Antoine,** which dates from the 13th century. Today private gardens extend over the area where the abbey buildings used to be, but the 12th century refectory is still standing. The interior is remarkable for its expansive space and glowing light. Today almost every surface is unpainted gleaming white stone; you must try to imagine the effect of the brightly painted frescoes that once covered the walls and ceiling. Don't miss the elaborately carved *chapiteaux* (capitals) at the tops of the columns inside the church; of special note is the one known as *"le moulin mystique"* (the mystical mill), which depicts a man pouring wheat into a mill while another collects the flour. ♦ By appointment. For information or a guided tour, call the tourist office: 86.33.23.69

7 Restaurant L'Espérance ★★★★$$$$
Superchef Marc Meneau's spacious establishment—by far the best restaurant in Burgundy—is just down the hill from Vézelay, and likewise is well worth the short detour from the main wine route. His place is a monument to French culinary innovation: Everything on the menu is delicious and surprising, yet a real departure from the nouvelle school of tiny portions and outlandish combinations. Try the *salade de l'homard aux herbes du jardin* (lobster in a salad with fresh garden herbs) or the *galette de truffe* (a truffle cake baked with butter). Notable entrées include *pigeon en crapaudine* (deboned grilled pigeon) and *le veau caramel* (roasted veal in caramel sauce). For dessert don't miss the *tarte à la semoule* (semolina tart with a caramel glaze) or the roasted figs with cumin ice cream. Chef Meneau is single-handedly bringing wine making back to Vézelay (most local vineyards were not replanted after the phylloxera disaster); the wine list, which offers one of the best selections of burgundies in France, includes his own Chardonnay white and a fruity red burgundy. The dining room feels like the ultimate greenhouse: Its roof is glass, and the enormous picture windows overlook an ample, flower-filled garden. ♦ Daily lunch and dinner July-Aug; M, Th-Su lunch and dinner, W dinner Apr-July and Sept-Dec; closed January-March. Reservations required far in advance. From Vézelay follow D958 south 2 km (1.25 miles) to the entrance to the village of St-Père-sous-Vézelay. 86.33.20.45; fax 86.33.26.15

At the Restaurant L'Espérance:

Hôtel L'Espérance $$$$ This member of the Relais & Châteaux group offers 13 small, old-fashioned rooms—perfect for a romantic rendezvous—in the same peach-pink stone building as the restaurant. Be sure to ask for a room with a garden view. There are also eight rustic rooms in an old stone mill at the other end of the garden, and 14 less expensive country-style rooms in a small modern building by the highway. If you require air-conditioning ask for the latter. A huge suite in the mill, reached by a private staircase, is the most popular. ♦86.33.20.45

7 Restaurant Le Pré des Marguerites
★★$ Here is Marc Meneau's cheery bistro alternative to his **L'Espérance** across the street. Gaze over a lawn planted with daisy beds (the restaurant's name means "daisy meadow") and savor the simple but exquisitely presented Burgundian fare. Try the *jambon persillé* (ham in a garlic-and-parsley jelly), the escargots, the sinfully rich *tourte de pomme de terre* (two-crust potato tart), the *jambon braisé au vin de Chablis* (ham braised in Chablis wine), and the *civet de canard* (long-simmered duck casserole). Everything is good, and the prices are amazingly low, especially if you stick with the fixed-price menus. The wine list is short but well chosen. Above the restaurant are 14 rooms and two suites, but they cost almost as much as the much nicer rooms in **L'Espérance** across the street. ♦ Daily lunch and dinner. Reservations recommended. St-Père-sous-Vézelay. 86.33.20.45; fax 86.33.26.15

8 Chambres d'Hôte Ferme de Forlonge $
Jacqueline and Bernard Noirot offer three rooms with private baths in a renovated stone farmhouse bed-and-breakfast. The homemade comforters on each bed, the dormer windows, the slanted ceilings, and the ancient, wood-roofed, geranium-bedecked *lavoir* (communal clothes-washing trough) on the grounds add romantic touches. Two rooms are in a first-floor wing, while the third—and best—is above, at the top of its own beautiful wooden staircase. The continental breakfast includes tasty homemade jams; for an extra fee, simple

evening meals with the family are served in a large dining room with massive ceiling beams and a big fireplace. ♦ From Avallon take N6 east 10 km (6.2 miles) to Cussy-les-Forges, then take D954 north 5.5 km (3.4 miles) and follow the signs to Sauvigny-le-Beuréal and the farmhouse. 86.32.53.44

9 Fromagerie Berthaut In the 16th century, local Cistercian monks began making a pungent cow's milk cheese that came to be known as époisses, after the nearby village of the same name. But 400 years later, the craft had been lost to rural flight to the cities and population losses incurred in the World Wars. Robert Berthaut began to revive it here in 1946, drawing on childhood recollections to re-create the cheese. Epoisses is now the village's main industry, and this spic-and-span shop—of which Berthaut is still the proprietor—is the best place to buy it. The cheese is the size and shape of camembert and bathed in *marc de Bourgogne* (a grapey eau de vie) as it ages; its taste is milder than its smell, and it's great picnic fare. Ask to see the slide show on how the cheese is made. ♦ M-Sa. From Avallon take N6 east 7 km (4.34 miles) to Cussy-les-Forges, then take D954 12.5 km (7.75 miles) to Epoisses. From Sauvigny-le-Beuréal, then take D954 4 km (2.4 miles) east to Epoisses. 80.96.44.44; fax 80.96.30.40

10 Abbaye de Fontenay (Fontenay Abbey) This immense 12th-century Cistercian abbey looms, solitary and independent, in a valley between Chablis and Dijon. A visit is well worth the 19-kilometer (12-mile) pilgrimage off the wine route—especially since wine lovers owe so much to the Cistercians, who were the first to make fine wines from vineyards along the Côte d'Or. Until the 16th century, the abbey was powerful and prosperous, home to more than 300 monks and converts. Then a decline set in, until it was converted to a paper mill during the French Revolution. The abbey was restored in the first part of this century, and the many fountains that gave it its name bubble once again in the surrounding gardens. The church here, consecrated in 1147, is one of the oldest surviving Cistercian churches in France; its unornamented style is typical of the order, which rejected the love of luxury that had developed in other medieval religious communities. Stroll through the magnificent cloister, with its long arcades, open courtyard, and massive stone arches and columns, and you'll forget about worldly luxuries too. ♦ Admission. Daily; guided tours on the hour. From Epoisses take D4 north 12 km (7.4 miles) to Senailly, then take D4E 6 km (3.7 miles) to Montbard; from Montbard take D32 northeast 5 km (3.1 miles) and follow the signs to the abbey. 80.92.15.00

La Varenne Cooking School

Noted cooking authority Anne Willan, the founder and director of **La Varenne Cooking School,** offers a series of tempting cooking classes at her beautiful **Château du Feÿ** in **Burgundy,** not far from the vineyards of **Chablis.** Students stay in huge, luxurious rooms within the château, which is surrounded by a 100-acre park and has tennis courts and a swimming pool. Three types of cooking courses are available: a one-week visitor program, a three-week intensive orientation program, and a five-week intensive professional program, which is open only to people in the food or restaurant business. All classes are taught by fine French chefs, with translations provided by bilingual assistants.

The one-week program includes four practical classes, a master chef demonstration, three wine tastings, visits with a cheese producer and an artisan baker, and four excursions highlighted by a vineyard visit. Students dine at two of France's finest restaurants, the **Côte St-Jacques** (★★★★$$$$; 86.62.09.70) in nearby **Joigny** and **Restaurant L'Espérance** (see page 65) in **Vézelay.** After a week, you too will be able to make typical Burgundian dishes like *jambon persillé* (ham in parsleyed gelatin), *feuilleté d'escargots à l'anis* (anise-flavored snails in puff pastry), *poulet au vin d'Irancy* (chicken in Irancy red wine), and a special chocolate cake. Fine wines are served at all meals.

The three-week program includes 20 practical classes (each about four hours long, ending with lunch or dinner); nine two-hour demonstrations; weekly tastings of wines from throughout France; and long excursions every Friday afternoon, including vineyard visits and tastings and visits to cheese makers, foie gras farms, and farmers' markets. Students will also have dinner in several fine restaurants. The cooking classes are organized around three themes: Fundamentals of French Cooking, French Pastry, and Contemporary French Cuisine. The course concludes with an exam, which leads to the La Varenne Intermediate Diploma.

The five-week professional course, limited to 14 students, involves about 40 hours per week in the kitchen and eight days (including two weekends) of excursions to different parts of Burgundy, Champagne, the Lyonnais region, and Paris. A practical exam leads to the La Varenne Professional Diploma. Alumni have praised this course highly.

All course fees cover the stay at the château, all meals and excursions, and pickup and delivery to Paris if desired. For further information, contact: La Varenne, Château du Feÿ, 89300 Villecien, France (9km/5.5 miles northwest of Joigny on N6). 86.63.18.34; fax 86.63.01.33. The US address is: La Varenne, c/o Janis McLean, La Varenne Representative, Box 25574, Washington, DC 20007. 202/337.0073, 800/537.6486; fax 703/823.5438

11 Château de la Motte, Sincey-lès-Rouvray ★★$ The Largy family offers hearty Burgundian fare in a creamy pink, turreted stone château that dates to the 13th and 14th centuries. The sumptuous fixed-price meals include an appetizer, a choice between two meat courses (such as rack of lamb or coq au vin), a cheese plate, and a choice of desserts, all for the usual tab at a mediocre steak joint back home. Everything—including the superb cheeses—comes from the Largy's farm or from farms nearby. Feast your eyes on the colorful garden when you come up for air. ♦ Sa dinner, Su lunch Easter-Dec. Reservations required. From Avallon take N6 east 20 km (12.4 miles) to Rouvray, then take D4 north about 3 km (1.8 miles) to Sincey-lès-Rouvray and follow the signs to the château. From Epoisses go 6 km (3.7 miles) southwest on D4. 80.64.71.13

Dijon

Dijon, a little over an hour from Paris on the *TGV,* is Burgundy's capital and a major commercial and industrial center in which roads, rails, and waterways converge. Surrounded by mustard fields and dominated by medieval architecture, Dijon is filled with attractions for both the wine fancier and amateur historian.

Founded as a Roman outpost called Divio, Dijon was repeatedly sacked and burned until 1015, when, under the rule of Robert the Pious, King of France, the city enjoyed about a century of calm before being almost completely destroyed by fire. But Dijon is a resilient city. Beginning in 1364, under Philippe le Hardi (Philip the Bold), it became the capital of the Duchy of Burgundy and a center for artists and scholars. The dukes were among the richest and most powerful rulers of the western world, and they filled Burgundy with palaces, abbeys, and vineyards that remain as witnesses to their extravagant lifestyle.

Wine funded much of the city's growth and even helped save Dijon from another attack. In 1513, 30,000 Swiss, German, and Franche-Comtois soldiers laid seige to the city, which had only 7,000 men to defend it. The governor of Burgundy, Monsieur de la Trémouille, wisely sent the invaders wagons loaded with wine, along with a few negotiators. A few hours later, the invading forces agreed to desist, for a fee. Today, wine's key role in Dijon's economy has been subsumed by—what else?—mustard, for which the city is world famous. While there, also be sure to try the *pain d'épices* (a honey bread similar to gingerbread).

12 Les Halles Centrales (Central Food Market) This lively market, a collection of individual stalls in a huge open building and along various streets nearby, is a great source for prime picnic fare. ♦ Tu, F-Sa morning. Bounded by Rue Bannelier and Rue C.-Ramey, and Rue Quentin and Rue Odebert. No phone

13 Fromagerie Simone Porcheret No market day is complete without a visit to this excellent cheese shop near **Les Halles.** All the great regional cheeses are available, including pungent époisses, delicate cîteaux (a centuries-old specialty of the monks of the **Abbaye de Cîteaux**), and chambertin, a more subtle type of époisses. ♦ Tu-Sa; M morning. 18 Rue Bannelier (between Rue Odebert and Rue des Godrans). 80.30.21.05

14 Bistrot des Halles ★★$$ Chef Billoux offers a moderately priced bistro alternative to his fine-dining establishment (see below), with inventive variations on Burgundian home cooking. Try the *terrine de poireaux et d'agneau* (leek and lamb terrine) or the *crème brûlée au pain d'épices* (crème brûlée with honey bread). The cuisine may not be as refined and innovative as at his flagship, and the wine list is shorter, but the atmosphere is friendly and the prices won't make you swoon. ♦ M-Sa lunch and dinner. Reservations recommended. 10 Rue Bannelier (between Rue des Godrans and Rue de Suzon). 80.49.94.15

15 Restaurant Jean-Pierre Billoux ★★★$$$$ Unquestionably Dijon's greatest chef, Billoux holds forth in an elegant, brightly lit space adorned with big mirrors in gilded frames, fine silver and china, and overstuffed chairs. On sunny days, tables are also available on the less formal terrace. The food is rich, but worth every calorie: Consider *salade de grenouilles à la gelée de perche* (frogs' legs salad with perch gelatin) and *poire rôti à la glace au pain d'épices* (roasted pear with *pain d'épices* ice cream). The wine list is outstanding, and the prices astronomical. To avoid spending a large chunk of your travel budget right here, opt for the fixed-price lunch menu served Monday through Friday. ♦ Tu-Sa lunch and dinner; closed two weeks in August and two weeks in February. Reservations required. 14 Pl Darcy (at Rue Devosge). 80.30.11.00; fax 80.49.94.89

16 Musée Grévin and Espace Grévin (Grévin Museum) Burgundy's answer to Madame Tussaud displays wax figures representing 20 scenes of local history and wine-making practices. In the same building is the **Espace Grévin,** a wine-tasting center with an exhibit about the different wines produced in Burgundy. Tastings (for a charge) include wines representing different varieties or different villages; the more you taste or the pricier your selections, the more you pay. ♦ Admission. Daily. 13 Ave Albert-1er (between Rue Hoche and Rue Nodot). 80.41.76.37

Restaurants/Clubs: Red   **Hotels:** Blue
Shops/ 🍃 Outdoors: Green   **Sights/Culture:** Black

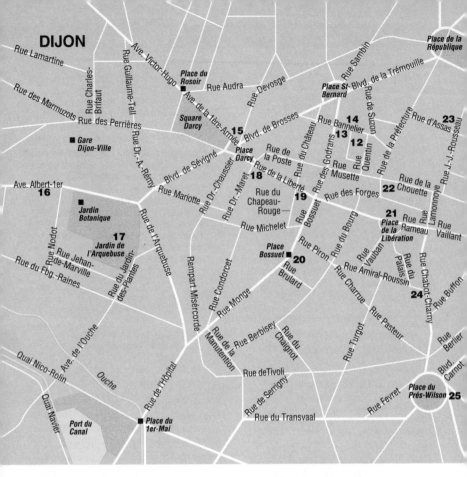

DIJON

17 Jardin de l'Arquebuse This huge public park is named for a group of soldiers—archers—who established their headquarters here in the 16th century. Half the park is devoted to a botanical garden, which was founded in the 18th century. Highlights include rare orchids and other plants in danger of extinction, many types of irises, medicinal herbs, and an aboretum with several 150-year-old trees, including a giant sequoia. You can picnic here as long as you keep to the benches and off the grass. ♦ Daily 7:30AM-dusk. Bounded by Ave Albert-1er and Rue Jehan de Marville, and Rue de l'Arquebuse, Rue du Jardin-des-Plantes, and Rue Nodot

18 Hôtel du Nord $$ Famous since the 19th century as a top Dijon hotel, this 29-room establishment has a friendly staff and a great central location. All the rooms are quiet and have private bathrooms, lots of heavy wood furniture, and flowery fabrics; some of the cheaper rooms are small, but comfortable and well equipped. There's a little wine bar/restaurant in the basement. All in all, it's a good deal. ♦ Closed late December–early January. Pl Darcy (at Rue Dr-Maret). 80.30.58.58

Within the Hôtel du Nord:

Caveau de la Porte Guillaume ★$$ If this place had a motto, it would probably be "Serve no good wine without something on the side." All the menu options include a selection of wines by the glass along with some charcuterie, bread, and cheeses. The least expensive choice includes three wines (such as a Bourgogne Aligoté white, a Moulin-à-Vent red beaujolais, and a Savigny-lès-Beaune red from the Côte d'Or); the most expensive includes two whites (such as a Chablis and a Meursault) and three reds (an Hautes–Côtes de Nuits, a Volnay, and a Santenay Premier Cru). Sip and nibble atop comfortable stools in a softly lit room with the arched stone walls and high ceilings of a wine cellar, surrounded by barrels and shelves of bottles. Full meals featuring Burgundian specialties are also served in a more formal dining room, but the wine-bar formula is the better deal. ♦ Daily lunch and dinner. 80.30.58.58

19 Grey Poupon As soon as you see the gold lettering and the big display windows filled with pots of mustard, you'll know you're in the right place. The selections range from the familiar to the *très* exotic, but all are powerful and fresh. Also for sale are lovely porcelain

reproductions of antique mustard crocks that make great souvenirs. ♦ M-Sa. 32 Rue de la Liberté (at Rue du Chapeau-Rouge). 80.30.41.02

20 Mulot & Petitjean Dijon's most famous source for a typical Burgundian edible, *pain d'épices*, a honey bread flavored with ginger. It's a bit dry, but keeps a long time; spread it with butter or soft cheese for good picnic fare. The shop also sells various brands of mustard, *cassis* liqueur, and numerous jams and jellies. ♦ Daily. 13 Pl Bossuet (between Rue Brulard and Rue Piron). Also at: 16 Rue de la Liberté (between Porte Guillaume and Rue du Chapeau-Rouge); 1 Pl Notre-Dame (at Rue des Forges). Phone for all three: 80.30.07.10

21 Palais des Ducs et des Etats de Bourgogne (Palace of the Dukes and States-General of Burgundy) For the best view of this medieval palace surrounded by opulent Renaissance-era buildings, stand just in front of the complex, near where the Rue Vauban enters the semicircular Place de la Libération (designed by **Jules Hardouin-Mansart,** the chief architect of Versailles). The stunning mosaiclike roof of brightly colored tiles is typical of the region's architecture. In the palace's left wing is the **Hôtel de Ville** (City

Hall); the right wing holds the **Musée des Beaux-Arts** (Fine Arts Museum) and a not-to-be-missed collection of paintings, sculpture, furniture, and other objects from the Middle Ages to the 20th century. Especially notable is the medieval **Salle des Gardes** (Guards Hall, where the dukes' guards ate), which contains Philip the Bold's elaborate 15th-century marble-and-alabaster tomb. The palace's splendid marble staircases and huge banquet halls are typical of medieval and Renaissance upper class dwellings. Behind the palace is the Place des Ducs de Bourgogne, from which you can see one of the palace's original Gothic walls, giving some idea of what it looked like in its medieval heyday. High above is the **Tour Philippe le Bon** (Philip the Good's Tower), built in the 15th century, with a terrace (reached by 316 steps) that overlooks the city's rooftops and steeples. ♦ Admission; free Sunday and holidays. Musée des Beaux Arts: M, W-Su. Tour Philippe le Bon: daily Easter–mid-November; Wed afternoon, Su, and holidays mid-November–Easter. Pl de la Libération (at the intersection of Rue de la Liberté, Rue Vauban, and Rue Rameau). 80.74.52.70

22 Rue des Forges and Rue de la Chouette (Street of the Blacksmith Shops and Street of the Owl) These winding cobblestone streets just behind the **Palais des Ducs** are among the city's most picturesque, lined with mansions (*hôtels*) built in medieval and Renaissance times. Note especially the creamy white, 13th-century **Hôtel Aubriot,** at 40 Rue des Forges (closed to the public): It's the birthplace of Hugues Aubriot, who served under Charles V and initiated the construction in Paris of such works as the Bastille palace (later a prison), many bridges over the Seine, including the Pont St-Michel, and the capital's first sewer system. On the blocklong Rue de la Chouette, which lies just north of and parallel to the Rue des Forges, is the splendid 17th-century **Hôtel de Vogüé,** with its tile roof that gleams blue, red, green, and gold. From the building's courtyard, you can view elaborate wall carvings of fruits, geometric shapes, and some human figures. The **Hôtel de Vogüé** is now home to Dijon's Bureau des Affaires Culturelles (Cultural Affairs Office), and visitors are allowed inside the courtyard Monday through Friday. ♦ From Rue de la Préfecture to Rue Lamonnoye

The *lavoir* (a communal clothes-washing trough) is a common site in Burgundy. Although no longer used for their original purpose, they were once *the* gathering place for villagers to meet for some juicy gossip.

Eat, Drink, and Be Merry in Burgundy and Beaujolais

Key grape varieties: Chablis: chardonnay. Burgundy Côte d'Or: pinot noir, chardonnay. Côte Chalonnaise: pinot noir, chardonnay, aligoté. Mâconnais: gamay, chardonnay. Beaujolais: gamay.

AOC Classification system: In **Chablis,** the farthest north of Burgundy's wine districts, wines are classified (in descending order of prestige) Chablis *grand cru,* Chablis *premier cru* (both referring to top vineyard sites, whose names appear on the labels), Chablis, or *petit* Chablis. On the **Côte d'Or,** there are also four main types of appellations, in descending order of prestige: *grand cru, premier cru* (both referring to top vineyard sites, whose names appear on the labels), *appellations communales* (labeled with the name of a village, such as **Nuits-St-Georges,** or a specific district, such as **Hautes Côtes de Beaune**), and finally a group of different wines with the regional Bourgogne appellation that differ according to grape variety (such as Bourgogne Passe-Tout-Grains made from specific percentages of pinot noir and gamay grapes) or type of wine (such as the bubbly white Crémant de Bourgogne). The four **Cotê Chalonnaise** wine appellations are (in descending order of prestige) *premier cru* (for top vineyard sites), specific *AOC* village name (such as **Givry**), the regional Bourgogne Côte Chalonnaise, and finally the simple Bourgogne regional appellation. In the **Mâconnais,** wines are classified (in descending order) by specific *AOC* village name (such as **Pouilly-Fuissé**) Mâcon-Villages (with grapes from several villages), Mâcon Supérieur (with a higher alcohol content than the last in line), or simple Mâcon. In Beaujolais, the top appellations are the names of the official *AOC* villages in the northern part of the region (such as **Juliénas**),

followed by Beaujolais-Villages (a blend of grapes from more than one village), Beaujolais Supérieur (with a higher degree of alcohol than the last in line), and simple beaujolais. The famous Beaujolais Nouveau, usually a simple beaujolais but sometimes made from grapes from a higher-ranking *AOC* vineyard, is a wine sold only one year after it was made and meant to be drunk within a few months.

Culinary specialties: With a capital named Dijon, it's only logical that mustard would feature prominently in Burgundy's hearty cuisine. Fish, chicken, and especially beef are often accompanied by a sauce of mustard, butter, cream, wine vinegar, egg yolks, and stock. Beef's ubiquity derives from its ability to stand up to a mustard sauce and from the Charollais steer (a white steer from the town of **Charolles**), which is said to provide the best aged beef in France. Below are some other delicacies of the Burgundy and Beaujolais regions:

jambon persillé: ham in wine-and-parsley gelatin

rosette: sausage

gougères: cheese puffs

boeuf bourguignon: beef stew with red wine sauce

escargots à la bouguignonne: snails in garlic butter

quenelles: fish mousse

coq au vin: cockerel in red wine

époisses: strong cow's milk cheese

---

23 Gautier Produits Régionaux Look no further for a reliable source of food and wine from all over Burgundy. Try the *crème de cassis,* the black-currant liqueur added to Aligoté white wine to make *kir,* Burgundy's classic cocktail. You'll also find a wide assortment of mustards, *pain d'épices,* and local crafts, including attractive baskets and pottery. ♦ Tu-Sa. 77 Rue Jean-Jacques-Rousseau (at Rue d'Assas). 80.67.17.19

24 Bibliothèque Municipale (Public Library) Since 1985, France's national library system has stocked here copies of all books published in France that deal with wine or food. Anyone can consult the collection, and it doesn't cost a *centime.* All the books are in French. ♦ M-F July-Aug; Tu-Sa Sept-Jun. 3-7 Rue de l'Ecole-de-Droit (at Rue Chabot-Charny). 80.30.36.39

25 Hôtel Wilson $$$ This 17th-century *relais de poste* (stagecoach stop) has been converted to a cozy 27-room hotel with a fine restaurant; it's far and away the most

charming place to stay in Dijon. The soundproofed rooms have country-style decor (lots of heavy woods and exposed beams) and well-stuffed armchairs, but white walls and floral fabrics lighten the effect. All rooms have well-equipped private baths. ♦ Closed 31 December. 10 Pl du Président-Wilson (at Rue de Longvic). 80.66.82.50; fax 80.63.87.72

Within the Hôtel Wilson:

Restaurant Thibert ★★★$$$ The pearl-gray-and-orange decor is sleek, and so is the food. Chef Jean-Paul Thibert specializes in ingenious, lightened renditions of Burgundian classics, such as *noix de Saint Jacques sur une purée de navets et de la truffe grise de Bourgogne* (sea scallops on a turnip purée with gray Burgundian truffles), *volaille de Bresse, poêlée de champignons et gousses d'ail confites* (Bresse chicken with sautéed mushrooms and caramelized garlic), or grilled fish accompanied by polenta with olives.

Don't miss the suberb assortment of local cheeses or the excellent desserts, which usually feature fruits and exotic spices. The outstanding wine list contains many affordable bottles. ♦ Tu-Sa lunch and dinner; M lunch; closed three weeks in August. Reservations required. 80.67.74.64

The Côte de Nuits

The area from just south of Dijon to just north of Beaune produces some of the greatest red wines in the world, including Romanée-Conti, Clos-Vougeot, Musigny, and Chambertin, but you would never know it by looking at the eight villages that make up the Côte de Nuits. Most of these towns are nondescript (save for a few stunning landmarks here and there), and are so quiet in the middle of the day that you might wonder whether anyone actually lives there. Stretches of the hectic N74—which runs through here—are downright drab.

But the glory of the local wine seems to emanate from the stone walls of the houses, on almost every other one of which hangs a *dégustation* (tasting) sign indicating that wines may be sampled there. Every village also has signs directing visitors to wine makers' cellars.

26 Domaine Bruno Clair For a Burgundy winery, this one has extensive holdings in several Côte d'Or appellations, but the winery itself is just outside Dijon in the village of Marsannay, a town whose wines have a centuries-long reputation. Unfortunately, Dijon's suburban housing developments are nibbling away at Marsannay's vineyards—but local wine makers, including Bruno Clair, are fighting to preserve Marsannay as an appellation and to upgrade the quality of the area's wines. Local wineries produce the dry, flavorful rosé for which Marsannay has long been known, and more and more are making reds, many of which are very good, at unbeatable prices. Most of **Domaine Clair**'s small annual production of rosé goes to local restaurants, but the estate also produces one of the best Marsannay red pinot noir wines. Three superlative choices are the Marsannay Les Grasses Têtes (from 30-year-old vines), the Marsannay Vaudenelles (from 20-year-old vines), and the fine Marsannay Longeroies (from 50-year-old-vines). Monsieur Clair also makes white wines from blends of chardonnay, pinot blanc, and pinot gris, aged in 20-percent-new-oak casks. His most highly rated wines are the reds from prestigious Côte d'Or appellations, such as Gevrey-Chambertin–Clos-Saint-Jacques, the Grand Cru Chambertin–Clos de Bèze, and the Premier Cru Gevrey-Chambertin Les Cazetiers. The Savigny-lès-Beaune Les Dominaudes from 50-year-old vines is superb, but it needs at least five years of bottle

aging. The red wines have a *cuvaison* (vatting) of about 15 days and are aged for about 18 months in oak casks, 25 percent of which are new; they are lightly filtered. This estate had slipped a bit from its great reputation in the 1950s and 1960s, but fortysomething Bruno Clair seems set to bring it back to the top ranks of Côte d'Or wineries. ♦ Free. By appointment. 5 Rue du Vieux-Collège, Marsannay-la-Côte (from Dijon go 2 km/1.25 miles south on N74 or D122; follow the signs to the winery). 80.52.28.95; fax 80.52.18.14

27 La Rôtisserie du Chambertin ★★★$$$$ Welcome to a restaurant twist on "Upstairs, Downstairs." On the ground floor of this vine-covered building, dignity hangs heavy in a formal dining room; upstairs is a casual bistro. In the dining room, meals are served on the finest of china. The menu focuses on traditional Burgundian fare, and does better with simple classics like coq au vin than with chef Jean-Pierre Nicolas's more complex creations. The wine list is sensational. The prices, however, will knock your socks off. Many find the chef's upstairs bistro alternative, **Bonbistrot,** more appealing. The decor and service are simple and informal, the dishes tasty (great coq au vin here as well), and the wine list affordable. Whichever you choose, take time before or after the meal to investigate the village itself, set at the base of the hills: There's a grand château and a Gothic church with a carved-wood interior. ♦ Tu-Sa lunch and dinner; Su lunch; closed two weeks in February and one week in August. Reservations recommended. Rue du Chambertin, Gevrey-Chambertin (from Dijon go 13 km/8 miles south on N74). 80.34.33.20; fax 80.34.12.30

28 The Hautes-Côtes Even the most determined wine taster needs a break occasionally, and the Hautes-Côtes (High Slopes) is the place to take it. In the Côte d'Or itself, vineyards spread out on low slopes leading down to a monotonous plain covered by more vineyards. But tiny D roads lead west from there to a wonderland of white stone villages clinging to steep hills covered with pine and oak trees; the vineyards are interspersed among woods, orchards, and cattle pastures. One route goes from Gevrey-Chambertin west on D31 for 10 kilometers (6.2 miles) to the village of Semezanges, where the road turns into D35. Follow this road south six kilometers (3.7 miles) to L'Etang-Vergy, turn left on D116, and follow the road three kilometers (1.8 miles) to the hamlet of Reulle-Vergy. Stendhal, a fan of Côte d'Or wines, in his novel *Le Rouge et le Noir* (The Red and the Black) named a château "Vergy" after this area. There's a small **Musée des Arts et Traditions**

Populaires des Hautes-Côtes (Museum of Local Arts and Traditions; Pl de la Fontaine, 80.61.42.93) here, with Bronze Age, Gallo-Roman, and medieval archaeological finds from the area, as well as exhibits on local wine making. There is an admission charge and you can visit Sunday afternoon or holidays without an appointment; otherwise call ahead. High on a hill above the village is a tiny 12th-century church, recently restored, with a few picnic tables and a pleasant hiking trail to a lookout point. Either return to D35 and follow it east nine kilometers (5.6 miles) back to Nuits-St-Georges, or continue south about 20 kilometers (12.4 miles) via the hamlets of Meuilley, Marey-lès-Fussey, Fussey, Echevronne, and Pernand-Vergelesses, to regain N74 at Aloxe-Corton.

28 Le Relais de Chasse $$ The welcoming Girard family runs a cozy bed-and-breakfast in a sprawling house. All four spacious guest rooms offer private baths and views of a garden filled with huge trees. Spanking-white bedspreads and floral-print drapes make the rooms cheery even on rainy days. The breakfasts alone are worth the price: eggs, breads, fruit, and homemade jams, served on an outdoor terrace in good weather. ♦ Chamboeuf (from Gevrey-Chambertin go 10 km/6.2 miles west on D31). 80.51.81.60; fax 80.34.15.96

29 Domaine des Lambrays Don't let the drab village of Morey-St-Denis deter you from a visit to this elegant wine estate, which produces some of the best wines of the Côte d'Or. If a vintage doesn't measure up to the Clos des Lambrays label's high standards, it is bottled as Morey-Saint-Denis Premier Cru, which is never bad either; the 1991 Morey-Saint-Denis is a bargain. The white stone mansion's magnificent vaulted cellars date from the 17th century, but are rarely open to visitors. As house *oenologue* Thierry Brouin points out, a true *cave* for storing wine shouldn't be opened any more than necessary, especially in summer; the wines suffer. Tastings are in a small room off an inner courtyard; outside, the mansion is surrounded by a peaceful garden with a huge cedar tree. ♦ Free. M-Sa. Appointment recommended. 34 Rue Basse, Morey-St-Denis (from Gevrey-Chambertin go 6.5 km/4 miles south on D122). 80.51.84.33; fax 80.51.81.97

29 Domaine Dujac Wine maker Jacques Seysses produces some of Burgundy's most complex, flavorful wines here. *Gourmet* magazine wine critic Gerald Asher has described them as "delicately plump," and thinks they may come close to what 18th-century burgundies might have been like.

The *grand cru* wines are aged in new oak barrels, while the *premiers crus* are in barrels that are 50 percent new oak; none is filtered. Depending on the vintage and the condition of the grapes, there is usually no destemming. Seysses says, *"Il ne faut pas séparer le veau de sa mère"* (You shouldn't separate a calf from its mother, or, leave those stems where they belong!). The wines are bottled after about 15 months in oak barrels. They are all good young, but also age well. In addition to the reds for which the winery is best known, some Morey-St-Denis white wine and a little rosé are also produced here. Look for the Bonnes Mares, Clos de la Roche, and Clos Saint Denis; the Gevrey-Chambertin Aux Combottes is also a good choice. ♦ Free. By appointment. 7 Rue de la Bussière, Morey-St-Denis. 80.34.32.58; fax 80.51.89.76

30 Clos de Vougeot Here is the very cradle of Burgundy's wine-making industry: the massive, walled 12th-century château that was once the **Abbaye de Cîteaux,** inhabited by the medieval monks who were forced to eke a living out of Burgundy's miserable terrain. (If you have to ask what their solution was, go directly to Champagne.) The monks lived here from the 12th century until the Revolution, when the building was seriously damaged. It was finally restored in the 19th century. Today **Clos de Vougeot** is the home of the *Confrérie des Chevaliers du Tastevin,* an exclusive brotherhood of wine makers whose elaborate initiation ceremony, modeled on a scene from Molière's play *La Malade Imaginaire* (The Imaginary Invalid), involves dressing up in fancy robes and drinking lots of wine in the château's original wine cellars. (The group's special label for wines that pass its tests is highly sought after by wine makers.) You can tour the château, including the wine cellars, the fermentation room with four gigantic 14th-century wine presses, an enormous 16th-century kitchen, and a spectacular monks' *dortoir* (dormitory), whose high ceiling is supported by massive wooden beams. There's no wine tasting, alas, because the château, though still surrounded by vines, no longer produces its own wine. The staff can be very snobbish. ♦ Admission. Daily. From Chambolle-Musigny take N74 south about 3 km (1.8 miles) to Vougeot and follow the signs to the château. 80.62.86.09

31 Château de Gilly $$$$ If you've just inherited a fortune, this member of the Relais & Châteaux group is a fine place to spend some of it. The turreted medieval building once belonged to the monks of the **Abbaye de Cîteaux,** located some 14 kilometers (nine miles) away, but there's nothing ascetic about the decor or services here. The 39 spacious rooms have every possible modern convenience, including superluxurious bathrooms, and the eight suites are bigger than most Parisian apartments. The decor varies, from a charming French Provincial room with an exposed-beam ceiling, dormer windows, and blue carpet and wallpaper, to an opulent Renaissance-style room with elaborately painted beams, tall windows, and a canopy bed. Breakfast includes delicious homemade breads. ◆ Closed February–mid-March. From Vougeot take D25 east about 3 km (1.8 miles) to Gilly-lès-Cîteaux and follow the signs to the château. 80.62.89.98; fax 80.62.82.34

Within the Château de Gilly:

Restaurant Château de Gilly ★★$$$
The monks' former wine cellars, an elegant space with white stone walls, vaulted ceilings, and floors of polished pinkish-white marble, have been converted to this brightly lit spot. The chef produces excellent versions of Burgundian classics, such as *oeufs en meurette* (poached eggs in red wine sauce) and *sandre poêlé à l'oseille* (pickerel sautéed with sorrel); the wine list is outstanding in rare burgundies. The building is surrounded by a four-acre Versailles-style formal garden; in fact, the "Sun King" (Louis XIV) himself once paid a visit. ◆ M-Tu, Th-Su lunch and dinner; closed February–mid-March. Reservations required. 80.62.89.98

32 Vosne-Romanée In this tiny, nondescript village is produced what is surely one of the most famous (and least attainable) wines in the world: Romanée-Conti. It is one of only three appellations in France with a single owner (the others are Château Grillet on the Côtes du Rhône and La Coulée de Serrant in the Loire Valley). The **Domaine de la Romanée-Conti,** which is in the center of town, owns the tiny La Romanée-Conti vineyard, as well as several other *grands crus* outside the village, including La Tache and part of Richebourg. It's almost impossible to visit the *domaine* (estate); groups are sometimes allowed if they reserve far in advance (80.61.04.57; no fax). And it's even

harder to buy a bottle of La Romanée-Conti wine here; the only way is to buy a case of the estate's extremely expensive *grands crus,* in which one bottle is Romanée-Conti. At least you can see the priceless La Romanée-Conti vineyard whence the wine came. It is surrounded by stone walls and reverently honored with a cross. A map next to the post office in the center of the village (on D109, the road leading into the village from N74) indicates where to find each of the great vineyards west of town. They are all reached by the appropriately named Route des Grands Crus, a vineyard access road that begins just south of the post office off D109. ◆ 3 km (1.8 miles) south of Clos de Vougeot on N74

Within Vosne-Romanée:

Domaine Jean Grivot Wine maker Jean Grivot and his son Etienne have fewer than 30 acres of vines, but these are scattered among 15 or so different appellations, an all-too-common situation for Burgundy's *vignerons.* Nevertheless, the winery, housed in a former *relais de poste* (stagecoach stop) turns out some of Burgundy's best wines. The *grand cru* reds all spend some time in oak (the exact amount depends on the vintage, but averages about 20 months), but the oak does not overwhelm the complex pinot noir taste. The wines are filtered very little or, in some vintages, not at all. All the wines here are good when young, but age well, too. Try the top-of-the-line Grand Cru Richebourg, if you can find any; it's produced in very small amounts. Other top-quality wines are the Nuits-St-Georges Les Boudots, the Vosne-Romanée Les Beaumonts (especially the 1990), the Vosne-Romanée Les Brûlées, and a very good Chambolle-Musigny La Combe d'Orveaux—not a *premier cru,* but from a vineyard that yields richly flavored wines that are sold at affordable (for Burgundy) prices. ◆ Free. By appointment. 6 Rue de la Croix-Rameau (follow the signs to the winery). 80.61.05.95; fax 80.61.32.99

33 Domaine Comtesse Michel de Loisy $$ Hobnob with royalty and learn about wine at the same time. Countess de Loisy, a registered *oenologue* (acquiring the title, which is quite prestigious, involves a difficult exam), offers four luxurious guest rooms in her centuries-old mansion. All have private baths and antique furnishings. She also organizes tastings and tours of Burgundy's finest wine areas and speaks excellent English. Her daughter Françoise de Loisy-Loquin produces wines from vineyards at Nuits-St-Georges and Clos de Vougeot, which you can sample here. The countess's two-day wine tours for small groups are worth the relatively high price. You arrive in the afternoon, have a tasting at one of the great local wineries, then have dinner and spend the night in the countess's home. After breakfast the next day, the countess gives a wine-tasting class, followed by a tour of several Côte de Nuits wineries, a light lunch, an afternoon tour of wineries in the Côte de Beaune, and a tasting of several rare vintages. The day ends with a gala dinner and another night *chez la comtesse,* and you leave after breakfast the following morning. While there, do notice the countess's good-luck charm atop the steep tile roof: a black ceramic cat, which escaped the Nazi gunfire that destroyed its ceramic companions of other colors. The countess believes the soldiers were afraid to shoot a black cat, and she has vowed never to remove it. ♦ Tastings for nonguests by appointment only. 28 Rue du Général-de-Gaulle, Nuits-St-Georges (from Vosne-Romanée go 2 km/1.25 miles south on N74; as you enter town, take a loop around the center by Rue Thurot, which becomes Rue du Général-de-Gaulle; the mansion's driveway begins just after the street changes names). 80.61.02.72; fax 80.61.36.14. Tasting room: 30 Rue du Général-de-Gaulle. 80.62.37.96.

33 Maison Faiveley This highly respected winery has vineyards all over Burgundy and operates as both *négociant* and wine maker. It uses strictly traditional methods, including handpicking the grapes. Many of the labels are marked *"Mis en bouteille à la main sans filtration"* (bottled by hand, no filtration), just one sign of the estate's commitment to quality. **Faiveley** is known primarily for its *grand cru* wines; it has vines in some of the best sites in Burgundy (including Corton and Chambertin), and the wines they yield are very expensive, but worth it. The winery also produces some great deals from *premier cru* and lesser sites; try the luscious Nuits-St-Georges Premier Cru Clos de la Maréchale, the Pommard Premier Cru Les Chaponnières (one of the unfiltered wines), or the Chablis Premier Cru Vaillons. Other good buys are the Rully whites and Mercurey reds from vineyards down south in the Côte Chalonnaise. Watch for the Faiveley name on restaurant wine lists; the wines are always reliable. ♦ Free. M-F by appointment. 8 Rue du Triboure, Nuits-St-Georges. 80.61.04.55; fax 80.62.33.37

Wine produced in Beaujolais accounts for two-thirds of the product of the vine from Burgundy.

34 Jean-Baptiste Joannet, Liquoriste Joannet, a former wine maker, now concentrates on producing fine liqueurs from fruits grown in the fertile Hautes-Côtes. His liqueurs are so intensely, deliciously fruity, who cares if the office is in a garage? Besides the classic *cassis* (black currant), *framboise* (raspberry), and *cérise* (cherry) liqueurs, the Joannet makes liqueurs of tomato, wild blackberry, and *pêche de vigne* (a particularly flavorful type of peach with red flesh). ♦ Free. By appointment. Rue Basse, Arcenant (from Nuits-St-Georges go 9 km/5.5 miles west on D25). 80.61.12.23

34 Maison des Hautes-Côtes This information center offers brochures and other publications (some in English) on what to see and do throughout the Hautes-Côtes area, organizes tastings of Hautes-Côtes wines, and operates a friendly restaurant serving simple, inexpensive dishes. ♦ Information center daily; restaurant M-Sa lunch and dinner; Su dinner. Marey-lès-Fussey (from Arcenant go 3 km/1.8 miles southeast on D8). 80.62.91.29

The Côte de Beaune

In the 20 languid hill towns that make up the Côte de Beaune, many of the same families, living in large, low, stone houses, have made the same wines for generations. The Côte de Beaune, which stretches from **Aloxe-Corton** to **Chagny,** is less visited by tourists than the Côte de Nuits, yet the villages are more picturesque, many of them scattered across small clefts in vine-covered hillsides. One town worth driving through is the charming hamlet of Aloxe-Corton, population about 200.

Wine has an ancient legacy here; even the emperor Charlemagne once owned vineyards in the region. Today, the vineyards just north and south of the town of **Beaune** (the area's capital) produce some fine red wines, including Aloxe-Corton, Auxey-Duresses, Pommard, and Volnay, and some incredibly rich-tasting whites that many consider to be the best white wines in the world: Corton-Charlemagne, Meursault, Puligny-Montrachet, and Chassagne-Montrachet.

35 Château Corton-André/Domaine Pierre André Without a doubt, one of the most elegant spots to taste wine along the Côte d'Or is this 15th-century château belonging to the Pierre André wine firm. The château's most distinctive feature is its roof of colorful tiles, many of them gleaming gold. The wines here come from both the Côte de Nuits and the Côte de Beaune; all are very good and you can taste several for free. Extensive tastings (with English spoken on request) of costlier wines are also given for a charge. ♦ Daily. From Nuits-St-Georges take N74 south 10 km (6.2 miles) to Aloxe-Corton and follow the signs to the château. 80.26.44.25; fax 80.26.43.57

35 Hôtel Clarion $$ This peaceful 10-room hotel with friendly management is in a renovated 17th-century mansion surrounded by vineyards, flower gardens, and pine trees. The spacious, contemporary rooms are decorated in pastels; all have private baths. One room (the best, and the most expensive) has a private garden terrace. There's no restaurant, but the great continental breakfast includes homemade jams and tasty breads. Baby-sitting services are available. ♦ Aloxe-Corton (follow the signs to the hotel). 80.26.46.70; fax 80.26.47.16

Pernand-Vergelesses

35 Pernand-Vergelesses Just west of Aloxe-Corton, past the vineyards used to make Corton-Charlemagne (the one great white wine produced north of Beaune), is the beautiful, hilly village of Pernand-Vergelesses. The tall white statue of Notre Dame de Bonne Espérance (Our Lady of Good Hope) watches over it from high on a hillside above. Originally a Celtic settlement called "Nan" (Celtic for "Spring"), the village was known to the Romans as Pernantum. Charles Martel had vines here, which he bequeathed to his grandson, the emperor Charlemagne. The village boasts a Romanesque church, many medieval houses, and one of the best views along the Côte d'Or: Follow the main road through the village and beyond it into pine woods, then take a right turn to reach a large picnic area on the hilltop behind the statue of Notre Dame de Bonne Espérance, where a spectacular vista of the Côte de Nuits and the Côte de Beaune spreads out before you. ♦ From Aloxe-Corton go 3 km (1.8 miles) west on D18

Within Pernand-Vergelesses:

Domaine Laleure-Piot Founded in the 18th century, this winery has been operated by the Laleure family for five generations. Frédéric Laleure is now the wine maker. From 14 hectares (34.5 acres) of vines (10 for red wine, four for white), the estate produces an excellent Corton-Charlemagne, the luscious, greenish-gold white wine that requires five to 10 years of bottle aging. The red Pernand-Vergelesse Premier Cru Ile-des-Vergelesses is, many wine critics say, one of the very best Burgundy reds being made today—and one of the most reasonably priced. The Corton-Charlemagne Grand Cru white is also superb (it's expensive, and very rare), and the red Pernand-Vergelesses "Villages" is a real bargain. The Laleures also produce some excellent everyday burgundies, a white Bourgogne Aligoté and a red Bourgogne Passe-Tout-Grains. The red wines are aged in

oak for 18 months, the whites for 12 months. Tastings are in an attractive room with exposed stone walls and stained-glass windows. ♦ Free. Open by appointment M-Sa. Rue de Pralot (follow the signs to the winery). 80.21.52.37; fax 80.21.59.48

36 Château de Savigny If you need a break from tastings, take a peek at this château's tiny museum of vintage cars. But if your heart is set on wine and only wine, don't despair: This fortified palace surrounded by vineyards also produces its own wines and houses a tasting center. Its long commitment to the fruit of the vine is evident in the inscription carved above one of the lichen-covered 17th-century stone doors leading to the château's park: *"Les vins de Savigny sont vins nourrissants, théologiques, et morbifuges"* (The wines of Savigny are nourishing, theological, and death-delaying), a holdover from the era when certain wines were prescribed as remedies for various ailments. Considering the recent reports on the benefits of wine drinking, maybe those early prescriptions weren't so far off. ♦ Free. Daily. From Aloxe-Corton follow N74 south 5 km (3.1 miles), then take D2 west about 4 km (2.5 miles) to Savigny-lès-Beaune and follow the signs to the château. 80.21.55.03; fax 80.21.54.84

36 Domaine Chandon de Briailles *"Grande famille, grande maison. Le Corton ne fait rien de mieux."* (A great family, a great winery. Corton doesn't get any better than this.) The prestigious *Hachette Guide des Vins 1994*'s wine critics were referring to this winery's outstanding 1990 Corton Les Bressandes, and to its noble lineage: Comte Aymard-Claude de Nicolay, who is in charge here, is related to the Chandon (as in Moët-et-Chandon) family of the Champagne region. The count sticks to tradition: Grapes are never destemmed, there's a three-week maceration in *cuves,* and the wines are filtered after the malolactic fermentation. The reds spend about 15 months in new oak. All Chandon de Briailles wines are known for their finesse, ability to age, and relatively low (for burgundy) prices. The top-of-the-line labels are reds: the Corton–Clos du Roi made from old vines, the Corton Les Bressandes from very old vines (average age around 35 years), and the very reasonably priced Pernand Ile de Vergelesses and Corton Les Marechaudes. The winery also produces very small quantities of Cordon Blanc, a rich white wine made completely from chardonnay grapes. Don't leave without exploring the formal gardens, which are so beautiful that Queen Elizabeth II made a special visit just to see them. Within the gardens is an 18th-century *folie* (small stone house) decorated with baroque stone carvings and topped with a colorfully patterned tile roof. ♦ Free. By appointment. Only the wine cellars, gardens, and tasting-sales office are open to visitors. 1 Rue Soeur-Govy, Savigny-lès-Beaune (follow the signs to the winery). 80.21.52.31; fax 80.21.59.15

37 Hostellerie du Vieux Moulin

★★★★$$$$ A restaurant named the Old Mill in a tiny hamlet on a scenic road in the Burgundy backcountry must be a cozy, casual old place, right? Well, it *is* in an old water mill. But the sleek, modern dining room, with its big windows overlooking the pretty Rhoin River, cries *"haute gastronomie,"* and at very *haute* prices (unless you stick to the cheapest of the three fixed-price menus). Young chef-owner Jean-Pierre Silva favors local products, but *what* products: wild morel mushrooms, lamb from nearby farms, and homemade vanilla ice cream served with a warm black currant–flavored brioche. It's no surprise that the wine list is exceptional too. ♦ Daily lunch and dinner; closed Wednesday and Thursday November-May. Reservations required far in advance. From Savigny-lès-Beaune follow D2 northwest 10 km (6.2 miles) to Bouilland and follow the signs to the restaurant. 80.21.51.16; fax 80.21.59.90

Adjoining the Hostellerie du Vieux Moulin:

Hôtel Le Vieux Moulin $$$ The Silvas offer 26 rooms and suites in an annex to their restaurant. The decor is appealingly rustic, with big windows overlooking the countryside; peace and quiet are guaranteed. The choices range from smallish, moderately priced rooms with showers to very large and expensive rooms equipped with showers, bathtubs, and private terraces. Guests have access to a heated swimming pool, a sauna, an exercise center (all the better to work off the calories consumed in the restaurant!), and a billiard table. ♦ Closed Wednesday and Thursday November-May. 80.21.51.16

38 Domaine Jean-Luc Maldant

This friendly young wine maker from a long-established wine-making family produced his first vintage in 1989 and has already become well known for his fruity, approachable white and red wines, all at excellent prices. The 1992 Savigny-lès-Beaune, ready to drink in 1995, is full of fruity pinot noir flavor, and the 1991 Cuvée La Commensale Savigny red, a more

complex wine, is a model of what can be accomplished with an unpromising vintage. Monsieur Maldant is a great source of information on Burgundy wines, and he speaks English. However, he travels a lot because he prefers to handle sales to restaurants himself, so call in advance to set up an appointment. Tastings are given in his cellars (under the family garage, which is adorned by a large Coca-Cola sign). ♦ Free. By appointment M-Sa. 4 Rue des Peinguets, Chorey-lès-Beaune (from Beaune take N74 north 7 km/4.3 miles to D24 east, and follow the signs to the winery). 80.24.19.38; fax 80.24.19.50

38 Domaine Tollot-Beaut et Fils

Since its vineyards were planted at the end of the 19th century, this winery has been in the hands of one family. The plain-looking white stucco building that houses the winery couldn't contrast more with the luscious wines: full of rich fruit flavor, they have a well-balanced spicy, toasty, vanilla taste that comes from having been aged in new oak. The vinification takes place in open wooden *cuves* (vats) in the old-fashioned manner, with constant punching down of the wine's *chapeau* (the thick layer of solids that forms on the must in the vats during fermentation). About half the grapes are destemmed; the reds are aged in wood for about 15 months, and are fined and filtered lightly. The top red wines here are Corton Les Bressandes, Corton, and the Beaune Premiers Crus Les Brèves and Clos du Roi. The Savigny Champs Chevrey and Chorey-Lès-Beaune are great values. So is the Aloxe-Corton Villages; it usually includes grapes from the winery's *premier cru* Aloxe-Corton vineyards, which yield such small amounts that it is not practical to bottle them separately. In effect, you're getting a touch of a *premier cru* wine for a *villages* price. ♦ Free. By appointment. Rue Alexandre-Tollot, Chorey-lès-Beaune (follow the signs to the winery). 80.22.16.54; fax 80.22.12.61

38 Château de Chorey

$$ The Germain family has set up six luxurious guest rooms, each with a private bathroom, in a lovely château located just outside Beaune. One of the rooms is a huge suite. All have antique furnishings, mainly from the 18th century, and are decorated in cheerful floral fabrics. The château, which dates from the 13th to the 18th centuries, harmoniously mixes rounded medieval towers, Renaissance wall carvings, and tall 18th-century windows, and it's surrounded by a walled flower garden punctuated by tall trees. Good continental breakfasts are served, but no other meals. The Germains produce their own excellent wine, which you can taste (and buy) here. ♦ Mar-Dec. Chorey-lès-Beaune. 80.22.06.05; fax 80.24.03.93

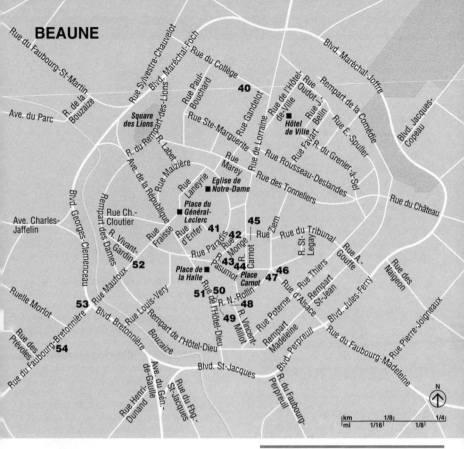

Map of Beaune with numbered locations including:

- Rue du Faubourg-St-Martin
- Rue Sylvestre-Chauvelot
- Blvd. Maréchal-Foch
- Rue du Collège
- Blvd. Maréchal-Joffre
- Ave. du Parc
- R. de la Bouzaize
- Square des Lions
- R. du Rempart-des-Lions
- Rue Paul-Bouchard
- Rue Ste-Marguerite
- Rue Gandelot
- Rue de Lorraine
- Rue de l'Hôtel-de-Ville
- Rue Oudot
- Rue J. Belin
- Rempart de la Comédie
- Rue E. Spuller
- Blvd. Jacques-Copeau
- Hôtel de Ville
- Rue Favart
- R. du Grenier-à-Sel
- Rue du Château
- Ave. Charles-Jaffelin
- R. Labet
- Rue Maizière
- Rue Marey
- Rue Rousseau-Deslandes
- Rue des Tonneliers
- R. Ave. de la République
- Rue Laneyrie
- Eglise de Notre-Dame
- Place du Général-Leclerc
- Rue Ch.-Cloutier
- Rempart des Dames
- R. Vivant-Gardin
- Rue Fraisse
- Rue d'Enfer
- Rue Paradis
- Rue Monge
- R. Carnot
- Rue Ziem
- Rue du Tribunal
- R. St-Legay
- Rue A.-Gouffe
- Rue des Naigeon
- Blvd. Georges-Clemenceau
- Rue Maufoux
- Place de la Halle
- R. Pasumot
- Place Carnot
- Rue Thiers
- Rempart St-Jean
- Ruelle Morlot
- Rue Louis-Very
- R. N.-Rollin
- Rue de l'Hôtel-Dieu
- R. Vincent-Millot
- Rue Poterne
- Rue d'Alsace
- Blvd. Jules-Ferry
- Rue Pierre-Joigneaux
- Rue des Prévoles-Bretonnière
- Blvd. Bretonnière
- Ave. du Gén.-de-Gaulle
- Rempart de l'Hôtel-Dieu
- Rempart Madeleine
- Blvd. Perpreuil
- Rue du Faubourg-Madeleine
- Rue du Faubourg-Bretonnière
- Rue Henri-Dunand
- Rue du Fbg.-St-Jacques
- Blvd. St-Jacques
- R. du Faubourg-Perpreuil

Numbered locations: 40, 52, 53, 54, 41, 42, 43, 44, 45, 46, 47, 48, 49, 50, 51

Scale: km / mi, 1/16, 1/8, 1/4

N (north arrow)

39 La Bouzerotte ★★$$ This friendly spot in a suburb of Beaune is a *vignerons'* hangout, and its popularity is easy to understand once you dig into the house omelette (made with bacon and potatoes) or a salad of greens the chef picked in his garden that morning. Heartier meals are also available, including Burgundian specialties like coq au vin and some fish dishes. In winter the big fireplace blazes; in summer tables are set on a tiny terrace. The wine list has a few inexpensive offerings and several more expensive ones, all from Burgundy or Beaujolais, and all excellent. ♦ Free. ♦ W-Su lunch and dinner; closed in August. Reservations recommended; no credit cards accepted. From Beaune take D970 northwest 6.5 km (4 miles) to Bouze-lès-Beaune and follow the signs to the restaurant. 80.26.01.37

Beaune

Right in the heart of Burgundy, Beaune is the most convenient base for touring the region. Although it is cursed with ugly suburbs filled with shopping malls, chain hotels, and the intersection of two frenetic autoroutes, it retains a beautiful, ancient center, with narrow streets, medieval houses, grandiose mansions, and a Romanesque church. Beaune also has the interesting **Musée du Vin de Bourgogne** (Wine Museum of Burgundy); **l'Atheneum,** a fabulous bookstore/market/ wine shop; the irresistible **Charcuterie Roger Batteault;** the colorful **La Halle** food market (in the center of town, next to the tourist office), where the region's bounty is displayed in abundance every Saturday morning; and a wine-tasting center on almost every block. That said, prices are high and tourists seem to outnumber the locals, especially in July and August. Still, Beaune is not to be missed.

A Gallic settlement and later a Roman outpost, Beaune was the official residence of the dukes of Burgundy until Philip the Bold moved his headquarters to Dijon in the 14th century. Nevertheless, through its residents' enterprise and its prestigious wine industry, Beaune continued to grow richer. To this day, a strong rivalry exists between the two cities, but as a capital of wine and the arts, Beaune wins hands down.

Restaurants/Clubs: Red   **Hotels:** Blue
Shops/ 🌳 Outdoors: Green   **Sights/Culture:** Black

Don't leave without visiting the town's chief landmark, the **Hospices de Beaune/Hôtel Dieu,** built as a hospital in 1443 and still a medical center today (though part of the building has been converted to a museum). The hospice still owns 58 hectares (143.2 acres) of vineyards—an incredible amount for Burgundy—that stretch from Aloxe-Corton to Meursault, much of which was donated by grateful nobles who were cured there. To benefit its ongoing charity work, the hospice holds the world's most famous wine auction every November: Les Trois Glorieuses. This "glorious" event is a grand excuse for ceremonies, wine tastings, and wine exhibits. Be forewarned: Hotel rooms around town are often booked a year in advance during this time.

40 Patriarche Père et Fils Don't be daunted by this company's motto—"the biggest cellars in Burgundy"—because the tour and wine tasting is one of Beaune's best. The winery was founded in 1780 and is now housed in a former 18th-century convent, where millions of bottles are stored in a labyrinthine maze of cellars. Guided tours of the cellars last about 40 minutes and conclude with an instructive tasting, which includes several types of *AOC* wines produced here. ♦ Admission. Daily; closed mid-December–March. 7 Rue du Collège (between Rue Paul-Bouchard and Rue Gandelot). 80.24.53.78

41 Musée du Vin de Bourgogne (Wine Museum of Burgundy) A must stop for wine lovers, the museum is housed in a 15th- and 16th-century stone mansion that once belonged to the dukes of Burgundy. The exhibits explain wine-making techniques, the history of wine making, the differences among wine presses (each locale seems to have developed its own type), and implements for working vines and harvesting grapes. Also here are works of art featuring wine, including the two magnificent Aubusson tapestries in an upstairs room. ♦ Admission. Daily Mar-Nov; M, W-Su Dec-Mar. Next to l'Eglise de Notre Dame (at 5 Rue d'Enfer, a cul-de-sac off Pl du Général-Leclerc). 80.22.08.19

42 Charcuterie Roger Batteault The fare here rises so far above typical charcuterie that the owner should coin a new term for his edible masterpieces. This is *the* source for picnic fare of the highest order. Don't miss the *jambon persillé* (which won a culinary gold medal in 1992, and it's obvious why), the two-crust meat pies, or the dense, flavorful sausage known as *rosette* (which also won a gold medal in 1992). The *jambon persillé* has a much more flavorful gelatin coating than at other places, maybe because it's made with white wine as well as some garlic and lots of parsley. It's available by the slice or as rounds of various sizes. Vegetarians will enjoy the delicious quiches and salads. ♦ Tu-Sa, Su morning Aug-Sept; Tu-Sa Oct-July; closed two weeks in February. 4 Rue Monge (between Place Carnot and Rue Pasumot). 80.22.23.04

43 La Vinothèque This store is an excellent source for wines from top Côte d'Or wineries; it represents not just the *négociants* (wine dealers), but also the *propriétaires-vignerons* (owners–wine makers). It has a greater selection of old vintages than you will ever find at the wineries, because French tax laws do not encourage wine makers to stock their older bottles (the rates go up every year the wine ages). Buying wines at a winery is always cheaper in France than buying in a wine shop, but the latter offers more choice and doesn't require an appointment. Some of the vintage *grand cru* wines on hand are very rare, very wonderful, and very, very expensive, but affordable bottles are always available too. The staff is knowledgeable and will ship large orders, but won't mind at all if you buy just one bottle. ♦ M-Sa. 4 Rue Pasumot (between Rue Carnot and Rue Monge). 80.22.86.35

Restaurants/Clubs: Red	Hotels: Blue
Shops/ ♣ Outdoors: Green	Sights/Culture: Black

Wines from Chambertin were the favorites of Napoleon and of John F. Kennedy.

Denis Perret

44 Denis Perret This reliable wine dealer is the official Beaune outlet for five *négociants propriétaires,* including the respected Bouchard et Fils. This spacious establishment purveys wines from hundreds of Burgundy's vineyards, in a wide range of vintages and prices, along with silver *tastevins,* corkscrews, glasses, and an assortment of locally woven baskets. If you haven't been able to find an old-enough-to-drink bottle of a great vintage at the *vignerons,* look for it here. ♦ M-Sa. English spoken. 40 Rue Carnot (at Pl Carnot). 80.22.35.47; fax 80.22.57.33

45 Tast' Fromage A delightful cheese shop in a four-story, 18th-century town house offers a selection of cheeses from all over France, but specializes in the cheeses of Burgundy. Epoisses (the deliciously smelly cheese bathed in *marc de Bourgogne,* a grapey eau de vie), chambertin (made by the same method, but a bit milder), delicate cîteaux (made by the order of monks who once owned **Clos de Vougeot**), and others are on hand; most are aged in the cellars below the shop. ♦ Tu-Sa. Rue Carnot (between Rue Ziem and Pl Carnot). 80.24.73.51

46 Beaune Choses *Choses* means "things," and the name of this gift shop is a pun on "Beaune" and its almost-homonym *"bonnes"* (good). It certainly lives up to the best of both words, with a wide selection of silver *tastevins,* baskets, and various items for the table, including Baccarat crystal and Christofle dinner services. The store will ship abroad, and the salespeople speak English. ♦ Daily. Pl Carnot (between Rue d'Alsace and Rue St-Legay). 80.22.11.56

47 Palais des Gourmets This luscious patisserie in the center of town bakes tempting tarts and other sweets, as well as fine, savory *gougères* (cheese puffs) in hefty sizes—great picnic fare. There are a few tables where you can have coffee or tea along with a treat, soaking up the heavenly aromas emanating from the ovens. ♦ Tu-Sa; closed in August. 14 Pl Carnot (at Rue d'Alsace). 80.22.13.39

48 Hôtel Le Central $$ Just down the street from the **Hôtel Dieu** and the tourist office in the heart of Beaune, this family-run place couldn't have a more convenient location. With wooden shutters and geranium-filled window boxes, it's the very image of a small hotel in provincial France. The 20 simple rooms are on the small side, but are comfortable, with private bathrooms. The management is very friendly. ♦ Closed late November–late December. 2 Rue Vincent-Millot (at Rue Nicolas-Rollin). 80.24.77.24; fax 80.22.30.40

Within the Hôtel Le Central:

Restaurant Le Central ★★$$ A pretty restaurant just steps from the **Hôtel Dieu** could easily be a tourist trap, but this one refused the temptation. Choices include typical Burgundian specialties as well as unusually seasoned dishes like *lotte au safran* (monkfish with saffron) and *rouget à la sauce vanille* (red mullet in vanilla-flavored sauce). The well-spaced tables and comfortably upholstered chairs add to the relaxed atmosphere. ♦ M-Tu, Th-Sa lunch and dinner; W, Su lunch; closed late November–late December. Reservations recommended. 80.24.77.24

49 Marché aux Vins Across the street from the **Hôtel Dieu,** this wine-tasting center was constructed on the foundations of a church dating from the 13th through 15th centuries. It offers about 40 different wines from Burgundy and Beaujolais in an unguided tasting. The entrance fee includes a glass, or, for a small extra charge, a *tastevin* (which you can keep) to look professional. Visitors stroll around two floors of wines, which are set out on barrels in groups of three open bottles; candles are available so you can check for sediment at the bottoms of the bottles. Buckets, rather than the usual gutters, are available for spitting out the tastes. Less expensive wines are displayed on the lower floor. A knowledgeable staff is on hand, but creates no pressure to buy. If you find you can't live without a case of Meursault 1988 from Patriarche Père et Fils, they will ship. The wines are not the grandest of *crus,* but the assortment is wide, and vintages range from three to 10 years old. This a good place to do your own "blind" tastings with a friend and compare different appellations and vintages. ♦ Admission. Daily. Rue Nicolas-Rollin (at Rue de l'Hôtel-Dieu). 80.22.27.69

50 L'Athenaeum de la Vigne et Du Vin This ultramodern cultural center and wine shop almost defies description, but is by far the best general shopping venue in Beaune, if not all of Burgundy. It is owned by *négociants-producteurs* Patriarche Père et Fils, Burgundy's largest *négociants,* along with the Paris-based book publisher Flammarion. Patriarche wines are for sale by the bottle in one wing of the shop and by the glass in a tiny wine bar, and seminars and other events are held here. The main draw, though, is the irresistible book department. Hundreds of books on wine (history, wine making, specific kinds of wine, and so forth), food, and travel are available in many languages; the wide assortment of books in English includes Robert Parker's guide to the wines of Burgundy, known locally as "The Bible." There are also many cookbooks and books on Burgundy, as well as French-language children's books and videocassettes. You can also pick up a *tastevin,* some Burgundian mustard or fruit liqueur, jams and other local products, and excellent maps of Burgundy's wine regions. ◆ Daily. 7 Rue de l'Hôtel-Dieu (at Rue Nicholas-Rollin). 80.22.12.00

HÔTEL

51 Hospices de Beaune/Hôtel Dieu The **Hôtel Dieu** is one of the most famous historic sites in France. Built as a hospital by Chancellor Nicolas Rolin in 1443, it still operates as an old-age home and medical center; only the **Hôtel Dieu** section, which has been converted into a museum, is open to tourists. The entrance (just across the street from the tourist office) leads to an inner cobblestone courtyard, the **Cour d'Honneur,** with elegant arcades that provide a spectacular view of the red, green, gold, and black tile roof and its many dormer windows. The roof has been so completely cleaned and restored that it almost looks too new to be the real thing, but it was built almost six centuries ago, and is not a Disneyland-style re-creation. Inside the museum, visit the huge **Grand'Salle,** or "Chambre des Pauvres" (Paupers' Room), a cathedral-like space with elaborately decorated ceiling beams; the walls are lined with curtained beds where indigent patients once lay. A kitchen staffed by mannequins dressed as nuns displays what must be tons of copper cooking utensils around the wide original fireplace. There is also a pharmacy whose glassed-in shelves contain rows of 18th-century porcelain herb containers. The chief work of art on display here is a vivid polyptych of the Last Judgment, a masterpiece painted by Flemish artist Roger van der Weyden in 1443; it's now in a small room of its own, but once hung in the chapel adjacent to the Grand'Salle. A magnifying glass hung in front of the painting is distracting, but allows you to view the meticulous detail of the figures, two of which represent Chancellor Rolin and his wife. ◆ Admission. Daily. Rue de l'Hôtel-Dieu (at Pl de la Halle). 80.24.45.00

52 Hôtel Le Cep $$$$ Beaune's best, this 49-room, three-suite hotel is housed in a restored Renaissance mansion within the city walls, not far from the **Hôtel Dieu.** The decor is extremely opulent—lots of draped fabrics, thick carpets, and heavily upholstered furniture—but not oppressive. The rooms are big, many with marble bathrooms, and each is different: For example, the Chambre Puligny has exposed beams, a lovely antique armoire, and richly patterned rugs; the Chambre Montrachet has a beautifully simple wooden floor and a very elegant canopy bed; the Suite Dames Hospitalières has regal magenta carpeting and bedspreads. A massive stone staircase leads from the interior roofed courtyard to the upper floors, and arched galleries overlook the courtyard on each floor. Stay here after you've won the lottery. ◆ 27-29 Rue Maufoux (between Rempart des Dames and Rue Vivant-Gardin). 80.22.35.48; fax 80.22.76.80

Adjacent to the Hôtel Le Cep:

Restaurant Bernard Morillon ★★★$$$$ One of the city's best (and most expensive) places to eat, it is adorned with elaborately painted ceiling beams and abundant bouquets of fresh flowers. The menu makes the most of the luxurious foods that will send your palate into ecstasy and your wallet into a decline, such as lobster, truffles, and morel mushrooms. It's all perfectly complemented by the great burgundies on the wine list. An almost-affordable fixed-price menu is available Tuesday through Friday. ◆ Tu dinner; W-Su lunch and dinner; closed three weeks in February and the last two weeks in August. Reservations required. 31 Rue Maufoux. 80.24.12.06

53 Hôtel de la Poste $$$$ An old *relais de poste* (stagecoach stop) just outside Beaune's ramparts has been converted into this sprawling white hotel. Despite that history, the

---

Restaurants/Clubs: Red   **Hotels:** Blue
Shops/ 🌱 Outdoors: Green   **Sights/Culture:** Black

30 rooms have modern decor and modern conveniences (mini-bars, televisions, and well-equipped bathrooms); service is friendly and the continental breakfasts are outstanding. The rooms in the front of the hotel overlook both the impressive ramparts and a noisy intersection that the soundproofed windows don't quite keep at bay. For complete quiet, ask for a room at the back of the hotel, where you'll have a view of the vineyards on nearby slopes above the tile roofs of the town. The in-house restaurant is reliable for traditional Burgundian dishes, but it's a bit overpriced, as is the long wine list. ◆ 1 Blvd Georges-Clemenceau (at Rue du Faubourg-Bretonnière). 80.22.08.11; fax 80.24.19.71

54 Restaurant Le Bénaton ★★$$ Standard Burgundian dishes are reinvented at this local favorite. Try the *raviolis aux escargots de bourgogne* (ravioli filled with local snails) and a *cuisse de lapin* (rabbit thigh) simmered for five hours in a sauce that includes crumbs of *pain d'épices*. Don't miss the great assortment of Burgundian cheeses. The excellent wine list is fairly priced (a rarity in this area) and the management is very friendly. The cheapest fixed-price menu is a bargain; it's offered weekdays and at lunch on Saturdays. Tables are set on an indoor terrace as well as in a small, modern dining room. ◆ M-W, F-Su lunch and dinner. Reservations recommended. 25 Rue du Faubourg-Bretonnière (between Blvd Bretonnière and Rue Jean-des-Vignes-Rouges). 80.22.00.26; fax 80.24.76.10

Elsewhere in the Côte de Beaune

South of Beaune, but continuing along through the Côte de Beaune, you'll find the quiet little wine villages of **Pommard, Volnay, Meursault, Puligny-Montrachet,** and **Chassagne-Montrachet.** Each has its own famous vineyards and its own superb wines. Reputed to produce the world's greatest white wine, the walled vineyard of **Le Montrachet** which lies between Puligny-Montrachet and Chassagne-Montrachet is an essential stop for the wine enthusiast.

55 Les Caves des Hautes-Côtes On the southern outskirts of Beaune, this good wine co-op is a perfect stop for tourists in a hurry to pick up a few bottles before leaving town. Set in a sprawling modern building, it has offerings from 180 wine makers based in the Hautes-Côtes region in the hills west of the Côte d'Or, although some of the wines come from Côte d'Or vineyards. Some of the *premier cru* and *grand cru* wines here tend to be disappointing, but the Hautes-Côtes de Nuits are very good, especially the Tête de Cuvée 1990, a fruity, rich red wine that can be enjoyed now or stored for another three years

or so. The staff is efficient and the prices are fair. ◆ M-Sa. 2 km (1.25 miles) south of Beaune on N74. 80.24.63.12; fax 80.22.87.05

56 Ballons de Bourgogne Here's a way to reach new heights in wine tasting—literally. Owner-manager Tom Sluder, who has a winery in Pommard, offers a combined hot-air balloon/wine-tasting tour, featuring several Pommard *domaines* that otherwise do not accept visitors. The balloon trips take about three hours, including transit to and from the liftoff site and inflating the balloon; the flight itself usually lasts about an hour, and traditionally concludes with a glass of Sluder's own wine upon landing. Wine tastings, wine-cellar tours, and château visits are included in some packages in conjunction with the balloon flight, but you do not travel to the sites by balloon. The view of Beaune and the Côte d'Or vineyards is spectacular. ◆ Flights daily, once in the morning and once in the evening mid-April–mid-Nov. Reservations recommended. Children under five are not allowed to fly except by special permission of the pilot. From Beaune take N74 south 3 km (1.8 miles) and follow the signs to Pommard and the Ballons de Bourgogne. 80.24.20.32; fax 80.24.12.87. For reservations from the US: Premier Travel, 4210 82nd St, Lubbock, TX 79423. 806/797.7799, 800/6.TRAVEL

56 Château de Pommard Wine maker Jean-Louis Laplanche, who is also a professor of psychoanalysis in Paris, runs a very proper establishment here. No easygoing chit-chat about the weather or the differences between US and French culture: The talk is of wine, and everyone's manners are very formal, including during tastings. The 19th-century, tile-roofed château, with an adjacent 18th-century farmhouse, is surrounded by an elaborate garden and by 20 hectares (50.6 acres) of prime vines (the largest number owned by an individual in Burgundy), all enclosed within walls. Visitors may tour the farm and wine cellars; a tasting of the great house Pommards is held at the end of the visit. Pommard and other nearby villages in the hills also offer great views of the vineyards, which are difficult to see from Beaune. ◆ Fee. Daily April–the third Sunday in November; other times by appointment. In Pommard follow the signs to D973 west and the château. 80.22.12.59; fax 80.24.65.88

56 Les Domaines de Pommard This simple wine shop and tasting center in the middle of the quiet little wine village of Pommard is operated by Bernard Dubreuil and Edith Boissière; they offer tastings and bottles of wines produced by 16 Pommard wineries, and many older vintages are available. The staff provides expert advice (though their English may be limited). This is a great place to sample different versions of one of Burgundy's most famous wines. ◆ Daily. Pl du Village, Pommard. 80.24.17.20

56 Domaine Jean Garaudet Wine critic
Robert Parker blew this tiny estate's cover
when he wrote that its fine wines were
Pommard's best-kept secret. Despite their
fame, Garaudet wines are still top quality and
still good buys. The Pommards are full, rich,
and mouth-filling; the top of the line is the
Pommard Les Charmots from a vineyard
planted in 1902. Garaudet uses little or no
filtration, and half (sometimes more) of the
barrels are new oak. Other good wines to try
here are the Monthélie and the Beaune–Clos-
des-Mouches. The cellars are beneath
Garaudet's 19th-century gray stone
farmhouse. ♦ Free. M-Sa; closed mid-
August–mid-September. Tastings of the
winery's more expensive wines are offered for
a charge by appointment. Rue de la Métairie,
Pommard (follow the signs to the winery).
80.22.59.77

57 Domaine Marquis d'Angerville This
winery in the tranquil village of Volnay became
a regional household word during the 1930s
and 1940s, when the present owner's father
began crusading to improve the quality of
local wines. He spoke vociferously against the
then-common practice among Burgundy's
wine makers of diluting *grand cru* and *premier
cru* wines with inferior grapes, but labeling
them *grand* and *premier cru* nonetheless.
Jacques d'Angerville has continued this
commitment to quality by rigorously
maintaining appellation standards and seeking
out clones from the best (not necessarily the
highest-yielding) pinot noir "parent" vines for
his own vineyards. The winery's top labels are
the Volnay–Clos des Ducs and the Volnay
Champans; the Volnay Taillepieds is also
good. All the grapes are destemmed, and all
the wines are aged in barrels that are one-
quarter new oak. Some have suggested that
filtering removes some of the punch, but
others love the characteristic delicacy of
d'Angerville reds. Added attraction: Since
Volnay is perched on a hilltop that overlooks
its vineyards, the views—especially toward
Meursault—are beautiful. ♦ Free. By
appointment. From Pommard take D973 less
than 1 km (a half-mile) south to Volnay and
follow the signs to the château. 80.21.61.75;
fax 80.21.65.07

57 Domaine Hubert de Montille Wine maker
Hubert de Montille practices law in Dijon,
returning to his garden-enclosed estate in
Volnay and his Pommard vineyards only on
weekends. But wine making is clearly more
than his hobby. Robert Parker has decribed
him as "a wine maker's wine maker," and
highly respected California-based wine
importer Kermit Lynch has said De Montille
wines are "so perfect, so pristine, they spoil
you for others." All the wines made here are
vin de garde (made for aging), and need at
least five years in the bottle. The top labels are
the Pommard Les Rugiens, Pommard Les

Pezerolles, and Pommard Les Epenots. The
wines are fermented with a high percentage of
stalks and aged about 18 months in oak
casks, some 30 percent of which are new oak.
None is filtered, but all are fined lightly.
Though some feel Pinot Noirs shouldn't be so
tannic, the *Hachette Guide des Vins 1994*
offered a spirited defense of the 1990
Pommard Les Rugiens: *"Doit-on être surpris
s'il porte une robe presque noire? (Hubert de
Montille est avocat) . . . . Le jury délibère et
note que ses arômes constituent des
circonstances bien attenuantes. Condamné à
un séjour en cave, incompressible et de 5
ans."* (Why should we be surprised that this
wine looks almost black? Hubert de Montille
is a lawyer [lawyers in France wear black
robes]. But the jury has deliberated and finds
that the aroma constitutes extenuating
circumstances. Condemned to five years in
the cellar, with no parole.) Some Chardonnays
are available here, too. ♦ Free. By
appointment. Rue du Pied-de-la-Vallée,
Volnay. 80.21.22.67; fax 80.42.85.78

57 Domaine Eric Boussey Carrying on the
tradition of his well-known local wine family,
this young wine maker has eight hectares
(19.7 acres) of vines from which he makes
several types of wines; he's gotten the most
praise for his red Monthélies and his
Pommard. Most of the wines here need long
aging. The Premier Cru Monthélie Les Riottes
1992 has a bouquet of black currants and is
expected to be excellent, but it will need
another six years or so in the bottle. The
Bousseys give tastings daily in a room
outfitted with a small bar and comfortable
chairs. It adjoins their wine cellars, just across
the courtyard from their modern white stucco
farmhouse. ♦ Free. Daily. Appointment
recommended. Grande-Rue, Monthélie (from
Meursault take D17E 2 km/1.25 miles west
and follow the signs for the winery).
80.21.60.70; fax 80.21.26.12

58 Domaine Guy Bocard On the other side of
a wide wooden gate is a friendly wine maker
with 8.5 hectares (21 acres) of vines from
which, like most independent *vignerons*, he
makes a wide range of wines: Bourgogne,
Auxey-Duresses, Monthélie, Meursault-
Villages, and Meursault Premier Cru (from the
Charmes and Genevières vineyards).
Monsieur Bocard greets visitors himself in the

small cellars next to his vine-covered 18th-century town house in the middle of Meursault. He is a great source of information about wine making, the Burgundy region, and what foods go with which wines (for those *premier cru* Meursaults, try *poularde au morilles*, guinea hen with morel mushrooms). The *premiers crus* are lovely, the Meursault Les Grands-Charrons is a rich, golden-yellow delight, and the simple Bourgogne Chardonnay is an absolute steal. ♦ Free. M-Sa. Appointments recommended. Parking in courtyard. 4 Rue Mazeray, Meursault (from Beaune go 6 km/3.7 miles south on N74; follow the signs to the winery). 80.21.26.06; fax 80.21.64.92

58 Domaine Joseph Matrot This highly respected winery is headquartered in an 18th-century white stone mansion with a couple of acres of vineyards reaching right to its back door. The family has been producing superb Meursaults and other wines for more than 30 years. Don't be fooled by the earring that wine maker Thierry Matrot sports: He's one of the Côte d'Or's most traditional wine makers, keeping yields very low and producing lushly flavored wines, particularly the Meursault Les Charmes. His Puligny-Montrachet Les Chalumeaux is also good. Among the best of the reds is the Blagny–La Pièce Sous le Bois, a wine described as "velvety." Other wines, all known for their full flavor, are Volnay-Santenots, Auxey-Duresses Village (a bargain), and simple Bourgogne reds and a Bourgogne Aligoté white. Like most of Burgundy's top wine makers, Monsieur Matrot is most opinionated about what foods to serve with each of his wines; for that opulent Meursault Les Charmes, deep-six your diet and go for something rich and creamy. ♦ Free. By appointment. 12 Rue Martray, Meursault. 80.21.20.13; fax 80.21.29.64

58 Hôtel Le Mont Mélian $$ The friendly young couple that runs this quiet 12-room hotel will do everything they can to help you enjoy your stay, including arranging for balloon trips in the vicinity and renting bicycles for tours of the local vineyards. All the rooms in the renovated 17th- and 18th-century house are spacious and have their original beamed ceilings; some have big skylights. Each room has a private bathroom (but two are across a corridor from the bedrooms), and two of the rooms have two double beds each. The continental breakfast includes fruit juice, a rarity in France. There's no restaurant. All in all, you get great value for your money here. ♦ 17 Rue de Lattre-de-Tassigny (at Rue de Rüdesheim), Meursault. 80.21.64.90

58 Hôtel Les Magnolias $$$ An elegant 18th-century mansion in the center of Meursault has been transformed into a luxurious 11-room, one-suite hotel. Each of the large, comfortable rooms is decorated with Laura Ashley–like fabrics and antiques, and has a private bath, television, and other modern conveniences. Continental breakfast is served, but there's no restaurant. ♦ Closed December–mid-March. 8 Rue Pierre-Joigneaux, Meursault. 80.21.23.23; fax 80.21.62.89

58 Château de Meursault Though other wine makers along the Côte d'Or point out that a real wine cellar shouldn't allow tourists to troop through it—especially during the summer heat—a visit and tasting here is very worthwhile, despite what it may do to the Meursault wines being stored nearby. Besides, the cellars themselves are a work of art: Vast and high-ceilinged, they are dramatically lit with spotlights that emphasize the chisel marks of the workers who quarried them in the Middle Ages. Aboveground, take a look at the Boisseaux family's restored 15th-century château, with turreted towers and an intricately patterned tile roof. The *"Paulée de Meursault,"* a wine festival, is held in the château on the third day (Monday) of Burgundy's most important annual celebration, the "Trois Glorieuses" wine auction. The château has vineyards in several Burgundian villages and produces not only Meursault but also Aloxe-Corton, Pommard Clos des Epenots Premier Cru, and Beaune Premier Cru, among other wines.
♦ Admission; charge includes a tour of the cellars and a tasting. Daily. Rue Moulin-Foulot, Meursault. 80.21.22.98

59 Domaine Leroy Lalou Bize-Leroy runs one of the most highly respected wineries in France in this two-story white stone château surrounded by vineyards and flower beds. She is both *négociante* and wine maker, and—this should say it all—was once the chief wine maker at the **Domaine de la Romanée-Conti.** *"Un vin signé Leroy, c'est la certitude de la perfection"* (The Leroy label on a wine is an assurance of perfection), proclaims GaultMillau's prestigious wine guide, *Le Vin.* Wine critic Robert Parker puts it this way: "You simply will never get a disappointing bottle of wine from Bize-Leroy." It's no wonder the prices are astronomical. The estate owns vineyards in several areas and produces sublime Richebourg, Savigny-lès-Beaune, Vosne-Romanée, Clos de Vougeot, Meursault, and Gevrey-Chambertin wines, among others; the Leroy Clos de Vougeot 1990 is considered one of the best burgundies to have been made in years. Bize-Leroy has used biodynamic techniques in her vineyards since 1989. Her vines are not cloned, no fertilizers or pesticides are used, and the grapes are cultivated according to the positions of the moon, planets, and stars, which are said to affect such factors as sap flow in vines. All Leroy wines are aged in oak and never filtered. Among the more affordable buys is a fruity Savigny-lès-Beaune Premier Cru Les Narbantons red from 60-year-old vines. Try to procure a bottle of the spectacularly rich and nutty 1990 Meursault Chaumes des Perrières from Bize-Leroy's **Domaine d'Auvenay** in Meursault. But don't get your hopes up: Only 288 bottles of this great wine were made. ♦ Fee for tasting the higher-priced wines. Tastings by appointment; sales M-F. From Meursault take D17E west 2 km/1.25 miles to Auxey-Duresses and follow the signs to the château. 80.21.21.10; fax 80.21.63.81

60 Auberge du Vieux Pressoir ★★$$; A friendly young Franco-British couple, Serge and Karen Demollière, operate this informal eatery in a tiny village on a hill above the Côte de Beaune. Among the house specialities are a mouthwatering *oeufs en meurette* (poached eggs in a rich, garlicky, red wine sauce) and delicious *boeuf bourguignon.* The big stone fireplace is always ablaze in winter; huge bouquets of fresh flowers decorate the dining room year-round. All the locals hang out here. The picturesque village is so small that you will have no trouble locating the restaurant; it's in a two-story white stone house in the center of town. ♦ Daily lunch and dinner June-Sept; Th-Su lunch and dinner in the off-season (usually Oct-Mar). Reservations recommended. From Auxey-Duresses take D973 south 5 km/3.1 miles and follow the signs to Evelle and the auberge. 80.21.82.16

60 Scenic Route through the Southern Hautes-Côtes-de-Beaune The southern Hautes-Côtes-de-Beaune seems to be in a totally different part of the country from the flat vineyard terrain around Pommard and Meursault just to the east. Here, tiny villages perch atop hills or nestle along one of the streams that crisscross the area; almost every resident has a patch of vineyard and some wine-making equipment in the cellar. From Evelle, travel downhill south for about half a mile on an unnumbered local road to the D17E

intersection, then turn north toward the village of Orches (home of a fruity, inexpensive rosé wine; a few local wine makers offer tastings). At the entrance to the village, a sign points out a walking trail to the *"vestiges romains"* (Roman ruins); these are ancient carved Roman stelae that apparently were part of a small temple next to a spring, which still gushes forth from the rocks. Picnic here, if you like, before retracing your steps down the trail. In the car, continue on the D17E along a ridge with spectacular views of the surrounding pine-covered hills; it all seems miles away from the often-hectic wine route, even in summer. Turn right toward the village of St-Romain, which is really two villages, one lower and the other perched on a cliff around the ruins of a château. St-Romain is known mainly as the home of Tonneleries François Frères, where many top wineries buy their barrels. Several wine makers in the village offer tastings of the light St-Romain reds and the lesser-known but very good Chardonnay whites, which are great buys. Bottles of wine on display and signs proclaiming *"dégustation"* will point the way to the tastings. Among the good wineries to seek out here are **Bernard Fèvre, Alain Gras, Domaine René Thévenin,** and **Domaine Henri et Gilles Buisson.** Follow D111 less than one kilometer (half a mile) back to D973 and travel south 2.5 kilometers (1.5 miles) to La Rochepot.

60 Château La Rochepot South of Beaune along the Côte d'Or is this imposing castle, without a doubt the most distinctive architectural landmark in the area. It was built in the 12th century, greatly expanded in the 15th century, and completely renovated following Revolution-era destruction. Perched on a rocky cliff, the château's pointed turrets and multicolored roof tiles can be seen from miles away; for the best view from afar, take tiny D35 from the village of Rochepot to St-Aubin and look left. The château's interior is also worth a visit; note the wrought-iron decoration of the well in the courtyard and the beautiful beams in the former Guards' Room. The view from here is great too. ♦ Admission. Guided visits M, W-Su. From Evelle take D973 south 2.5 km (1.5 miles) to La Rochepot, then follow the signs to the château. 80.21.71.37

61 Le Caveau de Chassagne-Montrachet One of the must stops along the Côte d'Or is this modern white building, where manager Jean-Paul Rateau has assembled bottles from 18 wine makers; they're all from the little village of Chassagne-Montrachet, which produces some of the world's finest white wines (and some good reds). Since wines from the neighboring village of Puligny-Montrachet are more famous, you can get some good deals here on wines that taste as sensational as the Pulignys. The *caveau* offers *dégustations* of several wines in a room with maps of Burgundy on the wall; listen to the locals chat about wine news while you drool over the list of what's for sale, which includes Bâtard-Montrachets and Chassagne-Montrachet "Les Chenevottes." The list also includes some simple Bourgogne Aligoté whites and Passe-Tout-Grains reds, but if you've never tried great Chassagne-Montrachet wines, this is the best place in the world to splurge. Top local wineries are represented, including **Ramonet, Jean-Marc Morey,** and **Lamy-Pillot.** The staff is friendly and low-key, and they offer expert advice; a copy of Robert Parker's book *Burgundy* is even on hand (in French) in case you don't have your own. This place likely has more aged vintages of these great wines than the wine makers' cellars, and the prices are very fair. Next door is a small supermarket, which is a good source for picnic items, and next to it is a pleasant little park in which to nibble on them. ♦ Daily. From La Rochepot take D973 south to N6 east, follow N6 8 km (5 miles) to D113A and follow the signs to Chassagne-Montrachet. 80.21.38.13; fax 80.21.35.81

61 Jean-Marc Morey The Morey family's cellars, beneath a white stucco house with a red tile roof, offer eminently reliable Chassagne-Montrachet white wines. They tend to be lush, full, and concentrated, with an intense chardonnay taste. One sip and you will understand, if you hadn't already, why everyone goes crazy over this grape. The best white wines here are the Chassagne-Montrachets from the Les Chaumées, Champs-Gains, and Les Caillerets vineyards. They generally do not need as much aging as some others from the village, so you'll be able to find bottles ready to drink here. The winery also produces a good Chassagne Champs Gains red and a fruity red Beaune Premier Cru Grèves. ♦ Free. Sales and tastings by appointment. 3 Rue Principale, Chassagne-Montrachet. 80.21.32.62; fax 80.21.90.60

61 Domaine Ramonet From the late Pierre Ramonet to his son André and *his* sons Noël and Jean-Claude—the generation now in charge—a dynasty of Ramonets has elevated this winery's reputation to the stuff of legend. Robert Parker has said the estate's great

wines "are Chardonnays about as profound and long-lived as one is likely to find." That is, if you can find them. Ramonet wines are so prized, and produced in such limited quantities that even great restaurants (and the governments of some countries) have been unable to procure them. Part of the wines' magic comes from the Ramonets' vines in some of France's top vineyards. Their holdings in the priceless Montrachet vineyard (where Ramonet vines have an average age of almost 70 years) would be enough to make any winery's reputation, but they also have vines in the great Bâtard-Montrachet, Chassagne-Montrachet Les Ruchottes (planted with 45-year-old vines), Chassagne-Montrachet Les Caillerets, and Chassagne-Montrachet Les Vergers vineyards. Any Ramonet wines with these labels will astonish with their intensity, fullness, and complexity. Traditional techniques are used in the cellars, located underneath the nondescript, purely functional stone winery. Wines are aged in 25- to 35-percent-new-oak casks for 18 to 20 months, and are lightly filtered. Yields are kept very low, another reason for the top quality. This is certainly the place to splurge on a sublime white wine. Just don't open your precious bottle too early; depriving one of these wines of the bottle aging it needs would be a crime. Ramonet wines are also available at **Le Caveau de Chassagne-Montrachet** (see page 84). ♦ Free. By appointment. 4 Pl des Noyers, Chassagne-Montrachet. 80.21.30.88; fax 80.21.90.38

Le Montrachet

62 Le Montrachet Between the villages of Chassagne-Montrachet and Puligny-Montrachet is a little hump of a hill known as Mont Rachet (Shaven Mountain) with a slope facing east. Here is where the grapes for the great local white wines are grown. The finest vineyards, renowned for centuries, range along the tiny D113A road, which leads north from Chassagne-Montrachet across the N6 to Puligny-Montrachet. Many vineyards are surrounded by ancient stone walls, with the vineyard name often carved on an arched entrance leading to the vines. The greatest vineyard of all is **Le Montrachet,** source of what many believe to be the best white wines in the world. Stroll around the narrow dirt roads through the vines here, and you will soon find that the light and air will begin to feel magical. If you buy a bottle of Chassagne-Montrachet or Puligny-Montrachet, you might want to drink it here and toast the source. ♦ 2 km (1.25 miles) east of Chassagne-Montrachet on D113A

Restaurants/Clubs: Red	**Hotels:** Blue
Shops/ 🌳 Outdoors: Green	**Sights/Culture:** Black

62 Domaine Leflaive The late Vincent Leflaive made this winery in the nondescript village of Puligny-Montrachet into one of Burgundy's most highly rated producers of white wines. It has been run since mid-1994 by Vincent's daughter, Anne-Claude Leflaive. Among the estate's absolutely reliable (and extremely expensive and hard to find) wines are the Grand Cru Chevalier-Montrachet and Bâtard-Montrachet; the Bâtard can be drunk a bit younger than the Chevalier, which needs six to seven years in the bottle. But both are the ultimate in Puligny-Montrachets: rich, complex, and full. The Grand Cru Bienvenues–Bâtard-Montrachet is another top wine, although some consider it a step below the estate's other *grands crus*. Then there are the *premiers crus:* Puligny-Montrachet Les Pucelles, Puligny-Montrachet Les Folatières, Puligny-Montrachet Les Chalumeaux, and Puligny-Montrachet Les Combettes. Les Combettes is a relative bargain, usually every bit as good as the *grands crus* but at *premier cru* prices—if you can find it; it's produced in very small quantities. **Domaine Leflaive** also makes a simple Bourgogne Blanc that is one of the best buys along the Côte d'Or. Anne-Claude Leflaive has been experimenting with biodynamics in one part of the vineyards since 1990 and believes, based on the results of her comparative testing, that this method of viticulture is definitely the way to go. She has said that she could not taste a difference between the 1990 Pulignys produced from biodynamic vineyards and those from conventional vineyards, but the 1991s from the biodynamic vineyards tasted better than the conventional ones, and the 1992 biodynamic wines were better still. ♦ Free. By appointment. Pl des Marronniers, Puligny-Montrachet (4 km/2.5 miles south of Meursault on N74). 80.21.30.13; fax 80.21.39.57

62 Hôtel Le Montrachet $$$ Those deciding to stay the night in town will find a friendly welcome and 30 quiet rooms in a three-story, 18th-century stone house with white shutters, right on the little village square. The rooms are comfortable (lots of flowery fabrics, soft carpets, and beamed ceilings), each with a private bath, telephone, and satellite TV. The best (and more expensive) rooms are the two large suites, especially the one with a mezzanine. ♦ Closed in December. Three nights for the price of two in November, January, February, and March. Pl des Marronniers, Puligny-Montrachet. 80.21.30.06; fax 80.21.39.06

Within the Hôtel Le Montrachet:

Restaurant Le Montrachet ★★$$$ Local specialties are featured here. Try the *salade de ris de veau au vinaigre de cidre* (salad of poached veal sweetbreads with cider vinegar), the *blanc de turbot braisé au*

Chardonnay et petits légumes (turbot braised in Chardonnay wine with early miniature vegetables), and the *pigeonneau de bourgogne laqué à l'hydromel* (Burgundian squab with a honey-based glaze). The wine list is outstanding, if you can afford anything on it. ♦ M-Tu, Th-Su lunch and dinner; closed in December. Reservations recommended. 80.21.30.06

62 Maison Olivier Leflaive Olivier Leflaive, nephew of the founder of the **Domaine Leflaive** (see left), began his *négociant* business in 1984 and has already made a name for himself. His Pommard or Volnay reds or the Rully and St-Aubin whites are all good deals. But the stars are definitely the local Puligny-Montrachet whites. Try the Puligny-Montrachet Les Garennes, a rich, grapey wine; the 1990 is ready to drink in 1995. Oak lovers enjoy Leflaive's wines, but others may find the oak taste too predominant. With its extremely discreet sign, the winery is easy to miss. Keep your eyes peeled for the sign on the east side of Place du Monument, the square in the middle of the village punctuated by a war memorial. The winery itself is an unobtrusive white stucco building that resembles a garage. ♦ Free. Sales and tastings by appointment. Pl du Monument, Puligny-Montrachet. 80.21.37.65; fax 80.21.33.94

62 Domaine Louis Carillon & Fils This wine-making family should win an award just for the elaborate wrought-iron sign, painted with their name, that hangs in front of the stone warehouse that shelters their cellars. Fewer and fewer Burgundy *vignerons* still bother to use this lovely and traditional way of advertising their wares. Carillons have been making wine from vines in the chalky clay soil of Puligny since 1520, so it's no surprise they favor traditional techniques and get maximum flavor and finesse out of their priceless 12 hectares (29.6 acres). Their wines include a Puligny-Montrachet Premier Cru, a Bienvenues–Bâtard-Montrachet, and a reasonably priced Puligny-Montrachet–Villages. The 1991s, with overtones of quince and apricot, are ready to be enjoyed in 1995. ♦ Free. M-Sa by appointment. Puligny-Montrachet (follow the signs to the winery). 80.21.30.34; fax 80.21.90.02

Lameloise

63 Lameloise $$$$ A walled, tree-filled garden surrounds this three-story stone mansion with a country atmosphere, despite its central setting in the busy town of Chagny. Inside, the decor is essentially modern, but 18th- and 19th-century furnishings are used as accents throughout. There are 20 huge rooms, some with terraces overlooking vineyards, and the breakfasts include fresh fruit, soft-boiled eggs, and homemade jams. The Lameloise family owns and operates the establishment, and they are perfect hosts. ◆ Closed late December–late January, and Wednesday July–mid-October. 36 Pl des Armes (at Blvd de la Liberté), Chagny (about 4 km/2.5 miles south of Puligny-Montrachet on N6). 85.87.08.85; fax 85.87.03.57

Within the Lameloise:

Restaurant Lameloise ★★★★$$$$ Chef Jacques Lameloise is in his element here, creating ultrarich, ultratraditional Burgundian dishes like escargots with lots of garlic and butter, *purée de pommes de terre truffée* (truffled mashed potatoes), and dark chocolate cake with *pain d'épices* ice cream. The dining room is formal but not stuffy, with antique furniture and fresh flowers everywhere. The wine list is one of the best in France, and boasts an absolutely incredible collection of burgundies. The Rully white wine is very good, and one of the best deals on the list. This place has earned three Michelin stars and is a member of the prestigious Relais & Châteaux group, so it's no surprise that you practically have to sell the family jewels to come here. But it just might be worth it. ◆ M-Tu, F-Su lunch and dinner, Th dinner mid-Oct–June; M-Tu, F-Su lunch and dinner, W-Th dinner July–mid-Oct; closed late December–late January. Reservations required far in advance. 85.87.08.85

The Côte Chalonnaise

The wine region that begins south of the Côte de Beaune at **Rully** and stretches to **Buxy** is named for the nearby bustling industrial center of **Chalon-sur-Saône**. The slope is broken up by small, picturesque valleys, with vineyards interspersed among fields and orchards.

Although following the Revolution—when France was divided into administrative departments—the Côte Chalonnaise was separated from the department of the Côte d'Or, local wine makers have always looked to Beaune for their wine-making style. Increasingly, distributors in France and abroad are offering Côte Chalonnaise wines as cheaper alternatives to the pricey Côte d'Or bottles.

The official village appellations include Rully, which produces some light reds, delicious whites, and a few Crémant de Bourgogne sparkling wines; Mercurey, where 93 percent of the vines are used to produce a fruity red wine made with pinot noir; Givry, which makes supple, flavorful reds and some whites;

and Montagny, specializing in whites made from chardonnay grapes; and Bourgogne Aligoté Bouzeron, a superior white burgundy made from aligoté grapes grown near the village of **Bouzeron.** The region also produces standard red and white burgundies, the best of which bear the appellation Bourgogne–Côte-Chalonnaise.

64 Domaine de la Folie After studying economics and international affairs in Switzerland for years, Xavier Noël-Bouton came home to make wine in the family mansion where his great-grandfather, Etienne-Jules Marey, invented cinematography. A passionate ambassador for the local wines, the amiable Noël-Bouton is also a fan of California wines. He makes light but intensely flavorful Rully red wines, such as the Rully Clos de Bellecroix, with its hints of red currants. He also makes delicious, fruity Rully whites, with overtones of peaches, that are aged one-third in oak; one such is the Rully Premier Cru Clos Saint Jacques, which is named for a medieval pilgrimage route to Santiago (St-Jacques) de Compostela that passed near the vineyards. The name of the golden stone estate, "La Folie" (Madness), has been cited since the 16th century; its origin apparently lies in sorcerer's rites that once were held here. Visitors are offered tastings in a recently restored wine cellar. ◆ Free. Daily. Appointment recommended. From Chagny take D981 south 2 km (1.25 miles) and follow the signs to Bouzeron and the winery. 85.87.18.59; fax 85.87.03.53

64 Domaine Dureuil-Janthial Raymond Dureuil-Janthial produces red and white wines of different types in his gray stone farmhouse. All the wines are worth a try, but Dureuil-Janthial is best known for his superb Rully whites that use grapes from vines up to 50 years old. He relies on strictly traditional methods: No artificial yeasts are used, and fermentation is in wood (one-fifth of which are new barrels). As he puts it, *"Notre principale caractéristique est que nous sommes restés trés attachés à la tradition de vinification que nous ont transmises nos ancêtres"* (Our key feature is that we have remained very faithful to the traditional wine-making procedures passed along to us by our ancestors). The wines are long-lived, but the estate keeps older vintages on hand, so you will be able to buy a bottle that is ready to drink. Tastings are given by family members, who are very welcoming. ◆ Free. M-Sa. 7 Rue de la Buisserolle, Rully (from Chagny take D981 south 4 km/2.5 miles and follow the signs to Rully and the winery). 85.87.02.37; fax 85.87.00.24

65 Hôtellerie du Val d'Or ★★★$$$ The rustic decor in this convivial family-run hotel/restaurant contrasts with chef-owner Jean-Claude Cogny's sophisticated, modern cuisine. You'll find lots of fresh vegetables and herbs, and a light touch with butter and cream in the sauces. Highlights include such regional dishes as *biscuit de brochet* (pike mousse) and *soupière de petits escargots* (a "stew" of tiny snails), or innovative treats such as *rouget sur une compote de légumes* (red mullet with mixed new vegetables). Don't even think of skipping the cheese assortment, which includes some of Burgundy's best, from cîteaux (made by the monks who once owned the **Clos de Vougeot**) to the delightfully smelly époisses. Luscious desserts include *poires caramélisées* (caramelized pears). The great wine list emphasizes local Côte Chalonnaise wines. The only drawback (besides the leisurely service) is the high cost, but the fixed-price menus are reasonable. ♦ W-Su lunch and dinner; Tu lunch; closed late August–early September and mid-December–mid-January. Reservations required. Grande-Rue, Mercurey (from Rully go 3.5 km/2.2 miles south on GR18). 85.45.13.70; fax 85.45.18.45

Adjoining the Hôtellerie du Val d'Or:

Hôtel du Val d'Or $$ The Cogny family offers 13 simple but very quiet and comfortable guest rooms, all with private bathrooms. This is a popular base for touring the Côte Chalonnaise vineyards, and reservations are required far in advance. ♦ Closed late August–early September and mid-December–mid-January. 85.43.13.70

65 Domaine de la Monette Paul Granger and his son Pierre-Emmanuel make mainly red wines along with some whites, all from vines between 20 and 60 years old. They favor traditional methods: no herbicides, slow fermentation, and long contact with the lees (sediment that forms in the barrel). Try the Velay Premier Cru white, the Mercurey Premier Cru Montaigu red, or the Mercurey Rouge Vieilles Vignes red, all excellent and at low prices. They still have several of their older vintages in stock. Visitors are greeted warmly, and tastings are in the wine cellars of the elegant old family house. ♦ Free. Daily. Appointment recommended. Rte de Touches, Touches (from Mercurey go 2 km/1.25 miles south on D978; follow the signs to the winery). 85.45.10.78; fax 85.45.29.04

66 Givry There are two reasons to come to Givry, west of Chalon. First and foremost, the town produces delicious reds and whites. Also, it is worth a visit to see the charming **Hôtel de Ville** (City Hall; Rue de l'Hôtel de Ville) built within a former 18th-century city gate, and the circular **Halles** (Pl Halle), an early-19th-century grain repository.

As in the Côte d'Or, the highest quality red wines in the Côte Chalonnaise are made from pinot noir and the whites from chardonnay, but the wines here have a lighter, fruitier taste and lower prices than their Côte d'Or counterparts. Some wineries are succumbing to temptation and producing more tannic Côte d'Or imitations to please the current market; try to seek out the more traditional wines, which can be a real pleasure to drink.

Among Givry's best wineries that accept visitors by appointment are **François Lumpp** at "Le Pied du Clou" (36 Ave de Mortières, 85.44.45.57) and **Domaine Thénard** (7 Rue de l'Hôtel-de-Ville, 85.44.31.36). In the hamlet of Poncey just south of the village is **Gérard Mouton** (1 Rue du Four, 85.44.37.99). Also visit the hamlet of Jambles, just southwest of Givry on D170, where you'll find **René Bourgeon** (Pl de Cereux, 85.44.35.85). Northwest of Jambles, route D48 in the Vallée des Vaux offers a lovely, scenic drive dotted with one perfect picnic spot after another. ♦ From Touches take a community road to D978, then take D978 southeast 6 km (3.7 miles) to D981. Take D981 south 4 km (2.5 miles) to Givry

Within Givry:

Parize et Fils This reliable winery produces both white and red Givry, but the reds are the real stars; the whites tend to need a long time in the bottle before they open up. Try the brilliantly red La Sauleraie 1991, with a powerful taste of raspberries. It's a superbly balanced wine that will age well. Tastings are in a small room in the winery, which is in a 19th-century stone farmhouse; an adjacent 19th-century building, once used for threshing hay, is now home to the aging vats. This is a good place to introduce yourself to fresh-tasting Givry wines, which may become your new favorites among affordable burgundies. ♦ Free. Daily. 18 Rue des Faussillons (from Chagny go 19 km/11.6 miles south on D981; follow the signs to the winery). 85.44.38.60; fax 85.44.43.54

67 Maison des Vins de la Côte Chalonnaise The only drawback to this modern wine center, which promotes Côte Chalonnaise wines, is that it's right in the middle of Chalon-sur-Saône, where you will inevitably get stuck in a traffic jam. But the wines here are worth the trouble. They are chosen in a blind tasting conducted each year by the region's wine makers. All regional wines are represented; you can taste three at a time for a fairly stiff fee (about $5 per person). Many tasty, inexpensive picnic wines are available by the bottle, such as Rully whites, Bourgogne Aligoté Bouzeron whites, and Givry and Mercurey reds. ♦ M-Sa. Promenade Ste-Marie (at the corner of Parque Georges-Nouelle), Chalon-sur-Saône (from Givry go 11 km/6.8 miles east on D69). 85.41.64.00

HÔTEL de GREUZE

68 Hôtel de Greuze $$$$ The place to go for luxurious accommodations, if you can afford it. A very quiet Relais & Châteaux establishment overlooking an abbey, it is surrounded by a gravel courtyard and a large garden. There are 20 spacious rooms and two suites with modern decor. All have thick carpets, comfortable beds with embroidered sheets, air-conditioning, and bathrooms with hair dryers and complimentary toiletries. Nonsmoking rooms—a rarity in France—are available. Breakfasts, which can be served in your room or in the breakfast salon, are fabulous, and so is the service. ◆ 5-6 Pl de l'Abbaye, Tournus (25 km/15.5 miles south of Chalon on N6). 85.51.77.77; fax 85.51.77.23

Adjoining the Hôtel de Greuze:

Restaurant Greuze ★★★$$$$ Jean Ducloux's lively establishment has long been a key stop on the Paris-Mediterranean route. The cuisine is resolutely traditional and is unlikely to change, even if Ducloux—who's been cooking for a half century—ever decides to retire. Try the *pâté en croûte* (pâté in a pastry crust), the *galettes de truffe* (a sinfully rich truffle cake), or the *quenelles de brochet* (ethereal pike dumplings, a classic French dish). The rich meals might be out of fashion today, but they never fail to please. The wine list is superb, particularly in fine beaujolais and Pouilly-Fuissés. The fixed-price menu (available Monday through Friday) is almost affordable; otherwise, prices are sky high. ◆ Daily lunch and dinner. Reservations required. Rue A.-Thibaudet (at Pl de l'Abbaye). 85.51.13.52; fax 85.51.75.42

69 Bouillot Ferronniers Inside a rambling warehouse, Michel Bouillot and his son Jean-Yves create elegant wrought-iron balconies, trellises, and other architectural treasures, as well as more portable creations. Most popular is the *rat de cave* (cellar rat), a wrought-iron candle holder with an elegant yet practical curve of a handle that looks nothing like a rat's tail. This type of candle holder has been popular for centuries—since at least AD 1000, when it is mentioned in manuscripts—to help

people find that perfect bottle in their pre-electricity wine cellars. Even if your "cellar" is a hall closet with its own light bulb, you won't be able to pass up one of these unique, traditional pieces. Visitors can watch the blacksmiths at work. ◆ M-F; Sa-Su by appointment. Rte de Chalon, St-Bonnet-de-Joux (from Tournus go 49 km/30.4 miles southwest on D14. From Cluny go 17 km/10.5 miles northwest on D7). 85.24.74.30; fax 85.24.70.61

70 Chambres d'Hôte La Ronzière $ Brigitte and Bernard Blanc have five guest rooms in their 150-year-old, lovingly restored bed-and-breakfast, previously a barn. All the rooms have private bathrooms and views of the surrounding hills, which are topped with pine and oak forests and slope into orchards and cattle pastures. Two of the rooms are on the ground floor and accessible to the disabled. Breakfast is served in a pretty dining room, and kitchen facilities are available to guests. Enjoy peaceful walks through the countryside in this seemingly out-of-the-way location that is just minutes from Cluny. ◆ Collonges (from Cluny take D981 north 6 km/3.7 miles and follow the sign to Collonge and the hotel). 85.59.14.80

71 Cluny Surrounded by unspoiled countryside, the town of Cluny is dominated by one of France's most famous historical sites, the **Abbaye de Cluny** (Abbey of Cluny). Founded by Benedictine monks in the 10th century and greatly expanded in the 12th century, it was under the direction of its abbé, Saint Hugues, that Cluny became a great center of learning, dubbed the "light of the world." In its heyday, it served as the world's largest Christian church and had dominion over 10,000 monks. But greed gradually proved the abbey's downfall; it was said that *"Partout où le vent vente, l'abbaye de Cluny a rente,"* ("Everywhere the wind blows, Cluny Abbey collects rents.").

After a long period of decline, the abbey became a casualty of the French Revolution and was almost completely destroyed. Today, only the right-hand supports of the original transepts remain from the church. But the village is worth visiting for its place in history and the **Musée Ochier,** where some relics from the abbey are housed. ◆ From Mâcon take N79 northwest for 21 km (13 miles) to Berzé-le-Châtel, then take D980 north for 5 km (3.1 miles)

Within Cluny:

Musée Ochier This 15th-century mansion, built for Abbé Jean de Bourbon, is filled with fragments of the Romanesque portal of the abbey's church, as well as several elaborately carved capitals from pillars that once supported part of the church's roof. The museum's collection also contains carved and gilded wooden chests, silver candelabra, and other items once used either in the abbey's church or in the rooms occupied by the notoriously luxury-loving Cluny monks. Some Gallo-Roman artifacts and 4,000 texts that were once part of Cluny's fabulous library, considered one of the medieval world's greatest, are also housed here. The building itself is a graceful three-story white stone structure with decoratively carved stone window frames and a gray tile roof. Admission includes a guided tour of the collection and a walking tour through the vestiges of the abbey itself, which lies just east of the museum. Next door to the museum is also a pleasant park (a good spot for a picnic, as long as you stay on the benches and off the grass). A climb up the **Tour de Fromage** (the Cheese Tower), which marks the former placement of the Abbey, provides good views of the city. ♦ Admission. Daily Apr-Aug; daily afternoon Sept-Mar. Parc Abbatial. 85.59.23.97

Hôtel de Bourgogne $$ The typical provincial French hotel, with geraniums in window boxes, comfortable beds, flowery drapes, a friendly (if rather formal) welcome, and a fine restaurant. It faces what's left of the abbey, and is perfectly located for touring the picturesque old center of Cluny. The 12 spacious rooms and three suites, all with private bathrooms, overlook either the abbey or a tranquil interior garden. The elegantly furnished suites are expensive, but the rooms are moderately priced. ♦ Closed mid-November–mid-March. Pl de l'Abbaye. 85.59.00.58

Within the Hôtel de Bourgogne:

Restaurant Le Bourgogne ★★$$ Pale pink walls, 18th- and 19th-century furniture, and lots of fresh flowers set the tone in this dining room. The cooking is strictly regional. Try the *salade tiède de ris de veau* (warm salad of sliced veal sweetbreads), the *noisettes de lotte à la moelle et pâtes fraîches* (fillets of monkfish with beef marrow and fresh pasta), and the tasty cheese assortment. The generous wine list includes many fine burgundies. The fixed-price menu served at lunch is a good deal; ordering à la carte can

Jura and Savoie

Both the Jura and Savoie regions once had many more vineyards than they do today; and though most of the vines that were devastated by phylloxera were replanted recently, many vineyards are still depleted. Both wine regions warrant a visit, though, because they are picturesque and off the usual tourist routes.

Jura

A green, hilly region whose vineyards were cultivated in Roman times, Jura produces red, dry white, rosé, and sparkling white wines from chardonnay, pinot noir, and various local grapes, including the black plousard (also spelled poulsard). The region's most famous wine is *vin jaune* (yellow wine, because of its color), a sweet sherry-type wine made from the local savagnin grape; it's aged in barrels for a minimum of six years, and used in making a local specialty, *poulet au vin jaune* (chicken in a cream sauce made with *vin jaune*). The rare *vin de paille* (straw wine) is a rich, sweet wine made from grapes left to dry on straw mats (or in special boxes, nowadays) until they are almost raisins. Henri Maire, the area's biggest producer, is based at **Château Montfort** near **Arbois;** he also hosts tastings daily at an outlet in Arbois (on Pl de la Liberté, at Rue de l'Hôtel-de-Ville, 84.66.15.27; fax 84.37.43.85). The Martin family's **Domaine de la Pinte** (on RN83, 2 km/1.25 miles south of Arbois, 84.66.06.47; fax 84.66.24.58) has excellent wines made from plousard and savagnin grapes; tours of the cellars and tastings are by appointment only. The Martins also operate a store, also called **Domaine de la Pinte** (Rue de l'Hôtel-de-Ville, Arbois, 84.37.42.62), where they offer tastings daily April through December. In the town of **Château-Chalon,** where the best *vin jaune* is said to be produced, the highly respected **Jean Macle** (Rue de la Roche, 84.85.21.85) holds tastings daily. For general information, maps, and lists of wineries open to the public in the Jura, contact the **Comité Interprofessionel des Vins du Jura** (Ave 44e R.I., Lons-le-Saunier, 84.24.21.07).

Savoie

The vineyards of the **Savoie** lie in the foothills of the **Alps,** south of Loc Léman (Lake Geneva). The region produces dry whites, sparkling whites, and some light reds from chasselas, gamay, jacquère, altesse (or rousette), bergeron (roussanne), and other local grapes. Most of these wines are light, refreshing, and made for quaffing at the local after-ski fondue parties; the better whites have been described as "bottled mountain air." The main vineyards are outside the pretty towns of **Thonon-les-Bains, Annecy, Aix-les-Bains,** and **Chambéry. Château de Ripaille** (just east of Thonon-les-Bains; follow signs to the winery, 50.71.75.12; fax: 50.71.72.55) produces a delicate, slightly bubbly dry white wine from chasselas grapes and is open for tastings daily. **Domaine Dupasquier** (79.44.02.23), in the hamlet of **Aix-Mai-Vigne** (which is in the commune of **Jongieux,** between Chambéry and Aix-les-Bains), produces a richly flavored Altesse dry wine called Marestel. Tastings are offered here on Saturdays when they are not harvesting grapes; in July and August the vineyard is usually open to the public from Monday through Saturday—any time of the year, the best bet is to call ahead. **Domaine du Prieuré Saint-Christophe** (79.28.62.10; fax 79.28.61.74) is another reliable winery. It lies outside Chambéry on the top of the hill that is the town of **Fréterive,** and provides tastings Monday through Saturday. For general information, maps, and lists of wineries open to the public, contact the **Comité Interprofessionnel des Vins de Savoie** (3 Rue du Château, Chambéry, 79.33.44.16).

get expensive. ♦ M, Th-Su lunch and dinner; W dinner; closed mid-November–mid-March. Reservations required. 85.59.00.58

Le Cellier de l'Abbaye Near the abbey and just down the hill from the **Hôtel de Bourgogne,** this small shop with a large display window has some regional food products on hand, but specializes in selling Burgundy and Beaujolais wines by the bottle; there's also a big selection of imported beers, in case anyone needs a break from the grape. ♦ M-Sa. 13 Rue Municipale. 85.59.04.00

Au Péché Mignon You can always diet tomorrow. Today, sample something rich from this irresistible pastry shop (its name means "besetting sin"). It's just steps from the abbey, on a street lined with beautiful medieval houses and dotted with tearooms and restaurants. In addition to the luscious sweets, try the huge, cheesy *gougères* (perfect for a picnic, along with some red wine) and excellent quiches. ♦ Tu-Su. 25 Rue Lamartine. 85.59.11.21

The Mâconnais

Overlapping slightly with Beaujolais, the Mâconnais begins in **Tournus** and heads south to **St-Véran,** bordered by the **Grosne** and **Saône Rivers.** The region's wines reflect the rich soil in this sunny valley, where vines and fruit trees thrive. The landscape and architecture hint of southern France.

The Cluny monks were the first to plant vines here. Most of the wines are white; 90 percent of them are produced by local cooperatives scattered throughout the hilly countryside. Roughly two-thirds of the vineyards use the native chardonnay grape. The greatest wines are the fruity, sometimes flowery whites from the villages of **Pouilly, Fuissé, Vinzelles, Loche,** and St-Véran. Pouilly-Fuissé, the popular white, is a blend of grapes from two of these villages. Mâcon-Villages and standard red and white burgundies are also produced in the region.

72 Maison Mâconnaise des Vins This center for the promotion of Mâconnais wines sells wine, gives tastings, provides brochures (some in English) on wine routes, and operates a restaurant serving simple local specialties and wine by the glass; the wines

are top-notch, but the food is overpriced. Another drawback is that busloads of tourists often disgorge to eat here. It's best to come for a tasting and some wine information, or to buy a bottle of wine and have a picnic in the countryside outside town (for example, along any of the pretty D roads just west of the village of Fuissé, the next stop on the route). ♦ Daily 8AM-9PM. 484 Ave de Lattre-de-Tassigny, Mâcon (from Cluny go 23 km/14.25 miles southeast along N79). 85.38.36.70

73 Domaine La Soufrandise A visit to this winery is a must. Pouilly-Fuissé wines are often overpriced and disappointing, but never here. In fact, dedicated young wine makers Nicolas and Françoise Melin have won several prestigious awards for their richly flavored Pouilly-Fuissé and Mâcon-Fuissé whites, some made from vines up to 70 years old. They produce Pouilly-Fuissé Vieilles Vignes, Pouilly-Fuissé Clos la Soufrandise (from the vineyards that surround the winery), and Mâcon-Fuissé. All are bargains, and the Mâcon-Fuissé is a steal. The Melins favor traditional Burgundian methods, including handpicking the grapes, aging partly in wood, and leaving the wine on its lees long enough to get the richest possible flavor. Their wines have been distributed on the East Coast of the United States since 1994, and are really worth watching for there. The winery is on the ground floor of the Melins' graceful stone house, which is covered with peach-pink stucco and surrounded by vines. It was once a convent, but the Melin family has owned it since 1835. Tastings are given in the wine cellars beneath the house. The Melins are also glad to suggest good picnic spots nearby. ♦ Free. By appointment. From Mâcon take D54 southwest 6 km (3.7 miles) to the adjoining villages of Pouilly and Fuissé and follow the signs to the winery in Fuissé. 85.35.64.04; fax 85.35.65.57

74 La Roche de Solutré A striking part of the landscape today, this rugged limestone cliff jutting up above vineyards just west of the villages of Pouilly and Fuissé may have been the death of tens of thousands of horses, whose ages-old skeletons were discovered at the cliff's base. Historians once believed the horses had been driven over the cliff, possibly by fire or stone age hunters, but the current theory is that the hunters attacked the horses beneath the cliff. Whatever happened, the many scenic roads around the cliff (such as D31 and D23 west out of Fuissé) have perfect picnicking spots at almost every turn, especially along a branch of the Grande Randonnée (official hiking trail) No. 76, which heads south where D31 turns into D23. You can also hike to the summit of the cliff from a small prehistory museum just above the hamlet of Solutré; on a really clear day, you can see the Alps, or so they say. ♦ 2 km (1.25 miles) west of Pouilly and Fuissé on D31

Parlez-Vous Français?

Since the French take great pride in their language, here are some phrases that will enable you to start communicating with them *en français*. When there is both a masculine and a feminine spelling, the feminine is in parentheses.

Bon voyage! (Have a good trip!)

Hello, Good-bye, and Other Basics

Hello/Good morning/Good afternoon	*Bonjour*
Good evening	*Bonsoir*
How are you?	*Comment allez-vous?*
Good-bye	*Au revoir*
Yes	*Oui*
No	*Non*
Please	*S'il vous plaît*
Thank you	*Merci*
You're welcome	*De rien* or *Je vous en prie*
Excuse me	*Excusez-moi* or *Pardon*
I'm sorry	*Je suis désolé(e)*
I don't speak French.	*Je ne parle pas français.*
Do you speak English?	*Parlez-vous anglais?*
I don't understand.	*Je ne comprends pas.*
More slowly, please.	*Plus lentement, s'il vous plaît.*
I don't know.	*Je ne sais pas.*
My name is	*Je m'appelle . . . .*
What is your name?	*Comment vous appelez-vous?*
miss	*mademoiselle*
madame, ma'am	*madame*
mister, sir	*monsieur*
good	*bon(ne)*
bad	*mauvais(e)*
open	*ouvert(e)*
closed	*fermé(e)*
entrance	*entrée*
exit	*sortie*
push	*poussez*
pull	*tirez*
today	*aujourd'hui*
tomorrow	*demain*
yesterday	*hier*
week	*semaine*
month	*mois*
year	*an*

Hotel Talk

I have a reservation.	*J'ai une réservation.*
I would like to reserve . . .	*Je voudrais réserver . . .*
a double room	*une chambre pour deux personnes*
a quiet room	*une chambre tranquille*
with (private) bath	*avec une salle de bain (privée)*
with air-conditioning	*avec la climatisation*
Are taxes included?	*Est-ce que les taxes sont comprises?*
Is breakfast included?	*Est-ce que le petit déjeuner est compris?*
Do you accept traveler's checks?	*Prenez-vous des chèques de voyage?*
Do you accept credit cards?	*Prenez-vous des cartes de crédit?*

Restaurant Repartee

Waiter!	*Monsieur!*
I would like . . .	*Je voudrais . . .*
a menu	*la carte*
a glass of	*un verre de*
a bottle of	*une bouteille de*
The check, please.	*L'addition, s'il vous plaît.*
Is the service charge (tip) included?	*Est-ce que le service est compris?*
I think there is an error in the bill.	*Je crois qu'il y a une erreur avec l'addition.*
lunch	*déjeuner*
dinner	*dîner*
tip	*service, pourboire*
bread	*pain*
butter	*beurre*
pepper	*poivre*
salt	*sel*
sugar	*sucre*
soup	*soupe*
salad	*salade*
vegetables	*légumes*
cheese	*fromage*
eggs	*oeufs*
beef	*boeuf*
chicken	*poulet*
veal	*veau*
fish	*poisson*
seafood	*fruits de mer*
pork	*porc*
ham	*jambon*
chop	*côtelette*
dessert	*dessert*

As You Like It

cold	*froid(e)*
hot	*chaud(e)*
sweet	*sucré(e)*
dry	*sec*
broiled, roasted	*rôti(e)*
baked	*au four*
boiled	*bouilli(e)*
fried	*frit(e)*

raw	cru(e)
rare	saignant(e)
well done	bien cuit(e)
spicy	épicé(e)

Thirsty No More

water	l'eau
coffee	café, express
coffee with steamed milk	café au lait
tea	thé
beer	bière
rosé wine	vin rosé
red wine	vin rouge
white wine	vin blanc
milk	lait
mineral water	l'eau minérale
carbonated	gazeuse
not carbonated	non-gazeuse
orange juice	jus d'orange
ice	glaçons
without ice	sans glaçons

Sizing It Up

How much does this cost?	Combien coûte-il?
inexpensive	bon marché
expensive	cher (chère)
large	grand(e)
small	petit(e)
long	long(ue)
short	court(e)
used	d'occasion
this one	celui-ci (celle-ci)
a little	un peu
a lot	beaucoup

On the Move

north	nord
south	sud
east	est
west	ouest
right	droite
left	gauche
straight ahead	tout droit
highway	autoroute
street	rue
gas station	station-service
here	ici
there	là
bus stop	l'arrêt de bus
bus station	gare routière
train station	gare SNCF
subway	métro
airport	aéroport
tourist information	informations touristiques
road map	carte routière
one-way ticket	aller-simple
round-trip ticket	aller-retour
first class	première classe
second class	seconde classe or deuxième
smoking	fumeur
no smoking	non-fumeur
Does this train go to . . . ?	Est-ce que ce train s'arrête à . . . ?
Where is/are . . . ?	Où est/sont ...?
How far is it from here to . . . ?	Quelle est la distance entre ici et . . . ?

The Bare Necessities

aspirin	aspirines
Band-Aids™	pansement adhésif
barbershop, beauty shop	coiffeur, salon de beauté
condom	préservatif
dry cleaner	teinturerie
laundromat, laundry	blanchisserie
letter	lettre
post office	bureau de poste
postage stamp	timbre
postcard	carte postale
sanitary napkins	serviettes hygiéniques
shampoo	shampooing
shaving cream	lotion à raser
soap	savon
tampons	tampons périodiques
tissues	mouchoirs en papier
toilet paper	papier hygiénique
toothpaste	dentifrice
Where is the bathroom?	Où est la salle de bains?
Where are the toilets?	Où sont les toilettes?
Men's room	WC pour hommes
Women's room	WC pour dames

Days of the Week

Monday	lundi
Tuesday	mardi
Wednesday	mercredi
Thursday	jeudi
Friday	vendredi
Saturday	samedi
Sunday	dimanche

Numbers

zero	zéro
one	un
two	deux
three	trois
four	quatre
five	cinq
six	six
seven	sept
eight	huit
nine	neuf
ten	dix

Beaujolais

Beaujolais is a stunning region of vineyard-covered granite foothills extending from the Massif Central, a wooded mountain range where some peaks reach 3,300 feet. In the small villages here, clusters of stone houses are accented by colorfully painted doors and shutters. The surrounding valleys are connected by tiny "D" and "C" roads, none of which heads in a straight line for very long, making speedy touring impossible. But meandering is part of the pleasure here, passing by vineyards and paying homage to their fruit. In this granitelike soil, the gamay grape is king.

Everyone knows of Beaujolais Nouveau, which has been marketed so well that on the third Thursday of every November, legions race to be the first in their town to uncork the fruity, young wine. But Beaujolais produces more than just fruity, light reds, especially in the north. Ten official *crus* from the northern part of the region are Beaujolais's best wines: St-Amour, Juliénas, Cénas, Fleurie, Chiroubles, Morgon, Brouilly, Côte de Brouilly; and, since 1988, Régnié. The last, Moulin-à-Vent, is a *cru* named not for a village, but for a now-defunct 300-year-old windmill standing in the middle of vines. The image has become a symbol of Beaujolais.

75 Domaine du Clos du Fief Jovial young wine maker Michel Tête comes from a long line of *propriétaires-viticulteurs* in Juliénas. He produces outstanding Beaujolais Villages and St-Amour wines as well as Juliénas, carefully respecting the natural styles of each. Recently he began making a Juliénas *cuvée prestige* partly aged in oak; this and some of the estate's other wines are distributed in the eastern United States and are worth looking out for. The winery's simple Juliénas is fruity and delicious (and inexpensive too); the 1993 vintage, ready to be drunk in 1995, is a very good year. Tastings are given by Tête or his wife in a large room in the fragrant, barrel-filled cellar of "Les Gonnards," their simple white stucco house. ♦ Free. M-Sa by appointment. From Mâcon take N6 south 9.5 km (5.9 miles), then take D95 west 6.5 km (4 miles) and follow the signs to Juliénas and the winery. 74.04.41.62; fax 74.04.47.09

Le Coq au Vin

75 Le Coq au Vin ★★$$ With bright blue shutters adorning the yellow stucco, this place is as cheerful outside as it is inside—where a flock of antique china chickens roosts on the mantel, and happy diners tuck into the hearty regional specialties. Try the *gâteau de foies grande-mère* (a cake of poultry livers prepared "grandma style," that is, simply and traditionally), which is made with just the right amount of chicken fat and a touch of

onion and garlic. There's also *pintade de Bresse au chou* (farm-raised guinea hen from the Bresse region, served with cabbage) and *andouillette beaujolaise* (tripe sausage, not for the faint-hearted). Wines are reasonably priced, including fruity Georges Duboeuf Beaujolais, Juliénas reds, and St-Véran whites. ♦ Daily lunch and dinner; closed most of January. Reservations recommended. Pl du Marché, Juliénas. 74.04.41.98; fax 74.69.68.41

75 Hôtel des Vignes $ Conveniently located at the edge of Juliénas and in the heart of Beaujolais, this quiet 20-room hotel makes for a pleasant stay. The rooms are simple but comfortable; most have private bathrooms, some with showers instead of bathtubs. Continental breakfast is served, but there's no restaurant. The management is very friendly, and the price is definitely right. ♦ Rte de St-Amour, Juliénas. 74.04.43.70; fax 74.04.41.95

76 Le Hameau du Vin Georges Duboeuf is known in France as "Monsieur Beaujolais" for his tireless efforts to promote his region's wines. He is credited with almost single-handedly launching (some would say foisting on a gullible public) the international craze for Beaujolais Nouveau. Still, you have to give Duboeuf credit: All wines with his label are inexpensive, flavorful, and easy to drink. His latest venture, this wine museum/tasting center/restaurant/boutique, opened in 1993 in what was once the village train station. Visitors take a very instructive 90-minute unguided tour through multimedia exhibits devoted to the different aspects of Beaujolais wine making. Films and exhibit labels are in French, but English-language exhibit brochures are available. The tour concludes with a tasting of several Duboeuf wines served with sausages and cheese. The wines are *"duboeufisés,"* as they say in Beaujolais: full of aroma and fruit flavor. A real plus is that you get to taste wines from all the Beaujolais appellations; don't miss the Fleurie and the Moulin-à-Vent. A huge sales area with a very competent staff is a great place to pick up a few bottles of the best. ♦ Admission. Daily; closed in January. Every day but Sunday, visitors can go to the tastings without touring the museum. From Juliénas take D266 south 7.5 km (4.65 miles) and follow the signs to "La Gare" in Romanèche-Thorins. 85.35.42.22; fax 85.35.21.18

77 Domaine Michel Chignard One measure of the quality of wines produced on this small estate is that they are on the wine list of superchef Joël Robuchon's Paris restaurant, **Robuchon,** widely considered the best in France. Monsieur Chignard has very old vines (40 to 80 years old) in Fleurie on the border of the vineyards of Moulin-à-Vent, an ideal Beaujolais location. The grapes are handpicked, and the wines are aged in small oak barrels rather than in stainless-steel tanks. They are very balanced, and more dense than many Fleuries—more like Moulin-à-Vent (the heaviest of the beaujolais), but still full of fruit flavor. Try the Fleurie Cuvée Speciale 1992, ready to drink in 1995. Tastings are in the pleasant wine cellar under the Chignards' ocher stucco house. ♦ Free. M-Sa by appointment. From Romanèche-Thorins go about 4 km (2.5 miles) west (follow the signs to Le Point du Jour, Fleurie, and the winery). 74.04.11.87; 74.69.81.97

77 Auberge Le Cep ★★★$$$$ This Beaujolais landmark offers elegant, old-fashioned cuisine in a festive dining room with exposed beam ceilings, white tablecloths, and fine silverware and china. Try the *ragoût d'écrevisses* (a stew of crayfish) and the *volaille fermière au vin de Fleurie* (farm-raised chicken in Fleurie wine sauce), then top it off with the *entremets glacé au moka et à la nougatine* (coffee and nougat ice cream)—you won't be disappointed. You may be shocked, however, by the very, very high prices. The management is trying to offer some more reasonable fixed-price menus; the least expensive of these is a good deal. The wine list has an outstanding selection of beaujolais. ♦ Tu-Sa lunch and dinner; Su lunch; closed mid-December–mid-January. Reservations recommended. Pl de l'Eglise, Fleurie. 74.04.10.77; fax 74.04.10.28

77 Hôtel des Grands Vins $$ It's hard to find a better spot than this quiet hotel as a base for touring the wineries of the upper Beaujolais. Some of the 20 rooms are small, but all are very comfortable and decorated—in contrast to the building's modern exterior—in 19th-century French style (overdone wallpaper and heavy wood furniture). All the rooms have good beds (although some are a bit short), private bathrooms, mini-bars, and TVs. There's also a swimming pool, and the front desk rents out bicycles. There's no restaurant, but continental breakfast is available, and the managers helpfully suggest places to eat. The 10 rooms on the ground floor are accessible to people with disabilities. All in all, a very good deal for the price. ♦ On D119E, Fleurie. 74.69.81.43; fax 74.69.86.10

78 Hôtel Au Chapon Fin $$$ In a tiny village, inside a 19th-century white stone mansion adorned with vividly planted window boxes, are 20 large, quiet rooms with private bathrooms. ♦ Closed Tuesday. Rue Paul-Blanc, Thoissey (from Mâcon take N6 south 10 km/6.2 miles, then continue on D32 east 5.5 km/3.4 miles and follow the signs to Thoissey and the hotel). 74.04.04.74; fax 74.04.94.51

Within the Hôtel Au Chapon Fin:

Restaurant Au Chapon Fin ★★★$$$ Chef Bruno Maringue has big shoes to fill. He is the grandson of famed chef Paul Blanc, who made this restaurant one of the best and most famous in France at the time. But Maringue, who is in his 30s, is already making a name for himself with lush dishes like *fricassée de volaille aux morilles à la crème* (chicken fricasee with morel mushrooms and cream), and Grand Marnier soufflé. Prices are high, except for the lunch menu. The wine list is superb, particularly in Mâconnais and Beaujolais wines. ♦ M, W-Su lunch and dinner. Reservations recommended. 74.04.04.74

79 Villié-Morgon and Morgon Many wineries are clustered in and around these adjoining villages, where one of the most popular Beaujolais wines, Morgon, is produced. Among the good ones to watch out for are **Domaine de la Chanaise** in Morgon (M-Sa; 74.69.10.20.) and **Louis-Claude Desvignes** in Villié-Morgon (visits by appointment; 74.04.23.35). Signs in the villages will direct you to both. ♦ 11.5 km (7 miles) west of Thoissey on D9

80 Hôtel Anne de Beaujeu $ The little market town of Beaujeu gave its name to the Beaujolais region. It makes a good base for discovering not only wine villages, but also the beautiful Beaujolais backcountry. This simple budget hotel in a converted private house is surrounded by a walled garden. It has seven spacious rooms, all with private bathrooms. ♦ Closed one week in August and mid-December–mid-January. 28 Rue de la République, Beaujeu (from Villié-Morgon and Morgon take D9 southwest 7 km/4.3 miles, then follow D37 west 6 km/3.7 miles to

Beaujeu and follow the signs to the hotel).
74.04.87.58; fax 74.69.22.13

Within the Hôtel Anne de Beaujeu:

Restaurant Anne de Beaujeu ★$$
Regional specialties are featured in this rustic
dining room with heavy ceiling beams and
floral curtains. A dish can't get more
traditional than *poulet de Bresse* (free-range
chicken from the Bresse region) or *cuisse de
grenouilles* (frogs' legs). The wine list
includes about 20 beaujolais, all reasonably
priced. Watch out, though; the tab can add up
if you order à la carte. ◆ Tu-Sa lunch and
dinner; Su lunch; closed one week in August
and mid-December–mid-January.
74.04.87.58

81 **Château Thivin** Wine maker Claude
Geoffray is the acknowledged master of
Brouilly wines; in fact, Geoffrays have been
making wines on this rambling estate since
1879. The long-prized vineyards here were the
property of Humbert III, lord of Beaujeu in the
12th century. Monsieur Geoffray produces
fine Côte-de-Brouilly, Brouilly, and Beaujolais-
Villages, but the stars are the Côte-de-
Brouillys from the blue granite slopes of Mont
Brouilly, an extinct volcano that looms over a
stretch of hilly Beaujolais countryside near the
winery. Côte-de-Brouilly is richer and riper
than regular Brouilly, and was made a
separate appellation in 1935. The château
presses its grapes by gravity (a slow process
said to result in more complex taste), and the
Côte-de-Brouillys are all aged in barrels. Year
after year, Geoffray's wines are full of fruity
flavor, rich and balanced; the 1992s are
excellent. You *can't* miss the vividly colored
labels, with the little vintage sticker that says,
*"L'Eclat de rire de la table, mis en Bouteille au
Château"* (A burst of laughter for the table,
estate-bottled). Visitors are greeted warmly in
a tasting room near the twin-towered château.
◆ Free. Daily. Appointments recommended.
From Beaujeu take D37 east 6 km (3.7 miles),
then take D43 south 4 km (2.5 miles) and
follow the signs to Odénas and the winery.
74.03.47.53; fax 74.03.52.87

Château de Pizay

82 **Château de Pizay** An immense white stone
château with sections dating from the 10th to
the 18th centuries houses this wine estate,
restaurant, and fine hotel. The château was
probably built on the site of a Roman villa,

since a Roman road passed nearby and the
estate is surrounded by perfect vineyard
terrain. The domain was mentioned in 1070 in
the charters of the **Abbaye de Cluny,** and
Pizay wines were renowned in the Middle
Ages. With 50 hectares (123.3 acres) of vines,
the winery offers a wide choice of beaujolais.
The unusual white beaujolais is delicate and
appealing; they also make fruity red
beaujolais, along with a full-flavored Morgon
and a Régnié that has a pronounced bouquet
of raspberries. Other wines include an
unusual Rosé d'Une Nuit, a rosé in which the
grapes macerate for only one night after
picking, and a Blanc-de-Blancs made from
chardonnay grapes. ◆ Fee for tasting if
traveling in a group of 10 or more. Tastings
M-Sa; closed late December–early January.
Appointment recommended. From Odénas
take D68E north 8 km (5 miles) and follow the
signs to St-Jean-d'Ardières and the château.
74.66.26.10; fax 74.69.60.66

Within the Château de Pizay:

Restaurant Château de Pizay ★$$$ It
may be overpriced, but you can't beat the
surroundings—especially in summer, when
tables are set on the château's elegant
outdoor courtyard with a view of the vines.
The menu features regional specialties
accompanied by the estate's wines. ◆ Daily
lunch and dinner; closed late December–early
January. Reservations recommended; hotel
guests have priority. 74.66.51.41; fax
74.69.60.66

Hôtel Château de Pizay $$$$ The hotel
offers 61 luxurious guest rooms of varying
sizes, all with private bathrooms. A swimming
pool and tennis courts are also on the
property. ◆ Closed late December–early
January. 74.66.51.41

82 **Maison des Beaujolais** This wine center,
in a typical Beaujolais golden stone building,
has many brochures on Beaujolais, including
lists of wineries that accept visitors. Tastings
of 12 Beaujolais wines are offered, and some
fine bottles are for sale here. There's a wide
range of prices, from the simplest beaujolais
to vintage appellations. The center contains a
small restaurant with rustic decor where you
can sample simple regional cooking. The six
fixed-price menus are all meat-oriented; you
might find sausage, beef in beaujolais wine
sauce, or coq au vin. ◆ Center: Tu-Sa 9AM-
9PM (no midday closing). Restaurant: daily
lunch and dinner. From St-Jean-d'Ardières
take D69 south 2 km (1.25 miles) and follow
the signs to the wine center. 74.66.16.46

83 **Domaine du Vissoux** Pierre-Marie
Chermette, a wine maker in his 30s, is already
recognized as one of the most reliable names
in southern Beaujolais, a region usually
known for simple "quaffing" wines that are
not always made with care. Chermette, in
contrast to many of his neighbors, favors

traditional methods that let the fruit shine through: little or no filtering, no artificial yeasts, no sulfur, and no chaptalization (the addition of sugar during fermentation to increase the alcohol content). This meticulous approach, and the many old vines in the estate's vineyards, bring **Domaine de Vissoux** wines closer in character to the village appellation beaujolais in the northern part of the region. The estate produces both reds and whites, and the fruity reds shine. New additions include wines from the prestigious Fleurie and Moulin-à-Vent appellations of northern Beaujolais, where Chermette recently bought vineyards. Visits and tastings are given in the golden stone winery by Monsieur Chermette or his wife, Martine. Their wines, which have won many awards but are still priced low, would be perfect for a picnic in the pretty countryside nearby; scout around for a spot in the village of Valsonne (about 10 km/6.2 miles west on D13). ♦ Free. M-Sa. Appointments recommended. From Villefranche-sur-Saône take D38 southwest 20 km (12.4 miles) to Le Bois-d'Oingt, then take D39 west 5.5 km (3.4 miles) to St-Vérand and follow the signs to the winery. 74.71.79.42; fax 74.71.84.26

Bests

Patrick Breuil
Owner, Hôtel Le Mont Mélian, Meursault

Discover the **Burgundy** region: visit the **Hautes-Côtes** area and the **Côtes de Beaune** by car, bicycle, balloon. See the **Hôtel Dieu** in **Beaune,** the **Palais des Ducs** in **Dijon,** and the region's châteaux. Try the rich and refined regional cooking, from a country-style snack to the finest cuisine of our great chefs. Leisure activities? Golf, tennis, swimming in local pools and lakes, all-terrain bicycle touring, walks; and don't forget the sound-and-light shows at the **Hôtel Dieu** in Beaune and the "Musical Encounters" classical music series held along the *routes des grands crus.*

Hester and Pascal Moreau
Wine Producers/Potters/Owners, Le Moulin, Poilly-sur-Serein, Burgundy

Burgundy is quite unspoiled—no industry, no ugly architecture. The landscape is lovely, with many old towns and villages and many small wine producers, like ourselves. The people are most friendly and open. Parisian hostility towards tourists is unknown here.

Wine is closely related to its *terroir,* and an excursion to some "caves," followed by a meal in a small village restaurant, may help you understand this. In this area, we have the Chablis white wines. All different, depending on the hill where they grow, but there are also some excellent small red *vignobles* (vineyards) known only to insiders, such as **Irancy** and **Coulanges.** (The bigger red burgundies are grown farther south.)

As far as culture is concerned, there are old churches and buildings in nearly every town. **Noyers,** a small medieval town along the river **Serein,** is one of the *plus beaux villages de France.* Farther west there is **Vézelay,** and **Ste-Colline** with its 13th-century basilica. East of Vézelay is the **Abbaye de Fontenay** (Fontenay Abbey), built by the Cistercian monks of **St-Bernard.** It has been declared a UNESCO world monument, mostly because it was never destroyed or rebuilt; it has remained untouched in a beautiful isolated valley ever since AD 1118. Not far from there, but some farther back in history, we'll come to **Alesia,** the hill where Julius Caesar beat Vercingetorix, the leader of the Gauls, in the year 60. When standing on the hill, with a copy of Caesar's diary (from the local tourist office) in your hand, it is not difficult to imagine the Roman camps below: nothing has changed in the setting. Burgundy is ancient country, with a smaller population now than ever before.

Gabriel Breen
Wine Merchant, Cave du Coux, Le Coux et Bigaroque

Most of our visitors here in the heart of **Périgord Noir (Dordogne)** say we are living in heaven. Situated east of **Bordeaux** along the banks of the **Dordogne River,** the Périgord Noir is renowned for its walled towns, its hilltop castles, prehistoric sites, and cave paintings. But the gastronomic delights of the region, including truffles, pâté de foie gras, and various duck and goose dishes, expose the *bon viveur* in us all. They are best appreciated if accompanied by the attractive wines of **Bergerac** to the west and of **Cahors** to the south.

A visit to **Château Belingard,** in the south of Bergerac at **Pomport,** is a must for those wishing to experience a little history and the finer Bergerac wines (including some excellent Monbazillac). The name "Belin-Gard" means the garden of the Sun God, and the buildings are on a 3,000-year-old Celtic site (complete with throne and sacrificial table). The family of the Count and Countess de Bosredon have been here for 200 years. Laurent and Sylvie (de Bosredon) are welcoming, with a pride in the fruits of their labor. Watch out for their *tête de cuvée* (top-of-the-line) Blanche de Bosredon 1990 rouge.

Not to be overlooked are the smaller properties that produce excellent wines. **Château Richard** at **Monestier** near the village of **Saussignac** is one worth looking for. Here you must taste the sweet wines, which can compare favorably with the best of the famous Sauternes, at a fraction of the price.

At **Cahors** (in the **Lot Valley**), very dark, rich, spicy red wines are produced from malbec grapes. Aside from the better-known properties of **Château de Chambert** and **Clos de Gamot,** again a tour of the smaller producers is always rewarding. Try Domaine de Theron 1989 or 1990, 100 percent malbec (auxerrois, as it's known locally).

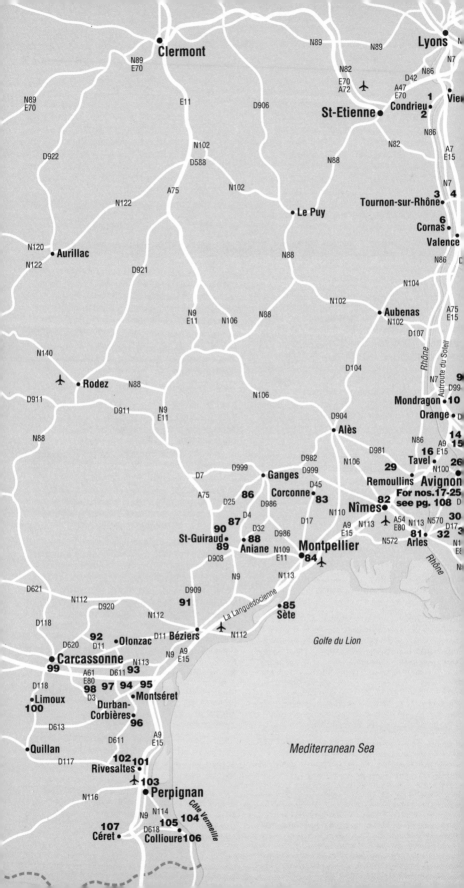

The South (The Rhône Valley, Provence, and the Midi)

There is a lot more to France's south than the Riviera's flashy discotheques, topless beaches, and pricey Parisian-style boutiques. The Rhône Valley, Provence, and the Midi, three adjoining regions in the south, have myriad ancient sites and stunning landscapes to discover: sun-baked hilltop villages; Roman citadels, bridges, and arenas; blinding white escarpments rising out of terra-cotta-hued soil; fields of thyme, rosemary, and lavender; and acres of olive groves and vineyards.

The sun in these regions has not only inspired some of the world's greatest painters, but also provided perfect conditions for some delicious, full-bodied reds, fruity rosés, dry and bubbly whites, and sweet fortified wines. Almost all of the Côtes du Rhône wines marry well with the indigenous food, which usually includes garlic and olive oil. Look for aïoli (a garlicky mayonnaise), bouillabaisse, *rouille* (a red pepper and garlic sauce), ratatouille, *pissaladière* (onion tart), and all manner of almond cookies.

The south of France has been home to good wine and food since 600 BC, when Phocaean sailors from Asia Minor set up camp in what is now **Marseilles.** They were drawn northward in their quest for wealth and power (as were the Romans after them) by the Rhône, France's mightiest river, whose source lies in the Swiss Alps. Sadly, much of the Rhône today is taken up with hydroelectric locks and dams, and the river now carries barges loaded with freight.

The Rhône Valley stretches from **Mâcon** to **Orange** (at the top of Provence), but its wine-producing region doesn't begin until **Vienne,** which lies in the upper half of the region, about 90 kilometers (56 miles) south of Mâcon. The valley makes a specialty of full-bodied, gutsy reds, two of which, Châteauneuf-du-Pape and Hermitage, can rival some of the greats of Bordeaux and Burgundy. The region is also the source for lesser known but excellent whites—sparkling, sweet, or dry—like the fabulously flowery but dry Condrieu.

The Provence region extends from the bottom of the Rhône Valley to the Mediterranean. The Romans occupied Provence for over 600 years, building villas, thermal baths, arenas, bridges, and other monuments, many of which still stand. While the area has become increasingly popular, there are still beautiful, untrampled hilltop villages and quiet country roads. The lively port city of Marseilles is the official capital of Provence, but the 14th-century town of **Avignon** is its true heart.

Provence offers some excellent art museums devoted to the works of the many artists who have fallen in love with the intoxicating light here, including Van Gogh, Cézanne, Gauguin, Matisse, and Picasso. The region has rocky soil and dry summers that produce intensely flavored vegetables and fruits, stunningly fragrant herbs, and some eminently quaffable, fruity rosés, which account for two-thirds of the production of the Côtes de Provence and the region's other *Appellation d'Origine Contrôlée (AOC)* vineyards. And of course there's the **Côte d'Azur**'s long stretch of sandy beaches along the Mediterranean.

The Midi encompasses the beautiful and often desolate areas of the **Languedoc** and **Roussillon.** And southwest of Roussillon is **Camargue**—an enormous marshland preserved as a botanical and zoological reserve—where wild ponies and cattle still reign, although sunbathers and Gypsies take over the preserve's new coastline resorts during the summer. The Midi is still known in the US more for its beauty than its wines, but there are some up-and-coming reds, whites, and rosés, especially the rich reds from the **Corbières** district in Languedoc. All in all, a tour through these enchanting areas in the south of France will offer something for everyone.

Getting to and around the Rhône Valley, Provence, and the Midi

Airports

Near Lyons, the **Aéroport International de Lyon-Satolas** (72.22.72.21) receives flights from Paris and other European cities. The airport is 20 kilometers (12.4 miles) east of Lyons. A bus leaves for Lyons approximately every 25 minutes.

The **Aéroport Marseille-Marignane** (42.78.21.00) is 29 kilometers (18 miles) northwest of Marseilles. It handles domestic and international flights, including US flights. A bus leaves every 20 minutes for the city.

In the Languedoc, **Aéroport Montpellier-Méditerranée** (67.20.85.00) is about seven kilometers (4.3 miles) southeast of the center of Montpellier. It services flights from Paris and other parts of France, as well as some from abroad. All major car-rental companies have offices in the airport. There is regular bus service to the city.

The **Aéroport de Nice–Côte d'Azur** (93.21.30.30), just seven kilometers (4.3 miles) from Nice, is one of the busiest in France, servicing many international flights, including ones from the US. All major car-rental companies have offices within the airport, and taxis are available to the center of Nice.

The **Aéroport de Toulon-Hyères** (94.22.81.60) in Toulon is 71 kilometers (44 miles) from St-Tropez. It services domestic flights only. Bus service is available to the city.

Car Rental

Avignon

Avis	90.82.26.33
Budget	90.87.03.00
Europcar	90.82.49.85
Hertz	90.82.37.67

Lyons

Avis	72.22.75.25
Budget	72.22.74.74
Europcar	72.22.75.27
Eurorent	72.22.75.59
Hertz	72.22.74.49

Marseilles

Avis	42.89.02.86
Budget	42.89.86.71
Europcar	42.89.51.65
Hertz	42.89.00.85

Montpellier

Avis	67.20.14.95
Budget	67.20.07.34
Citer	67.64.17.71

Nice

Avis	93.21.36.33
Budget	93.21.36.50
Eurodollar	93.21.36.47
Europcar	93.21.33.44
Eurorent	93.21.36.54
Hertz	93.21.36.72

Toulon

Avis	94.38.98.02
Budget	94.38.41.30
Europcar	94.58.06.22
Eurorent	94.58.04.27
Hertz	94.58.06.44

Trains

In Avignon, the *TGV* fast trains from Paris take three and a half hours. The *TGV* and several slower regional trains arrive at the **Gare d'Avignon** (Blvd St-Roch, at the Porte de la République, 90.82.50.50), which is within walking distance of most of the city's main sites. **Avis** has an office in the station, and other car-rental companies are nearby. Bicycles are also for rent here.

The Lyons station, **Gare de Part Dieu** (Rue Vivier Merle, at Rue de la Villette, 36.35.35.35), is two hours from Paris. All major car-rental companies have outlets in or next to the station.

Marseilles, four hours from Paris, is reached via **Gare Marseille-St-Charles** (Sq Narvik, at Blvd Gustave-Bordet, information 91.08.50.50; tickets 91.08.84.12). **Avis** has an office in the station.

Another station serving the Midi is Montpellier's **Gare SNCF,** in the center of town (on Rue Jules-Ferry, between Rue Maguelone and Rue de la République, 67.92.50.50). It's four hours and 20 minutes from Paris. All major car-rental companies have offices nearby.

Trains to Nice arrive at **Gare de Nice-Ville** (Ave Thiers, at Ave Gounod, 93.87.90.11) seven hours after departing Paris. **Avis** is just outside the station.

FYI

Visitors' Information Offices

Aix-en-Provence's **Office de Tourisme** (2 Pl du Général-de-Gaulle, at Ave Victor-Hugo and Ave des Belges, 42.16.11.70; fax 42.16.11.62) has much material in English on things to see and do in the city. Its bilingual *Guide Touristique* (Tourist Guide) contains typical Provençal recipes and a list of restaurants that serve them; hotels, sights, and sports activities are also detailed. The office also has plenty of information on local wines, as well as a boutique selling local crafts and comestibles. It is open Monday through Saturday.

Avignon's **Office de Tourisme/Festival d'Avignon** (41 Cours Jean-Jaurès, at Rue H.-Fabre; 90.82.65.11; fax 90.82.95.03) provides general information on the city, as well as information on, and tickets to, its highly rated—and extremely popular—summer arts festival. It also houses a branch of the **Maison des Vins,** which offers information on local wines and wineries. The office is open Monday through Saturday.

In Carcassonne, the **Office de Tourisme** (15 Blvd Camille-Pelletan, at Sq Gambetta, in the Ville Basse, 68.25.07.04) is open Monday through Saturday; there is no midday closing during July and August.

The **Comité Départemental du Tourisme du Var** (Conseil Général, Blvd Foch, Draguignan, 12 km/7.4 miles north of Les Arcs, 94.68.58.33; fax 94.47.08.03) is a regional tourism center with information on the Var *département*, which includes most of Provence and the Mediterranean coast stretching from Bandol almost to Cannes. Brochures detail special events, lodgings, campgrounds, and restaurants. The center is open Monday through Friday.

Marseilles's **Office de Tourisme** is just east of the Vieux Port (4 La Canebière, at Rue de la République, 91.54.91.11; fax 91.33.05.03) and is open daily.

The Montpellier **Office de Tourisme** is in the center of the city on Allée du Tourisme (at Pl de la Comédie and Ave F.-Mistral, 67.58.67.58). It is open Monday through Saturday (no midday closing).

Nice has an **Office de Tourisme** (Ave Thiers, at Ave Durante, 93.87.07.07), with information on the city—much of it in English—and low-priced city maps. The office is open from Monday through Saturday.

The Nîmes **Office de Tourisme** (6 Rue August, between Sq Antonin and Rue Général-Perrier, 66.67.29.11; fax 66.21.81.11) is open daily; there is no midday closing during July and August.

St-Tropez's **Office de Tourisme** (Quai Jean-Jaurès, at Rue de la Citadelle, 94.97.45.21) has a great deal of material (in English) on things to see and do in the area, as well as on restaurants and hotels; it is open Monday through Saturday.

Wine Organizations

In Aix-en-Provence, the **Syndicat des Coteaux d'Aix-en-Provence** (Maison de l'Agriculteur, Ave Henri-Pontier, between Allée des Musiciens and Allée des Muriers, 42.23.57.14; fax 42.96.98.56) promotes Coteaux-d'Aix wines. It has brochures, maps, and other publications (in French) on the wine and the local wineries open to the public. The center is open Monday through Friday.

Not far from Aix, the official headquarters of the professional Provençal wine makers' organization is one of the nicest wine centers in France. **La Maison des Vins des Côtes de Provence** (Les Arcs, 86 km/53 miles east of Beaurecueil on N7, 94.73.33.38; fax 94.47.50.37) offers a range of material on the wines of Provence, including maps, a booklet on wineries open to visitors, and a brochure on other activities and sights to enjoy during a wine tour. The typically Provençal building is a large, yellow stucco *mas* (Provençal-style farmhouse) with a red tiled roof and a wide entry gate. The center is open daily. It also operates an inexpensive restaurant (94.47.48.47) serving good, simple Provençal fare, and a wide selection of wines from throughout the region. The restaurant is open Tuesday through Saturday for lunch and dinner, and Sunday for lunch.

In Avignon, the **Comité Interprofessionnel des Vins des Côtes du Rhône** (Maison des Vins, 6 Rue des Trois-Faucons, between Pl St-Didier and Rue des Etudes, 90.27.24.00; fax 90.27.24.13) is the main information center for Côtes du Rhône wines. It provides brochures, maps, a booklet on wineries open to the public, descriptions of individual

appellations, as well as tastings. Wines are sold by the bottle. The office is open Monday through Friday.

The professional organization for the promotion of Languedoc wines, the **Syndicat des Coteaux du Languedoc/Mas Saporta** (Lattès, about 3 km/1.9 miles south of Montpellier on D58, 67.06.04.44) is housed in a *mas*. Open daily with no midday closing, it has considerable information on the region's wines and wineries; be sure to stop here before touring the region. It also runs a good, inexpensive restaurant (reservations 67.06.04.40), featuring local specialties and 65 Languedoc wines, which is open Monday through Saturday for lunch and dinner, and Sunday for lunch; reservations are recommended.

Minervois wines, one of the most respected Languedoc appellations, are the focus of the friendly **Syndicat du Cru Minervois** (10 Blvd Louis-Blazin, Olonzac, 55 km/34.1 miles west of Béziers on D11, 68.91.21.66). No tastings are offered here, but information and maps are, Monday through Friday.

Another important Languedoc appellation, hearty Corbières wines, are the specialty of the **Syndicat du Cru Corbières** (Lézignan-Corbières, follow D611 south 10 km/6.2 miles from Olonzac, 68.27.04.34; fax 68.27.31.66). Numerous brochures and maps are available, including the *Guide de l'acheteur des vins de Corbières* (Guide to the Buyer of Corbières Wines; in French), which lists all the local producers, their visiting policies, and price ranges. Also pick up the excellent "Routes du Cru Corbières" map, which has four itineraries that include historical sites as well as wineries. The center is open Monday through Friday.

Information on the newer Saint-Chinian appellation of Languedoc wines is available at the **Syndicat des Vins de Saint-Chinian** (Maison des Vins, Ave de la Promenade, St-Chinian, 28 km/17.3 miles northwest of Béziers on N112, 67.38.11.69; fax 67.38.16.33). Tastings are not usually offered, but there are lists of local wineries open to the public and bottles to buy. The center is open Monday through Saturday.

Phone Book
Hospitals

Aix-en-Provence	42.33.50.00
Avignon	90.80.33.33
Marseilles	91.38.60.00
Montpellier	67.33.90.50
Nice	93.03.44.08
Nîmes	66.27.34.09
St-Tropez	94.79.47.30

Police (nonemergencies)

Aix-en-Provence	42.93.97.00
Avignon	90.86.32.47
Marseilles	91.91.90.40
Montpellier	67.22.78.22
Nice	93.17.20.27
Nîmes	66.62.82.82
St-Tropez	94.56.60.30

The Rhône Valley

The Rhône Valley, whose capital is **Lyons,** is a fertile, steep valley running from **Mâcon** to **Orange,** with the Alps to the east and the Causses to the west. The valley was carved from the mountains by the powerful **Rhône River,** which has been used as a watery highway since 2000 BC. Beyond the valley's big cities (Lyons, **Valence,** and **Vienne**) lie lush forests, steep plateaus, and startlingly blue lakes.

The valley's wine-growing area is split into two distinct regions. The much smaller northern half, part of which is known as the **Côte Rôtie,** begins at **Ampuis** and follows the slope to Valence. For the next 70 kilometers (43 miles) there are no vineyards at all, just acres of orchards. The southern half begins at Orange and stretches down toward Avignon in Provence. The vineyards cling to the steep cliffside in hard, granite soil. This setting, combined with the strong sun, allows the tannic syrah grape to thrive and makes for full-bodied, gutsy red wines. Among the other grapes that grow here are grenache, carignan, mourvèdre, viognier, and rousanne.

1 Gilles Barge President of the Côte Rôtie growers association, Barge makes a highly rated Côte Rôtie wine using strictly traditional techniques. He does not favor leaving the wine for a long time in new oak, a practice he believes distorts the natural quality of this distinctive red. Every year Barge combines grapes from his various Côte Rôtie vineyard sites to produce one red Côte Rôtie wine made primarily from syrah grapes with a small amount of flowery viognier grapes "to bring finesse and a certain grace," as the winemaker puts it. Barge's wines vary with the vintage but are always a rich red color with concentrated flavor and pronounced fruit aromas with a hint of violets (the latter is the viognier's contribution). The winery is built above the cellars in the Barge family's modern farmhouse; the cellars may be toured on request. ♦ Free. Visits and tastings daily. Appointment recommended; open only to groups of five or more. Ampuis (from Lyons follow N7 south 31 km/19.2 miles to Vienne, then take N86 south 7 km/4.3 miles and follow the signs to the winery). 74.56.13.90; fax 74.56.10.98

2 Domaine Georges Vernay The leading wine makers in Condrieu, Georges Vernay and his son Luc use traditional techniques and do without herbicides to produce an extremely rich, aromatic white Condrieu, aged for six months in oak barrels. They also make some red Côte Rôtie and Saint-Joseph wines from syrah grapes, aged in oak for a year. Their highly praised Coteau du Veron white Condrieu is aged in oak, which some say overshadows the aromatic viognier grape taste. The simple Sainte-Agathe Côtes du Rhône and several *vins de pays* are great buys. The winery is in the Vernays' two-story white stucco house with a red tile roof; vine-covered hills rise all around. ♦ Fee for tastings. M-Sa. Visits to the cellars are available on request. Condrieu (from Ampuis go 5 km/3.1 miles south on N86). 74.59.52.22; fax 74.56.60.98

2 Hostellerie Le Beau Rivage $$$ Located in the tiny village of Condrieu (which is barely more than a cluster of red-roofed stone houses hugging a steep hillside between vineyards and the Rhône), this old-fashioned hotel is a great base for touring the northern Rhône Valley. The vine-covered mansion has long been a landmark on the route from Paris to the Mediterranean. Its 20 rooms and four suites are quiet and luxurious; most have views of the Rhône, and all have TVs, direct-line telephones, and mini-bars. The exuberant French Provincial decor includes intricately patterned wallpaper, with drapes and bedcovers to match. Some of the rooms are not air-conditioned, but the high ceilings and big windows keep things comfortable. ♦ Condrieu (follow the signs in the center of town). 74.59.52.24; fax 74.59.59.36

Within the Hostellerie Le Beau Rivage:

Restaurant Le Beau Rivage ★★★$$$ The excellent traditional cuisine served here includes *quenelles de brochet* (pike dumplings) and a casserole of beef and shallots. The food, however, is rivaled by the incredible view of the Rhône (in the summer, be sure to reserve a table on the terrace for the best sightlines). Even if you choose not to stay in the hotel, try to eat lunch here on a fine day; the spectacle of the Rhône flowing toward the Mediterranean should not be missed. Prices are high, except for a fixed-price menu available at lunch Monday through Friday. The superb wine list features Condrieu and Côte Rôtie wines. ◆ Daily lunch and dinner. Reservations required. 74.59.52.24

2 Château Grillet Owned by the Neyret-Gachet family, this estate is the smallest appellation in France, and one of only three with a single owner. Terraced vineyards curve in a sun-baked bowl around the medieval château, which is built of golden stone with a red tile roof. It has two massive, rounded towers whose tiny windows were once archers' lookouts. The wine, very expensive (partly because it's so rare), is unforgettable: The powerful dry white made from the viognier grape has luscious overtones of ripe peaches and apricots. The number of bottles produced per year depends on the vintage, but 12,000 is the maximum. The château itself is not open to visitors, but tastings are offered in a small outbuilding. ◆ Purchase required for tastings. By appointment. Verin (from Condrieu go 3 km/1.8 miles south on N86; follow the signs to the winery). 74.59.51.56

3 Hôtel du Château $$ Overlooking the Rhône and the Hermitage vineyards, this comfortable 19th-century mansion offers 14 quiet rooms. Some are on the small side, but all have private bathrooms, satellite TVs, mini-bars, and direct-dial telephones; ask for a view of the vineyards. The ultratraditional decor is a bit somber, with detailed wallpaper patterns and dark furniture. Wine tastings are offered at the in-house bar. ◆ 12 Quai Marc-Seguin, Tournon-sur-Rhône (from Verin go about 50 km/31 miles south on N86). 75.08.60.22; fax 75.07.02.95

Within the Hôtel du Château:

Restaurant du Château ★$$ Among the good traditional dishes featured are roast chicken, *boeuf en daube* (long-simmered beef), and a variety of fish. Four fixed-price menus are offered. ◆ Daily lunch and dinner Easter-Oct; M-F lunch and dinner mid-Nov–Easter; closed the first two weeks in November. Reservations recommended. 75.08.60.22

3 Chemin de Fer du Vivarais All aboard! This 19th-century narrow-gauge steam-engine tourist train chugs slowly (this is an all-day trip) through vineyards and orchards along the picturesque valley of the Doux River west of Tournon. There is usually a stop at Colombier-le-Vieux for the train to refill with water and the passengers to get a taste of the local wines. You can also arrange stops for visits to the Gorges du Doux or the town of Lamastre for lunch and shopping. ◆ Information: 2 Quai Jean-Moulin, Lyons. 78.28.83.34; fax 72.00.97.67

Restaurants/Clubs: Red	Hotels: Blue
Shops/ 🌳 Outdoors: Green	Sights/Culture: Black

4 Restaurant Jean-Marc Reynaud
★★★$$ Chef Reynaud excels with inventive variations on traditional classics. Try his saffron-flavored *cassolette de fruits de mer* (seafood casserole), the *poussin rôti désossé en sauce au vin* (roast young chicken, boned and served in wine sauce), and the delicious cheese assortment. In summer, meals are served on a garden terrace overlooking the Rhône, and in winter they are set before a roaring fireplace. The wine list has one of the best selections of Côtes du Rhône around. ◆ Tu-Sa lunch and dinner; Su lunch; closed the last two weeks of August and three weeks in January. Reservations required. 82 Ave Président-Roosevelt, Tain-l'Hermitage (across the river from Tournon). 75.07.22.10; fax 75.08.03.53

Above the Restaurant Jean-Marc Reynaud:

Hôtel Jean-Marc Reynaud $$ In a modern building on the banks of the Rhône are 10 comfortable, spacious guest rooms. All have contemporary decor, private bathrooms, color TVs, mini-bars, and direct-dial phones; some have balconies overlooking the Rhône. There's also a swimming pool. Breakfast is brought to your room on request. ◆ Closed three weeks in January. 75.07.22.10

4 Paul Jaboulet Aîné Founded in the early 19th century, this well-known family-run winery more than makes up for its charmless, modern building with its astonishing wines. Quite simply, it produces some of the best red and white Hermitage wines around. The powerful Domaine de Thalabert Crozes–Hermitage red wine is the estate's most highly praised bottle; it's made from 100 percent syrah grapes and has a bouquet of raspberries and blackberries. Drink it with game. The dark purple La Chapelle red Crozes-Hermitage is another fine wine; it too is made only from syrah grapes (from vines that average 35 years of age), but needs more time in the bottle. Among the best of the white Hermitage wines are the very aromatic La Mule Blanche and the Chevalier de Stérimberg (named for Gaspard de Stérimberg, the "hermit" of Hermitage—see "Major Appellations of the South," page 138). There are several other reds, whites (try the sweet white Beaumes-de-Venise), and rosés worth sampling, and even an eau-de-vie. The winery has vineyards all along the Rhône, and its range lets visitors take a tasting tour of the Côtes du Rhône's wines all under one roof. ♦ Visits and tastings by appointment. Les Jalets (on N7, just south of Tain-l'Hermitage). 75.84.68.93; fax 75.84.56.14

5 Cave des Clairmonts Three families who emigrated from North Africa founded this wine co-op, whose commitment to quality is a model for others in the region. They produce both red and white Crozes-Hermitage wines. The reds, made from syrah grapes, have strong bouquets and overtones of black currant and raspberry that go well with red meat; the whites, with overtones of honey and peaches, are perfect for a picnic in the surrounding countryside. ♦ Free. Visits and tastings M-Sa. Vignes-Vieilles, outside Beaumont-Monteux (from Tournon follow N7 south about 9 km/5.6 miles, then take D153 east about 4 km/2.5 miles and follow the signs to the winery). 75.84.61.91; fax 75.84.56.98

6 Domaine Jean Lionnet At this modern white stucco farmhouse, Jean Lionnet or a family member will provide a friendly welcome and an instructive tasting. Lionnet produces both sturdy, powerful Cornas reds and a Saint-Péray white made of 20 percent aromatic roussanne grapes; the latter is just

perfect as an aperitif, especially with foie gras. ♦ Free. Visits and tastings M-F. From Tournon take N86 south about 12 km (7.4 miles) and follow the signs to the winery just outside of Cornas. 75.40.36.01

6 Restaurant Ollier ★$ The focus at this friendly, rustic place is on simple, traditional French home cooking, including *gibier au Cornas* (game in Cornas wine sauce) and *filet de rascasse à la sauce Hermitage* (scorpion fish in a Hermitage wine sauce). The children's menu offers such favorites as *la viande du jour avec des pommes frites* (meat of the day with french fries) and *gratin de pomme de terre* (potatoes in a cheese sauce). The wine list is a dream, with many well-aged Cornas wines. ♦ M, Th-Su lunch and dinner, Tu lunch May-Sept; Th-Su lunch and dinner, M-Tu lunch Oct-Apr; closed the last two weeks of August and two weeks in February. Reservations recommended. On N86 in the center of Cornas. 75.40.32.17

7 Cave Clairette de Die Cellier Hannibal Still and sparkling Clairette de Die white wines—among the most popular sparkling wines in France—are produced at this excellent co-op. These wines, which are produced in the valley of the Drôme River, have been favorites for ages, literally: They were known to the Romans as *Dea Augusta,* and were rated by historian Pliny the Elder (in the first century) the best naturally sweet wines in the empire. The winery now produces mainly dry wines, to suit contemporary tastes. Try the bubbly Clairette Tradition Impériale. Many of the wines here are produced by organic methods. The co-op runs a small museum and wine exhibit on the premises, and gives friendly, informative tastings. ♦ Free. Daily. Die (65 km/40.3 miles southeast of Valence; from Valence take D111 south to D93 east and follow the signs to the winery). 75.22.02.22; fax 75.22.21.06

La Coqueto: Groupe Folklorique Provençal (Provençal Folklore Group)

On a mission to preserve **Provence**'s traditional culture, an organization near the old port in **Marseilles** offers a number of inventive programs that teach adults and children about the region's past and keep the culture alive. **La Coqueto** (12 Rue de la Bibliothèque, off Pl Jean-Jaurèz, 91.42.35.66, 91.41.34.28) mounts performances by folkloric dancers wearing traditional 19th-century Provençal garb; offers native cooking, theatre, and dance classes for children; broadcasts radio programs in the Provençal language; and, perhaps of most interest to the wine-route traveler, runs Provençal cooking classes. Teachers and students are friendly;

the classes are relaxed and open to anyone. They are held (in French) on the first Thursday of every month at 2:30PM and 7:30PM; call ahead for a reservation. The program is subsidized by the city of Marseilles, so students are asked to contribute only to the cost of the ingredients—which the entire class consumes after preparing. It's truly a bargain. Among the traditional recipes usually cooked up are *râgout d'aubergines aux anchois* (a stew of eggplant with anchovies), *barquettes aux oranges de Nîmes* (orange-flavored cookies as they are baked in Nîmes), and a classic *bourride* (fish soup with a garlic-mayonnaise sauce).

Provence

Provence (the Romans' *Provincia Romana*) is without a doubt the region of France most beloved by tourists, particularly sun-starved northerners who descend on the area in ever-growing numbers every season. Residents are hard put to preserve their traditional way of life, and especially their fragile landscapes, in the face of the onslaught, but local wine makers have held up well. Provence's rocky soil and dry summers produce full-flavored vegetables and fruits, potent herbs, a wide variety of olives (and olive oils), and an abundance of wine. Vines were probably planted here by Greeks in the sixth century BC, but it was the Romans—who stayed 600 years and covered the region with villas, thermal baths, arenas, and other monuments—who first produced wine on a large scale, most of it for export. In fact, until relatively recently Provence shipped much of its wine (especially the sharp but cheap and thirst-quenching rosés) abroad. But the last half of this century has seen a shift that favors quality over sheer quantity. Wine makers, led by dedicated owners of small estates, have been upgrading both the quality and image of the local product, and many fine wines can be found here (as well as many not-so-fine ones, often guzzled happily by easy-to-please tourists).

The **Rhône River** bisects Provence as it flows from the **Alps** northeast of Lyons all the way to the **Mediterranean**, but Provence's official **Côtes du Rhône** wine region designates those vineyards along either side of the river segment that runs from just south of Lyons to just south of **Avignon**. The wine region of **Côtes de Provence**—Provence's largest appellation—begins just south of Avignon and is centered around **Aix-en-Provence**, although Mediterranean coast vineyards from **Cassis** (east of Marseilles) all the way to **Nice** are also considered part of the region. The wines of the Côtes de Provence once were almost entirely rosé, but now include many fine whites and reds. Choices include Coteaux d'Aix-en-Provence from around the town of Aix; Coteaux des Baux-en-Provence from around the bleakly beautiful fortress town of Les Baux; Côtes du Luberon, from a picturesque region east of Avignon; and the tiny appellations (where fine small estates produce excellent wines) of Palette (near Aix-en-Provence), Bandol, Cassis, and Bellet (near Nice). Provence's riches extend well beyond its wines, however. Its clear light has attracted some of the finest artists of the last two centuries, whose works fill the excellent museums here. And those who sate themselves on fine wine and fine art can always unwind on the Mediterranean's long stretch of sandy beaches. But if you come here in July and August, reserve your hotels well in advance and be prepared for crowds and traffic jams along the coast.

8 Geneviève and Yvan de Chivré $ The friendly de Chivrés produce a fine Clairette de Die wine and also run a bed-and-breakfast in their tile-roofed farmhouse, which offers a taste of true country life. The eight simple but pleasant rooms (sleeping from two to four people each) all have private bathrooms, and guests are welcome to use a living room with a fireplace and refrigerator. Those on a tight budget—who don't mind a little company—should check out the three big dormitory-type rooms (eight beds each), with shared kitchen and bathroom facilities. If you happen to be traveling with your horse, it can stay here, too: This is an official *Relais-Equestre* (Equestrian Lodge) for people touring the countryside on horseback. It's nicely set near the banks of the Drôme, where there's a little swimming beach. Continental breakfast is the only meal served. ♦ On D164 in the hamlet of Aubenasson (look for the "Chambres d'Hôtes" signs), between the villages of Saillans and Crest. 75.21.53.81

9 Université du Vin de Suze-la-Rousse (Wine University of Suze-la-Rousse) If cellar tours and tastings leave you yearning to learn more, consider spending some time here. The university offers advanced training in all aspects of wines and wine making, including a diploma in vineyard law. Among the short-term courses are very serious Côtes du Rhône wine-tasting seminars, from beginning to advanced levels, which are offered on weekends (for about $300 per person). There's also a comprehensive library (some of the books are in English) and a computerized reference center, which you'll need to know French to use. The facilities may only be used by enrolled students or visited by groups with an appointment, but the university is still worth a stop for individual travelers: It's housed in a magnificent golden stone medieval château that became the property of the princes of Orange in 1175. The massive fortified outer walls and towers are signs that the château was built to withstand sieges, but the interior cobblestone courtyard and elegantly carved walls point to gracious living. For details about wine courses, which are given in French, write in advance (in English will do) to the university c/o Le Château, 26790 Suze-la-Rousse, France. ◆ Admission. Château M, W-Su 2PM-6PM; closed in November. University visits by appointment and for groups only. Suze-la-Rousse (from Orange take N7 and D26 north 22 km/14 miles to Bollène, then take D994 east 7 km/4.3 miles). 75.04.86.09; fax 75.98.24.20

10 La Beaugravière ★★$$$ Owner and chef Guy Jullien has put together one of the best wine lists on the Côtes du Rhône; it's no wonder his place has become a wine makers' hangout. Copious servings of such local specialties as *lapin rôti à la tapenade* (roast rabbit with olive paste) and an extravagant menu featuring truffles (Provence's black diamond) are perfect accompaniments to the wines. Don't let the rustic exterior of this restaurant fool you; the decor inside is quite elegant. A cozy conclusion to the evening is to stagger upstairs to one of the three simple but comfortable guest rooms, available only to those who dine in the restaurant. ◆ M-Sa lunch and dinner; Su lunch. Reservations recommended. Mondragon (from Suze-la-Rousse go 13 km/8 miles southwest on D994 and D26; from Orange go 16 km/10 miles north on N7). 90.40.82.54

11 Domaine des Tourelles Wine maker Roger Cuillerat's Gigondas 1991 received a special award from the prestigious *Hachette Guide des Vins 1994,* and is a great introduction to Gigondas. Cuillerat uses primarily grenache grapes (80 percent) with some syrah, cinsault, and mourvèdre, and favors strictly traditional methods. The wines have a long maceration (about two weeks) and are aged in oak; they need from five to 10 years of bottle aging, depending on the vintage, and should be uncorked two hours before drinking. The winery is in Gigondas, an ancient village of tile-roofed stone houses surrounded by steep vine-covered slopes; in small-town spirit, Cuillerat ages the wines in cellars under the village's **Café de la Poste.** The winery itself is in a 14th-century fortified stone château that was once a monastery; its

name comes from the two round towers (*tourelles*) on either side of the entrance. Tastings are in the cellars created by the medieval monks who once produced wine here. ◆ Free. Visits and tastings daily. Gigondas (from Orange take D950 southeast 10 km/6.2 miles, then take D977 north 8 km/4.9 miles, then take D8 about 3 km/1.86 miles south to D7 east, and follow the signs to the winery). 90.65.86.98; fax 90.65.89.47

Les Florets

11 Restaurant Les Florets ★★$$ The magnificent setting, in the midst of the stunning Dentelles de Montmirail hills, could almost distract you from the feast of Provençal specialties like beef braised in Gigondas wine and *tourte de lapereau au romarin et aux morilles* (double-crust rabbit pie with rosemary and morel mushrooms). The homey dining room is full of old-fashioned furniture, with such touches as a grandfather clock, copper cooking utensils hanging on the walls, and bouquets of fresh flowers on every table. In warm weather, get a table on the shady terrace overlooking the mountains and vineyards. No meal here is complete without a bottle of a local wine; some on the list are made by the owners, who offer tastings at their nearby wine cellars in Vacqueyras, **Domaine de la Garrigue** (90.65.84.60), about five kilometers (3.1 miles) away. ◆ M-Tu, Th-Su lunch and dinner; closed January-March. Reservations recommended. Rte des Dentelles-de-Montmirail, a tiny road going east from Gigondas. 90.65.85.01

Adjoining the Restaurant Les Florets:

Hôtel Les Florets $$ Some of the 15 simple guest rooms here have views of the surrounding vineyards; all have private bathrooms. The rooms are small but charming, decorated in ultratraditional French country style, with elaborately patterned wallpaper and matching bedcovers. Get out and go for a walk; the area is beautiful. This is a good base for touring the nearby wineries and picturesque villages. Continental breakfast is served, though, as in most of the country, it is not included in the price of a room. ◆ Closed January-March. 90.65.85.01; fax 90.65.83.80

Brother Timothy, a member of the Christian Brothers order and an avid corkscrew collector, credits Samuel Hensall, an English parson, with designing the first patented corkscrew in 1795.

11 Domaine de la Monardière Martine and Christian Vache make a fruity, flavorful Vacqueyras that doesn't need to stay in the bottle as long as many others, so you're sure to find some vintages here that are ready to drink. The excellent 1992 vintage Vacqueyras red has a fruity yet mineral taste, and is very full-flavored and mouth-filling. Another plus: The prices here are incredibly low—all less than $10 per bottle. The rambling two-story creamy yellow Provençal *mas* (farmhouse) that houses the winery is surrounded by vineyards. The reception room is in the oldest part of the house, which dates from the 17th century. Visits to the cellars are available on request. The winery is in the beautiful village of Vacqueyras, whose stone-and-stucco tile-roofed houses are set beneath the craggy peaks of the Dentelles de Montmirail (hills whose peaks are so jagged that they look like bits of *dentelle,* that is, lace). Vineyards and olive groves alternate on the slopes below the town. ◆ Free. Tastings daily. Appointment recommended. Vacqueyras (from Gigondas go 4 km/2.48 miles south on D7). 90.65.87.20; fax 90.65.82.01

11 Domaine de Coyeux Once head of a major corporation, Yves Nativelle found he just had to give in to his love of wine making. His sweet Muscat de Beaumes-de-Venise—one of the best examples of this wine around—is a delicate pale yellow and has a bouquet of apricots, peaches, and a touch of pepper. While many Muscats are made to be drunk within two years of bottling, the wines from this estate need more time in the bottle to develop their complex taste. The 1990, an excellent year that produced a particularly powerful wine, should really be saved to help you celebrate the turn of the century. Tastings are in a sunny room overlooking the vineyard. ◆ Free. M-Sa. Appointment recommended. Beaumes-de-Venise (from Vacqueyras go 4 km/2.4 miles east along D81). 90.62.97.96; fax 90.65.01.87

11 Château Redortier Etienne de Monthon produces red Beaumes-de-Venise, purple-black Gigondas, rosé, and white Beaumes-de-Venise. His estate, an 18th-century Provençal *mas* (farmhouse), lies beneath the spectacular Dentelles de Montmirail hills. The vineyards are planted in grenache (60 percent), syrah (20 percent), cinsault (15 percent), and other grapes. The award-winning fruity and spicy Beaumes-de-Venise reds need from five to 10 years in the bottle. An instructive tasting of many types of wine is offered. ◆ Free. Visits and tastings daily. Just outside Suzette (from Beaumes-de-Venise go 7.5 km/4.5 miles northeast on D90). 90.62.96.43; fax 90.65.03.38

11 Dentelles de Montmirail Excursion From the village of Suzette, take a tiny local road (unnumbered on maps; look for a sign to Château-Neuf and Vaison-la-Romaine) north through the craggy Dentelles de Montmirail hills. Between Suzette and the village of Vaison-la-Romaine are approximately 10 kilometers (6.2 miles) of scenic beauty. The views of the unspoiled Provençal countryside are unbeatable; the only problem with picnicking will be choosing which site is most perfect. Stop at Vaison-la-Romaine, a picturesque village of red-roofed stone houses and Roman landmarks (see below). From Vaison-la-Romaine take D977 and then the tiny D88 southwest 15 kilometers (9.3 miles) to Séguret, one of the most beautiful villages in Provence. Its tiny lanes, stone houses, and covered passageways have been restored, and many artists live and work here. A *crèche vivante* (Christmas tableau featuring live animals and local residents) is held here every Christmas and should not be missed. Take D79 from Séguret back to Gigondas.

Along the Dentelles de Montmirail excursion:

Vaison-la-Romaine Archaeology and history buffs won't want to miss this village, which was founded by the Voconces, a Celtic tribe who were conquered by the Romans in the second century. After the conquest, the village became part of Rome's Provincia Romana, and was a major trading center for centuries. The current village was built over much of the city's Gallo-Roman structures, but ongoing excavations have revealed some splendid ancient buildings around the village's edge. Many of these remains are fenced in, but can be visited as part of a trip to the museum devoted to Vaison's Gallo-Roman days (see below). Also check out the **Espace Vins** annex of the tourist office (Pl du Chanoine Sautel, at Rue de Gaulle, 90.36.02.11), where interesting tastings of Côtes du Rhône wines are held Wednesdays from 9:15AM to noon. Local comestibles are also for sale here, including *crème de myrtilles* (blackberry cordial) used to make a popular local aperitif, the *myro* (Côtes du Rhône rosé with a little *crème de myrtilles* mixed in). ◆ 10 km/6.2 miles north of Suzette

Within Vaison-la-Romaine:

Musée Archéologique Théo-Desplans (Théo Desplans Archaeological Museum) The collection includes some remarkable statues from the first through third century that were found nearby. There are also excellent maps showing what the village once looked like. The **Ruines Romanes** (Roman Ruins), including vestiges of a theater and some aristocratic houses with mosaics, are on both sides of Avenue de Gaulle. ♦ Admission includes museum and ruins. ♦ Daily. Museum: Quartier de Puymin. Ruins: Quartier de Puymin and Quartier de la Villasse. 90.36.02.11

Chambres d'Hôtes L'Evêché $ The Verdier family rents four comfortable guest rooms in an ancient house that was once part of a bishops' residence. All of the cozily rustic rooms have private bathrooms; two have bathtubs and the other two have showers. Peace and quiet are guaranteed. Continental breakfasts are served on a terrace with a view of the village. ♦ Rue de l'Evêché. 90.36.13.46; fax 90.36.32.43

12 Chambres d'Hôtes l'Escleriade $ Four rooms and one suite are available in the Gallo family's contemporary house, all with private bathrooms; two have showers rather than tubs. A great plus is the swimming pool. In summer, enjoy the continental breakfast on the terrace, where there's a great view of Mont Ventoux. Copious, typically Provençal meals are served on request in the evenings, and a simple village restaurant is nearby.
♦ Entrechaux (from Vaison-la-Romaine go 5 km/3.1 miles southeast; take D938 south about 3 km/1.86 miles to D54 east and follow the signs for "Chambres"). 90.46.01.32; fax 90.28.70.19

13 Domaine des Amouriers Jocelyn Chudzikiewicz, one of the most conscientious wine makers around, produces an award-winning Vacqueyras and an amazingly inexpensive Côtes du Rhône using the simplest possible equipment in her tiny cellars. Many of her vines are 40 years old; the vines are harvested in relays to insure that the fruit is perfectly ripe. All her wines are fruity, complex, and mouth-filling—and they're inexpensive, to boot. The winery, surrounded by vines, is one of the oldest you can visit along the Côtes du Rhône; the wrought-iron cross in one wall of the medieval stone house was set there by the *Templiers* (Templars), knights of a religious military order who once occupied the building. ♦ Free. Visits and tastings M-Sa. Appointment recommended. From Vacqueyras take D52 south 8 km/4.9 miles to Sarrians and follow the signs to the winery. 90.65.83.22; fax 90.65.84.13

"For a gourmet, wine is not a drink but a condiment, provided that your host has chosen it correctly."

Edouard de Pomiane, *Cooking with Pomiane*

14 Château de Beaucastel
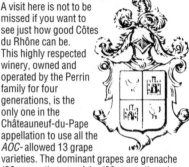
A visit here is not to be missed if you want to see just how good Côtes du Rhône can be. This highly respected winery, owned and operated by the Perrin family for four generations, is the only one in the Châteauneuf-du-Pape appellation to use all the *AOC*-allowed 13 grape varieties. The dominant grapes are grenache (30 percent), mourvèdre (30 percent), and syrah (10 percent) for the reds; only marsanne is used for the white Châteauneuf-du-Pape. The reds, with a bouquet of prunes, spices, bay leaves, and a bit of licorice, are always ranked at the top in tastings, and the white is considered by far the best white Châteauneuf-du-Pape in the appellation. For over 25 years the wines here have been produced organically, and they are never filtered. Harvesting is done manually, and each type of grape is pressed separately to preserve its special character. This winery illustrates how extreme care and a desire for authenticity pays off in the bottle. The operation is housed in a splendid 17th-century stone *mas* (Provençal farmhouse) with a red tiled roof, surrounded by a garden with a swimming pool, olive trees, and many flowers. The coat of arms of the Beaucastel family, who built the house and established the vineyards in 1687, is carved in stone in one of the château's reception rooms (with the exception of the sales and tasting room, the interior of the château is closed to the public). ♦ Free. Visits and tastings M-F. Beaucastel (from Orange take D68 10 km/6.2 miles south to Chateauneuf-du-Pape, then continue 7 km/4.3 miles northeast following signs to the winery on a private road). 90.70.41.00; fax 90.70.41.19

15 La Mère Germaine ★★$$ A favorite of the local wine-making community, this place features traditional Provençal cooking with some inventive touches, like an asparagus-and-crayfish terrine and *agneau de Provence à la crème d'ail* (Provençal lamb with garlic cream). There's a tasty cheese assortment, too. A fixed-price menu is served Tuesday through Friday and at lunch on Saturday. The cheerful decor includes bright fabrics, white chairs and tables, and plenty of flowers, all enhanced by a wonderful panorama of the vineyards. In the summer guests may eat on the shady outdoor terrace. Above the restaurant are six simple, moderately priced guest rooms with private bathrooms. ♦ Tu-Sa lunch and dinner; Su lunch; closed in January. Reservations required. Pl de la Fontaine, Châteauneuf-du-Pape (from Orange go 10 km/6.2 miles south on D68). 90.83.70.72; fax 90.83.53.20

Restaurants/Clubs: Red   **Hotels:** Blue
Shops/ ♣ Outdoors: Green   **Sights/Culture:** Black

15 Château la Nerthe The magnificent château on this estate is one of France's most beautiful. The oldest section of the immense, creamy yellow structure dates from the 16th century; it was expanded greatly in the 18th century. Topped with a well-weathered tile roof, it is what is known in Provence as a *bastide* (a large rectangular mansion with thick walls constructed by aristocrats). It has a wide terrace overlooking a garden filled with centuries-old trees and flowers. The château's long-renowned vineyards were celebrated by Provence's great 19th-century poet, Frédéric Mistral (he called La Nerthe wines *"royal, impérial, et pontifical"*). Today, the winery produces both white and red Châteauneuf-du-Papes. The whites are deeply fruity, with a flowery bouquet and a long-lasting taste—a revelation. The powerful reds are equally good, although they need years of aging. The Cuvée des Cadettes, made only in good years, is the top-of-the-line red. Be sure to ask for a vintage that's ready to drink if you don't have the means to store. Tastings are in a wine cellar overlooking the château's gardens. ♦ Free. Visits and tastings M-Sa. From Châteauneuf-du-Pape go 5 km (3.1 miles) east on D192. 90.83.70.11; fax 90.83.79.69

16 Domaine Maby The Maby family produces white, red, and rosé wines—all of which have won awards—from their vineyards within the Lirac and Tavel appellations. Try the Lirac white with a flowery, mouth-filling taste; the full, fruity reds (made from grenache, syrah, and mourvèdre grapes); and the excellent Tavel rosé from the La Forcadière vineyard—one of Tavel's best. The winery is in the Maby family's traditional stone *mas* with a red tiled roof. ♦ Free. Visits and tastings M-F. Rue St-Vincent, Tavel (from Châteauneuf-du-Pape go 15 km/9.3 miles southwest on D976; watch for right turn to Tavel). 66.50.03.40; fax 66.50.43.12

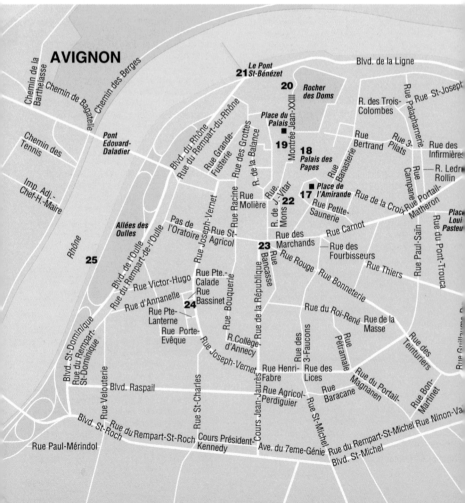

Avignon

The heart of Provence, Avignon's oldest claim to fame is that it was the papal headquarters in the 14th century. Bertrand de Goth, previously Archbishop of Bordeaux, moved the papal enclave to Avignon upon his election to the papacy in 1309. A series of six popes resided in the **Palais des Papes** (Palace of the Popes), one of the world's largest castles, before Gregory XI returned the papacy to Rome in 1377. When he was succeeded by a maverick Italian pope, the College of the Cardinals elected another pope in Avignon. With two popes reigning, the dispute became known as the Great Schism of the West. The Palace still looms over the city today.

Another landmark is the famous 12th-century **Pont St-Bénézet** (St. Bénézet Bridge), the "Pont d'Avignon" about which generations of French children have sung. A more recent cause for Avignon's renown is its prestigious summer art and music festival, *Le Festival d'Avignon,* which swells the city's population and traffic to the brink. The city is also known for its great emporiums: the food market on the **Place Pie** on Tuesday through Sunday morning, the *brocante* (used goods and antiques) market on the **Place Crillon** on Saturday, the *marché aux fleurs* (flower market) on the **Place des Carmes** on Saturday, and the *marché aux puces* (flea market) on the Place des Carmes on Sunday.

17 Hôtel de La Mirande $$$$ Ranked one of France's most elegant, this hotel provides every luxury you could possibly desire. Each of the 20 rooms and suites in this former palace has such amenities as a huge marble bathroom, silk curtains, opulent fabrics, paintings, and antique furniture; some of the suites are as big as apartments. All rooms are equipped with direct-dial phones, cable TV, mini-bars, safes, air-conditioning, hair dryers, robes, magnifying mirrors, and complimentary toiletries. Room service is available day and night. The public areas are adorned with old paintings, sculptures, tapestries, handmade carpets, and an antique parquet floor. There's a nice interior garden too. Although the facade dates from the 17th century, sections of the building are centuries older, from the time of the popes; it was apparently built on the site of a Roman theater. The hotel faces the most beautiful side of the splendid **Palais des Papes,** and if the popes could have lived here, they might not have gone back to Rome. The catch is that you practically need a papal budget to afford all this. ♦ 4 Pl de l'Amirande (at Rue du Vice-Legat). 90.85.93.93; fax 90.86.26.85

Within the Hôtel de La Mirande:

Restaurant La Mirande ★★$$$ The dining room boasts the same tastefully opulent decor as the main rooms of the hotel: paintings, antiques, and ancient tapestries. The atmosphere, though, is warm and welcoming, and the cuisine is mainly Provençal. Try the *filet de rouget* (red mullet, a delicious Mediterranean fish), *croustillant de pigeonneau au beurre de pistache* (crispy squab with pistachio butter), and a luscious *fondant au chocolat amer* (bitter chocolate cream) for dessert. Meals are served on a terrace in summer. Prices are high, but there are some moderate fixed-price menus. ♦ Daily lunch and dinner. Reservations required. 90.85.93.93

18 Palais des Papes (Papal Palace) Two adjoining palaces, both built in the early 14th century, form a massive fortified château that served as the papal headquarters from 1309 to 1377. It's unmissable, with tall crenellated towers and golden-yellow stone walls that blaze in the southern sun. From the outside, the **Palais Vieux** (Old Palace) is restrained and severe; the **Palais Nouveau** (New Palace), made more decorative with numerous stone carvings on its walls, hints at the extravagant lifestyles of the papal entourage. Inside are many works of art, frescoes, and magnificent tapestries, most dating from the days of the

popes. Next door is the 12th-century **Cathédrale de Notre Dame des Doms,** whose simple lines and more human scale contrast with the off-putting grandeur of the palace itself. The church, which has 15th- to 17th-century additions, contains the ornate Gothic tomb of Pope John XXII, whose remains were stolen during the Revolution. The church is flanked by the Rocher des Doms, a cliff with a garden on its summit and great views of the wide Rhône and of the city's beloved **Pont St-Bénézet.** ♦ Admission. Daily. Pl du Palais (on the northern edge of the city). 90.27.50.00

19 Le Petit Train Touristique A little "train" (it's on regular wheels, not a track) takes visitors on a tour of the old part of the city or from the **Palais des Papes** to the Rocher des Doms gardens; both trains leave from the Place du Palais, the wide square at the main entrance to the palace. ♦ Fee. Daily Mar-Oct, leaving approximately every half hour from 9AM-6PM. Pl du Palais. No phone

20 Musée du Petit Palais (Museum of the Little Palace) Across from the entrance to the palace is the **Petit Palais,** now an excellent fine arts museum. When the papacy arrived in Avignon in the 14th century, this building became the official residence of the archbishop while the **Palais des Papes** was being built for the pope. Its Renaissance touches were added during a 15th-century remodeling. The nearly 300 works of art that grace the museum, including 12th- to 16th-century paintings and sculpture of the Avignon School, were collected by Gian Pietro Campana, a 19th-century Roman count who helped himself to money at the bank in which he worked to purchase art. Alas, the count's love of art did him in, and he was imprisoned for embezzlement. His collection of more than 16,000 artworks was divvied up among the Louvre and many other museums. ♦ Admission. M, W-Su. Pl du Palais (at Montrée Jean-XXIII). 90.86.44.58

21 Le Pont St-Bénézet (St. Bénézet Bridge) Avignon's famous bridge was begun in 1177 and built over the next eight years by a Monsieur Bénézet, who claimed he had been given holy orders to build a bridge over the Rhône; to prove it, he effortlessly hauled huge stones to form the base of the arches. Or at least that's how the local legend goes. The bridge was originally 900 meters (984.2 yards) long and had 22 arches. Rebuilt several times, the bridge was almost completely destroyed by floods in the 17th century, but a bit of it remains. An ancient song known by every French child begins *"Sur le pont d'Avignon, on y danse, on y danse"* (On the bridge of Avignon, we all dance, we all dance), but the bridge was so narrow that only pedestrians and horses could negotiate it; any dancing must have taken place under, not on, the bridge. A small museum on the bridge's history has been set up in one of its support

columns on the banks of the Rhône. ♦ Admission. Daily Apr-Oct; T-Su Nov-Mar. Blvd du Rhône (at Blvd de la Ligne). 90.85.60.16

22 Christian Etienne ★★★$$$ The main dining room in this 14th-century mansion has medieval frescoes on its golden stone walls—a reminder of the building's opulent past: It has served as the **Palais du Maréchal de la Cour Romaine** (Marshal's Palace of the Roman Court), a pope's residence, and a town hall. Bringing it up to date, contemporary paintings also hang on the walls. In summer, tables are set on a terrace outside. The ever-changing menu has featured temptations like lobster ravioli, *ragoût de ris d'agneau* (a stew of lamb sweetbreads), *carré d'agneau rôti aromatisé d'une mignonette de poivre de sechuan et romarin* (roast rack of lamb flavored with a touch of Szechuan pepper and rosemary), and *homard entier au beurre d'orange* (whole lobster with orange-butter sauce). The delicious fixed-price vegetarian menu offers such specialties as *artichauts farcis en barigoule* (artichokes stuffed with spices and herbs), *millefeuille de tomates et aubergines* (puff pastry with tomatoes and eggplant), and a cheese assortment, followed by fennel sherbet for dessert. Other desserts include a sinfully rich chocolate cake with pine nuts. The superlative wine list contains the Côtes du Rhône's best bottles. ♦ M-Sa lunch and dinner. Reservations required. 10-12 Rue de Mons (near Palais des Papes). 90.86.16.50; fax 90.86.67.09

23 Restaurant Hiély-Lucullus ★★★$$$ In spite of the partial retirement of its longtime owner and chef, Pierre Hiély, this landmark restaurant maintains its high quality. The cuisine is pure Provençal, and although prices are rather high, the quality of the cooking is worth every franc. Don't miss the *râble de lapereau farci* (stuffed saddle of young rabbit), the *salade de homard à la tomate confite* (lobster salad with long-cooked, caramelized tomatoes), the excellent cheese assortment, and the irresistible dessert cart that includes ice creams made with herbs (such as mint) from chef Hiély's own garden. The cheapest of the fixed-price menus offers a reasonable alternative to the pricey à la carte selections, with a choice between two first courses and two main courses, and a choice of a dessert from the cart. A menu might start with marinated fresh mackerel or warm chicken-liver pâté with spinach, followed by salmon with sorrel sauce and mint butter or farm-raised squab roasted with vinegar. The excellent wine list includes many rare vintages available; the concentration is on Côtes du Rhône. ♦ Tu-Su lunch and dinner July-Sept; W-Su lunch and dinner, Tu dinner Oct-June; closed two weeks in January and one week in June. Reservations required. 5 Rue de la République (at Rue Bancasse). 90.86.17.07; fax 90.86.32.38

24 Hôtel Mignon $ The name means "cute," and this place is. The 16 rooms are small but quiet and sunny, decorated in cheerful Provençal style, and the management is very friendly. All rooms have private bathrooms; some have showers instead of tubs. There's no restaurant, which isn't really a problem in restaurant-rich Avignon. A catch: Rooms are on three floors, but there's no elevator. ♦ 12 Rue Joseph-Vernet (between Rue Bassinet and Rue Pte-Lanterne). 90.82.17.30; fax 90.85.78.46

25 Mireio Bateau Restaurant ★$$ Have lunch or dine and dance the night away as you cruise down the wide, powerful Rhône, enjoying the wonderful views of the **Pont St-Bénézet** and the **Palais des Papes.** This glass-topped floating restaurant seats 250, is air-conditioned, and operates all year long. Each cruise lasts 2.5 hours. Unfortunately, the quality of the food—which includes salmon, lamb, and *coquilles saint-jacques* (scallops)—doesn't measure up to the views. ♦ W-Su lunch and dinner. Lunch boat departs at noon; dinner boat departs at 9PM. Reservations required. Allée de l'Oulle, a quay on the Rhône just west of the center of Avignon. 90.85.62.25; fax 90.85.61.14

Avignon Environs

26 Le Ferme Jamet $$ In a 16th-century *mas* on the Ile de la Barthelasse (an island in the Rhône), this magical bed-and-breakfast is just north of Avignon but seems miles away from the city's bustle. There are five guest rooms with antique furnishings, two suites with modern furnishings, three rustic bungalows, and an authentic Gypsy wagon with beds— take your pick! The friendly owners have also installed a swimming pool and tennis court. This place is well known among the actors and artists who frequent Avignon's summer festival, so be sure to reserve well in advance for July or August. Breakfast is the only meal served, and it is not included in the price of a room. ♦ Ile de la Barthelasse, Avignon (from the center of Avignon take D900 west to D228 north and follow the signs to Le Ferme Jamet). 90.86.16.74; fax 90.86.17.72

Eat, Drink, and Be Merry in the South of France

Key grape varieties: syrah, viognier, marsanne, roussanne, muscat, clairette, grenache, rolle, chardonnay, cabernet sauvignon, mourvèdre, ugni, carignan, cinsault, and pinot noir.

Classification system: Wines in the south do not use any official *grand cru* or *premier cru* designations. The occasional bottle from Provence may be labeled *"grand cru classé,"* but this is only self-aggrandizement in a region without such classifications. The highest tier of wines from the area is the *Appellation Contrôlée (AC)*, and the next step down is the VDQS (*Vin Délimité de Qualité Supérieure,* or Delimited Wine of Superior Quality). The third level down—sometimes decent and sometimes awful—is the *vin de pays* (country wine).

Culinary specialties: Geography and history have conspired to bring strong Italian and Spanish influences to the cuisine of the south. The region is rich with olive trees, so naturally olives and olive oil feature prominently in the native dishes. Garlic has been called the "truffle of Provence" and can be found, along with tomatoes, in almost any dish of that region. Seafood is plentiful throughout the south because of the proximity to the coast; sardines and anchovies are particularly abundant, along with lobster, which is actually affordable. Here are some classic dishes for which the region is known:

aïgo buido (garlic soup)

aïoli monstre (garlic mayonnaise served with fish, snails, boiled vegetables, and more)

anchoïade (anchovy, olive oil, and garlic dip)

bouillabaisse (creamy fish stew)

bourride (fish soup with a garlic-mayonnaise sauce)

brandade de morue (potato and salt-cod puree)

cheeses of goat's and sheep's milk, including banon and roquefort

daube de boeuf provençale (long-simmered beef stew with red wine and orange peel)

salade niçoise (salad with tuna, anchovies, hard-boiled eggs, olives, and tomatoes)

soupe au pistou (vegetable soup with basil and garlic)

soupe de poisson avec sa rouille (fish soup with garlic mayonnaise flavored with saffron and red pepper)

tapénade (olive puree)

truffes du Ventoux (truffles from the Ventoux Mountains)

Restaurants/Clubs: Red   Hotels: Blue
Shops/ 🌳 Outdoors: Green   Sights/Culture: Black

27 Auberge de Cassagne $$$$ An official *Relais de Silence*, this hotel guarantees peace and quiet even during the crowded summer season. The 25 rooms and five suites are all very comfortable, and less opulently decorated than in most fine hotels in the region—not necessarily a bad thing. You'll find white walls, red tile floors, Provençal fabrics used for drapes and bedspreads, little balconies, and very well equipped bathrooms. All rooms have air-conditioning, direct-dial phones, mini-bars, safes, satellite TVs, and hair dryers. The rooms in the main building (a rambling Provençal former mansion) are moderately priced, as opposed to expensive; other rooms are in a separate building near the swimming pool, and the most expensive rooms and suites are in a third building, surrounded by its own garden. Summertime reservations are hard to come by. ♦ 450 Allée de Cassagne, Le Pontet (from the center of Avignon take N107 east to D62 south and follow the signs to the auberge). 90.31.04.18; fax 90.32.25.09

Within the Auberge de Cassagne:

Restaurant de Cassagne ★★★$$$ Among the tasty local specialties are a *terrine provençale* with eggplant, zucchini, tomatoes, and foie gras; *dorade et sa compotée de fenouil à l'huile d'olive vierge* (dorade, a Mediterranean fish, with a fennel purée seasoned with virgin olive oil); and *noisette et gigot d'agneau, petits cocos à la tomate et herbes de la garrigue* (fillet and leg of lamb with white beans seasoned with tomato and wild herbs). Try the crème brûlée or the fruits in puff pastry for dessert. The main dining room has a beamed ceiling, creamy yellow walls, and widely spaced tables; there's also a peaceful terrace. The wine list is outstanding, with many good wines offered in half bottles. ♦ Daily lunch and dinner. Reservations required. 90.31.04.18

28 L'Isle-sur-la-Sorgue This little village of small red-roofed stone houses and water-powered mills along the Sorgue River is an antiques-shopper's paradise, and well worth the drive from Avignon. The picturesque streets are lined with shops, most of them open Monday through Saturday; on Sundays, a *brocante* (used goods) market is held in the center of town. You'll find gaily colored Provençal fabrics, antique quilts and bedspreads, copper cooking utensils, salad bowls carved of olive wood, pottery and glassware, paintings, antique Provençal furniture, and much, much more. ♦ 23 km (14.2 miles) east of Avignon on N100

29 Pont du Gard A "must" excursion west of Avignon is a trip to view this bridge, one of the most spectacular Roman monuments in France. This two-level arched bridge across the Gardon River was built between AD 40 and 60, under the reign of Claudius. It was once part of an astonishing 50-kilometer (31-mile) aqueduct that brought water from a spring near the village of Uzès all the way down to Nîmes. The bridge's magnificent arches and its golden stone gleaming in the Provençal sun have inspired many writers and artists, including Jean-Jacques Rousseau, who wrote in his *Confessions* that the bridge so impressed him that he felt he had become a Roman. ♦ From Avignon take N100 15 km (9.3 miles) west to Remoullins, then take D981 northwest 5 km (3.1 miles)

On the Road to Aix-en-Provence

OUSTAU DE BAUMANIÈRE

30 L'Oustau de Beaumanière $$$$ Truly a dream destination, this member of the prestigious Relais & Châteaux group sits beneath a cliff on which the spectacular medieval fortress-village of Les Baux-de-Provence (often called Les Baux) perches. The longtime chef and owner, the late Raymond Thuilier, was instrumental in restoring the village (unfortunately, it has now become cluttered with tourist traps; come at dawn for the magical scenery and light, before the buses arrive). Monsieur Thuilier also turned his rambling 16th-century *mas* into one of the finest hotels and restaurants in France; his grandson, Jean-André Charial, carries on the tradition. There are 13 opulent suites and 11 big, luxuriously decorated rooms overlooking the swimming pool and gardens; the most peaceful are in a separate building, **Le Manoir**. Each room is unique, but all have big windows with fabulous views, some antiques, Provençal fabrics, and all the contemporary amenities, including mini-bars, direct-dial phones, satellite TV, complimentary toiletries, and huge bathrooms. One of the rooms has a huge, ancient fireplace and a canopy bed. The continental breakfasts are a delight. Tennis, horseback riding, and golf facilities are nearby, but you really come here to soak up the Provençal sun and get some peace, quiet, and pampering. A small shop sells the hotel's elegant edibles, such as fine olive oil and *tapenade*, an olive paste. ♦ Closed November-March. Val d'Enfer, Les Baux-de-Provence (from Avignon take D571 south 21 km/13 miles to St-Rémy-de-Provence, then take D5 south 7 km/4.3 miles to D27A west; from the intersection of D27A and D5 it's 2.5 km/1.5 miles to the center of Les Baux-de-Provence; the Baumanière is at the edge of town). 90.54.33.07; fax 90.54.40.46

Within L'Oustau de Beaumanière:

Restaurant Oustau de Beaumanière

★★★★$$$$ Elegant versions of Provençal cuisine are perfectly accompanied by wines from the impressive list, which includes those from the hotel's own winery. The ever-changing menu has offered such delights as *fricassée de légumes primeurs au beurre de truffes* (fricassee of vegetables with truffle butter), *ravioli de truffes aux poireaux* (leek and truffle ravioli), *salade de homard à la vinaigrette de basilic* (lobster salad with basil vinaigrette), *saint-pierre rôti entier à l'huile d'olive de la vallée des Baux et echalottes confites* (John Dory, a fine fish, roasted whole with local olive oil and caramelized shallots), *aiguillettes de canard rôti aux olives* (slices of roast duck breast with olives), and the most famous dish in the house, *gigot d'agneau en croute Raymond Thuilier* (leg of lamb in a crust as Raymond Thuilier made it). For dessert, try the *soufflé aux pistaches et au lait d'amandes* (pistachio and almond milk soufflé). ◆ M-Tu, F-Su lunch and dinner; W, Th dinner; closed mid-January–early March. Reservations required well in advance. 90.54.33.07

31 Château Romanin J.A. Charial, *chef de cuisine* at **Restaurant Oustau de Baumanière,** is part owner of a nearby winery that is well worth a visit. A convert to biodynamic agriculture, Charial avoids all chemical pesticides and weed killers in his vineyards, and times vineyard tasks according to celestial rhythms. Although the return to such traditional practices is now being adopted by some of France's most respected wineries, nowhere else is it accomplished in combination with such high-tech cellar facilities. The château's magnificent cellars look like a contemporary cathedral. They were designed with energy fields in mind, to promote the best possible conditions for aging the wine. The bottles are stored pointing 3° northwest, considered the most propitious position. Whether or not you take any of this seriously, you can't fail to be impressed by the cellars, surely among the most elaborate in France, and the wines (reds, whites, and rosés) are very good. Maybe Charial's energy fields account for the site's eons-long popularity: It was inhabited in the Bronze Age; was the scene of celebrations honoring the Greek goddess Artemis, and of Druids' rites (at this point, Romanin was already well known for its wines); and was the property of an aristocratic Roman, Claudius Postumus Dardanus, who perpetuated the wine-making tradition of the locale. Troubadours performed in the château in the Middle Ages. ◆ Individuals free; groups admission. Visits and tastings by appointment. Appointments must be made two weeks in advance; English-speaking guides available. From St-Rémy-de-Provence take D99 east about 4 km (2.5 miles) and follow the signs to the château. 90.92.45.87; fax 90.92.24.36

32 Auberge La Régalido $$$ In the heart of Provence, this country inn is in a restored olive-oil mill and operated by the Michel family. It's part of the Relais & Châteaux group. The 15 rooms are all elegantly decorated with antique furniture, beamed ceilings, Provençal fabrics, and the latest in modern comforts, including mini-bars and air-conditioning. Two rooms have balconies, five have private terraces; the others lack these charms, but overlook a flower-filled garden. Nearby (via the plane tree–shaded D33) is a picturesque windmill overlooking the countryside, where 19th-century writer Alphonse Daudet wrote his *Lettres de Mon Moulin* (Letters from My Mill). ◆ Closed in January. Fontvieille-en-Provence (from Les Baux-de-Provence go 10 km/6.2 miles southwest on D78 and D17). 90.54.60.22; fax 90.54.64.29

Within the Auberge La Régalido:

Restaurant Le Régalido ★★★$$$ The latest in four generations of restaurateurs, chef Jean-Pierre Michel offers fine, authentic Provençal recipes like *gratin de moules aux épinards* (mussel and spinach gratin) and *tranche de gigot à l'ail* (slice of leg of lamb with garlic). Tables are set in a majestic dining room with a vaulted stone ceiling, and on a flower-filled terrace. The wine list boasts a wide choice of Provençal wines. ◆ Daily dinner, W-Su lunch July-Sept; Tu-Su lunch and dinner Oct-June; closed in January. Reservations required. 90.54.60.22

33 Le Moulin de Jean-Marie Cornille Provence is olive-oil country, and this mill, where hundreds of growers bring their olives to be pressed, produces one of the best oils around. You can bring a bottle to be filled, or buy oil already bottled; real olive-oil addicts might want to haul the five-liter container home. Also for sale are some attractive serving bottles with special spouts. The staff isn't always friendly, but the oil is superb. ◆ M-Sa; closed the last two weeks of August. Maussane-les-Alpilles (from Fontvieille go 8 km/4.9 miles west on D17; follow the signs to the mill). 90.54.32.37

33 Lis Amelié This shop is an excellent source for Provençal crafts, especially pottery. The selection ranges from very expensive antique pottery and glass to charming, affordable modern pieces. Other local treats on hand include olive oil, *tapenade* (olive paste), honey, and wines. ◆ M, W-Su; closed mid-November–mid-February. Pont de Monblan, Maussane-les-Alpilles. 90.54.37.55

33 Ou Ravi Provençau ★★$$$ Everything is pure Provençal in this friendly spot, from the food to the decor to the waitresses' garb. Chef Jean-François Richard lets the food market in nearby St-Rémy-de-Provence guide his menu daily, but he usually includes *soupe au pistou* (vegetable soup with basil and garlic), rabbit sautéed with thyme, and picodon fermier (a goat cheese) marinated in spicy olive oil. Try the chestnut-and-prune ice cream for dessert. ♦ M, W-Su lunch and dinner; closed late November–late December and the last week of June. Reservations recommended. 34 Ave de la Vallée-des-Baux, Maussane-les-Alpilles. 90.54.31.11; fax 90.54.41.03

34 Mas Gourgonnier This winery is housed in a tile-roofed *mas* lost in a valley that is a little bit of paradise: olive trees, live oaks, fragrant rosemary—all the scents and colors of the Provençal countryside seem to be concentrated here. The Cartier brothers cultivate 40 hectares (98.8 acres) of vines (mostly grenache) using strictly organic methods. They produce a deeply fruity Coteaux-des-Baux rosé and a powerful red with overtones of truffles. Tastings are in the cellars, where you can also buy local olives, apricot juice, and wild rice. ♦ Free. M-Sa. Le Destet (from Maussane-les-Alpilles go 6 km/3.7 miles southeast on D17 to Mouriès, then go 4.5 km/2.8 miles north on D24). 90.47.50.45; fax 90.47.51.36

**CHATEAU
PONT ROYAL**
1993

35 Château de Pont-Royal In a big yellow stucco 18th-century *relais de poste* (stagecoach stop) with red shutters, charming Sylvette Jauffret, Provençale through and through, can entertain visitors for hours talking about how to make great rosés. Her full-flavored and aromatic Coteaux d'Aix-en-Provence rosés are among the region's best. Try the Grande Cuvée rosé made from 80 percent grenache and 20 percent syrah grapes; if you think rosés are just simple quaffing wines, this one will change your mind. Jauffret also produces an excellent red wine from grenache, cabernet, and syrah grapes, which needs about five years in the bottle. Tastings are in the lovingly renovated former stables of the inn, where the work of local artists is displayed and plays and concerts are often performed. Regional

edibles and pretty baskets are for sale here too. This is one of the best places in Provence for picnic provisions, as well as for excellent wines. ♦ Free. Visits and tastings Tu, Th-Sa 9AM-7PM; M, W 3PM-7PM; Su, holidays 9:30AM-noon. From St-Rémy follow D99 east 14 km (8.68 miles), then take N7 south about 20 km (12.4 miles) to Pont-Royal. 90.57.40.15; fax 90.59.12.28

36 Château de la Verrerie The deep red Côtes du Luberon produced here is proof that the lovely Luberon is more than scenic—it's also great wine country. Try the powerful and concentrated Grand Deffend, pure syrah, with overtones of blackberries and currants; the winery also produces good rosé and white wines. It is in a typical Provençal *mas* surrounded by lavender and vines. Tastings are in a wine cellar reached by way of a patio with a tinkling fountain. ♦ Free. Visits and tastings M-Sa by appointment only. Puget-sur-Durance (25 km/15.5 miles east of Avignon on D973; follow the signs to the winery). 90.08.32.98; fax 90.08.25.45

Aix-en-Provence

Provence's historic capital, Aix-en-Provence is one of France's most beloved cities. With its wide avenues lined with plane trees, its 17th- and 18th-century town houses, and bustling sidewalk cafes, Aix (as the city is often called) is the quintessential Provençal city. Founded in 122 BC as a thermal resort, **Aquae Sextiae** (the first Roman settlement in Gaul), it's still known as the *ville des eaux* (city of the waters). To this day, ornate stone fountains spout warm waters throughout the city, especially on **Cours Mirabeau,** Aix's main drag. The arts also figure prominently in the city's history. The Counts of Provence made Aix their base, and in the 12th century it became a center for troubadour music and poems. Aix is also Paul Cézanne's home town; one of his favorite subjects was the **Montagne Ste-Victoire,** a craggy mountain just east of the city.

The very popular **Les Deux Garçons,** a cafe patronized by such luminaries as Emile Zola and Jean Cocteau, is still doing business, along with many other cafes, on the elegant Cours Mirabeau. Don't miss Aix's many open-air markets, especially **Place Richelme**'s daily food market (a great source of picnic provisions and *calissons,* almond-paste-and-fruit cookies) and the *brocante* (antiques and used goods) market next to the **Palais de Justice** on Tuesday, Thursday, and Saturday.

Restaurants/Clubs: Red   **Hotels:** Blue
Shops/ ♥ Outdoors: Green   **Sights/Culture:** Black

37 Château de Gavelles The name of this winery comes from the Provençal word *gaveou*, a sheaf of vine clippings. The château is a *bastide* (an aristocrat's mansion) that once belonged to the archbishops of Aix. The current owners are James and Bénédicte de Roany; James de Roany is from an old wine family and is also the commercial manager of famed pastry chef Gaston Lenôtre's wine château in Anjou, in the Loire Valley. The vineyards here are planted in grenache, cinsault, syrah, mourvèdre, and cabernet sauvignon for the red and rosé wines they produce, and clairette de rolle for the white wine. All the wines are low-priced, and definitely worth a try. The fruity rosés would make a great match for aïoli, the Provençal garlic-laden mayonnaise that's served with vegetables and fish. ♦ Free. Visits and tastings daily by appointment. Puyricard (about 5 km/3.1 miles north of Aix-en-Provence on D14; follow the signs to the château). 42.92.06.83; fax 42.92.24.12

38 L'Atelier Paul Cézanne The renowned painter had his studio built on a hill overlooking downtown Aix and the Montagne Ste-Victoire, his eternal source of inspiration. The surroundings are not as bucolic as they were in the master's day, but the studio remains much as he knew it, complete with a number of everyday objects that give insight into his life. ♦ Admission. M, W-Su. 9 Ave Paul-Cézanne (between Ave Raymond-Poincaré and Ave de la Violette). 42.21.06.53

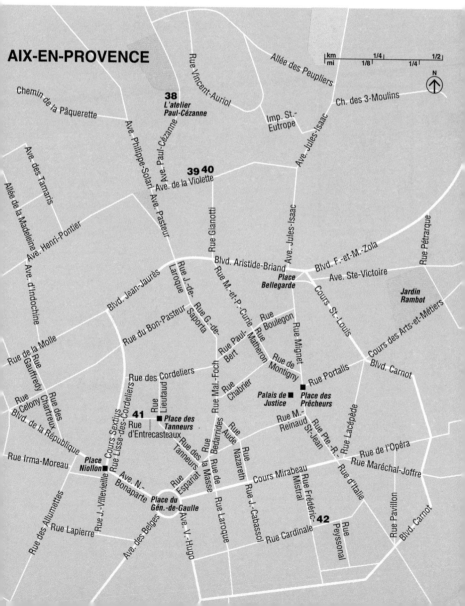

AIX-EN-PROVENCE

39 Le Clos de la Violette ★★★★$$$ Aix's finest restaurant just keeps getting better. It's set in a big white house with a terrace shaded by venerable chestnut trees. The cuisine is inventive, but true to Provençal traditions, with plenty of garlic, the freshest vegetables and fruits, and wonderful seafood specialties. Try the *langoustines à l'oignon fumé et ses ravioles de corail* (crayfish with smoked onions and pink ravioli), *coquilles saint-jacques en croustille à l'anis* (sea scallops with a crispy coating flavored with anise), *blanc de poularde fourré à l'ail confit* (farm-raised chicken stuffed with caramelized garlic), or the *agneau de lait en croûte d'herbes à l'ail rôti* (milk-fed lamb in an herb crust with roasted garlic). An extravagant all-truffle menu is served from December through March, when the local delicacy is in season. The wine list has many outstanding Provençal wines. ♦ Tu-Sa lunch and dinner; M dinner. Reservations required far in advance. 10 Ave de la Violette (between Ave Paul-Cézanne and Rue Gianotti). 42.23.30.71; fax 42.21.93.03

40 Villa Gallici $$$$ An absolutely fabulous place to stay. Although the building is new, it was built according to local architectural styles and looks as though it has been here, lost in its huge flower-filled garden, since the 18th century. The 15 luxurious rooms and two suites are elegantly decorated with Provençal fabrics and antiques, and all have private garden terraces; they seem more like guest rooms in a private château than hotel rooms. Antique sculptures and paintings abound, including Victorian candlesticks on the fireplace mantels in some rooms. All rooms have air-conditioning, satellite TV, direct-dial phones, mini-bars, and safes. The bathrooms are lavishly equipped, right down to the bathrobes and towels emblazoned with the villa's monogram in gold. The poolside terrace has elegant wrought-iron furniture with comfy cushions upholstered in more of those great floral Provençal fabrics. There is no restaurant, but light meals and drinks are served on the terrace or through room service. This place is sure to fulfill all your dreams of Provence. ♦ 18 Ave de la Violette (between Ave Paul-Cézanne and Rue Gianotti). 42.23.29.23; fax 42.96.30.45

41 Restaurant Le Petit Verdot ★$$ "Petit" is right: There are only 28 seats in this friendly place, but if you can get in, you'll love the simple Provençal dishes and meats cooked on a stone grill. The wine list is spectacular for such a small place, with many excellent wines served by the glass. The owner usually plays classic jazz records in the background. ♦ Daily lunch and dinner Sept-Jun; Tu-F, Su lunch and dinner, M, Sa dinner July-Aug. Reservations required. 7 Rue d'Entrecasteaux (between Pl des Tanneurs and Rue Lisse-des-Cordeliers). 42.27.30.12

42 Hôtel Cardinale $$ Near the Cours Mirabeau, this venerable small hotel has a family-style atmosphere. The building dates from the 18th century and much of the furniture is antique. All 24 rooms and seven suites (some smallish) are very comfortable, with big windows, pretty fabrics, private bathrooms, TVs, direct-dial telephones, and tables where you can have breakfast. Some of the tiny garret rooms on the top floor are impossibly romantic, with views of Aix's red tiled roofs. The best, though, are in an annex; most of these have kitchen facilities and one has a private patio with a fountain. There is no restaurant. ♦ Reservations recommended well in advance. 24 Rue Cardinale (between Rue Frédéric-Mistral and Rue Peyssonnel). 42.38.32.30; fax 42.26.39.05

Aix-en-Provence Environs

43 Château Simone Perched on a hillside covered with woods and vines just south of Aix, this gleaming white 16th-century château is straight out of a fairy tale, with towers, terraces, and a formal garden. And its wines are great too. The Rougier family, who bought the estate and replanted the vines after the phylloxera devastation, has been making wines in the area for almost 200 years; some of the vines are a century old. The Palette wines here are considered the best of the appellation, and are made by strictly traditional methods; no chemical herbicides, insecticides, or fertilizers are ever used. The red and rosé wines are made primarily from grenache, mourvèdre, and cinsault, but include syrah, manosquin, castet, cabernet sauvignon, and muscat noir. The white wines are made primarily from clairette, with some grenache blanc and ugni blanc. All grapes are picked by hand, sometimes in relays. Wines are aged in cellars that were dug out by monks in the 16th century. The outstanding, deep ruby red wines, which need six to 10 years of bottle aging, have a complex taste and bouquet described as combining ripe fruit (including prunes), vanilla, and truffles. The delicate rosés are fruity and fresh, and the elegant whites' flowery bouquet becomes more complex with age. ♦ Visits and tastings M–Sa. Meyreuil (from Aix take N7 2 km/1.2 miles east to the Pont des Trois-Saulets, then take D58H 2.5 km/1.6 miles southeast to Meyreuil and follow the signs). 42.66.92.58; fax 42.66.80.77

44 Mas de la Bertrande $$ This old-fashioned auberge at the foot of Ste-Victoire is the place to go for peace and quiet in the countryside—but it's just 10 kilometers (6.2 miles) east of Aix and a half-hour drive to the Mediterranean beaches. The 10 comfortable rooms (some of them a bit small) are decorated in typical Provençal style; all have private bathrooms and private garden terraces. The swimming pool is surrounded by a luxuriant garden. ♦ Closed mid-February–mid-March. Beaurecueil (from Aix take D46 east to D58 south, and follow the signs to the auberge). 42.66.90.09; fax 42.66.82.01

Within the Mas de la Bertrande:

Restaurant Mas de la Bertrande ★★$$ Chef and owner Pierre Bertrande serves excellent Provençal specialties in the dining room, and simple meals (including grilled meat and fish) on the poolside terrace. The fixed-price Provençal menu includes treats like *cuissot de lapereau farci aux olives des Alpilles* (rabbit thigh stuffed with Alpilles olives) or *rascasse et son velouté d'écrevisses* (scorpion fish with crayfish-cream sauce), followed with an assortment of local cheeses. The poolside grill offers lamb chops and salmon fillets; grilled *loup* (sea bass) or *daurade* (sea bream) are available with a week's notice. Bertrand knows many local wine makers and has an excellent choice of Coteaux-d'Aix wines on his list. ♦ Daily lunch and dinner mid-June–Sept; Tu-Sa lunch and dinner, Su lunch Oct–mid-June; closed mid-February–mid-March. Reservations required well in advance. 42.66.90.09

44 Le Relais Ste-Victoire ★★★$$$ This pretty auberge in Cézanne country offers elegant variations on Provençal specialties, such as *agneau confit aux flageolets* (long-simmered lamb with baby lima beans), fresh pasta with truffles and foie gras, and *méli-mélo de la mer sauce homard* (mixed seafood with lobster sauce). Finish with the *mousse au miel* (honey mousse, made from local honey). The wine list features an outstanding selection of hard-to-find vintages of the best Provençal wines. ♦ Tu-Sa lunch and dinner, Su lunch; closed one week in January, two weeks in February, and one week in November. Reservations required. 53 Ave Sylvain-Gauthier, Beaurecueil. 42.66.94.98; fax 42.66.85.96

Adjoining Le Relais Ste-Victoire:

Hôtel le Relais Ste-Victoire $$$ The 10 spacious guest rooms, all with private baths, are cheerily decorated with Provençal fabrics. Enjoy breakfast on a garden terrace. ♦ Closed one week in January, two weeks in February, and one week in November. 42.66.94.98

Nice

Glamorous Nice, capital of France's **Côte d'Azur,** is off the regular wine route, but is one of France's most vibrant cities. Large and cosmopolitan, Nice and its great wide beaches and boulevards can get overwhelmingly crowded in the summer. The most charming part of the city is **la Vielle Ville** (Old Town) next to the beach, a labyrinth of tiny streets filled with centuries-old town houses and inexpensive restaurants, many of them serving a local treat, *socca* (chickpea-flour pancakes). The city is also home to a few top art museums. A spectacular carnival celebrates Mardi Gras every spring, and a jazz festival takes place in July. The principality of Monaco is only an hour's drive east.

In the hills just northwest of Nice is one of the tiniest French wine appellations, Bellet. This area produces some very good, but quite expensive, white, red, and rosé wines.

NEGRESCO

45 Hôtel Négresco $$$$ One of the many palatial establishments lining the elegant Promenade des Anglais—Nice's main drag—this spectacular landmark hotel is the only one still privately held by Niçois hands. It was opened in 1913 by Henri Négresco, a Romanian who wanted to establish a hotel where his chums—rich aristocrats and royalty—would feel at home. But World War I transformed the hotel into a hospital, and brought Negresco's friends either death or ruin. Negresco himself died in Paris in 1920.

The present owners, the Augier family, remade the hotel into one of the world's most famous, and it was classified as a National Monument in 1974. The Royal Salon reception area has a turn-of-the-century glass-domed ceiling with the original crystal chandelier, designed and constructed by Baccarat; the floor is covered by the world's largest Aubusson carpet. It's undeniably grand; the decor is so opulent and filled with artwork that it feels more like a museum than a hotel. The 131 luxurious rooms are only *very* expensive; the 19 suites are *outlandishly* expensive. They're all filled with canopy beds, chandeliers, beautiful carpets, fine antique furniture, splendid views of the Mediterranean (in most rooms, so be sure to ask for a view), and every modern amenity. ♦ 37 Promenade des Anglais (between Rue de Rivoli and Rue de Cronstadt). 93.88.39.51; fax 93.88.35.68

Within the Hôtel Negresco:

Restaurant Chantecler ★★★$$$$ In accordance with the rest of the "palace," the decor features paneled walls, chandeliers, widely spaced tables with comfortable armchairs, and lots of fresh flowers. Service is excellent. The food is very good too. Chef Dominique Le Stanc specializes in fare with a regional accent; try the great risotto with morel mushrooms and baby lima beans, and

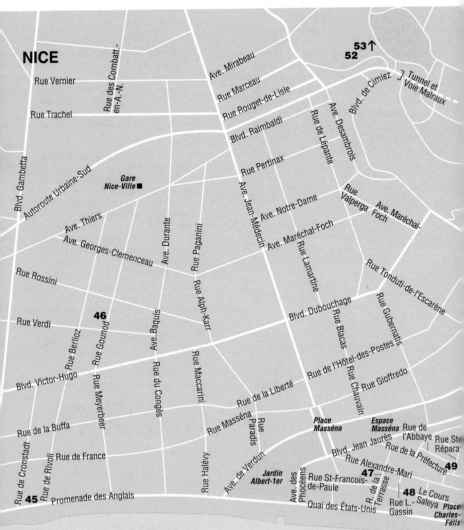

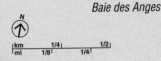

the artichokes stuffed with asparagus—an inspired combination. Fine seafood abounds, such as *rougets aux courgettes, tomates, et basilic en aïoli* (an earthy Provençal dish of red mullet with zucchini, tomatoes, and basil bound together with garlic mayonnaise). The wine list is exceptional, with many very rare, very expensive bottles, and a wide selection of Provençal wines. Prices are high, but the fixed-price menu lunch (wine included) is quite reasonable for the Côte d'Azur, especially since eating here lets you share in the hotel's grand history. ♦ Daily lunch and dinner; closed mid-November–mid-December. Reservations required. 93.88.39.51

La Rotonde ★★$$ The young and the young at heart will get a kick out this eatery with a merry-go-round theme. Pink banquettes are arranged in a somewhat circular plan, much like horses in a merry-go-round, and the place is filled with genuine merry-go-round horses that move up and down to calliope music. There are several fixed-price menus. Chicken and veal dishes are notable, but the desserts are especially good; try the *omelette norvégienne* (baked Alaska). ♦ Daily breakfast, lunch, and dinner. Reservations recommended. 93.88.39.51

46 L'Oasis $$ Right in the center of town, just down the street from the tourist office and train station, this aptly named placed offers a quiet little garden and 37 simple rooms. Unfortunately, the exterior—traditional Niçois yellow stucco with green shutters, wrought-iron balconies, and cafe tables under a tree near the front door—is much more charming than the interior, which is more like a typical US motel. The rooms are clean and comfortable, though, and have private bathrooms, TVs, and direct-dial phones. It's a good deal for the price, especially if you're just looking for a place to sleep. Breakfast is served, though it is not included in the price of the room. ♦ Reserve well in advance in July and August. 23 Rue Gounod (between Rue Verdi and Rue Rossini). 93.88.12.29; fax 93.16.14.40

47 La Mérenda ★★$$ This place in the old part of Nice is a must—if you can get in. It serves only local specialties, with the menu chalked up on a board each day. Among the goodies are ravioli, fried zucchini blossoms, and *stockfisch* (salt cod). No reservations are taken, so come early and stand in line. You'll be glad you did. ♦ Tu-F lunch and dinner; closed February and August. No credit cards accepted. 4 Rue de la Terrasse (at Rue Alexander-Mari). No phone

The pigments in wine are the same pigments that cause the red and blue colors in most fruits and flowers.

Restaurants/Clubs: Red	**Hotels:** Blue
Shops/ 🌳 Outdoors: Green	**Sights/Culture:** Black

48 Le Cours Saleya A pleasant pedestrian street in the old part of the city, it is the site of a colorful open-air food market—a great source of picnic provisions—Tuesday through Sunday mornings; a bric-a-brac and antiques market takes place here on Monday mornings. Many simple cafes and restaurants line the street. ♦ Between Rue L.-Gassin and Place Charles-Félix

49 Nissa Socca ★$ In the heart of old Nice, this rustic, friendly place on a pedestrian street always seems to be filled with Niçois having a good time. It's one of the best places in the city to try local specialties—not only *socca* but also *panisses* (a type of crepe made with chickpea flour), *beignets d'aubergines* (eggplant fritters), ravioli, and great thin-crust pizzas baked in a wood-fired oven. ♦ Tu-Sa lunch and dinner, M dinner; closed in January. Reservations recommended July and August. 5 Rue Ste-Réparate (between Rue de l'Abbaye and Rue de la Préfecture). 93.80.18.35

50 Musée d'Art Moderne et d'Art Contemporain (Museum of Modern and Contemporary Art) **MAMAC,** as the museum is often called, opened in 1990 under a cloud of scandal involving Nice's then-mayor, Jacques Médecin, who has since fled to South America. Fortunately he managed to push through the construction of this museum before leaving town. Conceived as a rival of Paris's **Centre Pompidou,** it is an imposing, fortresslike structure, but pleasant to visit; the terrace provides a great view of the city and a setting for Yves Klein's impressive outdoor sculpture. The collection contains works by the 1970s French avant-garde and by Americans (primarily from the 1960s), as well as more recent pieces. The **Grand Café des Arts** near the entrance is open until 1AM and has become a popular meeting place; it serves meals until midnight. ♦ Admission. Museum: M, W-Su; Cafe: M, W-Su lunch and dinner. Promenade des Arts (between Ave St-Sébastien and Ave St-Jean-Baptiste). 93.62.61.62

51 Hôtel Le Petit Palais $$$ This turn-of-the-century hotel is in the former home of early-20th-century French actor-director Sacha Guitry. Inside the creamy white stucco mansion are 25 rooms, all big and very comfortable; some have balconies and others have private garden-terraces. Peace and quiet are guaranteed, as is a great view of Nice and the bay from most rooms. The setting is a residential area well removed from the city center but near the suburb of Cimiez, where the **Musée Matisse** and the **Musée Marc Chagall** are. There's no restaurant. ♦ 10 Ave Emile-Bieckert (at Ave de Picardie), Carabacel. 93.62.19.11; fax 93.62.53.60

52 Musée Marc Chagall (Marc Chagall Museum) Nestled among olive groves and oak trees in the hills of Cimiez above Nice, this museum has such a perfect setting that you may not want to leave. It houses the world's largest collection devoted solely to Chagall; among the paintings is the great *Message Biblique,* 12 canvases on Biblical themes. There's a small cafeteria in the park surrounding the museum. ♦ Admission. M, W-Su. Ave du Docteur-Ménard (at Blvd de Cimiez), Cimiez. 93.81.75.75

53 Musée Matisse (Matisse Museum) In a 17th-century mansion in the suburb of Cimiez, in the hills north of the city near the well-preserved Roman arena, is the world's largest collection of Matisse's drawings and his 1947 masterpiece *Nature Morte aux Grenades.* Photographs of Matisse and his many artist friends are also displayed. ♦ Admission. M, W-Su. 164 Ave des Arènes-de-Cimiez (at Blvd de Cimiez). 93.81.08.08

54 St-Roman-de-Bellet The only Niçois wine is produced in the suburban village of St-Roman-de-Bellet. The vineyards here were almost completely overtaken by housing developments by the 1950s, when the Bagnis family of the **Château de Crémat** saved the appellation. Now they, the nearby **Château de Bellet,** and some smaller wineries are producing excellent white, red, and rosé wines from grapes that include the rolle (also called malvoisie) for the whites, the braquet for the rosés, and the folle noire (a black version of the ugni) for the reds, among other grape varieties. The whites are considered the stars of the appellation. These days, the highest marks go to **Château de Bellet** (in St-Roman-de-Bellet, 93.37.81.57; fax 93.37.93.83), a winery housed in a tile-roofed stone *mas* surrounded by vines. It can be visited daily by appointment. ♦ From Nice take D98 west 3.5 km/2.2 miles, then take D714 north 7 km/4.3 miles.

On the Road to Marseilles

55 St-Tropez Part of the Côte d'Azur, this coastal town has long been the playground for the rich and famous. It's not far from Aix-en-Provence and, for the curious, worth the trip. The ultrachic resort town boasts all the top couturier shops, expensive cafes (a café au lait can set you back $10), raucous discotheques, and lots of showy yachts and cars. While in town, be sure to try some of the area's very good rosés and some decent reds. ♦ 108 km (67 miles) southwest of Nice on N98

Within St-Tropez:

La Citadelle de St-Tropez (St. Tropez Citadel) Don't miss a visit to this 16th-century fortress perched on a hill above the city. The view of the city and its bay is spectacular. The citadel was occupied by the Italians and then the Germans from 1942 through 15 August 1944, when American troops, with the assistance of the residents of St-Tropez, recaptured it. The dungeon now houses a naval museum that exhibits model ships, guns, paintings, documents, and maritime objects. ♦ Admission. M, W-Su. On the eastern edge of town. 94.97.59.43

Galéries Tropéziennes Some items among this boutique's jumble will tempt you to bring the Mediterranean spirit back home. The inventory ranges from Provençal pottery, cheerfully colored table linens, and hammocks to authentic Mediterranean espadrilles and chic canvas beach bags. ♦ Daily. 56 Rue Gambetta (at Pl des Lices). 94.97.02.21

Jacqueline Thienot This antiques dealer is one of the most respected in the area. Her beautiful antique chests are anything but portable, but Thienot also sells bibelots, faience, wrought-iron objects, and other classy mementos. ♦ M-Sa; closed three weeks in November. 12 Rue Georges-Clemenceau (between Quai Suffren and Blvd Vasserot). 94.97.05.70

55 **Club 55** ★★$$$ Casual and chic, this spot run by chef-owner Patrice de Colmont and his wife is ideally located on the long, wide Plage de Pampelonne (Pampelonne Beach) in Ramatuelle. It's one of the in places to have lunch in the St-Tropez area, but not just a see-and-be-seen scene; the regulars tend to come here *en famille* (with their families) to enjoy the good cooking and lovely surroundings. An oasis of calm along the touristy Mediterranean—even during the summer—the terrace has bouquets of fresh flowers and views of the sea. Just steps from the Mediterranean, the kitchen focuses on fish; there's also a wide choice of inventive salads. A small boutique that sells beach gear adjoins the restaurant, and you can even arrange swimming lessons here. ♦ Daily lunch; closed mid-November–late December and early January–April. Reservations recommended. Plage de Pampelonne (from St-Tropez go 6 km/3.7 miles west on D93; follow the signs to the restaurant). 94.79.85.00, 94.79.80.14

Belieu

56 **Domaines de Bertaud-Belieu/Villa de Belieu** $$$$ A lavish corner of never-never land is hidden in an enormous garden on the St-Tropez peninsula; despite the proximity, it is spritually as far removed from St-Trop's crowds as you can get. The Mediterranean-

style **Villa de Belieu** (with pink-tiled roofs and creamy ocher walls) has been turned into an opulent hotel on the grounds of the **Domaines de Bertaud-Belieu**—a winery that produces very good red, white, and rosé Côtes de Provence. The 15 rooms and five suites are each decorated individually, from rococo to Art Deco; some have balconies or private gardens. All rooms are big, filled with antiques and trompe l'oeil murals (one representing erotic scenes from the Kamasutra, a medieval Indian epic poem on love), and equipped with every modern convenience, including air-conditioning. A tennis court and both indoor and outdoor pools are on the estate, as is a magnificent spa styled after Roman baths; it has been described as "a patio in Pompeii" (before the eruption of Vesuvius, presumably). A wall—guarded day and night—surrounds the estate's 10-acre park, excluding the real world. It's all tastefully gaudy with a touch of humor, and undeniably luxurious (and outrageously expensive). ♦ Presqu'île de St-Tropez (2 km/1.2 miles north of Gassin on Rte de St-Tropez). 94.56.40.56; fax 94.43.43.34

Within Domaines de Bertaud-Belieu/Villa de Belieu:

Restaurant Belieu ★★$$$$ Tables are set with fine china and antique silver, and white-gloved waiters tend to diners' every need. The Provençal cuisine focuses on seafood, and the wines are from the estate. There are several fixed-price, wine-included menus, but all are expensive. ♦ Daily lunch and dinner. Reservations required. 94.56.40.56

57 **Les Roches** $$$$ With its bougainvillea, hibiscus, rare cacti, and steep hillsides with stunning views of the azure sea, this hotel is set on a stretch of Mediterranean coast right off a picture postcard. Even in the height of summer, you can escape noise, bustle, and traffic here. Most of the 42 lovely rooms and five sumptuous suites overlook the sea; if you've had enough of the Mediterranean, take a dip in the big swimming pool or stroll in the private garden. ♦ Closed mid-November–Easter. 1 Ave des Trois-Dauphins, Aiguebelle (about 5 km/3.1 miles east of Le Lavandou and 23 km/14.2 miles southwest of St-Tropez along D559). 94.71.05.07; fax 94.71.08.40

Within Les Roches:

Restaurant Les Roches ★★★$$$ Although the sea views from the dining room and the terrace are spectacular, the real interest here—one of the most highly rated restaurants in Provence—is what appears on the plate and in the glass. The *rôti de lapin froid à l'aubergine brûlée* (cold roast rabbit with charred eggplant) and the many seafood dishes are particularly good; the wine list offers a hundred Provençal wines to choose from. ♦ Closed mid-November–Easter. Reservations required. 94.71.05.07

57 Le Jardin de Perlefleurs ★★★$$ Ask residents of Provence which local chefs produce authentic Provençal cuisine, and chef Guy Gedda is always mentioned. Gedda is an authority on Provence; his book, *La Table d'un Provençal,* gives not only recipes but also a portrait of the region he has loved for all his 60-odd years. This warm, friendly chef also founded La Tonnelle des Délices in Bormes-les-Mimosa, considered one of France's best restaurants while under his ownership. When he decided to retire from cooking a few years ago to concentrate on writing cookbooks and giving cooking classes, disappointed fans put up such an outcry that he created a small restaurant out of his home. Try to reserve a table on the terrace under the olive trees and enjoy Chef Gedda's *panisses* (chickpea-flour crepes), wonderful croutons rubbed with anchovies and herbs, sublime seafood dishes, rabbit tart, and crème brûlée with the inspired addition of local chestnuts. The wine list reflects where the chef's heart lies: He says, *"A l'exception du champagne, je n'ai que des vins de Provence (une centaine de domaines)"* (With the exception of champagne, I have only Provençal wines, from a hundred different wineries). ♦ Tu-Su lunch and dinner July-Sept; closed October-June. Reservations required far in advance; no credit cards accepted. 100 Chemin de L'Orangerie, Bormes-les-Mimosas (from Aiguebelle go about 5 km/3.1 miles west by local roads; follow the signs to Bormes-les-Mimosas). 94.64.99.23

Within Le Jardin de Perlefleurs:

Chef Guy Gedda's Ecole de Cuisine Provençale (School of Provençale Cuisine) Chef Gedda offers wonderful cooking classes in his home to professionals and amateurs alike (and he even speaks English!). His two- and three-day classes for amateurs are an excellent way to learn how to make regional specialties like bouillabaisse, *daube provençale* (a long-simmered beef stew), *fleurs de courgettes farcies* (stuffed zucchini flowers), *tarte aux pignons* (pine-nut tart), and dozens of other delights. ♦ Amateur classes W-F 10AM-5PM and Sa-Su 6PM-midnight June-Oct. No set schedule for professional classes. Reservations required far in advance; classes are limited to small groups. For course information contact Guy Gedda at 100 Chemin de L'Orangerie, 83230 Bormes-les-Mimosas. 94.64.99.23

57 Le Paradis $ A rarity for the area: a simple 20-room hotel that doesn't charge an arm and a leg, even in summer. The place is surrounded by a large garden, and it's just minutes from the sea. The small rooms are not paradisiacal by any means, but they are clean and comfortable and have private bathrooms and views of the garden. There is no restaurant, but breakfast is served.

♦ Closed October-March. No credit cards accepted. Reserve well in advance in summer. Breakfast not included in price of room. 62 Impasse Castellan, Bormes-les-Mimosas. 94.71.06.85

57 L'Escoundudo ★★$$ On a tiny street, this peaceful little eatery has a flower-bedecked terrace where you can feast on local specialties like *soupe de poisson* (fish soup), *sardines aux épinards* (fresh sardines with spinach), and *lapin sauté au polenta* (sautéed rabbit with polenta). Chef-owner Max Dandine's fixed-price menu has got to be one of the best deals along the Mediterranean. ♦ Closed mid-November–mid-December and January-February. Reservations recommended. 2 Ruelle du Moulin, Bormes-les-Mimosas. 94.71.15.53

58 Mas du Langoustier $$$$ Around the turn of the century, F.J. Fournier, a silver-mining ancestor of the present owners of this hotel, offered the Ile de Porquerolles—an impossibly beautiful island in the Mediterranean—to his young wife as a wedding present. Today, a room in the island's hotel must cost about as much as the island itself did back then—but if any hotel along the coast is worth these prices, this one is. Some of the 57 rooms and four suites are in a sprawling turn-of-the-century *mas* with ocher stucco walls and pale blue shutters; others are in a new but charming annex. All have been tastefully decorated and have wonderful views of the sea or a flower-filled garden. A few ground-floor rooms have private terraces overlooking the water. You can play billiards or rent a boat, swim in the Mediterranean or bicycle around the picturesque, pine-covered island, but there's not a disco anywhere in sight. Peace and quiet reign, and nightlife here is a stroll along the beach after a great dinner. ♦ Closed November-April. Ile de Porquerolles (20 km/12.4 miles southeast of Toulon, reached by helicopter or by ferries that leave several times daily from Giens, Port d'Hyères, Cavalaire, and Toulon; contact the hotel for schedule of crossings). 94.58.30.09; fax 94.58.36.02

Within Mas du Langoustier:

Restaurant Mas du Langoustier ★★★$$$ The excellent Provençal specialties include *langoustines au romarin* (crayfish with rosemary) and an opulent *bourride* (creamy, garlicky fish soup). The wine list includes wines produced nearby on the island by the **Domaine de l'Ile.** Prices are high, but the fantastic fixed-price menu (wine included) is really worth the trip to this isolated spot. ♦ Closed November-April. Reservations required far in advance. 94.58.30.09; fax 94.58.36.02

Domaine de l'Ile

58 Domaine de l'Ile When F.J. Fournier bought the island of Porquerolles in 1910, he planted 180 hectares (444.7 acres) of vines. Today one of his descendants, Sebastien Le Ber, is in charge of the family winery. The grapes are cultivated organically; no chemical insecticides, herbicides, or fertilizers are used. Grapes are picked manually, and yields are kept low. The red wines are made from grenache, mourvèdre, and syrah, and the rosés from grenache, cinsault, tibouren, and mourvèdre. These wines, particularly the excellent rosés, seem to radiate the charm of their *terroir*. ◆ Free. Visits and tastings by appointment. Ile de Porquerolles. 94.58.31.60; fax 94.58.31.03

59 Domaine de Terrebrune Housed in a *mas*, this winery is surrounded by olive trees, a flower-filled garden, and vineyards that slope down to the sea. The vines are cultivated organically, using natural yeasts in the traditional manner; the reds are aged in oak. They are made from grenache and cinsault mixed with mourvèdre, which gives a fruitier, more supple wine than the pure mourvèdre type. Don't miss the wonderful 1988 vintage. All Terrebrune wines are sure to please, though, and an additional draw is the restaurant on the premises (see below). ◆ Visits and tastings daily. Chemin de la Tourelle, just west of Ollioules via Rte du Gros-Cerveau (from Toulon go 3.5 km/1.86 miles north on D26). 94.74.01.30

Within the Domaine de Terrebrune:

La Table du Vigneron ★★$$ With a name like this, a restaurant is bound to serve great wines and good food to go with them, and that's just what this one does. The Delille brothers operate a friendly place that features Provençal specialties like *brandade* (a mixture of mashed potatoes and salt cod) and *anchoïade* (anchovy spread), along with grilled meats and their own fine Bandol wines. The spacious dining room has a beamed ceiling, whitewashed walls, a red tile floor, a big fireplace with a rotisserie, and huge windows opening onto a luxuriant garden. After dining, tour the wine cellars beneath the restaurant. ◆ Daily lunch and dinner. Reservations required. 94.88.36.19 (during meal times), 94.74.01.30

Restaurants/Clubs: Red   **Hotels:** Blue
Shops/ 🍃 Outdoors: Green   **Sights/Culture:** Black

60 Bandol This established vacation resort with an attractive coastline and a touch of understated elegance is also a major appellation. It's not just a place to drive through and taste the wine; you should stay the night at **La Ker Mocotte** or try a meal at **L'Auberge du Port.** ◆ 4 km (2.5 miles) west of Toulon on D559

Within Bandol:

La Ker Mocotte $$$ In a villa with a terrace overlooking the Mediterranean, this very comfortable 20-room hotel was once the home of Raimu, a popular actor who starred in many Marcel Pagnol films, including *La Femme du Boulanger* (The Baker's Wife). There's a swimming pool, a private beach, and a restaurant. The only catch is that the room rates in July and August double—as does the population of Bandol—and guests are required to eat in the restaurant then too. Off-season, it's a great bargain. ◆ Rue Raimu. 94.29.46.53; fax 94.32.53.54

L'Auberge du Port ★★$$ Seafood is on the menu and the sea is almost at your feet when you sip a glass of Bandol rosé on the terrace of this flower-filled restaurant. It's a hangout for local wine makers, whose best bottles are represented on the wine list. ◆ Daily lunch and dinner. Reservations required. 9 Allée Jean-Moulin. 94.29.42.63; fax 94.29.44.59

61 Domaine Tempier This magical winery is the fruit of one man's vision. When Lucien Peyraud married Lucie (known as Lulu) Tempier in 1936, her father gave the young couple some vineyards at the **Domaine Tempier**, his large tile-roofed Provençal *mas* on a hilltop overlooking a garden and vineyards. Seven years and four children later, amid wartime bombings and food shortages, Lucien bottled his first vintage. The winery is still located in buildings adjoining the Tempier home.

Over the years Lucien Peyraud was responsible for achieving appellation status for Bandol wines, for motivating neighboring wine makers to opt for quality, and for upping the required percentage of mourvèdre grapes in *AOC* Bandol wines to 50 percent. The mourvèdre, grown in Bandol for centuries, ripens late and has low yields, but wines made from it are immensely powerful, long-lived, and rich. Lucien has always favored traditional methods, which are now being carried on by his two sons: no herbicides or artificial yeasts, stemming because *"les tanins nobles sont dans le raisin"* (the noble tannins are in the grape, not the stems), and no use of new wood (because it masks the unique taste of mourvèdre). Red wines from some of the winery's prime vineyards are bottled separately: Cabassaou (100 percent 50-year-old mourvèdre vines), La Migoua, and La Tourtine. The reds can be drunk in their fruity youth, but will become even more complex with age; after 20 years in the bottle, they are sublime. The estate also produces a full-flavored rosé made to be drunk young.

There's another remarkable facet to this estate. Few wine makers in France so clearly convey the intimate relationship of wine and food, and the love that goes into making and enjoying fine wines, as do the Peyrauds of Domaine Tempier. Lulu Peyraud is a fine cook, whom Alice Waters (of the famed Chez Panisse restaurant in Berkeley, California) considers a mentor. This special wine-making family and Lulu's delectable recipes are the subjects of *Lulu's Provençal Table* (1994; HarperCollins), a cookbook by their friend and neighbor, food writer Richard Olney. As Olney puts it, "In Provence, cuisine and wine are as inseparable as Lulu and Lucien." ◆ Free. Visits and tastings M-F; Sa 9AM-noon. From Bandol go 6 km (3.7 miles) north on A50; follow the signs to the winery. 94.98.70.21; fax 94.90.21.65

62 Cassis Sit by the old port, watch the boats go by, drink a glass of white wine, and sample the Mediterranean's freshest fish. What more could you want on a vacation? According to the 20,000 or so Europeans who vacation here every year: nothing. The majestic views of the vineyards against the steep cliffs of Cap Canaille, a high cliff above the azure Mediterranean, make the stay complete. ◆ From Bandol take D559 25 km/15.5 miles west

Within Cassis:

Clos Sainte-Magdeleine For sheer beauty of location, this winery wins the grand prize. The vines are planted along the foot of Cap Canaille, and the vineyard boasts a stunning view of the Baie de Cassis. Georgina Zafiropulo and her husband François Sack produce richly flavored, mouth-filling white and rosé wines; François Sack says that since their wines are low in acidity, the focus is on *"onctuosité"* (unctuousness). The whites have overtones of preserved citrus fruits and honey, with an elusive hint of the sea; they are simultaneously light and full-flavored, a great match for simply grilled seafood. The whites are made primarily of marsanne grapes with a touch of ungi and sauvignon; the rosé is mainly mourvèdre. ◆ Free. Visits M-Sa. Ave du Revestel, on the eastern edge of Cassis at the foot of Cap Canaille. 42.01.70.28; fax 42.01.70.28

Hôtel Le Grand Jardin $ The garden of this budget hotel isn't as "grand" as all that, but the management is friendly, the 28 rooms are comfortable (all have private baths, mini-bars, and garden views), and you can have breakfast on a flower-filled terrace. ◆ 2 Rue Pierre-Eydin. 42.01.70.10; fax 42.01.33.75

Hôtel Royal Cottage $$$ Just steps from the beach and the port of Cassis, this small (21-room, four-suite) hotel is in a perfect location. The spacious rooms, all luxuriously decorated in contemporary style, have views of Cap Canaille or a garden. All rooms have private balconies or terraces and are equipped with mini-bars, safes, direct-dial telephones, and satellite TVs. The garden boasts a pool and a Jacuzzi. There's no restaurant—which can be an advantage in July and August, when guests at most places are required to take *pension* (meals). ◆ 6 Ave 11-Novembre, above the port by way of Ave Augustin-Isnard. 42.01.33.34; fax 42.01.06.90

Chez Gilbert ★★$$ A local institution, this rustic dining room is known for such seafood specialties as *brochettes de queues de crevettes* (shrimp brochettes), local fare like *pieds-et-pacquets* (a Marseilles treat made from lambs' feet and tripe—not for the faint-hearted), and a famous bouillabaisse (for two people minimum) that must be ordered a day ahead. **Chez Gilbert's** interior—all in blues—offsets the marine ambience of the port which the restaurant overlooks directly. ◆ M, W, F-Su lunch and dinner and Tu, Th dinner Apr-Oct; M, Th-Su lunch and dinner Oct-Apr. 19 Quai des Baux. 42.01.71.36

Restaurant La Presqu'île ★★★$$$ The great view from this Provençal villa of the sea and the port of Cassis sets the stage for the fine seafood. Choices include *salade de homard à la ciboulette* (lobster salad with chives) and *filet de loup aux olives noires* (sea bass with black olives). Some meat dishes are on hand for confirmed carnivores, and the wine list has many hard-to-find vintages of Cassis and Bandols. ◆ Tu-Sa lunch and dinner, M dinner July-Aug; Tu-Sa lunch and dinner May-June and Sept; closed October-April. Reservations recommended. Quartier Port-Miou. 42.01.03.77; 42.01.94.49

Monique Provence Monique Piche stocks her great gift shop with all kinds of items from the famous Soulëiado Provençal fabric company, pottery from the village of Uzès and elsewhere in the region, and other temptations. She also purveys the good Cassis wine, Domaine Couronne de Charlemagne, made by her husband, Bernard. ◆ M-Sa. 2 Rue Pierre-Eydin. 42.01.70.10

Corsica

The island of **Corse (Corsica)**, aptly nicknamed *"Ile de Beauté"* (Island of Beauty), lies in the Mediterranean about 160 kilometers (100 miles) off the **Côte d'Azur**. It has been part of France for centuries (Napoleon was born here), but has retained a language and culture all its own. Separatist groups are fighting to free Corsica from French rule, and bombings of French and other foreign buildings on the island have strained relations and caused a decline in tourism. It's a shame for travelers, because Corsica is without a doubt one of the most dazzling parts of France. Its coastline and interior are mainly unspoiled. Those arriving by boat can smell the island's herby *maquis* (undergrowth) and pine forests from miles away. Beaches are generally clean and lovely, and hill villages in the island's mountainous interior have been largely unchanged for centuries. The additional draw for the wine lover is that Corsica produces its own wines. Although they are often linked with those of nearby **Provence,** Corsica's wines are as unique as the island. Each area has its own grapes, which are rarely blended with grapes from other areas. Among the grape varieties grown here (some of which are not grown anywhere else) are sciacarello, grown near **Ajaccio;** nielluccio (the Italian sangiovese); vermentino (malvoisie, a white grape); muscat; and small amounts of barbarossa, aleatico, carcajolo, cordivarta, and élégante (grenache). Syrah and mourvèdre are beginning to be introduced. Most of the wines on Corsica are red, but some dry and sweet whites and a few rosés are also made.

Some excellent wineries lie near Corsica's major cities. They are open to visitors Monday through Saturday unless otherwise noted, but you may want to call ahead to be sure someone will be there when you arrive. Try **Clos Capitoro** (Rte Sartène, Pisciatella; from Ajaccio take N194 east about 12.5 km/7.75 miles, 95.25.19.61); **Domaine Comte Peraldi** (Chemin de Stiletto, Mezzavia; from Ajaccio take N193 north 6.5 km/4 miles, 95.22.37.30); **Clos d'Alzeto** (in Sari d'Orcino; from Ajaccio, take N193 north to D81 north, then take D201 east to D1 east, about a 48-km/30-mile trip, 95.52.24.67), which nestles in a lovely site between mountains and the sea; **Clos Landry** (Rte de l'Aéroport; from Calvi, take N197 south to D251 south, about a 7- km/4.3-mile

trip, 95.65.04.25); and **Domaine Culombu** (Chemin San Pedru, Lumio; 10 km/6.2 miles northeast of Calvi via N197, 95.60.70.68). At **Domaine de Torraccia** (Rte de Bastia, Lecci; 10 km/6.2 miles north of Porto Vecchio; 95.71.43.50; fax 95.71.50.03), you can also buy the estate's wonderful olive oil and stroll around the magnificent countryside.

One of the island's loveliest wine-growing areas is the beautiful **Cap Corse** peninsula in the north, where the unspoiled hilly landscape slopes above a turquoise sea. The main wineries here are clustered on or near D81 between the towns of **Patrimonio** and **St-Florent.** Two to try are **Domaine Leccia** (in Poggio d'Oletta, 95.39.03.22) and **Orenga de Gaffory** (in Patrimonio, 95.37.11.38), both of which are closed Satuday and Sunday in the winter. The charming estate **Antoine Arena** (95.37.08.27) is also in Patrimonio. Take the time for a leisurely drive all around the peninsula, stopping to enjoy its picturesque fishing villages, a swim, and a picnic overlooking the sea.

Among the reliable hotels on Corsica are **Château Calvello** ($; 95.37.01.15), a 16th-century château near Patrimonio that offers three bed-and-breakfast rooms and three fully equipped apartments that can be rented by the week; **La Jetée** ($; 95.35.64.46), a simple hotel in the village of Centuri-Port on Cap Corse whose restaurant serves the freshest possible seafood; **Les Roches Rouges** ($$; 95.27.81.81), in the village of Piana between Calvi and Ajaccio, which offers peace and quiet by the beach; and **Mare Monti** ($$; 95.61.73.06), a former mansion converted to a comfortable hotel, near Calvi.

For information on Corsica's wines, contact the **Groupement Interprofessionnelle des vins de l'île de Corse (GIVIC;** 13 Blvd du Fango, 20200 Bastia, 95.32.84.40). This organization publishes an excellent map listing all Corsica's wineries and their visiting policies.

The French national domestic airline, **Air Inter,** flies several times a day from Paris and other cities to Ajaccio, Bastia, and Calvi. Ferries for Corsica leave from several points on France's Mediterranean coast, including Nice and Marseilles; for information, call the **Société Nationale de Corse Maritime** (in Marseilles 91.56.32.00, in Paris 1/49.24.24.24).

---

63 Calanques When the traffic jams and crowds of the coast in summer make it seem that no unspoiled natural beauty is left along the Mediterranean, it's time to discover the *calanques*. The *calanques* are fjords between Cassis and Marseilles, inlets of turquoise water surrounded by dry, white, rocky cliffs. They were once covered with maritime pines, but many of these have been destroyed by forest fires; as a preventive measure, many of the cliffs are off-limits in very dry periods. At other times you can hike along the cliffs and

down to the water, or hire one of the many small boats to take you along the magnificent coastline and into the *calanques*. The area was declared a protected natural site in 1975 and has so far escaped development, but Marseilles's mayor has been proposing various tourist facilities here—a plan vigorously opposed by local environmentalists.

La Calanque de Port-Miou is the nearest to Cassis (about a 30-minute walk from the center of town, or drive to the head of a path where you will see signs leading you to La Calanque, the cliffs, and the water). Once you reach the "Col de la Gardiole" parking lot (about two miles west of Cassis), take the GR 98B national hiking trail to La Calanque de Port-Pin; a tiny beach, reached by a narrow path, sits at the base of the cliff here. Continue along to La Calanque d'En-Vau, which is the prettiest of all, with extremely rugged cliffs jutting out of the clear blue water; there's a small beach here, too. The two *calanques* closest to Marseilles, Sormiou, and Morgiou, are dotted by small villages inhabited mainly by Robinson Crusoe–types who live in fishers' huts without running water or electricity; a city bus (No. 20) from Marseilles travels to them. Always carry drinking water on a *calanque* visit, even if you're just planning a short hike. ♦ West of Cassis on GR98

64 Promenade de la Corniche This scenic coastal route (actually D559) offers some of the most spectacular views along the Mediterranean. There are lookout points along the way where you can stop the car and take pictures. The road turns into the lovely Promenade du Président-Kennedy just before reaching Marseilles. ♦ Runs from Cassis to Marseilles

Marseilles

Marseilles inspires strong emotion; it's a place people either love or hate, and by the time you leave you'll probably feel a little of both. This sprawling city, France's second-largest in population, is certainly not known for its wine production, but is the place where wines from the Rhône Valley, Provence, and Languedoc can all be found.

A lively melting pot of races and cultures since its beginning, Marseilles was founded by the Phocaeans in 600 BC. Over the centuries, it became an important port on the Mediterranean, but it wasn't until 1792 that Marseilles assumed profound importance in the national consciousness. That was when volunteer soldiers, in an effort to aid the Revolution, marched from Marseilles to Paris singing a song composed by a young officer, Rouget de Lisle. That song, "La Marseillaise," is now France's national anthem.

Modern-day Marseilles seems barely able to live up to that honor, as the city has horrendous traffic jams, a drug problem (one reason the film *The French Connection* was set partly here), a strong element of racism, and some unsafe areas, particularly around the **Porte d'Aix** and the **Rue Ste-Barbe.** But for a sample of all the passion, contrasts, and colors of southern France, Marseilles has no equal. The teeming old port is a wonderful backdrop to both the colors of the sea and the town's ancient stone buildings. The restaurants can be outstanding and the city

MARSEILLES

Mediterranean Sea

Bassin de la Grande-Joliette

Quai Jean-Charcot

Avant-Port de la Joliette

Rue de l'Anse-du-Pharo

Jardin du Pharo

Blvd. Charles-Livon

Rue des Catalans

Rue Charras

Ave. Pasteur

79

Ave. de la Corse

lays claim to the world's best bouillabaisse. And getting around is simple, if you keep out of cars: An efficient subway system runs throughout the city.

65 Château d'If (Yew-Tree Castle) On a small rocky island jutting out of Marseilles's bay, this 16th-century château was once used as a prison. The most famous (if fictional) of the prison's inmates was the Count of Monte-Cristo, incarcerated here by Alexandre Dumas. According to legend, the "man in the iron mask" was held prisoner here; although a cell is marked as having been his, the truth is that he never stayed here. The panoramic view from the old chapel terrace is magnificent. Also note the Huguenot carvings on the wall in some cells. ♦ Fee. Ferries depart for the island from the Quai des Belges in Marseilles on the hour 9AM-5PM May-Oct; 9AM, 11AM, 2PM, 3:30PM, and 5PM Nov-Apr

66 Le Vieux Port Marseilles's ancient port, founded in 600 BC, saw heavy maritime traffic until the 19th century. The north quay, with its labyrinth of medieval alleyways, was a hideout for members of the Resistance movement during World War II, and was heavily bombed by German forces in 1943. One of the city's

great sights is the fish market held daily along the Quai des Belges beginning at about 8AM. The freshest seafood is sold *"à la criée"* (the merchants tout their wares at the tops of their voices). A ferry travels several times a day (7AM-6:30PM) between the Quai du Port and the Quai de Rive-Neuve on the opposite side of the port; a one-way trip costs about a dollar and offers a great view of the city. *Le Petit Train de la Bonne Mère* (91.73.28.98), a sightseeing train, departs from the Vieux Port several times daily and runs up the hill to the **Basilica de Notre-Dame-de-la-Garde,** which overlooks the city; it's well worth the trip for the spectacular view, especially at sunset. Boats leave the Quai des Belges on the hour (9AM-5PM) for the Iles Frioul (Frioul Islands) southwest of the city; the islands offer a quiet retreat from the urban frenzy, and several simple restaurants. In summer, other boats leave the Quai des Belges for a four-hour round-trip tour of the *calanques,* the pristine fjords of the Mediterranean coast (departures at 2PM Wednesday, Saturday, and Sunday from mid-June through mid-September).
♦ Bounded by the Quai du Port and the Quai de Rive-Neuve

67 Le Panier One of the city's oldest neighborhoods and certainly its most picturesque is the ancient fishers' quarter, where immigrants from all over the Mediterranean region settled. The whole area is a hillside maze of tiny alleys, many of them connected by steep staircases on which prostitutes have traditionally stood. Today Le Panier is being gentrified; many of the ancient houses have been turned into shops, friendly bistros, and art galleries, and most of the prostitutes have moved elsewhere. Despite its former dangerous reputation, the area is now chic and safe, and the vivid images of Old Marseilles here will stay in your mind forever.
♦ Bounded by Rue Caisserie and Rue du Panier, and Rue de la République and Rue de l'Evêche

---

The oldest grape seeds discovered came from the Republic of Georgia; carbon dating has revealed them to be from 7000 to 5000 BC.

Restaurants/Clubs: Red   **Hotels:** Blue
Shops/ 🌳 Outdoors: Green   **Sights/Culture:** Black

Marseilles Nightlife

Days in the bustling port of Marseilles can be full—boating on the glistening water, wandering through ancient neighborhoods—but be sure to conserve some energy for exploring its active nightlife too. Below is some of the entertainment enjoyed most by the city's creatures of the night.

Ballet Roland-Petit (1 Pl Auguste-Carli, 91.47.94.88) is one of France's finest dance companies and the name of the theater it calls home. The season runs from May to October, although the troupe mounts occasional performances at other times.

Le Bar de la Marine (15 Quai Rive-Neuve, 91.54.95.42) is so picturesque it looks like a film set. And indeed it has been—scenes from some of Marcel Pagnol's films were shot here. Drinks and light snacks are served at low prices. Marseilles's artists comes here to chat over glasses of wine or *pastis* (anise-flavored aperitifs).

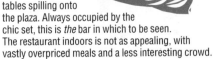

Bistro Thiars (★$$$; 13A Pl de Thiars, 91.54.03.94) has tables spilling onto the plaza. Always occupied by the chic set, this is *the* bar in which to be seen. The restaurant indoors is not as appealing, with vastly overpriced meals and a less interesting crowd.

Centre Julien (33 Cours Julien, 91.47.09.64), a former warehouse, is now a labyrinth of restaurants, theaters, and other venues offering jazz concerts, plays, dance, and fine-art exhibits.

68 **Centre de la Vieille Charité** (Old Charity Center) This suberb 17th-century building (designed by famed Renaissance architect **Pierre Puget**) was originally built to shelter the homeless and serve as a prison hospital, but today it houses an art museum. It is built of pink and white stone; in the center of the courtyard is a chapel topped with an ovoid cupola. The building was almost a ruin when the architect **Le Corbusier** successfully campaigned to have it made an official historic monument. After years of renovation, it reopened in its current incarnation in 1986. The museum mounts changing exhibits of contemporary art, and has permanent collections of African and American Indian art, and extensive exhibits on Mediterranean archaeology. After a visit, stroll around the picturesque streets nearby, including the Place des Moulins, the Rue des Muettes, and the Ruelle des Moulins. ♦ Admission. T-Su. 2 Rue de la Charité (between Rue de l'Observance and Rue Vieille-Tour). 91.56.28.38

69 **Le Jardin des Vestiges de la Bourse/Musée d'Histoire de Marseille** (Gardens of the Vestiges of the Stock Market/Museum of Marseilles History) During a 1967 construction project near the city's stock exchange (*la Bourse*), workers discovered the vestiges of the ancient port of Massilia, long thought to have vanished without a trace. In 1974 a wooden boat dating from the third century was discovered in the same area. Bits of the original ramparts and quays are exhibited here in a garden; here too is the history museum, with a well-organized, informative display of relics documenting the city's long past, including that ancient boat and a section of a sewer system installed here by the Romans. ♦ Admission. M-Sa noon-7PM. Rue Henri-Barbusse (between Rue Neuve-St-Martin and Rue Bir-Hakeim). 91.90.42.22

70 **La Canebière** This is Broadway and the Champs-Elysées all rolled into one, with the tacky excesses of the former and the chic shops of the latter—plus the mass of pedestrians and traffic jams of both. Choked with shoppers and workers during the day, the sidewalks empty at night. ♦ From Rue de la République to Sq de Verdun

71 **Pullman Beauvau** $$$ Ideally located overlooking the Vieux Port, this hotel once hosted George Sand, Chopin, and composer François Poulenc (who had his grand piano hauled up to the fifth floor). The whole place has been completely renovated and modernized, but the 72 spacious rooms, all sunny, comfortable, and quiet, contain some of the hotel's original antique furnishings. The chic bar is open until 1AM, and meals are available through room service, but there's no restaurant. All in all, a very good deal. ♦ 4 Rue Beauvau (at Rue St-Saëns). 91.54.91.00; fax 91.54.15.76

72 **St-Ferréol's Hotel** $$ A great value, this turn-of-the-century hotel near the Vieux Port has been totally renovated, and offers 19 rooms. Each is comfortable and quiet, but small, and has been given the name of a painter (Van Gogh, Gauguin). All have marble bathrooms, air-conditioning, direct-dial phones, and satellite TV; the more expensive rooms have Jacuzzis. The generous continental breakfasts include fresh orange juice, and the management is friendly. There's a small bar, but no restaurant. ♦ Closed late July–late August. 19 Rue Pisançon (at Rue St-Ferréol). 91.33.12.21; fax 91.54.29.97

73 **Chez Loury** ★★★$$ With Monsieur Loury in the kitchen and Madame in the dining room, this place near the Vieux Port has developed a loyal following. You'll see why once you taste the spectacular bouillabaisse, the *oursins rôtis* (roasted sea urchins) and, if you dare,

the *pieds-et-paquets* (lamb tripe and feet, a local specialty). The simply grilled fish is the freshest possible. The excellent choice of wines includes the finest of the south: Côtes du Rhône, Aix-en-Provence (Château Simone), Bandol (including Domaine Tempier), and Cassis. It all adds up to one of the best quality-price ratios in Marseilles. ♦ M-Sa lunch and dinner; closed the last two weeks in May. Reservations required. 3 Rue Fortia (between Rue St-Saëns and Cours d'Estienne-d'Orves). 91.33.09.73; fax 91.33.73.21

74 Les Arcenaulx ★★$$ This local favorite features authentic Marseilles cooking, such as *loup poché au vin rouge* (sea bass poached in red wine) and *sardines marinés* (marinated fresh sardines). The wine list, with many wines of the south, is very reasonably priced. The restaurant is part of a complex that includes a bookstore and an antiques shop. ♦ M-Sa lunch and dinner. Reservations required. 25 Cours d'Estienne-d'Orves (between Rue de la Paix and Rue Euthymènes). 91.54.77.06; fax 91.54.76.33

75 L'Ambassade des Vignobles ★★★$$$ Wine lovers must not miss having a meal at this place owned by a group of top restaurateurs and sommeliers. Each dish is served with a wine that will set it off perfectly; *lapereau au basilic* (young rabbit with basil) is paired with a full-flavored Château Simone white Palette from near Aix-en-Provence, for example. Choose between three fixed-price, wine-included menus, or order à la carte. The Provençal cuisine is excellent, as are the wines, and the setting (old stone walls and heavy ceiling beams) is lovely. ♦ M-F lunch and dinner, Sa dinner; closed in August. Reservations recommended. 42 Pl aux Huiles (between Rue de la Paix and Rue Fort-Notre-Dame). 91.33.00.25; fax 91.54.25.60

76 Patalain ★★★$$$ Local legend Suzanne Quaglia dishes up authentic Marseilles fare in her warm, cozy restaurant. Try her *filets de rouget à l'aubergine* (red mullet fillets with eggplant), *risotto aux coquillages* (shellfish risotto), and other regional specialties. ♦ M-F lunch and dinner, Sa dinner; closed mid-July–early September. Reservations required. 49 Rue Sainte (at Rue de la Paix). 91.55.02.78; fax 91.54.15.29

77 La Four des Navettes Marseilles's oldest bakery has been producing a local specialty, *navettes,* since 1781. These sweet, boat-shaped breads flavored with orange-flower water are baked here in a medieval bread oven. Delicious fresh, they also can be kept for up to a year in the metal boxes they're sold in; just heat them for a few seconds before eating. ♦ Daily. 136 Rue Sainte (between Rue Chantier and Rue Robert). 91.33.32.12

78 Ateliers Marcel Carbonel For a classic souvenir of Marseilles, visit this family-run workshop, which makes and paints *santons* (clay crèche figures) by hand. Some are nativity figures, but the best keepsakes are those that represent ordinary people from rural Provence: a woman holding a braid of garlic, a shepherdess with her flock, a fisherman, a robber, a man with a basket of chickens on his head, all wearing typical regional costumes of the 19th (or earlier) century. There are also models of buildings (a stable, a farmhouse, and the like) in which the figures can be displayed. The painstaking attention to detail makes clear why the family annually wins top awards at the "Meilleur Ouvrier de France" (Best French Craftsman) contest. The items are not designed for tourists; displays of *santons* are a cherished part of Christmas celebrations throughout southern France, and antique *santons* are popular collectibles. Visitors can watch the craftspeople at work here, but the figures are also sold in numerous shops in Marseilles. Just be warned: You may intend to buy one or two, but find you can't bear to leave without an entire collection. ♦ M-Sa; closed in August. 47 Rue Neuve-Ste-Catherine (at Rue Robert). 91.54.26.58

79 Résidence Le Petit Nice $$$$ An extravagant Relais & Châteaux establishment, this is by far the city's finest hotel. The sprawling white 19th-century villa has a stunning view of the sea and coastline. There are only 13 rooms and two suites, all spacious and elegantly decorated in a very contemporary style, with air-conditioning, TVs, mini-bars, safes, and other amenities. One of the suites has a sauna and a private terrace overlooking the sea; the other has a Jacuzzi with a golden fish-shaped faucet. No wonder the guestbook has been signed by the likes of Joan Baez. ♦ Closed January and the first week in February. About 2 km (1.25 miles) south of the Vieux Port on Corniche Kennedy, Anse Maldormé. 91.59.25.92; fax 91.59.28.08

Within the Résidence Le Petit Nice:

Restaurant Passadat ★★★★$$$$ One of the most highly rated in France, this restaurant features the fine cuisine of chefs Jean-Paul and Gérald Passédat, who excel in modern variations on local specialties. Try the *morue truffé à la marseillaise* (a mound of pureed salt cod studded with truffles) or the *agneau rôti au jus de thym* (roast lamb with thyme sauce). All the flavors are exquisite, but the portions will not please hearty eaters. The wine list is absolutely sensational, with a big selection of rare burgundies, of all things, as well as many wines from southern France. But be warned: Prices are sky-high. ♦ M-F lunch and dinner, Sa dinner; closed January and the first week in February. Reservations required far in advance. 91.59.25.92

80 La Cité Radieuse (Radiant City) Among **Le Corbusier**'s most famous projects, this building was designed as low-cost housing, with 350 apartments, a school, a hotel, sports facilities, and other services all under one roof. Built between 1947 and 1952, it was dubbed *"La Maison du Fada"* (The Lunatic's House), because its low, unfussy, long lines seemed bizarre at the time. Today it looks amazingly up-to-date, and airy in spite of its bulk. ♦ 280 Blvd Michelet (from Quai des Belges take La Canebière east to Cours St-Louis, then take Cours St-Louis, which eventually turns into Blvd Michelet, south 4.3 km/2.6 miles). No phone

Within La Cité Radieuse:

Hôtel Le Corbusier $ Fans of modern architecture shouldn't miss a stay in this **Le Corbusier**–designed hotel. The management is friendly, the 23 small and very simple rooms decorated in 1950s style are comfortable (although a bit scruffy these days), and the prices are low: just what the master had in mind, no doubt. ♦ 91.77.18.15

On the Road to Languedoc

81 Arles Founded in 49 BC, one of the town's major claims to fame is that it was home to Vincent van Gogh in the late 1880s. Although he stayed here only a year, Van Gogh helped turn Arles into a household name. The sun blazing down on its narrow streets and lush countryside inspired him to paint more than 200 canvases here in that brief time. The house where Van Gogh lived was destroyed during World War II, but there is now a cafe where his house used to be. **Le Café Van Gogh** ($; Pl du Forum, 90.49.83.30) serves coffee, tea, and light snacks. Though not on this route, for a complete Van Gogh tour, take D17 east 19 kilometers/12 miles, then take D5 north for 10 kilometers/6.2 miles to the town of **St-Rémy-de-Provence,** where the painter spent most of his final days cloistered in the hospital on the grounds of the **St-Paul-de-Mausole** monastery (Ave Le Roy, no phone). The cloisters and the chapel can be visited daily. There is no admission charge. There is also a **Centre d'Art Van Gogh** (Rue Estrine, opposite Town Hall, 90.92.34.72) completely devoted to the works of Van Gogh.

Arles also caught Pablo Picasso's fancy, and he donated more than 50 of his drawings to the town. All are on view at the **Musée Réattu** (10 Rue du Grand-Trieuré, at Quai Marx-Dormoy, 90.96.37.68). The museum is open daily and charges admission.

Roman ruins still stud the city, including the magnificent amphitheater, **Les Arènes** (which is still in use and seats over 25,000).

Just west of Arles begins one of the most wild, unspoiled parts of France, **La Camargue**

(90.97.00.97), a region of marshes that meets the sea. Most of the area is now a nature preserve which can be visited daily and is reachable by car. Birds and the famous Camargue wild horses, a tough, small, white breed, thrive here. Admission is charged. To get to the preserve from Arles take N570 three kilometers (1.9 miles) west to D36, then take D36 south toward Salin de Giraud and follow signs for **La Réserve Nationale de Camargue.** ♦ 90 km (55.8 miles) northwest of Marseilles on N568

82 Nîmes Another sun-baked city, colorful Nîmes has been admired for centuries; Celtic tribes built a menhir (standing stone) here 4,000 years ago. But the Romans were responsible for the city's most memorable landmark, its arena (see below). Nîmes's other great Roman relic is **La Maison Carrée** (Square House), which was built as a temple (see below). A not-to-be-missed annual event is the *Feria des Vendanges* (Grape Harvest Fair) held the third week of September; wine samples flow among the other festivities. ♦ 28 km (17.3 miles) northwest of Arles on E80-A54

Within Nîmes:

Nîmes Amphitheater Built between AD 50 and 100 for matches between gladiators, Nîmes's arena is still used for another blood-thirsty sport—bullfighting. Inspired by the Colosseum in Rome, the arena—with 20,000 seats—is one of the world's best-preserved Roman monuments. When the bulls and matadors aren't battling here, concerts and theatrical events are held; the arena has great acoustics, especially in winter, when a temporary roof covers it. ♦ Admission. Visits can be arranged through the Nîmes tourist office (66.67.29.11). Pl des Arènes (at Blvd Victor-Hugo and Rue de la République). Box office 66.67.45.76

La Maison Carrée (Square House) This beautiful creamy yellow stone temple was built between AD 3 and 5. Although known as the Square House, the columned building is actually rectangular. It now houses an anti-quities museum. ♦ Free. Daily (no midday closing) July-Sept; daily Oct-June. Pl de la Maison-Carrée (between Rue de l'Horloge and Rue Général-Perrier). No phone

Le Carré d'Art One of the finest libraries in France, this boasts some 300,000 books (a third of which can be borrowed) on all subjects. The building also houses the **Musée d'Art Contemporain** (Museum of Contemporary Art), whose 300 works include paintings and photographs from the 1960s and later. The museum's *centre de documentation* contains books, periodicals, and videos on France's contemporary art scene. ♦ Admission. Tu-Su (no midday closing). Pl de la Maison-Carrée (between Rue de l'Horloge and Rue Général-Perrier). 66.76.35.35

Restaurants/Clubs: Red	Hotels: Blue
Shops/ ♦ Outdoors: Green	Sights/Culture: Black

L'Orangerie $$ Housed in a converted *mas* with its own large garden and swimming pool, this hotel has real class. The 29 rooms and three suites are big, quiet—they've been soundproofed—and sunny; all are decorated in contemporary style and have private bathrooms, air-conditioning, satellite TV, mini-bars, and direct-dial phones. Some have views of the pool, others look out over a garden; several rooms have balconies. The ground-floor rooms are accessible to the disabled. Although the hotel is on the big highway that loops around the city, you won't notice once inside. It is well removed from the city center of Nîmes, but that can be an advantage in the heat and crush of summer. ♦ 755 Rue Tour-de-l'Evêque (at Blvd Président-Allende). 66.84.50.57; fax 66.29.44.55

Within L'Orangerie:

Restaurant L'Orangerie ★★$$$ Regional dishes like *brandade* (potato and salt-cod puree) with carpaccio are featured in this warm, yet sophisticated, place. The wine list offers many excellent wines from southern France. ♦ Daily lunch and dinner. Reservations recommended. 66.84.50.57

Languedoc

The name of this colorful former province in the southwestern corner of France means "language of *oc*." It refers to the dialect used in the southern half of the country during the Middle Ages, in which *oc* rather than *oui* meant "yes." While the people of this area no longer say *"oc,"* their accents are definitely not Parisian; you'll hear *"jardang"* for *"jardin,"* in a twang reminiscent of the southwestern United States.

With its lush fields, valleys, orchards, and vineyards, its beautiful beaches, and rugged **Cevennes Mountains**, Languedoc is filled with spectacular beauty. It also retains vestiges of its past rulers, especially the Romans. Languedoc is crowned by the historic city of **Montpellier**, which is famed for its university and for being the site of France's first medical school, which was founded in the 13th century. Although the fastest-growing city in France, Montpellier has preserved its charm, and is filled with public gardens and plazas.

Both Languedoc and Roussillon are known for their independent spirit (separatist movements often gain ground in local elections) and their wines: About one-fifth of France's wine comes from vineyards located in Languedoc's **Hérault** region alone. Vines were first planted here in the sixth century BC; later, the Romans planted vineyards on the slopes of the foothills rising from the coast, where yields were low but quality was high. But during the 17th century growers began to plant vines in the fertile lowland; yields increased dramatically, but quality was poor. Since then, most of Languedoc's wines have been cheap and inferior—until recently. The second half of the 20th century brought increasing competition from other countries making cheap wine, a decline in global wine consumption, and a soaring demand for high quality. The local vintners had to change their ways.

Many growers in Languedoc (and Roussillon), especially those with prime vineyards on hillsides, now strive for quality rather than quantity, and thousands of acres of vineyards in the too-fertile valleys have been pulled out and replaced with other crops. Plenty of cheap wine is still made in the region, but a search for dedicated wine makers will yield some surprisingly fine wines, all very reasonably priced.

Languedoc produces hearty reds (among the best of which are from the appellations Minervois and Corbières); still, sweet muscats and sparkling whites (including Blanquette de Limoux from near **Carcassonne**); and rosés. The Corbières region has led the way in upgrading the wines of Languedoc and Roussillon; many of its best vineyards are scattered around the villages of **Boutenac** and **Gasparets**. The Coteaux du Languedoc appellation fills the plains between **Narbonne** and Montpellier, producing wines that will be used mostly for blending. Keep an eye peeled for wines from the area known as **La Clape;** they are among the best in the region. With bottles in hand, find a nice match for them in **Roquefort,** in the **Causses** region, which produces the world-famous blue cheese.

83 Château de Lascaux Jean-Benoît Cavalier produces red, rosé, and (since 1993) white wines from his hillside vineyards above the pretty village of Vacquières. The word *lascaux* means "rocky cliff," which describes much of the local terrain. The Cavalier family has owned this estate since the 12th century, so it's no wonder the wine maker understands the potential of his particular *terroir* very well. He grows half syrah grapes and half grenache, which on this *terroir* produce intensely fruity wines. The red wines are made mainly from syrah (90 percent) from old vines. Cavalier says his focus is on *"finales"*—what's left in the mouth, rather than the first aromatic impressions—and he succeeds, particularly with the rich, intense, wood-aged Grande Cuvée red. When entering the old stone winery through its large gate, notice the elaborate iron cross just to the right. Tastings are in an 11th-century wine cellar. ♦ Free. Visits and tastings M-Sa. Appointment recommended. Pl de l'Eglise, Vacquières (from Nîmes take D999 west 31 km/19 miles, then take D45 south 6.5 km/4 miles to Corconne, then take D234 south 5 km/3 miles to Vacquières). 67.59.00.08; fax 67.59.06.06

84 Montpellier This southern city has all the bustle of a fast-growing university town. Its medical school—housed in a 14th-century Benedictine monastery—is the oldest in France, and the **Université de Montpellier** (University of Montpellier) has a prestigious viticulture studies program. A city of contrasts, it has wide avenues and narrow streets lined with stone buildings dating to the 13th century. Despite its charms, book hotel rooms in the marvelous countryside instead; the city can get hot and very crowded in summer. ♦ 51 km (31.6 miles) west of Nîmes on N113

Within Montpellier:

Jardin des Plantes (Botanical Gardens) Founded in 1593, these magnificent botanical gardens—France's first—should not be missed by plant lovers. They provide the perfect stroll amid the beauty and fragrance of local and exotic plants. ♦ Admission. Daily (no midday closing). Bounded by Blvd Henri-IV and Rue Bonnard, and Blvd Pasteur and Rue de St-Jaumes. 67.63.43.22

Cathédrale St-Pierre (St. Peter Cathedral) The 16th-century Wars of Religion completely destroyed all the churches in Montpellier—except this one. Its one Gothic arch rises between the two square towers that stand on either side of the main entrance. The ceiling in the simple 14th-century nave rises only 70 feet, quite low for a Gothic cathedral. The plain, primitive style derives from the cathedral's origins as a simple chapel that was part of the **Collège St-Benoît** (a priest-run children's school), which was established here in the 14th century; the *collège* no longer exists. ♦ Rue de Candolle (on the east side of the Jardin des Plantes). No phone

Musée Fabre (Fabre Museum) A fine collection of painting and sculpture is housed in this former mansion. Among the paintings are works by Ingres, David, and Delacroix. ♦ Admission. Tu-Su (no midday closing). Blvd Sarrail (at Rue Montpellieret). 67.14.83.00

85 Sète This colorful city west of Montpellier is France's busiest Mediterranean fishing port. The old port itself is a collection of brightly colored houses with balconies overlooking the sea, filled with restaurants that spotlight seafood (of course). Poet Paul Valéry and singer/songwriter Georges Brassens were both born here, and both celebrated the town in their works. Be sure to see the Tournament of the Joutes, which is played all summer and culminates at the end of August at the Fête de St-Louis. For exact dates, call the Sète tourist office (67.74.71.71). The object of the "war" between two teams in small boats—which has been fought since the 1600s—is to knock each other out of the boat and into the water. Musicians who bravely ride aside the battlers accompany the tournament with the *air des Joutes*, music written 300 years ago. ♦ 30 km (18.6 miles) southwest of Montpellier on N112

Within Sète:

Le Grand Hôtel $$ The most impressive features of this well-maintained, turn-of-the-century hotel are its lobby and its soaring, glass-topped central atrium onto which all the floors open. It offers 43 rooms and four suites, all with private baths; reserve well in advance for a top-floor room with a magnificent view of the port and sea. Most rooms are decorated in a vaguely Art Deco style with muted grays and blues, but a few have dizzyingly intricate wallpaper. All have air-conditioning, direct-dial phones, TVs, and mini-bars. Given the comfort level and location, it's a great deal—a steal in winter. The in-house restaurant features seafood, but is definitely not a reason to stay here. ♦ Closed Christmas–New Year's. 17 Quai de Lattre-de-Tassigny. 67.74.71.77; fax 67.74.29.27

La Palangrotte ★★$$$ The best restaurant in town specializes in seafood, including *morue fraîche au jus de veau* (fresh cod with veal essence) and *queues de langoustines en risotto aux fruits de mer* (rock lobster tails in a seafood risotto). The excellent wine list focuses on regional wines and offers many rare vintages. On nice days, be sure to reserve a table on the terrace, which overlooks boats bobbing on the water in the port. ♦ M-Sa lunch and dinner; Su lunch; closed one week in November and mid-January–mid-February. Reservations required. 1 Rampe Paul-Valéry. 67.74.80.35

86 Chambres d'Hôtes Bombequiols $ Anne-Marie Bouec's carefully restored medieval stone farmhouse is in a perfect setting, lost in the rugged countryside near St-Guilhem-le-Désert. Her bed-and-breakfast offers three very comfortable rooms and three suites, all with private bathrooms. A swimming pool, nine-hole golf course, and bicycles to rent are all on the property, and Bouec will prepare meals featuring local foods and wines on request. ♦ From St-Guilhem-le-Désert take D4 northeast 21.5 km (13.3 miles) to D1 south 5 km (3.1 miles) to St-André-de-Buèges and follow the "Golf de Bombequiols" signs). 67.73.72.67; fax 67.73.33.24

87 St-Guilhem-le-Désert Guilhem (born AD 755) was a victorious soldier and lifelong friend of the emperor Charlemagne. Charlemagne rewarded his friend's valor by making him Prince of Orange and presenting him with a relic of the "True Cross." Finally tiring of the soldier's life, Guilhem had an abbey built in a rugged area near the Hérault River, where he lived until his death. The abbey's church—which is in a square shaded by a grand plane tree—today displays the relic from the cross on the altar of St-Guilhem in the north apse of the church. The picturesque village named in Guilhem's honor that sprang up around the abbey has become an artist's colony; although both become clogged with summertime tourists, they are so beautiful they are worth the trip any time of year. ♦ 45 km (27.9 miles) northwest of Montpellier (from there take N109 northwest to D32, then take D27 northwest and follow the signs to St-Guilhem-le-Désert)

88 Mas de Daumas Gassac Aimé Guibert and his wife bought this estate—a modern red-roofed stone *mas* built on the site of a Gallo-Roman water mill—with no intention of making wines and no wine-making experience. But when a visiting geologist-archaeologist told them the land was ideal for wine making, they decided to establish a winery nonetheless. It is one of the most unusual in Languedoc. The unique soil of the vineyard, totally unlike surrounding terrain, contains high levels of iron, copper, and boron, and is made up of tiny pebbles that help conserve moisture in this very dry climate. The Guiberts decided to use uncloned root stocks and to keep yields extremely low. The combination of microclimate, *terroir,* and dedicated wine making here has resulted in outstanding wines. When the 1981 vintages won out over many of France's most famous reds in a blind tasting, *GaultMillau* magazine dubbed them the "Château Lafite of the Languedoc." Although the wines bear the simple Vin de Pays de l'Hérault appellation, they sell for nearly 10 times the price of a usual *vin de pays.* The grapes include petit manseng from the Jura region, viognier from the northern Rhône, marsanne, chardonnay, and cabernet sauvignon, as well as merlot, malbec, cabernet franc, syrah, and pinot noir. The wines are aged in Allier oak for about 18 months. The only drawbacks are the shocking prices, particularly for older vintages, and the limited quantities available. Daumas Gassac wines are on the list at the **Restaurant Le Mimosa** (see page 136). ♦ Free. Tastings and sales M-Sa Aug-Dec; closed January-July. Aniane (from Montpellier go 30 km/18.6 miles west on N109 to D32). 67.57.71.28; fax 67.57.41.03

Mas Jullien

89 Mas Jullien A not-to-be-missed stop on a Languedoc wine tour. Olivier Jullien is barely 30 but has already been dubbed Languedoc's most talented wine maker. Singlehandedly, he has done more than any other wine maker to restore Languedoc wines' reputation. "For 50 years, wine makers from this region were humiliated; my cellars are a cry of anger," he says. He is dedicated to producing *vins de terroir* using Mediterranean grapes adapted to each of his small vineyards. For his reds, he grows several grape varieties, including grenache, syrah, cinsault, mourvèdre, and carignan. His fruity, powerful rosé is made mainly from cinsault grapes. Of the wonderful, complex reds, try Les Depierre, which is full of finesse and needs about five years in the bottle, or Les Cailloutis, whose powerful bouquet suggests herbs and spices; it needs about 10 years in the bottle. He also makes excellent white wines, such as the well-named Vignes Oubliées (forgotten vines), which is made from carignan, grenache blanc, and terret. Jullien eschews the trend to age wines in new oak, which he says masks their authentic taste; his wines taste of the grapes and the special *terroir*. The winery is housed in the Jullien family's red-roofed stone-and-stucco *mas*. ♦ Free. Visits and tastings M-Sa 10AM-7PM July-Aug; M-Sa 2PM-6PM Sept-June. Jonquières (from St-Guilhem-le-Désert take D4 4.5 km/2.8 miles south to St-Jean-de-Fos, then take D141 6 km/3.7 miles west). 67.96.60.04; fax 67.96.60.50

89 Restaurant Le Mimosa ★★★$$$ This unspoiled region so captivated David and Bridget Pugh that they gave up their city lives (he worked as a musician, she as a ballet dancer) to open a restaurant here—a brave move, since they had no restaurant experience. They knew what they were doing, though, and have since won many accolades for the quality of the cooking (Bridget's department) and the wines on hand (David assembles the list). Settle into the spacious, high-ceilinged dining room to feast on the *cuisine du marché* (fare based on seasonal market offerings). The menu might include a *gratin de poivrons rouges et de fromage de chèvre au basilic* (red pepper, goat cheese, and basil gratin), *raviolis de champignons de bois au fumet de cèpes et aux deux asperges* (wild mushroom ravioli with two types of asparagus and cèpe-mushroom sauce), *noix de saint-jacques au cumin et à la coriandre fraîche* (sea scallops with cumin and fresh coriander), and *filet d'agneau rôti aux petits légumes de printemps et à la menthe fraîche* (fillet of roast lamb with spring vegetables and fresh mint). The cheeses are outstanding, and so are the desserts. The wine list, judged tops in the region, includes all the best local producers, as well as wines from other parts of France; David Pugh offers expert guidance on matching wines to food. ♦ Tu-Su lunch and dinner July-Aug; Tu-Sa lunch and dinner, Su lunch Sept-June. Reservations required. St-Guiraud (1.6 km/1 mile west of Jonquières and 40 km/24.8 miles northwest of Montpellier on N109). 67.96.67.96

LE SANGLIER

90 Le Sanglier $$ The name means "the wild boar," and you might even see one running near this ancient *mas* deep in the Languedoc hills (a boar trail passes nearby). The auberge, part of an 80-acre estate called the **Domaine de Cambourras,** is run by friendly owners Monique and Pierre Plazonet-Lormier. The 10 simple guest rooms are all very comfortable and have private bathrooms. Peace and quiet are guaranteed. A tiny path leads to a swimming pool set in the middle of rugged countryside that resembles America's Southwest. There's also a tennis court. Prices can get high during peak periods, when *demi-pension* (breakfast and one other meal) or *pension complète* (all meals) is required; be sure to check. ♦ Between St-Jean-de-la-Blaquière and Rabieux (from St-Guiraud take D130 2.5 km/1.5 miles south and follow the signs to Rabieux; from Rabieux take D144 north 3.5 km/2.2 miles to Le Sanglier). 67.44.70.51; fax 67.44.72.33

Within Le Sanglier:

Restaurant Le Sanglier ★$$ Local specialties are served in a cozy, rustic dining room where a fireplace roars as soon as the temperature drops. Steak, lamb chops, and duck breasts are grilled over *sarments* (vine cuttings); in keeping with the name, there's also a *terrine de sanglier* (wild boar terrine). Excellent local cheeses and very light desserts, including *mousse glacée au miel* (frozen honey mousse), round out the meal. Game is offered in the fall, and a fish dish is always on the menu. The Plazonet-Lormiers are fans of local wines, as the wine list shows. ♦ Daily lunch and dinner July-Aug; M, Th-Su lunch and dinner Mar-June and Sept–late Oct; closed late October–March. 67.44.70.51; fax 67.44.72.33

91 Château Coujan This winery, a large white stucco farmhouse with a red tiled roof, produces Saint-Chinian. The appellation has been official only since 1982, but the wine has a long history; it was mentioned in manuscripts dating from 1300, and the local vineyards were known in Roman times. The Guy family has been making wines here since 1868, and François Guy has played a key role in upgrading the reputation of Languedoc wines. The estate's *terroir* is unusual, with a lot of fossilized coral, and all its wines are aged in wood. The red wines, made primarily from mourvèdre and syrah grapes, have overtones of spices and cherries, with subtle tannins and wood. The Cuvée Bois Joli red is one of the estate's—and the region's—best. The rosé and white wines here are also excellent. The Coujan domain itself was once the property of a high-ranking Roman, and mosaics from that period can be seen in the estate's Roman chapel. ♦ Free. Visits M-Sa. Appointments recommended. Murviel (from Montpellier take A9 southwest 58 km/36 miles to Béziers, then take D19 15 km/9.3 miles northwest and follow the signs to the château). 67.37.80.00; fax 67.37.86.23

92 Château de Violet $$$ The best local hotel also produces one of the best Minervois red wines around (nonguests may come for tastings, too). Parts of the sprawling gray château date from the 11th century, but it was rebuilt mostly in the 17th and late 19th centuries. The 15 huge, elegant rooms and three suites all have private baths and offer peace and quiet. The room called l'Archevêque has a canopy bed, a little cocktail table surrounded by a settee and cozy chairs, extravagantly patterned floral carpeting and wallpaper, and a gilded statue of an archbishop standing in a nook. Other choices include a large two-bedroom suite that sleeps five people and has a private garden; **Les Couscounilles,** a separate two-bedroom house with private garden, which also sleeps five people; and the huge two-bedroom, three-bathroom **Suite de Villa,** which sleeps seven. The estate is surrounded by a large private park with a swimming pool. The moderately priced restaurant has a beamed ceiling, a huge fireplace, and big windows with views of the gardens, and the friendly hostess, Madame Faussié, serves simple regional dishes with a focus on duck. The château's own red, dry white, rosé, and late-harvest sweet white wines are all on hand. Wine-tasting weekends that include a tour of several nearby wineries are also available. ♦ Tastings M-Sa. Peyriac-Minervois (from Béziers take D11 44 km/27 miles west to Olonzac, then continue on D11 about 15 km/9.3 miles northwest). 68.78.11.44, 68.78.10.42; fax 68.78.30.01

93 Le Relais du Val d'Orbieu $$$ In a peaceful spot surrounded by vines, this 20-room hotel is a perfect base for touring Corbières wineries. The setting is a renovated water mill with flower-filled gardens. Some of the very comfortable rooms have balconies or private terraces, and all have direct-dial phones, mini-bars, satellite TV, and well-equipped private bathrooms. A swimming pool, tennis court, and driving range round out the amenities. The friendly owner/managers, Agnès and Jean-Pierre Gonzalvez, helpfully suggest things to see and do in the region. ♦ Closed one week in January, one week in February, and one week in November. Just northeast of Ornaisons (from Olonzac take D611 south 4.5 km/2.8 miles, then take D11 southeast 10 km/6.2 miles to D24; follow D24 2 km/1.2 miles southwest). 68.27.10.27; fax 68.27.52.44

Within Le Relais du Val d'Orbieu:

Restaurant Val d'Orbieu ★$$ There are two dining options here—a full-fledged menu in the formal restaurant and simple meals on the poolside terrace—both featuring regional cuisine. Try the *légumes de Provence en ratatouille, fondu de tomate au basilic* (ratatouille of Provençal vegetables in a tomato and basil sauce) or the *langoustines et crevettes en salade, huile d'olive et épices* (prawn and shrimp salad in olive oil with spices). The vegetables are usually from the Gonzalvezes' garden. There's also an excellent choice of local wines. ♦ Daily lunch and dinner; closed one week in January, one week in February, and one week in November. Reservations recommended. 68.27.10.27

CHATEAU
La Voulte-Gasparets

94 Château La Voulte-Gasparets The wines from this family-owned estate consistently garner top rankings in tastings of Corbières. The distinctive *terroir* is very stony, similar to Châteauneuf-du-Pape (except that here the stones are red), and the vines are very old; some of the carignan vines were planted in 1905. The Cuvée Romain Pauc 1990 is typical of this winery; it's powerful, with an herby, peppery bouquet, and has a very long finish (meaning the taste lingers). The great red wines are made from 60 percent carignan grapes, 30 percent grenache, and 10 percent syrah. The estate also produces rosés from 40 percent grenache, 30 percent cinsault, 20 percent carignan, and 10 percent syrah; the white wines are made from grenache (50 percent), macabeu, rolle, and bourgoulenc. All grapes are picked by hand and all the wines are aged in oak. The winery is in an ancient stone farmhouse covered with vines; the tasting room is in the former stables, another ancient stone building nearby. ♦ Free. Daily. Southwest of Ornaisons, between Gasparets and Boutenac on D161; follow the signs to the winery. 68.27.07.86; fax 68.27.41.33

The sun shines an average of 325 days a year in Roussillon.

Artists Dufy, Picasso, Chagall, Gris, Braque, and Matisse have all lived in Céret, a town in Roussillon, at some point in their lives.

Restaurants/Clubs: Red	**Hotels:** Blue
Shops/ 🌳 Outdoors: Green	**Sights/Culture:** Black

137

Major Appellations of the South

Some of France's most famous red wines are found in the **Rhône Valley:** big, long-lived, powerful Côte Rôtie, Hermitage, and Châteauneuf-du-Pape, all made predominantly from the syrah grape. Among the great whites are Hermitage *blanc,* Condrieu, and rare Château Grillet; there are also many lively rosés. Though **Provence** and the **Midi** are not as highly regarded for the fruit of their vines, they're working hard to improve quality and reputation. Bandol, Provence's most venerated appellation, produces some high-quality wines, and two VDQS wines of the Midi—Minervois from **Languedoc** and Corbières from **Roussillon**—were promoted to *Appellation Contrôlée (AC)* status in 1985. Below are some more details on the wines and appellations of the south.

Bandol

The reds of this appellation are generally considered Provence's best red wine. Made from at least 50 percent mourvèdre grapes, this wine can acquire a lot of character through bottle aging. Other grapes added into the mix are grenache, cinsault, and occasionally syrah. Descriptions tend to include the contrasting words herby, soft, and sweet. Bandol white wines are not as memorable. The best choices are the white wines that use some sauvignon blanc grapes, and they should be drunk as young as possible. The rosés, also best drunk young, have been overlooked—not because of their taste, which is exquisite, but because of their high price.

Château Grillet

This spectacular, very expensive white is harvested from three hectares (7.5 acres), one of the smallest *Appellations Contrôlées* in France. Made only from the viognier—no other grape is permitted—on one estate in the village of Vérin, it has been described as intense and fragrant (by Hugh Johnson, in his *Pocket Encyclopedia of Wine*) and compared to the essences of "apricots and slightly soured cream, spring blossom floating on the wind and honey tinged with tangerine spice" (by Oz Clarke, in his *Essential Wine Book*). The rarity of the grape drives up the price and, unfortunately, renders it unaffordable even for oenophiles.

Châteauneuf-du-Pape

This famous full-bodied wine is produced from stony white soil. The name comes from Pope John XXII, who built a summer palace in the area in the 14th century; the vineyards surrounding the palace, whose tower and a few crumbling walls still stand, were planted by the first of the Provence-based popes, Clément V. Although the area's rich red wine is best known, the flavorful white shouldn't be missed. The red wine is made primarily from grenache, with some mourvèdre, syrah, cinsault, and other grapes (up to 13 varieties are permitted by *AOC* standards). The white's primary grapes are the grenache blanc and clairette, accented by bourboulenc, picpoul, and roussanne. The wine makers of Châteauneuf-du-Pape are credited with initiating France's *AOC* system by establishing six criteria for true Châteauneuf-du-Pape wines in 1923; 13 years later the French government

adopted the idea of specific criteria as the basis for its national regulations.

Corbières

Having only received its *AC* designation in 1985, Roussillon's famous red wine is still a good buy, and the quality is usually high. The Corbières wines that have been aged in wood are particularly good, and more and more colorful fruity reds are being produced from carbonic maceration (fermenting in a closed vat). Some whites and rosés are also produced under the Corbières appellation, but with not nearly as much fanfare. The term "Corbières Supérieur" is applied to red and white only and simply designates a higher percentage of alcohol (and greater need for bottle aging).

Côte Rôtie and Condrieu

The most ancient vineyards of the Rhône Valley are on the **Côte Rôtie,** a steep slope that can only be worked by hand, not by tractor. The vineyards' stone terraces were originally built by the Romans, who prized Côte Rôtie in the first century. Set in a bowl of land, the vineyards get the full blast of the southern sun, hence the name "Roasted Slope." The slope is divided into the Côte Brune and the Côte Blonde— not, as local stories say, in honor of a brunette and a blond, but because some of the soil is brown from iron oxide, and some is creamy gold. All Côte Rôtie wines are aromatic, powerful reds (with hints of violets and raspberries) that linger long in the mouth. Made primarily from black syrah (a grape that is probably native to the Rhône Valley), they are usually rounded out with viognier. Adjacent to Côte Rôtie is **Condrieu,** where a totally different wine is made, yet another illustration of the importance of *terroir.* Condrieu is always white, made exclusively with the viognier grape. Produced on only 60 hectares (148.2 acres), Condrieu is rare and expensive, but unforgettable: its taste lingers very long, with overtones of apricots and violets.

Côtes du Rhône

Although the Rhône begins in the Alps and flows on to the Mediterranean, the wine region known as the **Côtes du Rhône** is limited to a 220-kilometer (140-mile) stretch of vineyards overlooking the river between **Lyons** and **Avignon.** The appellation Côtes du Rhône applies to over 80 percent of the wines of the Rhône Valley and is a more general appellation than Côte Rôtie or Hermitage. A label marked "Côtes du Rhône–Villages" indicates that the wine comes from a blend of any of 17 villages that have the best vineyard sites. When a bottle of Côtes du Rhône has an *AOC* village name on its label, such as **Gigondas,** it comes solely from that village and has not been blended with any other villages' product. These wines are typically of a higher quality than the blended ones.

Hermitage and Crozes-Hermitage

The vineyards in these adjacent appellations, probably first planted around the fourth century BC, were well known to the Romans and have been highly valued ever since. Louis XIV presented some to his cousin

Charles II of England, and Thomas Jefferson ranked white Hermitage as one of France's greatest white wines. The wine-loving "hermit" who gave the wines their name was a 13th-century crusader, Gaspard de Stérimberg, who probably claimed these priceless vineyards as payment for services he had rendered his king. The powerful reds, which need at least five years of aging, are made from syrah grapes; the whites from aromatic roussanne and nutty-tasting marsanne. Crozes-Hermitage produces both white and red wines; the fruity reds are less powerful (and cheaper) than Hermitage reds.

Minervois

These notable red and rosé wines grown primarily in Languedoc's **Aude Valley** made the grade and won an *AC* of their own in 1985. After four or five years in the bottle, the reds develop a rich, flavorful, earthy quality. The carignan grape provides a peppery flavor, which is softened by the prevailing raspberry effect. The growers who use some oak have a handle on how to perfect this wine. For the most part, it is produced cooperatively; big companies pooled their resources with the smaller local growers and came up with a reasonably priced and appealing wine.

94 Château Les Ollieux Romanis The Surbezy family has owned this estate since 1873; today, Françoise Surbezy and her son produce one of the top Corbières wines and other excellent reds. Their vineyards are planted 48 percent with carignan (most of the vines are very old), 30 percent grenache noir, 10 percent syrah, and some cinsault and mourvèdre. Be sure to try the nonfiltered reds, which intensely reflect their *terroir*. Vineyards have been cultivated here since Gallo-Roman times, and many relics from that period are displayed in the family's sprawling stone *mas,* which dates from the 19th century. Tastings are given in the ancient wine cellars. ♦ Free. Daily. From Gasparets take D123 south about 6 km (3.7 miles) to D613 west; follow the signs to the château. 68.43.32.61; fax 68.43.30.78

95 Abbaye de Fontfroide (Fontfroide Abbey) Hidden in the Corbières countryside, this Cistercian abbey of ocher and local pink stone is especially impressive at sunset. Founded in 1093, the abbey became part of the Cîteaux order in 1145. Its glory days were in the 12th and 13th centuries, although one of its 14th-century abbots (Jacques Fournier, 1311-17) was elected pope (Benedict XII). Over the centuries the abbey fell into ruins, and it was robbed during the Revolution, but it has gradually been restored. You can visit the main buildings, the peaceful cloisters, and the 12th- to 13th-century abbey church. ♦ Admission. Daily (no midday closing) mid-July–Aug; daily Sept–mid-July. From the Château Les Ollieux Romanis (see above) take D613 east about 14 km (8.7 miles) and follow the signs to the abbey. 68.45.11.08

96 Le Moulin ★★★$$$ Owner David Moreno is considered one of the best chefs in the region, and his restaurant has to be one of the most unusual-looking. A windmill with annexes built of roughly mortared stone, it looks from the outside like a ruined château. Moreno's seasonally changing menu features variations of regional specialties. You might find treats like *brandade en ravioles et infusion d'anchois* (ravioli made with salt-cod puree in anchovy sauce), *dos de saumon à l'infusion d'huile d'olive de Bize* (salmon in a Bize olive-oil sauce), *râble de lapereau et sa fricassée de légumes en aïoli* (young rabbit with vegetables and garlic mayonnaise), and great local cheeses. Find room for the delectable chocolate mousse soufflé with bitter-almond ice cream. The three fixed-price menus are interesting and reasonably priced. The wine list has a great choice of regional wines, particularly Corbières, also fairly priced. ♦ Daily lunch and dinner July-Aug; Tu-Sa lunch and dinner, Su lunch mid-Mar—June and Sept–mid-Jan; closed mid-January–mid-March. Reservations required. Durban-Corbières (12 km/7.4 miles south of Montséret on D611). 68.45.81.03; fax 68.45.83.31

97 Le Clos des Souquets $$ In a village halfway between the ancient town of Carcassonne and the sea, this modern hotel built in traditional *mas* style is a real find. Two of the rooms share a private swimming pool; the other three rooms overlook another pool, a garden, and the restaurant. All are comfortable and have private bathrooms. The rates are considerably lower than one would expect, which makes this one of the best choices in Languedoc-Roussillon (if you can get a reservation). To top it off, the management is very friendly. ♦ Closed November-April. Ave de Lagrasse, Fabrézan (about 13 km/8 miles northwest of Montséret on D611). 68.43.52.61

Within Le Clos des Souquets:

Restaurant Le Clos des Souquets ★$$ Various types of regional dishes are served here, but the focus is definitely on fish. Chef Philippe Julien is such a seafood fan that he has fish flown in from African waters twice a week so he can experiment with new varieties. The wine list is good, though short, and includes wines made by the hotel's owners. ♦ Daily lunch and dinner; closed November-April. 68.43.52.61

98 Domaine Baillat Friendly young wine maker Christian Baillat is the fourth generation of his family to make wine here, at one of the top Corbières wine estates. He uses mainly syrah and grenache to produce very fruity, aromatic, and powerful reds. The Cuvée Emilien Baillat is made from 100 percent syrah and looks almost black; it has a powerful, slightly herbal taste and needs lots of time in the bottle. There's also a rosé and a Corbières red made from syrah, grenache, carignan, and cinsault. Tastings are usually given by the wine maker, who will likely discuss some of his keenest interests: the need to upgrade the quality of Corbières and, perhaps, his favorite poets (Rilke and St. John Perse). The winery, one of the most unusual in France, was recently built in what was once the mill pond of a Gallo-Roman water mill. Vestiges of the mill were incorporated into a stone building where a tasting and sales room has been set up; one wall is 2,000 years old! ♦ Free. Visits and tastings daily by appointment. 2 Rue Montlaurier, Montlaur (from Fabrézan go 14 km/8.6 miles west on D114). 68.24.00.37; fax 68.24.00.37

99 Cité Médiévale de Carcassonne This mostly medieval fortified village—the largest in Europe—is one of the most magical places in France. One look at its massive, creamy yellow, double stone walls gleaming in the southern sun, its seemingly endless ramparts, and its narrow cobblestone streets with memorable views around every corner shows why local postcards say *"Il ne faut pas mourir sans avoir vu Carcassonne"* (You mustn't die without having seen Carcassonne). Legend has it that a woman named Carcas saved the city when Charlemagne held it under siege by throwing the residents' last remaining food—a fat pig—over the walls. The emperor's troops, thinking that the city must have plenty of food if it could discard such a pig, decided the siege was hopeless and left. Lady Carcas rang the town bells to let everyone know their troubles were over (*sonner* means "to ring"—hence, *Carcas sonne*). It's a good story, but actually the Romans gave the name Carcasso to a fort they built on this strategic spot in the first century BC. Occupied by Visigoths, Saracens, and many, many others over the centuries, the fortress, fallen into ruins, was restored in the mid-19th century by crusading architect **Viollet-le-Duc.** Don't miss the **Porte Narbonnaise,** the main gate in the city's interior walls, with its tall 13th-century turreted towers; **Les Lices,** a vast open space within the double fortress walls that usually provides an escape from the summer crowds; or the 13th-century **Pont Vieux** (Old Bridge), which spans the Aude

River and links the lower part of Carcassonne (*La Ville Basse*) with the medieval city. The whole place is spectacular at night. Sound-and-light shows are held regularly; the most magnificent is on Bastille Day (14 July). A medieval fair takes place the first two weeks in August, when villagers dress in medieval garb, musicians stroll while playing medieval instruments, dance and choral groups perform period dances and songs, and local food, drink, and craft producers peddle their wares as they might have done in the Middle Ages. There is an admission charge for the fair. ♦ Main entrance Voie Médiévale (at Pont Levis), Carcassonne (from Montlaur take D114 south 6 km/3.7 miles to D3, go northwest 15.5 km/9.6 miles to N113, then west 5 km/3.1 miles)

Within the Cité Médiévale de Carcassonne:

Château Comtal Built for Bernard Aton Trençavel, whose family ruled Carcassonne in the 12th century, this château adjoins the Gallo-Roman fortifications. It contains two courtyards, the huge Cour d'Honneur (the château's main entrance), and the smaller Cour du Midi. Since different owners added to the château over the centuries, there is now a hodgepodge of architectural styles. The Cour d'Honneur provides a great view of the château's facade, with its Romanesque base, Gothic middle section, and Renaissance half-timbered upper section. The château also houses the **Musée Lapidaire** (Lapidary Museum), which displays finely sculpted stone items from various epochs, all discovered in or near the Cité, and other treasures. A theater festival is held in the Cour du Midi in July and August (contact the tourist office for more information). ♦ Admission. Daily. Rue Viollet-le-Duc. 68.25.01.66

Basilique St-Nazaire (St. Nazarius Basilica) Only the nave remains of the original church built on this spot in the 11th century. Blessed by Pope Urban in 1096, when construction began, the nave is a model of restrained Romanesque architecture with its simple lines and round arches. It contrasts with the other parts of the church, which were built in the 13th century to replace destroyed sections of the older building and feature Gothic arches and elaborate stone carvings. The church's main treasure, its magnificent stained-glass windows, dates from the 13th and 14th centuries. The facade was restored (and modified) in the 19th century by **Viollet-le-Duc.** ♦ Rue St-Louis. No phone

Hôtel de la Cité $$$$ Definitely the best place to stay in Carcassonne, this Neo-Gothic landmark hotel has hosted many celebrities.

The 23 ultraluxurious rooms and three suites provide every modern comfort. Each spacious room is furnished with antiques and boasts lots of windows offering great views of either the city or an interior garden. There's a swimming pool next to the ramparts, a fantastic view of the Cité, and, on a rare perfectly clear day, a glimpse of the snowcapped Pyrénées to the west. ♦ Closed mid-January–mid-February. Pl de l'Eglise. 68.71.60.60; fax 68.71.50.15

Within the Hôtel de la Cité:

Restaurant La Barbacane ★★★$$$$
The vast dining hall, covered with fleurs-de-lys and coats of arms, may look a bit Disneylandish to some, but a taste of chef Michel del Burgo's creations will dash any qualms. He favors regional and Mediterranean dishes and uses only the finest ingredients. The menu changes regularly but might include such delights as *ravioles de jeune fenouil parfumés à l'anchois de Collioure au jus d'olive, basilic, et huile d'olive* (ravioli stuffed with young fennel in a sauce of local anchovies, olive juice, basil, and olive oil); grilled *loup* (sea bass) with tiny spring vegetables and truffle juice; and roast free-range chicken stuffed with wild mushrooms. The stellar desserts range from a *soufflé au chocolat noir avec sauce chocolat blanc au Grand Marnier* (dark chocolate soufflé with a white-chocolate–Grand Marnier sauce) to a *grosse tomate farci de fruits frais et secs* (large tomatoes stuffed with fresh and dried fruits, served warm). The wine list is every bit as outstanding, with 1,500 wines, including a hundred Languedocs. ♦ Tu-Sa lunch and dinner, Su lunch; closed mid-January–mid-February. Reservations required. 68.25.03.34

99 Hôtel Mercure la Vicomté $$ A link in the ever reliable Mercure chain, it is in a modern building decorated in contemporary style, perfectly located near the Porte Narbonnaise; some rooms offer views of the ramparts. The 58 rooms and three suites are all soundproofed and have private bathrooms, air-conditioning, mini-bars, and satellite TVs. There's a big swimming pool, friendly management, and a good restaurant too, making this one of pricey Carcassonne's best deals. ♦ 18 Rue Camille-St-Saëns, Basse Ville, Carcassonne. 68.71.45.45; fax 68.71.11.45

Sieur d'Arques

100 Les Caves du Sieur d'Arques Nestled in the quiet little town of Limoux, this winery is best known for its Blanquette de Limoux, a bubbly white wine produced using champagne techniques. Limoux's may be the oldest sparkling wine in the world: Monks in the nearby **St-Hilaire Abbey** produced a sparkling wine in 1531, by trapping the bubbles with a strong cork and inducing the crucial second fermentation inside the bottle. This winery's Blaners Brut is intense and has a long finish, with hints of apricots and acacia blossoms. It also produces *vins de cépages* (still wines made from a single grape variety, such as chardonnay). On sunny days tastings are on the terrace. ♦ Free. Visits and tastings daily May-Oct; M-F Nov-Apr. Ave du Mauzac, Limoux (from Carcassonne go 24 km/14.8 miles south on D118). 68.31.14.59; fax 68.31.62.48

100 Maison de la Blanquette ★$$ Among the local specialties here, try the foie gras, cassoulet, or the hearty salad topped with *gésiers confits* (duck or goose gizzards preserved in goose fat and sautéed). Blanquette de Limoux wines are served by the glass or bottle. ♦ M-Tu, Th-Su lunch and dinner. Reservations recommended. Promenade de Tivoli, Limoux. 63.31.01.63

Roussillon

Sandwiched between the Pyrénées to the south and the Mediterranean to the east, Roussillon is one of France's loveliest areas, although some of its coastline has been spoiled by intense tourist-industry construction. The region was once an official province that spread into Spain. In fact, its proximity to Spain made it the subject of a centuries-long tug-of-war, during which it was alternately French and Catalonian.

The redbrick city of Perpignan and especially the beautiful fishing villages of **Collioure** and **Banyuls**, favored by many artists in the early part of this century, are well worth a visit. Olive oil, fruit, and wine are the region's chief products. Roussillon produces red, white, and rosé wines. It is most famous, however, for its *vin doux naturel,* a portlike drink made mostly with muscat grapes.

DOMAINE CAZES

101 Domaine Cazes Surrounded by cypress trees and vineyards, this winery is housed in a big stone farmhouse with a red tiled roof. It's operated by the enterprising Cazes brothers, Bernard and André, who produce a wide range of wines from 165 hectares (407.7 acres) of vines. Their very good Vin de Pays Chardonnay white has encouraged other growers to try the grape here. They also produce sweet white wines, including one of the region's best naturally sweet Muscat-de-Rivesaltes; the *vieux* (old) and *très vieux* (very old) vintages are exceptional, particularly the *très vieux* Cuvée Aimé Cazes Rivesaltes 1973, aged in wood. This amazing sweet wine has an intense bouquet of walnuts, honey, oranges, and prunes. Another unusual wine to try is a dry Muscat, the Canon du Maréchal, which also has an intense bouquet. Their Côtes de Roussillon Villages, aged in wood, is a powerful, rich red wine. ◆ Free. Visits and tastings M-Sa July-Aug; M-F Sept-June. 4 Rue Francisco-Ferrer, Rivesaltes (from Limoux take D118 south 27 km/16.7 miles to Quillan, then take D117 east 68 km/42.2 miles to Rivesaltes).

101 Domaine de Joliette In this hilly area overlooking the sea, four generations of the Mercier family have made wines the traditional way, including handpicking the grapes. André Mercier, now head of the family, produces whites, reds, rosés, and sweet Muscat de Rivesaltes wines. The top-of-the-line wines are named for family members. Try the Cuvée Laurence 1992, a rich, slightly flowery white (named for André's daughter-in-law); it's made from macabeu and grenache grapes. Other good bets are the supple, mouth-filling red Cuvée Romain 1991 (named for a grandson) and the deep ruby red, fruity, mouth-filling Cuvée André Mercier, named for the wine maker himself. The labels of the special *cuvée* wines suggest the foods that would best accompany each one; consider the advice golden. Mercier's vineyards include grenache, carignan, muscat, and macabeu vines that are over 40 years old, as well as syrah and mourvèdre that have been planted more recently. The winery is a cluster of white stucco outbuildings adjoining the wine maker's large stone farmhouse, all set amid a landscape scattered with maritime pines, olive groves, and vineyards. Tastings are in a pleasant room in the wine cellars. ◆ Free. M-Sa. Rte de Vingrau, just east of Montpins (9 km/5.5 miles northwest of Rivesaltes on D12). 68.64.50.60; fax 68.64.18.82

102 Château de Jau This estate has much to attract the wine-route traveler. First of all, the wines are very good; second, many different types may be sampled: reds, dry whites, rosés, and sweet Muscat de Rivesaltes. White grape varieties cultivated on the estate include malvoisie, macabeu, vermentino, muscat, and grenache blanc; among the red grapes are carignan, syrah, and mourvèdre. From its vineyards nearer the coast, the estate produces Banyuls and Collioure red and rosé wines under the Clos de Paulilles label. The château here is a two-story brick-and-stone building with shutters at its windows; the winery is composed of several modern buildings with red tiled roofs. The winery also operates a restaurant here with lunch daily from 15 June through 30 September. It serves moderately priced regional dishes, accompanied by wines from the estate. Reservations (68.38.91.38) are required. Ask to see the exhibit of international art. ◆ Free. Tastings offered in the cellar M-F year-round; tastings offered in the restaurant daily 15 June-30 Sept. About 10 km (6.2 miles) west of Rivesaltes on D117; follow the signs to the château. 68.38.91.38

103 Perpignan The ancient capital of the Counts of Roussillon and the Kings of Majorca is in many ways more Catalonian than French. Don't miss the **Palais des Rois de Majorque** (Palace of the Kings of Majorca) or **Le Castillet** (see below for both). ◆ About 153 km (95 miles) south of Montpellier on A9

Within Perpignan:

Palais des Rois de Majorque (Palace of the Kings of Majorca) This sprawling medieval structure—a remarkable remnant of Spanish rule—is enclosed by ramparts. Its arched interior courtyard has Romanesque galleries on the ground floor topped by Gothic galleries above. Also here is the remarkable Flamboyant Gothic **Chapelle Ste-Croix** (Holy Cross Chapel), built at the beginning of the 14th century; it's really two chapels, one on top of the other. The lower level is the **Chapelle de la Reine** (Queen's Chapel), where royal ladies once worshiped; it has many medieval frescoes of the *Vierge à L'Enfant* (Virgin with Child). Many of the frescoes in the upper chapel, known as the **Chapelle Haute**, are trompe l'oeil windows. ◆ Admission. Daily. Ave G.-Brutus (at Ave des Baléares). 68.34.48.29

Le Castillet The city's most beloved monument, this redbrick fortress has tall towers whose windows sport elaborate wrought-iron grillwork. It houses the **Casa Pairal,** an excellent museum dedicated to Catalan arts and culture—which shows you just where Perpignan's heart lies. From the top of the tower, reached by 142 steps that start in the museum, is a great view of the city and surrounding countryside. ♦ Free. ♦ M, W-Su. Pl du Castillet (at Rue du Castillet). 68.35.42.05

Park Hotel $$$ This modern hotel has 67 comfortable rooms, some of them quite luxurious, and friendly management. The decor is contemporary. All the rooms have well-equipped bathrooms, mini-bars, satellite TVs, direct-dial phones, and air-conditioning. The less expensive rooms are on the small side. In addition to the gourmet **Le Chapon Fin** restaurant, there is a very good, moderately priced eatery, the **Bistrot du Park**, that offers French home cooking with Catalan accents. ♦ 18 Blvd J.-Bourrat (at Rue des Mimosas). 68.35.14.14; fax 68.35.48.18

Within the Park Hotel:

Restaurant Le Chapon Fin ★★★$$$ The chef, who trained with Paris's culinary master Joël Robuchon, learned his lessons well: At what is considered Perpignan's best restaurant, he produces unusual, intensely flavored variations on regional dishes, such as fillet of beef with grilled foie gras. His seafood concoctions include *saint-jacques rôties à la crème d'oursins* (sea scallops roasted with sea urchin puree). The wine list emphasizes regional wines and is reasonably priced. ♦ Tu-Sa lunch and dinner, M dinner; closed three weeks in January and the last two weeks of August. Reservations required. 68.35.14.14

Restaurant Casa-Sansa ★★$$ A meal at this friendly place will transport you to Barcelona. It has typical Catalan decor—whitewashed walls, dark wood tables, copper utensils on the walls—and is *the* place for authentic Catalonian cooking, along with some well chosen Roussillon wines. Don't miss the *calamars* (squid) and various seafood and lamb dishes. ♦ Tu-Sa lunch and dinner, M dinner. Reservations recommended. 2 Rue Fabriques-Nadal, just south of Le Castillet. 68.34.21.84; fax 68.35.02.78

"If wine disappeared from the realm of human production, I think it would leave a void, an absence, a defection in human health and intellect, that would be much more horrible than the excesses for which wine is always said to be responsible."

Charles Baudelaire, *Du vin et du haschisch* (Of Wine and Hashish)

Restaurants/Clubs: Red   **Hotels:** Blue
Shops/ 🌳 Outdoors: Green   **Sights/Culture:** Black

104 La Côte Vermeille (Vermilion Coast) This stretch of coastline is one of the most pristine in Languedoc-Roussillon, and a beautiful route winds along by the sea. It passes through Banyuls, a famous wine village, and Collioure, one of France's most beautiful fishing ports. The Fauvists and, later, Picasso loved Collioure; a little exploration shows why. Just wander its winding medieval streets lined with houses whose balconies overflow with flowers; stroll the Sentier de la Moulade, a walkway at the edge of the picturesque bay; or swim in the sea in the blazing clear light that inspired generations of painters. The main industry here is still anchovy fishing, followed closely by tourism; Collioure can get very, very crowded in August. Not-to-be-missed events in Collioure are its *Sardanes* (Catalan dances, held regularly in the village squares between May and September); the *Festa Major* (held every 16 August), with a bullfight and spectacular fireworks display; and the *Procession de la Sanch,* a religious procession by torchlight on Good Friday. To tour the Côte Vermeille, drive along N114, which just skirts the sea, and don't miss the spectacular view from Cap Rederis, west of Banyuls. Good picnic spots lie all along the way. ♦ On N114 stretching from Argelès-Plage (20 km/12.4 miles south of Perpignan) to Cerbère on the Spanish border

105 Les Templiers $$ Whatever you do, don't bypass the Pous family's friendly hotel. The many painters who worked in the village in the early 20th century usually stayed or ate here, and they paid their bills with works of art that still hang in every nook and cranny. Unfortunately, the most valuable works (including a few Picassos) were stolen a few years ago, forcing the owners to store several others, but many paintings are still on display. The 54 comfortable rooms, all decorated in Catalan style, are very reasonably priced; ask for one with a view of the port. ♦ Closed one week in November and most of January. Reservations recommended well in advance. Quai Amirauté, Collioure (about 25 km/15.5 miles south of Perpignan on N114). 68.98.31.10; fax 68.98.01.24

Within Les Templiers:

Restaurant Les Templiers ★★$$ Since it's set in a fishing village, it's only right that the menu should focus on seafood. Don't miss the great *soupe de poisson de roche au fenouil* (fish soup with fennel). ♦ Tu-Sa lunch and dinner, Su lunch; closed one week in November and most of January. Reservations required. 68.98.31.10

106 Banyuls-sur-Mer The most southerly seaside resort on France's Mediterranean coast, this village is also famous for Banyuls wine, a heavy fortified wine which is often compared to port. The vines are grown on slopes terraced in by dry stone walls. The French like to take family holidays here by the sea. ♦ 9 km (5.6 miles) south of Collioure on N114

Within Banyuls-sur-Mer:

Domaine de la Rectorie The Parcé brothers, Thierry and Marc, make red Banyuls wines, primarily from old vines, that are consistently ranked among the best in the area. The Parcés are passionate defenders of the Banyuls appellation, which is currently being threatened by real-estate developers. (The coast is too pretty here to be safe.) The Domaine de la Rectorie red from their vineyards near Collioure is a full-flavored, well-balanced wine made from grenache, mourvèdre, carignan, and syrah grapes; it's aged in oak and needs time in the bottle. They also make a good, fruity Collioure rosé. But the most unusual wines produced here are the *vins doux naturels* (naturally sweet red wines), made primarily from late-harvest grenache grapes. These wines have been made in Banyuls for generations, traditionally for the wine makers' own use, and need long aging to develop their potential; they are like fine port, and are a perfect match for well-aged roquefort. Try the fine Cuvée Léon Parcé *vin doux naturel,* aged for a year in oak. Yields from all the Parcé vineyards are kept very low, resulting in complex, full-flavored wines. The vineyards themselves are spectacular; rows of vines cling to a steep slope held in place on terraces by myriad stone walls. Tastings are in a 19th-century stone villa, reached through a large gate opening onto a garden courtyard. Ask to visit the wine cellars; they are enclosed in brick bunkers built by German forces during World War II. ♦ Free. Tastings daily. 54 Ave du Puig-del-Mas. 68.88.13.45; fax 68.88.18.55

Picnic Provisions Pick up all the fixings for a fresh, homey lunch right in the center of Banyuls-sur-Mer, where a family sells *produits locaux* (local products, in this case honey, cheeses, milk, and Muscat-de-Banyuls wine) from the courtyard of their home. ♦ No fixed hours, but someone is usually here to assist. 58-60 Ave Puig-del-Mas. No phone

107 Céret This tiny, colorful medieval village in the foothills of the Pyrénées is Catalonian through and through; *corridas* (bullfights) and *sardanes* (street dances with costumed participants) are held here regularly. Céret is known for its early-ripening vegetables and fruits (especially cherries) and, most of all, for its artists: In the early 20th century, avant-garde artists, friends of the resident Catalonian sculptor Manolo, often gathered in the village or traveled up from nearby Collioure. Céret was known then as the "Mecca of Cubism." ♦ 36 km (22.3 miles) west of Collioure on D618

Within Céret:

Musée d'Art Moderne Céret (Céret Museum of Modern Art) One of France's best modern art museums, it contains works by Matisse, Chagall, Maillol, Dalí, Juan Gris, Manolo, Miró, Picasso, and Tapiès (each of the latter two has a room devoted to their works); there are also many works by more recent artists, including Viallat and Manessier. The collection is housed in a contemporary space, with lots of natural light. ♦ Admission. Daily July-Oct; M, W-Su Nov-June. 8 Blvd Maréchal-Joffre, in the center of Céret. 68.87.27.76; fax 68.87.31.92

Les Feuillants ★★★$$$ In a beautiful turn-of-the-century villa with a terrace shaded by plane trees, this delightful establishment is one of the region's best. It's run by Didier and Marie-Louise Banyols (he's the chef; she's the sommelier). Feast on elegant Catalonian dishes like *soupions vinaigrette à l'ail doux et petits artichauts violets* (little octopus in a vinaigrette with sweet garlic and baby artichokes), *poivrons rôtis aux anchois de Collioure* (roast peppers with fresh Collioure anchovies), or rack of lamb in a salt crust. Marie-Louise Banyols has put together one of Languedoc-Roussillon's finest wine lists. Simpler, moderately priced dishes are served in a brasserie section. There is also a pleasant bar. Adjoining the restaurant are one pretty guest room and two luxurious suites—all expensive, but worth it. ♦ Tu-Sa lunch and dinner, Su lunch; closed in February. Reservations required. 1 Blvd de La Fayette. 68.87.37.88; fax 68.87.44.68

Bests

Stephanie & Phil Kimmel
Wine Importers

Village restaurant we enjoy: **Le Mimosa** in **St-Guiraud,** near **Lodève.** Run by an English couple, situated in a lovely historical structure in a tiny village. Superb food and wine list that's a who's who of quality local producers.

Good restaurant in **Montpellier: La Pomme D'Or.** Small, simply appointed city restaurant. Professional service and very nicely presented cuisine.

Carole Courtelon
Owner, Domaines de Bertaud-Belieu winery and the Villa de Belieu hotel, Gassin

Have lunch in one of the restaurants on **Plage de Pampelonne** (Pampelonne Beach) in nearby **Ramatuelle** (such as **Voile Rouge, Tahiti, Club 55, Jumeaux, Liberté, Bora-Bora, Tahiti Plage, Tropicana,** or **Aqua**). Visit the charming Provençal village of **St-Tropez,** as well as **Gassin, Grimaud,** Ramatuelle, and **Port-Grimaud.**

William Hardy
Wine Maker/Director, Domaine de la Baume, Servian

Marseilles: Sitting in **Le Vieux Port** restaurant on the banks of the canal, sipping Noilly Prat vermouth before dining on local shellfish.

Pezenas: A sunny Saturday morning in this ancient town's market, retracing the steps of Molière, who lived here in the 17th century.

Béziers: *Feria* (festival) time in August. Bullfighting festival with four days and nights of feasts (paella and sangria), dancing, and singing and partying in the streets to Spanish flamenco music.

Sète and **Agde:** A picnic on the Mediterranean coast between these two coastal towns, drinking Chais Baumière Chardonnay and dining on oysters and grilled sardines, followed by duck breasts and the local roquefort cheese, washed down with a red wine from **St-Chinian.**

What better place to make wine than in the sunny Mediterranean, with its wonderful food and friendly locals! (Unless it is Australia, of course, but that's another story!)

Estelle Daure
Director, Château de Jau, Clos de Paulilles

The **Prieuré de Serrabone**, for the impressively sober design of the priory itself and for the grandiose landscape around it. **Casa Sansa** and **L'Opéra Buffe** are two charming restaurants on tiny streets in old **Perpignan**, both with cafe tables outside. **Les Clos de Paulilles** has one of the rare unspoiled landscapes along the Mediterranean.

Lulu Peyraud
Created, with her husband Lucien, the Domaine Tempier, Le Plan-du-Castellet

The *AOC* appellation of Bandol includes seven villages: **St-Cyr, Bandol, Sanary, Le Beausset, Le Castellet, Ollioules,** and **La Cadière.** In addition to the attraction of its wines, **Bandol** offers its beaches and the pleasures of windsurfing and sailing in dinghies and sail boats, not to mention fishing for tuna and many other kinds of fish. You can also visit the inland area, where you will discover charming villages like **Le Castellet, Le Cadière, Signes,** and **Méounes** that deserve to be better known.

Patrice de Colmont
Owner, Club 55, Ramatuelle

A drive through the **St-Tropez** peninsula. From St-Tropez take the route toward the **Phare de Camarat;** from this lighthouse you will have a wonderful view of **Plage de Pampelonne** (Pampelonne Beach) and the **Ile de Porquerolles.** Then go to **Ramatuelle** and **Gassin** by way of the **Moulins de Paillas de Gassin,** then go down toward the sea by way of the **Château de Bardeyrolles,** where you can taste excellent wines. Come to St-Tropez at the end of September or beginning of October for the Nioulargue Regatta (one of the most beautiful regattas in the world, bringing together historic and contemporary vessels). Visit the **Annonciade Museum** in St-Tropez, which has one of the world's best collections of Impressionist paintings. Visit the naval museum in St-Tropez's citadel, which has an entertaining exhibit on the maritime history of St-Tropez, as well as a beautiful view of the bay. Don't miss the Provençal market on the **Place des Lices** in St-Tropez every Tuesday and Saturday morning.

Jean-Marc Banzo
Chef/Owner, Le Clos de la Violette, Aix-en-Provence

Visit the **Montagne Ste-Victoire,** which inspired Cézanne. Buy lavender and local products in the **Luberon** region. Visit the Mediterranean, such as the **Calanques** near **Cassis.** Try the golf club of **Calas Cabriès.** Visit the parks and gardens in nearby châteaux and fortified villages.

François and Georgina Sack
Wine Makers, Clos Ste-Magdeleine, Cassis

Visit the **Calanques** (fjords between **Cassis** and **Marseilles**), the port of Cassis, the **Cap Canaille** (a high cliff plunging into the sea), the many local wineries with tasting rooms, and the numerous beaches.

Etienne de Menthon
Wine Maker, Château Redortier, Suzette

The **Dentelles de Montmirail,** a chain of mountains whose name comes from the Latin *mons mirabibilis* (admirable mountain). The **Château Redortier** vineyards are in the heart of these mountains. The famous Provençal markets, such as the ones in **Vaison la Romaine** on Tuesday mornings and in **Carpentras** on Friday mornings: all the aromas and flavors of Provence brought together in a single spot. The restaurant **Le Four à Chaux** near the hilltop village of **Barroux** serves excellent French cuisine in a cool and pleasant setting; summer is the best time to go there.

Anthropologists found the skull of a Caune de l'Argo man—believed to be 500,000 years old—in Tautavel, a small wine village in Roussillon.

"There is not the hundredth part of the wine consumed in this kingdom that there ought to be. Our foggy climate wants help."

Jane Austen, *Northanger Abbey*

Restaurants/Clubs: Red   **Hotels:** Blue
Shops/ 🌳 Outdoors: Green   **Sights/Culture:** Black

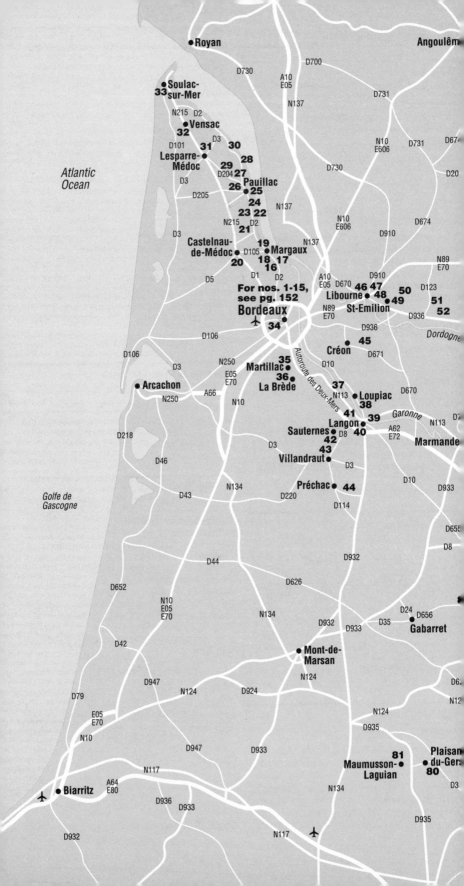

Bordeaux and the Southwest

Bordeaux and the Southwest

The landscape of Bordeaux and the Southwest is the most varied of any of France's wine regions, ranging from dense pine forests to verdant pastures to golden beaches. The beautiful countryside is dotted with medieval villages precariously perched upon hilltops, and sliced by innumerable rivers. In fact, the name of the region's chief city, Bordeaux, derives from *"bord des eaux"* (on the edge of waters). Here the **Dordogne** and **Garonne** meet to form the mighty **Gironde**, which flows like a lifeline from the city of **Bordeaux** northwest to the Atlantic. Many lesser rivers, such as the Tarn, also carve their way through the region's forests and vineyards, and picturesque villages cluster along their banks. The soft light here seems always to be filtered through river mists. The region's bounty is apparent in the local food markets, which are heaped with wild *cèpes* (mushrooms), truffles, glistening foie gras, and ropes of garlic, and it's celebrated by numerous festivals of wine, food, crafts, music, and art.

But the wine is what draws most here. The magnificent countryside is filled with wine châteaux great and small, famous and unknown. Vineyards were established relatively late in the **Bordelais**, the region surrounding Bordeaux. It wasn't until the first century that a hardy grape variety resistant to harsh winters was discovered and planted by wealthy Roman settlers. Medieval monks elevated wine making to an art here in the 12th century, during the reign of Henri Plantagenêt, King of England, and his wife, Eleanor of Aquitaine, whose dowry included most of southwestern France. Legend has it that the Plantagenêts so prized Bordeaux wine that a thousand barrels were commonly consumed during big celebrations, and anyone caught stealing grapes had his or her ear cut off. Until the French repossessed Aquitaine in 1453, English fleets loaded with textiles, metals, and foods arrived twice a year to trade their cargo for Bordeaux wine, which the English called "claret."

The Bordelais, as the region around Bordeaux is called, boasts a tremendous output of a large variety of high-quality wines, more than half of which are exported. The Bordelais is known the world over for its fine bottlings of wines from grapes that include cabernet sauvignon, cabernet franc, merlot, petit verdot, malbec, sauvignon blanc, semillon, and muscadelle. The region's most famous wines are from the **Médoc**, a flat, formerly marshy peninsula northwest of Bordeaux whose wines, a relatively small percentage of the region's production, are what most people think of as Bordeaux wines. The Médoc's wine estates were formally classified for the 1855 Paris Exhibition into *grands crus* (great growths) ranging from the highest, *premier grand cru* (first growth), to *cinquième grand cru* (fifth growth). Out of about 2,000 vineyards in the Médoc at the time, 62 were classified. The five châteaux ranked then as first growths were (and remain) **Château Lafite**, **Château Margaux**, and **Château Latour** (all from the Médoc), and **Château Haut-Brion** and **Château d'Yquem** (which are located in the nearby Garonne valley east of Bordeaux). The list remained unchanged until 1973, when **Château Mouton-Rothschild**, in the Médoc, was promoted from second to first growth. A vineyard ranked in 1855 has the right to call itself a *grand cru classé* (an officially classed great vineyard). These produce some of the world's greatest reds.

Many of the lower-ranked wines are now considered as good if not better than some of the higher *crus*. **Château Lynch-Bages** in **Pauillac** was originally classified a fifth growth, but is now considered equal to higher ranked wines. Indeed, those wines classified fifth growth were never fifth-rate. As Alexis Lichine wrote in his *New Encyclopedia of Wine and Spirits,* all the vineyards that were classified "are the absolute cream of the vineyards which, as a group, are probably the world's finest in red wine." In 1977, in an effort to provide some standard for judging the many fine châteaux that were not included in the original 1855 classification, an organization of Médoc vineyard owners classified over a hundred wines below the classed growths as *crus grands bourgeois exceptionnels, crus grands bourgeois,* and *crus bourgeois.* Here again, the rankings aren't always a reliable indicator of quality: You'll find some *crus bourgeois* that taste like *crus classés,* while others are more deserving of their lower status.

Although the famous wine villages in the Médoc such as **Margaux** and Pauillac are musts on any visit, lesser-known regions in Bordeaux are also worth exploring. Just southeast of Bordeaux at the edge of the Garonne is **Graves,** named for its gravelly soil. This is where the first wine was produced in the Bordelais. A little farther east along the Garonne are **Barsac** and the untrampled **Sauternes,** both of which make luscious sweet white wines. Between the Garonne and the Dordogne Rivers is **Entre-Deux-Mers** (literally, between two seas), known for its production of excellent dry whites. East of Bordeaux is the area's architectural jewel, the medieval village of **St-Emilion,** surrounded by its own priceless vineyards. Further east in unspoiled hill country is the **Côtes de Castillon,** which makes wine that is both undiscovered and a great value. The nearby town of **Bergerac** produces some heady reds as well as dry and sweet whites, such as Monbazillac.

Keep in mind that the top-rank châteaux of Bordeaux venerate wine almost religiously, and they expect visitors to share their passion. Those who have a sincere interest in wines or in learning more about them will be given an instructive introduction to fine wines; those who approach these châteaux with nothing more in mind than knocking back a few glasses will likely receive a chilly welcome. Also keep in mind that many of the most famous châteaux are open to visitors by appointment only, so it's best to plan ahead.

Getting to and around Bordeaux and the Southwest

Airport

Bordeaux's busy airport, the **Aéroport International de Bordeaux-Mérignac** (56.34.50.50), which handles over two million passengers a year, is located on the southwestern edge of the city, 11 kilometers (seven miles) from the center of Bordeaux by D106. All major car-rental companies have offices in the airport. Several flights arrive daily from Paris on **Air Inter** (the French national domestic airline), as do international flights from various destinations. Currency exchange is available, as are taxis and buses to the city center that stop at the train station.

Car Rental

Bergerac

Citer	53.57.73.70
Europcar	53.27.13.00
Hertz	53.57.19.27

Bordeaux

Avis	56.91.65.50
Budget	56.91.41.70
Hertz	56.91.01.71

Cahors

Avis	65.30.13.10
Budget	65.30.19.20

Europcar	65.22.35.55
Hertz	65.35.34.69
SNCF	65.22.50.50

Gaillac

Gayet	63.57.15.47
Molinier	63.57.23.54

Pauillac

Shell	56.59.04.53

Trains

The **Gare de Bergerac** (Ave du 108e-Régiment-d'Infantrie, between Cours Alsace-Lorraine and Blvd Victor-Hugo, 53.57.26.71) has a **Europcar** and **Hertz** office within the station. The best route from Paris is to take the *TGV* to Bordeaux and transfer there for the regular train to Bergerac, 100 kilometers (62 miles) farther.

In Bordeaux, the **Gare SNCF St-Jean** (Rue Charles-Dumercq, southeast of the city center and near the Garonne River, 56.91.50.50) receives *TGV* trains from Paris (a three-hour trip) and other cities, along with regional trains. **Avis** has an office within the station, and other car-rental companies have offices across the street.

The **Gare de Cahors** (Pl Gambetta, at Rue J.-Murat, 65.22.50.50) is six hours from Paris by ordinary train. **Avis, Hertz,** and **SNCF** operate car-rental offices at the station. The fastest route to Cahors is via the *TGV* from Paris (a four-hour trip) to the **Gare de Montauban** (Ave Roger-Salengro, at Ave Mayenne, 63.63.50.50), 60 kilometers (37 miles) south of Cahors. From Montauban, Cahors is a short train or bus ride away.

The trip from Paris to the **Gare de Gaillac** (Pl de la Gare, at Ave Georges-Clemenceau, 63.57.00.23) takes about eight hours by regular train. A much more efficient route would be to take the *TGV* to Montauban and connect by train or bus to Gaillac, 50 kilometers (31 miles) southeast of Montauban.

The train station in Pauillac (Pl Verdun, at Maréchal-Joffre; 56.59.04.53) is approximately four hours from Paris. You can rent cars at **Shell,** next door to the station.

FYI

Visitors' Information Offices

Bordeaux's **Office de Tourisme** (12 Cours du 30-Juillet, on Pl de la Comédie, Bordeaux, 56.44.28.41; fax 56.81.89.21) has a wealth of information (most of it available in English) on what to see and do here. They also provide free city maps, reserve hotel rooms, and organize guided city tours. The office is open daily.

St-Emilion's **Office de Tourisme** (Pl des Créneaux, 57.24.72.03) provides many maps and brochures (most of them in English) on the village and on nearby wine châteaux that are open to visitors. Ask for a copy of the *"Guide des Vins du Saint-Emilion,"* which lists all local wineries and their visitation policies (in French, with easy-to-follow symbols). The office also gives guided tours of wine châteaux, including tastings, every day at 2PM and 4:15PM in July and August; it also arranges concerts followed by wine tastings in local wine châteaux several times a year. The office is open daily.

Wine Organizations

The friendly operator of the tiny **Maison de Vin de Barsac** (Pl de l'Eglise, Barsac, 56.27.15.44) wine center has provided a little bar where you can chat (in French, anyway) about the sweet white local wines and enjoy a complimentary tasting of a few of them. Information on this small Sauternes appellation is available, and bottles of wines from Barsac and its neighbor, Sauternes, are for sale. The center is open daily.

The **Comité Interprofessionnel des Vins de la Région de Bergerac** (Professional Council on Bergerac Wines; 2 Pl du Docteur-Cayla, Bergerac, 53.57.12.57) makes its home in a lovely former cloister in Vieux Bergerac. This is an excellent place to become informed on the whole array of Bergerac appellation wines, which include reds, whites, and rosés; no tastings are given. It is open Monday through Friday.

The **Maison du Vin de Bordeaux** (Bordeaux House of Wine; 3 Cours du 30-Juillet, at Allée d'Orléans, 56.00.22.88; fax 56.00.22.77) offers a wealth of information on Bordeaux wines and organizes tours of and tastings at the châteaux that produce them. Within its flatiron-shaped building are changing exhibits on wine making; special tastings are held with a registered sommelier for a fee. The organi-

zation, which is open Monday through Saturday, also distributes free brochures and maps in English.

In the same building, the **Conseil Interprofessionnel des Vins de Bordeaux** (**CIVB**; Interprofessional Council on the Wines of Bordeaux; 1 Cours du 30-Juillet, at Allée d'Orléans, 56.00.22.66; fax 56.00.22.82) can provide more in-depth information on Bordeaux wines, most of it in English. Ask for the free booklet *"Découverte Médoc,"* which lists (in French, but with code symbols explained in English) all the Médoc wine châteaux and their visiting policies, and notes where English is spoken. The **CIVB** also manages the **Ecole du Vin de Bordeaux** (Bordeaux Wine School), which offers excellent courses on Bordeaux wines for nonprofessionals. A three-day course in English is held once every June and again in July. (An optional fourth day includes a vineyard tour accompanied by an oenologist.) Reservations are required far in advance. The center is open Monday through Saturday.

Between Bordeaux and St-Emilion lies **La Maison de la Qualité** (20 km/12.4 miles east of Bordeaux on N89, near Beychac-et-Caillau, 56.72.90.99). Here an official *Appellation d'Origine Contrôlée (AOC)* body decides what titles local wines can put on their labels (or whether they can call themselves "Bordeaux" at all). The friendly and competent staff offers free tastings of many different types of Bordeaux wines; one way to plan a wine route is to come here first to taste your way around the region. The **Maison** offers a guided visit of a typical Bordeaux wine cellar, informative publications on the region's wines, and an audiovisual display that describes the Bordeaux appellation and the mission of the **Maison de la Qualité;** however, no wines are for sale. It is open Monday through Friday from September to June, and Monday through Saturday in July and August.

In the center of Gaillac, the **Maison des Vins** (Pl de l'Abbaye St-Michel, 63.57.15.40; fax 63.57.20.01) offers tastings and a wealth of information on Gaillac's many wines. There's history here, too: It's located in the **Abbaye St-Michel,** the ancient monastery (dating to AD 972) where Gaillac's *"vin du coq"* was first made. It's open Monday through Friday.

Maison des Vins de Graves (2 Rue François-Mauriac, Podensac, 5 km/3.1 miles west of Barsac on N113, 56.27.09.25) is an efficient wine center that provides a number of printed materials, many in English, on Graves wines. Ask for the free brochure *"Les Graves Accueillent"* (Graves Welcomes You), which lists (in French, but with easy-to-follow symbols) all the Graves châteaux that accept visitors. Tastings are available, and a variety of Graves are for sale by the bottle. The center is open daily.

The **Maison de Vin de Margaux** (Pl La Trémouille, Margaux, 20 km/12.4 miles south of Pauillac on D2, 57.88.70.82) distributes brochures and other information on the wines produced near the village of Margaux, but its main function is to sell bottles from a variety of local producers. It has one of the best selections in the region, and is a great place to find an excellent, reasonably priced bordeaux that has actually aged enough to be ready to drink. It is open Monday afternoon, and Tuesday through Saturday.

The **Office de Tourisme et Maison du Vin de Médoc** (La Verrerie, Pauillac, 56.59.03.08; fax 56.59.23.38) is an extremely helpful tourist office/wine information center at the edge of the Gironde River. It's a great source for all kinds of useful brochures and other information about the Médoc, much of it in English. Another plus: Bottles of wine from all over the region are for sale at cost; look for the older vintages that may no longer be available at the châteaux. The staff also organizes visits to area châteaux, some of them by horse-drawn carriage. The office is open daily.

St-Emilion's **La Maison du Vin** (Pl Pierre-Meyrat, 57.55.50.55) is one of the best wine centers in France. It organizes wine tours and tastings year-round and sells all manner of wine-related accoutrements—from guides to local wine châteaux to fancy corkscrews and carafes. Look for the kit called *Nez au Vin* (Nose for Wine), which holds 12 tiny bottles of scents found in wine (musk, cinnamon, truffles, and so on) that help budding connoisseurs train their noses. There are also exhibits on wine making. The biggest draw, though, is the center's vast collection of St-Emilion wines from the best producers, sold at cost; many old vintages are available. The English-speaking staff is knowledgeable and helpful. The center is open daily.

The **Maison du Vin de St-Estèphe** (Pl de l'Eglise, St-Estèphe, 56.59.30.59) is small, but offers a wide selection of the rich, distinctive St-Estèphe wines, with many vintages represented. The very friendly staff provides maps and excellent information on the wines. In addition, a mini-museum displays old wine cellar tools and runs an audiovisual presentation on local wine making. A large map of the local vineyards, with all the châteaux marked, is painted on an outside wall. The center is open Monday through Saturday from April to January; there is no midday closing in July and August.

Maison de Vin de Sauternes (Rue Principale, Sauternes) sells bottles from a range of vintages and has a bar where you can sip local wines, all at wholesale prices (which still isn't always cheap). This center doesn't bother to print up brochures, lists of châteaux that accept visitors, or even copies of its price list. But the great lineup of Sauternes at the bar is sufficient reason to visit. The center is open Monday through Saturday.

Phone Book

Hospitals

Bergerac	53.63.88.88
Bordeaux	56.79.56.79
Cahors	65.20.50.50
Gaillac	63.42.50.50

Police (non-emergencies)

Bergerac	53.57.61.02
Bordeaux	56.99.77.77
Cahors	65.35.27.00
Gaillac	63.57.00.50
Pauillac	56.59.00.76
Sauternes	56.63.06.17

Bordeaux

No matter where a wine route leads in France's Southwest, it will probably begin in Bordeaux, only three hours from Paris by *TGV* (France's "very fast" trains). It was founded by a Celtic tribe in the third century BC and has grown into the largest French city devoted to the business of wine. Bordeaux is plagued by noise, pollution, and heavy traffic that makes it impractical as a base for touring the wine country, but some interesting sights are worth seeing before leaving town; the city has been making a concerted effort to refurbish its medieval center, and Bordeaux is slowly beautifying.

1 Château Chartrons $$$$ Don't expect a medieval castle—this "château" is actually several converted 19th-century wine warehouses, but it's still one of the city's finest hotels. In the heart of the Chartrons district, near the Cité Mondiale du Vin, the hotel has a Victorian facade that belies its ultramodern, extremely luxurious interior. The 143 rooms and seven suites are equipped with every imaginable amenity, including mini-bars, high-tech bathrooms, air-conditioning, and soundproofing. In addition to the gourmet restaurant **Novamagus** (see page 153), there's a bistro featuring simple regional dishes at moderate prices. Plan your tasting trip over a glass of fine Médoc in the cozy wine bar, or check out the regularly scheduled tastings of fine bordeaux held in the hotel's own wine cellars. The desk will book bus tours or arrange a car, either with a driver or a simple rental, for touring the local châteaux. ♦ 81 Cours St-Louis (between Rue Prunier and Rue Barreyre). 56.43.15.00; fax 56.69.15.21

Within the Château Chartrons:

Restaurant Novamagus ★★$$$ There is nothing quaint about this huge space with big columns; it has the look of a shopping mall. That said, the food is good, with regional specialties like *lamproie* (eel), mussels, roast duck, and all the luxurious goodies typical of the southwest, including foie gras. The real draw, though, is the excellent wine list, which features a wide assortment of bordeaux from many vintages. Still, the prices may make you head for the hotel's more reasonable bistro. ♦ Daily lunch and dinner. Reservations recommended. 56.43.15.00

2 Musée des Chartrons (Museum of Chartrons) For a museum devoted to the wine trade, the setting could hardly be more appropriate: an elegant, gray stone house built in 1720 by Francis Burke, an Irish wine dealer. With exhibits on how wine was bottled and on the role of sailing ships in the wine trade of centuries past, this is a good place to get a feel for Bordeaux's long history as a wine center. Climb the staircase with a spectacularly elaborate wrought-iron railing to the *"plancher."* Traditionally, that was the upper level of a wine cellar, where labels were applied to the bottles. Here, the *plancher* is an exhibit space for a marvelous collection of wine bottles and labels from many eras. ♦ Admission. Tu-Sa. 41 Rue Borie (between Cours St-Louis and Cours Balguerie). 56.81.52.99

3 Cité Mondiale du Vin et des Spiritueux (World Wine and Spirits Complex) This vast trade center for all things intoxicating occupies several restored wine *chais* (aboveground wine cellars) in Chartrons, Bordeaux's historic wine-dealing district. Many of the facilities at the core of the five-acre complex (a cluster of ultramodern buildings around a courtyard) are closed to nonprofessionals, but there's plenty to interest the amateur. Investigate the small museum on Bordeaux wines, which features a surprisingly intriguing display of soil samples from Margaux, Graves, and other key wine-growing areas. (It's hard to believe that samples like the one from Graves, which looks like mostly rocks, are actually ideal for creating the fabulous stuff that springs from them.) The bookstore, **Vigne-Table**, stocks several books in English on Bordeaux wines, as well as a nice selection of maps; the wine store has several fine older vintages. ♦ Daily. 20 Quai des Chartrons (between Cours Xavier-Arnozan and Rue Latour). 56.01.20.20; fax 56.01.71.00

Within the Cité Mondiale du Vin:

Hôtel Claret $$$ What this ultracontemporary hotel, a member of the Best Western chain, lacks in the way of traditional charm it makes up for in location. Right in the center of the Cité Mondiale du Vin, it's a great choice for wine-loving visitors to Bordeaux. All 97 rooms are air-conditioned, with large, private bathrooms, comfortable beds, and cable TV. Business services are exceptionally good—one reason the hotel tends to be filled with conference-going wine professionals. One of the best breakfast buffets in Bordeaux is served on a terrace overlooking the Cité and the ancient rooftops of Chartrons beyond. The traditional restaurant/bar is overpriced, but the sensational wine list is one of Bordeaux's best. ♦ 56.01.79.79; fax 56.01.79.00

4 Aliénor Loisir See the region from the water, as centuries of sailors and other river travelers have seen it. This company organizes cruises up the Garonne and Gironde on its very comfortable, big-windowed boat, the *Aliénor;* the dinner cruises are especially enjoyable. The various cruises travel north down the Gironde all the way to Pauillac (six hours round-trip); south up the Garonne to Cadillac (five hours round-trip); up the Dordogne to Libourne, with a side trip by bus to St-Emilion (4.5 hours round-trip); and to other destinations. ♦ Hangar 7, Quai Louis-XVIII (between Allées de Chartres and Allée de Bristol). 56.51.27.90

5 Esplanade des Quinconces At 12 hectares (30 acres), this square is said to be the largest in Europe. Laid out between 1818 and 1828, it presents an enormous expanse of vibrant gardens stretching down to the Garonne. At the end farthest from the river is the **Colonne des Girondins** (Girondins Column), erected in 1895 to commemorate the famous political party from Bordeaux that played a key role in the Revolution until Robespierre sent all 29 Girondin representatives, singing "La Marseillaise," to the guillotine. ♦ Quai Louis-XVIII (between Allées de Chartres and Allées d'Orléans)

6 Hôtel des Quatre Soeurs $$ Wagner aficionados will want to stay here; the master did, twice, in 1849 and 1850. Right in the center of town, the hotel was built in 1840 of the local gray stone, and has been kept up-to-date with amenities such as air-conditioning, mini-bars, TV sets, and modern bathrooms in its 35 comfortable rooms. There's also valet service. Some of the rooms overlook one of Bordeaux's busiest streets; request a quieter one facing the interior courtyard. A supremely opulent Napoleon III bar, with dark woods, ornate gilt-framed mirrors, and plush armchairs, is open almost around the clock (from 6:30AM to 2AM) even to nonguests. The bar offers a light menu, and continental breakfast is served, but there's no restaurant. ♦ 6 Cours du 30-Juillet (between Allées d'Orléans and Rue Esprit-des-Lois). 57.81.19.20; fax 56.01.04.28

6 Vinothèque Temptation strikes hard at this fantastic wine store, with an awe-inspiring display of every kind of Bordeaux wine you've ever heard of. Even jaded oenophiles may find a few surprises among the vast selection of producers and vintages. Prices are higher than they would be direct from the châteaux, but, unlike the châteaux, the store stocks several older vintages. It's also the best place to purchase wines from those châteaux that do not allow visitors or (like **Château Haut-Brion**) only sell wholesale. The friendly owner, Noël Lagrue, can also offer advice on affordable, but still excellent, bottles. In short, this is *the* source for all the wines you won't be picking up en route through the vineyards themselves. ♦ M-Sa. 8 Cours du 30-Juillet (between Allées d'Orléans and Rue Esprit-des-Lois). 56.52.32.05

7 Grand Théâtre The rival of Paris's Opéra (considered by many proud Bordelais its undisputed superior), this theater was designed by **Victor Louis,** and completed in 1780 on the site of the former Gallo-Roman forum and temple. Its noble Neo-Classical facade, with its colonnade of Corinthian columns crowned by 12 statues (representing the nine Muses and Juno, Venus, and Minerva), has reigned over the Place de la Comédie ever since. The interior of the theater is equally majestic. In fact, an impressed Charles Garnier adopted the design of its monumental staircase and its dome in his plans for the Opéra. ♦ Admission. Except for scheduled performances, the theater is open only for a one-hour guided tour, by arrangement with the tourist office (12 Cours du 30-Juillet, on Pl de la Comédie, Bordeaux, 56.44.28.41; fax 56.81.89.21). Pl de la Comédie (between Rue Esprit-des-Lois and Cours du Chapeau-Rouge). 56.44.70.71; to reserve seats for performances 56.48.58.54

8 Grand Hôtel Français $$ In a converted 19th-century town house with ornate wrought-iron balconies, this quiet, comfortable place is a member of the reliable Best Western chain. Conveniently located just steps from all of Bordeaux's major sights and shopping areas, the five-story gray stone building contains 35 sunny, spacious rooms with contemporary decor and amenities to match—all have air-conditioning, mini-bars, and well-equipped private bathrooms. There's no restaurant. ♦ 12 Rue du Temple (at Cours de l'Intendance). 56.48.10.35; fax 56.81.76.18

9 La Chamade ★★★$$$ Don't be put off by the decor—1970s high-tech, with a tad too much emphasis on black, all of it clashing with the vaulted ceiling and stone walls of the original 18th-century structure. It's worth putting up with a little aesthetic transgression to taste chef Michel Carrère's wonderful regional cuisine. This is the place to try a quintessential Bordeaux specialty: *lamproie* (eel) from the Gironde, cooked slowly in red wine sauce and served with delicious caramelized leeks (from January through March, *pibale,* succulent baby eels, are often on the menu). The *ris d'agneau* (lamb sweetbreads) from the Pyrénées are also excellent, and for dessert there's a crème brûlée—*formidable*. The wine cellar offers a fabulous selection of bordeaux at reasonable prices. The tab gets hefty if you order à la carte, but the prix-fixe menus offer great value. ♦ M-F, Su lunch and dinner, Sa dinner Sept-June; M-F lunch and dinner July-Aug. Reservations recommended. 20 Rue Piliers-de-Tutelle (between Rue St-Rémi and Rue Ste-Catherine). 56.48.13.74

10 Place de la Bourse This jewel of Bordeaux squares was built between 1730 and 1755 by the father-and-son architectural team of the **Jacques** and **Jacques-Ange Gabriel** (who designed Paris's Place de la Concorde around the same time). Facing the quays on one side, it's surrounded on the other three by magnificent buildings from the period, including the former **Hôtel de la Bourse** (Stock Exchange), now the home of Bordeaux's **Chambre et Tribunal de Commerce** (Chamber and Court of Commerce). ♦ At the intersection of Quai de la Douane and Rue St-Rémi

11 Porte Cailhau (Cailhau Gate) This turreted gate, the traditional entrance to Vieux Bordeaux, is all that remains of a former medieval seneschal's palace. Its name comes from the Gascon word for *"cailloux,"* or "pebbles," recalling the mounds of pebbles from the Garonne that once piled up at the foot of the gate after being used as ballast by passing ships. In 1495 the gate was rebuilt as a monument to Charles VIII's victory at the Battle of Fornoue, where he was aided by many of Bordeaux's nobility. ♦ Admission. Daily 2PM-6PM July–mid-September; Sa 2PM-6PM only the rest of the year. North of Pont de Pierre (at Quai Richelieu)

Restaurants/Clubs: Red   **Hotels:** Blue
Shops/ ♣ Outdoors: Green   **Sights/Culture:** Black

12 Cathédrale St-André Begun in the 11th century, this cathedral took the next 400 years to complete; it continued to be modified up through the 18th century. As a result, this most beautiful of Bordeaux's churches represents a variety of architectural styles, and its facade is a fantastic confection of statues, gargoyles, and pillars. (The west side of the cathedral is completely devoid of ornamentation, because at one time it abutted the city's ancient ramparts.) The 13th-century **Porte Royale** (Royal Portal) was built during the reign of Louis IX (St. Louis) as an entrance opened only for royal visits. It's a doorway fit for a king, or a saint: Its 10 celebrated statues of apostles inspired **Viollet-le-Duc,** the 19th-century architect, to reproduce them in his restoration of the Cathédrale de Notre Dame de Paris. Standing apart from the cathedral is its Gothic bell tower, the **Tour Pey Berland,** named after the 15th-century archbishop who built it and topped by a 19th-century gilded copper statue of the Virgin. The interior of the cathedral conveys a marvelous sense of light and space; the nave, the first part of the church to be built, has Romanesque foundations, while the vaulted ceiling overhead is 15th-century Gothic. ♦ Pl Pey-Berland (at the end of Cours d'Alsace et Lorraine). 56-52-68-10

13 Musée d'Aquitaine (Aquitaine Museum) Ensconced in a restored Victorian building, this well-organized museum honors the long history (encompassing the art, agriculture, commerce, and daily life) of the ancient province of which Bordeaux was a part. This rich land, comprising most of southwestern France, was used by the 12th-century queen Eleanor (Aliénor in Old French) of Aquitaine as a dowry in her two royal marriages—first to Louis VII of France, then to Henry II of England. Yet the region was old when Eleanor inherited it, as the displays here show. There's an impressive array of prehistoric relics, as well as a remarkable collection of Gallo-Roman artifacts, including a magnificent bronze statue of Hercules. Separate sections of the museum focus on the Middle Ages through the Renaissance, and on the modern period—from 1715 to the present. The excellent displays on the history of regional wine making from 1750 to 1950 in themselves warrant a visit. Don't miss the huge early-19th-century grape press from the Graves region. ♦ Admission; free Wednesday. Tu-Su; closed 1 May. 20 Cours Pasteur (between Cours d'Alsace et Lorraine and Cours Victor-Hugo). 56.01.51.02

14 Grosse Cloche (Great Bell) This unofficial symbol of Bordeaux looks out over the old city from the top of an ancient gate, first built in the 13th century and embellished during the 15th. Now rung only on rare occasions of national significance, the bell once was used not only to chime the hours, but also to celebrate holidays, to mourn deaths, to announce the all-important grape harvest, to warn the townspeople of danger, and to incite them to action during times of rebellion against outside rule. It was this last function that once cost the town its beloved bell: In 1548, when the French king wanted to punish the unruly Bordelais, he had it removed for the next eight years. ♦ Cours Victor-Hugo (at Rue St-James)

Cognac

Cognac, the world's most imitated brandy, can only legally be called cognac if it is made in an area north of Bordeaux that comprises most of the *départements* of the **Charentes.** Romans grew wine here, and in the 17th century, the Dutch began importing the local wines to distill into *brandewijn* (the "burnt wine" from which comes the word "brandy"). Soon after, it occurred to local growers to distill it themselves. And so the cognac industry was born.

The brandy begins as a thin white wine from ugni blanc (known locally as st-emilion) grapes. It's distilled twice in an alembic—a kind of still—and aged in Limousin oak. Since cognac is usually a mixture of brandies of different ages, no vintage appears on a cognac bottle. In the town of **Cognac** itself, where many producers and dealers are based, a black fungus that lives on the fumes given off by the brandy as it ages can be seen on walls and roofs.

Professionals advise that cognac be "tasted" with a sniff rather than a sip. High on the list of producers to visit are **Hennessy** (1 Rue de la Richonne, at Quai de la Charente, Cognac, 45.35.72.72), **Rémy Martin** (Domaine de Merpins, 2.4 km/1.5 miles southwest of Cognac on D732, 45.35.76.66; fax 45.35.02.85), and **Courvoisier** (2 Pl du Château, Jarnac, 45.35.55.55;

fax 45.35.55.00). At **Delamain** (7 Rue Jacques-et-Robert-Delamain, next to Place de l'Eglise, Jarnac, 45.81.08.24; fax 45.81.70.87), a single family has produced one of France's best cognacs for 15 generations. However, it's open only by appointment to visitors who want to learn more about the product, not necessarily taste it. **Cognacs Ragnaud-Sabourin S.A., Domaine de la Vôute** (in Ambleville, 17 km/10.5 miles south of Jarnac by D736 and D49, 45.80.55.61; fax 45.80.50.13) is run by Patricia Sabourin, who has won many awards for her cognacs. The **Bureau National Interprofessionel du Cognac** (23 Allée du Champ-de-Mars, between Rue Edith-Cavell and Pl Edouard-Martell, Cognac, 45.35.60.00; fax 45.82.86.54) is open Monday through Friday and has brochures, maps, and other information on the producers in the region.

If you decide to stay in the area, consider going where local cognac producers celebrate their special occasions. **L'Hostellerie des Pigeons Blancs** (★★$$$; 110 Rue Julyaves-Brisson, Quartiers St-Jacques, Cognac, 45.82.16.36) is an elegant restaurant with rich regional cuisine, complemented by 30 excellent Cognacs (all expensive). It's housed in an inn with three simple but comfortable guest rooms (with private baths) upstairs.

15 La Tupiña ★★★$$$ Some critics rank this homey, unassuming bistro, with its golden stone facade cheerfully trimmed in turquoise, among the best restaurants in France. The dining room is decorated with red, white, and blue Basque linens, and there's a big fireplace where chickens and beef are always roasting and rich soups, bean dishes, and stews sit and simmer. The menu suffers no shortage of seafood dishes and southwestern French fare, all of it wonderful and served in trencherman's portions. Chef-owner Jean-Pierre Xiradakis is committed to *"la sauvegarde des traditions:* *sud-ouest avant tout!"* (preserving traditions: the Southwest above all!), and his renditions of typical regional specialties are superb. Try the charcoal-grilled *magret de canard* (duck breast) or the *carré d'agneau de Pauillac* (rack of Pauillac lamb). The wine list—if not the best in the Bordeaux region, then a close contender—has about 200 bordeaux, with many from small vineyards that are excellent values. ◆ M-Sa lunch and dinner. Reservations recommended. 6 Rue Porte-de-la-Monnaie (between Rue Carpenteyre and Rue Camille-Sauvageau). 56.91.56.37

The Médoc

The Médoc, a flat peninsula bounded by the **Gironde River** and the **Atlantic**, stretches north from the city of Bordeaux. Along with Burgundy and Champagne, the Médoc is one of France's three most famous wine regions, source of most of the great wines known around the world as bordeaux. Made primarily from cabernet sauvignon grapes and aged in French oak casks, Médoc wines need time in the bottle to reveal their charms; always ask whether the wine you are tasting (or buying) is ready to drink, or when it will be.

The area offers much to discover, from its sparsely populated southern half (known as the **Haut-Médoc**) covered with marshes and pine forests, to golden sand beaches lined with small resorts, to quiet villages of simple 18th- and 19th-century stone houses. But the real draw is the wine produced here, much of it by wineries housed in opulent 18th-century *chartreuses,* the low-slung stone manor houses typical of the Bordelais. Hidden behind high walls and ornate wrought-iron gates, each elegant wine estate has its own *chai* (above-ground wine cellar) and luxuriant garden. The Médoc's great wineries are found on a gravelly strip of reclaimed marshland along the banks of the Gironde, an unlikely-seeming provenance for the likes of Château Margaux and Château Lafite-Rothschild. The main wine route here is the picturesque D2, which leads from Bordeaux through Margaux and Pauillac to the village of Saint-Vivien-de-Médoc, near the Atlantic. In this area, each row of grape-vines culminates with a rose bush. The roses have been planted for practical rather than aesthetic reasons: The rose is susceptible to many of the same diseases that attack the vine, but reveals symptoms more quickly and visibly.

Until very recently the Médoc did little to promote tourism, and a visitor's only recourse was to stay at a friend's château. Fortunately for those of us who cannot claim such friends, some inns and restaurants have opened in the area. Many châteaux now welcome visitors to tour their wineries, although most require an appointment. And in early April, during a "Portes Ouvertes" weekend, the doors of a number of otherwise inaccessible Médoc châteaux are opened to tourists.

16 Château Giscours An imposing 19th-century mansion, the château sits to the side of a grand expanse of vineyards, which were ranked as a *troisième cru* in 1855. Set in the middle of one of the best beds of gravelly soil in the Margaux appellation, its 270 hectares (667 acres) of vines are planted with cabernet sauvignon (65 percent), merlot (15 percent), and a mixture of cabernet franc, petit verdot, and malbec (20 percent) grapes. The Tari family bought the château after World War II, when it had gone into a decline, and have since restored its dense and powerful wines to their historical distinction. And the Taris are as accomplished at greeting visitors as they are at making wine. They offer a guided tour of the property, complete with an informative lecture and video presentation. In the summer, take in one of the polo matches that are held on the lawn, or stroll through the magnificent stands of rhododendron in the park behind the château; there's also a lovely, man-made lake, installed on the theory that water evaporating from it would benefit the vines. The lucky few who manage to get reservations can stay in one of the three luxurious guest rooms in what were once the stables; dinners for groups of six or more are served by prior arrangement. The Taris also organize luxurious, all-inclusive, four-day or weekend tours of the Bordeaux wine regions between April and October. ♦ M-F. English spoken. Labarde (from Bordeaux go about 14 km/8.7 miles north on D2). 57.88.34.02; fax 57.88.30.91

17 **Château Siran** Elegant red wines that are considered to be among the best in the Médoc are produced at this superb 18th-century mansion near Margaux. Its vineyards are mostly classed *cru grand bourgeois exceptionnel,* with some that were classed among the second growths in 1855. Altogether, the château comprises 250 acres of vineyards and produces not only its namesake Château Siran wines, but also its second labels, Bellegarde and Château St-Jacques, from vineyards near Labarde and Cantenac. Since 1981, it has housed its very old vintages in an underground nuclear-bomb shelter (you can never be too careful). The estate has a long and illustrious history; the archives of the village church in nearby Macau document that its founder, Guilhem de Siran, took an oath of allegiance to a powerful *abbé* (abbot) in 1428. It was later owned by the counts of Toulouse-Lautrec (the painter's ancestors) and, since 1848, has been in the hands of the Miailhe family. The tour includes a tasting, a visit to the cellars, and a look at the château's collection of wine labels designed by contemporary artists, wine bottles from the 17th and 18th centuries, and, somewhat incongruously, 19th-century faïence. ♦ Free. Daily. Siran (about 3.5 km/2 miles south of Margaux on D2; follow the signs to the winery). 57.88.34.04; fax 57.88.70.05

18 **Château Cantenac-Brown** Classed a *troisième cru* in 1855, this 77-acre estate within the Margaux appellation suffered a steady decline until 1987, when energetic new management (and major investments) brought it back into the top ranks of Médoc wines. As *Gourmet* magazine's wine critic Gerald Asher has written, the 1990 vintage

alone "should help reestablish this classed growth's reputation." The 1990 has a deep, profound color that reflects the quality of its bouquet, which suggests cocoa, coffee, and new wood. The wine is both supple and powerful, very mouth-filling. This vintage really demands more time to age, but earlier vintages are available. The estate is named for the village of Cantenac and for John Lewis Brown, a British bordeaux merchant who established the vineyards here in the early 19th century. The château is a big redbrick building that wine expert Alexis Lichine described as looking like an English boarding school. At least it has a pretty garden. ♦ Free. Visits and tastings M-F; Sa-Su by appointment. From Siran follow D2 west about 2.5 km (1.5 miles) to Cantenac, then take D105E west about 2 km (1.25 miles) and follow the signs to the château.

19 **Château Margaux** At the end of a sedately beautiful alley of plane trees, this magnificent château, built in 1802 in quintessential Empire style, greets the visitor with a grand pillared facade that's perfectly in keeping with the dignity of its wines. It was one of the four châteaux ranked *premier cru* in 1855, but its wines had been revered by aficionados for at least a century before then. Its legendary vintages from these 209 acres of vineyards have sealed the reputation of the whole appellation. The sublime reds, which are known for their luxuriously complex perfumes and their concentrated, very balanced depth of color and flavor, are many experts' favorite Médoc wines. The Pavillon Blanc wines, made from sauvignon blanc grapes, are also widely considered the best white wines the Médoc has to offer. Don't make the common mistake of confusing other wines in the Margaux appellation with the ones from this château. These occupy a higher plane altogether, with prices to match, but you'd have a hard time finding anyone who would complain they weren't worth it. Visitors get a tour of the château's imposing *chai,* one of the largest in the region. The château also has its own cooperage, where the barrels for storing wine are made. Watch the staunch workers building barrels by hand, often before a roaring fire, and be transported to another time. ♦ Free. M-F; closed in August and during harvest. Appointment required; English-speaking guides available on request. Rte des Grands Crus, just before the village of Margaux. 57.88.70.28; fax 57.88.31.32

19 **Le Relais de Margaux** $$$$ Built in the 18th century of the creamy, pale stone indigenous to the area, this 28-room, three-suite luxury hotel is surrounded by its own 40-acre park, complete with a swimming pool and tennis courts. The rooms, decorated in contemporary style, are spacious, with every modern amenity; the best of them overlook a

Château La Tour-de-Mons

flower-filled interior courtyard. The continental breakfast features excellent homemade breads; afternoon cocktails are served on a pleasant stone terrace. The location is perfect for touring the Médoc châteaux. The only problem: If you can afford to stay here, you may as well buy a château of your own. ◆ From Margaux go 2 km (1.2 miles) east on D105; follow the signs to the hotel. 57.88.38.30; fax 57.88.31.73

Within Le Relais de Margaux:

Restaurant Relais de Margaux ★★$$$ Overlooking a delightful garden (where tables are set in the summer), it has a short but varied menu designed to set off its list of (surprise!) incredible—and incredibly expensive—wines. The menu depends on the season and the market, but might include *agneau de Pauillac en écrin de sel* (Pauillac lamb in a salt crust) or *magret de canard lissé de miel et d'épices* (duck breast with a coating of honey and spices). The prix-fixe lunch menu served weekdays is a relative bargain. ◆ Tu-Su lunch and dinner mid-May–Sept; Tu-Sa lunch and dinner, Su lunch Oct–mid-May. Reservations recommended. 57.88.38.30

19 Château Lascombes Once owned by a group of American wine lovers, including Alexis Lichine, this château is a gray stone mansion covered with vines, much warmer and cozier-looking than most of the Médoc châteaux. It is in the Margaux appellation (ranked a *deuxième cru* in 1855), and was originally a feudal holding of the dukes of Duras. Its 240 acres of vineyards, which adjoin those of **Château Margaux,** produce wines that have a light quality with a hint of violets. They are made from 65 percent cabernet sauvignon, 30 percent merlot, and the rest cabernet franc and petit verdot grapes. The grapes are still handpicked, and 20 to 50

percent (depending on the vintage) of the wine is aged in new oak. The wines mature fairly early for Médoc wines, but also age well. If any of the excellent 1988s are on hand, snap them up. The tour of the château is very informative and well organized, and ends with a tasting. ◆ Free. Daily June-Oct; M-F Nov-May. From Margaux go 2 km (1.25 miles) north on D2; follow the signs to the château. 57.88.70.66; fax 57.88.72.17

19 Château La Tour-de-Mons Run by the same family for over three centuries, this château is one of the sleepers along the Médoc wine route: A *cru bourgeois* within the Margaux appellation, it can usually be relied on for both quality and reasonable prices. The 35 hectares (86 acres) of vines, many of them quite old, produce wines that tend to have a pronounced bouquet of toasted vanilla and fruits; they are full in the mouth, with what some say is a hint of coffee. The château itself is spectacular—right out of a fairy tale—with one crenellated tower and another with a tall, pointed roof. ◆ Free. M-Sa. Marsac (from Margaux go about 4 km/2.5 miles north on D2). 57.88.33.03; fax 57.88.32.46

20 Château du Foulon $$ In what is surely one of the most magnificent establishments to come under the heading of "bed-and-breakfast," the charming Vicomte and Vicomtesse de Baritault offer four guest rooms near all the great Médoc wine towns. Their 19th-century, Neo-Classical, pale stone château is surrounded by a well-groomed 100-acre private park, full of ancient, stately oaks and crossed by a lovely stream. Two of the rooms are really huge suites (one sleeps four, the other three); both have private bathrooms. The other two rooms are regular doubles, one with a private bathroom, the other with its own bathtub, but the WC (toilet) down the hall. All the rooms are large, comfortable, and elegantly furnished in traditional style, with dark wood furniture and the occasional antique. ♦ Reservations required. Castelnau-de-Médoc (from Margaux go 10 km/6.2 miles west on D105; follow the signs to the château). 56.58.20.18; fax 56.58.23.43

CAP LÉON VEYRIN

21 Château Cap-Léon-Veyrin The Meyre family has been making wine here for five generations, and the current generation, Maryse and Alain Meyre, produces a very good Listrac (one of the Médoc village appellations). It's made from 60 percent merlot, 37 percent cabernet sauvignon, and three percent petit verdot grapes; the dominance of merlot gives the wines a rich, fruity quality. The wines have won many top awards, but still sell for reasonable prices. In addition, the Meyres are extremely knowledgeable sources of information on the local wines (they also speak English). ♦ Tastings M-Sa. Donissan (from Castelnau-de-Médoc go about 9 km/5.6 miles north on N215; follow the signs to the château). 56.58.07.28; fax 56.58.07.50

Within Château Cap-Léon-Veyrin:

Hôtel Château Cap-Léon-Veyrin $ The Meyres rent seven simple but very comfortable rooms in their home, which is not so much a château as a manageably sized mansion, a 19th-century white stone building with tall white shutters and a red tile roof. The rooms are small, but have cheerful floral wallpaper, antique furnishings, and private bathrooms. Breakfast is included, and excellent dinners are served on request. The couple will also arrange visits to nearby châteaux, and are full of suggestions of other things to see and do in the area. If you come during the *vendanges* (grape harvest), you can even help pick. All in all, a stay here is a wonderful introduction to the real life of the Médoc. ♦ Reservations required. 56.58.07.28; fax 56.58.07.50

"I rejoice, as a moralist, at the prospect of a reduction of the duties on wine. It is an error to view a tax on that liquor as merely a tax on the rich. Prohibition of its use to the middling class is condemnation of them to poison whiskey."

Thomas Jefferson, *Letters*, 1818

Restaurants/Clubs: Red   Hotels: Blue
Shops/🌳 Outdoors: Green   Sights/Culture: Black

1990
CHATEAU
MAUCAILLOU

MOULIS

APPELLATION MOULIS CONTROLÉE

MIS EN BOUTEILLE AU CHATEAU

DOMAINES DU CHATEAU MAUCAILLOU
PROPRIÉTAIRE A MOULIS-EN-MÉDOC · GIRONDE · FRANCE

PRODUCT OF FRANCE   PRODUIT DE FRANCE

21 Château Maucaillou Built in 1875 in a hodgepodge of earlier architectural styles, this lovely ocher château may once have cut an odd figure, but has settled into its garden-filled setting quite well. Its 55 hectares (136 acres) of vines were planted in the 15th and 16th centuries—very early for the Médoc. The terrain is made up of the large, shiny pebbles (*cailloux*) that gave the château its name; they are excellent for retaining heat and helping the grapes ripen. The *cru bourgeois* wines produced here are *cru classé* quality. Those with the Château Maucaillou label are made from 62 percent cabernet (mostly cabernet sauvignon, some cabernet franc), 32 percent merlot, and six percent petit verdot; they're full-tasting and well rounded. Other wines produced here include La Dame de Maucaillou, a white Sauvignon, and La Rosée de Maucaillou, a light rosé that's perfect for picnics. The château also offers classes in wine tasting and even helicopter tours of the Médoc. ♦ Free. Daily. Near Médrac, southeast of Donnisan (from Donissan take a community road 3 km/1.9 miles south to Listrac-en-Médoc, then go east about 5.5 km/3.4 miles on D5[E2] and follow the signs to the château). 56.58.01.23; fax 56.58.00.58

Within the Château Maucaillou:

Musée des Arts et Métiers de la Vigne et du Vin (Museum of the Arts and Professions of the Vine and of Wine) The Dourthe family, which owns **Château Maucaillou,** has put together one of France's best museums on wine making, housed in one of the château's outbuildings. A visit begins with a film (in French) on wine making, and is followed by some very interesting exhibits on wine-making methods past and present. Among the items on display are a gnarled vine planted in 1820, a cork-making machine, vineyard tools dating from the 19th century, and 16th- and 17th-century oak casks. One of the most intriguing exhibits is the *orgue à arômes* (scent organ), an instrument that emits the different aromas of wine. A visit to the ultramodern tanks and other equipment in current use concludes with a generous tasting, accompanied by a commentary (most of the guides speak English). A small shop here sells bottles of the château's wines. There's a restaurant that serves simple meals (by reservation only), but beware: It's often overrun by tour groups who have reserved *en masse.* ♦ Admission. Daily. 56.58.01.23; fax 56.58.00.88

22 Château Ducru-Beaucaillou On a hill overlooking the Gironde, this splendid 18th-century château was originally built in the traditional *chartreuse* (charterhouse) style, with golden stone and a red tile roof. The two square towers were added in the 19th century. The château's name, which means "the growth of the beautiful pebble," is fitting, because its topflight wines spring from 49 hectares (120 acres) of mostly gravel, one of the best wine *terroirs* in the region. The vineyards, in the St-Julien appellation, were classed *deuxième cru* in 1855, and produce some of the finest wines in the Médoc. In fact, many critics say these are the first among *deuxième cru* wines, what some call "super-seconds," and that they represent the quintessential St-Julien wine. Both the Château Ducru-Beaucaillou and its second label, La Croix-Beaucaillou, are supple, full-bodied wines that can be counted on to please, regardless of the vintage. ♦ Free. By appointment; closed August and during harvest. Beaucaillou (5 km/3.1 miles south of Pauillac on D2). 56.59.05.20; fax 56.59.27.37

23 Château St-Pierre One of the sleepers of the Médoc, this château in the St-Julien appellation has produced wines since the 17th century and was classed a *quatrième cru* in 1855. It fell into decline until 1981, when it was purchased and resurrected by Henri Martin, patriarch of a highly respected bordeaux-making family and mayor of St-Julien-Beychevelle for over 40 years. The château, which dates from the 18th and 19th centuries, is one of the most impressive on the Médoc wine route, a three-story Neo-

Classical affair, built of creamy white stone and stucco with a square tower. Today its wines, produced from a relatively small 20 hectares (50 acres) of vineyards, are considered among the Médoc's best, but are still priced reasonably. They are made in the classic Médoc manner from 70 percent cabernet sauvignon, 25 percent merlot, and five percent cabernet franc grapes. Several older vintages are usually available, as are the estate's other wines, Château Haut-Beychelle-Gloria, Château Bel Air, and the supreme wine, Château Gloria (see below). ♦ Free. M-F by appointment. St-Julien-Beychevelle (5 km/3 miles south of Pauillac on D2). 56.59.08.18; fax 56.59.16.18

23 Château Gloria The angels blowing trumpets on its label are appropriate; Château Gloria is a wine worth celebrating (if you can afford it). It is made of 65 percent cabernet sauvignon, 25 percent merlot, five percent cabernet franc, and five percent petit verdot, from vines ranging from 20 to 80 years old. Again we have the late Henri Martin (see **Château St-Pierre,** above) to thank for the marvelous Château Gloria *cru bourgeois*

Château St-Pierre

wines. To create them, he patiently bought up, almost row by row, 45 hectares (110 acres) of vines scattered around St-Julien on some of the area's finest *terroirs*. Many believe their quality is further evidence that the ranks of the *crus classés* should be reshuffled. **Château Gloria** itself is a 19th-century manor house that shares **Château St-Pierre**'s grounds; visitors may tour the château, as well as the modern *chais*. ♦ Free. M-F by appointment. St-Julien-Beychevelle (5 km/3 miles south of Pauillac on D2). 56.59.08.18; fax 56.59.16.18

23 Château Talbot Classed a *quatrième cru* in 1855, this large estate in the St-Julien appellation was named for the English commander who was defeated in the 1453 battle that put an end to both the Hundred Years' War and British domination of Aquitaine. The château is a one-story 18th-century mansion dominated by a square tower and surrounded by gardens. Owned by Jean Cordier, one of Bordeaux's foremost *négociants* (wine dealers), the château's 100 hectares (250 acres) of vineyards produce sturdy, yet supple wines that many feel deserve an even higher ranking. The château also bottles a second label, Connétable Talbot. ♦ Free. By appointment; closed August and during harvest. From St-Julien-Beychevelle take D104E west about 3 km (1.8 miles) and follow the signs to the château. 56.73.21.50; fax 56.73.21.51

Pauillac

Pauillac, the Médoc's largest town, is itself nondescript, but is surrounded by some of the world's greatest and best-known wine châteaux, including **Château Lynch-Bages, Château Latour, Château Pichon-Longueville, Château Lafite-Rothschild,** and **Château Mouton-Rothschild.** A few have decided to open their massive iron gates to the public; as for the others, you can always view their priceless vines from the road. Take the time to drive along the little vineyard roads and soak up the light and air that have helped to produce Médoc's greatest concentration of *grand cru* wine estates.

24 Château Latour Just across a small ravine from the last of the St-Julien vineyards, this first of the Pauillac châteaux was one of the four 1855 *premiers crus*. It was renowned as early as the 16th century, even earning a mention in Michel de Montaigne's *Essais*. The château itself dates only from 1881; it's a simple, two-story affair, whose relatively small size is  likely explained by the fact that no right-minded wine grower would encroach on the priceless vines here any more than necessary. The round stone tower (*tour*) of the château's name still stands at the edge of the vineyard's 60 hectares (150 acres); it also appears on the wine's label. It was once part of a medieval fortification built to protect the locals from pirate attacks. The rest of the fort, which stood on the site of the *chais*, was destroyed during the Hundred Years' War. A persistent legend has it that a vast fortune in gold pieces was concealed in the old fort's moat; the story has gained some credence since the discovery of documents in the Tower of London that refer to a treasure here. But it also could be that the treasure is and always has been simply rock—the fabulously stony *terroir*. An 18th-century owner of the château, the Marquis de Ségur, even had glittering, polished bits of quartz from the vineyards sewn to his garments; this prompted Louis XV to describe the Marquis as "the richest man in my kingdom. His soil produces nectar *and* diamonds."

More recently, the château spent several years in the hands of a group of British investors, but returned to French ownership in 1993. The estate has always been known for its integrity and adherence to the highest standards. It still retains its very old vines for as long as possible; that makes for finer wines, but far lower yields than the average vineyard would need to survive economically—one reason these wines are so expensive. Yet they are invariably outstanding, even in years that send the rest of Bordeaux back to the drawing board. Many believe the *terroir* here (and at the other first-growth Pauillac estates) is the most perfect on earth for cabernet sauvignon grapes, which make up a large portion of the wines—about 80 percent. The wines are rich, full-bodied, almost imposing, and require a long time in the bottle. The château's second label, Les Forts de Latour, is excellent, too, though still expensive. The lucky few who get appointments here will be treated to a very informative tour and a tasting. ♦ Free. By appointment. From Pauillac go about 3 km (1.8 miles) south on D2; follow the signs to the château. 56.59.00.51; fax 56.59.23.49

24 Château Pichon-Lalande The 60 hectares (148 acres) of vineyards adjoining **Château Latour**'s here were classed *deuxième cru* in 1855. Not long before, they had been part of one huge estate, belonging to the Pichon family, barons of Longueville, that included the lands of **Château Pichon-Longueville-Baron** (now simply called **Château Pichon-Longueville**) across the way. But in the 19th century the estate was split by inheritance between Sophie, the Comtesse de Lalande, and her brother, the Baron de Pichon; the two estates have been separately owned ever since. Though both are second growths, many feel **Pichon-Lalande** has the edge. The wines are excellent, sometimes a bit lighter and headier than other Pauillacs, and very dependable. The estate also produces a second label, Réserve de la Comtesse. The lovely 17th-century château has an elegant reception room with a spectacular view of the vineyards of Pauillac and St-Julien; on display is a collection of wine glasses and other wine-related objects. ♦ Visits free; tastings only with purchase. M–F by appointment. From Pauillac go about 3 km (1.8 miles) south on D2; follow the signs to the château. 56.59.19.40; fax 56.59.29.78

24 Château Pichon-Longueville Unlike its sister château, **Pichon-Lalande** (see above), this *deuxième cru* château does not encourage visitors, but accepts them by appointment. The talented Jean-Michel Cazes, who owns **Château Lynch-Bages,** has run this estate on behalf of its official owners—his family's large insurance company—since 1987. Thanks to his efforts, what some critics judged to be less-than-stellar wines (compared to celestial top Pauillacs) have become things of the past. The 31 hectares (77 acres) of vines produce wines that are deep purple and well balanced, with a complex, woodsy bouquet of vanilla, fruits, and many other scents. The second label, Les Tourelles de Longueville, is also outstanding. The 1851 château is a striking mishmash of architectural styles (the predominant one seems to be Neo-Renaissance), with two stone towers shaped like Egyptian obelisks. ♦ Visits and tastings free. By appointment. From Pauillac go about 3 km (1.8 miles) south on D2; follow the signs to the château. 56.73.17.17

24 Château Cordeillan-Bages $$$$
Perfectly located amid a cluster of great Médoc wine châteaux, this luxurious hotel is housed in a lovely 17th-century château of golden stone, surrounded by gardens and vineyards. Inside are 21 rooms, four suites, a fine restaurant, and even a highly rated wine school. The rooms are huge, decorated in elegant, contemporary style, with muted but cheerful colors (for example, the honey-colored room adorned with gold-and-white curtains). All have sumptuous bathrooms, satellite TV, direct-dial phones, jacks for computer modems, safes, and mini-bars. The pampering at this Relais & Châteaux member makes it worth the (very) high price; absolutely splurge on it if this is your once-in-a-lifetime trip to the Médoc and you can afford to. ♦ Closed late December–February. Bages (from Pauillac go 2 km/1.25 miles south on D2). 56.59.24.24; fax 56.59.01.89

Within the Château Cordeillan-Bages:

Restaurant Cordeillan-Bages ★★★$$$
The elegant dining room overlooks the surrounding vineyards, and in nice weather, you can dine on the two outdoor terraces just steps from the vines. The chef focuses on inventive variations on regional specialties, including the famous Pauillac lamb. Dishes include a *petit ragoût d'asperges et de morilles* (a little stew of asparagus and morel mushrooms), *saint-pierre au laurier* (John Dory—a fine fish—with bay leaves), and *ris de veau aux carottes* (veal sweetbreads with carrots). Prix-fixe menus present excellent opportunities to sample the haute cuisine and elegant atmosphere at moderate prices. The wine list is absolutely sensational—some say one of the best in France—and the cellar is open for visits. ♦ Tu–Sa lunch and dinner, M dinner, Su lunch Feb–mid-Dec; closed late December–January. Reservations required far in advance. 56.59.24.24

Ecole de Bordeaux This highly rated wine school is directed by Pierre Paillardon, voted the best young sommelier in France in 1979 and the best Paris sommelier in 1986. It offers a variety of classes, all available in English, including a simple introduction to wine tasting, a *"mono-cépage"* (single grape variety) tasting, a tasting of four wines with lunch at the restaurant, and a five-day course that involves tastings at châteaux throughout the region. Guests of the hotel are invited to certain free courses. ♦ Reservations recommended. 56.59.24.24; fax 56.59.01.89

24 Château Lynch-Bages Ranked a *cinquième cru* in 1855, this Pauillac château is nevertheless considered the equal of many higher-ranked châteaux (it's beaten many of them in blind tastings)—and its wines are priced accordingly. Since 1933 the 70-hectare (175-acre) estate has been in the hands of the Cazes family, which has brought it to the top ranks of Médoc vineyards. (The Cazes also own the **Château Cordeillan-Bages,** the **Château Pichon-Longueville,** and, in St-

Estèphe, the **Château d'Ormes-de-Pez**.) The wines are absolutely outstanding, very aromatic, complex, and perfectly balanced. The second label, Château Haut-Bages Avérous, is also exceptional, and much more affordable. The 19th-century château is set back from the vineyard road on the side away from the river. It is named for a former owner, the Irishman Thomas Lynch, who settled here in the 18th century and established a family that became prominent in the region. "Bages" is the name of another very old wine-growing family of the area, whose name also went to the hamlet in which the château is located. ♦ Free. Visits M-F. Appointment recommended. Bages. 56.73.24.00; fax 56.59.26.42

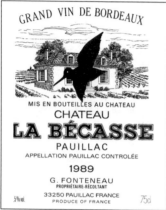

24 Château La Bécasse Founded late by Médoc standards, in 1966, this reliable Pauillac château has already made a name for itself. The wines are made from 55 percent cabernet sauvignon, 36 percent merlot, and nine percent cabernet franc, from vines with an average age of about 35 years. Grapes are picked manually, and all the wines are aged in oak, 35 percent to 40 percent of it new. The château (a modern house) produces only about 25,000 bottles per year, which makes its wines difficult to find anywhere else—and they are definitely worth trying. ♦ Free. M-Sa. Bages. 56.59.07.14

24 Château Croizet-Bages In the heart of the Pauillac appellation, this small *cinquième cru* estate is made up of the domains of two old Médoc families—the Bages estate, which dates from the 16th century, and the Croizet estate, from the 18th century. But even with this august heritage, the estate lacks the aristocratic relic of a château; there's just a modest 18th-century house where the manager lives. The wines are made from 21 hectares (52 acres) of vines, 70 percent cabernet sauvignon, 20 percent merlot, and 10 percent cabernet franc. The resulting potions are very powerful, with a ruby red color and an almost spicy bouquet, with a

touch of truffles. The same owners produce two other wines, Château Rauzan-Gassies (from an estate in the Margaux appellation) and Château Bel-Orme-Tronquoy-de-Lalande (an excellent value from vineyards in St-Seurin-de-Cadourne). Visitors are given a friendly, informative tour of the 18th-century stone *chais*, whose atmosphere is dramatically enhanced by candlelight and classical music in the background. The attractively laid out garden offers pleasant rhododendron-lined walks. Martine Mandé, the very competent public relations director, can arrange guided tours of the area, including tastings, and participation in the *vendanges* (grape harvest), with tastes of the new wine; she also organizes buffet dinners with, of course, the estate's wines on hand. ♦ Free. Visits M-F mid-June–early Sept; by appointment only Oct–mid-June. For information on tours and special events, contact Madame Mandé (56.59.66.69). Bages. 56.59.01.62

25 Hôtel de France et d'Angleterre $$ Located in the center of Pauillac—and smack in the middle of some of the world's greatest vineyards—this modest but comfortable 29-room hotel is a good base for a foray around the appellation. The main building is a three-story 19th-century stone house adorned with wrought-iron balconies overlooking the Gironde. Some less charming (though still adequate) rooms are in a motel-like, modern annex that overlooks an interior garden. All rooms have private bathrooms, TV sets, and telephones. A pleasant terrace is the perfect spot for afternoon tea or (what else?) a leisurely glass of bordeaux. ♦ Closed late December–mid-January. 3 Quai Albert-Pichon (opposite Port de Plaisance), Pauillac. 56.59.01.20; fax 56.59.02.31

Within the Hôtel de France et d'Angleterre:

Restaurant Hôtel de France et d'Angleterre ★$$$ This dining room is saddled with a pretentious (and overpriced) menu of regional dishes. Stick to the simpler fare, like the excellent Pauillac lamb, or the prix-fixe menus; you're likely to get a good meal for the price. ♦ Daily lunch and dinner June-Sept; Tu-Sa lunch and dinner, Su lunch Oct-May. Reservations recommended. 56.59.01.20

25 Médoc Cycle The relatively flat terrain in the Médoc makes it great for touring on two wheels, and a labyrinth of vineyard-access roads winds throughout the Pauillac country-side, just begging to be explored. There's no better way to get close-up views of the area's hallowed vines. This friendly bike shop rents bicycles at reasonable rates, by the day, weekend, or week. In summer, reserve in advance. ♦ Tu-Sa. 6 Rue du Maréchal-Joffre, Pauillac. 56.59.02.29

25 Château Batailley Occupying 45 hectares (110 acres) in the Pauillac appellation, this *cinquième cru* château is a lovely, 18th-century, golden stone mansion surrounded by formal French gardens planted in the late 19th century. The main entrance is flanked by two imposing stone lions. The wines are excellent—and an excellent value—although they lack the complexity of some of the more famous, higher-ranked Pauillac wines. ♦ Visits free; tastings only with purchase. M-F; Sa-Su afternoons. From Pauillac take D206 west 3 km (1.8 miles) and follow the signs to the château. 56.59.01.13; fax 56.00.00.70

26 Château Pontet-Canet The Tesseron family, who also own **Lafon-Rochet** in St-Estèphe, bought this Pauillac château after it suffered from indiscriminate management in the early 1970s. They tightened up the reins and have turned it into yet another *cinquième cru* estate that many say rates a second- or third-growth classification—and the wine prices reflect its unofficially recognized quality. The wines are made predominantly from cabernet sauvignon grapes (about 75 percent), with some merlot, resulting in full-bodied wines with a bouquet of vanilla and ripe fruit; they are best when given plenty of time to mature. The second label is Les Hauts de Pontet. Traditionally one of the biggest producers in the Médoc, the estate encompasses 75 hectares (185 acres) of prime *terroir*. A narrow drive lined with shade trees leads to the 18th-century, golden stone château, which is charming in its simplicity, with white shutters and clean lines. Vine-covered outbuildings with claret-colored shutters, and a beautiful rose garden add to the quietly graceful ambience. Visitors are welcome to drop by without reservations—a rarity among top Médoc châteaux. ♦ Free. Daily. From Pauillac take D2 north to D205 west and follow the signs to the château. 56.59.04.04; fax 56.51.64.05

26 Château Mouton-Rothschild This famed château has the distinction of being the only Médoc château to change rank since the 1855 classification seemingly wrote them in stone. It was originally classed *deuxième cru*—at which point its owner, the baron Nathaniel de Rothschild, came up with the disgruntled motto, *"Premier ne puis, second ne daigne, Mouton je suis!"* (I can't be first, I won't be second, but I *am* Mouton!). After more than a century of the family's furious lobbying, the French government elevated the château to *premier cru* on 21 June 1973. Then-owner Baron Philippe de Rothschild declared, *"Premier je suis, second je fus, Mouton ne change"* (I am first, I was second, but Mouton never changes). The château is now run by the baron's daughter, the baroness Philippine de Rothschild; the family also produces wines from its other estates, including the *cinquième*

cru **Château d'Armailhac** (formerly known as the Château Mouton Baronne-Philippe), just up the road.

The château itself is relatively small, leaving all the more room for the wine facilities. But the grand *chai* is stunning: Rank upon rank of barrels fill its vast length (900 feet), which leads to a backlit seal of Mouton on the far wall. The *caves*, a rare feature in a Bordeaux château, are also breathtaking. Beneath vaulted ceilings covered with ancient mosses are stored over 100,000 bottles of priceless bordeaux, including every vintage back to 1859.

The châteaux's renowned wines are made according to the strict standards of quality set by Baron Philippe. Composed of 75 percent cabernet sauvignon, they are very hard and tannic when young. In time, though, they become positively magnificent, even brilliant. For many years the wine labels have borne images of works by famous painters; the 1990 vintage sports a Francis Bacon, who might qualify as an Old Master by the time the wine comes into its own! ♦ Admission. By appointment; closed in August. English-speaking guides available on request. From Pauillac take D2 north about 2.5 km (1.5 miles) just past the D205 turnoff and follow the signs to the château. 56.59.22.22

Within the Château Mouton-Rothschild:

Musée du Vin de Mouton (Museum of the Wines of Mouton) Here is perhaps the world's greatest collection of wine-related art and artifacts from around the globe and every era. Painstakingly gathered by Baron Philippe de Rothschild and his wife, Pauline, the items include priceless wine vessels such as Egyptian alabaster cups, faïence wine bottles from medieval Persia, and 17th-century Venetian-glass goblets, together with paintings, tapestries, and other objects, all beautifully displayed. ♦ By appointment

26 Château La Fleur Milon A reliable *cru bourgeois* château that produces good wines at reasonable prices. They are full-flavored and balanced, tasting of ripe fruits with a hint of leather. The château is a rambling stone farmhouse built during the 19th century; unlike most of its Bordeaux brethren, it accepts visitors—very warmly, at that—and offers tastings without appointments. ♦ Free. M-F. From Pauillac take D2 north to D205 west and follow the signs to the château. 56.59.29.01; fax 56.59.23.22

26 Château Lafite-Rothschild One of the most respected Médoc names, this *premier cru* château has 90 hectares (222 acres) of vineyards that have produced fine wines for the last 800 years. According to one theory, the château's name comes from Gombaud de Lafite, who might have produced some of the earliest of these noble wines in the 13th century. Another theory is that "Lafite" stems from its commanding location atop the highest hill in Pauillac; an old Gascon word, *la hite,* means "the height." Whatever the derivation, the name and the wine became synonymous with nobility. It was the only wine served at dinners given by Louis XV's mistresses, the Marquise de Pompadour and the Comtesse du Barry, and it was said to be the king's favorite wine. Lafite's prestigious reputation also dazzled Nazi field marshall Hermann Göring, who declared that he would claim the château and vineyards as his personal spoils when Germany won World War II.

Luckily, the current owners remain the ubiquitous Rothschilds, actually a different branch of the family than the owners of **Mouton-Rothschild** and **Armailhac.** (Back in the 19th century, when Nathaniel Rothschild was toiling to make his great Mouton wines, his brother James caught the fever and bought **Lafite.**) The talent for wine producing seems to be hereditary, for these Rothschilds rival their cousins across the way. In the past, the

Mouton Rothschilds and the **Lafite** Rothschilds competed every year, informally but aggressively, to see whose wines could fetch the higher prices. In the 1970s, when they began to price themselves right out of any market, the two branches settled into a less public, more comradely rivalry.

As a wine-producing property, **Lafite** is as old as France's Gothic cathedrals, but the exquisite château dates from the 17th century. Shaded by cedars, it's surrounded by a Louis XIV balustrade. Visitors (no more than six at a time) are taken through a massive, rather forbidding new circular *chai* designed by Spanish architect **Ricardo Bofill.** A formal tasting follows the visit, and clearly demonstrates what all the fuss is about. These wines are often described as majestic—deep purple, exquisitely balanced, with a complex bouquet—and they need a very long time to arrive at their peak—sometimes 30 years or more. The château bottles an excellent second wine, Moulin des Carruades. It also possesses the oldest known bottle of Médoc still in

Eat, Drink, and Be Merry in Bordeaux and the Southwest

Key grape varieties: cabernet sauvignon, cabernet franc, merlot, petit verdot, malbec (also called auxerrois and cot), tannat, sémillon, sauvignon, muscadelle.

Classification system: Conceived at the Paris Exhibition of 1855, the Bordeaux classification ranked (by price, since that seemed to be the best measure of value) only those wines that were most esteemed at the time: the whites of **Sauternes,** the reds of **Médoc,** and Haut-Brion of **Graves.** The most desirable category in the Médoc is *premier grand cru,* followed by *deuxième grand cru, troisième grand cru, quatrième grand cru,* and *cinquième grand cru.* Sauternes wines were divided into only three categories, and the top category, *premier grand cru* (first great growth) has only one stellar member, Château d'Yquem; the other two categories are *premier cru* and *deuxième cru.* Haut-Brion was the only Graves château classified, and it was named a *premier grand cru.* There is no classification in **Pomerol. St-Emilion'**s vineyards received their first official classification in 1955; a new version was instituted in 1986. It is as follows: St-Emilion and St-Emilion *grand cru* are the two St-Emilion appellations. The superior wines in the latter category have been classified as St-Emilion *grand cru classé* and, at the very top in the ranking, St-Emilion *premier grand cru classé* (of which there are now 11 châteaux, divided into "A" and "B" lists). This classification, last revised in 1986, is revised every 10 years following periodic tastings; wine estates that violate strict classification standards can be demoted at any time. Each of five villages near St-Emilion has the right to hyphenate the names of the village with the name St-Emilion on wine labels but cannot use the name St-Emilion alone.

Culinary specialties: In this region, menus are studded with items cooked *à la Bordelaise,* but such dishes will differ from restaurant to restaurant. At some places the term will refer to a sauce of wine, butter, tomato, shallots, and herbs; at others, to a *mirepoix* sauce (carrots, onion, celery, ham, and herbs reduced to liquid form). Still others will simply dot such a dish with *cèpes* (large fleshy mushrooms) or artichokes and potatoes. Though the contents may be a mystery, all of the choices are delicious. Below are some additional morsels that figure prominently in the local cuisine:

agneau de Pauillac (baby lamb from Pauillac)

cassoulet (white bean and meat casserole)

confit de canard (duck preserved in duck fat)

entrecôte à la bordelaise (steak with shallots, bone marrow, and red wine)

entrecôte aux sarments (steak grilled over vine cuttings)

escargots bordelaises (snails stewed with pork, garlic, shallots, and red wine)

foie gras d'oie and *foie gras de canard* (goose or duck foie gras)

huîtres (oysters)

lamproie (lamprey eel from the Gironde)

lou kencous (hot sausages)

moules de bassin (mussels from the Arcachon basin south of Bordeaux)

truffes (black truffles)

existence—its own 1797 vintage. ♦ Fee for tasting. Tu-Th 2PM-4:30PM; closed in August and during the grape harvest. Appointment required. From Pauillac follow D2 north about 4 km (2.5 miles) to the château. Appointment 1/42.56.33.50, orders or information 56.73.18.18; fax 56.59.26.83

27 Château Cos Labory One of five classed-growth châteaux within the St-Estèphe appellation, it was classed a *cinquième cru* in 1855, but some say the wines deserve a higher ranking. The château's vineyards are spread across 15 hectares (37 acres) on the border of St-Estèphe, neighboring **Château Cos d'Estournel** and Pauillac's **Château Lafite.** The wines are typical of their appellation, whose heavier soil (with more clay and less gravel) produces big, well-rounded wines that lack some of the delicacy of the Pauillacs. The château is a small 19th-century manor house typical of the region; what's atypical is the giant sequoia tree, imported from the US in the 19th century, that looms over the entrance to the driveway. ♦ Free. By appointment. From Pauillac go 5 km (3.1 miles) north on D2. 56.59.30.22; fax 56.59.73.52

27 Château Cos d'Estournel With a prime location on the border of the Pauillac and St-Estèphe appellations, this château was classified *deuxième cru* in 1855, but has long been regarded as one of the greatest of the great second growths. In fact, an arched gate built on the property in 1830 is inscribed (in Latin), "Traveler, stay thy steps, and on the hillside contemplate these peerless vines; they are monuments worthy of thy gaze. O taste and see how delectable this pure wine, how wondrous its bouquet, and give praise to God, the creator of such great blessings." High praise, indeed. And now, under the direction of Bruno Prats, the 57 hectares (140 acres) produce some of the best Cos d'Estournels ever—between 180,000 and 400,000 bottles each year. Aged in oak casks, the wines are made from about 60 percent cabernet sauvignon, 38 percent merlot (a relatively high percentage for the Médoc), and two percent cabernet franc; the vines are 35 years old on average. Cos d'Estournels are a bit lighter and more supple than other great St-Estèphes, but still rich and long-lived. The château's second label is Château Marbuzet, a very reliable *cru bourgeois* wine that many say is on par with the *crus classés;* it has a particularly appealing bouquet of ripe fruit, vanilla, and a touch of prune.

The château itself is without a doubt the most unusual in the Médoc: Its 19th-century builder imported architectural features from all over the world, especially the Orient, giving it the appearance of some fantastic Chinese temple. The huge wooden doors at the entrance came from the palace of the Sultan of Zanzibar. The

little pagodas that adorn the vineyard walls were used as gun emplacements by German troops during World War II. Tours of the château are available in English, and are accompanied by an audiovisual presentation. ♦ Free. By appointment. From Pauillac take D2 north about 5 km (3.1 miles) and follow the signs on the right to the château. 56.73.15.50; fax: 56.59.72.59

27 Château Haut-Marbuzet Near Cos d'Estournel's **Château Marbuzet** vineyards, this château (a *cru grand bourgeois exceptionnel*) competes neck and neck with its neighbor for critical acclaim (no doubt confusing consumers in the process). The wines, which contain an unusually high amount of merlot (60 percent), are produced with special care and aged in all-new oak casks; the results are very mouth-filling, with a powerful bouquet that has hints of tobacco. The château's second label is Château Tour de Marbuzet. Instead of a single château here, a *hameau* (hamlet) of 18th-century stone buildings sits amid the estate's 38 hectares (94 acres) of vines. Visitors are given an instructive tour of the *chais* and a tasting. ♦ Free. M-Sa by appointment. About 7 km (4.4 miles) north of Pauillac via D2, then D2E; follow the signs to the château. 56.59.30.54; fax 56.59.70.87

27 Château Montrose Although classed *deuxième cru* in 1855, this fine estate's wines are not as expensive as most other second growths. They are full and powerful, with a distinctive gamey bouquet, and they age extremely well. The château also bottles a second wine, La Dame de Montrose. The château, an attractive white villa, is set amid 67 hectares (166 acres) of vineyards overlooking the Gironde. ♦ Free. By appointment. About 9 km (5.6 miles) north of Pauillac; take D2, then D2E; follow the signs to the château. 56.59.30.12

27 Château St-Estèphe/Château Pomys These neigboring *cru bourgeois* châteaux in a hamlet near St-Estèphe date from the 19th century and are surrounded by their vineyards; under one ownership, tours and tastings are given at both. The wines of **Château St-Estèphe** are made from 55 percent cabernet sauvignon, 30 percent merlot, 10 percent cabernet franc, and five percent petit verdot and malbec; they are considered superior to those of **Château**

Pomys, which are made with a higher percentage of cabernet franc grapes. ◆ Free. Visits and tastings M-F mid-May–mid-Sept; M-F afternoon Jan–mid-May; by appointment mid-Sept–Jan. Leyssac (from Pauillac go about 6 km/4 miles northwest on D2). 56.59.32.26; fax 56.59.35.24

Within Château Pomys:

Hôtel Château Pomys $$ A lovely golden stone edifice surrounded by its own park, it offers 10 luxurious guest rooms. All are spacious, decorated in typical French Provincial style, and have private baths and large windows overlooking the gardens; they're very reasonably priced for the Médoc. Breakfast is included, but there's no restaurant. For tighter budgets, a small, well-equipped campground is also on the property. ◆ Reservations recommended well in advance. 56.59.73.44

28 Chambres d'Hôtes Leemann $$
Françoise Leemann offers one big, luxurious guest room with private bathroom, TV, minibar, and automatic kettle (a rare amenity in France for the deprived tea drinker) in her 19th-century town house in the quiet wine village of St-Estèphe. Leemann, who speaks English, is a great source of information about the Médoc. She also provides a copious breakfast, and will even produce orange juice and eggs for her American visitors. Evening meals are available by request. ◆ Reservations required. In the center of St-Estèphe (from Pauillac go about 11 km/6.8 miles north on D2E). 56.59.72.94; fax 56.59.39.58

28 Château Calon-Ségur Don't pass this one by. The northernmost of the Médoc *crus classés,* this *troisième cru* château was owned in the 18th century by the Marquis de Ségur, who also owned **Château Lafite** and **Château Latour.** His motto, *"Je fais du vin à Lafite et à Latour, mais mon coeur est à Calon"* (I make wine at Lafite and Latour, but my heart is at Calon), is inscribed over the gateway to the château. To signify the marquis's special affection for this estate, the wines bear a heart shape on their labels, and the château's second label, Marquis de Ségur, perpetuates his memory. The estate has been called the greatest of the third growths, and is often ranked above many second growths. The wines made here may not match those of **Lafite** and **Latour,** but they are consistently excellent, mouth-filling and well balanced, with a dark, intense color that reflects their taste. The vines are very old, left as long as possible before being replaced, which partly explains the wines' complexity. The beautiful château, a grand, elegant structure with twin towers, dates from the 17th century; it is surrounded by lush gardens, with 50 hectares (123 acres) of vineyards beyond. The château also has an interesting *cave* (wine cellar), unusual for this region of *chais.* No wines are sold here to individuals, though. ◆ Free. By appointment. Just outside St-Estèphe, on the northern edge of the village. 56.59.30.08; fax 56.59.30.27

Château Sociando-Mallet

28 Château Sociando-Mallet A highly recommended stop on any Médoc wine tour. When Jean Gautereau bought this 30-hectare (75-acre) estate in 1969, it was a mess: *"Il pleuvait dans le cuvier, des herbes hautes poussaient entre les ceps, et je ne connaissais rien à la vigne"* (The vats were full of leaks, the vineyards were overgrown with tall weeds, and I knew nothing about wine making). Since then the *cru grand bourgeois* has come a very long way. *Gourmet* magazine's wine critic Gerald Asher cited the 1990 Sociando-Mallet as one of the best wines he tasted in a recent trip to the Médoc; Robert Parker, in his book *Bordeaux,* also ranked the château among the top Médoc estates. One reason for its success is the vineyard's excellent location on one of the last gravelly outcroppings in the Haut-Médoc, but it could never have been achieved without Gautereau's passionate conviction that *"Le vin naît par la dégustation, pas par des chiffres"* (Wine is a matter of taste, not statistics). The care given to the wine production here is rare for an unclassed growth: The wines are filtered very lightly, macerated for a month, and aged in oak (about half of it new) for about 15 months. The resulting wines are very powerful, almost black, and they age extremely well. The château's second label, Demoiselle de Sociando, is also excellent. Visits and tastings are given in a magnificent brick *chai* with a beautiful view of the Gironde. ◆ Free. M-F; Sa morning by appointment. From St-Estèphe go about 3 km (1.8 miles) north on D2E; follow the signs to the château. 56.59.36.57; fax 56.59.70.88

Restaurants/Clubs: Red   **Hotels:** Blue
Shops/ 🍴 Outdoors: Green   **Sights/Culture:** Black

29 Association Farfadet Sport This small association of bicycle and wine enthusiasts organizes excellent guided bike tours of Médoc châteaux every year during the *Portes Ouvertes* (Open Doors) weekend in early April, the only time that many great châteaux accept casual visitors. Other bike tours are offered at other times. The various tours range from about seven miles to 40 miles, offering options for everyone from the casual peddler to the dedicated decathlete. Participants may bring their own bikes along or rent them on the spot, and receive a souvenir T-shirt and a bottle of wine (naturally, a Médoc). ♦ Rte de Bourdin, Vertheuil (from St-Estèphe go about 5 km/3.1 miles west on D204E). 56.41.99.30

30 Château Loudenne One of the most beautiful in Bordeaux, this lovely pink-and-white château is set amid a large park crisscrossed with pleasant paths and sporting a croquet lawn, all overlooking the Gironde outside St-Estèphe. The 49-hectare (120-acre) estate has been owned by the English firm Gilbeys since the late 19th century, and it does have a British air about it. Informative tours are offered, including tastings of its *cru grand bourgeois* wines, which include a pleasant, dry Sauvignon Blanc. But the real draw here is the excellent wine school (see below). ♦ Free. Visits and tastings M-F, Sa-Su 2PM-5:30PM July-Aug; M-F Sept-June. St-Yzans-de-Médoc (from St-Estèphe go about 11 km/6.8 miles north on D2E and D2). 56.09.05.03; fax 56.09.02.87

Within Château Loudenne:

L'Ecole du Vin du Château Loudenne (Wine School of Château Loudenne) A highly instructive three-hour class, given in French or English, takes in the château, the ins and outs of viticulture, and the entire process of turning grapes into wine; it concludes by tasting the fruits of this fascinating art. A more in-depth weeklong course is also offered. There's also a small wine museum on the premises. ♦ Fee. Apr–early Oct. Reservations are required several months in advance. For course brochures in English, contact: Charles Eve, Ecole du Vin, Château Loudenne, 33340 St-Yzans-de-Médoc, France

"There is not a corner nor a burrow in all my body where this wine doth not ferret out my thirst."

Rabelais, *Gargantua*

CHÂTEAU La Tour de By

30 Château La Tour de By The *tour* (tower) of this château's name is a former lighthouse that once helped passing ships negotiate the Gironde; today it's surrounded by a sea of vines, 58 hectares (144 acres) in all. This *cru bourgeois* estate's wines are full-flavored and long-lived—and, what's more, they're reasonably priced. The 1990 should make a perfect bottle for celebrating the turn of the century. In addition to its reliable wines, the château offers one of the most informative tours of any in the Médoc; it includes a visit to the lovely *chais* and a small museum, a slide show on wine making, and a tasting. ♦ Free. M-F. English spoken. From St-Yzans-de-Médoc take D2 north 7 km (4.3 miles) to D3 west and follow the signs to the château. 56.41.50.03; fax 56.41.36.10

The Médoc's Atlantic Coast

For a breath of fresh sea air after trooping through winey-smelling cellars, head for the Médoc's coast, where pine groves and dunes shelter a long stretch of public beach. Two of the most popular seaside communities near the Médoc châteaux are **Soulac-sur-Mer,** 49 kilometers (30 miles) from Pauillac, and **Montalivet-les-Bains,** 41 kilometers (25 miles) from Pauillac. Soulac-sur-Mer is a lively, family-oriented resort town of converted fishers' houses with brightly painted shutters. It gets especially crowded in the summer, however.

Montalivet-les-Bains is known for its beach, officially designated *naturiste* – it's a low-key nude beach frequented mostly by families. From the nearby village of **Vendays-Montalivet,** eight kilometers (five miles) inland, drive here via D102 or take the bike trail that parallels D102 and ends in a pine grove with a pretty picnic area at the edge of the beach community.

31 Château Layauga $$ Ideally placed for touring the wineries of the northern Médoc (the Bas-Médoc), this delightful hotel is also only 15 kilometers (nine miles) or so from the Atlantic beaches. It's a good place to relax after hitting the Médoc vineyards and before heading back along the nearby fast route (N215) to Bordeaux. Inside the pretty 17th-century château are seven enormous guest rooms decorated in Louis XV style, with cheerful fabrics, comfortable furniture, and large, well-equipped private bathrooms. The entire setting is tranquil, but the most peaceful rooms look out over a lush lawn and a little pond. Given the shortage of decent rooms in the Médoc and this hotel's special charm and comfort, it is a real find. ♦ Reservations recommended far in advance. Gaillan-en-Médoc (from Pauillac take D204 20 km/12.4 miles northwest to Lesparre-Médoc, then follow N215 north about 2 km/1.25 miles). 56.41.26.83; fax 56.41.19.52

Within the Château Layauga:

Restaurant Château Layauga ★★★$$$
Chef-owner Philippe Jorand favors treating the finest products (such as truffles, the freshest seafood, game in season, and foie gras) simply, to allow their inherent sublime flavors to shine through. Try the *truffe en feuilletage* (truffle in a pastry) or the *sauté de homard au poivre doux* (sautéed lobster with sweet peppers); the desserts are wonderful; save room for a soufflé or tart, either one served warm. The outstanding wine list offers something in the neighborhood of 500 choices, about half of them bordeaux. The catch is the prices. But if you stick to the cheapest prix-fixe menu and avoid temptation when ordering wine, you can still have a great meal without blowing your budget. ♦ Daily lunch and dinner. Reservations required. 56.41.26.83

32 Moulin de Vensac *Moulins* (windmills) still dot this windswept region, but this 19th-century windmill is one of the rare few that still grinds flour in the traditional fashion. An informative 45-minute tour gives a step-by-step explanation of the centuries-old process of turning wheat into flour. ♦ Admission. M-Sa Mar-May, Oct-Nov; M-F June, Sept; closed July-August and December-February. From Lesparre-Médoc take N215 north about 13.5 km (8.3 miles) to Vensac and follow the signs to the windmill. 56.09.45.00

33 Hôtel La Dame de Coeur $ You can't miss this hotel; near the beach in Soulac-sur-Mer, it sports a 15-foot-tall mosaic of *La Dame de Coeur* (The Queen of Hearts) herself. Within are 16 functional, spacious, and very affordable rooms. They are clean and quiet, with private bathrooms. A small restaurant serves basic regional cuisine. ♦ Closed Sunday. 103 Rue de la Plage, Soulac-sur-Mer. 56.09.80.80

The Garonne Valley

Graves

The Graves wine district stretches from Bordeaux along the south bank of the **Garonne**'s terraced valley; it's filled with pine forests, farms, and the gravelly soil (**graves**) that gave the area its name. Graves once produced primarily sweetish white wines, but now is known mainly for its dry whites and top-quality reds. (Graves surrounds the smaller regions of Sauternes and Barsac, but since those wines are so distinctive they have separate *AOC* categories.) Although the same grapes are grown here as in the Médoc, these wines are a bit more rustic, with spicy or smoky overtones.

First cultivated by the Romans, Graves vineyards began garnering acclaim in 1300, when Pope Clement V (then the archbishop of Bordeaux), established his own wine domain here; today it's known as **Château Pape-Clément.** Graves wines also caught the attention of the famous London diarist Samuel Pepys, who wrote in 1663 that he had tasted "a sort of French wine called Ho Bryan that hath a good and most particular taste that I ever met with." That was Château Haut-Brion Pepys enjoyed, and all these centuries later it is still one of the top Graves wines.

Except for **Château Haut-Brion,** the only Graves estate to be included in the 1855 Médoc classification, Graves châteaux weren't classified until 1959. At that time 15 châteaux (once more, including Haut-Brion) were honored, some for their red wines, some for whites, some for both. In 1987, the northern part of the Graves appellation, where some of its finest wines are produced, formed a new appellation, Pessac-Léognan. The southern part of the region continues to use the name Graves.

34 Château Haut-Brion The wine that Pepys praised so highly back in the 17th century is still the Graves region's most famous red wine. **Haut-Brion** is the oldest of the great Bordeaux estates and the only Graves estate to be included in the 1855 classification, which ranked it right at the top, a *premier cru.* Both its red and white wines, now officially part of the Pessac-Léognan appellation, also made the 1959 Graves classification. The château's history as a wine-growing estate dates to the 14th century, but its wines first achieved international renown in the 16th century, when its owner, a wealthy Bordeaux merchant named Jean de Pontac, began distributing them widely. By the late 17th century, the enterprising Pontac family had hit upon a surefire way of sealing Haut-Brion's already vast popularity in England. They opened a tavern in London, the Sign of Pontac's Head, which served only Pontac family wines; it became a favorite hangout of Defoe, Dryden, and Swift. Several illustrious centuries later, in 1935, the château was purchased by American banker Clarence Dillon, and his estate still owns it, as well as the redoubtable Graves estates **Château La Mission-Haut-Brion, Château Laville-Haut-Brion,** and **Château La Tour-Haut-Brion.**

Three flags—the US, the French, and the new European Union flag—fly at the entrance of the noble 17th-century château, which

169

overlooks 44 hectares (108 acres) of surrounding vineyards. The red wines here are fruity, earthy, and velvety, very full in the mouth. With their sumptuous bouquet (which has been described as suggesting coffee, spices, and leather) and intense flavor, Haut-Brion reds are unusual in that they're good almost anytime: Age gives them complexity, but they can be savored even when young. The white wines, made in small quantities, and the second label, Château Bahans-Haut-Brion, are also formidable. The *chais* are open to the public—one spectacular room, with massive stone pillars and exposed beams, contains long rows of barrels lit by a large, wrought-iron candelabra hanging overhead—and a tasting is part of the tour. The visitors' center includes displays detailing Haut-Brion's history. Unfortunately, no wines are sold directly to individuals here. ♦ By appointment. 133 Ave Jean-Jaurès (N250) (about 5 km/3.1 miles southwest of Bordeaux city center). 56.00.29.30

34 Château Pape-Clément As the château's name implies, Pope Clement V held sway over this domain in the 14th century, but he would probably be scandalized by the 19th-century, faux-Gothic extravanga of a château that stands here now. Just ignore the château and concentrate on the estate's fine wines. The *cru classé* reds and equally well bred whites (the estate didn't produce white wines when the classification was made in 1959) are among the best Graves on the market—and some of the most expensive. The grapes are grown on 27 hectares (67 acres) of vineyards that are now part of the Pessac-Léognan appellation. The 1989 red has an ink-dark color and a complex bouquet of figs, blackberries, and a bit of vanilla; like the other reds here, it's best left corked up awhile (until at least the turn of the century). The excellent, aromatic 1992

white wine, made from sauvignon blanc and sémillon, is ready to be enjoyed right now. ♦ Free. M-F by appointment. 157 Ave du Docteur-Marcel-Penard, Pessac (on the southwestern edge of Bordeaux, on N250). 56.07.04.11; fax 56.07.36.70

35 Château Smith-Haut-Lafitte Best known for its fine red wines, which made the cut in the 1959 Graves classification, this famous wine château has recently received special praise for its white wines; both now fall into the relatively new appellation of Pessac-Léognan. The Cathiard family, which took over the 49-hectare (122-acre) domain in 1991, has restored the magnificent 18th-century manor house, built brand-new cellars, abandoned the use of chemical weed killers, and made the selection of grapes much more strict; all their efforts are restoring the reputation that was beginning to go by the wayside before they came along. The 1992 white wine, made completely from sauvignon grapes and aged in new oak, is rich, intense, and balanced; it can be enjoyed in 1995, but will be even better in a few years. The reds, made from cabernet sauvignon with some merlot and cabernet franc, have a rich, ruby color and an intensely fruity bouquet. Visitors are welcomed to a tasting and sales center inside the château and are free to tour the *chai*. ♦ Admission. M-F by appointment. Martillac (from Bordeaux take N113 southeast about 8 km/5 miles to Martillac and follow the signs to the château). 56.30.72.30; fax 56.30.96.26

36 Château de Labrède This 15th-century Gothic château is noteworthy not only for its spectacular beauty, but also because it was the birthplace (in 1689) and home of Charles-Louis de Segondat, baron of Montesquieu, one of the philosophers whose writings formed the basis for modern democracy. The

Ballooning Over France

Though the countryside of France is beautiful on foot, its splendor and grace are even more impressive when seen from above. Whether you choose an elegant picnic flight or a novelty ride in a balloon shaped like a birthday cake, don't miss the bird's-eye view.

Most flights last from one to 1.5 hours (allow three hours, including preparation and transport to and from the balloon), and are followed by a wine or champagne toast. Some companies combine balloon tours with on-the-ground activities. For example, a three-day hotel-barge cruise in **Burgundy** includes one balloon flight, and a one-day wine-tasting excursion in Chablis or the Loire Valley includes a balloon flight. Tours in English can usually be arranged. Below are a few reliable companies:

France Montgolfières 6 Pl de la Gare, Vermenton, 89270 Burgundy. 86.81.64.93; fax 86.81.62.25. Central reservations in Paris: 1/40.60.11.23; fax

1/45.58.60.73. In the Loire Valley, contact Jane Adamson in Monthou-sur-Cher: 54.71.75.40; fax 54.71.75.78

Champagne Air Show 15 *bis* Pl St-Niçaise (at Blvd Victor-Lambert), 51100 Reims. 26.82.59.60; fax 26.82.48.62

Club Tonus Montgolfières 36 Rue Léo-Lagrange (between Canal de l'Aisne-à-la-Marne and Parc Léo-Lagrange), 51100 Reims. 26.82.80.04; fax 26.49.08.52

Ballons de Bourgogne In Burgundy: 80.24.20.32; fax 80.24.12.87. For reservations from the US: Premier Travel, 4210 82nd St, Suite 222, Lubbock, TX 79423. 806/797.7799, 800/6.TRAVEL

austere château lies on the border of the Landes forests, surrounded by green meadows and a wide, placid moat. Montesquieu loved this place above all others and he produced wines here, which he sold very profitably to the English. In fact, Montesquieu got the idea for the gardens (which remain as he designed them) in England; in a letter to a friend, he boasted of them, "Here, nature can be found in her dressing gown, just having gotten out of bed." Visitors to the château can see Montesquieu's bedroom, with most of its original furnishings, and the great, drafty, and vaulted library, where it's not difficult to imagine the philosopher, his fingers numb with cold, scribbling his lofty thoughts. ♦ Admission. M, W-Su afternoon July-Sept; Sa-Su afternoon Easter-June and Oct–mid-Nov; closed mid-Nov–Easter. La Brède (from Bordeaux take N113 southeast 11 km/6.8 miles, then follow D108 southwest 3 km/2 miles to La Brède). No phone.

37 Château de Chantegrive The Lévêque family consistently produces excellent red and white Graves, as well as a rosé, from this 87-hectare (215-acre) estate; they also make a sweet white Cérons wine from vines planted in the official Cérons *commune.* All of the château's wines are produced by traditional methods, without chemical weed killers. The red wines are made from 55 percent cabernet sauvignon, 35 percent merlot, and 10 percent cabernet franc, while the dry whites are 50 percent sémillon, 40 percent sauvignon, and 10 percent muscadelle. Try the top-of-the-line dry white, the Cuvée Caroline, with delicious overtones of quinces and plums, and the top-of-the-line red, the full-flavored Cuvée Edouard; both are aged in oak. Visitors may tour the estate's modern *chais;* the *chai à barriques* (aboveground barrel cellar) is filled with long rows of wooden barrels containing

the precious, aging wine, and the vaulted stone ceiling of the *cave de vieillissement* (aging cellar) soars over racks and racks of bottles. Incidentally, the name "Chantegrive," which means "song of the thrush," pays tribute to the bird that loves to feed on ripe grapes in these vineyards. ♦ Free. M-F, Sa morning. From Bordeaux take N113 southeast about 24 km (15 miles); the château is just east of the village of Virelade, between Virelade and Podensac. 56.27.17.38; fax 56.27.29.42

Premières Côtes de Bordeaux: Loupiac and Ste-Croix-du-Mont

The Premières Côtes de Bordeaux is a 50-kilometer (30-mile) strip of gorgeous vineyards sloping along the steep northern banks of the **Garonne**—on the wrong side of the tracks, according to the Bordeaux classification system. The region's more successful neighbors—the great vineyards of Sauternes, Barsac, and Graves—lie just yards away across the river, but can command much higher prices for their wines. The reason lies at least partly in the weather patterns; the thick fogs that roll over Sauternes, aiding the development of the "noble rot" that distinguishes its grapes, amass here much less often. Nevertheless, this region's Loupiac and Ste-Croix-du-Mont appellations have made a name for themselves (though it's not a familiar one across the Atlantic) by producing Sauternes-style wines, many of them quite good, at far lower prices. More recently, ambitious growers here have tired of keeping up with the Joneses and have begun planting different grape varieties. So far their efforts have been mostly rewarded, with some fine reds and dry white wines worth keeping an eye on.

Domaine du Noble

38 Domaine du Noble The friendly Déjean family have been making wine here near the village of Loupiac for five generations. Their ancient house is perched high on a hill and reached by a steep road twisting through vineyards, with a beautiful view of the countryside from the top. The Déjean's wines are a real find. Their specialty is the traditional Loupiac sweet white wine; it's made Sauternes-style, with grapes from vines that are a whopping 40 to 100 years old! The 1990, a great year for the region, is sublimely balanced and rich, and sells for about half the price of one of its counterparts across the river in Sauternes. Unless you're a licensed oenologist, you'll probably never know it isn't the real thing. ♦ Free. Visits M-Sa by appointment. Loupiac (37.5 km/23.3 miles southeast of Bordeaux city center on D10; or from Bordeaux take A62 about 26 km/16 miles to the turnoff for D117 north, cross the river to Cadillac, about 4.5 km/2.8 miles, where you'll pick up D10 southeast for the last 2.5 km/1.6 miles to Loupiac). 56.62.99.36; fax 56.76.91.31

38 Château La Rame Florence and Yves Armand produce a highly rated Ste-Croix-du-Mont sweet white wine using traditional Sauternes techniques. They warmly welcome visitors to an attractive tasting room in the château's former stables, and their enthusiasm for their estate and the whole difficult business of making these wines is infectious. The château is an elegant 18th-century stone manor house that surveys its vineyards—and the spectacular sweep of the Garonne Valley—from atop a steep hill. The vineyards are planted in 75 percent sémillon and 25 percent sauvignon, with vines averaging 60 years of age. If you get a chance, taste the rich Ste-Croix-du-Mont Réserve du Château 1990, one of the best vintages around here in years. With its mouth-filling taste and suggestions of mangoes and apricots, this wine won a *coup de coeur* (special appreciation) award from the prestigious Hachette wine guide. As good as many wines from the true Sauternes appellation, it makes an excellent, economical substitute for its often exorbitantly priced

Saint-Macaire

cousins. ♦ Free. Visits M-F. Ste-Croix-du-Mont (from Loupiac go about 3 km/2 miles southeast on D10; follow the signs to the château). 56.62.01.50; fax 56.62.01.94

39 St-Macaire This medieval village overlooking the Garonne is one of the region's most picturesque. Stroll around the 12th-century ramparts, built when the city was founded; the southern gate offers a fine view of the river below flowing past the limestone cliff on which St-Macaire is built. The Place du Marché-Dieu in itself is worth a trip here. It's surrounded by houses dating from the 14th through the 16th centuries; most are built of pale golden stone and topped with roofs containing *embans,* arches supported by columns. ♦ From Ste-Croix-du-Mont go about 5.5 km/3 miles southeast on D10. From Bordeaux go 50 km/31 miles southeast on A62; it's just across the river from Langon

Within St-Macaire:

Restaurant L'Abricotier ★★$$ In an old stone house on the edge of St-Macaire, this cheerful dining room is bedecked with fresh flowers, white tablecloths, and the occasional well-placed antique; during the summer, tables are set on a pretty garden terrace shaded by an ancient plane tree. The cooking is strictly regional, with some inventive touches. Try the river fish, including *alose* (shad) in the spring and *lamproie* (eel). The *petits-gris aux pieds de porc* (tiny snails with pigs' feet), *flan d'asperges aux langoustines* (asparagus and crayfish custard), and *aiguillettes de canard au fumet rouge* (slices of duck breast with red wine sauce) are other specialties. The caramelized pears make a divine finale. ♦ M, W-Su lunch and dinner, Tu lunch. Reservations recommended. 2 Rue Bergoeing. 56.76.83.63

40 Restaurant Claude Darroze ★★★$$$ Claude Darroze admirably carries on the tradition of his father, the great chef Jean Darroze. Housed in an ancient *relais de poste* (stagecoach inn), this excellent restaurant has earned two Michelin stars for its unusual variations on regional classics, such as *huîtres farcies glacés au sabayon au Sauternes* (stuffed oysters with Sauternes-based zabaglione). It is *the* place to sample a favorite local dish, *lamproie de la Gironde* (eel from the Gironde), beautifully done here. There's a superb wine list too. ♦ Daily lunch and dinner; closed most of January and mid-October–early November. Reservations required. 95 Cours Général-Leclerc, Langon (50 km/31 miles southeast of Bordeaux on A62). 56.63.00.48; fax 56.63.41.15

At the Restaurant Claude Darroze:

Hôtel Claude Darroze $$ In the old days, the location made this a logical stop on the stagecoach route; today, Claude Darroze's elegant little hostelry is an excellent base for touring the wineries of Entre-Deux-Mers and Sauternes. The 14 good-sized rooms are decorated in homey, French country style, but are equipped with all the modern conveniences and private bathrooms. The breakfasts are both plentiful and outstanding. ◆ Closed most of January and mid-October–early November. 56.63.00.48; fax 56.63.41.15

Sauternes

The rare golden wine of Sauternes is always described with such expressions as "sunshine in a glass" and "nectar of the gods." Its luscious sweetness and high alcohol content derive from an unusual process. The grapes (mostly sémillon, with sauvignon blanc and sometimes a little muscadelle) are left on the vine to soak up the morning mists and the warm sun until Botrytis cinerea bacteria sets in, causing *pourriture noble* (noble rot) to develop and sugar to concentrate. This grape decay is the secret of a fine Sauternes but the degree of rot is crucial, so all grapes in Sauternes are picked by hand in stages, and if even after this care the grapes don't have the required amount of natural sugar, the wine cannot be labeled sauternes at all.

The district comprises five villages, one of which is Sauternes itself. The appellation is known the world over for one wine: Château d'Yquem. This golden-hued potion is so rare and expensive that most of us will never taste it. In mediocre years, no Château d'Yquem is released; even in a *good* year, the yield is approximately one glass of wine per vine. It was at Château d'Yquem that the effect of extreme noble rot was discovered in 1847, when the grapes were left exceptionally late on the vine. The result was so unusual that the château didn't even release the wine, but Russia's Grand Duke Constantine tasted this vintage 12 years later and immediately offered a fortune for it, changing the style of Sauternes forever. (Unfortunately, you need to have the status or wherewithal of Grand Duke Constantine to even get near the grand Château d'Yquem today; luckily, neighboring châteaux are more welcoming.)

The village of **Barsac** is the largest of the five *communes* that make up the Sauternes appellation, and as such it is permitted to put its own name on its wines, sometimes in addition to the Sauternes name. Barsac produces sweet white wines in the same manner as its more famous neighbor, but they cost far less. The terrains in the Barsac appellation are not as prestigious as those in Sauternes, and perhaps are not quite as ideal for the production of these wines; nevertheless, Barsac produces some of the finest sweet whites in the region, a little lighter than Sauternes. To reach Barsac from Bordeaux, take A62 southeast about 26 kilometers (16 miles) to the intersection with D117 north; take D117 four kilometers (2.5

miles) to Cérons, then N113 southeast along the river three kilometers (1.8 miles) to Barsac.

Given the price tags sported by its wines, you might expect the village of Sauternes itself to be the pinnacle of high-class elegance, with fancy boutiques and multistarred restaurants. In fact, it's just the opposite, a quiet hamlet lost in the middle of vineyards and woodlands. To reach Sauternes from Bordeaux, take A62 to the same turnoff as for Barsac, but instead, go south on D11 to Landiras. At Landiras, pick up tiny D125 southeast, following signs to Sauternes.

41 Château de Malle If you're thinking "when you've seen one Renaissance château, you've seen them all," this treasure of a palace will prove otherwise. Enter the estate through an ornate wrought-iron portal (which is pictured on the château's wine labels), beyond which lies a perfectly proportioned château topped by a slate mansard roof and flanked by horseshoe-shaped wings, each ending in a massive round tower. It is surrounded by terraced gardens in the Italianate style popular when the château was built in the early 17th century. The Comtesse de Bournazel, a descendant of the orginal owner, lives here now, and she graciously opens it to visitors; it's filled with period furnishings and works of art, including a rare collection of trompe l'oeil silhouettes. But there's more to **de Malle** than meets the eye; refined palates will find plenty to keep them occupied too. The château has the unique privilege of possessing vineyards, 50 hectares (124 acres) in all, that overlap both the Graves and Sauternes appellations. Its Sauternes were classified one of the 14 *deuxième cru* estates in 1855, and they're still considered among the best. Tastings include both red Graves and the excellent Sauternes. ◆ Admission; tastings offered with purchase. Daily (no midday closing) July-Aug; daily Easter-June, Sept–mid-Nov; closed mid-Nov–Easter. Appointment required. Just south of Preignac (from Sauternes take D8 about 6 km/3.7 miles north. From Bordeaux take A62 southeast about 30 km/18.6 miles to D8, the turnoff for Preignac; follow the signs to the château). 56.62.36.86; fax 56.76.82.40

"What precisely differentiates a perfect bourgeois growth in Pauillac from its seignorial neighbor— or a Vosne-Romanée from La Tache? It is the same thing that separates de Hooch from Vermeer. It can only be sensed, but one knows that between the two is an abyss; the one is terrestrial, the other divine. And the mystery remains intact."

Richard Olney, *Simple French Food*

Restaurants/Clubs: Red   **Hotels:** Blue
Shops/ 🌳 Outdoors: Green   **Sights/Culture:** Black

42 Le Saprien ★★★$$$ This golden stone edifice, a former private house, now houses a restaurant with a terrace overlooking the Sauternes vineyards. Chef Jean-Luc Garriques favors *cuisine du marché* (a menu inspired by what's best in the market on any given day) and specializes in typical southwestern French fare; his *lamproie au Sauternes* (river eel cooked in Sauternes) and *foie gras à la gelée de Sauternes* (foie gras in a gelatin made with Sauternes) are two local variations worth trying. An extensive selection of Sauternes is available by the glass, a rarity almost anywhere in the world but here. The prix-fixe menus are worth checking out for those on a budget. ♦ Tu-Sa lunch and dinner, Su lunch. Reservations recommended. Rue Principale, Sauternes. 56.63.60.87; fax 56.76.68.92

42 Le Millesime At this small wine shop, cordial owners Gilles Telesfort and Michel Trijasson give tastings and provide information on the wines of Sauternes and of the Bordeaux region in general. The place is stocked with many varieties of bordeaux from several vintages. ♦ Daily. 11 Rue Principale, Sauternes. 56.76.66.67; fax 56.76.62.56

42 Auberge Les Vignes ★★★$$ The very picture of a simple village auberge in provincial France, this low-key spot has it all: checkered tablecloths, an open fireplace, authentic country cooking, and reasonable prices. The regional specialties include *salade frisée aux gésiers de canard confits* (curly endive salad with duck gizzards), *entrecôte grillée sur les sarments de vignes* (steak grilled over vine cuttings), and *omelette aux cèpes* (omelette with boletus mushrooms). For dessert, try one of the delicious, homey offerings, like the *tarte aux pommes* (apple tart). The excellent wine list offers Sauternes by the glass. ♦ Tu-Su lunch and dinner. Reservations recommended. Pl de l'Eglise, Sauternes. 56.76.60.06

42 Château Guiraud Although ranked among the 11 *premiers crus* in the 1855 Sauternes classification, this vine-covered, 18th-century château had fallen into decline by the time the Narby family took it over in 1981. Today it's considered one of the top five Sauternes producers. The château's 85 hectares (210 acres) of vines—planted in 65 percent

sémillon and 35 percent sauvignon—grow right next to Château d'Yquem's vineyards. The grapes are treated in the time-honored Sauternes manner: They are carefully harvested when "noble rot" has left enough sugar in the grapes for a potential 20-percent alcohol content; absolutely no sugar is added (a process called chaptalization, often resorted to by less scrupulous producers); and at least 50 percent new oak is used to age the wine each year. The resulting wines are sublime, and they age beautifully. The château also produces a small amount of red and dry white wine. Visitors get a warm welcome at the tasting room inside the château. The beautiful *chais* are built of golden stone. ♦ Free. Daily. English spoken. Follow the signs from Pl de l'Eglise, Sauternes. 56.76.61.01; 56.76.67.52

42 Château de Commarque $$ Now a charming bed-and-breakfast run by its British owners, this château set among the vineyards just outside Sauternes was built in the Middle Ages as a "fortified farm." The eight sizable rooms (including one duplex suite) are decorated in French Provincial style and have a simple elegance; they all overlook the quiet central courtyard and have private bathrooms. A pleasant restaurant in the former winery features regional cuisine, fish dishes, and a few local specialties that make delicious use of Sauternes wine. There's also a swimming pool on the premises. ♦ Reservations required; English spoken. Follow the signs from Sauternes. 56.76.65.94; fax 56.76.64.30

42 Chambres d'Hôtes Péringuey $ The friendly Péringuey family offers four simple but comfortable guest rooms, each with a private bathroom, in a farmhouse just outside Sauternes. Guests may use the swimming pool in summer. There's no restaurant, but breakfast is included in the room rate. ♦ Reservations required; English spoken. Brouquet (about 4 km/2.5 miles from Sauternes; take D125 east and D8 south; follow the signs to Brouquet). 56.76.60.17; fax 56.76.61.74

43 Château de Villandraut One of the most famous châteaux in the Bordeaux region, it was built near Sauternes in the 14th century by Pope Clement V, who was born nearby. Although it's an imposing *château-fort* (fortified château) typical of France's war-plagued Middle Ages, the elegant interior shows that the pope liked his comforts too. His likeness is carved in stone on a wall in a room in one of the towers (he's the bearded one sitting between two angels). The tops of the towers afford a splendid view of the Landes forest. ♦ Admission. Daily 3PM-6PM June-Sept; Sa-Su 3PM-6PM Oct-May. Villandraut (from Sauternes go 8 km/4.9 miles south on D8). 56.25.31.39

44 Château de Cazeneuve This spectacular château near Sauternes was begun in the 11th century, with significant additions in the 14th and 17th centuries. Property of the Seigneurs d'Albret (rulers of the ancient region of the Pays d'Albret) since the 13th century, it is still occupied by their descendants, the Sabran-Pontevès family. (Other notable Albrets include Henri IV, who lived here with his wife, Marguerite de Valois; Louis XIII, one of Henri's Bourbon descendants, stayed here in 1620.) The current owners have won several awards for their extensive renovation of this sprawling place and its interior decoration (which drew on the family's considerable store of antiques); be sure to look into the marvelous medieval kitchen. The accommodating Sabran-Pontevès open the château and its lovely formal gardens to visitors. For groups, they also hold special tastings of fine bordeaux (by reservation), and arrange dinners and entertainment in the château. ♦ Admission. Daily July-Aug; Sa-Su Easter-Oct; groups only, by appointment, Nov-Easter. About 4 km (2.5 miles) east of Préchac via D9; take D114 south from Villandraut about 7 km/4.3 miles to Préchac; at Préchac, take D9 east, following signs to the château. 56.25.48.16; fax 56.65.27.87

Along the Dordogne: Bordeaux to Bergerac

Entre-Deux-Mers

Although its name means "between two seas," this wine-growing appellation is actually sandwiched between two rivers—the **Dordogne** and the **Garonne.** Some say the name refers to the two seas of vineyards that flank the region. Within the "V" formed by the rivers lies a patchwork landscape of rolling hills and woodlands scattered with little villages, farms, and vineyards. Entre-Deux-Mers also has many splendid architectural treasures, particularly châteaux and fortified villages dating from the Hundred Years' War.

Anyone who thinks of the wine from this district as just a simple dry white to quaff with seafood is in for a pleasant surprise: Many of them are complex and very good, as well as reasonably priced. In Entre-Deux-Mers, a visit to a winery usually means a friendly tasting with the wine maker in his cellar under the family house.

45 Hostellerie Château Camiac $$$$ Among the *hautest* of hotels in the Entre-Deux-Mers region, this early-19th-century château, an imposing white edifice with mock-Renaissance towers, is surrounded by a gorgeous 14-acre park. It has two sumptuous suites fit (both in decor and price) for a potentate, and 19 double rooms. Seven of the lavishly comfortable rooms are in the château itself; they have beautiful views of the countryside, though the contemporary decor isn't particularly charming. The other 12 rooms are in an annex called the *Relais;* smaller, but with the same decor and amenities, they cost about half the price of the château rooms. Just a 30-minute drive from Bordeaux, the hotel is well located for touring the four great wine districts of Graves, Sauternes, St-Emilion, and Entre-Deux-Mers, and it even organizes wine-tasting tours of nearby châteaux. Those who just want to relax and enjoy the peaceful atmosphere right here will appreciate the large swimming pool, tennis courts, horseback riding, and fine restaurant on the premises. ♦ Créon (about 26 km/16 miles east of Bordeaux; take D113 and then D14 east to Créon, then take Rte de Branne/D121 north, and follow the signs to the château). 56.23.20.85; fax 56.23.38.84

Within the Hostellerie Château Camiac:

Restaurant Château Camiac ★★$$$ Many of the inventive dishes here feature ingredients as luxurious as the surroundings: foie gras with lentils and *filet de barbue aux poireaux avec jus de truffes* (brill with leeks and truffle juice), for example. The excellent wine list focuses, naturally, on bordeaux. The dining room has two huge fireplaces that warm the restaurant in chilly weather, but its contemporary decor is more sleek than cozy. If the weather is nice, ask for a table on the terrace, which has a splendid view of the château's gardens. The prix-fixe menus are the way to go here; ordering à la carte gets expensive fast. ♦ Daily lunch and dinner July-Aug; M, Th-Su lunch and dinner, W dinner mid-Mar–June, Sept–mid-Jan; closed mid-January to mid-March. Reservations required. 56.23.20.85

CHATEAU DE CASTELNEAU
ENTRE-DEUX-MERS
APPELLATION ENTRE-DEUX-MERS CONTRÔLÉE
12% vol   1992   750 ml
MIS EN BOUTEILLE AU CHATEAU
VICOMTE LOÏC DE ROQUEFEUIL, RÉCOLTANT A SAINT-LÉON - GIRONDE - FRANCE
PRODUCE OF FRANCE   L 92 E 1

45 Château de Castelneau When Viscount Loïc de Roquefeuil and his wife, Diane, arrived here in 1987, most of the vineyards had been abandoned. Gradually, they resuscitated this fine estate, and now they produce both red and white wines, all aged in wood. The well-rounded, full-flavored reds are similar to St-Emilions and do well with age. The classic Entre-Deux-Mers white is a fresh-tasting but complex wine with a bouquet of toast and peaches. It's made from 85 percent sémillon grapes from vines whose average age is 30 years. It is one of the best dry white Entre-Deux-Mers wines on the market, yet is sold at an unbelievably low price. The winery's second-label red, Château Seignouret, a lighter wine than the Château de Castelneau–label wines, is another excellent value. The vineyards surround a medieval fortified château, which is perched on a hill; it's dominated by two round, turreted, 14th-century towers and was built by Soudan de Pressac, a nobleman who served the English crown when this was still an English territory. ♦ Free. Visits daily. Appointment recommended; English spoken. Near St-Léon-Château-Neuf (about 24 km/14.8 miles from Bordeaux; take D936 and then D671 east; at La Sauve, take D239 north, then D140 toward Blésignac; follow the signs to the château, south of D140). 56.23.46.23; fax 56.23.46.31

CHATEAU

La Grave

46 Château La Grave Using biodynamic techniques designed to preserve the ecology of the *terroirs,* Paul Barre makes Fronsac appellation wines here; under the Château La Fleur Cailleau label, he produces the more prestigious Canon-Fronsac appellation wines from nearby vineyards, also cultivated biodynamically. Both are lesser-known, underappreciated wines in the star-studded universe of Bordeaux appellations. Like all Fronsac and Canon-Fronsac wines, these are made from a high percentage of merlot grapes, combined with cabernet sauvignon; they have a rich bouquet and full taste, but need about five years in the bottle before they reveal their best. La Grave has an intense bouquet of spices and a touch of licorice; La Fleur Cailleau has a lovely fruity, woodsy bouquet. The château is an ancient, rambling stone farmhouse, parts of which date all the way back to the 13th century. The delightful Barres accord visitors an especially warm welcome. ♦ Free. Tastings and visits daily. Appointment recommended. Fronsac (from Libourne go 2 km/1.25 miles west on D670. From Bordeaux go 25 km/15.5 miles east on N89; follow the signs to the château). 57.51.31.11; fax 57.25.08.61

Pomerol

Once a stop on the pilgrim route to Santiago de Compostela (some road markers still bear the Maltese cross), the town of Pomerol is now known for its rich red wines, all produced with a high percentage of merlot grapes. Pomerol's most famous winery is **Château Pétrus,** which does not accept visitors. Its deep, dark, intense wines are perhaps the Rolls-Royces of the Bordelais, commanding up to three times the price of the grandest Médoc châteaux. Two other highly regarded, though only slightly more affordable, local wines to try are Château Latour à Pomerol and Vieux-Château-Certan, both stocked at the headquarters of the leading proprietors and *négociants* (merchants) of Pomerol, St-Emilion, and Fronsac wines, **Ets. Jean-Pierre Moueix** (54 Quai du Priourat, Libourne, 57.25.01.23).

47 Château Rêve-d'Or The "golden dream" of making fine wine has guided the Vigier family for generations; today, the son and grandson of master wine maker Maurice Vigier are helping to carry on the tradition. The Vigiers use strictly traditional techniques, handpicking the grapes (to avoid the dirt and mice that machines tend to pick up along with the grapes, says Maurice Vigier) and using no herbicides. The Vigiers stand apart from many other Bordelais producers in their staunch disapproval of the practice of aging in new oak, which they believe masks a wine's unique taste. The château's 1990 vintage is a bargain and can be drunk now or kept for a decade. Visitors to the family home are offered a tasting in a simple room adjoining the *chais;* ask to see Maurice Vigier's cherished chunk of *crasse-de-fer,* the iron-rich limestone that forms the bedrock of Pomerol's vineyards and is said to give the wines a characteristic overtone of truffles. ♦ Free. Visits M-Sa by appointment. Pomerol (from Libourne go about 2 km/1.25 miles northeast on N89; follow the signs to the château, which is actually a small white house). 57.51.11.92; fax 57.51.87.70

48 Château La Croix de Gay For six generations, this 12-hectare (30-acre) winery in the Pomerol appellation has been operated by the Raynaud family (now one of the daughters has her own winery nearby, **Château Faizeau,** which produces excellent St-Emilion wines). Try La Fleur de Gay, a 100 percent merlot wine that some say approaches Château Petrus in complexity and finesse (but, fortunately, not in price). Some older vintages are also available here, including a wonderful 1990. The small stone manor house is surrounded by gardens and enclosed by a wrought-iron fence; it also has an underground *cave,* rare for the region. ♦ Free. Visits and tastings daily. Appointment

---

Restaurants/Clubs: Red   **Hotels:** Blue
Shops/ 🌳 Outdoors: Green   **Sights/Culture:** Black

Armagnac, A Detour into Brandy Country

Armagnac, an eau de vie distilled from grape juice, was the mother's milk of the ancient province of **Gascony.** However, it was already being produced in the 1300s—centuries before the first Cognac was made. The main difference between the two: Armagnac is distilled only once, whereas Cognac is distilled twice, which gives Armagnac a lower alcohol content and a more pronounced flavor and aroma. Another difference is the oak used for aging; the local oak used for Armagnac gives it a pronounced woodsy, smoky flavor, whereas Cognac uses the milder Limousin oak. Many who have tried Armagnac say they'll never go back to Cognac again. Unlike Cognac, it is still mainly in the hands of small producers; taste around to find your favorites.

Armagnac country makes up most of what is now the *département* of the **Gers,** and overlaps the *départements* of the **Landes** and **Lot-et-Garonne;** it's a lovely, sparsely populated (there are more ducks and geese than people), and untouristed rural region of rolling hills, huge oak trees, and stunning medieval villages and châteaux. The region is divided into three official zones for Armagnac production: **Bas-Armagnac** (also called "Black Armagnac" for its dark oak forests) whose Armagnac is said to have the most finesse; **Ténarèze,** an ancient stop on the route from the Pyrénées to Bordeaux, which produces a gutsy Armagnac; and **Haut-Armagnac** (also called "White Armagnac," perhaps because of its chalky soil), the least flavorful of the three types.

One of the most beautiful villages in the area is **La Bastide d'Armagnac,** where several highly rated Bas-Armagnac producers are established. Look for **Domaine Boignères** (Rte du Fréche, 58.44.80.28) and **Domaine Martine Lafitte** (Rte du Fréche, 58.44.80.28). These two producers are mother and daughter, and are located next to each other; they are open by appointment only. A short distance away is **Domaine Laberdolive** nearby (follow the road to Cazaubon/Barbotan for 8 km/5 miles, turn left onto small, unnamed road, and look for the "Laberdolive" sign at the corner on the left, 58.44.81.32; fax 58.44.86.03), which is open Monday through Saturday. Other producers to watch out for are **Domaine d'Ognoas** (in Arthez d'Armagnac, 3 km/1.8 miles northeast of Villeneuve de Marsan, 58.45.22.11), open Monday through Friday from

October through April, and Monday through Friday and from 2PM through 5PM on Saturday and Sunday from May through September; **Domaine de Jouanda** (in Arthez d'Armagnac, follow the signs, 58.45.21.41), open daily, but call ahead; **Trépout** (12 Chemin de Ronde, at Ave du Stade, Vic-Fezensac, 62.06.30.44) open Monday through Saturday by appointment; and **Domaine de Sans** (in Cazeneuve, 62.09.90.36), open daily, but call ahead to arrange a visit with Monsieur Théaux. **Domaine Le Basque** (in Lannemaignan, 8 km/5 miles south of Roquefort on D934 south, 62.09.65.25; fax 62.09.69.16) is worth a visit, but requires an appointment. Last, but not least, there's **Samalens** (on Rte de Panjas, Laujuzan, 9 km/5.5 miles west of Noagaro, 62.09.14.88), which is open Monday through Saturday.

The town of **Condom** houses the **Musée de l'Armagnac** (2 Rue Jules-Ferry, 62.28.31.41), with exhibits on how grapes are grown and how Armagnac is made; an audiovisual presentation on the process is shown on request. The museum is open daily from June through September (but if you visit in the off-season, the tourist office will open the museum for you!). In August, several villages in the region hold rousing celebrations, and **Mauvezin,** a village with much of its medieval heart intact, holds a garlic festival on the third Monday in August. An Armagnac festival, the *Foire aux eaux-de-vie d'Armagnac,* is held in **Eauze** in late May or early June every year; a colorful food market takes place on the **Place de l'Eglise** every Thursday morning. For more information (in French) about Armagnac, contact the **Bureau National Interprofessionel de l'Armagnac** (Pl de la Liberté, 32800 Eauze, France, 62.09.82.33; fax 62.09.77.46).

recommended. Pomerol (from Libourne go about 2 km/1.25 miles northeast on N89; follow the signs to the château). 57.51.19.05; fax 57.74.15.62

St-Emilion and Its Environs

Perched high atop a vineyard-cloaked hill, St-Emilion wins many people's vote for favorite Bordelais village. With its steep, narrow, cobblestone streets, tiny golden houses, magnificent medieval church carved out of

the hillside by Benedictine monks, and great vistas over the surrounding vineyards, it has been designated a historic landmark. It's hard to believe this beautiful spot was the site of many violent battles during the Hundred Years' War, the 16th-century Wars of Religion, and the French Revolution. Through it all, St-Emilion remained a stopover for pilgrims on the way to Santiago de Compostela. Today it is besieged by pilgrims of another sort—tourists—who walk about by the busload, often munching on local macaroons, and sipping in wine-tasting centers which occupy almost half the town's buildings.

Still, the magic of this place remains intact. To get a feel for it, splurge on a hotel room in the village and explore the steep cobblestone alleys in the early morning or evening, have a drink in the **Place du Marché**, and check out the great view from the ramparts next to the **Eglise Collégiale**'s belfry. If you visit during the grape harvest you may see red-robed members of the Jurade, a secular society formed in 1199 that still oversees the local wine industry; the grape-picking season officially begins with the Jurade's ceremony atop the 13th-century Tour du Roi.

With 13,000 acres, the St-Emilion district is Bordeaux's largest wine district. Although many people in the United States think of the wines of St-Emilion as being just another version of the famous bordeaux wines of the Médoc, in fact St-Emilion produces a very different kind of wine. The Médoc peninsula's soil and climate are ideal for growing the cabernet sauvignon grape, a tannic variety that needs long bottle aging and is the dominant grape used in great Médoc wines like Margaux and Pauillac. In St-Emilion, with a different climate and soil, the merlot grape is the star, with aromatic cabernet franc and occasionally some cabernet sauvignon grapes playing supporting roles. This means that, in general, St-Emilion wines have less punch, especially when they are young, than Médoc wines do, but the best St-Emilions (considered to be those from vines on the sandy plateau just north and west of the village or from a gravelly area, known as the *graves,* in the direction of Pomerol) tend to be fuller, fruitier, more aromatic and less astringent than Médoc wines; in short, easier to enjoy. The wines from the lower slopes of the plateau, known as the *côte,* tend to be rounder and have more body but in general lack the finesse of the plateau and *graves* wines. What further sets St-Emilion apart from the Médoc and from all other Bordelais wines is its classification system. St-Emilion was not part of the 1855 Bordelais classifications; its own system, first instituted in 1955, with a new so-called "simpler" version instituted in 1986, can mystify the outsider. Basically, St-Emilion has two official appellations, just plain St-Emilion (applying to wines produced in the village itself and in eight villages nearby) and St-Emilion *grand cru.* Within the latter category, though, are a group of superior wines singled out and classified (in 1984, with the ranking made official in 1986) as *grand cru classé* or the more prestigious *premier grand cru classé,* both of which were once separate appellations. All these categories are strictly controlled (to prevent wineries from labeling a bottle of St-Emilion as a *grand cru classé* when it's in fact ranked only a *grand cru,* for

example). This classification of the *grand cru classé* and *premier grand cru classé* wines is revised every ten years based on several tastings made by the Jurade. The last such revision was made official in 1986, and resulted in 74 *grand cru classé* wines and 11 *premier grand cru classé* wines. To add to the complexity, two of the *premier grand crus classé* wines are, as *Gourmet* magazine's wine editor Gerald Asher puts it, "more *premier* than their peers." The *premier grand cru classé* wines were divided in 1986 into "A" and "B" lists, with two estates—Château Ausone and Château Cheval Blanc—on the "A" list and the others on the "B" list, for reasons only the Jurade, perhaps, understands. Any winemakers caught violating the system (for example by putting *grand cru classé* grapes into a *premier grand cru classé* wine) can have their wines demoted at any time. In addition to the St-Emilion appellations are five appellations for nearby villages, each of which can label its wines with its village name followed by St-Emilion (such as St-Georges-St-Emilion) but cannot use the St-Emilion name alone. The main effect of all this on wine fanciers is that *grand cru classé* and *premier grand cru classé* St-Emilion wines are never cheap, but their quality, guaranteed by up-to-date and carefully controlled classification, will probably never disappoint. For bargains, sample lower-ranked wines that are reasonably priced, but buy with care: St-Emilion has a reputation for overpricing.

49 Le Train des Grands Vignobles A little train on wheels departs from St-Emilion's **Eglise Collégiale** to take visitors down tiny lanes (some of them private) that wind through nearby vineyards. Commentary is provided in French and English. The whole thing may seem hokey, but the close-up look at the vines is worth the 35-minute trip. Children love it. ♦ Fee. Daily June-Nov; Dec-May by appointment only. Reservations required for groups of 25 or more. St-Emilion. 57.51.13.76; fax 57.51.01.99

49 Eglise Monolithe The only church of its kind in Europe, this monolithic edifice was carved out of the solid limestone plateau on which the village rests. It was built from the ninth through the 12th centuries from various grottoes and quarries that already existed. Enter through the striking 14th-century Gothic portal that's set right into the cliff wall facing the town's main square; its tympanum is decorated with scenes of the Last Judgment and the Resurrection of the Dead. The vast space the church's builders managed to hew into the depths of rock, and the precision with which they achieved it, with regular rows of pillars supporting the vaults, is awe-inspiring. Another feature possibly unique to this church is that it has not one, but three naves. ♦ Admission. The church is open only for 45-minute guided tours, offered daily. For information, contact the St-Emilion tourist office (57.24.72.03). Pl du Marché, St-Emilion. No phone

49 Tour du Roi (King's Tower) On a hill opposite the one on which the **Eglise Monolithe** perches, this decidedly secular edifice was part of a fortress built by England's Henry III in the 13th century. Originally used as a dungeon, the tower offers a breathtakingly beautiful view from its summit. It is from this height that red-robed members of the Jurade, an ancient society that oversees the local wine industry to this day, proclaim the *ban des vendanges,* the beginning of St-Emilion's grape harvest. ♦ Admission. Daily. Rue du Couvert (at Rue de l'Ermitage), St-Emilion. 57.74.44.55

BAR DE LA POSTE

49 Bar de la Poste ★$$ A pleasant, casual place for a simple lunch of crepes or an omelette and salad. Its location is ideal, with outdoor tables stretching onto the Place du Marché beneath an enormous old acacia tree. Wines are available by the glass, but their prices may keep you sipping cider or beer—blasphemous though that may seem in this town. Under the same management, the wine shop next door, **La Tour des Vins,** specializes in old—even antique—vintages. It advertises bottles dating "from 1881 to today." ♦ Daily lunch and dinner. Pl du Marché (at Rue de la Cadène), St-Emilion. 57.24.70.76

49 Hostellerie de Plaisance $$$ Well worth the splurge, this elegant hotel hugs the steep limestone hill in the center of town. The typical 17th-century St-Emilion building, white stone with a weathered pink tile roof, houses 12 rooms. Some have private balconies, others have their own tiny gardens on cliffside terraces overlooking the rooftops of the village. All are decorated with an eye toward traditional, understated elegance (some have tasteful gold wallpaper and heavy antiques) and have private bathrooms and contemporary amenities. ♦ Closed in January. Pl du Clocher, St-Emilion. 57.24.72.32; fax 57.74.41.11

Within the Hostellerie de Plaisance:

Restaurant Hostellerie de Plaisance
★★$$$ This cozily elegant place may be one of the prettiest in France, with creamy yellow walls, red-and-gold upholstery, lots of lush greenery, and great views of town. Its food draws considerable praise too: Michelin has awarded it one star for traditional dishes such as *blanquette de filets de sole* (sole in a rich cream sauce), *terrine de girolles et ris de veau, coulis de tomates aux aromates* (a terrine of chanterelle mushrooms and veal sweetbreads with an herbed tomato sauce), and *filets de canard gras au foie frais et raisins* (duck breast with fresh foie gras and grapes). The wine list is excellent, but resist temptation; it's wildly overpriced. ♦ Daily breakfast, lunch, and dinner; closed in January. 57.24.72.32; fax 57.74.41.11

49 Restaurant Francis Goullée ★★★$$$ Many say this posh yet convivial spot is the best in town. The chef specializes in south-western French cuisine. Foie gras, wild mushrooms, duck, and game in season often figure prominently, and he handles them all with delectable expertise. The wine list has an impressive selection of bordeaux, with an emphasis on St-Emilion wines. Although it's right in the center of this wildly popular town, and would succeed no matter what it served, this restaurant admirably adheres to the highest standards, never letting the great food and service slide. The prix-fixe menus are an excellent value. ♦ Daily lunch and dinner; closed 1-15 August. Reservations required. 27 Rue Guadet, St-Emilion. 57.24.70.49; fax 57.74.47.96

49 Le Logis des Remparts $$ This charming hotel built of the local golden stone is in the medieval heart of St-Emilion. Its elegant lobby features a spectacular spiral stone staircase that leads to 15 comfortable rooms. The decor is cozy French country—flowery wallpaper, comfortable furniture, even quaint little writing desks. All the rooms have private bathrooms and windows that look out on the village's narrow, Gothic streets or over the vineyards that cover the slopes east of town. There's no restaurant, but breakfast is served in a lovely interior courtyard, and a little bar is open to guests. ♦ Closed late December–late January. 18 Rue Guadet, St-Emilion. 57.24.70.43; fax 57.74.47.44

"To own ten hectares in Burgundy is to be a major figure in your village. In Bordeaux, such a holding would push a château well down the local pecking order."

Hugh Johnson and Hubrecht Duijker, *The Wine Atlas of France*

♦ Fee for tastings. Visits and tastings by appointment. Just south of St-Emilion; follow the sign to the château east of D122. 57.55.43.43; fax 57.24.63.99

49 Château du Moulin St-Georges Year after year, the Vauthier family produces excellent wines from this *grand cru* estate (which is surrounded by the vineyards of more famous *premier grand cru classé* and *grand cru classé* St-Emilion châteaux whose wines are proportionately pricier). The wines are consistently rich and full, with overtones of spices and ripe, red fruit; all are aged in oak. A small tasting center and shop in front of the *chai* gives visitors a chance to try several vintages (if any of the 1986 is on hand, snap it up). These dependable, reasonably priced wines are a welcome relief in a village full of inflated price tags. ♦ Free. Tastings daily. Just south of St-Emilion on D122; follow the signs to the château. 57.24.70.26; fax 57.74.47.39

49 Château Pavie Classified at the top of the St-Emilion ladder in 1955 and as one of St-Emilion's *premiers grands crus classé* in 1986, this great estate went through a slump in the 1960s and early 1970s, but since the late 1970s has made a comeback worthy of its long and illustrious history. The vines occupy 37 hectares (92 acres) of prime wine-growing area on the St-Emilion *côtes*—the steep limestone slopes just outside town. They've been turning out palate-pleasing wines since the fourth century, but it wasn't until the 18th century (when the elegant stone manor house was built) that they (and the other great estates of the area) finally achieved renown. They certainly deserve all the attention they get: Pavie wines, with their deep luster and dense taste, have a subtly elegant bouquet suggesting spices and fruits; they're exceptionally well balanced. It's no wonder the wines are so sought-after (and so very expensive). Visitors may tour the *chais*.

49 Château Pavie-Macquin Though this estate's 10 hectares (25 acres) of vineyards no longer belong to the great **Château Pavie** (see above) farther up the *côtes*, they garnered a *grand cru classé* ranking on their own in 1955. Since 1986, wine maker Maryse Barre (mother of Paul Barre of Fronsac's **Château La Grave**) has consistently produced exceptional St-Emilions for the owners, the Corre-Macquin family. Maryse Barre officially retired in 1994 but intends to continue overseeing operations here. Albert Macquin, who oversaw wine making here in the late 19th century, was a local hero of sorts—he was one of the first growers in the area to graft American rootstock onto vines debilitated by the onslaught of phylloxera. Maryse Barre continues the tradition of innovation, cultivating the vines biodynamically. Robert Parker, in his book *Bordeaux,* described the 1989 Pavie-Macquin as superbly balanced and "fabulously concentrated," with a bouquet and taste that hint at raspberries; he also noted that these are some of the few good St-Emilions to be had at reasonable prices. The unusual wine label bears as a logo a hangman's noose, which the French consider good luck: At one time, the hill these vineyards occupy was the site of St-Emilion's public executions. ♦ Free. Visits and tastings by appointment. Just south of St-Emilion; follow the signs to the château east of D122. 57.24.74.23, 57.51.26.44

49 Château Bernateau Although this family-run winery lies at the edge of the St-Emilion appellation, its *grand cru* wines bear the unmistakable stamp of St-Emilion quality. The 1990 vintage is a powerful, rich, and well-

Château Pavie

balanced wine that will age very well; it was ranked by the prestigious *Hachette Guide des Vins* in 1994 as providing the best quality-to-price ratio of all the 1990 St-Emilions listed. Other vintages to pounce on are the 1986 and the 1988. The château is a modest stone farmhouse with two 18th-century wings built in an age-old local fashion with clay and fieldstone. Wine maker Régis Lavau welcomes visitors, but warns that they may have trouble finding the place on the winding back roads ("We wonder whether whoever laid these roads out was sober when he did it"). At least you'll have a lovely time getting lost: The countryside around here is gorgeous, with rolling hills and vineyards interspersed with pine groves, all of it sloping down to the wide Dordogne. ♦ Free. Visits by appointment. In the hamlet of St-Etienne-de-Lisse (from St-Emilion go 6 km/3.7 miles southeast on D245; follow the signs to the château). 57.40.18.19; fax 57.40.27.31

49 Château-le-Chatelet The vineyards of this appealing 18th-century Neo-Classical château (whose name, fittingly, means "little castle") stretch over the high, flat plateau west of St-Emilion. The wines produced on this *grand cru classé* estate are made up of 30 percent merlot, 40 percent cabernet sauvignon, and 30 percent bouchet grapes. They're supple, ready to drink young, and they won't break the bank. ♦ Free. Daily mid-June–mid-Sept; by appointment mid-Sept–mid-June. Appointment recommended. From St-Emilion take D243 2 km (1.25 miles) northwest, and follow the signs to the château. 57.24.70.97

50 Château St-Georges Just north of St-Emilion, in the satellite appellation of St-Georges–St-Emilion, this stunningly beautiful château perches on a hill overlooking its 51 hectares (125 acres) of vineyards. No relation to **Moulin St-Georges** (see page 180), it was built in the 18th century by **Victor Louis,** Louis XVI's favorite architect; its series of stately wings connects four round feudal towers that remained from an earlier structure. For over a century, the Desbois family has been producing wines here that are as magnificent as the château itself. Wine

critic Oz Clarke has called Château St-Georges one of the few outperforming St-Emilions (wines that cost relatively little for what they offer) still around. Typically for St-Emilion vineyards, these are planted in 75 percent merlot and 25 percent cabernet franc and other grapes. The high percentage of merlot makes the wines drinkable while still young, but these are sturdy enough to peak after about 15 years in the bottle. This is one of the very few châteaux in the area that sells only to individuals rather than to distributors. ♦ Free. Tastings and sales M-F. Appointment required for tours. St-Georges-de-Montagne (from St-Emilion go about 4 km/2.5 miles north on D122). 57.74.62.11; fax 57.74.58.62

50 Ecomusée du Libournais (Museum of Libournais Culture) Obviously put together carefully with limited means, this small museum is one of the most informative in the region on the traditions of the Libournais, the area around St-Emilion. Among the several exhibits on wine making are displays on the region's viticultural practices over the past centuries and the effects on local life of the phylloxera disaster that wiped out the grape harvest. In an unassuming stone house in a sleepy village just north of St-Emilion, it's a great place to escape the town's touristy bustle and get a thoughtful overview of the area's very long history. ♦ Admission. M-F, Sa-Su 2PM-7PM mid-Mar–mid-Nov. St-Georges-de-Montagne (from St-Emilion go 4 km/2.5 miles north on D122). 57.74.56.89

50 Château de Roques $ Just outside a tiny village, this early-19th-century château is now a bed-and-breakfast whose owners extend a warm welcome. The 18 rooms are comfortably old-fashioned, some with massive old armoires; room No. 4 has a picture-perfect view of the surrounding vineyards. The rooms are scattered among the château, a wing, and an annex 1.5 kilometers (a mile) away. Some are equipped only with showers and sinks, sharing a WC (toilet). Two dormitory-style rooms accommodate up to four people—good for those traveling in a group and on a budget. Hearty, country-style meals are available with advance notice, and the owners also give free tastings of the château's own wine. They rent bicycles for jaunts around the countryside, too. ♦ Closed Christmas–early January. Lussac (from St-Emilion go 8 km/4.9 miles north on D122). 57.74.69.56; fax 57.74.58.80

The Côtes de Castillon

Just east of St-Emilion, the Côtes de Castillon is a peaceful region of green hills, the highest in the Gironde *département,* most of which are dotted with tiny villages. Each town has its own lovely Romanesque church, the most beautiful of which is in the village of **Petit-Palais-et-Cornemps.** A perfect picnic spot lies just around the bend of almost every turn of the "D" roads here. The area takes its name from its principal town of **Castillon-la-Bataille** on the **Dordogne;** the "battle" in its name refers to a clash between British and French troops in 1453 that brought an end to the Hundred Years' War and British domination of the southwest. The battle is re-created every July and August on open ground near the **Château de Castegens** by about 600 costumed residents of the village of **Belves-de-Castillon.**

Côtes de Castillon wines are some of the best affordable red wines to be found anywhere in Bordeaux. The Côtes de Castillon is one of two areas in the catch-all Bordeaux Supérieur appellation (the other is nearby Côtes de Franc) that have earned the right to put their own names on the wines. As in St-Emilion, the wines use a high percentage of merlot grapes, and as a result they're prime for drinking in just a few years.

51 Château de Pitray A highly recommended stop on any wine lover's itinerary, the imposing Victorian Neo-Gothic château surrounded by a gorgeous park complete with a swimming pool, was built in 1868, but its 25 hectares (62 acres) of vineyards have been around centuries longer. The vines here, many of which reach the venerable age of 25 years, produce an award-winning, estate-bottled red wine from a mixture of 69 percent merlot, 28 percent cabernet franc, and three percent pessac grapes. The delicious results rival many wines from more famous châteaux, but are more reasonably priced. If you get a chance, try the 1986, with its intriguing hint of truffles. A visit here is a particular pleasure; the Count and Countess de Boigne, who speak English, warmly receive visitors in one of the château's breathtakingly beautiful *salons.* ◆ Free. By appointment Apr-Oct, and occasionally at other times. 12 km (7.5 miles) east of St-Emilion (take D243 east to D123 north and east to Gardegan; follow the signs to the château). 57.40.63.38; fax 57.40.66.24

52 Château de Montaigne Fans of the eponymous 16th-century essayist (who, in fact, coined the word "essay" with his erudite, subjective reflections that he called *"essais,"* or trials) shouldn't miss a pilgrimage to the master's home, where he lived his entire life. Unfortunately, the château Montaigne inhabited burned down in the 19th century and was subsequently rebuilt (it's not open to visitors); but what's left may very well be the most important part—from the admirer's standpoint, anyway—a small stone tower where Montaigne retreated to ply his pen. On the top floor is the beautiful circular library where he wrote, with windows overlooking the expanse of peaceful countryside and beams on which Montaigne painted inspirational Greek and Latin phrases. When he tired of one, he would rub it out and put another in its place—some of his last selections are still visible. The gardens of the château are also open to visitors; the path through them leads along the edge of the high plateau occupied by the château, with the checkerboard of vineyards, meadows, pine forests, and orchards spread out below. And, though it's not the main draw here, the château does sell bottles of its own quite respectable wine. There's a guided tour of the tower approximately every hour (times are posted at the château); visitors aren't permitted to explore it on their own, so be prepared to while away some time in the gardens if you arrive between tours. Visitors customarily tip the guide. ◆ Admission. Daily July-Aug; W-Su Sept-Dec, Feb-June; closed in January. St-Michel-de-Montaigne (from Pitray take D123 and D17 south to Castillon-la-Bataille; then take D936 east and D9 north, and follow the signs to the château). 53.58.63.93

52 Hôtel Le Jardin d'Eyquem $$ In a quiet village that almost belongs more to the 16th century (when famed essayist Michel de Montaigne occupied the castle here) than the 20th, this comfortable hotel is ensconced in a sprawling, restored old house built of golden stone with a red tile roof. The five spacious, sunny rooms are done in updated French Provincial style, with cheerful floral prints. They all have private bathrooms and TV sets, and some even have kitchenettes. There's also a swimming pool surrounded by a garden. Breakfast is served, but there is no restaurant. ◆ Closed December-March. Reservations recommended well in advance. St-Michel-de-Montaigne (from Pitray take D123 and D17 south to Castillon-la-Bataille; then take D936 east about 5 km/3.1 miles; then D9 north about 3 km/1.9 miles). 53.24.89.59

The Southwest

Bergerac and Its Environs

Just east of St-Michel-de-Montaigne begins the *département* of the **Dordogne,** which roughly corresponds to the ancient province of **Périgord.** In addition to producing many very good, affordable wines, this region is one of France's loveliest, a land of steep green hills and some of the country's most magnificent rivers, first among them the mighty **Dordogne.** The countryside is scattered with graceful houses built of warm golden stone, spectacular prehistoric cave paintings, medieval châteaux and churches, and picturesque fortified villages (known as *bastides*) that overlooked the battles of the Hundred Years' War. A combination of relatively poor farmland and great natural beauty has shifted the region's economic focus from agriculture to tourism—in July and August, it shows. But if you avoid the main roads, you'll find peace and quiet here, even at the height of the season.

An exception may be in the busy, prosperous town of Bergerac, whose ancient streets are perennially snarled in traffic. If you're driving, ignore signs for *centre ville* (center of town) and make for the port, a wide paved area overlooking the Dordogne, where you'll find a free parking lot and a walking path along the river. Then head for the center of **Vieux Bergerac,** the quaint old section of town, which is filled with medieval buildings. (Those interested in historical accuracy should know that, despite the myriad references to Cyrano de Bergerac—half the restaurants in town seem to have taken his name!—the real Cyrano, a 17th-century poet and soldier, was born in Paris and never set foot here.) The **Musée du Vin et de la Batellerie** (Museum of Wine and River Craft; Rue des Conférences, 53.57.80.92) has displays on the history of Bergerac's role as a wine-making and shipping center. The museum is open Tuesday through Saturday, and on Sunday from 2:30PM to 6PM. There's an admission charge. Stop by the **Place du Marché-Couvert,** where from Tuesday through Saturday a covered market is filled with stalls laden with cheeses, fresh fruits and vegetables, meats, bread, and wine that make for a spectacular picnic down by the port; be advised: There's a long midday closing.

Once labeled as bordeaux, Bergerac wine now has its own appellation, with several smaller appellations grouped within it. Historically, Bergerac was known for its sweet white wines, but tastes have changed; now the production is dominated by reds (Bergerac and powerful Pécharmant), some good dry whites, called *Bergerac sec,* which make excellent accompaniments to seafood, and a few sweet white wines, the best and most famous of which is Monbazillac.

53 Le Cyrano ★★$$ This quintessential French country eatery is in a two-story golden stone house with green shutters and cheerful window boxes. Jean-Paul Turon, the owner of this popular spot, roams the dining room, amiably greeting his guests. Bourgeois only in the most comforting culinary sense, the menu offers generous, straightforward regional dishes, such as a succulent *magret*

de canard (grilled duck breast). The wine list is strong on southwestern varieties, including some excellent Monbazillacs; try one with the nougat soufflé for dessert. There's also a marvelous cheese assortment. The prix-fixe menus offer the same satisying fare at more modest prices. ♦ Daily lunch and dinner May-Oct; M-Sa lunch and dinner, Su lunch Nov-Apr. Reservations recommended. 2 Blvd Montaigne, Bergerac. 53.57.02.76; fax 53.57.78.15

Above Le Cyrano:

Le Cyrano $ The price is unquestionably right for these 11 smallish but serviceable rooms. They are clean and quiet, and all have private bathrooms. The rooms are available only on a *demi-pension* plan (with breakfast and one other meal included); breakfast is served in an enclosed terrace. ♦ 53.57.02.76

53 Delpérier Frères Grands Vins The friendly owner of this small wine shop in the covered market knows the local wines inside and out, and offers a wide selection. Follow his recommendations for rich, inexpensive Bergerac or Pécharmant reds and surprisingly good Bergerac white wines. The Pécharmant Ma Réserve, made by a local wine co-op, is a good (and inexpensive) introduction to the hearty red wine of the Pécharmant appellation; many critics say it's tops among the smaller appellations that make up the Bergerac *AC.* Its label shows wine being loaded onto boats in Bergerac's port in the old days. ♦ Tu-Sa. Between Pl du Marché-Couvert and Pl du Foirail, Bergerac. 53.63.08.85

53 Musée du Tabac This remarkably fascinating museum, the only one in France devoted solely to tobacco, serves as a reminder that this currently discredited plant once played as important a role in Bergerac's economy as wine now does. Housed in the stately Renaissance **Maison Peyrarède,** the museum traces the history of tobacco from the 15th century, when a few Native American tribes were the world's only smokers, to the present, with tobacco a staple crop with an all-too-global demand. Displays cover everything from the effects of tobacco on society and politics, the cultivation and trade of the plant over the centuries, and the many methods people have devised to enjoy that nicotine high. Even if you never touch cigarettes, you'll find this an intriguing glimpse into the culture of smoking. ♦ Admission. Tu-Su. 10 Rue Ancien Pont, Bergerac. 53.63.04.13

183

54 Château de Monbazillac Perched on a cliff overlooking the Dordogne valley, this gray granite château looks like a fairy-tale vision, with its moat, immense round towers, crenellated battlements, and steeply angled tile roof. Built around 1550, it's surrounded by a large park and by the vineyards that produce the Bergerac region's famous sweet wine, which put the entire region on the map for centuries. (One legend describes how the pope asked a group of pilgrims in medieval Rome where their home was. When they answered "Bergerac," the pope expressed confusion, until one of his attendants interjected, "It's near Monbazillac, Your Excellency.") The château is owned by a wine co-op, which is responsible for maintaining the high quality of the wine. The tasting center is right in front; try the 1990 Monbazillac, one of the best vintages in recent memory. It can be enjoyed now or kept at least a decade. Cyril Forget, the resident oenologist, speaks English and dispenses expert advice. Although Monbazillac wines are similar to Sauternes, they are not as sweet and therefore are more appropriate with foie gras or the local walnuts than with dessert, he says. Guided tours are given of the elaborately furnished château, filled with period antiques. It also contains three museums—one on Huguenot culture (Bergerac and the surrounding region were a Protestant stronghold during the 16th-century Wars of Religion), one on crafts, and the third on wine. ♦ Admission charge for tour; tasting is free. Daily. Monbazillac (from Bergerac go 8 km/4.9 miles south on D13). 53.63.65.00; fax 53.63.65.09

Within the Château de Monbazillac:

Restaurant du Château de Monbazillac
★$$ In the château's restored 17th-century *chais*, this pleasant eatery has a tasteful, contemporary ambience. The extensive menu features such regional specialties as *confit de canard aux cèpes* (slow-cooked duck preserved in duck fat with boletus mushrooms) and *désossé de pigeon aux truffes* (boneless squab with truffles), as well as fish dishes, and, not surprisingly, a number of creations using Monbazillac wine. In summer, ask for a table on the terrace and enjoy the view of the château, a beautiful remnant of the Renaissance. ♦ Daily lunch and dinner July-Aug; Tu-Su lunch and dinner Sept-June. 53.58.38.93, 53.63.65.03; fax 53.57.82.50

55 Ferme de Séjour La Barabie $ A bed-and-breakfast on a working Dordogne farm offers five rooms in the rambling stone farmhouse. They are simple, but comfortable and quiet, with private baths; two accommodate three people and another sleeps four. The excellent country breakfasts feature touches such as homemade jams. During the off-season (November through April), friendly hostess Marie-Jeanne Archer gives classes (in French) in regional cuisine and in foie gras production—something you might prefer not to know about in such detail (it's a cruel process, from the bird's point of view). The farm also has bicycles for rent. ♦ Two-night minimum; reservations recommended far in advance. Rte de Ste-Alvère, La Monzie-Montastruc (from Bergerac go 7 km/4.3 miles northeast on N21; follow the signs to the farm). 53.23.22.47, 53.23.22.26

Within Ferme de Séjour La Barabie:

Restaurant Ferme de Séjour La Barabie
★★$ For visitors who call well in advance, Marie-Jeanne Archer cooks up ample portions of such regional specialties as cassoulet (a hearty, flavorful stew of white beans and meats) and *magret de canard* (grilled duck breast). Meals are served in a rustic, wood-beamed dining room that's nicely suited to the hearty country fare. ♦ M-Tu, Th-Su; closed the last week of December-January. Lunch and dinner by advance reservation only. 53.23.22.47

56 Le Vieux Logis $$$$ Near the banks of the Dordogne, this Relais & Châteaux establishment has been called the most beautiful hotel in the Périgord; it's certainly one of the most expensive. An ivy-covered 17th-century Carthusian monastery built of the local ocher stone, it's surrounded by a formal French garden. The 19 luxurious rooms boast lots of floral fabrics, exposed beams, Oriental rugs, and fresh flowers everywhere; there are also five huge, opulent suites. One of the most appealing is decorated in blue, yellow, and white; it has a canopy bed in its own alcove, a yellow couch, delicate floral wallpaper and drapes, and heavy whitewashed ceiling beams. Other rooms have a more rustic look, some with big open fireplaces. No modern convenience has been overlooked, starting with mini-bars, safes, and giant bathrooms. A swimming pool graces the elegant garden, and there's a billiard room. Henry Miller, that member of Paris down-and-outers, once stayed a whole month here (in room No. 4) proving that he liked his comforts (as well as the local wines). ♦ Reservations recommended well in advance. Trémolat (34 km/21.1 miles east of Bergerac; take D660 east to Lalinde, then D29 east, then D28 north to Trémolat; follow the signs to the hotel). 53.22.80.06; fax 53.22.84.89

Within Le Vieux Logis:

Restaurant Le Vieux Logis ★★★$$$
Although this excellent restaurant is set in a rustic former tobacco-drying shed with stone walls and an exposed-beam ceiling, the table settings, food, and service are anything but down-home. Chef Pierre-Jean Duribreux prepares superb regional cuisine, which around here means that duck, foie gras, truffles, and meaty *cèpes* (boletus mushrooms) take leading roles. His one-Michelin-star specialties include *pomme de terre farcie de ris de veau à la truffe* (baked potato stuffed with veal sweetbreads and truffles)—a delight not to be missed—*oeuf mollet au caviar* (soft-cooked egg with caviar), *tarte "minute" aux cèpes* (a quick-cooked tart of boletus mushrooms), and *petite salade de homard à l'huile de truffes* (lobster salad with truffle oil). Other seafood dishes are also quite good. The cheese assortment is wonderful, but a dessert from the chef's old family recipe is unforgettable: the *timbale de crème de chocolat* (a gooey, creamy chocolate custard), which will make chocolate lovers swoon. The wine list is outstanding, with an especially fine selection of local wines. In summer tables are set on a pretty terrace next to a brook that meanders through the property. The prices are not as high as you might expect, and the prix-fixe menus are a downright steal. ♦ Daily lunch and dinner. Reservations required. 53.22.80.06; fax 53.22.84.89

57 **Cave du Coux** A real find. Friendly Irishman Gabriel Breen has opened this gem of a wine store in a tiny village on the banks of the Dordogne. He knows everything—but everything—about the local wines, and is committed to offering good values. Free tastings are provided, and you can buy many of the local wines right out of the barrel; others are available in bottles. Breen has an especially good selection of organically produced wines, and he also offers a variety of top-quality regional foods, including foie gras, pâté, and *confit de canard* (slow-cooked duck preserved in duck fat). He even organizes tours in English of Bordeaux wineries, and will ship cases of wine abroad. ♦ M-Sa 9AM-9PM; Su 9AM-1PM. Coux-et-Bigaroque (from Trémolat go about 12 km/7.4 miles east on D31 and D51). 53.29.46.62

58 **Château de Castelnaud** The partially restored ruins of this once-great fortress still command perhaps the most spectacular view of the Dordogne in this region of sublime sightlines. On one side lies the valley of the Céou, on the other that of the Dordogne; from the far bank, the imposing **Château de Beynac** stares the château down, as it has done since the turbulent Middle Ages, and the village of La Roque-Gageac hugs the cliffs below it. **Castelnaud** was built in the 12th century and was occupied in the 13th by

Simon de Montfort, the tireless and merciless leader of the Albigensian Crusade that laid waste to much of southern France. But the château wasn't fully fortified with battlements and bastions until the 14th century, just in time for the Hundred Years' War. It spent most of that century in the hands of the English, while the French bivouacked across the way in **Beynac**. Castelnaud's museum displays a video of a modern re-creation of one of the many sieges it withstood—this one the assault by the French Army of King Charles VII that took place on 17 October 1442. There's also an interesting collection of medieval arms and armor. The castle's keep is still furnished with the original 14th- and 15th-century pieces. ♦ Admission. Daily. From Coux-et-Bigaroque follow D703 east about 22 km (13.6 miles) along the Dordogne; just past the village of Beynac-et-Cazenac, take the Castelnaud Bridge (D57) across the river to the château. 53.28.94.94

58 **Château des Milandes** This picturesque 15th-century château was once the home of the American performer Josephine Baker, who gained fame in the Paris cabarets of the 1920s. Here, she lived out her dream of adopting many children from all races and nationalities and raising them together to show that peace and understanding between the world's peoples were not just idealistic fantasies. The château is furnished with a gorgeous array of 17th-century antiques and paintings, and contains a small museum on its own history and on Baker's life. All around the château lie its beautiful, well-planned French gardens. ♦ Admission. Daily (no midday closing) and W, Sa until midnight July-Aug; daily mid-Mar–June, Sept–mid-Nov; closed mid-November–mid-March. Just east of Beynac-et-Cazenac, take the Castelnaud Bridge (D57) across the river, then D53 west 5 km (3 miles), follow the signs to the château. 53.29.50.73

La Plume d'Oie

59 **Auberge La Plume d'Oie** ★★★$$ This place is in one of the most enchanting of a string of picturesque villages along this stretch of the Dordogne, where the ancient golden stone houses are arranged in tiers along the base of a steep cliff overhanging the river. The lovely dining room has exposed beams, a tile floor, a wall of golden stone with a big, modern fireplace, and large windows with a view of the Dordogne. The friendly, English-speaking owners serve inventive dishes that make excellent use of high-quality local ingredients; *poêlé de foie gras au*

vinaigre de Modène (foie gras sautéed with Modena vinegar), *coquelet rôti aux morilles et pâtes fraîches* (roasted young chicken served with morel mushrooms and fresh pasta), and *fricassée d'escargots et de cèpes* (sautéed snails and boletus mushrooms) might appear on the menu. The wine list is exceptional, and very reasonably priced, as are the prix-fixe menus. Upstairs are four pretty, inexpensive guest rooms, all with private bathrooms; they are reserved for patrons of the restaurant, who can happily stagger to bed after a fine meal. ◆ M-F, Su lunch and dinner, Sa dinner July-Aug; Tu-Su lunch and dinner Sept-June. Reservations required. La Roque-Gageac (about 5 km/3 miles east of Beynac-et-Cazenac on D703). 53.29.57.05; fax 53.31.04.81

60 Domme Perched high on a cliff, Domme is an ancient *bastide,* one of the fortified towns that sprang up in this part of France during the 13th and 14th centuries. It was built in 1281 by a nervous King Philip the Bold, after a furious spurt of *bastide*-building on the part of the local power, Alphonse of Poitiers. Perhaps the most exhilarating view to be had here is from the **Belvédère de la Barre** (Barre Belvedere), a terrace overlooking the Dordogne just off the town's main square, the Place de la Halle. Below, the river lined with poplars winds its way through the valley, with hills beyond cresting the horizon. From here, too, you can see the **Château de Beynac** and La Roque-Gageac, as well as a number of other medieval landmarks. Visit the **Grottes,** caves that once served as hiding places for the townspeople during times of war. The entrance to the caves is on Place de la Halle; they're open daily, from October through March from 2PM to 6PM only. There's an admission charge. Another fine panorama is to be seen along the **Promenade des Falaises** (Cliff Walk), a path that runs along the north side of town and begins at the exit to the **Grottes.** You can continue along the **Promenade des Falaises,** circling around the town to the **Promenade des Remparts,** which follows the line of the city's ancient fortifications. And don't overlook the town itself—its charming narrow streets are crowded with the typical golden stone houses of the region, enlivened by wrought-iron outer staircases and balconies adorned with flowers and climbing vines. ◆ Take D703 east past La Roque-Gageac and go south on D46, crossing the Dordogne, to reach Domme

61 Sarlat-La-Canéda The bustling, beautiful market town of Sarlat is capital of the Périgord-Noir (Black Perigord), so called because of the area's dense forests of live oaks. The old quarter of the city has some of the best-preserved medieval buildings in France, constructed mostly of the attractive

ocher stone so prevalent in the region, with roofs of sun-bleached red tile or gray slate. Traffic can be a problem in July and August, so it's best to find a parking place and explore the wealth of interesting sights on foot (you'll see public parking lots on the way from Domme, just before the outer edge of the old quarter). The Rue de la République, built in the 19th century and called the *"Traverse"* by locals, slices down the center of the Gothic jumble of Vieux Sarlat (Old Sarlat). To the east of the Traverse, the Place du Peyrou is bordered by some of the most remarkable of the town's many landmarks. The Renaissance **Maison de La Boétie** (Pl du Peyrou), was the 16th-century home of Etienne La Boétie, a famous magistrate in the Bordeaux Parliament, as well as translator, poet, and essayist—all at quite a tender age (he died at 33). Still, La Boétie is perhaps best known as the close friend of Michel de Montaigne; his death prompted Montaigne to write his famous *Essay on Friendship.*

Facing La Boétie's house is the **Cathédrale St-Sacerdos,** a mélange of Gothic and Romanesque styles; be sure to explore the complex of courtyards, 12th-century chapel, and former cemetery, now a garden, reached through the south doorway. On the far side of the garden stands the curious **Lanterne des Morts** (Lantern to the Dead), a tower capped by a conical roof, where, legend has it, St. Bernard performed a miracle in the year 1147. Farther north is the Place des Oies (Geese Square), where a lively, not-to-be-missed food market is held on Saturday morning, as it has been for centuries. Overlooking the square is the meticulously restored **Hôtel Plamon.** The 14th-century home of a wealthy family of cloth merchants, it is actually a group of connected buildings that line the Rue des Consuls leading out of the Place des Oies. Note the three beautifully traceried Gothic windows that look out on the street from the second floor. ◆ 14 km/8.7 miles from Domme; take D46 north 1 km (.6 miles) to D703 northeast; after 3 km (1.9 miles) pick up D46 north again, and take it 10 km (6.2 miles) more to Sarlat

---

When tasting wine, choose a glass that is clear, so that the color and clarity of the wine are visible. The stem was developed to allow you to hold the glass without cupping your hand around the bowl, which would affect the temperature of the wine. The stem also facilitates rotating the wine around the glass, a practice designed to activate the wine's oxygenation and to stimulate the release of its bouquet.

Restaurants/Clubs: Red   Hotels: Blue

Shops/ 🌳 **Outdoors:** Green   **Sights/Culture:** Black

61 Hostellerie de Meysset $$ Atop a hill just outside Sarlat, this simple auberge in an old, ivy-bedecked stone manor has 22 comfortable (though smallish) rooms and four large suites overlooking a park. The rooms are decorated in charming French Provincial style, and all have private bathrooms. The peaceful terrace, with its view of the flower-filled gardens, is a great place to have a drink and unwind after a day of sightseeing in Sarlat. ♦ Closed October-April. Reservations recommended well in advance. Argentouleau (from Sarlat go 3 km/1.8 miles northwest on D6). 53.59.08.29; fax 53.28.47.61

Within the Hostellerie de Meysset:

Restaurant Hostellerie de Meysset
★★$$ A cozy, rustic place, with very good regional cuisine. Try the *coeurs d'artichauts à l'émincé de foie gras tiède* (artichoke hearts with slices of warm foie gras), the *magret de canard et sauce au goût de noix* (grilled duck breast with walnut sauce), or the *émincé de cèpes* (sauté of boletus mushrooms). The wine list is short, but includes some good regional offerings, and the service is very friendly. Check out the prix-fixe lunch menu, which includes wine. ♦ M-Tu, Th-Su lunch and dinner, W dinner; closed October-April. Reservations recommended. 53.59.08.29

62 Huilerie du Moulin de la Tour One of Périgord's many *huile de noix* (walnut oil) mills, this family-owned operation offers an interesting tour in addition to selling its products, which also include *huile de noisettes* (hazelnut oil). If you've never tried fresh walnut oil, run—don't walk—to this or any other local mill. The bottled stuff that fetches top dollar stateside pales in comparison to the freshly pressed oil; it is very perishable, at its peak only when straight from the mill. The hazelnut oil is a delicacy in its own right. ♦ Free. Daily. Ste-Nathalène (from Sarlat go 9 km/5.5 miles northeast on D47). 53.59.22.08

63 Lascaux II (Cave Paintings) On 12 September 1940, four village boys attempting to rescue a dog stumbled upon an enormous cave covered with hundreds of vivid paintings of bulls, horses, deer, and ibex. Since then, Lascaux has become perhaps the most famous prehistoric site in Europe and one of France's foremost treasures. The original cave was closed in 1963 to protect the fragile paintings; instead, visitors see **Lascaux II,** a meticulous reconstruction. To duplicate the 17,000-year-old originals, the paintings were done in natural pigments by artists from Paris's Ecole des Beaux-Arts. Don't be discouraged from visiting these latter-day substitutions. They've been executed with such care that they seem like the genuine article—and the originals are among early

humankind's masterpieces. ♦ Admission. Daily July-Aug; Tu-Su Feb-June, Sept-Dec; closed January. From Sarlat take D704 north 26 km (16.1 miles) to Montignac and follow the signs to Lascaux II. 53.51.95.03

63 Espace Cro-Magnon (Cro-Magnon Park) It may sound like a hokey tourist attraction, but this outdoor theme park near the Lascaux caves is oddly moving. Realistic-looking mannequins re-create Cro-Magnon life, busying themselves with daily tasks around replicas of the tepeelike tents they probably inhabited. The park is also stocked with the live animals commonly depicted in the cave paintings, including stags, wild boar, and bison, as well as scale models of extinct creatures like woolly mammoths. The overall effect is more Smithsonian than Six Flags, and provides some interesting perspective on the people whose paintings still survive in the Lascaux caves. ♦ Admission. Daily (no midday closing) July-Aug; Tu-Su Feb-June, Sept-Dec; closed in January. Le Thot (from Lascaux go 6 km/3.7 miles south on D65). 53.50.70.44

64 Ferme-Auberge Danie, Guy, et Gilles Dubois $ The delightful Dubois family opens its farm (and hearts) to visitors who want a real taste of Périgord country life. They offer five very comfortable, inexpensive guest rooms, and with advance notice will serve fantastic evening meals for the price of a salad and sandwich at a Paris café. The Dubois also hold demonstrations on foie gras production (not a lesson everyone will enjoy). For wider-ranging culinary interests, they also stage a series of *Weekends Culinaires*. Informal classes are given around a chosen theme— for instance, during a *weekend du cochon*, participants will learn to cure a ham or make blood sausage. Another frequent theme focuses on that staple of the Périgordine farmyard, the goose, with *confit d'oie* (goose preserved in its fat), foie gras, and *jambon d'oie* (goose "ham") likely to appear on the syllabus. The weekend officially begins on Thursday after lunch, and includes ample meals featuring the region's typical country fare. Even if you can't linger here, stop by to pick up some of the farm's many food products, available in cans or jars.

◆ Reservations required. Peyrenegre (29 km/18 miles north of Sarlat; from Montignac take D704 north, then D62 southeast to La Cassagne, and follow the signs to Peyrenegre and the farm). 53.51.04.24; fax 53.51.11.22

65 Rocamadour During its heyday in the Middle Ages, this tiny village (population 650) ranked next in importance only to Rome and Jerusalem as a pilgrimage site. Perched on a sheer cliff 500 feet above the Alzou Canyon, the town became a major pilgrimage destination in 1166, when remains hailed as those of an obscure saint—St. Amadour—came to light here. According to legend, the saint was actually Zaccheus, a disciple of Christ and husband of St. Veronica. Persecuted in Palestine, the couple fled here, and when St. Veronica died, Zaccheus retreated to this high, rocky plateau, where he lived as a hermit until his death (which would explain St. Amadour's and the town's names, from the Latin *roc amator,* meaning "lover of rocky cliffs"). Soon after St. Amadour was unearthed, miracles began to be reported here, and the town quickly became a destination for pilgrims, including the English King Henry Plantagenêt (who was mysteriously cured of an ailment here), St. Bernard, St. Louis, Blanche of Castille, and Louis XI. Today, the stream of worshipers has become a torrent of tourists. But if you arrive via the village of L'Hospitalet, where the first sight of Rocamadour precariously clinging to the gorge takes the breath away, you'll see why visitors, religious or secular, would be willing to make the trip here.

Rocamadour's modern-day pilgrims support an amazing number of tacky souvenir shops, but most of this desecration is confined to the village's main street. Make your way through it all to the 216 steps of the **Escalier des Pèlerins** (Pilgrims' Stairs; Pl de la Carreta, off Rue de la Couronnerie), remembering when you start to pant that pilgrims once climbed these stairs on their knees and in chains. At the top is the Parvis des Eglises, a small square surrounded by seven chapels, where begins the **Cité Religieuse.** Here, the history of Rocamadour's religious fervor remains vivid in such impressive medieval buildings as the 11th- to 13th-century **Basilique St-Sauveur;** the **Chapelle St-Michel,** with its famous frescoes of the Annunciation; St. Amadour's crypt; and the **Chapelle Miraculeuse.** Suspended from the ceiling of the latter is a bell that is said to ring of its own accord to foretell miracles. Farther still up the cliff stands the 19th-century **Château,** where the chaplains of Rocamadour now live. From the ramparts that surround it is an awe-inspiring view of the surrounding countryside. But after the hubbub of the sights every tourist must see, an early-morning or evening stroll around Rocamadour's quiet back streets is perhaps the best way to experience the sense of magic that medieval pilgrims must have felt here. ◆ From Sarlat take D704 southeast 26 km (16 miles) to Gourdon, then D673 northeast 34 km (21 miles) to Rocamadour

66 Domaine de la Rhue $$$ Although it's just minutes from Rocamadour, this charming hotel seems miles away from anywhere. It's run by a friendly young couple, Eric and Christine Jooris, who offer 11 guest rooms and one suite in the converted stables of their magnificent château. But there's no trace of livestock in the stables now: A large, elegant living room boasts a beamed ceiling, an enormous fireplace, and a wide staircase that leads to the rooms. Eminently comfortable, they too have beamed ceilings and are decked out in cheerful, light-colored fabrics. All are equipped with private bathrooms, and some have TV sets, mini-bars, and even private gardens. A swimming pool is also on the premises. Excellent continental breakfasts are served, but there's no restaurant. However, the Joorises can suggest several good places to eat in the area. To top it all off, they run a company nearby that offers hot-air balloon tours of the region. ◆ Closed mid-November–Easter. La Rhue (from Rocamadour go 7 km/4.3 miles north on D673 and N140). 65.33.71.50; fax 65.33.72.48

Cahors and Its Environs

Nestled in a loop of the **Lot River,** the beautiful town of Cahors, once the capital of the ancient province of **Quercy,** has accumulated a store of medieval and Renaissance treasures since its founding in the time of the Gauls. Its most famous landmarks are the **Pont Valentré,** one of the few remaining medieval fortified bridges in France, and the Romanesque **Cathédrale St-Etienne** (Pl Chapou, 65.35.27.80). The latter's north door is decorated with unusually fine 12th-century carvings depicting the Ascension. Among the town's other must-see sights are the truffle market held every Saturday morning from November through March in the **Allée Fénelon** and the lively food market held Wednesday and Saturday mornings year-round in **Place Chapou.**

Surrounded by vineyards planted along the steep banks of the Lot, Cahors is perhaps most famous for its wines, all red, which the city has produced since at least the seventh century AD. Known over the centuries as vin noir (black wine) for its very dark red color, the distinctive Cahors wine is made primarily of auxerrois grapes (the local name for cot or malbec grapes) with a little merlot and jurançon added for roundness. At their best, the wines are sturdy and tannic, but with a fruity finish; they're best when left to age a long while in the bottle, and are well worth the wait. For a beautiful view of Cahors and its vineyards, head for **Mont St-Cyr**, just south-east of town; a pretty, moderately difficult hiking trail (GR 36) leads from the Pont Louis-Philippe right to the summit. Signs are posted to indicate the trail, and a map is available from the tourist office (Pl A.-Briand, off Blvd Gambetta, 65.35.09.56). The hike takes about an hour and 40 minutes round-trip.

67 Restaurant Marco ★★★$$ Ask anyone in Cahors for a great place to eat, and most will name this lovely place in a vine-covered house just north of the city. The cooking is regional, but with new variations, which have garnered the place one Michelin star. Consider the *pied de cochon à la truffe* (pig's foot with truffles—a bit of poetic injustice, since pigs often are put to work locating truffles); delectable foie gras prepared a variety of ways; and duck pot-au-feu, a long-simmered stew. The wine list commands respect, with several excellent regional choices, including some rare Cahors vintages. The prix-fixe menus are a very good, economical way to go. Adjoining the restaurant are four very comfortable, moderately priced guest rooms overlooking a swimming pool; all have private bathrooms. ♦ Daily June-Sept; Tu-Sa lunch and dinner, Su lunch Oct-May; closed January–early March and the last week in October. Reservations recommended. Lamagdelaine (from Cahors go 7 km/4.3 miles northeast on D653). 65.35.30.64

68 Pech-Merle Grotto As at Lascaux, village boys uncovered this treasure—enormous caverns east of Cahors filled with magnificent prehistoric paintings—in 1922. The most impressive of these are the spotted horses and prints of human hands in the **Galerie des Peintures** (Gallery of Paintings) cave and a frieze of mammoths and bison in the **Salle de la Colonne Brisée** (Hall of the Broken Column). Visitors view a film on the paintings before they move on to the real things (unlike at Lascaux, these are authentic, not reconstructions). ♦ Admission. Daily; closed December-March. Be sure to wear nonslip shoes, and bring a sweater. Cabrerets (32 km/19.8 miles northeast of Cahors; take D653 east to D662 and follow the signs to Cabrerets and the caves). 65.31.23.33

69 Château de Mercuès $$$$ Perched above the Lot Valley, this romantic, 13th-century château, with its four crenellated towers, once belonged to the Bishops of Cahors. It's now a member of the Relais & Châteaux group, and is *the* splurge hotel along the Cahors wine route. The 25 rooms and seven suites are all large and lavish, with huge marble bathrooms and all the up-to-date amenities, including direct-dial phones, mini-bars, and satellite TVs. The rooms are done up in French Provincial style, with exposed beams and the occasional half-timber wall reflecting the château's venerable age. Each room is unique: One has an antique four-poster bed, another is a split-level suite in one of the towers. Also on the premises are two tennis courts, a huge and beautiful swimming pool, and lovely French gardens; horseback riding facilities and a golf course are nearby. Another plus for wine lovers is that the château produces its own Cahors wine and offers tastings in the 13th-century wine cellars dug out of the cliff on which the château stands. ♦ Closed November-March. Mercuès (from Cahors go 5 km/3.1 miles northwest on D911). 65.20.00.01; fax 65.20.05.72

Within the Château de Mercuès:

Restaurant Château de Mercuès ★★★$$$ Inventive versions of local specialties as well as excellent seafood—a rarity in this region—are the draws here. Try the *sandre poêlé et gratiné aux herbes, tête de cèpe farcie* (pickerel sautéed with herbs, served au gratin with a stuffed boletus mushroom) or the *civet d'oie à la Quercynoise, gros macaroni au foie gras* (slow-cooked goose with macaroni in foie gras sauce). The cheese assortment is especially good, but save room for the delicious desserts, some made with the local *pruneaux* (prunes). The wine list is outstanding in Cahors wines. ♦ Closed November-March. Reservations required. 65.20.00.10

70 Le Relais des Champs $ Strategically placed for touring the Cahors wineries, this hotel in a tiny village overlooking the Lot River has 16 quiet, simple, and very inexpensive rooms (some without private baths). A quaint little restaurant on the premises serves hearty, uncomplicated regional specialties such as cassoulet (a bean stew with sausage and duck). ♦ *Demi-pension* (breakfast and one other meal included in the room rate) required July-August. Reservations recommended. Caillac (from Mercuès go 4 km/2.4 miles west on D10). 65.30.91.55

70 Château de Lagrezette The most striking château of the Cahors region also produces one of its best wines. It's a 16th-century fairy-tale castle from central casting, with tall turrets, creamy white walls, and pink-gold tile roofs. Its owner, the CEO of Cartier, has made sure everything here, including the wine, is of the highest possible quality; new *chais* have recently been installed at a cost of about $2 million. The wines, which come from vineyards that have been here since 1503, have the deep red color, the concentrated earthy flavors, and the tannic character typical of Cahors wines. Visitors get a guided tour of the *chais,* followed by a tasting. ♦ Free. M-Sa July-Aug; M-F Sept-June. Caillac (from Mercuès go about 1 km/.6 miles west; follow the signs to the château). 65.20.07.42; 65.20.06.95

71 Château Eugénie The Imperial Court of Russia once owned part of the vineyards here, which is why one of the wines is called Cuvée des Tsars. Today, the Couture brothers own the estate, a stone farmhouse with vineyards spreading over terraces above the Lot River. In 1982, the Coutures set out to produce a wine exactly the way their grandfather had made the prizewinning 1929 vintage: They thinned out the grapes in July, harvested when the juice was at 14 degrees of potential alcohol, and aged the wine two years in oak. Naturally, they named it Cuvée de l'Aïeul (Ancestor's Vintage), and it was a smashing success, regarded as one of the best-ever Cahors wines. Since then, the Coutures reprise this wine only in promising years, but, in general, all their wines are reliable. ♦ Free. Daily July-Aug; M-Sa Sept-June. Rivière-Haute (from Cahors go 15 km/9.3 miles west on D8). 65.30.73.51; fax 65.20.19.81

72 Clos de Gamot/Château du Cayrou Lovers of rich, full-flavored reds should not miss a stop at the Jouffreau family's two properties in the Lot Valley. **Clos de Gamot,** where they make their home, is surrounded by the vines that produce their best Cahors wines. The family also acquired **Château du Cayrou** in 1971; its wines are more fruity and direct, pleasant when drunk after a shorter time in the bottle than many other Cahors need. Both vineyards' wines are highly respected in the region, but the real star is Clos de Gamot, with its classic Cahors weightiness and depth of color, and its overtones of truffles and cassis; it's the perfect partner for game dishes or such robust regional dishes as cassoulet. Some of the vines used to make this top-of-the-line wine date back to the 1880s, when Lucien Jouffreau, grandfather of the current owner, saved the vineyard from ruin during the phylloxera scourge by grafting his last remaining healthy vines onto resistant American rootstock. It's not every day that you can sample wines from 100-plus-year-old vines. Also look for a wine that will debut by 1996: Clos St-Jean, which is made from vines that were cloned from **Clos de Gamot**'s oldest vines and, in a daring experiment, not grafted to American rootstock. The Jouffreaus favor strictly traditional wine-making practices, which is not surprising since the family has been making wine in the region since the 13th century, and at **Clos de Gamot** since the 17th century. They don't use chemical weed killers and always harvest by hand over a period of eight to 10 days to make sure every grape is picked when perfectly ripe. All wines are aged from 18 to 24 months, sometimes longer, in oak. Architecturally, **Château du Cayrou** is the standout: It's an attractive structure of golden stone, built in a horseshoe shape around a wide lawn, with architectural features back to the 14th century. Tastings are offered at both estates. ♦ Free. Clos de Gamot daily, preferably by appointment. Château du Cayrou M-Sat Easter-October; the rest of the year by appointment. From Rivière-Haute take D8 west about 10 km (6.2 miles) and follow the signs to Clos de Gamot. Château du Cayrou is about 5 km (3.1 miles) west of Clos de Gamot off D8. Phone for both 65.22.40.26; fax 65.22.45.44

"I didn't know what Bordeaux wine was before I made this trip. I thought of it as what you added one-third Hermitage to before shipping it to England or somewhere else. The true Bordeaux has an astonishing bouquet and is less coarse than what we think of wine of this name."

Marie-Henri Beyle (Stendhal), *Journal de voyage de Bordeaux à Valence en 1838*

73 Château Triguedina The Baldès family has been making wine on this estate since 1830, and the vines range from an impressive 25 to a venerable 60 years old. All the wines regularly win medals, but the Prince Probus red, made entirely of auxerrois grapes from 50-year-old vines, is the star attraction: So dark it's almost black, it has overtones of cinnamon, old leather, and anise. The much-praised Château Triguedina is a slightly lighter wine made from 25-year-old vines. To really shine, both of those wines need to age for some time, but the Domaine Labrande, which has a rich bouquet, can be drunk earlier. A wide stone staircase leads up to the vine-covered château, which is a typical example of Lot Valley architecture. Jean Baldès and his son Jean-Luc have put together a little wine museum in the cellars on the history of Cahors wines, and about the eight generations of their family who have made them here. This is a great place to learn about the special character of the *vin noir* of Cahors. ♦ Free. Visits M-F. Appointment recommended. Puy-l'Evêque (from Cahors go 29 km/18 miles west on D911. From Rivière-Haute, go about 22 km/13.6 miles west on D8). 65.21.30.81; fax 65.21.39.28

74 Château de Bonaguil Between 1480 and 1520, just as his contemporaries were beginning to build the serene Renaissance pleasure palaces of the Loire, a local overlord named Bérenger de Roquefeuil fortified this 13th-century castle to the hilt. In a paranoid frenzy to defend the baronies he had brutally seized from neighboring lords, he included every ingenious device of defense or attack the French had learned while fighting the Hundred Years' War. He made the fortress almost siege-proof, capable of sustaining a garrison of several hundred defenders. But no one ever tested De Roquefeuil's might; perhaps everyone else was tired of battle. One of the largest castles in France, it's the archetypal medieval fortress—something Hollywood might film when it's lashed by rain and lit by lightning. Indeed, it is said to be haunted by De Roquefeuil's daughter, who was forced by her father to marry a cruel old man instead of her young lover. Her ghost has been sighted, wringing her hands and lamenting her lost love, only on—what else?—dark and stormy November nights. A tour provides a fascinating glimpse into the warlike Middle Ages, with some of the finest medieval military architecture still in existence. The castle looms forbiddingly over the tiny village of Bonaguil from a high cliff surrounded by lush green forests. For the best view of the whole ensemble, park the car along the tiny unnumbered road leading from the village of St-Martin-le-Redon (just north of Puy-l'Evêque) to Bonaguil. The picturesque village below the castle is itself well worth a stroll; there, in the parking lot by **Le Cellier**

restaurant (you can't miss it) you can also pick up Grande Randonnée hiking trail No. 36, which passes behind the château and is studded with good picnic spots. ♦ Free. Daily; closed November–mid-March. From Puy-l'Evêque take D911 west 15 km (9 miles), then take D673 north 6.5 km (4 miles), then D158 west to the château. 53.71.39.75

74 Les Bons Enfants ★★$ Set in an old water mill, this pleasant place at the base of the **Château de Bonaguil** has a friendly, relaxed atmosphere, a lovely terrace shaded by weeping willows (with a great view of the château), and, best of all, excellent Périgord home cooking. Try the *gésiers confits aux pommes* (duck gizzards with apples) or the *canard au citron* (duck with lemon). The weekday prix-fixe lunch menu, which includes wine, is a steal; you could pay more for picnic fixings. In an adjoining building are three very simple guest rooms, available only to those who dine here. ♦ Daily lunch and dinner; closed mid-November–mid-February. Reservations recommended in summer. At the foot of the château, Bonaguil. 53.71.23.52

75 Hôtel Les Chênes $$ Just outside the medieval city of Pujols, this unpretentious hotel offers 21 quaint, traditionally decorated rooms with flowery wallpaper and private bathrooms. It is surrounded by a park with a swimming pool. Part of the *Relais de Silence* organization, it guarantees peace and quiet. There's no restaurant, but breakfast is served, and neaby is a fine restaurant, **La Toque Blanche** (see below). ♦ Pujols (46 km/28.5 miles from Puy-l'Evêque; take D911 west 43 km/26.7 miles to Villeneuve-sur-Lot, then D118 3 km/1.8 miles south to Pujols; follow the signs to the hotel, on the far side of Pujols). 53.49.04.55; fax 53.49.22.74

La Toque Blanche

75 La Toque Blanche ★★★★$$$ Although the dining room in this former private house commands a stunning view of the countryside and the medieval village of Pujols perched on a nearby hill, the prime attraction here is the cuisine, which has earned this place a Michelin star. Taste for yourself just how good southwestern French cooking can be; try the rich *terrine de foie gras de canard* (a meaty pâté of duck foie gras) or the *magret grillé aux poires confites* (grilled duck breast with caramelized pears in wine sauce). The seafood, such as *filet de turbot au fumet de vin des côtes de Buzet* (fillet of turbot in Buzet wine sauce), is also expertly prepared. The wine list is an excellent match for the menu, with an especially fine selection of bordeaux and Cahors. Ordering à la carte can run up

How to Read a French Wine Label

French wines are bottled and labled under the strict supervision of the *Institut National des Appellations d'Origine*. Deciphering the information provided on the label can be difficult unless you know the rules (which do on occasion change). On the four

Appellation Contrôlée (Controlled Label of Origin, appreviated *AOC* or *AC*) labels shown below—each slightly different in terms of region and required disclosures—we have demonstrated how to identify some of the terms you will encounter.

Alsace

Grape variety, allowed only if the vine is made from a single variety

Brand, name, and address of bottler (required)

Alcohol content (required)

For export to US distributor

Appellation (required)

Volume (required)

Required for export to some countries

US practice; no mention of this appears in France.

Champagne

Brand (required)

Type of wine in terms of sugar content (required)

Alcohol content (required)

Appellation (required)

The winery's name for this particular wine; optional, and not governed by *AOC* laws

Address (required; implies "bottled by the owner at this address")

Volume (required)

There is no mention of *"appellation contrôlée"* on any champagne label, because any bottle legally bearing the word "champagne" is *AOC* champagne.

Bordeaux

Brand (optional) — CHATEAU PAPE CLÉMENT

Classification (optional) — GRAND CRU CLASSE DE GRAVES

Appellation (required) — APPELLATION PESSAC-LEOGNAN CONTROLEE / PESSAC · LEOGNAN

Vintage year (optional) — 1986

Name and address of bottler (required) — Sté MONTAGNE & Cie PROPRIÉTAIRE À PESSAC-GIRONDE

"Bottled at the Château" (optional) — MIS EN BOUTEILLE AU CHATEAU

Alcohol content (required after 1988) — 12,5% vol.

Volume (required) — 37,5 cl

PRODUCT OF FRANCE

Burgundy

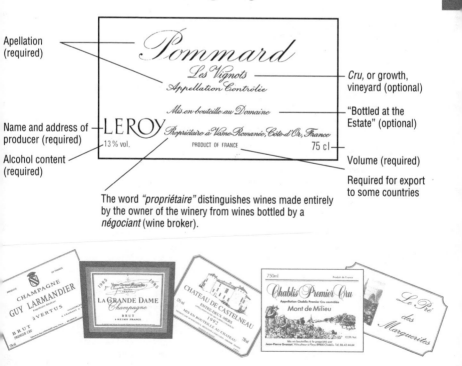

Apellation (required) — Pommard

Cru, or growth, vineyard (optional) — Les Vignots / Appellation Contrôlée

"Bottled at the Estate" (optional) — Mis en bouteille au Domaine

Name and address of producer (required) — LEROY / Propriétaire à Vosne-Romanée, Côte-d'Or, France

Alcohol content (required) — 13% vol.

PRODUCT OF FRANCE

Volume (required) — 75 cl

Required for export to some countries

The word *"propriétaire"* distinguishes wines made entirely by the owner of the winery from wines bottled by a *négociant* (wine broker).

the tab alarmingly fast, but the prix-fixe menus are quite reasonable. ◆ Daily July-Aug; Tu-Sa lunch and dinner, Su lunch Sept-June; closed one week in June and one week in December. Reservations required; nonsmoking room available. Pujols (look for the sign on the southern edge of town). 53.49.00.30; fax 53.70.49.79

76 Chambres d'Hôtes Les Huguets $$ Edward and Gerda Poppe rent five guest rooms in their restored 18th-century stone farmhouse, which is adorned with a red tile roof and blue shutters. The traditional French country rooms are comfortable and have private bathrooms. On the grounds are an inviting swimming pool, edged in local stone, and two impressive 500-year-old oak trees; the hotel also has a sauna. The Poppes, who are Dutch and speak English, will provide healthful dinners on request, such as rabbit with prunes served with organic vegetables from their own garden. They're also full of excellent, friendly advice on things to see and do in this picturesque area. ◆ Take N21 south of Villeneuve-sur-Lot and follow the signs to the hotel. 53.70.49.34

Gaillac

Though not a well-traveled spot on the wine route, the Gaillac wine district is worth a visit. About 90 kilometers (54 miles) southeast of Cahors, near the fascinating Languedoc town of Albi, this wine-making center on the banks of the **Tarn River** is one of the most productive in France, continuing a nearly 2,000-year-old tradition. In the 12th century Benedictine monks produced Gaillac wines that were exported widely and dubbed *vin du coq* (wine of the rooster) for the rooster featured in the Gaillac coat of arms, which appeared on the labels. Once known for its sweet white wines, Gaillac broadened its range in this century to conform to contemporary tastes. A wide variety of grapes are now planted around Gaillac: duras, gamay, syrah, and negrette for the vigorous, rustic reds and piquant rosés; and mauzac, muscadelle, ondenc, sémillon, sauvignon blanc, and len de l'el (a regional grape whose name derives from *loin de l'oeil*—"out of sight") for the whites.

With a recent upgrade in quality, Gaillac wines have enjoyed something of a renaissance in the past few years. The area's best-known (and best, many say) wines are its sparkling whites, or Gaillac Mousseux, produced both by the champagne method and by a regional variation, the *méthode gaillaçoise*. Don't confuse these beguiling, bubbly wines with the weak imitation called Gaillac Perlé produced by some local co-ops. And don't overlook the quite respectable sweet white

wines, the best of which bear the label Gaillac Premières Côtes. As good as they are, many of these wines are rarely seen outside the area. A roisterous annual wine festival, the Cocagne des Vins, is held in town on the first or second weekend in August.

77 Domaine de Gradille, "La Grouillère" $ Lyne and Denis Soulié offer five guest rooms in their rambling stone farmhouse near Gaillac. All the rooms are comfortable and charmingly decorated, usually spruced up with bouquets of fresh flowers. Two of the rooms have private bathrooms; the other three have private baths, but share a toilet. The Souliés prepare excellent meals on request, and they also make delicious fruit liqueurs; guests have been known to spend long, tranquil evenings sampling them on the terrace. Nearby is a pristine lake for swimming. The Souliés speak English and happily share their considerable knowledge of things to see and do in the area. ◆ Reservations recommended. From Gaillac take D999 west 4 km (2.4 miles) and follow the signs for "Chambres d'hôtel." 63.41.01.57, 63.57.14.89; fax 63.57.43.73

78 Hostellerie du Vieux Cordes $$ In the heart of the picturesque medieval village of Cordes, this attractive hotel is well located for visiting Gaillac wineries. The restored ancient house, on one of Cordes's steep, winding cobbled streets, has 21 simple but comfortable rooms; all have contemporary decor and private baths, and are very quiet. Be sure to ask for a room overlooking the valley (*"avec vue sur la vallée"*); the panorama is spectacular. ◆ Closed in January. Rue de la République, Cordes (24 km/14.9 miles north of Gaillac on D922). 63.56.00.12

Within the Hostellerie du Vieux Cordes:

Restaurant Hostellerie du Vieux Cordes ★$ Don't be put off by this delightful place's quirks; they are more than offset by the ambience, food, and low prices. The first is the large, laminated menu; featuring glossy photos of dishes, it looks like something from a US truck stop. The second is its insistence on serving only salmon and duck, whose virtues are humorously extolled in purple prose on one side of the menu. (The excellent daily specials are exempt from the salmon/duck requirement, and feature other regional meat and fish dishes.) Despite the limited ingredients, the chef achieves a delicious variety; consider, for example, the *jambonnette de canard en crépinette de chou* (boned and stuffed duck thigh, cooked in a cabbage leaf). The wine list features several Gaillac entries. In fine weather, request a table on the romantic terrace, which is overhung with ancient wisteria vines entwined around wrought-iron trellises and boasts a beautiful view. ◆ Daily lunch and dinner. 63.56.00.12

79 Cave de Técou This highly respected wine co-op near Gaillac has been instrumental in upgrading the area's wines from simple *vins de table* to ones worthy of the appellation they now bear. The co-op buys grapes from about 220 growers, then mixes them carefully according to the characters of their original *terroirs*. The resulting reds, rosés, and dry and sweet white wines are bottled under three labels: Tradition, the simplest, least expensive wines; Séduction, the next step up, with grapes culled from the best vineyards and vintages; and Passion, the top-of-the-line label, made from the pick of the crop and always aged in oak. Two excellent choices are the 1990 Passion red, made from the local fer servadou (or braucol) and merlot grapes, and the 1992 Passion white, made primarily from sauvignon. But decide for yourself: Tastings are offered in a shop at the entrance to the cellars. ♦ Free. M-Sa. Técou (8 km/4.9 miles from Gaillac; take D964 south to D16 east and follow the signs). 63.33.00.80, fax 63.33.06.69

Madiran

Southwest of the Gaillac vineyards, on the edge of the famous Armagnac brandy-producing region, tourists become rarer and the landscape grows more rugged: Dense, verdant oak forests cloak steep hills, with grapevines planted on the lower slopes. Amid this terrain lies Madiran, one of the four districts that make up the wine-producing region of the western **Pyrénées.** As a wine-growing area, Madiran had almost become extinct by the end of World War II. But determination and modern technology brought it back to life, and now its red wines are considered some of the best in the Pyrénées. In the vineyards flanked by the **Adour River,** the local tannat grapes grow, along with some cabernet sauvignon, cabernet franc, and other grapes. The tannat give the Madiran wines their characteristic tannic bite. Small wineries are scattered throughout the region, all hung with signs offering *dégustation* (tasting); stop in for an authentic taste not only of Madiran's wine, but of its everyday life too.

80 La Ripa Alta ★★★$$ A visit to this sensational place on the main square of a picturesque *bastide* (fortified village) is a fitting reward for trekking all the way down to Madiran country. Friendly chef Maurice Coscuella has been delighting guests for many years with his rich southwestern dishes, which make the most of the local triumvirate of duck, foie gras, and rich red wine. Coscuella's motto is *"Quod sapit nutrit"* (What pleases nourishes best) and you'll certainly walk out of here well nourished and pleased by such treats as *pastilla de homard au foie gras* (pastry with lobster and foie gras), the regional classic *confit de canard aux haricots blancs* (duck preserved in its fat and cooked with white beans), *feuilleté de ris d'agneau aux cèpes* (puff pastry filled with lamb sweetbreads and boletus mushrooms), or *escalopes de foie de canard aux raisins* (warm foie gras with grapes). Somehow, try to save room for the great cheese selection and wonderful desserts. The wine list is one of the area's best, ranging from fine bordeaux to well-chosen Madirans to some great Armagnacs; it includes a few excellent rare vintages, such as a 1976 Château Latour from the Médoc and a 1952 La Tache burgundy. With all this, the prices seem almost too good to be true: This is one of the least expensive high-quality restaurants in France, and the prix-fixe menus are bargains. ♦ Daily June-Oct; Tu-Su early Nov, mid-Dec–May; closed mid-November–mid-December. Reservations required. 3 Pl de l'Eglise, Plaisance-du-Gers (from Toulouse take N124 west 79 km/49 miles to Auch; from Auch the trip totals 54 km/33 miles on N124 followed by D943 west, which becomes D946; at the tiny village of Beaumarchés, take D3 north to Plaisance). 62.69.30.43; fax 62.69.36.99

Above La Ripa Alta:

Hôtel Ripa Alta $$ The Coscuellas offer 12 homey, comfortable, and quiet guest rooms and two suites, with preference given to those who dine at their restaurant. The decor includes floral wallpaper and drapes and wooden armoires; some rooms have TV sets and mini-bars. All have private bathrooms. This is a good base for touring the seldom-explored Gers, as well as Armagnac and Madiran country. ♦ 62.69.30.43

81 Vignobles Alain-Brumont Monsieur Brumont is one of France's most respected *vignerons,* and a visit to his domain is worth the considerable detour off the usual wine route. He has almost single-handedly upgraded the quality and image of the Madiran appellation, time and again outclassing his competitors with his uncanny talent for and devotion to his métier. Acting on sheer intuition in 1992, he hired all the workers he could find to harvest his grapes in three days instead of the usual two weeks; days later, torrential rains ruined many other producers' vintages. And when other local wine makers gave up on the tannat grape to shift to the fashionable cabernet sauvignon, Brumont stayed loyal; he has proved that with proper treatment this variety can yield suberb wines that are quintessentially Madiran. The richly flavored reds age well and are a perfect match for the spicy, hearty cuisine of this region. Try the Bouscassé Vieilles Vignes 1989, with its overtones of raspberries and mushrooms, and the Château Montus, the estate's premier wine, which is produced from vineyards nearby. The Château Montus 1985 took second place only to the Château Haut-Brion Premier Cru bordeaux in a blind tasting held in 1991, and bested *cinquième cru* Château Lynch-Bages, among other high-flying bordeaux entries. A tasting follows a tour of the cellars. ♦ Free. Visits M-Sa. Maumusson-Laguian (from Plaisance take D946 west to D935 north, then D136 west; follow signs for Maumusson-Laguian). 62.69.74.67; fax 62.69.70.46

82 A La Belle Gasconne ★★★$$ In the heart of old Gascony, not far from Armagnac, this archetypal provincial French auberge in a 14th-century mill boasts irresistible fare that has earned it a Michelin star. Friendly chef-owner Marie-Claude Gracia's regional cuisine will make you toss any diet resolutions out one of the quaint little windows. Some of the dishes on the ever-changing menu include foie gras in many guises, *tourte de légumes* (vegetable tart), *rognons de veau* (veal kidneys), and *cassoulet maison* (the hearty regional stew of beans, duck, and pork). One seasonal treat is described as *alose cuite à l'ancienne, au vin blanc et à l'oseille très doucement, deux heures, au four* (shad cooked the old-fashioned way, with white wine and sorrel, for two hours, in the oven). For dessert don't miss the prune-and-Armagnac flan or Gracia's sensational chocolate cake. The wine list is impressive, with many local wines as well as some real finds from elsewhere in France, including a wide selection of Sauternes and a superb 1985 Château Haut-Brion. ♦ Daily July-Aug; Tu-Sa lunch and dinner, Su lunch Feb-June and Sept-Dec; closed January and one week in December. Reservations recommended. Poudenas (from Mont-de-Marsan take D932 north, then D933 northeast for 43 km/27 miles; at Lapeyrade, take D24 southeast 11 km/7 miles to Gabarret, then take D656 20 km/12 miles north). 53.65.71.58; fax 53.65.87.39

Above A La Belle Gasconne:

Hôtel Auberge La Belle Gasconne $$ Here are six romantic guest rooms and one suite, all with private bathrooms and views of the picturesque Gélise River. Each is individually decorated: For example, the Gabrielle d'Estrées suite, named for a mistress of King Henri IV, is outfitted in Renaissance style, with exposed beams and pretty floral bedspread and drapes; the Andalouse room has a black, white, and red bathroom done up in tiles from Andalusia. The inn also boasts a swimming pool. On winter weekends, owner Marie-Claude Gracia gives cooking classes so that guests can return home with an invaluable souvenir–the ability

to reproduce some of the exquisite recipes from her restaurant. ♦ Reservations required far in advance. Closed January and one week in December. 53.65.71.58

Buzet

At the northern edge of Armagnac country, between the banks of the **Garonne** and the **Landes** forest, lies this small but important wine region. Relatively near the Bordeaux region, Buzet has made a name for itself by growing the same red grape varieties that predominate in Bordeaux—cabernet sauvignon, cabernet franc, merlot, and malbec—then producing bordeaux-style reds for much lower prices. The appellation does produce some decent white wines, but as in Bordeaux, it's the reds that count.

83 Les Vignerons de Buzet About 98 percent of the wines produced in Buzet come from this highly respected wine co-op, which has one of the most popular tasting centers in the southwest. Nearly 100,000 people visit every year—but never fear, there's always plenty of room. Try the splendid red wines, including the excellent Cuvée Napoléon, aged in new oak barrels, or the top-of-the-line Domaine du Château de Gueyze. Made from 40 percent merlot, 35 percent cabernet franc, and 25 percent cabernet sauvignon, the latter has pleasing notes suggestive of prunes, ripe fruit, and chocolate. Some very good white and rosé wines are also on hand. Be sure to check out the small wine museum. ♦ M-F; Sa morning. From Agen 30 km (18.6 miles) northwest, or from Bordeaux 95 km (59 miles) southeast; take the Bordeaux-Toulouse autoroute (A62) to the exit (*sortie*) for the towns of Damazan and Aiguillon. Pass through the village of Damazan (a 13th-century fortified town) and follow the signs to the hamlet of Buzet-sur-Baïse, 5 km (3.1 miles) south on D108; the shop is just outside the village. 53.84.74.30; fax 53.84.74.24

When buying a white Bordeaux, one can tell whether the wine is sweet or dry without even seeing the label. In this region, a bottle made of green glass always indicates a dry wine.

"Il n'y a pas de bons vins, il n'y a que des bonnes bouteilles." (There are no good wines, only good bottles.)

French proverb.

Restaurants/Clubs: Red **Hotels:** Blue
Shops/ 🍃 Outdoors: Green **Sights/Culture:** Black

Xavier Planty
Château Guiraud, Sauternes

A day in the **Sauternes:** Drive past **Château d'Yquem, Filhot, Suduiraut,** and **Fargues.** Visit **Château de Malle** (17th century).

Drive to **Roquetaillade** castle—the oldest lived-in castle in France—with its outstanding interiors. A must! If you are lucky, you will meet the English viscountess for an enchanting visit. Don't forget the farm, its live animals, and its ca. 1850 rooms.

Visit **Villandraut,** its shady square, with local cafes and restaurants. Visit the impressive ruins of the castle built by Pope Clement V, **Château de Villandraut.** Canoe rides on the **Ciron.**

Visit **St-Macaire,** a medieval town of charm. Stroll through the deserted streets, and imagine the bustle 700 years ago.

Visit **Cadillac** (its name has given us the famous car of the same name) to see its castle and the fortified town walls.

Restaurants: **Claude Darroze** (Langon), **Le Saprien** (Sauternes).

Hotels: **Claude Darroze, Valmont, Château d'Arbieu, Relais de Fampeyre.**

Jean-Luc Baldès
Wine Maker, Baldès & Fils, Château Triguedina, Vins de Cahors, Puy l'Evêque

Visit **Puy-l'Evêque,** a picturesque village on the **Lot River.** You can camp along the Lot near a small beach, and there are hotels in the village. You can also visit a porcelain factory and watch a craftsman who creates hand-blown glass. There are many good restaurants in the area. Visit the **Château de Bonaguil,** the **Château Fort de Grezels,** and **St-Cirq-Lapopie,** named one of the "most beautiful villages of France" by the French Government Tourist Board, about 50 kilometers to the east of Puy-l'Evêque. In summer, you can cruise down the Lot in a boat; in winter, visit the truffle market in **Lalbenque.**

Patricia Sabourin
Cognac Producer, Cognacs Ragnaud-Sabourin S.A., Domaine de la Vôute, Ambleville

First of all, visit the Romanesque churches of the **Charente** and **Charente-Maritime** *départements* (administrative districts). They are everywhere, and the Roman art they contain is exceptional. The Atlantic Coast near **Royan** (a beach resort) is beautiful and a great place to swim. And finally, visit cognac producers and taste cognacs and Pineau de Charentes.

Claude Marco
Owner/Chef, Restaurant Claude Marco, Lamagdelaine

Lamagdelaine has tennis courts and the **Lot River,** which you can cruise down. See the **Port Valentré** in **Cahors** nearby, and take the scenic route down the Lot valley. Visit **St-Cirq-Lapopie,** one of the most beautiful villages of France, and the **Cabrerets** grotto, **Pech-Merle.** Don't miss **Rocamadour,** the second most important site in France. The Lot has surprises around every turn: the Lot, a land of marvels!

Alix de Pitray, Comtesse de Boigne
Wine Maker, Château de Pitray, Gardegan

Visit the medieval village of **St-Emilion,** with its winding streets lined with shops that sell prestigious wines. See the tiny 11th-century church in the village of **Parsac,** perched on the top of a hill. Near a Neo-Gothic château is the ancient tower where Michel de Montaigne wrote. Take a walk past the vineyards of the **Château de Pitray** when they are turning red and gold in autumn, and also through the fields and forests nearby, where you may see deer; the **Périgord** is not far away. Practice golf at the village of **Gardegan'**s driving range in an unspoiled, mysterious landscape.

Jean-Luc Lacoste
Organizer, All-terrain Bicycle Trips, Médoc

Take bicycle rides through the **Médoc** vineyards with stops at châteaux for tastings; ride to the local marshes, forests, and beaches. The prettiest wine châteaux are **Château Lafite-Rothschild, Cos d'Estournel, Château Margaux,** and **Château Pichon-Longueville.** Don't miss the forests in **Landes** and the Atlantic Coast beaches.

Christian Le Morvan
Owner, Le Jardin D'Eyquem Hotel

The tower at **Château de Montaigne** must be seen. The castle has been destroyed, but the tower where essayist Michel de Montaigne wrote is still there!

St-Emilion is renowned for its wines, but its medieval architecture is also delightful.

Each appellation in this region has a *maison du vin* (wine center) where free tastings allow you to discover the wines produced in that district.

Enjoy open food markets in **Castillon** on Mondays, **Ste-Foy** on Saturdays, and **Libourne** on Sundays.

The English *bastides* (walled towns) are fascinating. The closest are **Libourne, Ste-Foy-la-Grande,** and **Sauveterre-de-Guyenne.** Each of them is slightly different, though they were built on the same pattern.

The Loire Valley

The abundantly fertile **Loire River** valley, studded with glittering châteaux and medieval villages, yields some of the best wines in France. Sunny, but also moist and mild, the region produces around 80 varieties, including some rare breeds like the Coteaux du Layon's Bonnezeaux, a white Sauterne-type wine from near **Angers.** The *Val de Loire* (Loire Valley) is endlessly praised by the French for its serenity and for the sweetness of its air. Here, they say, is the place to taste the *douceur de vivre* (sweet life). Yet it is within easy reach of Paris: Angers, the center of the valley's main wine-making section, is only 90 minutes away from the French capital by *TGV* (fast train).

The "Loire Valley" that most Americans know is the region around **Tours,** known as **Touraine,** where the valley's most famous châteaux are found. But the river itself is 1,000 kilometers (621 miles) long, flowing from its source in the mountains of south-central France near **Puy-en-Velay** all the way to the Atlantic near **Nantes.** Châteaux are actually found all along the Loire but are concentrated around Tours and Angers, the area that tends to draw not only the greatest tide of château lovers but also wine tasters, because this is where many of the valley's wines are produced. This stretch of the valley stands up well to crowds, though, the proof being that the French still consider this true France, where the beret, bicycle, baguette, and bottle of wine still rule. And they say the purest French is spoken here.

Although the standard image of the valley is a collection of carefully tended fields and vineyards, there are also huge forests all along the river's length. It was these game-rich forests that drew kings and aristocrats here. The châteaux provide visual drama and historic reference points to the languidly pretty landscape. A country lane lined with poplars or thick stands of oak and pine may suddenly open onto a gleaming, turreted château. The Loire was peppered with noble residences throughout the Middle Ages and Renaissance, some of them converted from ancient forts; more recently, quite a few have been converted to museums or hotels.

Most châteaux stand near or at the heart of medieval villages, whose old are built of the same goldish white *tuffeau* (tufa) stone and topped with the same blue-gray slate roofs as the châteaux. A few local inhabitants live in cave houses known as troglodyte dwellings whose stone facades usually resemble elegant châteaux. These were originally dug out to extract building stones, particularly for the valley's great Renaissance châteaux. The uninhabited caves are often used to grow edible mushrooms or store wines.

The châteaux of the Loire vary enormously in size and bombast, but three stand out. From west to east, they are **Azay-le-Rideau**, near Tours, **Chenonceau**, south of **Amboise**, and **Chambord**, near **Blois**. Azay-le-Rideau, on a wooded island, hugs a quiet moat, fed by the **Indre River**, that reflects the château's four delicate corner towers. The graceful, many-galleried **Château de Chenonceau** straddles the **Cher River** at Chenonceaux village. And the largest castle in the Loire Valley, **Château de Chambord**, was built as an unapologetically grand hunting lodge for France's King François I in the 16th century. Then there are noble ruins, like **Château de Chinon**, between **Samur** and Tours, where Joan of Arc met with King Charles VII of France in 1429.

Because the Loire River is flood-prone, vines are grown well away from it, usually on slightly elevated, sloping hills. In land unsuitable for grape-growing is *bocage*, ancient farmland divided by hedgerows and small clumps

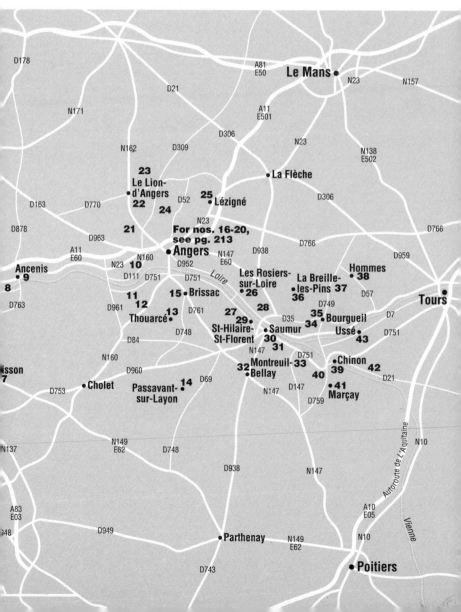

of trees, particularly northwest of Angers. Golden fields of grain, sunflowers, and corn throughout the valley are sustained by the Loire and its numerous tributaries—among them the Indre, Cher, **Vienne**, and **Maine.** The four major wine-producing areas of the Loire are, from west to east, the **Pays Nantais** (around Nantes), **Anjou** (around Angers), **Touraine** (around Tours), and the upper Loire's **Sancerrois** district, which stretches on either side of the river's great bend at the city of **Orléans.**

Some of the best-known types of wine produced in the region are the dry white Muscadet from the lowlands near Nantes, still and sparkling white Saumurs and Vouvrays from the mid-Loire Valley, and pale, flinty, white Sancerre from the upper Loire Valley. The region also produces many other excellent wines including Sauternes-like Quarts de Chaume; dry Savennières white; fruity Rosé d'Anjou; light reds including Saumur-Champigny, Chinon, and Bourgueil; and some smaller appellations. The climate is too cool for some grapes, but many do well here: muscadet (officially, melon de

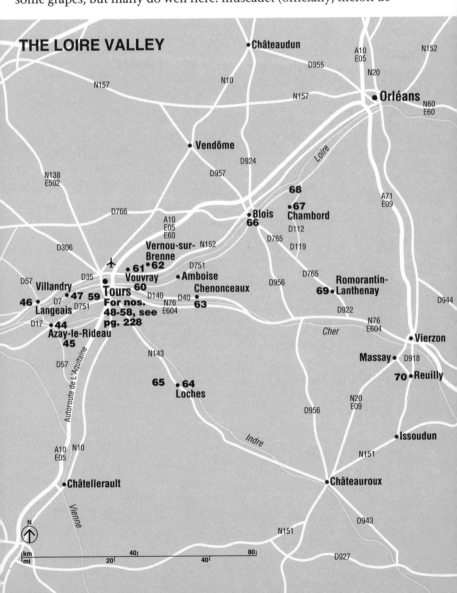

bourgogne), sauvignon, cabernet franc (known as breton), chardonnay, gamay, malbec (also known as cot), and especially the native chenin blanc (also known as pineau de la loire).

Wine tasting along the Loire is often a matter of seeking out *"dégustation"* or *"vin, vente directe"* signs that will lead you right to a wine maker. Except for a few large Saumur concerns producing sparkling wines, most Loire wineries are small, many of them relying heavily on individual clients—mostly Parisians who visit annually to stock their cellars.

The Loire Valley boasts some of France's finest hotels (reserve far in advance for July and August, the high season), many of them in converted châteaux. And the restaurants make wonderful use of the region's excellent wines, fish, dairy products, vegetables, fruits, game, and farm-raised meats and poultry. The markets abound with the local specialties; look for clusters of shallots, creamy goat cheese, rosy-skinned Anjou pears, strands of garlic bulbs, and golden, coiled loaves of an eggy bread known as brioche.

Visitors also can partake of the area's architectural and archaeological treasures, from castles to prehistoric dolmens, medieval churches and abbeys, and troglodyte dwellings. The Loire Valley has long been a magnet for writers, artists, and vacationing royalty, especially during the heyday of the Valois kings (14th through 16th centuries). François Villon, Pierre Ronsard, François Rabelais, Leonardo da Vinci, René Descartes, Cardinal Richelieu, Honoré de Balzac, Julien Gracq, and Alexander Calder have all resided here, as have the "Bon Roi René" ("Good King René," Duke of Anjou and Provence in the 15th century), Eleanor of Aquitaine, and the Plantagenêts. Modern-day visitors will find much to enjoy here too.

Getting to and around the Loire Valley

Airports

The **Aéroport International Nantes Atlantique** (40.84.80.00) is about 10 kilometers (6.2 miles) southwest of Nantes by the Route de Pornic. Currency exchange is available 24 hours a day. A bus goes from the airport to the train station in Nantes from 6AM to 11PM approximately every half hour on weekdays and every hour evenings and weekends, but the schedule varies depending on flights; call (40.29.39.39) to confirm times.

The **Aéroport Tours–St-Symphorien** (47.54.19.46) is seven kilometers (4.3 miles) northeast of the center of Tours. The airport services primarily domestic flights, but international flights arrive and depart here occasionally. No buses or trains run between the airport and Tours, but taxis are available for the 10-minute trip.

Car Rental

Angers

Avis	41.86.00.24
Europcar	41.88.80.80
Hertz	41.88.15.16

Chinon

Europcar	47.93.03.67

Nantes

Avis	40.74.07.65, 40.89.25.50
Europcar	40.47.19.38
Hertz	40.89.69.04

Tours

Avis	47.20.53.27, 47.44.61.61, 47.29.21.49
Europcar	47.64.47.76
Hertz	47.20.40.24

Trains

In Angers, the **Gare SNCF** (Pl de la Gare, at the intersection of Rue Marceau and Rue Faidherbe, information 41.88.50.50, reservations 41.88.43.18) is a few blocks south of the château. About 11 *TGV Atlantique* trains travel daily to and from Paris's Gare Montparnasse; the trip takes about 1.5 hours. Bicycles can be rented in the station. Car-rental companies have offices either in the station or just across the street from its main entrance.

In Nantes, the **Gare SNCF Nantes Sud** (2 Quai Lourmel, at Pl de la Gare, 40.08.50.50) is south of the **Jardin des Plantes**. There are 21 *TGV* trains to and from Paris's Gare Montparnasse; the trip takes about two hours. **Avis** has an office in the station. Non-*TGV* trains arrive at the adjacent **Gare SNCF Nantes Nord** (Blvd Stalingrad, at Rue S.-Baudry, 40.08.50.50). An underground passageway connects the two stations.

Two train stations service Tours. The **Gare SNCF St-Pierre des Corps** (47.20.50.50) is in the suburb of St-Pierre des Corps about two kilometers (1.2 miles) from the main Tours station. Several *TGV* trains run daily between St-Pierre des Corps and Paris's Gare Montparnasse; the trip takes only an hour. There is an **Avis** office in the station. A shuttle transports passengers between this station and the **Gare SNCF Tours** (Pl du Maréchal-Leclerc, between Rue de Nantes and Rue Edouard-Vaillant, 47.20.50.50). The information office in this station is particularly helpful. **Avis** (47.20.53.27) has an office in the station, and other car-rental companies have offices nearby.

The **Gare SNCF** (Pl de la Gare, at Ave Gambetta, 47.93.11.04) in Chinon does not service *TGV* trains. Trains and buses run between Chinon and Tours.

FYI

Visitors' Information Offices

The **Comité Départemental de Tourisme de l'Anjou** in Angers (Maison du Tourisme, Pl du Président-Kennedy, at Blvd du Général-de-Gaulle and Blvd du Roi-René, 41.88.23.85; fax 41.88.36.77) has a plethora of free information on Anjou, most of it available in English. Be sure to ask for a copy of the *Guide du Visiteur* (Visitor's Guide), which provides useful details in French and English on all sorts of activities and sites in Anjou. They also publish a brochure listing bed-and-breakfasts throughout the region. Adjoining the office is a *gîte* rental bureau (41.20.09.99; fax 41.88.36.77), where you can arrange to rent completely furnished farmhouses for a week or weekend. Both offices are open Monday through Friday.

The **Office de Tourisme** in Chinon (12 Rue Voltaire, at Rue Docteur-Gendron, just below the château, 47.93.17.85) provides maps and brochures on things to see and do in the city, and also rents bicycles. The office is open Monday through Saturday; there's no midday closing from May through August.

The Nantes **Office de Tourisme** (Pl du Commerce, between Rue des Gorges and Rue Gaston-Veil, 40.47.04.51) is open Monday through Saturday.

The **Office de Tourisme** in Tours (78 Rue Bernard-Palissy, at Blvd Heurteloup, 47.70.37.37) is open daily November through April, and Monday through Saturday May through October.

Wine Organizations

The **Maison des Vins de Bellevue/Comité Interprofessionnel des Vins de Nantes** (Bellevue Wine Center/Professional Organization for Nantes Wines; 40.36.90.10; fax 40.36.95.87) in La Haye-Fouassière (10 km/6.21 miles southeast of Nantes on N149) is the place to go for general information about local wines and wineries, including a booklet listing local producers' visiting policies. Wines of various vintages are sold and tastings are offered. The office is open daily June through September, and Monday through Friday October through May.

The **Maison du Vin de l'Anjou** (Anjou Wine Center; 5 *bis* Pl du Président-Kennedy, at Blvd du Général-de-Gaulle and Blvd du Roi-René, 41.88.81.13; fax 41.86.71.84) in Angers is a well-run wine center. Wine lovers should definitely stop here. The friendly staff offers tastings of Anjou wines and bottles of local wines for sale, and several maps and brochures with addresses and visiting hours of local wineries are available in English. Since Anjou produces one of the largest varieties of wines of any region in France, this place has quite a selection to sample. The office is open Tuesday through Sunday April through September, Tuesday through Saturday October through March.

The **Maison du Vin de Saumur** (Saumur Wine Center; 25 Rue Beaurepaire, between Rue Gambetta and Rue d'Orléans, 41.51.16.40) in Saumur is an excellent wine center. It serves as the headquarters of two professional organizations that oversee the quality and promotion of Saumur wines, as well as a place for the public to discover these wines. Located on a lively shopping street in the center of town, it has a cozy stand-up bar where you can sample the wares. Many wines—including bubbly Saumur *blanc* and red Saumur-Champigny—are available by the bottle; several older vintages are represented. The center also has maps and brochures on local wineries. It is open Monday through Saturday June through September, Tuesday through Saturday October through May.

The **Comité Interprofessionnel des Vins de la Touraine et du Coeur Val de Loire/Maison des Vins de la Touraine** (Professional Organization for Wines of the Touraine and the Heart of the Loire Valley/Touraine Wine Center; 19 Sq Prosper-Mérimée, at Rue Nationale, 47.05.40.01) in Tours is an efficient wine organization that has many publications in English on the region's wines, including free brochures on each of the Touraine appellations. The center sells a larger, very comprehensive French-language booklet, the *Guide Touristique du Vignoble Touraine–Val de Loire* (Tourist Guide to Touraine–Loire Valley Vineyards), that lists wineries throughout the region that are open to visitors, as well as useful phone numbers and addresses of hotels and local sites. It even mentions which wineries have English-speaking staff, and includes some recipes for typical Touraine

dishes like *rillons de lapereau au Vouvray sec* (rabbit spread made with dry Vouvray). The wine center, which does not sell wine or offer tastings, is open Monday through Saturday.

Phone Book

Hospitals

Angers	41.35.36.37
Chinon	47.93.75.15
Nantes	40.08.33.33
Tours	47.47.47.47

Police (nonemergencies)

Angers	41.73.56.10
Chinon	47.93.04.05
Nantes	40.37.21.21
Tours	47.31.37.37, 47.60.70.67

On the Road to Anjou

1 Nantes It has a Gothic cathedral, a large château, and an old section dating from the Middle Ages, but Nantes lost a lot of its charm to World War II bombings and has been heavily developed since then. Its port has made many resident sea merchants wealthy, so the city has a number of grand, leafy boulevards with king-size homes. And because old trade routes linked Nantes to Portugal (and to Africa and Charleston, SC), some of the architecture shows Iberian influences. The swamps around the town were shored up to support a good network of roads, and a number of canals also traverse the region. Near Nantes, at the mouth of the Loire River, is the home of the melon de bourgogne grape (also called muscadet) and the Muscadet family of dry white wines. Muscadets that come from south of the Loire are more favored, and get the Muscadet de Sèvre-et-Maine appellation.

Nantes was a seat of virulent pro-Royalist versus anti-Royalist rivalry in the 18th century, when a slave trade also thrived here. Officially the capital of the Loire-Atlantique *département* and the center of countryside known as the Pays Nantais, Nantes used to be part of Bretagne (Brittany). That region's spirit really hasn't left it, which explains the town's impressive **Château des Ducs de Bretagne** (Palace of the Dukes of Brittany), a storehouse of regional history and handicrafts. Modern-day traffic, shipyards, apartment towers, and shopping outlets do encroach these days, but the **Château** and the genteel old residences of the Ile de Feydeau (one of several historic districts) are worth a visit. Easy to find is the elaborate **Cathédrale**

St-Pierre et St-Paul, one of the most beautiful in France. Nantes is known for its seafood, and almost any restaurant's *plateau des fruits de mer* (seafood platter) will be laden with deliciously fresh shellfish. ♦ 377 km (233.7 miles) southwest of Paris by A11

Within Nantes:

Cathédrale St-Pierre et St-Paul (St. Peter and St. Paul Cathedral) Built between 1434 and 1872, this medieval-Renaissance cathedral has two massive square towers on either side of its elaborately carved Flamboyant Gothic central portion. Among the many biblical carvings on the portal above the cathedral's main entrance is a very lifelike St. Peter in the center. Proceed inside and look up at the cathedral's vaulted interior. Its 37.5-meter-high (123-foot) ceiling is truly remarkable—and higher than that of the Cathédrale de Notre Dame de Paris. In the right transept is the marble tomb of the Burgundian duke François II and his wife Marguerite de Foix, sculpted from 1502 to 1507 by Breton artist Michel Colombe. Commissioned by the couple's daughter, Anne of Brittany, it is considered one of the glories of the French Renaissance, not only for the artistry of its carvings but for its complex Renaissance symbolism. The tomb's two reclining figures represent the duke and duchess. At their heads are two angels symbolizing a heavenly welcome; at François's feet are two lions, representing Power, and at Marguerite's feet is a greyhound, representing Fidelity. Four figures stand around the white marble base on which the figures rest: a male figure holding a scale represents Justice; another, wearing a helmet and carrying a sword, represents Force; a woman carrying a clock to represent well-measured actions stands for Temperance; and a woman with two faces—one old and the other young—is Prudence. Above the tomb are 16 niches with statues of saints, above which are 16 statues representing mourners, all of whom have lifelike faces which were probably based on contemporaries of the duke and duchess. The tomb is illuminated by light filtered through modern stained-glass windows (which took 12 years to complete) representing the Breton saints. Don't miss the lovely Place de la Psalette garden just behind the church—it's a wonderful place to stroll. ♦ Pl St-Pierre (at the intersection of Rue du Roi-Albert and Rue Mathelin-Rodier). No phone

Château des Ducs de Bretagne (Palace of the Dukes of Brittany) This former fortress was turned into a luxurious residence for Brittany's rulers at the end of the 15th century, and was the birthplace of Anne of Brittany, who later married Charles VIII at the **Château de Langeais** (see page 226). Don't miss the lovely wrought-iron decorations on the well in the central courtyard, or the small museum devoted to regional folk art and crafts within the château. The Loire once lapped against the château's southern and eastern walls; quays weren't built here until the 19th century. ♦ Admission. Daily July-Aug; M, W-Su Sept-June. 1 Pl Marc-Elder (at the intersection of Rue du Château and Rue Prémior). 40.57.18.15

Ile de Feydeau Until 60 years ago, this chic residential district was an island, but then the canals that surrounded it were filled in and turned into streets. Private 18th-century stone mansions adorned with lovely wrought-iron balconies line the streets. Although now part of the mainland, this great place for a quiet stroll will always be called an *île* (island) by the Nantais. ♦ Bounded by Cours F.-Roosevelt, Cours d'Estienne-d'Orves, and Rue G.-Veil

Hôtel de la Duchesse Anne $$ Located near Nantes's main train station, this 72-room hotel was *the* place to stay in the city in the early 20th century; today it is one of the city's best deals. A modern annex has been added, but ask for one of the rooms in the renovated, older part of the building (Nos. 220 to 320); they're spacious, less expensive, and have more charm than those in the annex (particularly No. 216, which has a good view of the cathedral). Breakfast is served in a pleasant dining room, and a restaurant serves traditional (but overpriced) French cuisine. ♦ 3-4 Pl de la Duchesse-Anne (between Cours John-F.-Kennedy and Rue Henri-IV). 40.74.30.29; fax 40.74.60.20

Le Pressoir ★★$$ With a name like "the grape press," you'd expect this old-fashioned restaurant in a former mansion to have a great wine list, and it does. Oddly, the selection is stronger in wines from other regions along the Loire than in the local Muscadets. Several

wines are served by the glass; all go wonderfully with the traditional food served here. Try the *bar de ligne au beurre citronne et au cerfeuil* (bass with lemon butter and chervil) or *joues de boeuf braisées au vin rouge* (beef cheeks braised in red wine). ♦ Tu-F lunch and dinner; Su lunch; closed in August. Reservations recommended. 11 Allée Turenne (at Cours John-F.-Kennedy). 40.35.31.10

2 Le Domaine d'Orvault $$$$ This is *the* splurge address in Muscadet country. Housed in a sprawling two-story Spanish-style mansion with white stucco walls, pink tile roofs, and a few wrought-iron balconies, this 24-room, two-suite hotel has a modern and very elegant interior; its huge rooms have all the modern conveniences, plus big windows overlooking the gardens. The sprawling suites offer cozy armchairs that are wonderful for unwinding after a long day of sightseeing. There's a tennis court and health center, but no pool. The good continental breakfasts featuring homemade breads and jams are a great way to start the day. ♦ Closed mid-February–mid-March. Reservations required. Chemin du Marais-du-Cens, Orvault (from Nantes follow N137 north about 2 km/1.25 miles to the exit for D42 west and follow the signs). 40.76.84.02; fax 40.76.04.21

Within Le Domaine d'Orvault:

Restaurant Le Domaine d'Orvault
★★★$$$ Considered one of the best restaurants in the Nantes area, both for its formal, elegant atmosphere and its refined traditional French cuisine. The menu focuses on local seafood, but all items are well prepared—and presented so beautifully that you might not want to disturb the arrangements on your plate. Try (if you can afford to) the *homard Breton aux cèpes* (Breton lobster with cèpes) or the *rognons de veau rôtis en venaison avec son poêlée de girolles* (veal kidneys in a rich sauce with sautéed chanterelle mushrooms). Ordering à la carte gets expensive fast, but guests staying in the hotel for at least three days can arrange a *demi-pension* that allows them to order anything on the menu at a fixed price. More moderate fixed-price menus also are available. The wine list has an exceptional choice from the Loire Valley. The dining room offers nice views of the gardens. ♦ Daily dinner; Tu-Su lunch; closed mid-February–mid-March. Reservations required. 40.76.84.02

3 Château de Chasseloir and Château du Coing de St-Fiacre Wine maker Bernard Chéreau and his family have two wine estates within the Muscadet-du-Sèvre-et-Maine appellation, both of which produce some of the best Muscadet wines around. The **Château de Chasseloir** is the main winery; the 18th-century *tuffeau*-stone château has one turreted tower remaining from a 16th-century château that stood on the same spot and was almost completely destroyed during the French Revolution. The classy-looking winery is surrounded by its great vineyards, where some gnarled, century-old vines grow. From these *vieilles vignes* (old vines), the Chéreaus produce several intensely flavored Muscadets that are definitely worth investigating. Among the wines here, all *sur lie* (aged on their lees), are the excellent Comte de Leloup Ceps Centenaires sur Lie; they are named for the Count of Leloup, a previous owner of the estate who probably planted the *ceps centenaires* (century-old vines) here. Another excellent wine to try is the Moulin de la Gravelle sur Lie Grande Cuvée Don Quichotte 1992, a very well balanced, flavorful wine. It's named for the ancient *moulin* (windmill) that still stands in one of the vineyards and for that charger after windmills, Don Quixote. At **Château de Chasseloir** you can also taste the wines produced at the nearby **Château du Coing de St-Fiacre,** an estate run by Bernard's daughter, Véronique Chéreau. This château, surrounded by woods and vineyards, is a two-story *tuffeau* structure dating from the 17th century; the central portion is flanked by two square towers that were added in the 19th century. Somehow the architectural styles fit together to make this one of the most elegant-looking châteaux in the Muscadet wine region. Véronique Chéreau produces full-flavored Muscadets, all *sur lie,* some of which are aged in new oak. Each winery has tastings and sales rooms, but the other parts of the châteaux are closed to visitors. ♦ Free. Tastings and sales daily; visits by appointment. St-Fiacre-sur-Maine (from Nantes follow N149 east about 9 km/5.5 miles to La Haie-Fouassière, then go south on D63 about 3 km/1.8 miles and follow the signs). Château de Chasseloir 40.54.81.15; Château du Coing 40.54.80.21; fax 40.54.81.70

4 Louis Métaireau et ses Vignerons d'Art Louis Métaireau and his "artful wine makers" are among the most reliable sources for Muscadet. Métaireau, the driving force, and a group of associated wine makers sample each other's wines in blind tastings and ruthlessly decide whose should be sold to distributors as bulk wine and whose can be given one of the group's labels. Their goal is, as Métaireau puts it, *"Le retour aux valeurs sérieuses et traditionnelles"* (the return to serious and traditional values) to make fine, classic Muscadet. And they do. Try the Métaireau Grand Mouton Muscadet sur Lie from the organization's collectively run vineyards, part of an estate known for its wines since the Middle Ages, and the Muscadet-sur-Lie One, a particularly rich wine that the makers say is perfect with lobster. The top of the line is the Grand Mouton with the word "huissier" stamped across the label. This wine is taken off its lees by gravity, not pumping, and is unfiltered; a *huissier* (a legal official) observes the proceedings to guarantee that this traditional method is used. ♦ Free. M-F; Sa by appointment. La Févrie (about 8.5 km/5.3 miles east of St-Fiacre on D76). 40.54.81.92; fax 40.54.87.83

5 Domaine Bruno Cormerais The wines from this estate are consistently ranked among the top Muscadets. Made from very old vines planted near the banks of the Maine River, the wines have a powerful, almost floral nose with overtones of violets, and have a long finish (meaning that the taste lingers). The modern tasting and sales room adjoins the Cormerais family's white-stone farmhouse. ♦ Free. Visits and tastings daily by appointment. La Chambaudière (from La Févrie follow D76 east 2 km/1.25 miles to D7 south about 6 km/3.75 miles and follow the signs). 40.03.85.84; fax 40.06.68.74

6 Château de la Preuille This golden stone château, originally a feudal fortified structure, dates from the 13th and 15th centuries; its most distinctive features are two round towers topped with pointed turrets. Admire the château from the door of the adjoining wine cellar, where tastings are given, with a glass of fine Muscadet-sur-Lie in hand. Philippe and Christian Dumortier took over this domain in 1986 and have been investing in new equipment and upgrading their wines ever since; they favor strictly traditional practices such as harvesting by hand and fermentation with natural yeasts. The vines here have an average age of about 40 years, one reason for the complexity of the estate's wines. Try the Tête de Cuvée-sur-Lie 1990, with overtones of honeysuckle, hazelnuts, and almonds. *Bon Appétit* magazine ranked **Château de la Preuille**'s 1990 Muscadet-sur-Lie among its top 10 wines of the month in February 1993, and American wine critic Robert Parker has said it is one of the best Muscadets he has ever tasted. This château's wine is the only one of its appellation to be kept in the cellars of the Palais de l'Elysée (Elysée Palace) in Paris (the official residence of the president of France). ♦ Free. Tu-Sa. From La Chambaudière follow N137 south for about 6 km (3.7 miles) and follow the signs for the château. 51.46.32.32

Restaurants/Clubs: Red   **Hotels:** Blue

Shops/ 🌳 Outdoors: Green   **Sights/Culture:** Black

7 La Bonne Auberge ★★★$$$ A local favorite, in a stone house covered with vines in a village near Nantes, it features traditional French cooking with an accent on luxurious treats like lobster, foie gras, and truffles. The ultralight *millefeuille de homard* (puff pastry with lobster) bursts with chunks of lobster, and the chocolate soufflé makes a delectable dessert. This is also a great place to discover some rare Muscadets. The wine list includes some superb Loire Valley wines, and the wine steward's advice is dependable. The fine meals don't come cheap, though, especially if you stray from the fixed-price menus. For a special bargain (about a third the price of ordering à la carte) order the prix-fixe lunch Tuesday through Friday. ♦ Tu-Sa lunch and dinner; Su lunch; closed two weeks in February and most of August. Reservations required. 1 Rue O.-de-Clisson (at Rue F.-Albert), Clisson (from Nantes go 20 km/12.4 miles south on N149, or 10 km/6.2 north of the Château de Preuille on D54). 40.54.01.90; fax 40.54.08.48

8 Les Jardins de la Forge ★★★$$$ In a lovely old house on the Loire, chef Paul Pauvert prepares traditional cuisine using only the finest products, such as *sole fourée d'un mimosa d'huîtres* (oyster-stuffed sole) and *salade de saint-jacques à l'huile de truffe* (sea scallops salad with truffle oil). Don't miss his excellent *beurre blanc* (white butter) sauce, served with various Loire River fish. The wine list has a fantastic selection of Loire Valley wines, with many rare yet affordable bottles. The vast glassed-in veranda provides a great view of the ruins of the **Citadelle de Chamtoceaux,** which was demolished in a seige in 1420. ♦ M, Th-Sa lunch and dinner; Tu, Su lunch; closed most of February and three weeks in October. Reservations recommended. 1 *bis* Pl des Piliers, Chamtoceaux (from Nantes go 20 km/12.4 miles east on D751 or N23. From Clisson follow N149 west to N249 west, then take either D751 or N23). 40.83.56.23; fax 40.83.59.80

9 Hôtel du Val de Loire $ This modern hotel, located just yards from the banks of the Loire, is surrounded by vineyards. Its 40 rooms are smallish, but well equipped; all have private bathrooms. The management is friendly. There's also a simple, inexpensive restaurant. ♦ Jarrier-d'Ancenis (on N23 between Nantes and Angers, about 2 km/1.2 miles east of Ancenis). 40.96.00.03; fax 40.83.17.30

Eat, Drink, and Be Merry in the Loire Valley

Key grape varieties: melon de bretagne (muscadet), chenin blanc (known locally as pineau de la loire), sauvignon blanc, cabernet franc, chardonnay, gamay, malbec (also known as cot), and some pinot noir (from around Sancerre).

Classification system: There are no *premier crus* or *grand crus* within this region. The top ranked wines here are the *Appellations Controlées* (Controlled Label of Origin). Generally, the more specific the appellation cited on the label, the higher quality the wine. **Sancerre, Muscadet, Anjou,** and **Touraine** all have their own appellations, but the best wines name a specific village within one of these areas, and the very top appellations specify a vineyard, such as tiny La Coulée de Serrant in Anjou.

Culinary specialties: Charcuterie, game, wild mushrooms (especially from the Sologne region), fruits, and early vegetables are all Loire regional delights. Here are a few others you may not be familiar with:

alose: shad and other river fish, including salmon and various tiny fish served fried, called *friture*

asperges: asparagus

beurre blanc: a sauce made of butter, vinegar, and local shallots

fromages de chèvre: goat cheeses (especially good in summer)

pâté aux prunes angevin: two-crust plum tart from Anjou

poires: pears

rillettes: shredded pork

rillons: long-cooked chunks of pork

tarte tatin: upside-down apple pie

soupe aux orties: nettle soup

Anjou

ust east of Nantes begins the Anjou region of the Loire Valley, headed by Angers and hailed for its "douceur de vivre;" it's considered one of the "sweetest" places in France to live because of its temperate climate, fertile soil, and tradition of elegant living. Numerous grassy isles dot the Anjou stretch of the Loire until fairly far inland. Joachim du Bellay, a 16th-century poet, described life in his native Anjou as "la douceur angevine" (douceur means both "softness" and "sweetness" and angevine is the adjective for Anjou). The description holds true today: Anjou remains a land of soft light filtered through the mists from its many rivers, of gentle breezes coming from the Atlantic just a few miles to the west, of green and gentle rolling hills—a land where life is sweet.

The rich soil of Anjou produces some of the best vegetables and fruit in France (like the Poire William pear), and a greater variety of wines are made in Anjou than in any other region along the Loire. The broad range of Anjou appellations includes reds, whites, and rosés. Anjou-Villages, an appellation covering some four dozen villages' output, includes some of the area's better dry reds (and some recent, fruitier renditions) made with cabernet franc and cabernet sauvignon grapes. Anjou whites such as Anjou Blanc also hail from here, and use chenin blanc, chardonnay, and sauvignon blanc grapes. The best local whites have their own appellations, such as Coteaux du Layon (see "Major Appellations of the Loire Valley" on page 210) and the rare and splendid dry white, La Coulée de Serrant (see below).

Anjou's ancient capital, the medium-sized city of Angers, was founded around the first century BC by a tribe of Gaulish fishermen and hunters whom the Romans (who took over later) called the Andigaves. The strategically placed settlement at the confluence of the **Maine** and **Loire Rivers** was successively dominated by Romans, Normans, and Vikings. From the 10th to the 13th centuries the region was controlled by the Foulques dynasty of feudal lords, the last of which was Geoffroi V, dubbed Plantagenêt because he liked to wear a branch of genêt (yellow Scotch broom) in his cap. His line included Henri II, later King of England, Henri's wife Eleanor of Aquitaine, and their son Richard the Lionhearted, all of whom lived part of their lives in Anjou and are buried there. The "Bon Roi René" (Good King René), Duke of Anjou and Provence in the 15th century, is still honored throughout the region. His passions—flowers, the arts, fine architecture, and horses—live on here: All the local villages are covered with flowers, Angers holds a highly respected arts festival every July, Anjou has many magnificent châteaux, and the French national riding school is based in the region, at **Saumur**.

10 Savennières La Coulée de Serrant/Château de la Roche-aux-Moines Nicolas Joly's **Savennières** estate includes La Clos de la Coulée de Serrant, one of only three appellations in France with a single owner (the others are Romanée-Conti in Burgundy and Château Grillet on the Côtes du Rhône). When you taste the wine you'll see why the seven-hectare (17.2-acre) **La Coulée de Serrant** vineyard, where grapes have been grown for 600 years, has been made an appellation in itself. A very dry Chenin Blanc white, it has a bouquet of honey, apricots, and preserved fruits, and has been described as combining sensuality, power, and delicacy. No wonder it's considered one of the world's greatest wines. As if that were not enough of a draw, the estate is one of the most beautiful along the Loire. Visitors drive along a hilly gravel road through vineyards and woods to arrive at the **Château de la Roche-aux-Moines,** a white stone and stucco 18th-century château surrounded by a garden overlooking vineyards that slope steeply down toward the nearby Loire. Joly also produces superb Savennières Becherelle and Savennières Clos de la Bergerie–Roche-aux-Moines from his family's **Château de la**

Roche-aux-Moines vineyards. The Becherelle is made from a vineyard that had been destroyed by phylloxera and replanted by Joly beginning in 1982; it has a lovely bouquet of hazelnuts. The small tasting and sales room on the ground floor of the château is filled with family mementos.

All wines made on the estate for the past 13 years have been produced biodynamically, as is guaranteed by the Demeter reference on their labels. If you get a chance to meet the charismatic owner, he is sure to win you to the biodynamics cause. He says the time has come to remember that *"avant d'être bon, un vin doit être vrai"* (before a wine can be good, it has to be authentic). To maintain his own wines' authenticity, Joly avoids using any insecticides, weed killers, or commercial fertilizers that might destroy natural elements in the soil. The vines are cultivated by hand and the soil is worked by horse-drawn plows (biodynamics is definitely labor-intensive). The only fertilizer used is manure from cows Joly raises himself (so he can control what they eat). Joly also takes movements of the planets, sun, and moon into account when he times plowing, harvesting, or other basic vineyard tasks; grape growers have successfully done so for centuries, and recent scientific experiments on the effects of planetary and solar changes on grape vines back him up. In the cellar, Joly avoids all practices that would change the nature of his wines, including using artificial yeasts, fining (removing sediment) with egg whites, heavy filtering, using centrifuges, or flash-freezing. All his wines are aged in 600-liter (131-gallon) old oak barrels; the shape of the barrel itself enhances the wine's development, he believes. There's no fancy lighting here, either, because powerful electrical currents have been found to affect fermentation. All this may sound odd, but the formula works. Joly's vines are healthier than ever, and many tasters agree that the wines he has made biodynamically are even better than wines previously made on the estate. Joly, who dared to try this radical approach on his priceless vineyards, also has an MBA from Columbia University; you can be sure his wine-making colleagues listen when he talks about what biodynamics means in economic terms. ♦ Free; 250-franc minimum purchase required for tastings. M-Sa (no midday closing); appointments preferred. Clos de la Coulée-de-Serrant (between Epiré and Savennières, 12 km/7.4 miles southwest of Angers on D111). 41.72.22.32; fax 41.72.28.68

Nowhere in France is a greater proportion of land devoted to producing wine than in the tiny village of St-Fiacre-sur-Maine in Pays Nantais.

10 Château de Chamboureau The hamlet of La Roche-aux-Moines was the site of a battle in 1214 during which Louis VIII drove Jean-sans-Terre out of Anjou and Poitou, consolidating the crown's holdings in western France. Vineyards on this historic site yield the grapes wine makers Pierre and Yves Soulez use to make their version of Savennières La Roche-aux-Moines: It is pale gold, with an intense bouquet of flowers and minerals, full-tasting but very dry; the 1989s are ready to be savored in 1995. Other fine wines produced on the estate include a rich, sweet Quarts de Chaume; the demi-sec Clos du Papillon; and a light red Château de Chamboureau made from cabernet sauvignon grapes. ♦ Free. Tastings by appointment. La Roche-aux-Moines (just outside Savennières on D111 west of Angers. About 2 km/1.2 miles north of Clos de la Coulée-de-Serrant; follow the signs). 41.77.20.04; fax 41.77.27.78

11 Domaine des Baumard Practice makes perfect: The Baumard family has been making wines on this estate since 1634, and all the Anjou wines they produce are highly rated. The star is the fine, pale gold Quarts de Chaume, like a Sauternes with a bouquet of apricots and peaches; it ages extremely well. Other wines include a Rosé de Loire; a bubbly Crémant de Loire; a ruby pink Cabernet d'Anjou rosé; the luscious, sweet Clos de Sainte-Catherine Coteaux du Layon (a great buy); and the dry white Clos du Papillon Savennières. Housed in **Logis de la Giraudière,** a late-17th-century stone dwelling, the winery provides tastings in an elegant room with a beamed ceiling and 17th-century frescos that were discovered under layers of plaster when the house was remodeled 30 years ago. Members of the Baumard family greet visitors. ♦ Free. Visits and tastings M-F. 8 Rue de l'Abbaye, Rochefort-sur-Loire (from Angers take N160 10 km/6.2 miles south to Murs-Erigné, then go 12 km/7.4 miles west on a stretch of D751 known as the "Corniche Angevine"). 41.78.70.03; fax 41.78.83.82

11 Auberge de la Corniche ★★$$ Perched on a hill overlooking the Anjou countryside, near where the Layon enters the Loire and right where the Layon River wine route begins, this restaurant is a great favorite of locals. Its exterior resembles a run-down village bar, but the cozy interior (as well as the food) will make you glad you came. Regional specialties include various kinds of river fish with *beurre blanc* sauce and *veau sauce crème champignons* (veal with mushroom-cream sauce). On nice days diners can sit on the shady terrace to enjoy the countryside and the fine Anjou and other Loire Valley wines on the list here. ♦ M, Th-Su lunch and dinner; Tu lunch; closed in February. Reservations required. La Haie Longue (25 km/15.5 miles southwest of Angers on D751). 41.78.33.07

12 St-Aubin-de-Luigné This village is the site of a wine fair held on the third weekend in July. **La Sète des Vins Millésimés** (41.78.33.28) is a little wine center next to the *Mairie* (City Hall), where you can taste the local production. ♦ 3 km (1.8 miles) southeast of La Haie Longue on D125

12 Musée de la Vigne et du Vin d'Anjou (Museum of Anjou Vines and Wine) This small museum in the village of St-Lambert du Lattay has displays on grape varieties, wine tools, and the effects of the phylloxera disaster; a worthwhile vineyard walk begins at the museum and and gives a close-up view of the vines. ♦ Admission. Daily Apr-Oct; closed November-March. Pl des Vignerons, St-Lambert du Lattay (5 km/3.1 miles southeast of St-Aubin on D125). 41.78.42.75

13 Auberge de la Contrêche ★$ A friendly couple runs this lovely auberge in a tiny hamlet along the Layon wine route. They serve homemade local products in a tastefully rustic and spacious dining room. The offerings depend on the market and season, but the charcuteries are always excellent, as are superbly prepared fish dishes like *truite de mer* with *beurre blanc* (sea trout with white butter sauce) and the fresh vegetables—be sure to order the stuffed mushrooms. Upstairs are three simple guest rooms, where you can have a quiet night and an excellent complimentary continental breakfast featuring homemade jams. ♦ Tu-Su lunch and dinner; closed mid-September–early October. Reservations recommended. Contrêche (take D125 10 km/6.2 miles southeast of St-Lambert du Lattay and follow the signs to Contrêche). 41.87.48.18

13 Domaine de la Petite Croix Alain Dénéchère is the third generation of his family to produce wines from old vines in the small but highly rated Bonnezeaux appellation. His Vieilles Vignes 1992 Bonnezeaux is a deep gold with a fresh but powerful bouquet, one of the best of this Sauternes type of wine now being made. It makes a fine aperitif. The sweet, grapey flavor of the magical "noble rot" makes clear why it is called *noble*. The winery is in a modern building behind Dénéchère's simple white farmhouse on a hilltop surrounded by vines.

♦ Free. Visits and tastings daily. Appointment recommended. On D199, 2.5 km (1.5 miles) southwest of Thouarcé; follow D125 4 km (2.5 miles) south of Contrêche and follow the signs to Thouarcé, then look for the signs to the winery. 41.54.06.99; fax 41.54.30.05

13 Château de Fesles The Boivin family and Gaston Lenôtre, the famed pastry chef and gourmet foods purveyor, co-own this estate with vineyards in the Bonnezeaux appellation. The winery is located in a tiny hamlet atop a hill. Drive up a road leading through vineyards to reach the two-story 18th-century château, which Lenôtre has painted a pale pink, reminiscent of the sugary decorations on a birthday cake. No color scheme can mar the spectacular view of miles of Layon Valley vineyards you'll find here, though. Don't miss the massive 400-year-old oak tree near the château's entrance. The château is closed to visitors; sales and tastings are in the nearby former stables, which no 19th-century equine resident would recognize today. There is one long room, with a table for wine tasting at one end and a display of decorative creations made of sugar by Lenôtre and fellow *pâtissiers* (pastry makers) at the other. These rather garish displays (one is a three-foot-long azure fish) are presumably edible; all are enclosed in glass cases. Through a glass wall you can view an adjoining room that's lit with dim golden light and filled with oak barrels. Next to this room and also visible through the glass are the ultracontemporary computer-controlled stainless-steel vats. Visitors can tour both rooms on request. After buying half of the Boivin family's interests, Lenôtre swept through the domain like a whirlwind, buying new vineyards, improving facilities, and promoting the wines. He has also bought two other wine estates in the area, **Château de la Roulerie** and **Château de la Guimonière** (neither is open to the public). This ambitious investment has resulted in many different types of wines that visitors can try. The top of the line here, the Château de Fesles Bonnezeaux, is a superb Sauternes-like sweet white wine—and much less expensive than Sauternes. Another good sweet wine produced here is the Château de la Roulerie Coteaux du Layon. The domain also produces Cabernet d'Anjou (a fruity, almost red rosé), lighter Rosé d'Anjou, a Chardonnay, a dry white wine, and a light Anjou red wine. ♦ Free. Daily. Fesle (2 km/1.24 miles east of Thouarcé on D199; follow the signs). 41.54.14.32; fax 41.54.06.10

Restaurants/Clubs: Red   Hotels: Blue
Shops/ 🌳 Outdoors: Green   Sights/Culture: Black

14 Château de Passavant Run by the David family for five generations, this winery is now overseen by the children of well-known wine maker Jean-Noëlle David, who retired in 1994. The magnificent family château overlooking the Layon River was built in the 12th century by feudal lord Foulques Nerra. A rambling stone structure with many towers, surrounded by a large garden, it is reached by crossing an ancient stone bridge spanning what was once a moat and is now a tiny road. The vineyards are planted mainly with chenin blanc (pineau de la loire) for the white wines and cabernet france and sauvignon for the reds. Among the wines are a red Anjou Villages with a deep purple color and fruity taste, made from particularly old vines, and a sweet Coteaux du Layon that is consistently ranked among the best of this local specialty. The winery also makes rosé, dry white Anjou, and a bubbly Crémant de Loire, all excellent. If you buy a bottle of the Coteaux du Layon, be sure to ask the Davids when you should drink it; it needs long aging. Tastings are in the 13th-century wine cellars. ♦ Free. Daily by appointment. Rte de Tancoigné, Passavant-sur-Layon (from Thouarcé follow D125 south to Martigné-Briand, then take D167 south to Tigné, D84 east to St-Georges-sur-Layon, D178 south to Les Verchers-sur-Layon, D170 south to Passavant, and follow the signs to the château). 41.59.53.96; fax 41.59.57.91

15 Château de Brissac This imposing *tuffeau* stone château surrounded by a beautiful park has been in the same family since it was built in the 15th century. One of the 17th-century residents decided to rebuild the château in a contemporary style, but died before the job was completed. That's why half the facade looks late Renaissance and the other half 15th century. The château still has most of its original furnishings, including gorgeous Aubusson tapestries. Elaborately painted 17th-century ceilings and beams adorn several rooms. There's even a theater, built in the 19th century for family use. Tastings of local wines are offered in the vast wine cellars. ♦ Admission. Daily (no midday closing) July-Aug; M, W-Su Apr-June, Sept-Oct; closed January-March, November-December. Brissac (15 km/9.3 miles south of Angers on D761). 41.91.22.21

Major Appellations of the Loire Valley

Approximately 80 different types of wine are produced in the Loire Valley. Though the climate is too cool for some grapes, the ones that thrive in this region contribute to some of France's highest quality wines. The appellations the Loire is known for include such classic white wines as Muscadet, Sancerre, Pouilly-Fumé, Savennières, Saumur Mousseux, and Coteaux du Layon. Some outstanding reds also are made here, including Bourgueil, Chinon, and Saumur-Champigny.

Bourgueil

Made primarily from cabernet franc (breton) grapes, the Bourgueil and St-Nicolas-de-Bourgueil wines come from adjoining villages on the border of **Anjou** and **Touraine** that are officially part of Touraine. These wines are deep purple, fruity and, in good years, long-lived. They should be drunk cool (not cold). St-Nicolas-de-Bourgueil has a reputation as the better of the two, but in fact the determining factor is not village of origin, but *terroir* site: The best wines tend to come from vineyards on the slopes above both villages.

Chinon

The wines of Chinon are generally red. They are made primarily from the cabernet franc grape (here called the breton), age well, have a very spicy, fruity flavor, and should be drunk at a cool cellar temperature. Some dry whites and rosés are also produced in the area, but the reds are the stars.

Coteaux du Layon

Producing some of the finest sweet white wines in France, the **Layon Valley** is a very quiet, rural region south of the Loire along the banks of the small **Layon River.** The best of its wines—Quarts de Chaume and Bonnezeaux—can approach Sauternes in finesse and richness, but at an extremely reasonable cost. The name "Quarts de Chaume" dates from the Middle Ages, when feudal lords reserved the right to the best quarter (*quart*) of all grape harvests; around here, the best *terroir* was near the hamlet of **Chaume.** The grapes for these wines are picked late, giving them a chance to develop the "noble rot" used in making Sauternes; yields are among the lowest in France. Though these wines are best after about 10 years in the bottle and the 1990 vintage probably should not be drunk before the turn of the century, 1990 Côteaux de Layon whites have already been ranked 20 out of 20 for excellence by one prestigious French wine guide. The key villages on the "Route des Vins du Layon" (a signposted local wine tour) are **Rochefort-sur-Loire** (where many places provide tastings), Chaume, **Beaulieu, Rablay, Faye, Thouarcé, Bonnezeaux,** and **Martigné-Briand.**

Muscadet

Muscadet (whose name comes from the grape, not the village) is produced in **Nantes** in the western Loire Valley. When you order a glass or carafe of house white wine in a French bar or bistro (especially a bistro that features seafood), you will usually be served a Muscadet. It was practically unknown outside its own region before 1930, when a group of Parisian sommeliers toured the area and developed a fondness for the wines; only then did Muscadet begin appearing on the capital's wine lists. The inevitable result of its popularity was the production of cheaper, inferior Muscadets that eroded the wine's reputation. Today, Muscadet wines face stronger competition from inexpensive white wines from other parts of France and elsewhere in Europe. In an effort to make a new place for themselves on the market, Muscadet's producers are trying to upgrade the wine without destroying its natural characteristics: freshness, dryness, and simplicity. Muscadet wines have a tendency to oxidize; to prevent this, and to give the wine more flavor, the best of them are bottled *sur lie* (on the lees), which involves leaving the wine to ferment along with its sediment for a while, then bottling it directly from the vat. By law, wines sold as *sur lie* must be bottled by 30 June. Some wineries ferment in oak, while others believe oak masks Muscadet's natural qualities. Most wineries experiment with different types of yeast. Since so many types of Muscadet are being produced today (most of them inexpensive), a tour of the local wineries can lead to some delightful discoveries.

Pouilly-Fumé

A famous wine made from the sauvignon blanc grape, Pouilly-Fumé has fanned disagreement about everything but its quality. Some say the *fumé* refers to its smoky flavor; others say it refers to the smoky appearance of the grapes as they ripen. Searching for the proper description for the exciting flavor of this wine, aficionados have compared it to gunflint, to fresh-roasted coffee, to gooseberries, to litchi nuts, elderflowers, and even to asparagus. All of the excitement over this delightful liquid has driven up the prices. Even the more ordinary wines from this appellation cost dearly. Many of the vineyards have soil called silex, which accentuates the flinty taste.

Sancerre

One of France's greatest, most famous, and most expensive white wines (there are also Sancerre reds and rosés, but their quality is not as high). This appellation is located in one of the prettiest of the wine towns, set on a hill with breathtaking views of the Loire Valley. The growers are scattered both on the hilltops and in surrounding villages, which produce some of France's most deliciously refreshing white wines. A favorite of Henry IV and Louis XVI, Sancerre fell out of style for a while, then came back in the 1970s. Particularly notable are the wines from the hamlets of Bué, Chavignol, and Ménétréol. The whites—like Pouilly-Fumé, which is harvested only eight kilometers (five miles) away—are made from the sauvignon blanc grape. The reds and rosés are made from pinot noir grapes.

Saumur-Champigny

This spicy, fruity red Anjou wine, drunk cool (the cool of a true wine cellar, not cold), has been made for centuries, but was little known outside the area where it was produced. Now it is becoming increasingly popular throughout France, especially in Paris; it is seen as a more complex, tastier version of beaujolais, another approachable red wine drunk cool. Made of cabernet franc (breton) grapes with a little cabernet sauvignon and/or pineau d'aunis, Saumur-Champigny is produced in a small area around the village of **Champigny** east of **Saumur.** The cabernet franc grape was first planted here in the 17th century by Abbé Breton at **Abbaye Royale de Fontevraud** (Royal Fontevraud Abbey), which is why the cabernet franc is known locally as the breton. Saumur-Champigny is usually served with charcuterie, roasted poultry, game birds, and cheeses. It's a great picnic companion; if you wrap the bottle in wet newspaper and keep it so that the water evaporates, the wine will be the right temperature—or cool it in the Loire River while you sit on its banks.

Saumur-Mousseux

This bubbly wine, a champagne type, is made primarily from chenin blanc grapes and aged in cellars carved out of the *tuffeau* stone that is used to build the local châteaux. Maybe that's what gives it its elegant aura. It has been prized internationally since the 12th century, when the Plantagenêts brought some of it with them to the English court. Sparkling Saumur is served as an aperitif or with dessert.

Savennières

This small Anjou appellation near **Angers** shows the versatility of chenin blanc (known locally as pineau de la loire). Here, just across the Loire from vineyards where sweet wines are produced from the same grape, chenin blanc is turned into an exceptional white wine that has an incredibly rich bouquet and taste, but is extremely dry. Produced in very small quantities, these wines are hard to find abroad. Savennières wines were once sweet, but an *Appellation d'Origine Contrôlée* decree of 1952 specified that they are to be dry. Low-yield harvests and a high alcohol content explains their intense taste and aging potential. Savennières wines have been prized for centuries; Louis XI compared Savennières to "drops of gold." The star of the Savennières area is the tiny appellation within it, La Coulée de Serrant.

BOURONEL

PIONET
1992

KITTI HOMME

Angers

On a bluff overlooking the confluence of the Loire and Maine Rivers (the Maine is fed by the great Sarthe and Mayenne Rivers to the north), market-filled Angers is split between the old and the new. The castle on its heights, Château d'Angers, has 17 round towers and a museum containing the stunning Tapisserie de l'Apocalypse (Tapestry of the Apocalypse). The ancient center of town, which lies between the château and the Cathédrale St-Maurice, has several medieval houses lining narrow, twisting streets. Taken over by the Romans and later by the Normans, Angers lived through an especially illustrious period under the Counts of Anjou, from the 10th to the 12th century.

Today, Angers is still bustling. Much of it is contemporary, though, with a large student population (there is a university here) and a lively cultural life. At the end of January the Festival des Vins de la Loire (Festival of Wines of the Loire) takes place here, and the well-attended Anjou Festival of visual and performing arts is held each July.

16 Château d'Angers Angers's massive château is an almost perfect example of feudal architecture. Built between 1228 and 1238, it is dark gray with bands of white *tuffeau* stone. It has 17 towers, each approximately 150 feet high. The towers were once higher and topped with conical roofs, but Henri III ordered the château destroyed when the Angevins went against him during the *Guerres de Religion* (Wars of Religion) in the 16th century. The soldier in charge of the job had already knocked off the tops of the towers when the king's sudden death saved the château from further destruction. The turrets have not been rebuilt, giving the towers a massive, chunky shape atypical of Loire châteaux. Renaissance-style gardens have been planted in the former moats. The château's great treasure, however, is the magnificent 14th-century *Tapisserie de l'Apocalypse* containing 76 vividly colored tableaux that represent the biblical revelation. The tapestry is displayed in a museum within the château. ◆ Admission. Daily. Promenade du Bout-du-Monde (between Promenade du Port-Ligny and Pl du Président-Kennedy). 41.87.43.47

Restaurant Le Toussaint

17 Restaurant Le Toussaint ★★★$$ This excellent restaurant housed in a *tuffeau* stone mansion decorated with red awnings and geranium-filled window boxes is ideally located facing the château. It is set with heavy tablecloths and fine glassware and silver, and enlivened by paintings, lots of fresh flowers, and brightly painted walls and ceilings. The overall effect is cozy elegance. The dining room is always filled with well-groomed locals and Parisians feasting on chef Michel Bignon's delicious regional cuisine. Try any of his very fine treatments of Loire fish, including *alose* (shad), served with excellent *beurre blanc* sauce. The menu changes according to the season and the market. Game is featured in the fall; Bignon also likes to experiment with delicious "forgotten" vegetables and herbs, all grown locally, such as parsnips, physalis, and chervil. For dessert, try the great *millefeuille aux fruits exotiques* (puff pastry with tropical fruits) or the local specialty, *cremêts d'Anjou* (fresh cream drained until dense and served with sugar and fresh fruits). Prices are very reasonable for the quality; the fixed-price menus are incredibly good values. The wine list, one of the best in the region, boasts an excellent selection of Bordeaux and Loire wines. ◆ Tu-Sa lunch and dinner; Su lunch; closed most of August. Reservations required. 7-9 Pl du Président-Kennedy (at Rue Toussaint). 41.87.46.20; fax 41.87.96.64

18 Musée des Beaux-Arts (Museum of Fine Arts) Located in the 15th-century **Logis Barrault,** this museum houses the complete works of 19th-century sculptor David d'Angers. There's also a fine collection of paintings by other French artists. ◆ Admission. Daily. 10 Rue du Musée (between Rue Toussaint and Rue St-Aubin). 41.88.64.65

19 Cathédrale St-Maurice Built during the 12th and 13th centuries, this beautiful Gothic cathedral is a fine example of Angevin vaulting. The single nave, with the first Gothic vaulting built in Anjou, was the widest at the time it was built. The Aubusson tapestries that line the walls, the 12th-century stained-glass window of the *Virgin in Majesty,* and the stained-glass window of St. Christopher with a dog's head are not to be missed. ◆ Pl Monseigneur-Chappoulie (between Rue St-Christophe and Montée St-Maurice). 41.86.88.18, 41.87.58.45

By regulation of the European Economic Community, the label on a *vin de table* may not indicate any geographic region, grape utilized, or vintage.

Restaurants/Clubs: Red   Hotels: Blue
Shops/ 🌳 Outdoors: Green   Sights/Culture: Black

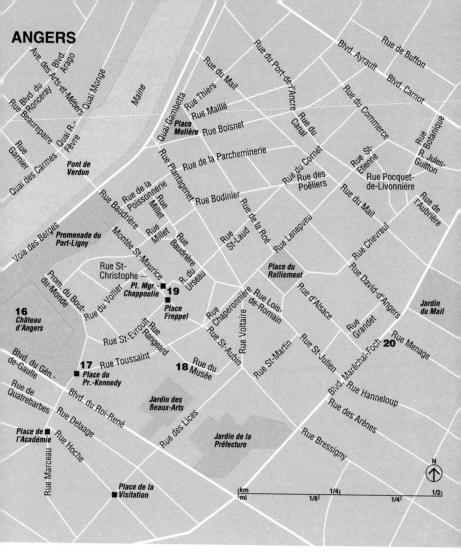

ANGERS

Rue de Buffon

Blvd. Ayrault · Blvd. Carnot

Ave. des Arts-et-Métiers · Blvd. Arago

Quai Monge

Rue du Ronceray · Rue Beaurepaire

Rue Garnier

Quai des Carmes · Quai R.-Fèvre

Maine

Rue du Mail

Rue Thiers
Rue Maillé

Quai Gambetta

Place Molière · Rue Boisnet

Rue du Port-de-l'Ancre

Rue du Commerce

Rue du Canal

Rue Botanique · Rue R. Jules-Guitton

Pont de Verdun

Rue de la Parcheminerie

Rue du Cornet
Rue des Poëliers

Rue St-Étienne

Rue Pocquet-de-Livonnière

Rue de l'Aubrière

Rue Plantagenet

Rue de la Poissonnerie

Rue Baudrière

Rue Bodinier

Rue du Mail

Voie des Berges

Promenade du Port-Ligny

Rue Millet

Montée St-Maurice

Rue Millet

Rue Baudrière

Rue St-Laud

Rue de la Roë

Rue Lenepveu

Rue Chevreul

Rue David-d'Angers

Rue St-Christophe

Prom. du Bout-du-Monde

Rue du Vollier

Pl. Mgr.-Chappoulie

R. du Urseau

19

Place du Ralliement

Rue d'Alsace

Jardin du Mail

16
Château d'Angers

Place Freppel

Rue St-Evroult

Rue Rangeard

Rue Chaperonnière

Rue Lois-de-Romain

Rue Voltaire

Rue St-Aubin

Rue Grandet

20

Rue Ménage

Blvd. du Gén.-de-Gaulle

17 Rue Toussaint
Place du Pr.-Kennedy

18 Rue du Musée

Rue St-Martin

Rue St-Julien

Blvd. Maréchal-Foch

Rue de Quatrebarbes

Blvd. du Roi-René

Rue Delage

Jardin des Beaux-Arts

Blvd. Rue Hanneloup

Rue des Arènes

Place de l'Académie

Rue Hoche

Rue des Lices

Jardin de la Préfecture

Rue Bressigny

Rue Marceau

Place de la Visitation

km / mi — 1/8 — 1/4 — 1/4 — 1/2

N

20 Hôtel d'Anjou $$ Built in 1842 and now completely renovated, this cozy 53-room hotel, a member of the Best Western chain, is one of the best places to stay in Angers. The interior of the white stone structure is decorated in dark woods, with lots of antique furniture and floral fabrics; the spacious rooms all have private bathrooms, mini-bars, cable TV, and good beds. There's a private garage for hotel guests, and room service is available. The location is ideal; it's right in the center of town, within walking distance of the **Château d'Angers** and the train station.

♦ 1 Blvd Maréchal-Foch (at Rue Ménage). 41.88.24.82; fax 41.87.22.21

Within the Hôtel d'Anjou:

Restaurant La Salamandre ★★$$$
Heavy wood paneling and golden salamanders painted on dark green walls grace this Neo-Gothic dining room. You might expect the cooking to mirror the dark, heavy decor, but just the opposite is so: The chef produces innovative dishes with a light touch, such as *gratin de sole au Savennières* (sole gratin with Savennières wine sauce) and *sabayon d'huîtres au vin de Layon* (oysters in an egg-based sauce made with Layon wine). The wine list has a good selection of Loire wines. ♦ M-Sa lunch and dinner. Reservations recommended. 41.88.24.82

Actor Gerard Depardieu—who lists his profession as *vigneron* (wine grower)–has wine fields and makes wine in Anjou.

On the Road to Saumur

21 Château du Plessis-Macé Built as a fortress in the 11th century, this gleaming white *tuffeau* stone château was totally remodeled and expanded into a luxurious residence in the 15th century by Louis de Beaumont, a friend of Louis XI (who often stayed here). The imposing outer walls and wide moat are part of the legacy from its fortress days. Jousting matches were once held on the wide inner courtyard, while aristocrats watched from a magnificently carved *tuffeau* stone external balcony—one of the few of its kind remaining in France. Tour the chapel with its rare 15th-century wood carvings, the reception rooms, dining room, and the king's bedchamber; all are furnished with antiques. ♦ Admission. Daily July-Aug; Tu-Su June, Sept; Tu-Su afternoon Mar-May, Oct-Nov; closed December-February. From Angers take N162 northwest 10 km (6.2 miles) and follow the signs to Plessis-Macé. 41.32.67.93

22 Chambres d'Hôtes Auguste and Jacqueline Bahuaud $ The Bahuauds rent three very spacious, comfortable double rooms, all with private baths, in a peaceful 18th-century white stone manor house on the banks of the tranquil Mayenne River. All the rooms are furnished with family antiques. The house, like the others in this lovely village, is surrounded by a flower-filled garden. In fact, the village, with picturesque quays along the river, is one of the prettiest in the area. Have tea on the hotel terrace and watch the boats go by. The Bahuauds do not serve meals, but restaurants are nearby; the couple are happy to offer suggestions of things to see and do in the area. ♦ Closed November-Easter. 2 Rue de l'Ecluse, Grez-Neuville (4 km/2.4 miles north of Plessis-Macé on N162; watch for the signs for the *"Chambres d'hôtes"*). 41.95.68.49

23 Maine-Anjou Rivières Floating down the peaceful Mayenne, sipping a glass of local wine, and watching the cows, ducks, horses, and occasional fishers on the banks is the ideal way to experience the quiet rhythms of Anjou. René Bouin's operation rents over 40 fully equipped houseboats that let visitors do just that. No permit is needed to pilot these boats down the rivers of Anjou (or in other parts of France; **Maine-Anjou Rivières** has links with boating companies throughout the country). Most sleep seven to eight people (some accommodate as many as 20) and are new and extremely comfortable, with separate bedrooms, a panoramic-windowed captain's cabin, and decks that have space for bicycles (which you can rent along with the boat). All have electricity, heating, full bathrooms, equipped kitchens, and running water. The *Louisiane,* which sleeps six to eight, has a twin hull and is accessible to persons with disabilities because its decks sit low in the water. You can rent a boat for a day, a weekend, a week, or more, from March to November. A boat that sleeps six rents for about $1,500 a week in July and August; it's discounted up to 45 percent in the off-season. Even if you don't want to rent a boat, come here to picnic along the Mayenne. You can also visit two other Bouin operations. Carrying on a 600-year family tradition, he maintains a working flour mill on the banks of the river. And the rustic but excellent **Restaurant La Table du Meunier** (see below) is also in the family. ♦ Le Moulin, Chenillé-Changé (7 km/4.3 miles northeast of Le Lion-d'Angers on D287). 41.95.10.98; fax 41.95.10.52

Next door to the boat docks and mill:

Restaurant La Table du Meunier ★★$$ Run by René Bouin's wife, Madeleine, this friendly place is in a lovely restored stone building, a former walnut-oil mill, on the banks of the Mayenne. There are several fixed-price menus; the least expensive includes pâté, a light first-course fish dish, *poulet à l'angevine* (chicken in cream sauce with mushrooms), a cheese plate, dessert, Anjou wine, and coffee. ♦ Daily lunch and dinner July-Aug; W-Su lunch and dinner mid-Feb–June, Sept–mid-Jan; closed mid-January–mid-February. Reservations recommended. 41.95.10.83; fax 41.95.10.52

> "Nobody has ever been able to find out why the English regard a glass of wine added to a soup or stew as a reckless foreign extravagance and at the same time spend pounds on bottled sauces, gravy powders, soup cubes, ketchups, and artificial flavorings. If every kitchen contained a bottle each of red wine, white wine, and inexpensive port for cooking, hundreds of store cupboards could be swept clean forever of the cluttering debris of commercial sauce bottles and all synthetic aids to flavoring."
>
> Elizabeth David, *French Country Cooking*

23 Château de Briottières $$ François de Valbray, his wife, and their five children live in a lovely 18th-century château that has been in the family for six generations. The friendly, English-speaking De Valbrays make guests also feel at home in their home, one of the best château bed-and-breakfasts in France. The white, U-shaped building has a gray slate roof typical of the Loire Valley; the château is surrounded by an 80-acre private park that virtually guarantees serenity. The 10 spacious, comfortable guest rooms are furnished with double canopy beds or twin beds in an elegant, but homey, style. Each room looks out on the peaceful countryside, and has a telephone and a private bath; some have working fireplaces. There's also one very reasonably priced single room. Excellent dinners are served on request; guests can dine with the family or at individual tables. François de Valbray describes the cuisine as "our grandmothers' cooking," which in the Loire Valley means that dishes feature the freshest local fish and farm-raised poultry, an excellent selection of cheeses, and seasonal fruits and vegetables. A heated swimming pool, billiards room, and fishing are on the premises. Tastings of Loire Valley wines can be arranged. Bicycles are available for rent, and an 18-hole golf course, horseback riding center, and tennis courts are nearby. ♦ Reservations required. From Chenillé-Changé follow D78 east to Marigne, then take D190 south to Champigné. From Angers take N162 northwest to Le Lion-d'Angers, then D770 northeast to Champigné; follow the signs to the château. 41.42.00.02; fax 41.42.01.55

24 Château de Plessis-Bourré This stunning building of chalk-white *tuffeau* stone with blue-gray slate roofs is everyone's idea of a Loire Valley château, from its wide, shimmering moat to its massive, rounded towers with conical roofs at each corner. Yet, like all Anjou châteaux, this one is rarely crowded with tourists. Jean Bourré, Louis XI's finance minister, had the place built for himself beginning in 1468. With its high walls and the 130-foot-long stone bridge across the moat, the château looks from the outside like the invincible fortress it was meant to be, but

within is evidence that Bourré also loved the good life. Tour the several antiques-filled reception rooms, and don't miss the **Salle des Gardes** (Guards' Chamber); its ceiling, painted in the late 15th century, shows allegorical figures such as "Fortune" and "Truth." ♦ Admission. Daily (no midday closing) July-Aug; M-Tu, F-Su, and Th morning mid-Feb–June, Sept–mid-Nov; M-Tu, Th-Su afternoon late Dec–mid-Feb; closed mid-November–late December. D500 (from Champigné follow D190 south to Cheffes, then take D74 west to Ecuillé and follow the signs). 41.32.06.01; fax 41.32.06.72

CHATEAU DE NOIRIEUX

24 Château de Noirieux $$$$ If you're looking for a magnificent setting and money is no object, you can't go wrong here. This splendid hotel's 19 huge guest rooms are luxuriously decorated and have all the modern conveniences: opulent private bathrooms, mini-bars, satellite TVs, safes, and big windows overlooking the gardens. There's a magnificent salon with a huge fireplace and a terrace with views of the Loir River, a tributary of the Loire. Guests stay in either the 18th-century château (the larger, more expensive rooms are here) or in a 15th-century manor house nearby. The rooms in the château span decorating history from Louis XV to 18th-century Neo-Classical (Regency) to Art Deco, while those in the manor house are done in cheerful French Provincial style. A lovely 16th-century chapel sits on the estate's 18 acres of parkland; guests also have use of a swimming pool (in season) and tennis court. You can rent bicycles here too. ♦ Closed late January–March. 26 Rte du Moulin, Briollay (from Ecuillé take D107 south to D109 and continue east to Briollay. From Angers follow D52 north about 14 km/8.6 miles). 41.42.50.05; fax 41.37.91.00

Within the Château de Noirieux:

Restaurant Château de Noirieux
★★★$$$ The huge light-filled dining room has yellow drapes and tablecloths, a white marble floor, and big windows overlooking the gardens and the Loir River. Chef Gérard Côme favors classic cuisine, lightened to suit contemporary tastes. Try the river fish in *beurre blanc* sauce, *sandre rôti et farci au foie gras* (roast pickerel stuffed with foie gras), and *filets de boeuf à l'armagnac et sauce poivrade* (beef fillet with armagnac and pepper sauce); the *soufflé chaud au chocolat amer* (hot bitter chocolate soufflé) is a marvelous way to end any meal. The extensive wine list

has an excellent choice of Loire Valley wines. This establishment has one of the best quality-price ratios in the Loire Valley. ♦ Tu-Sa lunch and dinner, Su lunch Apr-June, Sept–mid-Jan; M-Sa lunch and dinner, Su dinner July-Aug; closed mid-January–March. 41.42.50.05

25 Château de Préfontaine $$ Marie-France O'Neill offers four sumptuously decorated guest rooms in her white stone 18th-century château. All the rooms have private baths; two of them, Persane and Empire, are actually huge suites. O'Neill will prepare meals on request; offerings include *saumon au beurre blanc* (salmon with white butter sauce) and *tarte tatin* (upside-down apple tart) for dessert. In summer, she serves dinner outside in the garden. ♦ 25 km (15.5 miles) northeast of Angers on N23; follow the signs to Lézigné. 41.76.97.71

26 Auberge Jeanne de Laval ★★★$$$ This fine family-run hotel/restaurant is one of the best places in Anjou to sample the local specialty, river fish with *beurre blanc* sauce. The auberge, a vine-covered stone house adorned with geranium-filled window boxes, became famous under the reign of master chef Albert Augereau, a mentor to Paris's great chef Joël Robuchon. Things have come full circle, because Michel Augereau, Albert's son, trained with Robuchon before taking command of the kitchen here. The result is superb cuisine—regional flavor with contemporary touches. Try the *écrevisses au vin de Saumur* (crayfish with Saumur wine sauce), the *panaché de ris et rognons de veau aux girolles* (mixture of veal sweetbreads and kidneys with wild mushrooms), and any of the delicious desserts. The comfortably elegant dining room has a friendly staff that gives good advice on wine; the list boasts one of the region's best selections of Loire wines (collected over generations by the auberge's owners). ♦ Tu-Su lunch and dinner. Reservations required. 54 Rue Nationale, Les Rosiers-sur-Loire (30 km/18.6 miles southeast of Angers on D952). 41.51.80.17; fax 41.38.04.18

Behind the Auberge Jeanne de Laval:

Hôtel des Ducs d'Anjou $$ The Augereau family runs this hotel, whose 10 comfortable rooms are clustered around a flower-filled interior courtyard; all have traditional furnishings and private baths, and two rooms have been equipped for people with disabilities—a rarity for a small hotel in this area. Delicious continental breakfasts are available. ♦ Closed Monday October-May. 41.51.80.17; fax 41.38.04.18

27 Notre Dame de Cunault This Romanesque church built from the 11th through 13th centuries was part of the **Abbaye de Cunault** (Cunault Abbey), a powerful Benedictine monastery founded in 847. Little remains of the abbey except for the church, but what a legacy it is! Don't miss the elaborately carved portals, the 11th-century bell tower, or the astonishing *chapiteaux* (capitals) above the columns lining the church's vast interior. The artisans who carved these stone artworks must have been laboring for the glory of God—the only explanation for the intricate details that mere mortals can barely see from the ground without binoculars! Classical music concerts are held daily at 5PM in July and August either here or in the nearby **Eglise de Trèves**. ♦ Trèves-Cunault (3 km/1.8 miles south of Les Rosiers-sur-Loire on D751). 41.67.92.44

27 Le Prieuré $$$$ This former priory, an ancient *tuffeau* structure overlooking the Loire, is considered one of France's finest hotel/restaurants (it's part of the Relais & Châteaux group). Among the 35 guest rooms are several enormous suites; all are elegantly decorated and equipped with luxurious bathrooms, mini-bars, satellite TVs, and other amenities. Some rooms have spectacular views of the Loire; others look out on the pretty gardens. There's a heated pool, and an *"école de dégustation,"* a class in wine tasting. The continental breakfasts include delicious pastries as well as big bowls of fresh fruit. ♦ Closed January-March. Chênehutte-les-Tuffeaux (8 km/4.9 miles northwest of Saumur on D751). 41.67.90.14; fax 41.67.92.24

Within Le Prieuré:

Restaurant Le Prieuré ★★★$$$ When you walk into the bar/salon of this spacious, elegant dining room to have an aperitif, you'll be so dazzled by the view of the Loire that you may forget to order; the beautiful terrace (meals are served here in summer) shares the spectacular view. Chef Jean-Noël Lumineau offers delicious regional cuisine, with many dishes featuring sauces made from local wines. Try the *suprême de bar au chou, sauce* *vin de Chinon* (fillet of sea bass with cabbage and Chinon wine sauce) or the *foie gras frais de canard en terrine avec gelée au vin de Layon* (fresh foie gras with an aspic made from Layon wine). The list boasts a stunning collection of Loire Valley wines, along with a good choice of bordeaux. For a good deal, come for lunch Monday through Friday, when a fixed-price menu (including wine) is served. ♦ Daily lunch and dinner; closed January-March. Reservations required. 41.67.90.14; fax 41.67.92.24

28 Chambres d'Hôtes La Croix de la Voulte
$$ Helga and Jean-Pierre Minder, a friendly couple with many good suggestions of things to see and do, rent four spacious rooms with private bathrooms. Their 15th- to 17th-century white stone house, a former hunting lodge, is surrounded by a huge garden with a swimming pool. The guest rooms are in an annex to the main house, but it's an old annex; the room called Anjou and the one called Touraine have huge 15th-century fireplaces. Others have high beamed ceilings and lovely Louis XIV fireplaces. ♦ Closed mid-October–Easter. 2 km (1.25 miles) west of St-Lambert-des-Levées on Rte de Boumois (D229). 41.38.46.66; fax 41.38.44.66

29 Musée du Champignon (Mushroom Museum) A *mushroom* museum? Yes, because the little fungi have long been a key part of the local economy. About 70 percent of the small white mushrooms known all over France as *champignons de Paris* (they were once cultivated in quarries in the capital) are now grown in the *tuffeau* caves around Saumur (usually fertilized by elite manure from thoroughbreds at the nearby **Ecole Nationale de l'Equitation,** the national riding school). A shop within the museum proffers local products (many made, of course, with mushrooms) and books on the Saumur region. Take the half-hour tour through a maze of *tuffeau* caves to see how mushrooms grow. ♦ Admission. ♦ Daily (no midday closing) mid-Mar–mid-Nov; closed mid-November–mid-March. St-Hilaire-St-Florent (just west of Saumur on D751). 41.50.31.55

29 Saumur Vol à Voile Look ma, no engines! With its gentle breezes and warm-air thermals, the Loire Valley is great glider country. Anyone between the ages of 12 and 99 can glide over the Loire with an instructor from this friendly company (some speak English). Discover how quiet and calming it can be to fly without a motor, especially here—the views of the meandering Loire and surrounding countryside are spectacular. The flights last from 10 to 30 minutes, depending on wind conditions, and cost around $50 per person. ♦ Fee. Daily (no midday closing) July-Aug; Sa-Su and holidays Mar-June, Sept; closed October-February. Aérodrome de Saumur, Rue du Clos-Pointu, St-Hilaire-St-Florent. 41.50.82.44; fax 41.53.42.88

29 Ecole Nationale d'Equitation/Le Cadre Noir (National Riding School) French-speaking guides (some will translate into English) lead tours of this training center for cavalry officers and top equestrians. You can visit the stables, watch magnificent horses being exercised, and, if you're lucky, see members of the elite Cadre Noir riding team practicing their famous *cabrioles* ("airs above the ground"). It's a caper in which the horse—with its rider—hovers with all four feet off the ground for a few seconds. The Cadre Noir performs here periodically throughout the year. ♦ M 2:30PM-4PM and Tu-Sa Apr-Oct; closed November-March. Terrefort, a suburb of St-Hilaire-St-Florent. 41.53.50.50, 41.53.50.60; fax 41.67.63.08

Crottin de Chavignol

One of the Loire Valley's most famous cheeses is the tangy, round little goat cheese made in and around **Chavignol,** a village near **Sancerre.** The crottin de chavignol has been written about since the 16th century, and was no doubt first made long before then. The name *crottin* is said to be derived either from a slang word for "droppings" or from the word for an ancient oil lamp that had the same shape as the cheese. The cheese is the perfect picnic food, along with a loaf of bread, some fruit, and a bottle of Sancerre. Several Sancerrois *fromageries* (cheese dairies) are well worth a visit: **Dubois-Boulay,** in the center of Chavignol (48.54.15.69); **Michel Denizot,** also in the center of Chavignol (48.54.01.62); and **Chèvrerie des Garennes,** where you can help milk the goats around 5PM every day if you like, on D955 outside Sancerre (48.54.03.85). The real star is **Ferme La Brissauderie,** on D923 near the hamlet of Jarsot. This farm produces what many believe to be the best crottin de chavignol in France; the restaurant of Paris's chic **Hôtel Georges V** is a customer. All the above operations are family-run farms; they don't have regular visiting hours, but someone is usually on hand to greet customers and offer tastings of the cheeses. There is no admission charge.

29 Le Clos des Bénédictins $$ There's nothing monkish about the decor or cuisine in this hotel/restaurant overlooking Saumur, although it *is* classed by the French tourist office as a *Relais de Silence*, meaning that peace and quiet are guaranteed. The contemporary building is built in traditional Angevin style, with white walls and a gray slate roof. The 23 spacious rooms have modern decor and conveniences, including private bathrooms and TVs; some suites are especially convenient for parents traveling with children. There's also a swimming pool. The hotel offers several theme packages (including room, meals, wine, aperitifs, and travel to sites); activities include performances by the elite riding team at the national riding school or visits to wineries and a tasting class. The packages are discounted 20 percent between mid-October and mid-March. ◆ Closed one week in November and mid-December–mid-January. Rte de l'Ecole Nationale d'Equitation, St-Hilaire-St-Florent. 41.67.28.48; fax 41.67.13.71

Within Le Clos des Bénédictins:

Restaurant Le Clos des Bénédictins
★★$$ This intimate restaurant features sure-to-please dishes like *crêpes de langoustines au vieux Layon* (crayfish crepes with a Layon wine sauce) and dark chocolate soufflé, plus a great selection of Loire Valley wines. ◆ Closed one week in November and mid-December–mid-January. Reservations required. 41.67.28.48

29 Maison Bouvet-Ladubay Established in 1851 and now owned by the Taittinger Champagne concern, this winery is *the* place to try bubbly Saumur white wine. It is made from 95 percent chenin blanc and five percent chardonnay grapes using the *méthode champenoise* (champagne method). The winery is set in an 18th-century white stone mansion overlooking a cobblestone courtyard and surrounded by high stone walls. The wines here are delicate, yet aromatic and fruity; try the Brut de Blanc or the top-of-the-line Cuvée Trésor Brut. The winery also produces still white Saumur, as well as several reds that include Saumur Rouge, Saumur-Champigny, Bourgueil, and Chinon. A visit begins with a tour of the wine cellars, which were hollowed out of *tuffeau* stone caves, and ends with tastes of the wide range of wines produced here. The winery also gives tasting classes for an in-depth look at the local wines. Also within the winery is the **Centre d'Art/Art Concept,** an elegant exhibit space devoted to contemporary art, and a 19th-century theater where plays, concerts, and conferences are held. ◆ Free. Daily (no midday closing). On D751, St-Hilaire-St-Florent. 41.50.11.12; fax 41.50.24.32

Saumur

Set at a slight southward dip in the **Loire** 54 kilometers (36 miles) east of Angers, the provincial Anjou town of Saumur has two passions: horses and wine. An excellent museum of equestrian arts is housed in the 14th-century **Château de Saumur,** a former fortress that soars above the town atop a stark promontory. The many-turreted castle has been famous since it first appeared in the medieval illuminated manuscript *Les Très Riches Heures du Duc de Berry* (Hour Book of the Duke of Berry). Below, an arched bridge connects the lower town to an inhabited island, the **Ile d'Offard.**

For centuries Saumur was a thriving Huguenot trading center, but it declined after the 1685 revocation of the Edict of Nantes, which sent many Protestants into hiding. The town revived a century later when France decided to establish an elite military riding school here. During World War II, cadets and officers from the school managed to hold off Nazi forces for 48 hours, using only their horses and dummy guns. Today the school, the **Ecole Nationale de l'Equitation** (see page 217), is the home of the celebrated **Cadre Noir** riding team.

The local wine industry also fuels the town's economy, producing many robust Saumur whites, Saumur-Champigny reds, and sparkling Saumurs. To go with its well-loved fruity wines, the town still produces about 70 percent of France's edible mushrooms. Trains from Angers and Tours arrive at the small **Gare SNCF de Saumur** (41.88.50.50) on the north bank of the Loire.

30 Château de Saumur This splendid 14th- to 15th-century château built of gleaming white *tuffeau* stone perches on a bluff high above the banks of the Loire; its dozens of towers and turrets can be seen for miles. The château was built as a sparely decorated fortress; it was later a residence of the Bon Roi René (Good King René), Duke of Anjou and Provence in the 15th century, who greatly improved the interior by adding decoratively carved stone fireplaces, elegant tapestries, and elaborately painted ceilings. Today it is filled with period furnishings and contains an art museum as well as the **Musée du Cheval** (Horse Museum). The latter includes a fine collection of sporting prints, including many by British artists. The grounds around the château are a good spot for an off-the-grass picnic. ◆ Admission. Daily (no midday closing) mid-June–mid-Sept; daily Apr–mid-June, mid-Sept–Oct; Tu-Su Oct-Apr. Just east of the center of Saumur. 41.51.30.46; fax 41.67.78.35

30 Hôtel Anne d'Anjou $$ Right at the foot of the bluff on which stands the **Château de Saumur** lies this elegant 18th-century white stone mansion with views of the Loire. It has a beautiful interior staircase with intricately curved wrought-iron railings, and an elaborate wrought-iron balcony that wraps above the main entrance. The government has classified the whole building a national historic monument. The 50 rooms (all with private baths) are elegantly decorated and comfortable; some rooms are accessible to people with disabilities. The most luxurious room is No. 102, whose restored decor dates from Napoleon's time. There is no restaurant, but breakfast is served in a flower-filled courtyard shared with the **Restaurant Les Ménestrals**. ♦ Closed late December–early January. 32-34 Quai Mayaud (at the Quai des Etats-Unis, just down the hill from the Château de Saumur). 41.67.30.30; fax 41.67.51.00

30 Restaurant Les Ménestrels ★★$$$ Chef Christophe Hosselet prefers light dishes with inventive touches, like *râble de lapin dans son jus au gingembre et à la coriandre fraîche* (rabbit with ginger and fresh coriander) and *langoustines rôties aux tomates confites et beurre d'oursins* (roast crayfish with caramelized tomatoes and sea urchin–butter sauce). Try the apple tart with cognac sherbet for dessert. The wine list has a great choice of Loire Valley wines, but it's a bit overpriced, as is the restaurant. The cheapest of the fixed-price menus (served only at lunch Monday through Friday) is a good deal, though. The restaurant, housed in a *tuffeau* stone building with exposed beams and stone walls, is decorated in contemporary style. ♦ Tu-Sa lunch and dinner, M dinner, Su lunch Oct-Apr; Tu-Sa lunch and dinner, M, Su dinner May-Sept. Reservations recommended. 11 Rue Raspail (near the Hôtel Anne d'Anjou). 41.67.71.10

30 Charcuterie-Traiteur Girardeau Top-quality picnic items are temptingly on view through big plate-glass windows. You'll find various salads (some vegetarian) and such traditional charcuterie specialties as excellent ham, *rillaux* (long-cooked chunks of pork, a Loire Valley specialty known as *rillons* in Touraine), *rillettes* (shredded pork), sausages, and pâtés—not for cholesterol watchers. Top-quality quiches and *plats cuisinés* (cooked meat and vegetable dishes) are also available. But the main attraction for the wine-lover is the stock of wines from the Loire Valley and from all over France. Owner Gérard Girardeau calls himself an *antiquaire en vins* (rare wines dealer); check out the 1945 Château Pétrus Pomerol and the Romanée-Conti to see why. ♦ M-Sa; closed two weeks in July. 53 Rue St-Nicolas (at Rue d'Orléans). 41.51.30.33

30 Dolmen de Bagneux This dolmen is one of the most remarkable megalithic monuments in Europe. Built approximately 5,000 years ago, it is made up of 16 huge stones arranged in two 60-foot rows about 20 feet apart; four other huge stones are laid over them as a roof, about nine feet off the ground. Unfortunately, the dolmen is now surrounded by a white wooden fence, so you can only see it if you pay. ♦ Admission. 56 Rue du Dolmen, Bagneux (south of Saumur on N147/D960, follow the signs to the dolmen). No phone

On the Road to Touraine

31 Château de Villeneuve One of this historic estate's former owners died fighting in the American Revolution with the Marquis de Lafayette. It is now owned by the Chevallier family, who completely restored the elegant *tuffeau* château, which dates partly from the 16th and mainly from the 18th century (and is closed to the public). Known for its delicate white Saumur wine made from chenin blanc, the winery has branched out into a red Saumur Champigny that now is ranked among the best of that appellation. Try the 1989 Saumur-Champigny Vieilles Vignes (the vines are about 30 years old) with its rich overtones of blackberries and currants. The white, made from chenin blanc grapes from 35-year-old vines, also is very good. Tastings are held in a modern room above the wine cellars. ♦ Free. Visits and tastings M-Sa. 3 Rue Jean-Brevet, Souzay-Champigny (6 km/3.7 miles south of Saumur on D947). 41.51.14.04; fax 41.50.58.24

32 Montreuil-Bellay This picturesque town south of Saumur was built as a fortress by feudal lord Foulques Nerra in 1025 (most of the ramparts remain). It has an elegant 15th-century château that's off the beaten tourist track and makes a delightful visit, especially if you bike here from Saumur along pretty D160 and an unnumbered road that winds through vineyards along the Thouet River. ♦ 20 km (12.4 miles) south of Saumur on D160 or N147

Within Montreuil-Bellay:

Château de Montreuil-Bellay Built of *tuffeau* stone that has weathered to a buttery gold, this 15th-century château has all the classic accoutrements: tall turret-topped towers, 11th-century fortifications, a moat, and a drawbridge. One of its most unusual features is the huge medieval kitchen, which is still in working order and filled with copper cooking utensils. Also unique are the private wine-storage closets in some of the opulently furnished bedrooms once reserved for noble guests. The château's terrace and gardens overlook the Thouet valley and the vineyards of Saumur-Champigny. ♦ Admission. M, W-Su and Tu afternoon July-Aug; M, W-Su Apr-June, Sept-Oct; closed November-March. 41.52.33.06

Musée de l'Artisanat et des Traditions (Museum of Crafts and Traditions) One of the best of the small museums along the Loire dedicated to local traditions, this includes exhibits on wine-making tools and domestic objects from the past. The beautiful mansion (closed to the public) next door dates from 1428. ♦ Admission. Daily Mar–mid-Oct; W, Sa afternoon, Su mid-Oct–Feb. Pl du Marché, near the Château de Montreuil-Bellay. 41.52.34.44

Splendid Hôtel $ A sprawling white stone building near Montreuil-Bellay's château, this hotel has very friendly management and 60 simple, smallish, and reasonably priced rooms. All are decorated in the typical cheery French Provincial manner (flowery fabrics, heavy wood furniture) and have private bathrooms; some have views of the château. There's a swimming pool and a pretty garden. ♦ 139 Rue du Docteur-Gautrez. 41.53.10.00

Within the Splendid Hôtel:

Restaurant Splendid-Relais de Bellay ★$$ This friendly place is a big favorite among the locals; try the *cuisse de canard au vinaigre de cidre* (duck thigh in cider vinegar sauce) or the fish with *beurre blanc* sauce. ♦ Daily lunch and dinner Apr-Sept; M-Sa lunch and dinner, Su lunch Oct-Mar. Reservations recommended. 41.53.10.00

33 Abbaye Royale de Fontevraud (Royal Fontevraud Abbey) Built of *tuffeau* stone that has weathered to gray, this abbey was founded in 1101 by Robert d'Arbrissel, a former hermit sent by the pope to bolster the church in western France. D'Arbrissel set up an unusual organization for the abbey: Its head would always be chosen from among the nuns living there (even though monks also were in residence). A series of highly intelligent women, most of them aristocrats who entered the convent after being widowed, made the abbey a center of learning and spirituality for many centuries. The Plantagenêts heavily endowed the abbey, and 15 of them are buried here in splendid tombs, including Henry II, Richard the Lionhearted, and Eleanor of Aquitaine—who spent her last years in the abbey. The building was badly damaged during the French Revolution and made into a prison by Napoleon (a function it served until as recently as 1963), but it has been carefully restored. Don't miss the kitchen with its elaborate external chimneys—the only Romanesque kitchen remaining in France—and the herb garden with the same kinds of plants that would have been grown during the abbey's heyday. ♦ Admission. Daily (no midday closing) June–mid-Sept; daily mid-Sept–May. Follow D947 east from Saumur or D751 west from Chinon, and follow the signs to Fontevraud. 41.51.71.41

33 Auberge de l'Abbaye ★★$ This friendly restaurant in an ancient stone building is a fine, casual place to sample typical regional dishes. Try the *pâté en brioche* (pâté in a golden pastry crust) or, simplest of all, a grilled steak, accompanied by a glass of local wine. The fixed-price menus are all great deals. ♦ M, Th-Su lunch and dinner, Tu lunch; closed February and most of October. Reservations recommended. 8 Ave Roches, Fontevraud. 41.51.71.04

"I feast on wine and bread and feasts they are."

Michelangelo

"Wine, the most delightful of drinks, whether we owe it to Noah, who planted the vine, or to Bacchus, who pressed juice from the grape, goes back to the childhood of the world."

Anthelme Brillat-Savarin, *La Physiologie du goût* (The Physiology of Taste)

Restaurants/Clubs: Red   **Hotels:** Blue
Shops/ 🌳 Outdoors: Green   **Sights/Culture:** Black

Touraine

Said to be the birthplace of the French Renaissance, the Touraine region is rich in produce, game, châteaux (about 300 of them), formal gardens, and literary history. The best-known wines of Touraine are the light, fruity reds, Bourgueil and Chinon. The white Vouvrays, all from the chenin blanc grape, are extremely varied in flavor, and some, known as Vouvray Mousseux, are sparkling.

Although centered around modern **Tours**, and now the most visited section of the Loire Valley, Touraine is an ancient province whose traditional character still thrives. Touraine has been prized for its gentle climate, fertile soil, natural beauty, and abundant game ever since Renaissance aristocrats set up residence here. They followed the lead of François I, who commissioned an enormous second home in Touraine in the 16th century, the 440-room **Château de Chambord.** (Two of Molière's plays were first produced there after having been commissioned by Louis XIV.) Most of Touraine's châteaux, like those in Anjou, are built of the local white *tuffeau* stone, and are known for their fanciful towers and elaborate interiors. Touraine also is the site of the most beautiful Renaissance-style gardens in France (formal, with flowers and vegetables and fruits), on the grounds of the 16th-century **Château de Villandry.** Exquisite goat cheeses are made on local farms, too (watch for the fromage de chèvre fermier signs throughout the region).

34 Manoir du Port Guyet $$ Geneviève Valluet offers three large, comfortable guest rooms, each with a private bathroom, in her 15th-century manor house (a previous guest—under prior ownership—was the poet Pierre de Ronsard). The lovely house, built of white *tuffeau* stone with the typical Loire Valley slate roof, has large windows offering fine views of the surrounding garden and vineyards. Valluet, who speaks English, will prepare excellent meals on request. ♦ 2 km (1.25 miles) west of Bourgueil on D35. 47.97.82.20

35 Domaine des Géléries This small winery is set in a simple, modern white home just outside the village of Bourgueil. The Rouzier-Meslets produce a supple, fruity, full-flavored wine from just six hectares (14.8 acres) of vines. Although their Bourgueils have won many awards, they're very inexpensive. This is a perfect wine to accompany a picnic of cheese and bread; just find a sunny spot overlooking the nearby Loire. You can tour the nearby cellars if someone is available to take you through. ♦ Free. Tastings daily. Les Géléries (5 km/3.1 miles north of the Loire at the intersection of D749 and D35, follow the signs to Bourgueil; from Bourgueil take D635 northeast and watch for signs to the winery). 47.97.72.83

35 Domaine de la Coudraye Conscientious wine maker Yannik Amirault produces a different wine from the vines on each of the *terroirs* on his 10 hectares (24.7 acres)—five in Bourgueil, five in St-Nicolas-de-Bourgueil—to preserve the *terroirs'* originality. His St-Nicolas-de-Bourgueil Les Malgagnes, made from old vines growing on the slopes above the village, is one of the winery's best. It has a rich, mouth-filling, fruity taste with hints of currants. Other excellent wines are the Bourgueil Le Grand Clos and the St-Nicolas-de-Bourgueil Les Graviers. All grapes are picked manually; filtration is kept to a minimum, and in some years not used at all. Though these wines can be drunk after two years in the bottle, they also age very well. Tastings are given at a big wooden table in a ground-floor room of the family's house. You can visit the nearby cellars if someone is available to give an impromptu tour. ♦ Free. M-Sa. La Coudraye (take Rte du Moulin Bleu 3 km/1.85 miles north of Bourgueil). 47.97.78.07; fax 47.97.94.78

36 Ferme Apicole d'Anjou (Angevin Bee Farm) The Girard family are beekeepers based in a tiny village in the middle of a pine forest north of the Loire. They produce several types of *miel* (honey), both liquid and creamy, along with honey spreads, candies, and beeswax items. The *miel de forêt* (forest honey) is dense, dark, and sensational. Someone is usually on hand in the small shop behind the modern farmhouse to greet you and offer tastes. The pine forest around the village has many pretty spots for a picnic. ♦ Daily. Follow N147 north from Saumur, turn right onto D10, take D85 north, and continue to La Breille-les-Pins. 41.52.02.89

37 La Butte de l'Epine $ Make your way through a dense pine and oak forest just a few miles north of the Bourgueil vineyards to find a lovely 17th-century manor house and a warm welcome from the Bodet family. Their bed-and-breakfast has two guest rooms with private bathrooms and showers. If you're looking for peace and quiet, you're sure to find it here. Another reason to stay: the copious continental breakfasts served in the flower-filled dining room. The many hiking trails in the vicinity will help you work off some of the calories. ♦ On D64, just north of Continvoir (13 km/8 miles north of Bourgueil on D15). 47.96.62.25

38 Le Vieux Château $$ Part of this 15th-century yellow stone château surrounded by a moat lies in picturesque ruins; the rest has been luxuriously restored. All of the five huge guest rooms have private bathrooms, telephones, and televisions; one of the rooms sleeps four. The friendly English-speaking hosts, the Hardys, provide good complimentary continental breakfasts, and serve meals in the evenings on request. ♦ Hommes (10 km/6.2 miles northeast of Continvoir on D69). 47.24.95.13; fax 47.24.68.67

39 Chinon The wines of Chinon are produced near the birthplace of François Rabelais—who must have drunk quite a lot of them in his time, since he mentions them often in his writings. The town itself, high on a cliff above the confluence of the Loire and the pretty Vienne River, is one of the most charming along the Loire—especially at sundown, when the *tuffeau* stone of the houses here seems to turn to gold. Two not-to-be-missed annual events: a medieval fair featuring 2,000 locals in period costume dancing in the streets to ancient music (first weekend of August); and the *Marché à l'ancienne,* a turn-of-the-century-style food market and antiques fair (third Saturday in August). ♦ 25 km (15.5 miles) east of Saumur (follow D947 to D751 to D749)

Within Chinon:

Château de Chinon This impossibly romantic castle, perched on a hill overlooking the quiet Vienne River, is now mainly in ruins, but remains one of the most memorable châteaux along the Loire. From a distance it looks as it did in the Middle Ages, since its ramparts are intact. But inside, in place of staterooms you'll find lawns with scattered ruins and interior walls exposed to the elements. A few structures are still in good condition and furnished with medieval and Renaissance antiques. The château was the site of a historic meeting between Joan of Arc and France's Charles VII in 1429. Legend has it that the king tried to trick Joan by dressing as an ordinary aristocrat and putting a courtier dressed as the king in his throne. As soon as Joan entered the room, she walked straight to the real king and bowed. All that remains of the room where the two met is one tall white stone wall with an elaborately carved stone fireplace. On the grounds, which provide magnificent views of the Vienne and nearby vineyards, is a clock tower whose clock, known as Marie Javelle, has been striking the hours since 1399! Leaving the château, stroll down Rue Jeanne-d'Arc, a steep and narrow cobblestone pedestrian street that leads to the medieval heart of Chinon. At the foot of the street is a re-creation of a stone well that Joan supposedly used to dismount her horse when she began her walk to meet the king. ♦ Admission. Daily (no midday closing) mid-Mar–Oct; daily Nov, Feb–mid-Mar; M-Tu, Th-Su Dec-Jan. On the western edge of Chinon. 47.93.13.45

Musée du Vin et de la Tonnellerie

(Museum of Wine and Barrel Making) This little museum adjacent to Chinon's tourist office exhibits an amazing array of tools used in wine making in past centuries; a tasting of local wines is provided. ♦ Admission. M-W, F-Su Apr-Sept; closed October-March. 12 Rue Voltaire. 47.93.25.63

 Plage de la Belle Laveuse The "beach of the pretty washerwoman," a 60-foot stretch of tree-shaded sandy beach on the Vienne just outside Chinon, is a great place for a picnic and a dip in the placid river. There's even a little drinks-and-snacks stand open in summer. ♦ Around 3 km (1.5 miles) southeast of Chinon on the Promenade des Docteurs-Mattrais

---

"Knowledge of wines is a lifetime hobby, and the only way to learn is to start drinking and enjoying them, and comparing types, vintages, and good marriages of certain wines with certain foods."

Julia Child, *Mastering the Art of French Cooking, Vol. I*

Restaurants/Clubs: Red   **Hotels:** Blue
Shops/ ♣ Outdoors: Green   **Sights/Culture:** Black

Hôtel DIDEROT

Hôtel Diderot $ Past a huge, ancient gate lies an 18th-century vine-covered house, which opens onto a courtyard. This quiet hotel boasts exceptionally friendly management and 27 comfortable rooms cheerfully decorated with bright bedspreads and some antique furniture; all have private bathrooms. Although there's no restaurant, excellent continental breakfasts are served in a large room with beamed ceilings and a 15th-century fireplace. This hotel is a great deal, especially for a tourist mecca like Chinon, so reserve well in advance. ♦ Closed mid-December–mid-January. 4 Rue Buffon (at Rue J.J.-Rousseau). 47.93.18.87; fax 47.93.37.10

Restaurant Au Plaisir Gourmand

★★★$$$ Chinon's best restaurant is located in an ancient house built of white *tuffeau* stone right in the center of town. Chef Rigollet, who usually greets diners as they enter, favors regional dishes; try the excellent *salade tiède de langoustines* (warm crayfish salad), the *gâteau de pommes de terre* (potato cake), the *lapereau à l'ancienne* (rabbit cooked in traditional style, with wine sauce), and a delicious side dish of *champignons en duxelles* (mushrooms sautéed with shallots and herbs). The wine list has an admirable selection from Chinon, with many older and hard-to-find vintages. ♦ Tu-Sa lunch and dinner; Su lunch; closed in February. Reservations required. 2 Rue Parmentier (at Quai Charles-VII). 47.93.20.48; fax 47.93.05.65

Domaine Couly-Dutheil Look north from the ramparts of the **Château de Chinon** and you will see this winery, considered one of the best in Chinon, stretched out before you. A long gravel path leads through vines to the elegant white 18th-century manor house (closed to visitors) atop a vineyard-covered hill. The vineyard here, one of the many around Chinon that the estate owns, is the Clos de l'Echo, source of one of the best Chinon red wines. The vineyard's name comes from an actual echo on the hill. To see for yourself, walk from the small tasting and sales center at the foot of the vineyard up the one-lane Rue de l'Echo to a spot on the hill marked *"ici l'écho"* (here is the echo). Here, try out an old Chinon tradition: Facing the valley, shout, *"Les femmes de Chinon, sont-elles fidèles?"* (Are the women of Chinon faithful?). You should hear the echo answer, *"Elles?"* (The women?). Then shout, *"Oui, les femmes de Chinon"* (Yes, the women of Chinon), and the echo should respond, *"Non."* (Sometimes noise from the town interferes with the phenomenon.) Head back to the Couly-Dutheil sales and tasting center. The Clos de l'Echo red is the main attraction—a fruity, rich, spicy wine that just keeps getting better over time. Be sure to drink it at a cool cellar temperature rather than at normal room temperature; it tastes too acidic when warm. If any of the 1989 vintage is on hand, snap it up. Ask the very helpful staff whether the wines you taste (or buy) are considered ready to drink (many people come here to stock their cellars). Also try the Clos de l'Olive, a red from a vineyard at the edge of Chinon, and a fruity but dry white wine made from chenin blanc grapes from the family's Les Chanteaux vineyard. ♦ Sales and tasting center: daily July-Aug; M-F, Sa 9AM-noon Sept-June. Winery: M-F, Sa 9AM-noon. Tastings are not offered when the weather is too hot; the center is not air-conditioned and heat destroys the wines' taste. Sales and tasting center: Rte de Tours (at Rue de l'Echo). Winery: 12 Rue Diderot (between Rue Buffon and Pl Jeanne-d'Arc). 47.93.05.84; fax 47.93.28.58

Rue Voltaire In the center of the medieval section of the city, this pedestrian street is lined with beautiful medieval houses, some of them half-timber, others built of white stone with elaborate decorative carvings. Many have been turned into shops and restaurants. ♦ Runs from Rue Haute-St-Maurice to Rue J.J.-Rousseau

40 La Devinière The name of this ancient, picturesque, gray stone farmhouse comes from an incongruously gruesome fact: On this spot, in Celtic and Roman times, *devins* (oracles) would slaughter geese and predict the future by reading their entrails. There's more history here, too: Writer François Rabelais, who celebrated the joys of the table and grape, spent most of his childhood in this house. (Local legend holds that he was born here in 1494, but he was likely born in nearby Chinon.) You can visit Rabelais's bedroom and a little museum with exhibits on his life and work. Don't miss the 16th-century bed and massive original fireplace in one bedroom, or the date—8 April 1509—carved into a window frame in another room; they say it was the work of the young François himself. Just down the road (the tiny D117) is the pretty village of Lerné with its houses built of golden stone. The setting for some hilarious scenes in Rabelais's burlesque novel *La vie inestimable de Gargantua* (Gargantua's Inestimable Life), Lerné was known in Rabelais's day for its *fouace*, a brioche-like bread that can still be found in bakeries throughout the area. ♦ Admission. Daily (no midday closing) May-Sept; daily mid-Mar–Apr; M-Tu, Th-Su Oct-Nov, Feb–mid-Mar; closed December-January. From Chinon take D749 south to D751 west, then take D759 south and follow the signs to La Devinière. 47.95.91.18

41 Château de Marçay $$$$ A stay in this place right in the heart of Touraine's château country is a splurge you'll never regret. Parts of the château, including its vast wine cellars, date from the 12th century, when a fortified castle was built here by Etienne de Marçay, a knight who served at the court of Henry II of England. Transformed into a luxury hotel in 1973, this Relais & Châteaux member has a total of 38 guest rooms, 27 in the main château (23 are ultraluxurious and roomy, and four are smaller) and 11 in a connecting building which are smaller. The rooms are decorated in typical French Provincial style with antique furniture and flowery wallpaper. Most rooms have huge bathrooms, satellite televisions with CNN, and telephones; some have private terraces. There are three floors, and, happily, an elevator. An annex has smaller, simpler, much more affordable, but still luxurious rooms. On the château's private parklands are a heated swimming pool and a tennis court. The hotel will arrange hot-air balloon trips, and rents bicycles to guests. A special attraction for wine lovers: The château produces its own excellent Chinon wine from only 1.7 hectares (4.1 acres) of vineyards. ♦ Closed mid-January–mid-March. Marçay (6 km/3.7 miles south of Chinon on D116). 47.93.03.47

Within the Château de Marçay:

Restaurant Château de Marçay
★★★$$$$ Among the delicacies here are *petit gris à l'ail* (tiny local snails in garlic sauce) and *côte de veau en cocotte aux fèves et morilles* (veal chops in a casserole with fava beans and morel mushrooms). The fixed-price menus help you get by on less than a week's pay; check out the one that includes wine, which is served at lunch Monday through Friday. The restaurant's greatest draw, though, is its mind-boggling, 35,000-bottle cellar. All the great Loire wines are represented, many from hard-to-find vintages, along with wines from other regions, including such miraculous offerings as a 1919 Château Margaux. You don't even want to know what that one costs! ♦ Daily lunch and dinner July-Aug; Tu-Sa lunch and dinner, Su lunch mid-Mar–June, Sept–mid-Jan; closed mid-January–mid-March. Reservations required. 47.93.03.47

Restaurants/Clubs: Red   **Hotels:** Blue
Shops/ ✿ Outdoors: Green   **Sights/Culture:** Black

42 Domaine Bernard Baudry Bernard and Henriette Baudry make superlative Chinon red wine on their 25-hectare (61.8-acre) estate. The winery is in the Baudrys' home, a white stone building overlooking a wide expanse of vineyards that slope down to the placid Vienne River. (They're not far from the birthplace of Rabelais, who would have greatly appreciated these wines.) The wine cellars have been hollowed out of a cliff behind the house. Bernard Baudry has several *terroirs,* many with very old vines, and treats each differently according to its special character. Try Les Grézeaux Chinon red. It comes from 35- to 60-year-old vines and is aged in wood from the region, resulting in elegant overtones of cinnamon, leather, and spices. The Domaine Bernard Baudry (from 30- to 35-year-old vines) and Les Granges are also excellent. The Baudrys also produce a light Chinon rosé that makes a great picnic wine. ♦ Free. Visits and tastings daily; closed mid-August–early September. 13 Coteau de Sonnay (D21), Cravant-les-Coteaux (10 km/6.2 miles east of Chinon on D21). 47.93.15.79; fax 47.98.44.44

42 Chambres d'Hôtes Pallus $$ This pretty 18th-century house offers three elegant guest rooms with antique furnishings, private baths, and views of surrounding vineyards. One room has an exposed-beam ceiling and a large desk, just in case you want to record your wine notes. There's also a pool. Barbara and Bernard Chauveau, the English-speaking owners, are also antiques dealers; they may just have that perfect thing you've been searching for, or can find something to your liking. ♦ Pallus (12 km/7.5 miles east of Chinon on D21). 47.93.08.94; fax 47.98.43.00

42 Domaine de Beauséjour Gérard Chauveau gave up architecture in favor of his passion for wine making. He and his son David produce excellent Chinon red wines—already winning awards—from 24 hectares (59 acres) of vines. The 1990 is a real bargain, with its rich, spicy fruitiness. Tastings and sales are in a spacious modern building surrounded by vineyards. Unlike many small wineries, this one keeps several older vintages on hand for you to try. Another plus: You can stay here (see below). ♦ Admission. Visits and tastings M-Sa. Panzoult (just east of Cravant-les-Coteaux on D21). 47.58.64.64; fax 47.95.27.13

Within Domaine de Beauséjour:

Chambres d'Hôtes Domaine de Beauséjour $$ The Chauveaus rent three moderately priced guest rooms in their lovely white manor house. On a hill overlooking the vineyards and the Vienne River, it is reached by a driveway leading from the tasting center. One of the rooms, a spacious suite, is actually in a separate tower on the opposite side of the garden; it has cheery yellow curtains, stone walls, slate-tile floors, and fine antique furniture. The rooms in the main house also have antique furnishings and are very comfortable. All have private bathrooms and views of the vineyard or the swimming pool, which guests are free to use. Madame Chauveau, who's responsible for the attractive decor, serves complimentary continental breakfasts on a terrace with fine views of the vines. ◆ 47.58.64.64; fax 47.95.27.13

43 Château d'Ussé This château is straight out of a fairy tale (or a Hollywood back lot). The roof seems to sprout literally hundreds of turrets and chimneys, delicately displayed in front of the Chinon forest. (You would never know that one of France's biggest nuclear power plants is practically next door, so try not to think about it.) For the best view, stand about 600 feet in front of the château on the little bridge over the Indre River. Most of the château dates from the 15th century, but some structures in the interior courtyard are from the 17th century. A guided tour takes you through the opulently furnished reception rooms, including an exhibit of elegant clothing from past centuries. There are many good picnic spots along little D16 at the opposite end of the bridge from the château. ◆ Admission. Daily mid-Mar–mid-Nov; closed mid-November–mid-March. 13 km (8 miles) northeast of Chinon on D7. 47.95.54.05

Maisons Troglodytes (Cave Dwellings)

All along the **Loire,** from **Angers** to **Tours,** but especially just east of **Saumur,** you will find *maisons troglodytes* (cave dwellings) that have been carved out of the cliffs of white *tuffeau* (tufa) stone once quarried for building the local châteaux. If "troglodyte" brings to mind primitive creatures and open fires, think again: Many of these cave dwellings are elegant private homes with delicately carved stone facades that just happen to be backed up against a cliff; within the cliff itself, the owners have wine cellars, and often a place to raise mushrooms.

For a taste of the cave life, the following are especially worth a visit:

Village Troglodytique Rochemenier (Louresse-Rochemenier, 41.59.13.15; fax 41.59.35.13) is a whole village of cave dwellings. Guided tours are available in English. Each dwelling charges an admission fee and is open daily from April to October. From November to March, they are only open on Saturday and Sunday from 2PM to 6PM.

Even more unusual is **Troglo'Tap** (Le Val Hulin, 41.51.48.30), a "factory" that still makes a 19th-century Loire Valley specialty, *pommes tapées* (pounded apples). These apples are sliced, pounded, and dried, and can be kept for years; they were often taken on board sailing vessels. Pour a little red Anjou wine over them and wait until they soften up before eating. Packages of the apples are for

sale here to those who take the tour, which includes a tasting. The cave is cold, so be sure to bring a sweater, even in summer. An admission fee is charged. The cave is closed from mid-November until Easter; call for hours at other times.

The **Moulin de la Herpinière** (Turquant, 41.51.75.22) is one of the few working windmills left in a region that once was filled with them. At the base of the mill is a museum of tools from yesteryear, housed in a tufa cave. The museum is open daily from May through October; the rest of the year it is open only to groups. There is an admission charge.

And for luxury-loving cave dwellers, there's the **Domaine des Hautes-Roches** ($$$$; 86 Quai de la Loire, Rochecorbon, 47.52.88.88; fax 47.52.81.30), an 11-room hotel and restaurant partly carved out of caves overlooking the Loire. The huge rooms are opulently decorated and not at all cavelike. The hotel is closed from late January to mid-March. The restaurant of the same name (★★★$$$$) is rated as one of the Loire Valley's most inventive, and has a sublime wine list.

M. BLUM

44 Château d'Azay-le-Rideau The 16th-century château of Azay is an elegant, seemingly delicate structure surrounded by a wide moat that is actually part of the Indre River. Wander the grounds, explore the beautiful English garden, and be transported to a lovelier time. The château's exterior is prettier than its interior, although the staircase inside is worth a look (it's one of the earliest built as a ramp rather than a spiral). The château can best be admired (and photographed) from the picturesque village of Azay, whose ancient stone houses nestle along the banks of the Indre. A spectacular sound-and-light show with music, lasers, and commentary is held at the château just after sundown every evening in summer. ♦ Admission. Daily (no midday closing) Apr-Sept; daily Oct-Mar. 14 km (8.6 miles) east of Ussé on D17. 47.45.42.04

44 Canoe-Kayak Rentals Michel Verdier rents canoes and kayaks for exploring the calm Indre, a perfect way to experience the ancient rhythms of the Loire Valley. ♦ Daily 1PM-6PM. Reservations required. Boats leave from a small beach on the Indre near the château. 47.45.37.59, 47.45.40.85

44 Cycles Leprovost Bicycling is a wonderful way to discover the village of Azay. This shop rents and repairs bikes. ♦ M-Sa. 13 Rue Carnot, Azay. 47.45.40.94

45 Vannerie de Villaines A group of wicker weavers formed a *vannerie* (wickerwork) cooperative here in 1849 at the instigation of the local curé, and it's still going strong. Today the co-op's 80 weavers account for about a third of France's total wicker production. They even grow their own osier (a kind of willow), cut it during the winter, sort it by size, and age it in an artificially stepped-up process. In the spring, they strip the bark and soak the shoots for several hours. Only then can the wicker be woven. Their craftsmanship is sensational. Check out the bread baskets that are big enough to hold several baguettes; some are on wooden stands intended for bakers' displays. The tall baskets on wheels are meant to hold dozens of loaves, and the small baskets with special linings are for loaf risings. In addition to infinite styles of baskets (including the perfect one for a picnic), the weavers produce wicker silverware holders, lampshades, and chairs, tables, and screens; all are for sale here. ♦ Daily Apr-Sept; M-Sa, Su 2PM-7PM Oct-Mar. Take D57 south 5 km (3.1 miles) from Azay, and follow the signs to Villaines-les-Rochers. 47.45.43.03

Muscadet is the only appellation to specify a maximum alcohol content.

Restaurants/Clubs: Red Hotels: Blue
Shops/ 🌳 Outdoors: Green Sights/Culture: Black

46 Château de Langeais Although this château is officially in the Touraine, a donjon (castle keep) on its grounds was built in the 10th century by the Anjou feudal lord Foulques Nerra, ancestor of the Plantagenêts; it's the oldest surviving donjon in France. The main part of the château was built for Louis XI in just four years (1465-69). This, and the fact that the château has never been rebuilt or expanded, make it a unique monument to 15th-century architecture; most other local châteaux have a mishmash of architectural styles. One of its 20th-century owners, Jacques Siegfried, is responsible for the painstaking restoration and refurnishing of the interior in authentic 15th-century fashion. The château gives a real taste of aristocratic life as it was lived along the Loire 500 years ago. You'll see beautiful tapestries from Flanders, portraits of various nobles, huge carved stone fireplaces, and massive Renaissance furniture. ♦ Admission. Daily (no midday closing) July-Aug; daily mid-Mar–June, Sept-Oct; Tu-Su Nov–mid-Mar. Guided visits of about 45 minutes are given several times a day. On the north bank of the Loire near Langeais, halfway between the châteaux of Ussé and Villandry. 47.96.72.60

47 Château de Villandry Built in 1536, this splendid château has a classic turreted tower and an elegant *tuffeau* stone main portion topped with a tall slate roof. It contains an excellent collection of paintings, most from the Renaissance, and a magnificent 13th-century ceiling of gilded cedar wood, brought here in 3,000 pieces from a Spanish mosque by one of the château's previous owners. In spite of these attractions, the main reason to come here is to tour the spectacular garden. It was designed in the early part of this century as an authentic example of a 16th-century French garden. One of France's greatest gardens, and the only one of its kind in the country, it's planted on three levels. The highest, closest to the château, has a large body of water in which the château is reflected. The next level has ornamental plants designed to represent aspects of love, including blood-red flowers that reflect the suffering it can bring, and plants arranged in the shape of horns (the Renaissance symbol of cuckoldry). The lowest level is devoted to herbs, vegetables, and medicinal plants common to French gardens of the period. A stroll through the garden, with the château looming above against a background of trees, is like a trip to the Renaissance. ♦ Admission. Daily (no midday closing) mid-Mar–mid-Nov; closed mid-November–mid-March. Villandry (10 km/6.2 miles northeast of Azay on D7). 47.50.02.09; fax 47.50.12.85

47 Le Prieuré des Granges $ Antiques dealer Philippe Dufresne has five guest rooms in an elegant house (ca. 17th through 19th centuries) set amid a seven-hectare (17-acre) garden. Each of the rooms is decorated with antiques (Louis XII, Louis XIV, or more romantic periods) and has a large window facing the garden. All have private baths and telephones, and guests may use the lovely swimming pool. Dufresne, who speaks English, is a great source of information about antiques hunting and other things to see and do in the area. Another plus is its location: close to all the major Loire Valley châteaux. ♦ Savonnières (follow D7 2 km/1.2 miles east from Villandry). 47.50.09.67; fax 47.50.06.43

Tours

Tours's ugly industrial suburbs will come as a shock to those who think the Loire Valley is made up solely of châteaux and picturesque villages. But sheltered near the city's heart are an ancient Gallo-Roman district with crumbling walls and a cathedral district crowded with wonderful Gothic architecture. Steeped in Renaissance history and still a French cultural center, Tours is considered the geographic center of the Loire château region, and attracts many visitors. The city originated in the first century, when the Romans built a fortress, **Caesarodunum,** at the strategic meeting point of the **Loire** and **Cher Rivers.** The site had once been controlled by a local Gallic tribe, the Turons, from whom the modern city gets its name.

The ancient city center holds plenty of treasures, many restored after the German bombardments of June 1940. Clustered near the **Place Plumereau** (filled with cafes, and a great spot for coffee or a glass of wine) are the city's main architectural landmarks, including the **Cathédrale St-Gatien** (built from 1170 to 1574, which explains its jumble of styles); the **Cloître de la Psalette,** with vestiges of a Gallo-Roman tower; the 11th-century **Eglise St-Julien; Rue Colbert,** the main axis of Caesarodunum, now lined with Renaissance houses; and **Rue Briçonnet,** with several medieval and Renaissance dwellings. **Rue de la Scellerie** and **Rue de Cygne** both have many antiques shops. Also here are several wine experts' associations and the **Musée des Vins de Touraine** (Museum of the Wines of Touraine), which offers a historic look at this noble art and related subjects.

48 Musée des Vins de Touraine (Museum of the Wines of Touraine) This elegant museum is housed in the former wine cellars of the 13th-century **Abbaye St-Julien,** in the ancient center of Tours. Exhibits cover the history of wine making, wine and food, related crafts such as barrel making, and other topics. The setting is impressive, but the exhibits, all locked under glass, are somewhat lifeless. ♦ Admission. M, W-Su. 16 Rue Nationale (at Rue Colbert). 47.61.07.93

48 Eglise St-Julien (St. Julien Church) Above the wine museum is the abbey's church. Built of *tuffeau* stone weathered to shades of gray, the exterior is a showcase of Gothic architecture. Most of the the building dates from the 13th century, but note the 11th-century entrance portal. The sober interior of high Gothic arches in carved stone contrasts with a set of vivid stained-glass windows designed by artist Max Ingrand in 1960. ♦ 16 Rue Nationale (at Rue Colbert). No phone

49 Confiserie Tourangelle/Poirault This candy shop's specialty is the *livre tournois,* named for a unit of money used in Touraine for centuries and immortalized here in chocolate, orange, and coffee cream. Also try the prunes stuffed with plum and apricot purée and glazed with rum. ♦ Daily. 6 Rue Nationale (between Rue Colbert and Pl Anatole-France). 47.05.42.00

50 Le Canotier ★★$$ Chef Valerie Bardet's bistro has quickly become a local favorite. Try the hearty *terrine de queue de boeuf au foie gras* (oxtail and foie gras terrine) and the *soufflé chaud et froid au chocolat* (hot and cold chocolate soufflé). ♦ Tu-Sa lunch and dinner; M dinner; closed late February–early March and late December–early January. Reservations required. 6 Rue des Fusillés (between Pl de la Résistance and Rue du Commerce). 47.61.85.81

51 Hôtel Le Francillon $$$ An ancient mansion built mainly of white *tuffeau* stone has been converted to a 10-room, one-suite luxury hotel in the heart of Tours. The facade is lovely, with a tall half-timbered column wedged between walls of white stone. Inside, however, everything is decorated in beige-and-pink contemporary style. Some of the rooms are on the small side, but all are cozy and comfortable, with private bathrooms and large windows. A 20-percent discount is offered Friday through Sunday. ♦ 9 Rue des Bons-Enfants (at Pl de Châteauneuf). 47.66.44.66; fax 47.66.17.18

Within the Hôtel Le Francillon:

Le Francillon ★$$$ This formal restaurant serves traditional French haute cuisine, including *ragoût de légumes aux trois poissons* (vegetable stew with three fishes)

and *agneau au miel et vinaigre de cidre* (lamb with honey and apple-cider vinegar). Desserts include homemade sorbets and a grapefruit terrine. The restaurant is good but overpriced; its location, however, is very convenient. ♦ Daily lunch and dinner. Reservations recommended. 47.66.44.66

Chez Laurent ★$$ Billed as *"la cuisine d'autrefois"* (cooking of the past), the simple, traditional dishes at this bistro include seafood platters, roast chicken, *pavé de boeuf au roquefort* (steak with roquefort), and *cuisse de grenouille* (frogs' legs). ♦ Daily lunch and dinner. Reservations recommended. 47.20.32.33

Au 50 ★$ A buffet of cold dishes—charcuterie, salads, and vegetables—is served at a fixed price of 50 francs per person (hence the name); drinks are not included. It's a nonsmoking restaurant—a rarity in France. ♦ Tu-Sa lunch. 47.20.32.33

52 Marché à la Brocante (Used-Goods Market) Come early to this lively flea market for the best pickings. Typical finds include 19th-century French porcelain; antique copper cooking utensils; handmade lace tablecloths and curtains (mainly from the 19th century); turn-of-the-century women's clothing, including delicate white blouses with handmade lace; silver candelabras and serving pieces; books, paintings, and drawings from many periods; and a wide assortment of furniture and decorative objects. Some items are much too large to tuck into a suitcase but others are small enough to tote home. ♦ W, Sa; many vendors close for lunch between 1PM and 2PM. Pl de la Victoire (at Rue du Grand-Marché). No phone

53 Grammont-Motocycles This reliable shop rents bicycles. They're not a great way to get around Tours (too much traffic), but are perfect for an escape to the countryside. ♦ M-Sa. 93 Ave de Grammont (between Rue Alfred-de-Vigny and Rue Eupatoria). 47.66.62.89

54 Chez Jean-Michel Restaurant à Vins Le Charolais ★★$$ Friendly chef Jean-Michel Montagu, once a sommelier in some of France's best restaurants (and at Bouley in Manhattan), now owns his own bistro. He serves excellent traditional dishes, with a focus on meats; if you like beef, you'll love the *entrecôte à la moelle* (steak with beef marrow) and the *steak tartare*. He always offers *"le poisson du marché"* (whatever fish looked good in the market that day). First courses include *oeufs en meurette au vin de Chinon* (a Burgundian dish of poached eggs in red wine sauce, here made with Chinon wine). The food is very good, and, as you might expect from someone with Montagu's credentials, the wine list is outstanding—one of the most complete and reasonably priced along the Loire. Several wines are available by the glass. The fixed-price lunch menu offers a full meal for the price many city establishments in France would charge for a sandwich. ♦ Tu-Sa lunch and dinner; M dinner. Reservations recommended. 123 Rue Colbert (between Rue de la Barre and Rue Jules-Moineaux). 47.20.80.20

55 Cathédrale St-Gatien/Cloître de la Psalette (St. Gatien Cathedral/La Psalette Cloisters) These adjoining Tours *tuffeau* landmarks were built from 1170 to 1574, which explains their jumble of styles, a surprisingly harmonious history in stone of Gothic architecture. The cathedral's apse shows the spare lines of early Gothic style, its transept and nave reflect the increasing use of decorative lines typical of mid-Gothic architecture, and its facade is an example of late Gothic (Flamboyant) style. Added to the mixture is a Gallo-Roman wall, on which rests the church's Romanesque main tower, and a Renaissance spiral staircase. Inside the cathedral are superb stained-glass windows dating from the 13th to the 15th centuries, which miraculously survived the heavy bombing Tours suffered during World War II. Adjoining the cathedral is the elegant 15th-century **Cloître St-Gatien**, known as "La Psalette." (The cloisters were named for the fact that one of the canons in residence always chanted psalms during mass.) The cloisters have three main wings. The oldest, **L'Aisle Ouest** (West Aisle), dates from 1460. It has a library on an upper level reached by a lovely spiral staircase dating from the 16th century. The library itself has an elegant vaulted ceiling and 13th- to 14th-century frescoes brought here from the ruins of a small church in a nearby village. ♦ Cathedral free; La Psalette admission. Daily. Pl de la Cathédrale (between Rue de la Scellerie and Rue Albert-Thomas). 47.05.05.53

56 Musée des Beaux-Arts (Museum of Fine Arts) Housed in the 17th- to 18th-century former palace of the archbishop is an impressive collection of paintings by such artists as Rembrandt, Rubens, Degas, and Delacroix. ♦ Admission. M, W-Su. 18 Pl François-Sicard (between Rue des Ursulines and Rue de la Scellerie). 47.05.68.73

Restaurants/Clubs: Red	**Hotels:** Blue
Shops/ 🌳 Outdoors: Green	**Sights/Culture:** Black

57 Hôtel Mirabeau $ Set in a 19th-century mansion, this pleasant budget hotel is not far from the train station. Most of the 25 comfortable rooms have private baths. There's no restaurant, but room-service meals are available. ♦ 89 *bis* Blvd Heurteloup (at Rue de Châteaudun). 47.05.24.60; fax 47.05.31.09

58 Hôtel Jean Bardet $$$$ This Relais & Châteaux member offers opulent extras—including a chauffeured Rolls-Royce to pick up guests at the train station or take them on château or winery tours! The hotel is a large white mansion on the north bank of the Loire, surrounded by a six-acre park. All of its 16 rooms and five palatial suites have views of the surrounding gardens, and some contain working fireplaces. All have private bathrooms; the marble bathrooms in some of the suites are as big as small apartments. The elegant decor updates traditional French style; for example, the Louis XV–style chairs are made of light-colored wood and upholstered in white. There's also a swimming pool. The only drawback (other than the astronomical price) is the sometimes chilly welcome. ♦ Closed late February–early March. 57 Rue Groison (at Rue de Trianon). 47.41.41.11; fax 47.51.68.72

Within the Hôtel Jean Bardet:

Restaurant Jean Bardet ★★★$$$$ This is *the* gastronomic temple of Tours, and is considered one of the best of its kind in France. Chef Bardet's dishes range from the most sophisticated *homard breton au vieux Vouvray épicé au gingembre frais et citron vert* (Brittany lobster with a sauce of aged Vouvray, fresh ginger, and lime) to the earthiest *petites anguilles de Vendée aux champignons* (tiny Vendée eels with mushrooms). Bardet is famed for his *gésier de canard et homard rôti au vin de Graves* (duck gizzards and lobster roasted with Graves wine) and *pintadeau fermier truffé* (farm-raised squab with truffles). The fabulous wine list includes many Loire wines, with a focus on Vouvrays and Bourgueils. The choices—and the prices—will make you swoon. ♦ M-Sa lunch and dinner, Su lunch May-Sept; Tu-Sa lunch and dinner, Su lunch Oct–mid-Feb, mid-Mar–Apr; closed mid-February–mid-March. Reservations required. 47.41.41.11; fax 47.51.68.72

59 Le Noble Joué ★$ This wine bar and restaurant on the outskirts of Tours has a good selection of Touraine wines by the glass. It's a great place to have a casual lunch and sample a few local wines before heading off to visit the nearby wineries. ♦ Tu-Sa lunch and dinner; M lunch. Reservations recommended. 86 Blvd de Chinon, Joué-lès-Tours (a suburb about 5 km/3.1 miles southwest of Tours on D751). 47.53.57.97

On the Road to the Upper Loire Valley

60 Château de la Bourdaisière $$$ This classy bed-and-breakfast has some lineage. It was built over a 14th-century structure at the command of François I for his mistress Marie Gaudin. Gabrielle d'Estrées, Henri IV's mistress, was born in the château. And today's owners are Prince Philippe Maurice de Broglie and his brother Prince Louis Albert de Broglie. The enormous château is surrounded by a 100-acre park, which includes a formal garden in the Versailles style, a swimming pool, tennis court, and several friendly deer. The 10 guest rooms and two suites are luxuriously decorated and have private bathrooms (two rooms with showers but no tubs are less expensive). Ask for the impossibly elegant Gabrielle d'Estrées room, with a canopy bed and blue-green floral wallpaper and drapes; the Catherine de Médicis suite, decorated in cheerful yellow, is also sumptuous. Although there is no restaurant, dinner can be arranged for groups. The château is also open for guided visits from mid-March through mid-November. ♦ English spoken. About 8 km (5 miles) east of Tours on D751 or D140, then follow the signs to Montlouis. 47.45.16.31; fax 47.45.09.11

61 Vouvray Just outside Tours sits the village of Vouvray amid its vineyards. Vouvray's famous wines, made primarily from the chenin blanc (pineau de la loire) grape, are produced in still and bubbly varieties; the still wines are dry, semidry, or sweet (*moelleux*). All Vouvrays have a pronounced fruity taste. The dry wines go very well with fish and local goat cheeses; the sweeter and sparkling varieties are usually served as aperitifs or with desserts. The village has numerous cave dwellings dug into its cliffs; many are used by the vinters as *caves* (wine cellars). ♦ 9.5 km (5.9 miles) east of Tours on N152

Within Vouvray:

Le Virage Gastronomique A wonderful source for picnic provisions, including a great selection of local goat cheeses (at their peak during the summer) and *rillettes* (shredded pork), a Touraine specialty. ♦ Daily 8AM-8PM (no midday closing). 25 Ave Brûle (N152) on the southern edge of Vouvray. 47.52.70.02

Ecomusée du Pays de Vouvray, L'Espace de la Vigne et du Vin (Museum of Vouvray Culture, Wine, and the Vine) In an ancient house in the village are exhibits on local customs, traditional crafts and lifestyles, and wine making. Guides demonstrate how to use the ancient vineyard tools on display. An instructive tasting at the end of the visit includes several Vouvray wines; children are offered grape juice. ♦ Admission. Daily (no midday closing) mid-Mar–mid-Nov; daily mid-Nov–mid-Mar. 30 Rue Victor-Hérault. 47.52.76.00

Domaine Huet Noël Pinguet took over this Vouvray estate—one of the best places in the area to try the full range of the local wines—from his father-in-law, Gaston Huet. Visitors are greeted in a small, modern office in front of the winery's cellars, which are carved out of the *tuffeau* that is the bedrock of Vouvray. Pinguet produces his wines biodynamically, as the official Demeter reference on their labels attests. He says he can't explain why biodynamics works, but he knows his vines have been healthier and his wines more complex since he switched to that approach. Both the dry and semidry Vouvrays produced here are superlative. Try the Vouvray Demi-Sec Clos du Bourg or any of the 1989s, which the wine maker considers his "vintage of the century." Haut-Lieu, Mont, and Clos du Bourg are the three top vineyards from which the wines are made. You can visit the cellars if someone is available to guide you. ♦ Free. Tastings daily by appointment. Manoir du Haut-Lieu, Vouvray (follow the signs to the winery). 47.52.78.87; fax 47.52.66.51

Jean-Claude Aubert This wine maker's operation is located in the Vallée-Coquette (literally, the coquettish valley), a region Balzac loved. He described it in one of his novels as being "delicious because it winds around, curves, is reborn with each step you take and gets more beautiful the farther you travel along it." Balzac would no doubt have appreciated Aubert's dry Vouvray, with its bouquet of exotic fruits, almonds, and chestnuts. You will too. ♦ Free. Visits and tastings daily. 10 Rue La Vallée-Coquette (follow the signs to the winery). 47.52.71.03; fax 47.52.68.38

Vallée-Coquette Follow in Balzac's footsteps with a walk in the lovely countryside on Vouvray's western edge. Next to the church parsonage at 2 Rue Victor-Hugo is a small stairway leading uphill; take it to reach a walking trail that heads past a cemetery and through vineyards. The summit yields a great view of the Loire. Continue along the (only) path to a T-shaped intersection and turn left to join the GR3 hiking trail (part of a nationally numbered walking route system), which follows along a cleft between vineyard-covered hills through the Vallée-Coquette. The trail loops north and then southwest back to the D1, which will lead you back to Vouvray. The whole walk is around five kilometers (3.1 miles) and is not strenuous; about half of it is along the little D1 road and the rest is on the GR3, a dirt road occasionally shared by a tractor. Keep your eye out for the occasional cars or tractors that may be on the road. ♦ Western Vouvray

Barging through France

If glimpses of river winding through countryside leave you longing for more, consider spending the night on the water. Several companies in France rent fully equipped houseboats that can go head-to-head with any luxury hotel. The barges come in a variety of sizes, and are outfitted with full kitchen and bathroom facilities. Bicycles can usually be rented along with the boat. Barging down one of France's many canals or quiet rivers, pausing to bike through tiny villages ashore, is an exeptional way to discover the French countryside. You can cruise the many rivers of the western **Loire Valley**—including the **Maine, Mayenne,** and **Sarthe,** as well as the **Loire** and the **Loir.** Or try the **Canal de Bourgogne;** the

Canal de la Marne au Rhin, which leads from the **Marne River** all the way to the **Rhine** in Alsace; or the earliest French "wine route," the **Canal du Midi,** built mainly to transport wine between the Mediterranean and Bordeaux.

Maine-Anjou Rivières, located north of Angers in the Loire Valley, is one of France's best barge-rental companies and is also the central reservations center for similar companies throughout the country. Call or write to request a brochure (English spoken): Maine-Anjou Rivières, Le Moulin, Chenillé-Changé, 49220 Le Lion d'Angers, France. 41.95.10.83, 41.95.10.98 (dial 16 before either number if calling from Paris); fax (16) 41.95.10.52.

M. BLUM

62 Vallée de la Brenne This pretty route for cyclists or those traveling by car runs from the village of Vernou-sur-Brenne to the village of Château-Renault. The tiny road (D46) follows along the banks of the tranquil Brenne River 16.5 kilometers (10.4 miles), and there are great picnic spots all along the way. The most scenic part of this road is the 6.5-kilometer (four-mile) stretch between Vernou-sur-Brenne and Reugny. ♦ Follow D1 east from Vouvray about 4 km (2.5 miles) to Vernou-sur-Brenne, where the route begins; then take D46 16.5 km (10.4 miles) to Château-Renault

63 Château de Chenonceau This château is at the top of almost everyone's list of favorite Loire Valley châteaux. Built from 1513 to 1521, with its splendid gallery spanning the Cher River, it's not as imposing as the **Château de Chambord** (see page 234) nor as delicately pretty as the châteaux of Azay or Ussé, but it has more soul. You can still feel the presence of the powerful women who lived here, including beautiful Diane de Poitiers, the mistress of Henri II, who gave her the château in 1547. She was ousted by the queen in 1559, after Henri died in a jousting match. With the castle to herself, Catherine de Médicis held shockingly extravagant parties here. In the 18th century, the château hosted such luminaries as Jean-Jacques Rousseau. **Chenonceau** produces its own wine (a light red), but you can only visit the 16th-century cellars nearby by forming a group (there's a charge). There's a little restaurant where you can pick up a simple lunch to eat at the tables outside, and a sound-and-light show every evening from mid-June to mid-September. Beauty has its price: This is the most-visited château in France after Versailles, so expect crowds. ♦ Admission. Daily (no midday closing). Chenonceaux (35 km/21.7 miles southeast of Tours on D40; follow the signs to the château). 47.23.90.07

63 Le Bon Laboureur et Château $$ This landmark is *the* place to stay in Chenonceaux, so be sure to reserve well in advance if you want to stay here. A rambling vine- and flower-covered house in the center of the village, it is everyone's postcard-perfect image of a provincial French hotel. There are 34 rooms and two elegant suites. Ten rooms are above the restaurant in the renovated main building; the others are in three modern cottages that overlook the hotel's pool or a large garden. All rooms are comfortable and have private bathrooms (and a somewhat impersonal, but top-notch, modern decor). The garden in back boasts a swimming pool, and the hotel also rents bicycles. ♦ Closed mid-November–mid-March. 6 Rue du Docteur (at Rue de la Roche), Bretonneau, Chenonceaux (follow the signs to the château). 47.23.90.02; fax 47.23.82.01

Within Le Bon Laboureur et Château:

Restaurant Le Bon Laboureur et Château ★★★$$$ The fare served in the dining room of the main building is rich and ultratraditional, such as *coquilles saint-jacques aux cèpes* (sea scallops with cèpes), *croustillant d'agneau à l'ail* (crusty roast lamb with garlic), and a great *gâteau au chocolat* (chocolate cake). The elegant traditional decor matches the cuisine. You'll find bouquets of fresh flowers, thick white tablecloths, and the finest china and silverware. Summers offer outdoor dining on a tree-shaded patio. Service is superb and the atmosphere is convivial rather than formal or stuffy. ♦ Daily lunch and dinner; closed mid-November–mid-March. 47.23.90.02

Gourmandises de Touraine ★★$$ This informal restaurant is housed in one of the modern cottages adjoining the hotel's garden, behind the main hotel building. It has a rustic but cheery decor, with simple wooden tables and colorful tablecloths, and offers such

Château de Chenonceau

home-style local specialties as *rillettes* (pork spread), *rillons* (long-simmered chunks of pork), and river fish served in rich sauces made with Vouvray wine. ◆ Daily lunch and dinner; closed mid-November–mid-March. Reservations recommended. 47.23.90.02

64 Loches Even in July and August, when tour groups clog the roads and towns along the château trail, the little medieval town of Loches usually provides a respite from the crowds. Its strategic position on a cliff above the valley has attracted settlers since pre-Roman times. Henry II, Richard the Lionhearted, and other Plantagenêts lived here. But the most famous resident was Agnès Sorel, Charles VII's mistress, who was known as the *Dame de Beauté* (the Lady of Beauty). She had generously endowed a local nunnery, but after her death the nuns objected to the sinful woman's burial here; the king said he would bury her elsewhere if they returned the money she had given them. She was buried here.

The heart of Loches is its medieval city, which perches on a small plateau that provides splendid views of the surrounding countryside. No cars are allowed here: Reach the plateau by steps that lead from a parking lot at the intersection of Mail Droulin and Rue Balzac to the massive **Porte Royale** (Royal Gate), a 13th-century gate flanked by two 15th-century towers. Beyond these lie the **Cité Médiévale**, a collection of picturesque medieval houses, either half-timber or *tuffeau* with elaborate stone carvings. Beneath the town sprawls a lovely landscape dotted with prime picnic spots, especially around the pretty village of Chanceaux-près-Loches to the northwest or in the public garden in the village of Beaulieu-lès-Loches to the east. ◆ In the Indre Valley south of the Loire, 40 km (24.8 miles) southeast of Tours by N143

Within Loches:

Château de Loches and Donjon The medieval city is bounded on the northern edge of the plateau by the 14th-century **Château de Loches** and on the south by the **Donjon.** Among the château's claims to fame is that Joan of Arc met with Charles VII here on 3 and 5 June 1429. You can visit the vast room with a huge open fireplace where their meetings took place. Also within the château is the tomb of Charles's mistress, Agnès Sorel, whose beauteous visage is carved in alabaster (the tomb was desecrated more than three centuries later by revolutionaries who mistook her for a saint). In the same room is a portrait of the Virgin by Jean Fouquet, who supposedly used Sorel as the model for the Virgin's face, along with a beautiful triptych by Fouquet. The 11th-century **Donjon** was built by feudal lord Foulques Nerra (ancestor of the Plantagenêts); hike up to the top (157 steps) for a spectacular view. ◆ Admission (one ticket covers the château and the donjon). Daily (no midday closing) July-Aug; daily mid-Mar–June, Sept; M-Tu, Th-Su Feb–mid-Mar, Oct-Nov; closed December-January. Enter through the Porte Royale. 47.59.01.32

M. Schmitt This small shop rents bicycles for exploring the picturesque countryside. Call ahead during the summer to make sure the type of bike you want is still available. ◆ M-Sa Mar-Oct; Tu-Sa Oct-Mar. 7 Rue des Moulins. 47.59.02.15

Hôtel George Sand $$ Named for one of Loches's famous fans, this place has 20 simple, comfortable rooms, all with private bathrooms (the cheaper rooms have showers instead of tubs). The hotel is a former *relais de poste* (stagecoach stop) that dates from the 15th century, and has exposed beams in the ceilings. The cheerful French Provincial decor includes white curtains and flowery wallpaper. Be sure to ask for a room overlooking the Indre River; the others face a noisy street. ◆ Closed late November–late December. 39 Rue Quintefol (across from the château). 47.59.39.74; fax 47.91.55.75

Within the Hôtel George Sand:

Restaurant Le George Sand ★$$ Good traditional cuisine, with a wide choice of fixed-price menus; the lowest-priced menus are actually the best. Try the river fish *au beurre de Chinon* (a butter and Chinon wine sauce). In summer, you can dine on a lovely terrace looking out on the Indre River. ◆ Daily lunch, afternoon tea, and dinner; closed late November–late December. 47.59.39.74

65 Restaurant La Belle Epoque ★$ This friendly eatery in a little vine-covered house has such good, simple cuisine as *salade avec des rillons chauds* (salad with warm chopped pork), *coq au vin de Chinon,* and *andouillettes* (small sausages). Local artists' works are on display. It's in a tiny picture-postcard village far removed from tourist crowds most of the year. ◆ Tu-Sa lunch and dinner; Su lunch; closed in September. Reservations recommended. Chanceaux-près-Loches (5 km/3.1 miles northwest of Loches on D21). 47.59.38.16

"Don't ask me anymore why I love Touraine. I don't love it the way one loves his cradle, nor as one loves an oasis in the desert; I love it the way an artist loves art."

Honoré de Balzac, *Le Lys dans la vallée* (The Lily in the Valley)

Restaurants/Clubs: Red   **Hotels:** Blue
Shops/ ● Outdoors: Green   **Sights/Culture:** Black

66 Château de Blois In the center of what is now a bustling little town, halfway between Chartres and the Sologne region south of the Loire, stands the medieval stronghold of the Counts of Blois. From this massive, fortified château, the counts held off attacks from various adversaries (particularly Foulques Nerra, the Anjou feudal lord), and ruled not only the Blois region, but also Chartres and part of Champagne. Charles of Orléans ruled here in the 15th century. After losing one wife in childbirth and another during his 25-year imprisonment in England after the Battle of Agincourt, Charles returned to Blois and remarried. In 1462, at the age of 71, he finally fathered a son, the future King Louis XII. Louis loved Blois and spent much of his reign here with his wife, Anne of Brittany. François I set up house here (and in the nearby château of Amboise) in the 16th century, and his architects added what many consider to be the château's most beautiful wing; it is famous for a splendid exterior spiral staircase with elaborate stone carvings. All the royal residents left their mark: The château contains examples of aristocratic French architecture from feudal times to the 17th century. Visitors may tour the château's vast interior, whose many reception rooms and bedrooms are furnished as they were in the past. Don't miss Catherine de Médicis's old room—it has 237 carved wooden panels that conceal secret hiding places (the guide will open a few for you). One wing has a portrait gallery; among the fine paintings hangs a Rubens portrait of Marie de Médicis. ♦ Admission. Daily (no midday closing) mid-Apr–Sept; daily Oct–mid-Apr. Guided tours of around 45 minutes are given daily; English-speaking guides are usually available in summer. Blois (64 km/39.7 miles northeast of Tours on A10). 54.78.06.62

67 Château de Chambord After a long drive through a dense forest, you turn a corner— and this grandiose, gleaming white *tuffeau* castle suddenly spreads out before you as in a dream. François I actually ordered this immense Renaissance château, the biggest along the Loire, to be built as his hunting lodge. The surrounding forests, part of the region known as the Sologne, are still known for their abundant game. Louis XIV and Molière often stayed here. Visitors today can tour the huge park (surrounded by the longest wall in France, 32 kilometers/19.8 miles) and the château's interior, which is richly furnished. It is famous for its central stairway with two ramps—built to allow a person to descend on one side and not see, or be seen by, someone ascending the other. Climb the stairs to the upper terraces, where you can get a close view of the elaborate multiturreted and slate-tiled roof. An annual music, theater, and dance festival is held at the château in early September. ♦ Admission. Daily (no midday closing) July-Sept; daily Oct-June. Chambord (16 km/10 miles east of Blois on D33). 54.50.40.18

Hôtel du Grand St-Michel

67 Hôtel du Grand St-Michel $$ This cozy hotel has a great location: It faces the **Château de Chambord,** so you can enjoy the view long after the tour buses have gone. Inside the large white-stone-and-stucco building are 40 simple but comfortably decorated rooms; all have private baths. Ask for a room with a view of the château. Note that guests staying here in July or August are charged for breakfast and at least one other meal per day in the restaurant (see below). ♦ Closed mid-November–late December. Facing the Château de Chambord. 54.20.31.31; fax 54.20.36.40

Within the Hôtel du Grand St-Michel:

Restaurant du Grand St-Michel ★$$ The traditional regional specialties (including game dishes in winter and good goat cheeses in summer) are pleasant, but you'll find no gastronomic inventiveness here. The view of the château is spectacular in the evening—ask for a window table. ♦ Daily lunch and dinner. Reservations recommended in summer. 54.20.31.31

67 Ecuries du Maréchal de Saxe (Maréchal de Saxe Stables) Equestrians can relive the days of the royal hunt with a ride through the forest of Chambord; others might want to arrange a one-hour drive through the forest in a luxurious antique coach, complete with coachman. An equestrian pageant with riders in Renaissance costumes is held here in summer. ♦ Fee. Daily, hours vary. Reservations recommended. Chambord, near the entrance to the château. 54.20.31.01

"Have you noticed how bread tastes when you have been hungry for a long time? Jesus Christ, how good it was! As for the wine, I sucked it all down in one draught, and it seemed to go straight into my veins and flow round my body like new blood."

George Orwell, *Down and Out in Paris and London*

Restaurants/Clubs: Red   **Hotels:** Blue

Shops/ 🌿 Outdoors: Green   **Sights/Culture:** Black

Biodynamics: Back to the Future

Biodynamics (*biodynamie*) is not only an idea whose time has come, but one that has come just in the nick of time for the world of wine making. For the last few decades, vineyards in France and elsewhere have been bombarded with tons of chemical fertilizers, insecticides, and fungicides. These were first hailed as a means of making vineyard cultivation—always a risky business—much more predictable and profitable. But the long-term problems brought about by their use are beginning to come to light. One, of course, is the effect on the wine drinker of consuming wines made from chemically treated grapes. There are other negative consequences too: Vines subjected to strong doses of heavy-duty fertilizers and insecticides tend to lose their natural immunities and become, ironically, even more vulnerable to disease. And, even more disturbing for the wine connoisseur, wines made from grapes grown in chemically treated vineyards can lose their special character. It's only logical: What separates a great vineyard from a mediocre one is a complex balance of soil quality, sun exposure, microclimate, and the unique qualities of the vines. Chemically tampering with this balance changes the quality of the wine, and not for the better. Chemically treated grapes are even proving to be incapable of forming their own natural yeasts, another key element in a wine's special taste. And chemically treated grapes are producing wines that do not age as well as they once did, a real problem in places like the **Médoc,** where the cabernet sauvignon–based wines need a long time in the bottle.

For all these reasons, many French wine makers have switched to organic agriculture in the past few decades, but with very mixed results. Deprived of the chemicals that have been protecting them, grapes become so vulnerable to disease that a whole crop can be lost. That's not a risk owners of great vineyards want to take. And a lot of organic wines just don't taste very good. But there's an alternative: biodynamics. This approach employs some of the methods of organic agriculture, but goes much further to preserve the special nature of a vineyard's soil and microclimate and to achieve a proper balance among the four elements that affect the life of the vine—earth, water, air, and heat.

In the biodynamic approach, even so-called organic fertilizers and insecticides are avoided, because they could destroy microscopic elements of the soil or vine that contribute to the vineyard's authentic character. The poverty of vineyard soil—which results in low yields, but better wine grapes—is maintained in the biodynamic approach; fertilizers, usually animal manures, are used only sparingly. Techniques include spraying the vineyard with a diluted solution containing quartz crystals to intensify the light the vines receive from the sun; spraying with a mild nettle

solution to perk up circulation of sap; and spraying with a gentle valerian "tea" to bring heat to the vines, if such help is needed. And the biodynamic grower takes into account other forces that affect the vines, such as the phases of the sun, moon, and planets, and even electromagnetic fields. Our ancestors made wine in this way for centuries, by tradition and instinct. Now, many of France's top wine makers are returning to the practice by design, and succeeding. According to one of them, Nicolas Joly of **La Coulée de Serrant**—source of one of France's rarest and greatest white wines—the time has come to shift the focus from popular and stylish wines to authentic wines that reflect their particular *terroir,* microclimate, and vintage.

No authentic wine is ever like any other wine, nor even like itself in other vintages. The life of the vine always shines through, if it is allowed to. All this may sound like New Age idealism, but the proof is on the vine and in the bottle: Biodynamically raised grapes tend to be more disease-resistant than grapes grown using other methods, and biodynamic wines tend to have more individual character than standard wines. Highly respected French wine makers who have adopted biodynamics include Joly, those at **Domaine Leflaive in Puligny-Montrachet** (in some of its prime vineyards), and Lalou Bize-Leroy, a producer of great burgundies at her **Domaine Leroy.** Wines made from biodynamically grown grapes have the right to a "Demeter" certification on their labels, which indicates that all the vines in the vineyard used to make the wine have been cultivated biodynamically for a minimum of three years.

French wine lovers, faced with the fact that many of their favorite wines have been losing their identities over the past few years, have been quick to accept biodynamics. One of France's best wine stores, **Caves Taillevent** in Paris, has opened a special section for biodynamic wines, and they've become top sellers. When you try them, you'll notice right away that they don't taste like any other wines. And there are no artificial chemicals mixed in with the bouquet.

68 Auberge La Chaumette $ This archetypal vine-covered French Provincial hotel has 19 simple but comfortable rooms that overlook either the garden or a quiet street. ♦ Closed late December–mid-January and Sunday evening mid-January–early April, mid-November–late December. Muides-sur-Loire (6 km/3.7 miles northeast of Chambord on D112). 54.87.50.97; fax 54.87.01.02

Within the Auberge La Chaumette:

Restaurant La Chaumette ★$ Here are regional dishes, with an accent on river fish; they also serve a very inexpensive fixed-price, wine-included lunch menu. Selections, which change seasonally, might include *rillettes* (shredded pork spread on bread), *alose au beurre blanc* (shad with white butter sauce), and *tarte tatin* (upside-down apple tart). There's a covered terrace for summertime dining. ♦ Daily lunch and dinner mid-Apr–mid-Nov; M-Sa lunch and dinner, Su lunch mid-Jan–mid-April, mid-Nov–late Dec; closed late December–mid-January. Reservations recommended. 54.87.50.97

69 Grand Hôtel du Lion d'Or $$$$ If you're looking for an absolutely fabulous place to stay between the vineyards of Touraine and those of the upper Loire Valley—expense be damned—this is it. Owners Marie-Christine and Didier Clément (she's a writer, he's the chef) have chosen a rather isolated corner of the world, a great find for travelers. The 13 luxurious rooms and three spectacular suites in this former *relais de poste* (stagecoach stop) have been decorated with taste and charm. The style is contemporary, with some old-fashioned touches: exposed ceiling beams, statues, prints on the walls, and luxurious comforters on the beds. The best (and most expensive) rooms have views of a lovely garden. You'll probably find a copy of one of the hostess's books on the bedside table, perhaps *Colette et George Sand* or *Colette Gourmande* (which includes recipes for the foods Colette wrote about). The delicious breakfasts feature homemade jams and wonderful breads. There's a lovely, flower-filled interior patio, but no pool or tennis courts. Come here simply to relax—and to enjoy the hotel's marvelous restaurant (below). ♦ Closed mid-February–March. 69 Rue Georges-Clemenceau, Romorantin-Lanthenay (about 90 km/55 miles east of Tours on N76; 30 km/18.6 miles south of Chambord on D765). 54.76.00.28; 54.88.24.87

Within the Grand Hôtel du Lion d'Or:

Restaurant du Lion d'Or ★★★★$$$$ Chef Clément transforms the excellent products of his local network of cheese makers, mushroom gatherers, fishers, hunters, and farmers into a wide range of sumptuous fare. Some dishes are as simple as can be, such as incredibly tender *côte de boeuf de la Coutancie* (steaks from beer-fed cattle); some are extremely old-fashioned, based on recipes from ancient cookbooks; and some are up-to-the-minute, like the *rouget barbet au potage de vinaigre, fenouil, et citronnelle* (red mullet with vinegar, fennel, and lemon grass). Don't miss the *vol-au-vent aux morilles* (puff pastry filled with morel mushrooms) or the irresistible cheese assortment. Desserts are delicious and innovative; try the *flan de poires au curry et caramel* (pear flan with curry and caramel). The wine list features a wide selection from the Loire Valley. Every morsel is superb, but it all costs dearly; even the prix-fixe lunch menu's tab surpasses some restaurants' top price. ♦ Daily lunch and dinner; closed mid-February–March. 54.76.00.28

69 Pâtisserie Gérard Frédéric The pretty little town of Romorantin-Lanthenay boasts a pastry shop with a fine version of that regional specialty now popular all over France: *tarte tatin*. This upside-down apple tart with caramel glaze is best served warm with a dollop of crème fraîche, if you dare. ♦ Tu-Su. 38 Rue Georges-Clemenceau (between Rue Notre-Dame and Rue de Verdun), Romorantin-Lanthenay. 54.76.12.37

69 Hôtel d'Orléans $$ This friendly hotel/restaurant is especially popular in fall and winter, when the menu features game dishes, wild mushrooms, and other local treats. Any time of year, it has a convivial hunting-lodge atmosphere, with stag and boar heads on the walls. The 10 simple, comfortable rooms all have private bathrooms. The restaurant has a number of good fixed-price menus, the cheapest of which is a steal. ♦ Closed Sunday and most of December. Hotel and restaurant reservations required. 2 Pl du Général-de-Gaulle, Romorantin-Lanthenay. 54.76.01.65; 54.76.07.44

Restaurants/Clubs: Red	**Hotels:** Blue
Shops/ 🌳 Outdoors: Green	**Sights/Culture:** Black

The Sancerrois: Sancerre and Pouilly-sur-Loire

The Loire arcs through the Sancerrois and Orléanais countryside east of the Touraine, making a big loop west near Orléans. A few light white wines from chardonnay grapes, like Clos de St-Fiacre, and an earthy rosé from the pinot meunier, Gris Meunier, are produced near Orléans, the area's largest city, but these are primarily simple "quaffing" wines. Farther south, the main wine-producing area of the upper Loire Valley, around the villages of **Sancerre** and **Pouilly-sur-Loire** is known as the Sancerrois. Excellent whites are produced here, as well as some light reds and rosés from the prized sauvignon blanc and pinot noir grapes. One of the best of the whites has the Sancerre appellation. Perched on a steep hill that seems to rise out of nowhere to dominate the surrounding countryside, Sancerre is one of the most picturesque villages along the Loire. It is topped by a 14th-century ruin, the **Tour des Fiefs** (Tower of Feudal Estates), which is all that remains of the residence of the Counts of Sancerre. Once a Roman stronghold, Sancerre also has an ancient city gate called the **Porte César** (Caesar's Gate). The town looks down over villages tucked into valleys, and great sweeps of agricultural land (in this part of France, the phrase *mon fief* means "my property"). The surrounding **Collines de Sancerrois** (Sancerre Hills) are threaded with twisting, difficult-to-navigate country lanes. Between hedgerow divisions, sheep and other pasture animals graze in the shade of chestnut and elm trees. Pouilly, to the east, sits among flatter fields, giving easier access to the surrounding countryside and to the vineyards.

The sauvignon blanc grapes are used nowhere else in France as successfully as they are here. Sancerre white wines tend to have a flinty, yet almost floral bouquet and go well with shellfish and the tangy local goat cheese, *crottin de chavignol* ("goat droppings" from Chavignol). Pouilly-sur-Loire's wines (Pouilly-Fumé and a less interesting variety known simply by the name of the village) are produced in heavier soils and have a denser body, suitable with poultry and white meat as well as with fish. Rosé and red wines from the pinot noir grape are also produced in Sancerre, but fail to match the quality of the whites. Unfortunately, the recent surge in Sancerre wines' popularity has led to the production of inferior Sancerres sold at inflated prices; buy carefully.

Southwest of Sancerre are three other small wine districts that are definitely worth getting to know: **Ménétou-Salon**, which produces white, red, and rosé wines similar to Sancerre's, but often just as good and always less expensive; **Reuilly**, which produces a bone-dry white wine and a delicious gray-pink rosé (made from the pinot gris grape) that is considered one of the best rosés along the Loire; and **Quincy**, which produces mainly fruity, well-balanced white wines.

70 Guy Malbête This wine maker produces what many French wine critics consider the best Reuilly rosé wine, which means it is one of the best rosés made along the Loire. His Pinot Gris 1992 has a fresh, lively, but also complex taste; one critic has compared it to "nectar gathered by bees" (it's a dry wine, but that's a wine critic for you). In addition to his outstanding rosés, Malbête also produces excellent reds and whites. Tastings are in the Malbêtes' white-stone-and-stucco house above the wine cellars. ♦ Free. Visits and tastings by appointment. Bois St-Denis (55 km/34.1 miles southeast of Romorantin-Lanthenay; take N76 east to Vierzon, N20 south to Massay, then D75 south to Reuilly, and follow the signs to the winery). 54.49.25.09

71 Georges Chavet et Fils The Chavet family has been making wines in Ménétou-Salon at least since 1750, so it's no surprise they consistently produce excellent, award-winning wines. Their fine whites are made from sauvignon blanc grapes; their rosés and reds from pinot noir. All their wines are known for complex bouquets and flavors; for example, the 1992 white has suggestions of bitter orange, mint, and yeast. It's great as an aperitif or with fish. The red wine can be drunk young, when it's fruity and pleasant, but it gains in complexity after two or three years in the bottle, becoming rich and mouth-filling. The rosés are great summertime wines, perfect for a picnic. All the wines here are offered at amazingly low prices for such high quality. Visitors are taken to a tasting and sales room in a modern building above the cellars, which can be toured on request. ◆ Free. Visits and tastings daily. From Romorantin-Lanthenay take N76 east to Mehun-sur-Yèvre, then take D68 east to St-Martin d'Auxiny, where you take D59 north and follow the signs for Ménétou-Salon and the winery. From Bourges take D11 north about 30 km (18.6 miles) to Ménétou-Salon. 48.64.80.87; fax 48.64.84.78

72 Domaine Dauny No chemical cocktails here: Wine makers Christian and Nicole Dauny organically produce excellent wines from old vines (30-40 years), "Perhaps for the pleasure of being able to ride the tractor without wearing a mask," as Christian says. Daunys have been making wines here since 1683, so organic agriculture is nothing new to them. The Daunys make white Sancerre from sauvignon blanc, and red and rosé Sancerres from pinot noir. The top of the line are the Clos du Roy whites from vines that are over 25 years old, and the Sancerre Rouge Vieilles Vignes from vines with an average age of 40 years. A simple modern building near the entrance to the cellars serves as a tasting and sales center. Visits are available. ◆ Free. Daily visits, tastings, and sales (no midday closing). Call ahead to be sure someone will be there to greet you. Champtin, Crézancy (from Bué follow D955 west to D22). 48.79.05.75; fax 48.79.02.54

73 Clos de la Poussie This is one of the most spectacular-looking vineyards in France: The vines grow in a steep natural amphitheater whose sides slope 60° or more. The white wines are among the best Sancerre *blancs;* the 1991 has a hint of rum in its bouquet. The estate also produces red Sancerres with an oaky taste that should please fans of oak, even though it isn't typical of this region's wine. ◆ Free. Visits and tastings by appointment. Bué (about 3 km/1.8 miles south of Sancerre on D955). 48.54.20.14; fax 48.54.01.63

73 Le Caveau ★$ This unpretentious wine bar and restaurant just outside Sancerre is a great place to sample the local wines, accompanied by snacks of local goat cheeses or charcuterie. Simple regional dishes tend toward the Burgundian, such as *oeufs en meurette* (poached eggs in red wine sauce). ◆ M-W, F-Su lunch and dinner. Reservations recommended. In the center of Bué. 48.54.22.08

74 Sancerre This picture-postcard hilltop town was once the site of a Gallo-Roman fortress and a medieval fortified château belonging to the Counts of Sancerre. Unfortunately the structures were torn down in the 17th century by Henri de Bourbon, ruler of the nearby province of Berry, to punish the Sancerre counts for their Protestantism. The fortress and château were replaced by white-stone, slate-roofed mansions and more humble houses, most of which were occupied by families who made wine from the vineyards surrounding the village. Several medieval and Renaissance houses still line Sancerre's narrow cobblestone streets. ◆ 46 km (28.5 miles) northeast of Bourges on D955

Within Sancerre:

Domaine de la Moussière/Alphonse Mellot Alphonse Mellot, a *vigneron-négotiant,* is known as "Monsieur Sancerre," both for the quality of the wines he produces and distributes and for his efforts to promote Sancerre's wines. His wines are produced from 50 hectares (123 acres) of vines that take a hundred workers over 20 days to harvest by hand. Mellot is known to listen to tapes of Pavarotti and jazz as he works in the cellars with his vintages; maybe that is what gives them their opulent flair. The winery is a sprawling white stucco-and-stone building in the center of Sancerre; a little shop provides tastings and wine sales (wine is sold in the cellars when the shop is closed). The Mellots also operate a simple, inexpensive restaurant next door, **Le Restaurant d'Alphonse,** with (you guessed it) a great selection of Sancerres. ◆ Free. Cellars by appointment; shop M, Sa-Su. 3 Rue Porte-César. 48.54.07.41; fax 48.54.07.62

Hôtel Panoramique $$ As its name suggests, this modern hotel atop a hill has wonderful views of the countryside. Although decorated in an unremarkable contemporary style, the 58 rooms and two suites are very comfortable and have private bathrooms. The swimming pool in the lovely garden is a welcome plus on a steamy summer day. The real reason to come here, though, is that splendid panorama of Sancerre's vineyards; be sure to ask for a room *"avec vue sur le vignoble"* (with a view of the vines). ◆ Closed in January. Remparts des Augustins. 48.54.22.44; fax 48.54.39.55

Within the Hôtel Panoramique:

Restaurant La Tasse d'Argent $$ This dining room has one of the best views along the wine route: Two walls of glass provide a spectacular, uninterrupted vista of vine-covered hillsides. The chef favors fish and meats in sauces made with Sancerre wines, including *poulet au Sancerre* (chicken in red Sancerre wine sauce) and fish in white wine sauce. The wine list is very good; unfortunately, the quality of the cooking fails to match that of the view. ♦ Daily lunch and dinner; closed in January. Reservations required. 48.54.01.44

La Pomme d'Or ★★$$$ A local favorite, this friendly restaurant has a superb wine list, with a focus on Sancerres. The excellent regional cuisine emphasizes seafood; the *salade de langouste à la ciboulette* (rock lobster and chive salad) and the *truite saumoné aux saint-jacques* (salmon trout with sea scallops) are particularly good. Don't miss the cheese assortment or the *fondant au chocolat*—a gooey, sinful cross between cake and mousse. Most dishes are simple rather than inventive but the ingredients are all top-notch. ♦ Tu-Sa lunch and dinner, Su lunch; closed late December–early January. Reservations required. Pl de la Mairie. 48.54.13.30

Restaurant de la Tour ★★$$ Housed in a 14th-century mansion, the stunningly beautiful dining room has an ancient beamed ceiling and a view of surrounding vineyards. All of the chef's delicious seafood dishes have an original touch—a little ginger or lime, or even meat essence in the sauces. You'll also find some good meat and poultry dishes, like the *fricassée de volaille au vinaigre* (chicken in vinegar sauce) and the *lapin à la crème d'ail* (rabbit with garlic puree). The fine wine list emphasizes Sancerres (naturally). Among the many lower-cost fixed-price menus is a *menu rapide* (quick menu) with one main dish and a dessert. ♦ Daily lunch and dinner. Reservations recommended. 31 Pl de la Halle. 48.54.00.81

Esplanade de la Porte César (Caesar's Gate Esplanade) This long walkway at the base of the village's former ramparts begins at the **Porte César** (Caesar's Gate). The view of the surrounding vineyard-covered countryside is superb from here. ♦ Northern edge of Sancerre

Tour des Fiefs (Tower of the Fiefs) This 15th-century tower, a cylindrical dungeon, is all that remains of the medieval château that Henri de Bourbon destroyed in the 17th century. It is closed to the public. ♦ East of Rue St-Dénis

Le Beffroi (The Belfry) The Counts of Sancerre built this 60-foot-tall tower in the 16th century to house their church bell. But the bell was among the first casualties in the battle between the Protestant counts and the Catholic royals. Soon after the belfry's completion, Catholic troops seized the giant gong and transported it to Bruges, Belgium, where it remained for 400 years. Though it was returned to Sancerre in 1990, and is now back in the belfry, the ill-fated bell is not rung; it has been silenced by three newer ones. And they call this progress? ♦ In the center of Sancerre

74 Auberge à la Ferme/La Ferme de l'Estang ★★$ A hearty, informal meal in this farmhouse restaurant is like a visit with a friend in the country. Home-style fare is served on long wooden tables: Try the *chavignol en croûte* (the local goat cheese in a pastry crust), the *poulet au Sancerre* (chicken cooked in Sancerre wine), or the *filet de brochet Sancerrois* (pike fillet cooked in Sancerre wine sauce). And to drink? Any wine you like, as long as it's Sancerre. ♦ Daily lunch and dinner Easter-Sept; closed October-Easter. Reservations required. Ménétréol-sous-Sancerre (take D307 4 km/2.5 miles south of Sancerre and follow the signs to the auberge). 48.54.22.63

75 Maison Henri Bourgeois The Bourgeois family are *négociants* as well as wine makers. Their own wines are exceptional; try the Monts-Damnés white (named for "damned mountains" near Chavignol, thus cursed because they are so hard to work) and the La Bourgeoise white made of grapes from very old vines. Tastings are offered in underground cellars beneath a small modern building facing the Monts-Damnés. ♦ Daily (no midday closing) Feb-Dec; M-F (no midday closing) Jan. Chavignol (5 km/3.1 miles west of Sancerre on D183). 48.54.21.67; fax 48.54.14.24

76 Hôtel de Pouilly $$ Having spent four years in California, Robert Fischer, the manager of this cozy hotel, appreciates when American guests stay here. His establishment is an official welcome center in the French national tourist office's "See France Person-to-Person" program. All 23 comfortable, quiet rooms have views of the Loire, private baths, mini-bars, telephones, and satellite TVs (with CNN and other channels). The garden in back has a children's play area. Fischer makes excellent suggestions of things to see and do in the area (including a visit to the nearby historic town of La-Charité-sur-Loire). This place is a great find. ◆ Charenton (from Pouilly-sur-Loire take N7 2 km/1.2 miles southeast. From Sancerre take D4 6 km/3.7 miles east to N7 and continue southeast on N7 for 9 km/5.6 miles). 86.39.03.00; fax 86.39.07.47

Within the Hôtel de Pouilly:

Restaurant Relais Grillade ★★$$ Each of the three fixed-price menus here features very traditional country cooking, including game in season and Loire fish dishes. Try the *terrine de lapin maison* (the house rabbit pâté), the *truite aux amandes* (trout with butter and almond sauce), the cheese plate, and such traditional desserts as chocolate mousse. The wine list has a good choice of local wines. In summer, meals are served on a garden terrace; if you have children, you can send them to play in the garden and keep your eye on them while you finish your meal. ◆ Daily lunch and dinner. Reservations recommended. 86.39.03.00

76 Domaine Masson-Blondelet This highly respected small estate (just 13 hectares/32.1 acres of vineyards) produces both Sancerre and white Pouilly-Fumé wines. Try the excellent Pouilly-Fumé "Les Angelots," which has a pleasant mineral taste. The rich Pouilly Tradition Cullus is made from grapes from old vines and is aged in new oak, which will please oak lovers. The Villa Pollus has a lovely pale yellow color and a delicate taste. The Masson-Blondelets like to work with individual customers and have opened a little wine shop/tasting center in the middle of Pouilly; it's a modern building over an entrance to the estate's wine cellars, which you can visit on request. ◆ Free. Tastings M-Sa. 1 Rue de Paris, in the center of Pouilly-sur-Loire. 86.39.00.34; fax 86.39.04.61

Bests

Barbara Chauveau
Owner, Chambres d'Hôtes Pallus, Cravant-les-Côteaux

The **Loire Valley** conjures up images of magnificent châteaux, abundant orchards, light-bodied wines. It has been called the "playground of kings" and "the garden of France." It is the historical heart of the nation.

The Renaissance wonder of **Château d'Azay-le-Rideau,** the fortified giant of **Château de Langeais,** the towering ruins of **Château de Chinon,** all have a place in the embattled story of the **Touraine.**

Prince Philippe Maurice de Broglie
Owner, Château de la Bourdaisière, Touraine

Given the richness of the **Touraine,** I propose a type of "theme" visit inspired by the heritage of the region: "Live like a king!" Your itinerary should include not only the châteaux and gardens that have given the **Loire Valley** its reputation as "château country," but also intense moments such as wine tasting, gastronomic pleasures, or the discovery of other elements of the region's culture.

Château visits: **Château de Chenonceau** built for the mistress of Henri II that later became the property of the Duc César Vendôme, recognized natural son of Henri IV and Gabrielle d'Estrées; **Château d'Ussé** belonging to the Marquis de Blacas; and the **Clos Lucé** in **Amboise,** the house in which Leonardo da Vinci died, and which now contains an exhibit of some of his inventions.

Visits to gardens: the **Château de Villandry,** a unique testimony to Renaissance garden style.

Visits to wineries, such as the **Château de Valmer** (in **Vouvray**), the property of the Count and Countess of Saint Venant. The cellars in **Montlouis-sur-Loire** are also worth discovering.

A gourmet dinner at **Restaurant Jean Bardet** in **Tours** (the restaurant of one of France's best chefs) or a sampling of the gastronomic pleasures of the region at one of our simple bistros.

Discovery of our region's culture: the **Donjon Millénaire des Aigles** (Ancient Eagles' Tower) in **Montrichard,** with its exhibit on the ancient art of falconry.

A balloon flight originating from the **Château de la Bourdaisière.**

A visit to the mushroom cellars of **Bourré.**

All this represents what I believe would make for an enriching and unusual visit to the Loire Valley.

Michel Bodet
Bed-and-Breakfast Operator, La Butte de l'Epine, Continvoir

The **Loire Valley,** with its banks of pink sand and its marvelous sunsets, is a marvelous region that the kings of France chose for its gentle climate. Here the kings hunted, practiced gallantry, played, and built splendid châteaux, such as **Chenonceau, Chambord, Blois, Amboise** (where Leonardo da Vinci lived), **Langeais, Chinon, Ussé, Villandry** and its very beautiful gardens, **Azay-le-Rideau,** and many, many others. The wines are delicious: the fruity reds of **St-Nicolas-de-Bourgueil** and **Champigny,** the more full wines of **Bourgueil** and **Chinon.** After a few years in a tufaceous limestone cellar, they rival some Bordeaux. The white wines here are Vouvray and Montlouis; the sweet and fruity ones are served chilled as aperitifs or with foie gras. The dry white wines are marvelous with fish and shellfish. How lovely it is to live in the **Touraine!**

Wine Glossary

appellation: the geographic region a wine's grapes are grown in.

Appellation d'Origine Contrôlée (*AOC* or *AC*; Controlled Label of Origin): on the label of a French wine, a guarantee of the highest quality vineyard, grape variety, and vinification methods. In France these standards are regulated and enforced by the *Institut National des Appellations d'Origine.*

astringence (astringency): a sharp taste derived from acid content and tannin.

barrique (barrel).

blanc (white): white wine.

blanc de blancs: champagne or sparkling wine made from white grapes only.

blanc de noirs: champagne or sparkling wine made from dark-skinned grapes.

blending: mixing wines to achieve the best quality or to obtain uniform quality year after year. See *"cuvée."*

body: A wine with substance, or body, fills the mouth. Body depends on the unique combination of alcohol and tannin present. It is a characteristic of all great red wines, though great white wines may lack it. When young, some wines have excessive body.

Bordeaux mixture: a mixture of copper sulfate and slaked lime used as a fungicide spray in many parts of Europe. When applied, it gives vineyards a blue-green tinge.

Botrytis cinerea: a parasitic fungus that attacks grapes. In certain climates, it causes grapes to develop gray rot and spoil; in others, such as that of Sauternes, the Botrytis cinerea causes white grapes to wither, their skin to become soft and flaccid, and their juice to evaporate, leaving behind an extremely sweet sort of grape concentration that gives Sauternes and other sweet wines their distinctive taste. These wines are some of the sweetest white wines in the world. The fungus and its effect are also known as *pourriture noble* or noble rot.

bouchonné (corky or corked): wine that has been spoiled by a bad cork.

bouquet: the perfume of a wine when it is first opened (the later, more lingering odor, is its aroma).

breathing: having contact with air. Most red wines need to aerate, or breathe before serving, in order to develop a full bouquet. Simply uncorking the bottle lets very little air enter; some wines need to spend time in a carafe for sufficient contact with the air.

brut: indicates very dry champagne.

case: a case of wine contains twelve 24- to 26-ounce bottles or 24 half bottles; a case of champagne holds 24 half-bottles (splits), 12 full bottles, six 1.5-liter magnums, or three 3-liter jéroboams.

cave (cellar): wine cellar.

cépage (type of vine): grape variety (i.e., chardonnay or pinot noir).

chai (aboveground wine cellar): any place above ground where wine is stored in casks. This term is used particularly in Bordeaux, where most wines are stored in *chais.*

chapeau (hat): the thick layer of solids that forms on the must in the vats during fermentation.

chaptalisation (chaptalization): the addition of sugar to fermenting wine must, which builds up the alcohol content.

charnu (fleshy): full in body.

claret: another name for red bordeaux—used in the UK and sometimes in the US.

climat (climate): used in Burgundy to refer to a vineyard. That region has such a diversity of soil composition and exposure to sun, rain, and wind that each parcel of land is considered to have its own climate.

clone: a group of individual plants propagated asexually from a single source.

clos: a walled vineyard, or one that once was enclosed by a wall. This term is used mainly in Burgundy.

collage (fining): a technique used before bottling to rid wines of suspended particles, often done with egg whites or albumen-type substances.

commune (township or parish): often to designate the official place name, or *Appellation Contrôlée,* of a particular wine. Margaux, for example, is a *commune.*

corsé (robust, full-bodied).

côte (slope).

coteau, coteaux (hillside, hillsides).

Coteaux Champenois: appellation for still wines produced in Champagne.

courtier (wine broker).

cru (growth): denotes a single vineyard. See *"grand cru," "grand cru classé,"* and *"premier cru."*

cuvaison: the process of leaving the wine in vats for a period of time.

cuve (vat): a container in which wines are fermented.

cuvée (the contents of a wine vat): denotes a particular selection, crop, or barrel of wine. When used in the context of champagne, the word refers to a blend of champagnes, or a special lot of wines.

dégorgement, dégorgé (disgorging, disgorged): removing sediment from a bottle of champagne; a champagne that has had its sediment removed. See *"récemment dégorgé."*

dosage (chaptalization): the process of adding sugar or aged wines to a bottled wine, usually employed in making sparkling wines.

dur (hard): sometimes used to describe a wine that lacks suppleness.

égrappage (destemming): the process by which grape stems are removed before the grape juice is fermented. Destemming reduces tannin in the wine, since tannins are particularly concentrated in stems.

équilibré (balanced): refers to the harmony achieved between the different characteristics of a wine when they are considered as a whole.

estate-bottled: wines that have been bottled where they have been produced. The French terms that appear on wine labels to indicate that the wine is estate-bottled are *mis en bouteilles au château, mis au domaine, mis en bouteilles au domaine, mis du propriétaire, mis à la propriété.*

étiquette (label).

ferme (hard): refers to a wine that is hard, tannic, and not ready to drink.

fermentation: the same word in French and English, it indicates the decomposition of sugar into ethyl alcohol and carbon dioxide.

fermentation malolactique (malolactic fermentation): secondary fermentation, caused by the conversion of malic acid into lactic acid and carbon dioxide. If this happens in the barrel, it reduces acidity; if it happens when the wine is in bottle, it can make the wine gassy.

filtration: the same word in French and English, meaning the process by which wine is rid of sediment. Also referred to in French as *filtrage.*

fine champagne: not a champagne, but a prestigious type of Cognac; *"une fine"* is the popular French expression for a glass of Cognac.

finesse: breed, delicacy, discretion.

fining: see *"collage."*

floraison (flowering): refers to the tiny green grape buds that form when vines flower.

flûte: a tall, thin champagne glass.

foudre (a large cask): the vessel used for maturing, storing, and transporting wines.

fût (cask or barrel).

goût de terroir: a particular taste imparted by a wine's vineyard (it doesn't mean the wine tastes like dirt).

grand cru (great growth): the highest classification for a vineyard in Burgundy; used less formally in Alsace, Bordeaux, and Champagne.

grand cru classé (classed great growth): an officially classified great vineyard.

grand vin (great wine): although it freely appears on wine labels, it is not an official term and gives no indication of wine quality.

gras (fat): refers to a big wine that contains much natural glycerine, and lacks the hardness that would give it body.

haute qualité (high quality): an unofficial expression sometimes seen on a wine label, which is no guarantee of quality.

hotte: a long basket carried on the back, used in grape picking.

kir: a popular French aperitif, usually made with a simple white burgundy, such as one made from the Aligoté grape, and crème de cassis liqueur.

levure (yeast).

lie (lees): the sediment or dregs left at the bottom of a wine cask after racking.

liquoreux *(rich and sweet).*

liter: a standard liquid measure in the metric system; it equals 1.05 US liquid quarts.

mâché (chewed): refers to a wine that tastes tired from excessive racking or handling.

maderized: refers to wines that have lost their freshness and have acquired a brown tinge and an unpleasant musty taste as a result of age, poor storage, or oxidation. Sulfur dioxide combined with the milk protein casein is sometimes added to white wines to protect them against maderization.

maître de chai: the person in charge of vinification and aging of all the wine made on an estate (usually used in Bordeaux).

millésimé: refers to wine from a particular vintage year.

mis en bouteilles au château, or *au domaine:* an indication on a wine label that the wine is estate-bottled.

mousseux (sparkling wine).

moût (must): crushed grapes before they ferment and become wine.

négociant, négociant-éleveur (wine dealer): a merchant or broker who buys wine at various levels of completion from grape growers. The dealer may then put finishing touches on the wine, bottle it, and sell it with his or her own label.

nerveux (nervous): used to indicate an assertive, vigorous wine.

noble rot: see *"Botrytis cinerea."*

nose: a wine's bouquet.

oaky: refers to a slightly sweet, vanilla taste that wine acquires after aging in oak barrels or casks, especially those made from new, rather than aged, oak.

oxidation (oxydation): overexposure of wine to air.

pétillant: refers to wine that is slightly sparkling.

pichet (pitcher): the vessel used to serve simple wine or cider in restaurants.

piqué: refers to vinegary wine.

pourriture noble: see "Botrytis cinerea."

premier cru (first growth): designates that the quality of the vineyard is second tier after *grand cru* in Burgundy; the top Bordeaux wine classification is *premier grand cru* and applies to a *domaine* rather than a vineyard.

propriétaire-vigneron: someone who both owns vineyards and makes wine, often used in Burgundy.

race: distinction and breeding in a wine.

racking: the draining or pumping of wine off its lees from the barrel in which it has been maturing into a new, clean one. This process is usually repeated several times as the wine ages.

récemment dégorgé (RD; recently disgorged): on a champagne label this indicates that the wine has been aged with its sediment for longer than usual, which usually means it will have a richer, more complex flavor.

robe (dress): the appearance of the wine, particularly its color and clarity.

rouge (red).

sans année: nonvintage, usually applied to champagne.

sec (moderately dry): less dry than brut, but more dry than demi-sec (half dry) or doux (sweet) wine, used mainly in reference to champagne or other sparkling wine.

séché (dried out): usually applied to oxidized wines.

sélection de grains nobles (selection of noble grapes): appears on the labels of wines from Alsace. Indicates that the grapes have been picked one by one, to harvest only those that have developed "noble rot."

sève (sap).

tanin (tannin): an important component of wine, derived from grape skins, pips (seeds), and stems, and also from the oak barrels in which the wine is aged. Tannin provides character and long-lasting quality, but excessive tannin in a wine makes it harsh.

tastevin: a small, flat cup with a ring handle and raised indentations, traditionally made of silver, in which wine is tasted in Burgundy. The shape and silver color of the tastevin reflects light and thus helps the taster to see the wine's color, especially in a dark wine cellar.

tirage: the act or process of drawing wine from barrels.

tonneau (a large barrel): in Bordeaux, the term is a unit of measure. It refers to four *barriques,* or barrels, and contains 900 liters (237 gallons).

varietal wine: wine made from a single grape variety.

vieilles vignes (old vines): the older the vine, the more intense the flavor of the grape and the lower the yield from the vineyard. Any wine labeled *"vieilles vignes"* is bound to be one of a winery's best wines.

Vins Délimités de Qualité Supérieure (*VDQS;* Delimited Wines of Superior Quality): a step below *Appellation Contrôlée* wines.

vendange (grape harvest).

vendanges tardives (late harvest): a term used on a wine label (usually for wines from Alsace) to indicate that the grapes have been harvested late to allow their natural sugars to develop to the maximum; the wine will be naturally sweet.

verjus: the very acidic juice from grapes that result from a late or second flowering; often used for cooking or to add acid to wines produced in the first-flowering grapes.

vigne (individual grape vine): wine makers often use the term to indicate a certain parcel of a vineyard.

vigneron: one who is both a wine maker and a winegrower.

vignoble (vineyard).

vin (wine).

vin de coule (wine from the first pressing).

vin de cuvée (champagne from the first pressing).

vin de garde: wine that ages well, can be kept a long time, and will, if not improve, at least not deteriorate.

vin de pays (country wines): The French government began regulating these wines in 1968 in an effort to raise the overall quality of basic table wine production. Though the lowest category among the *AC* wines—one notch below *VDQS*—these wines have been promoted from *vin de table,* and some superb wines are in this category.

vin de presse: a harsh wine made from pressing the grape residues after the grapes have been pressed.

vin de primeur (young wine).

vin de queue: inferior wine made from juice obtained through pressing the stalks.

vin de table: a wine that may be a blend of wines from several years, grapes, or regions. If grapes from more than one country have been used, it must be stated on the label, but acknowledging a more specific geographical region, grape type, or vintage is not permitted. These wines have not received even the lowest recognition afforded by the French government: *vin de pays.*

vin de tête (the best wine): in Sauternes, refers to wine from the first crushing.

vin doux naturel (naturally sweet wine): no sugar is added to make these wines sweet, but they are often fortified with brandy.

vin fin (fine wine): not an official designation, it guarantees nothing about the quality of the wine when it appears on a wine label.

vin gris (gray wine): a pale type of rosé.

vin mousseux (sparkling wine).

vin ordinaire (common wine).

vinage: the technique of adding alcohol to wine to increase its alcohol content.

vinification, vinifié (wine making, made into wine): when the expression *"vin vinifié et élevé par"* is followed by the name of the producer on wine labels, the *"vinifié"* means that the wine has been pressed and fermented at the winery.

vintage: The year the grapes were picked and the wine was produced. Wines produced from a blend of wines from different years are nonvintage.

vrac, en vrac (bulk): refers to wine procured from the wine maker in bulk containers, then packaged by the seller. It is sold to the consumer in small barrels or jugs, or in bottles with corks but no labels.

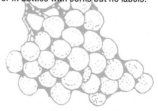

Index

Index

Index

Restaurants

Only restaurants with star ratings are listed below. All restaurants are listed alphabetically in the main (preceding) index. Always call in advance to ensure a restaurant has not closed, changed its hours, or booked its tables for a private party. The restaurant price ratings are based on the average cost of an entrée for one person, excluding tax and tip.

★★★★ An Extraordinary Experience
★★★ Excellent
★★ Very Good
★ Good

$$$$ Big Bucks ($150 and up)
$$$ Expensive ($50-$150)
$$ Reasonable ($20-$50)
$ The Price Is Right (less than $20)

Index